M

398.41 WITHDRAW
Ra

ENCYCLOPÆDIA OF SUPERSTITIONS

ENCYCLOPÆDIA
OF
SUPERSTITIONS

by

E. and M. A. RADFORD

<small>WITH A FOREWORD BY</small>
SIR JOHN HAMMERTON

GREENWOOD PRESS, PUBLISHERS
WESTPORT, CONNECTICUT

The Library of Congress cataloged this book as follows:

Radford, Edwin, 1891–
    Encyclopaedia of superstitions, by E. and M. A. Radford.
With a foreword by Sir John Hammerton. New York,
Greenwood Press ₁1969₁

    269 p. 24 cm.

    Reprint of the 1949 ed.
    Bibliography : p. 265–269.

    1. Superstition—Dictionaries. 2. Folk-lore—Dictionaries.   I. Rad-
ford, Mona Augusta (Mangan) joint author. II. Title.

BF1775.R3   1969b   398.3'7'03   70–88993
SBN 8371-2115-9   MARC

Library of Congress   70 ₁3₁

Originally published in 1949 by the Philosophical Library, Inc.,
New York

Reprinted with the permission of the Philosophical Library, Inc.

Reprinted in 1969 by Greenwood Press, Inc.,
51 Riverside Avenue, Westport, Conn. 06880

Library of Congress catalog card number 70-88993
ISBN 0-8371-2115-9

Printed in the United States of America

FOREWORD

HAVING had the opportunity of examining the typescript of this latest compilation of Mr. and Mrs. Radford, it gives me pleasure to say a word by way of appreciation of an excellent idea well carried out. There was need for some such work of reference on superstitions, covering the whole world in an encyclopædic way, rather than a cyclopædia of beliefs peculiar to one country or one people. For although there have been many odd volumes touching the subject in haphazard fashion, and one can find a good deal about superstitions in the celebrated compilations of Dr. Brewer, his *Dictionary of Phrase and Fable*, for instance, in Chambers's *Book of Days*, with its many occasional references, in general encyclopædias without number, books devoted to the explanation of curious customs, and so forth, I think this is, if not the first encyclopædia devoted entirely to its specific subject, certainly the first that has come under my notice.

The most noteworthy feature of the Radfords' book is the skill with which its compilers have succeeded in observing the rather fine distinction between superstition and custom. Having myself edited a considerable work some years ago on *Manners and Customs of Mankind*, I did not then take any particular care to exclude superstitions where these underlie or are the remote origins of the multitude of customs which are observed by different peoples all over the world, customs which in many instances can be traced and related to others in widely separated regions of the globe.

But while no difficulty is presented to an editor whose main concern is to bring together a large and representative selection of manners and customs, a very real difficulty does present itself to editors who aim at assembling a really comprehensive record of the superstitions, and nothing but the superstitions, still prevailing amongst the races of mankind to-day, and especially to identify their existence and observance with totally unrelated groups of the human race.

To judge to a nicety where a superstition is the prime cause of custom and to concentrate upon the prime cause rather than upon the resulting custom must have involved a very considerable amount of judgment in making many of the decisions as to what should become an entry in an encyclopædia so highly specialized. This judgment is very successfully exemplified in the volume now before the reader. And the skilful manner in which the method of presentation for ready reference has been here effected will scarcely be denied.

To the reader who is unskilled in the study of superstition this work will, in my opinion, come as a surprise on his discovering the widespread diffusion of superstitious beliefs still obtaining at this day in every aspect of social life among both the civilized and the savage, and to those who have given any thought to the origins of superstitions this work cannot fail to prove of real value as a reference book; but whether it be regarded as an orderly collection of reading for the curious which will provide much entertainment as well as instruction, or as a work of reference, I feel sure the general opinion will be that the compilers have hit the mark they aimed at, and have achieved a skilful and valuable piece of work on which they are to be congratulated.

J. A. HAMMERTON

PREFACE

S O M E years ago the idea occurred to us that there was need for a work containing as complete a collection as possible of British superstitions presented in encyclopædic form, giving easy and quick reference to the reader.

There were, and are, in existence many excellent books on Folklore which review customs and superstitions of our people, but none containing in one volume a comprehensive catalogue. Moreover, all have a laborious indexing system necessitating voluminous notes and research.

We accordingly began collecting and authenticating all the superstitions we could trace. The task occupied more than four years, and is brought to a conclusion with the presentation of this volume, containing more than two thousand superstitions of Britain ranging over the past six hundred years, and extending down to the present day.

Individual classification has been carried out, and the title headings enable the reader to obtain within a few minutes the list of beliefs attached to any one subject—and, where it is possible to present it, the origin, or possible origin, of the belief.

Care has been taken to distinguish between superstition and custom. Except in one or two instances, where the line of demarcation is barely distinguishable, customs have been omitted as lacking any spiritual origin. The "maypole" is an exception since, though more of a custom than a superstition, its origin, in all probability, lies in the ancient worship of the Tree Spirits by our people.

Early in our examination of beliefs prevalent in Britain, and of superstitions as a whole, we were confronted with a succession of coincidences in the form of exactly similar spiritual remedies for disease in these islands and in countries which, at the time, were uncivilized judged by Western standards. Deeper research was undertaken; as a result several hundred examples of this correlated belief are given in this volume.

They raise a topic of peculiar and fascinating interest—whether, indeed, there are such things as "British" superstitions, or whether, *on the contrary, those superstitions are world-wide, inherent in all peoples of the world in exactly identical forms of fear, of avoidance, and of remedial measures?*

Take, as an example, childbirth. To ensure easy labour for a woman it was the custom in North-west Argyllshire, Scotland, to open every lock in the house. Regard this in the light of the Roman custom of presenting women in labour with a key as a charm for easy delivery. The Argyllshire custom could be stretched into a corruption of the Roman key by reason of the occupation of these islands by the Romans, and the consequent copying of custom and beliefs; but what can be said in explanation of the beliefs of the natives of the Island of Salsette, near Bombay, and of parts of Java, or Chittagong in the East Indies where, from the earliest times, all doors were opened to ease a mother in her labour?

Equally with the days following the birth. Ancient Scottish belief, dating beyond the sixteenth century, entailed that the closest watch had to be maintained over the babe lest evil spirits wreaked their will; and no person must pass between the infant and the fire during the first eight days of its life. The Greeks held that a child must not be left alone for eight days after birth; the Danes that fires in the house must not be extinguished for eight days.

When Western man penetrated into the island of Saparoca and Hanockoe, and in Nyassaland, and delved into their ancient superstitions, it was found that so long as native memory had existed the people at childbirth had known that a light must be kept burning until the eighth day of a new-born babe's life in order that the spirits should not harm the infant.

Even more marked are the examples of homœopathic magic. In Britain in the sixteenth and seventeenth centuries superstition encouraged the belief that a child could be relieved of whooping cough by its elders passing it through an arch of brambles formed by one branch of the parent stem having made root in the earth. The peoples of the area round about Lake Nyassa had, at the same period, a cure for such ailment of the chest: the sufferer was made to pass through an arch formed by bending down a branch of a bush and inserting the free end in the ground.

A child with a rupture was, in Britain, at one time passed three times through a sapling, the stem of which had been cleft longitudinally with an axe, and the halves of which were held apart for the ceremony. In Uganda, the Medicine Man from time immemorial had split a tree stem and held the two halves apart while a sufferer stepped through the opening.

The M'Bengas of Western Africa on the birth of twins planted two trees; henceforth, it was believed, the lives of the children were bound up with the trees; if the trees withered and died, the children withered and died with them. In Britain the belief existed in strong measure that the health, and even the life, of a child passed through a cleft tree for rupture depended upon the progress of the tree; if the cleft, bound together, would not heal, the rupture in the child would not heal. Should the tree wither and pine away, so would the child pine away.

In a Sussex village when a portion of land changed hands and the new owner announced his intention of cutting down a row of trees, the population protested in horror; for years their children had been passed through those trees, the sides of which showed plainly for all to see the scars left by the cleavings. They protested that to kill trees would be to spell the death of their children.

A farmer near Birmingham throughout his life would not have a bough lopped or a branch clipped of a tree through which forty years earlier he had been passed for rupture. He maintained that to do so would mean that the rupture would return, mortify, and he would die.

In the heart of darkest Africa, in the jungles of Central America, the Tree Spirits were the gods, beneficent or otherwise. British people for generations nailed their headaches to a tree in the shape of a lock of hair wrapped round a nail which was then driven into the bark; they lost their headaches, the tree gained it. The hill tribes of South Mirazapur, as did other races discovered long after the practice in Britain, in like manner believed that they could transfer their evils to the beneficent Tree Spirits.

What explanation can be offered of this correlation of superstition in civilized and uncivilized countries?

Communications of people?

In the thirteenth and fourteenth centuries—and between countries some of which had not then been discovered?

Between the peasants of the Scottish Highlands and the wild natives of the M'Bengas?

Is the alternative the presence of a sameness of fear inherent throughout the human race; a mysterious sameness of escape also inherent from primitive times?

The authors in the following pages have given tabulated lists of superstitions immediately beneath the classified headings, and have enlarged and illustrated them in the text beneath.

Where no source is mentioned it may be assumed that the beliefs enjoyed general circulation. Where a county or area are named, the practices described were prevalent in the places mentioned.

Our thanks are acknowledged to the many people who have so kindly supplied us with details of superstitions and beliefs within their ken; to the authors of works mentioned in the bibliography; to Mr. C. E. Leese, for Cornish beliefs; to many correspondents; and last, but by no means least, to Sir John Hammerton, who not only wrote the foreword, but so kindly helped with suggestions.

EDWIN and MONA A. RADFORD

Hampton Court
Surrey, England

1947

ACCIDENTS

Accidents are most frequent when the broad bean is in flower.—East Midlands.

For many years the people in the rural areas of the East Midlands held firmly to this belief, and they took special precautions to avoid injury during the few weeks that the broad bean was flowering.

In Yorkshire it was held by old country people that the beans contained the souls of the departed, and even to-day a bean shape is associated, in some connection, with death—a relic of the seventeenth and eighteenth centuries.

As to the origin, it is likely that the belief or connection of beans with death is a revival, in the seventeenth century, of the earlier Roman occupation, for during the three days in May when the Romans held a festival in honour of the ghosts, the head of each family arose at the dead of night, and having made certain magic signs to ward off ghosts, he threw black beans over his shoulders without looking behind him. As he did so he repeated: "With these beans I redeem me and mine." The ghosts, following unseen at his heels, picked up the beans and left him and his family alone.

Similarly in Japan, on the last night of the year, the head of the family, clad in his ceremonial robes, went through all the rooms of the house at midnight carrying a box of beans, from which he scattered a number in each room pronouncing a form of words, the meaning of which was "Go forth, demons." Thus was the house rid of demons and ghosts, which latter are, of course, associated with death.

ACORN

If a lady carries an acorn in her pocket or bag, she will be blessed with perpetual youth.—Sussex.

For generations British people of rural areas, in reply to this superstition handed down by word of mouth, carried acorns about their person—and steadily grew old and wizened! But the failure of one did nothing to exterminate the belief; it seemed only to stir others to further efforts.

The belief is not yet dead. On 8th August, 1946, the authors received a letter from a woman living at Worthing in Sussex. It read:

"Do you know that if women carry an acorn, they will never grow old? This is an old English custom dating back to the days of the Norman Conquest."

There seems nothing to link the Normans with the charm of the acorn. On the contrary, the superstition probably existed long before the Normans. The acorn comes, of course, from the oak, and the oak was a sacred tree to the Druids. No ceremony or rite of the Druids took place without the aid of the oak and the mistletoe.

Students, too, may remark with interest that there are in the Vatican and the Lateran statues of a figure, one of the decorations of which is a necklace of acorns. The figure, strangely enough, is that of the goddess Artemis. She was the Ephesians' embodiment of the wild life of Nature, revered on the mountainside and in the swampy lowlands, in the rustling woods and the rippling springs. She was the goddess of fecundity, though not of wedlock; and it may be that it was in this sense of perpetual youth that the superstition was originally born.

ADDER

Kill the first adder you see in the spring and you will triumph over your enemies.—General.

Let an adder go alive and bad luck will attend you.

Hang an adder skin over the chimbly (chimney) and it will bring you good luck.—Leicestershire.

Hang an adder's skin in the rafters and your house will never catch fire.

The authors doubt whether any insurance company, shown the hanging skin, would be prepared to accept a lower premium for the fire risk!

Most of the adder superstitions belong to those areas of Britain where forest land, interspersed with open common, abounded, particularly in the New Forest. It is probable that the origin of the hanging skin insurance against fire lies in the South European gipsies, who came to England about the year 1100.

It was a gipsy custom on the evening of Easter Sunday to place herbs and simples in a wooden vessel together with the dried carcase of a snake, which every person present must have touched with his, or her, fingers. The herbs were then burned.

By the ceremony which followed all evil was supposed to have been expelled from the tribe. Fire was an evil of the Fire God.

In many parts of England it was held

that a cast adder's skin drew out thorns from a body. The same people held that adders dreaded the ash tree, and a blow from an ash stick would kill an adder outright—which no other weapon would do. If any other wood was used, the adder would not die until sundown.

ADDER BITES

To cure an adder bite, repeat verses one and two of Psalm lxviii.

The dead body of an adder, bruised on the wound it has made, is an infallible remedy for the bite.—Cornwall.

In Devonshire the remedy resorted to was to kill a chicken and thrust the bitten part of the person into the bird's stomach. There it had to remain until the chicken was cold. If the flesh of the bird, when cold, assumed a dark colour, then the cure was effected; if the flesh retained its natural colour, the poison had been absorbed into the system of the bitten person.

In this connection it is interesting to note that when a native of the Hottentots in the Kat River settlement, on the eastern frontier of Cape Colony, was bitten by a snake, feathers were plucked from the breast of a fowl and a small incision made in the skin. The wound was applied to the incision on several separate occasions until the fowl died. It was believed that the fowl gradually died as it absorbed the venom abstracted from the wound by its body.

How the superstition came to Britain from the Hottentots, or from Britain to the Hottentots—if it did—is a matter of interesting conjecture.

Wales had a rather remarkable method of overcoming the adder's venom. It was held that if a person bitten could leap across the nearest water before the reptile vanished, he would lose the venom, and not die. By water was not meant, necessarily, a stream; if only over a small rain-pool in the roadway, the charm worked.

In Somerset the bite of an adder was best cured, it was believed, by tying a circlet of ash twigs round the neck of the patient (see ADDER, above), and in other parts of the country the remedy was the expensive one of wrapping the bitten person in the reeking skin of a newly killed sheep.

ADDER STONES

Adder stones, carried in the pocket, will cure all maladies of the eyes.—Wales.

To prevent a child having the whooping-cough, hang an adder stone round its neck.—Superstition recorded in Scotland as far back as 1699, and still extant in remote parts of the Highlands.

Adder stones are also called Serpents' Eggs and Snake Eggs. They were held in high esteem by the Druids. According to them the peculiar virtue resident in the stones was that they secured success in law-suits, and free access to kings and rulers. Many adder stones are still preserved as charms in those rural areas of Britain where the Celtic population still lingers. In some parts of Wales the stones go by the name of Gleini na Droedh and Glaine nan Druidhe (the Magician's or Druid's glass).

The legend behind the properties of the stones is that they were believed to have been made by serpents. The snakes, it was said, gathered together in a wriggling, slimy mass to generate the stones from their slaver, and shoot them into the air from their hissing jaws. It is a curious omission in superstition that such stones, thus made, were never associated with the curing of a serpent's bite.

The gathering time of the snakes was held, in Cornwall, to be on Midsummer Eve; in Wales, on the eve of May Day. So recently as the early 1900s the authors were told, in all seriousness, by people in the Principality that they had witnessed such a congress of snakes, and had seen the magic stones in the midst of froth.

The stones are of various colours—green, pink, red, blue and brown. There are a number still preserved in several museums in the country; and many of these are perforated. It was held that the perforation was caused, after the stone had been conflated by the serpents generally, by one of the serpents sticking its tail through the still viscous glass.

The test of the genuineness of an Adder Stone was to throw it into a moving stream; if genuine it floated against the current, and no weight attached to it could make the stone sink.

AGATE

If bitten by a poisonous insect, press an agate on the spot; and the bite will come to no harm.—General.

Put an agate on the head of a person suffering from the fever, and the fever will depart.

It is likely that behind this superstitious belief lies a portion of the world-wide belief, both in civilized and heathen countries, that evil can be transferred to stones.

See WARTS.

For superstitions concerning other precious stones, see GEMS.

AGNES

Persons named Agnes always go mad.

For many years in rural North Lincolnshire no native-born child was given the name Agnes, the result of this remarkable belief. Even in the authors' lifetime the name was taboo in Lincolnshire.

When, or how, the superstition originated is lost in antiquity. It is, of course, as complete nonsense as the belief that any boy christened George will never be hanged. Yet this question has been asked of the authors a hundred times, the phrase going, as a rule, "You can't tell me of any person with the Christian name George who has been hanged for murder." In point of fact we can give the names of half a dozen Georges who have fallen at the hangman's hands. George Smith, the "Brides in the Bath" murderer," was one.

AGNES' EVE, ST.

(21st January)

Upon St Agnes' Eve you should take a row of pins and pull out every one, one after the other, while saying a Paternoster. Stick a pin in your sleeve and you will dream of him you are going to marry. —General belief held in the days of Robert Burton (1577-1640) and mentioned by him in his *Anatomy of Melancholy;* and by Aubrey in *Miscellanies.*

Before going to bed say: "Fair St. Agnes, play thy part. And send to me my own sweetheart. Not in his best or worst array. But in the clothes he wears every day. That to-morrow I may him ken. From among all other men.—Durham.

"And on sweet St. Agnes' night. Please you with the promised sight. Some of husbands, some of lovers. Which an empty dream discovers."—Ben Jonson's version of the old belief, generally prevalent (1573-1637).

The St. Agnes tradition was a little more strict throughout Yorkshire and other parts of Durham. There young girls desirous of dreaming about their future husbands had to abstain from eating and drinking or even speaking during St. Agnes' Eve, and not even touch their lips with their fingers. They had, still in silence, together to make "dumb cake," the ingredients of which—flour,

salt, water, etc.—must have been supplied in equal proportions by their friends, who had also to take equal shares in baking and turning the cake, and taking it out of the oven. The cake had then to be divided into equal portions and each girl, taking her share, had to walk backwards up the stairs, finally eat it and jump into bed. She might then confidently expect to see her future husband in her dreams.

In Northumberland girls, after a day's fasting and silence, boiled an egg apiece, extracted the yolk, filled the cavity with salt, ate the egg, shell and all, and recited a couplet to St. Agnes. Another Northumbrian husband vision (and also a wife vision) could be gained on this night by swallowing a raw herring, bones and all.

Finally, in the North, all these arduous pursuits in search of a glimpse into the future could be broken by a single kiss—and young wags had a lively time on St. Agnes' Eve kissing all girls they suspected of "being in preparation for husband-gazing."

The origin of the love portent on this night lies in the life and death of the saint. St. Agnes was a Roman virgin and a martyr to the Christian faith in the reign of Diocletian (A.D. 245-313). The Gospel for her day in the Missale ad Usum Sarum (1554) was the Parable of the Virgins.

St. Agnes, for her Christian belief, was condemned to be debauched in the public stews before being beheaded. But her virginity was, according to legend, miraculously preserved by thunder and lightning from heaven. The account, which appears in the *Miracles of the Saints,* states that when Agnes refused to marry Procopius, the son of a Roman Prefect, the Prefect gave her the choice of marrying his son or serving in the Temple as a Vestal Virgin. She declined both.

The Prefect then ordered her to be led naked through the streets, proclaimed a strumpet, and left in a brothel. God, says the account, sent his angels, who presented her with a white robe; and her chamber in the brothel was brilliantly illuminated with celestial light. Many entered the chamber with evil intent, but went away converted to the new faith. Last of all Procopius entered; as soon as he laid hands upon her he fell dead.

After her execution her parents, going to lament and pray at her tomb, saw a vision of angels, among them their daughter, beside whom was standing a lamb. As a result, St. Agnes is generally depicted accompanied by a lamb. The Portiforium ad Usum Sarum declares that Agnes was the daughter of immaculate parents, that she was deeply versed in magic, and that Christ was her spouse.

AGUE, CURE OF

To cure the ague, eat, fasting, seven sage leaves, seven mornings running.

Wrap a spider in a raisin and swallow. The ague will disappear.—Common in all parts of the country.

Take a good dose of elixir and hang three spiders round the neck, and the ague will be driven away.—Berkshire charm related by Ashmole, the English antiquary, as having been tried successfully by himself.

To cure the ague, visit at midnight the nearest cross-roads five different times, and there bury a new-laid egg. With the egg you will bury the ague.—A charm mentioned by Douce as prevalent in Exeter.

Break a salted cake of bran and give it to a dog when the fit comes on, by which means the malady is supposed to be transferred to the dog.—*The Gentleman's Magazine*, 1787.

If you would be rid of the ague, go by night alone to a cross-roads, and just as the clock is striking midnight turn round three times and drive a large nail into the ground up to the head. Walk backwards from the nail before the clock has finished the twelfth stroke. The ague will leave you, but will go to the person next to step over the nail.—Suffolk superstition of the 1600s.

Down the ages and in many lands this nailing and pegging of evils, and their transference to objects, animate and inanimate, has been regarded as a powerful charm against witchery—and nearly all the ills in mediæval times were attributed to bewitching. Ague has always been a disease deemed peculiarly open to the influence of charm. In Central Africa natives who could have had no knowledge whatever of the charms practised in Britain neverthelesss nailed the disease into trees in order to rid themselves of it. Pliny, in his *Natural History*, xxviii, 63, records it as a practice of the early Romans. More will be said of this transference of evil later in this volume. Meanwhile, mention may be made here of a North Country cure of the ague, re-

corded by Henderson. On the advice of an old farm labourer she took his knife, cut off a lock of her hair, wrapped the tress round a large pin and put the pin in the bark of an aspen tree, saying: "Aspen tree, aspen tree, I prithee shake instead of me." She explained: "I've niver had t'shakking fra that day to this."

Henry Wickham describes a document cure which was found round the neck of a dead man at Hurstpierpoint, Sussex. It was inscribed on a paper and is given here in the original spelling:

When Christ came upon the cross for the redemption of mankind, he shook and his Rood trembled. The Chief Priest said to him "Art thou afraid, or as thou an ague?" He sid unto them I am not afraid neither have I an ague, and whosoever believeth in these words shall not be troubled by anny feaver or ague. So be it unto thee.

The date on the paper was 1708; and the charm was prevalent in the Border and northern counties of Britain at the time.

Another "document" was described in *Notes and Queries* by a clergyman who, having heard a woman had been subject to the ague, but had had no return of it since she had worn a spell for the cure, explained to her the sinful nature of such superstitions, and asked her to put away the spell. For a long time she refused, saying that if she removed the spell the ague would return. At last, however, she yielded to the priest's exhortation, took off the spell and handed it to him. He opened it and read the contents to her as follows:

"Ague, farewell.
Till we meet in hell."

The woman, a respectable widow, was horrified and declared that she would rather have the ague.

It was a belief in Devonshire that you could give away your ague by burying under your neighbour's threshold a bag containing the parings of a dead man's nails and the clippings of some of the hairs of his head; the neighbour would be afflicted by your ague until the bag was removed.

In Somerset and the adjoining counties the sufferer shut a large spider in a box and left it there to die. As it died, so did the ague. In Flanders the spider, imprisoned between the two halves of a walnut, was worn round the sufferer's neck; and still is in the more remote parts.

In Wales the remedy was to cross water to a hollow willow tree, breathe into the hollow three times and then stop up the hole and go home without looking round or speaking a word. You would be cured.

In Lincolnshire the ague was charmed away by nailing three horse-shoes on the foot of the bed of the sufferer, with a hammer placed cross-wise over them. The idea was that when the "Old 'Un" came to shake the patient the horse-shoes plus the charm would "fix him safe as a church spire." The charm was to take the "mell" (hammer) in the left hand, tap the horse-shoes with it and say:

"Father, Son and Holy Ghost,
Nail the Devil to the post.
Thrice I strikes with holy crook.
One for God, one for Wod,
And one for Lok."

The remarkable combination of Christianity and heathenism in the charm will be noticed, for Wod and Lok stand for the old Scandinavian gods, Woden and Loki.

An extraordinary story of an ague "charm" is related of Sir John Holt, Lord Chief Justice of the King's Bench in 1709. Holt, who was a wild youth in early days, on one occasion visited with some friends a country inn. There he found the daughter in an attack of ague, and the mother anxious at the recurrence of the attacks in spite of the fact that she had spent much money on doctors. Holt, promising her that the attacks should never occur again, wrote a few words on a piece of parchment, rolled it up, and directed that the child should wear the parchment on her wrist, it to remain there until she was well. The child had no more attacks during the week that Holt and his friends remained at the inn. The mother, duly thankful, refused to accept any payment for the accommodation given to Holt.

Many years later, when Holt was a Judge, he went on circuit in the county, and one case before him was that of a reputed witch, charged with practising witchcraft. The prosecution stated that she had a spell with which she could either cure cattle which were sick or destroy those that were well. She had, it was said, been detected using the spell which was now at the convenience of the Court. Upon this Judge Holt asked that it should be given to him. The spell was in a dirty ball, wrapped in several rags, and bound with pack-thread.

He opened it, to find inside the parchment of his own boyhood joke.

After a moment's thought, he told the jury of the incident, and explained that the so-called witchcraft charm was the parchment he had written. The result was that not only was the woman freed, but it was the last prosecution for witchcraft undertaken in the county. The account is given in Pettigrew's *Medical Superstitions*.

We will conclude the cure of ague with a quotation from *A Closet for Ladies and Gentlewomen*, published in 1611:

"Make a posset with white wine and take away the curd. Take horse-dung from a stone horse as hotte as you can get it from the horse and strain it with the posset drink, and put a little methridate and cardus benedictus and unicorn's horne—and if you have no unicorn's horne then put ivorie or sea-horse tooth and give it to the sicke to drink fasting in the morning. Use this two or three mornings."

ALL SOULS' DAY

If two people walk round a room at midnight and in the darkness going contrariwise, they will never meet, and one of the two will be spirited away.

All souls in Purgatory are released for twenty-four hours from this eve. On this night they are free.—Gaelic belief.

"A soul cake, a soul cake. Have mercy on all Christian souls for a soul cake."—Old chant to visitors calling at any house on 2nd November.

This is the day of remembrance for the dead. It was believed by Catholics of mediæval times, and the superstition became general throughout Europe, that on this day the dead returned and for a time lingered among their living kin. Throughout the country, as late as the end of the nineteenth century, soul cakes were baked and given to all callers at a house, the invitation to eat being couched in the chant given above, making it virtually impossible to refuse to pray for the departed members of the household.

In Shropshire, up to the end of the seventeenth century, it was the custom to have on the dining-table a large pile of soul cakes, and visitors to the house, of whatever degree, took one on leaving.

In Staffordshire, Cheshire, Lancashire and Monmouthshire peasants spent the day "a'Souling," proceeding from one house to another. In Herefordshire the soul cakes were of oatmeal, and any who received one had to reply to the giver: "God have your soul, beens (has beens?) and all."

In Wales poor people spent the day begging for bread. This, a custom within a superstition, was a survival of the Middle Ages when the poor begged bread for the souls of their departed relatives and friends. Down to the middle nineteenth century Whitby, in Yorkshire, made soul mass loaves—small, round loaves which were sold for a farthing each, and bought mostly as presents for children. In Aberdeenshire soul cakes were called "Dirge Loaves," and were presented to visitors.

In the island of St. Kilda a large cake was baked in the form of a triangle, furrowed round.

This thought for the dead is almost world-wide in its application. In Caichi (Ecuador) Indians prepare provisions and set them on a table in the local Catholic church. They become the property of the priest who then says Masses for the dead. After the service, the Indians proceed to the cemetery. There, with pots of Holy Water and burning candles, they prostrate themselves in front of the graves of their ancestors.

Now note, for comparison, how similar is the Festival of the Dead in Cambodia (Indo-China). On the last day of the month Phatrabot (Sept.-Oct.) cakes and sweetmeats are put out. Incense is burned and candles lighted to ancestral shades, who are invited: "Oh, all you our ancestors who are departed, deign to come and eat." A fortnight later tiny boats made of bark are loaded with sweetmeats, coins and smoking incense and, each with a lighted candle, are set floating as the sun goes down. The souls, it is believed, embark in them to return to their own abode. In Cochin-China ancestral spirits are similarly propitiated. Even the Dahomans of West Africa "set a table" on one given day. In Persia, on the five days called Farwardajan, the people put food and drink in the halls of the dead. Thus, savage and civilized remember their dead.

The soul cakes survived in Britain until the late nineteenth century; the day itself is still celebrated by prayers "for the dear departed" in both Roman Catholic and Anglican churches.

Its origin? Like most of these Christian feasts it is a survival of a much earlier pagan feast—in this case the pagan Festival of the Dead. The early Christian Church, unable to suppress it and keep their converts, connived at it, but gave to it a religious turn. It was Odilo, the Abbot of the Cluny Benedictine monastery who, in A.D. 998, ordained that a solemn Mass should be said on 2nd November each year for the dead "who sleep in Christ." That was the start of the Christian festival. Generations before in ancient Egypt, on the 17th of the month of Athyr (corresponding to our 13th-16th November) the dead Osiris was feasted.

ANDREW'S WELL, ST.

To know if a sick person will die of the sickness send a woman with a wooden dish to St. Andrew's Well. If the dish, laid softly on the surface of the water, turns round sun-ways, the patient will recover. If otherwise, the patient will die.

The St. Andrew's Well mentioned is in the village of Shadar, Isle of Lewis. And the superstition of the verdict of the waters was widely held and practised.

In a French version of the romance of Bevis of Hampton, there is an allusion to the pilgrimage on foot to St. Andrew's Well as of equal efficacy to that of Mont St. Michel in Brittany for the cure of certain physical troubles.

ANGELS

The fossil bones of the Saurians, found in Northern Yorkshire, are called Fallen Angels.

The bones are supposed to belong to the angels who were cast out of heaven for their rebellion.

ANIMALS

If fruit trees are planted without a dead animal being buried under their roots they will not bear crops.—General.

Incredible though it may seem this absurd belief was still held in parts of this country as recently as the year 1946. The authors were approached in August of that year by a Middlesex woman who had just purchased a house and was proposing to stock the garden with fruit trees. She had, she said, been assured by a neighbour that the trees would come to no good unless a dead animal was buried under the roots.

The authors' researches suggest that the belief arose not from any superstition, but from the practice, in Derbyshire, of burying dead animals under fruit trees in the orchards. They do not, however, put this forward as an origin, though it may be held that there is some truth in the assertion that the trees might bear better crops from the practice, not from superstition, but from the value of the manure!

See CAT, DOG, HORSE, etc.

ANTS

It is unlucky to destroy a colony of ants.—Cornwall.

When ants are unusually busy, foul weather is at hand.—General country belief.

If you place a piece of tin in a bank of Muryans at a certain age of the moon it will be turned to silver.—Cornish tin miners' belief.

Ants' eggs are an antidote to love.

The Cornish peasants' name for the ant is a muryan. They were held to be the "small people" (fairies) in their state of decay off the earth.

In what way ants' eggs are applied to the person desiring to fall out of love has not, so far as the authors know, been handed down.

APOPLEXY

Place a sharpened hatchet on the threshold of the house of a sufferer from apoplexy, and he will be cured.—Wales.

APOSTLE SPOONS

He was born with a silver spoon in his mouth.—General saying.

In other words his parents, or relatives, were wealthy. The superstition, if superstition it may be called, arose from the ancient custom (15th-16th century) of sponsors at a christening giving spoons as presents to their god-child. These were usually Apostle Spoons, so-called because the figures of the Apostles were chased or carved on the tips of the handles.

Opulent sponsors gave the whole twelve spoons, and *silver* ones at that. Those in middling circumstances gave a lesser number; and the poorer classes aped their wealthy neighbours by giving a single and *metal* spoon.

It is in allusion to this custom that Cranmer professes to be unworthy of being sponsor to the young princess. Shakespeare makes the King reply: "Come, come, my Lord, you'd spare your spoons."

APPLE

Stand in front of a looking-class with an apple. Slice the apple into nine pieces, stick each piece on the point of a knife and hold it over the left shoulder while looking into a mirror. The spectre of your future husband will appear—to take the apple.—General country Hallowe'en belief.

NOTE: A variation is to eat eight slices of the apple and throw the ninth to your expected husband—in the mirror.

Let a girl pare an apple on Hallowe'en and fling the skin over her left shoulder. She will read in the twists the initials of her future husband's name.—General.

To eat an apple without first rubbing it, is to challenge the Evil One.—Surrey superstition.

The authors have for many years followed the last superstition. Not from any superstitious belief, but as a matter of simple hygiene, since the apple while on the tree has been exposed to all the impurities of the air and insects, as well—in modern times—as the spraying with insecticides of a poisonous character. The origin of this superstition would seem to be the sound common sense of some sensible person.

Apples played a large part in Sussex Christmas festivities in the olden days. Single people of either sex fastened each an apple to a string which had, then, to be twirled in front of a hot fire. Whichever apple first fell off, its owner was held to be on the point of getting married. This, it may well be believed, in mixed company caused not a little heartburning. The owner of the last apple to fall was doomed to remain a spinster, or bachelor, for life.

While the origins of the apple twirling and the paring are not known, that of the throwing over the shoulder the parings and reading the twists would seem to have come from the blood-stained smoke of Baal's fire. The oak-wreathed Druids drew conclusions of the future by watching the writhings of their victims, whether animal or human, under their knives, and the way they fell in their death agony. So a less blood-thirsty age deals in apple skins, in the placement of tea-leaves in a cup, or molten lead poured into water to reveal the future by its fallen shape.

It is passing strange that in this country the apple is not associated with fecundity—a superstition that has been held in other hands from earliest times.

APPLE HOWLING
See APPLE TREES.

APPLE PIPS

A maid should take an apple pip, and, naming one of her avowed lovers, put it in the fire. Should the pip make a noise in bursting from the heat, it is a proof of love. If it is consumed without a crack, the avowed lover has no real regard.—Old Suffolk.

Identically the same superstition prevailed in Durham and the Border Counties. The belle of the village could occupy an entire evening in this form of love delineation!

APPLE TREES

If the sun shines through the apple trees on Christmas Day, there will be an abundant crop the following year.—Derbyshire.

To ensure a good apple crop, a piece of toast should be placed in a fork of the biggest tree in the orchard.—Somerset and Cornwall. This rite was supposed to propitiate the spirits which watch over apple trees.

If an apple remains on the tree until the spring, a member of the family owning the tree will die.

Should an apple tree bear at the same time blossom and fruit nearly mature, there will be a death in the family.

The placing of toast in a fork of an apple tree was part of the ceremony of "Wassailing the Apples," observed for many years at Carhampton, near Minehead, Somerset. (It was still preserved up to shortly before the World War of 1939-45). Men of the village formed "Wassail parties," and proceeded to certain orchards, where they were joined by the farmer and his men. These, standing round the trees, sang the old wassail song, the last verse of which ran:

Old apple tree, old apple tree,
We've come to wassail thee.
To bear and to bow apples enow,
Hats full, caps full, three bushel bags full,
Barn floors full, and a little heap under the stairs.

The superstition was followed, also, in Sussex, Devonshire and Cornwall, with the difference, in Cornwall, that the apple crop being intended for cider, that beverage was drunk by the wassaillers, the dregs afterwards being thrown over the trees. The wassail time, in each case, was the Yule-tide season—usually on Twelfth Night. It was known, locally, as apple howling (or "yuling").

At Keston and Wickham, however, similar ceremonies took place during Rogation Week, at which young men met together, and with an outcry of noises ran into orchards, encircled trees, and chanted:

Stand fast root, bear well top;
God send us a yowling sop.
Every twig apple big
Every bough apple enow.

In return for the incantation the men expected money or drink. In the unlikely event of neither being proffered, they returned and anathematized the trees!

Now the origin of all this seems to belong to age-old perambulations of pagans, who made prayers to their gods for the blessing of fruit. We have referred to the local name given to wassailing in Sussex and Devonshire as "apple yuling." The pagans supplicated Eolus (sometimes written Æolus, in Greek and Roman mythology, the God of the Winds) for his favourable blasts. The festival of Eolus was the winter solstice—about 25th December. From Eolus to Yule is a short step.

Hereford, another cider country, has a saying, or it had, that unless the orchards are christened on St. Peter's Day the crop will not be good.

The christening was the pouring of a glass of cider over the apple trees, or the orchard.

Two other superstitions associated with apples are: that apple blossom flowing in Autumn means death to someone in the house of the owner of the tree (this is a Cheshire belief); if a crab apple overhanging a well blossoms out of season there will be more births and marriages than deaths, say the people in Welsh country areas. Lastly, is an old general belief:

A blossom upon the apple tree
when the apples are ripe,
Is a sure termination to somebody's life.

It may be of interest in passing to point out that many German peasants think that the after-birth of a cow must be hung in an apple tree, otherwise the cow will not have a calf next year; and in connection with this should be mentioned an old Yorkshire belief in Cleveland that when a mare foals the placenta must be hung in a thorn tree, or bush, to secure luck with the foal.

See TREE WORSHIP.

APRIL

A cold April gives bread and wine.—Old country belief.

If the first days of April be foggy, it

prognosticates that there will be floods in June.

A cold April was regarded by our country forefathers as luck for farming operations. One of their beliefs was that "A cold April the barn will fill."

Thunder on April the First (All Fools' Day) was welcomed on the principle that

If it thunders on All Fools' Day
It brings good crops of corn and hay.

And, of course, we all know the rhyme that March winds and April showers bring forth May flowers.

APRIL FOOL

On the first day of April,
Hunt the gowk another mile.
              —Scotland.
"April fool . . . April fool.—Everywhere.

Hunting the Gowk represents the more elaborate 1st April custom. It is more common in Scotland, but occasionally prevalent in England. The fooled youth was dispatched with a couplet in a sealed envelope to a particular person. That person, opening the letter, and reading the joke. rewrote it, or merely enclosed it in a fresh envelope, and dispatched the messenger to another address, and so on, *ad infinitum* until the "fool" realized his predicament.

In England the more popular "fooling" was to send a youth for some "pigeon's milk;" to a bookseller for the "History of Eve's Mother," or a left-handed knife from the ironmonger. The vogue has nowadays pretty well died out, modern young people being a little too wide-awake.

The origin? The practice seems to have come to Britain from France, which country took the lead (in 1564) in moving the new year from what is now known as Lady Day (25th March) to the present 1st January. From the earliest period of history people of all nations made a practice of bestowing gifts upon their friends on New Year's Day. As the old New Year's Day, 25th March, fell so often in Holy Week, the Church uniformly postponed the celebrations until the Octave—1st April. When, therefore, New Year's Day was transferred to 1st January, people in France paid mock visits to their friends on 1st April, with the object of fooling them into the belief that that date was still the first day of the new year. That is the usually accepted origin.

But an immemorial custom among the Hindus at the Huli Festival (held about the same time of the year—1st April) was to send people on errands that were bound to end in disappointment. Even before this was the ancient practice of celebrating with rites and merriment the period of the Vernal Equinox on the day when the new year of Persia anciently began.

Readers may be interested in the story of the most tragic April Fooling of any time—the rape of the Sabines by the Romans. The latter, finding that they could not obtain women from their neighbours by peaceful addresses, made use of stratagem. They initiated certain games to be performed in the beginning of April (according to the Roman calendar) in honour of Neptune. Upon receiving notice of the games, the bordering inhabitants flocked to Rome to see the celebrations, whereupon the Romans went out into the country, seized a great number of the Sabine virgins, and ravished them.

APRON

For a fisherman to meet a woman wearing a white apron as he is walking to his ship to go to sea will bring bad luck during the voyage.

The ill-luck can, however, be averted if the fisherman returns home, and waits for one tide.

This was a widely held superstition along the Yorkshire coast; and at such times as tides were favourable, and smacks and trawlers were like to put out, fisherwives eschewed white aprons.

The suggestion still pertains in certain villages of the county.

ARCHES

Throughout the superstition practices of almost every country, use of an arch is universal. In Britain the passing of a child, or person, under an arch of brambles, was regarded (together with certain words of ritual) as a certain cure for whooping cough, blackheads, boils, and rheumatism, among other diseases.

A child with rickets was passed through a split trunk of an elder or ash tree, kept open with a wedge, forming, again, an arch. For whooping cough in a child, another remedy was to pass the child underneath the belly of an ass, once more the arch theory.

Now compare the superstitions of, first, Bulgaria, where when whooping cough is prevalent in a village, an old woman will scrape the earth from under a willow tree, after which, all the children creep through the opening thus made. In the Lake Nyassa country, when sickness is rife, sufferers crawl through an arch formed by bending a branch down and inserting the free end in the ground.

In Uganda, a tree stem is split and the split held open by the Medicine Man while the sick person steps through. There are certain directions as to clothes, but it is the arch which is the main theory of the operation.

In France, in Germany, among the Ovambo of South-West Africa, the arch is paramount. Highlanders of Strathspey used to force all their sheep and cattle through an arch of rowan tree, on All Saints' Day, and Beltane. In Oldenburg, a cow giving little or no milk is passed through a hole made by a branch.

The instances can be multiplied in a hundred countries. When the Kayans of Borneo are returning from a journey which has been dogged by ill-luck, they fashion an archway of boughs, light a fire under it, and pass through in single file.

What is the origin which made the arch so universally accepted a safeguard? The authors suggest that it was, in all probability, the acceptance of the idea that all illness is an evil spirit, pursuing the sufferer; and that the arch was what a door has become to-day—something that can shut out a pursuer. Thus, to pass through the arch, having made certain ritual preparations beforehand, is to give the slip to the dangerous pursuer and reach sanctuary on the other side.

ARVALS

Come, bring my jerkin, Tubb, I'll
be to the Arvil
Yon man's dead seny scoun, it makes
me marvil.

The Arval was a thin, light and sweet cake (called Arval bread) distributed in the North of England at funerals—in other words, a funeral loaf. It was sometimes distributed to the poor by the relatives of the deceased; but its real reason was to sustain the friends and relatives of the dead to whom the corpse was exposed, as Hazlitt puts it, "to exculpate the heir and those entitled to the possessions of the deceased from fines and mulcts to the Lord of the Manor, and *from all accusations of having used violence;* so that the persons then convened might avouch that the person died fairly and without any personal injury." The people of the older days were a suspicious lot.

NOTE: Arthel (corrupted to Arval) is a British word. In Wales it was written Arddel. It signified, according to Doctor Davies's dictionary, asserere, "to avouch."

Origin: The origin of these funeral feasts has been stated to be the Roman occupation of Britain. The authors question the likelihood, since the Roman Arvals were ceremonies intended to ensure the fertility of the soil, and particularly in relation to the corn crops, the *Fratres Arvales* (Roman Brethren of the Ploughed Fields) being a college of priests whose business it was to perform the rites deemed necessary for the growth of the corn.

On the other hand, Cecrops, the mythical founder of, and first King of, Athens, is said to have instituted funeral feasts for the purpose of renewing decayed friendships among old friends. Whether there exists any connection directly between the funeral feasts of Cecrops and the arvals of the North Country of Britain, history has failed to show.

A Northern Britain funeral feast of nearer affinity to Cecrops is that more recent than the Arvals, known as "buryin' him' w' ham."

ASCENSION DAY

If it rains on Ascension Day, though never so little, it foretells a scarcity that year, and sickness, particularly among cattle.

If it be fair, then, to the contrary, there will be pleasant weather, mostly till Michaelmas.—Weather superstition, generally held.

The figure of a lamb appears in the sky in the East on this day.—Old Devonshire superstition.

To hang an egg laid on Ascension Day in the roof of your house preserves the house from all harm.—Rife in the early sixteenth century throughout Britain.

If work is continued on Ascension Day, an accident will occur.—Superstition once widely held in Bangor (Wales) and other areas.

Superstition dies hard; but on two occasions the management of Lord Penrhyn's slate quarries, near Bangor, succeeded in overcoming the belief that there would be accidents if work continued in the quarries on Ascension Day. But for two years in succession an accident *did* occur. The holiday was then resumed at the insistence of the workmen. It is not, of course, persisted in in these more enlightened times.

The belief that the figure of a lamb

appears in the sky in the East on this morning appears to have been prevalent mostly in the Exeter area of Devonshire. It was so deeply rooted that (says an authority of the time): It hath frequently resisted, even in intelligent minds, force of the strongest argument."

It was the custom of many villages around Exeter to "Hail the Lamb" on Ascension morning, expeditions being made at dawn to a high spot where the sky was unobstructed by trees.

An Ascension Day superstition in the villages near York in the early nineteenth century was for children to lay rushes (or "sehhs") on their doorsteps. It is of passing interest to note that in Cologne (Germany) in pre-Reformation days, the streets on this day were strewn with short twigs of fir branches and other green things for an annual procession.

At Tissington, Derbyshire, the inhabitants are wont to dress their healing well on this day. It seems on a par with the practice in parts of Switzerland, where girls climb the towers of their churches and ring all the bells in order to ensure a good harvest of flax. The girl who swings her bell the highest will get the longest sheaf of flax.

In Sicily Ascension Day was believed to hold marvellous charms of healing. People who suffered with goitre gathered at midnight to bite the bark from the trunk of a peach tree. The biting had to be done at the moment that the clocks struck midnight. The malady, it was believed, was passed into the sap of the tree, and the subsequent behaviour of the tree—whether its leaves withered or not—was a guide to whether the patient was to be cured or not.

See GOITRE, WELLS.

ASHEN FAGGOT, THE

Since time immemorial it has been a Christmas Eve custom in Somerset and Devon to "burn the Ashen Faggot," in local inns and taverns, as in King Alfred's time.

Custom ordains that the faggot—it must be of ash wood—should be hooped round with nine bands of the same wood. Each time a band cracks with the heat, the *watching* company regale themselves with a mixture of cider and egg. In 1945, and the five years previous, the egg was mostly missing.

A superstition attached to it was that nine of the unmarried company might each choose a hoop band. The band which first bursts indicated that whoever had chosen it would be the first to be married. These last two points—the refreshment and the marriage—may account for the emphasis laid on the necessity for *watching* the faggot during the burning. The breaking of each band was the signal for a fresh toast.

As for the origin: Legend has it that the Blessed Virgin, being cold in the scanty shelter of a stable on the first Christmas Eve, St. Joseph collected a bundle of sticks to make a fire, and chose ash twigs because he knew they were the only green ones that would burn. This, however, has nothing to do with Devon or Somerset; and local Somerset tradition says that King Alfred's men, being cold and weary on the night before the battle of Ethandune, were overjoyed at finding ash, common in that particular neighbourhood, as it would burn easily, although green. They accordingly cut and tied faggots of ash, and burned them.

ASHES

Before going to bed on New Year's Eve spread the ashes of the raked-out fire smoothly over the floor. Should the toes of a footprint next morning be seen pointing to the door a member of the household will die during the year; should the toe be pointing away from the door, there will be an addition to the family.—Manx uplands.

Ashes from the May Beltane fires, placed in a person's shoes, will protect the wearer from great sorrow or woe.—Wales.

From the earliest times the charm of ashes has been a powerful one. People of all nations, civilized and savage, have seen in them the germ of fertility.

Not only were the ashes of more or less sacred fires gathered and mixed with the seed at sowing—this was a practice in many parts of Britain, at the great fire festivals—but they were also scattered on the fields after the seeds had been planted, and when it was growing.

The Hallowe'en and Midsummer Fires of England and Scotland in earlier days were used for this purpose.

In the Isle of Man on Midsummer Eve fires were lighted in the villages, to the windward of the fields, in order that the smoke and ashes might blow over the crops and magnify them.

In the North of England, particularly in Northumberland, down to the middle of the nineteenth century, when the Midsummer Fires were lit, villagers ignited torches at the blaze, and with them made a circuit of their crops, letting the smoke and the ash from the torch fertilize their lands and crops.

Braemar Highlanders performed the same evolutions at the time of the Hallowe'en fires, the lighted torches ensuring, they believed, the fertility of the crops. In other parts of Scotland ashes from the fires were scattered round the borders of the fields, a symbolic scattering on the crops.

In most of the Catholic countries of Europe, ashes of the Easter bonfires were mixed with ashes from the consecrated palms and then mixed again with the seed to be sown for the next harvest.

In Germany the ashes of the bonfires were mixed with the drink of animals in order to make the animals thrive. In Auvergne on the first Sunday in Lent bonfires were kindled and the ashes were scattered by villagers across their fields and also placed in fowl nests, in order that there should be ensured good crops of corn and eggs.

In Poitou, the ashes of the great bon-fires were regarded by the peasants as a preservative from thunder and lightning damage; and the same belief was held in parts of Wales and England. In India ashes of bonfires were regarded as talismans against devils and demons. It should be emphasised, too, that much of the ash sprinkling and the use of ashes in other ways in Scotland was thus applied; if scattered on the land, it was held to protect the land from the ill-wishing of witches.

So much for the civilized races; what of the savage? It was the custom of some of the Orinoco tribes of Indians to disinter after a year the bones of a dead tribesman, burn them and scatter the ashes to the winds. It was held by them that the ashes thus scattered turned to rain and thus refreshed and fertilized the lands of the family.

The Marinios of Bechuana tribes each year sacrificed a human being to their crops. The preference was for a short, stout man. He was taken to the fields where he was attacked and killed amongst the wheat. After his blood had coagulated in the heat of the sun, it was burnt, together with the frontal bone and the brain and some of the flesh, and the ashes scattered over the land to fertilize it. The remainder of the body was eaten.

Indians of the Vancouver Island believed that the ashes of wasps rubbed on the faces of warriors before they went into battle made them as pugnacious as wasps. They believed, too, that the ashes of flies, given internally to their women, made them as prolific as flies.

Now, where did all this begin? Whence came this ritual of ashes as a fertilizer for the fruits of the earth?

On the 15th of April each year the chief Roman Vestal sacrificed pregnant cows to the Earth Goddess. Unborn calves were torn from their mothers' wombs, burnt, and the ashes kept and scattered at the shepherds' festival of the Parilia. The sacrifice was a fertility charm designed to quicken both the seed in the ground and the seed in the wombs of cows and ewes. Was this the origin?

Then how did it come to the tribes of Bechuana, or the Orinoco? Not from the Romans, who never went there.

ASH LEAVES

To find an even ash will mean good luck.—General.

A sprig of ash (with the triple leaves) worn on the breast will give prophetic dreams.—Wales.

A garter made from the green bark of the mountain ash is a charm against witches and the devil.—Wales.

If you catch a mouse and shut it alive in a hole in a pollard ash, you will shut up your bad luck.

The failure of the crop of ash keys portends a death in the Royal family within a year.—General.

An even ash is the name given to an ash leaf with an even number of leaflets. It should be placed at once in the button-hole, or worn in the hat. Mountain ash is the name for rowan (q.v.).

Ash keys are the winged seeds of the ash. In connection with the superstition quoted above, it may be noted that there were no ash keys in the year in which Charles I was beheaded.

Ash leaves in superstition were another love delineation. The method was for a maiden to take an ash leaf with even fronds (if she was fortunate enough to find one), and recite the lines:

Even ash, I pluck thee.
In my bosom I put thee.
Hoping this night my true love to see.
Not in his vest, not in his best,
But in the clothes he wears every day.

On putting the ash leaf under her pillow that night she might expect to dream of her future husband. This was rife as a superstition in Yorkshire.

ASH SAP

To prevent witches, fairies and other imps of darkness from attacking a new-born baby, give ash sap to the child.—Scottish Highlands.

Rowan ash and red thread, keep the Devils frae their speed.—Scottish.

It is unlucky for herdsmen to carry a stick not made from ash.

There was a sound reason for the Scottish Highland custom of giving ash sap to newly-born babies, apart from the superstitions of aid against witch-craft. Ash sap acts as a powerful, but harmless, astringent. However, the belief is not of the antiseptic results, but that, should the child not be given the sap of the ash, fairies might "change" it, or, possibly, steal it altogether.

The superstition of the ash herding stick (it was especially prevalent in the district of Buchan, Aberdeenshire) was that ash had the magic of being *sure* not to strike the cattle in a vital place when thrown at them, which a stick of any other kind of wood *might* do.

In passing, it might be noted that in the same areas it was the practice of farmers' wives to tie a piece of red worsted thread round the tails of their cows before they were first turned out to grass in the spring. By so doing, it was held that the cows were protected from the Evil Eye, or from being "elf shot" by fairies, etc. Hence the couplet quoted above.

ASH TREE

Bury the first parings of a child's nails under an ash tree, and the child will turn out a fine singer.—West Northumberland.

Rub your warts with a piece of bacon, cut a slit in the bark of an ash tree, and slip the bacon under the bark. The warts will disappear from your hand, and reappear as knobs, or excrescences on the bark of the tree.—Cheshire.

Pass a child with rickets or a rupture through a cleft ash tree, and a cure is certain.—General belief.

The cleft ash tree as a cure for rickets or rupture, particularly the latter, was a superstition universal in this country. The operation was carried out as follows:

A young ash sapling was split, longitudinally, for the space of some six feet, and held open by wedges. The ruptured child was then passed, naked, through the fissure, three times (at least). The time of the passing had to be sunrise.

The ceremony performed, the wedges were taken out, and the tree bound up. Clay and mud were plastered over the lines of the fissure. It was held that as the cleft in the tree closed and healed up, so would the rupture in the child also close and heal. If, however, the tree remained rifted, and did not heal, the rupture would remain with the child.

There was a more sinister side to the superstition—that should the tree die, the child, also, would die. And this was stated to hold good all through life; so that, should the tree die when the child had grown to manhood, the rupture of which he was cured as a child would return, and mortification and death would ensue.

It sounds incredible, but as late as the second half of the enlightened nineteenth century, this remedy for rupture was in common use in a number of places in Sussex. This county had a more elaborate ritual than other places. It was held, for instance, that the remedy would not be effective unless the ash was sound at heart, and was split with an axe. The child, too, had to be passed through the cleft three times three (i.e., nine times) on every morning for nine successive days, and must have been attended by nine persons, each one of whom, in turn, "passed" the child.

There stood for many years an ash tree on the road from Hockley House to Birmingham, on the side of Shirley Heath, which was a Mecca for this cure. Another tree was on a farm nearby, of which the owner, one Chillingworth, would not permit a branch to be touched with the lopping axe, since his son had been passed through it when a year old, and it was held that the life of that son depended on the life of the tree. The son at this time was nearly forty years of age.

In the early nineteenth century a row of ashes were standing in a farmyard near the middle of the village of Selborne. They were each marked by long seams and cicatrices down their sides, the result of the clefts made for this "passing" of children.

In Wales, the superstition ordained that the tree should be a "maiden" (i.e., one that had never been lopped or cut); that the split should be made east and west; that the child should be passed through head foremost by a maiden, and taken out at the other side by a boy.

In parts of Surrey a holly tree was sometimes used instead of an ash; and in parts of Wales an oak tree.

What psychological explanation can be given of the fact that among the M'Bengas of Western Africa, when two children are born on the same day, the villagers plant, and dance round, two trees, and hold that, henceforth, the life of the children are bound up with the trees? If one of the trees withers, or dies, they are sure that the child will die.

The Wajagga, of East Africa, and certain groups in Sierra Leone hold a similar belief. The Maoris of New Zealand plant a sapling over the spot where the navel string of a child is buried; and hold that as the tree grows or withers so will the child prosper or die.

In the Canton of Aargau, Switzerland, an apple tree was of old planted for a boy, and a pear tree for a girl—and were said to have the same properties of life and death.

NOTE: It is worth remembering that the Yggdrasil, the world tree of Scandinavian mythology, was an ash.

ASH WEDNESDAY

Wherever the wind lies on Ash Wednesday, it continues throughout Lent.—Norfolk.

"Ye shall begyn your faste upon Ashe Wednesday. That daye must ye come to Holy Churche and take ashes of the priestes hondes, and thinke on the wordes well that he sayeth over hedes."

The religious aspect of Ash Wednesday has almost entirely divested the day of any superstitions or customs except those of the laying on of ashes and the sackcloth of repentance.

Whatever may be the custom to-day in such churches (mostly Roman Catholic) where ashes are still used in the rite, in the olden days the ashes were made from the branches of brushwood or the palms consecrated the year before. They were cleaned, dried and sifted for this purpose.

A still more ancient custom is referred to by Lord North in his *Forest of Varieties* (1645): "The ancient discipline of sackcloth and ashes, on Ash Wednesday is at present supplied in our church by reading publicly on this day the curses denounced against unrepentant sinners, when the people are directed to repeat an Amen at the end of each malediction." It is recorded that many people on this day kept away from church because of the point of view that the unrepentant sinners they may be called upon to curse were, more often than not, their own neighbours.

On Ash Wednesday morning at Henfield (Sussex) children used to bring to school twigs from ash trees. Those who did not do so were liable to be pinched by their fellows. Further, the twig had to show no white; the place where it was broken off, therefore, had to be dirtied or inked over. Nor was any white on the dress to be shown—for instance, the edge of a handkerchief. There were similar rules and regulations at Selmestone, and in an Oxfordshire village.

ASPARAGUS

It is unlucky not to leave always one stem of asparagus in the bed to blossom.

We can believe it—for the seeds thus lost would have to be purchased.

ASPEN TREE

To cure a fever, insert the parings of the patient's nails into an aspen tree, and then plaster up the hole to prevent the fever getting out again.

The shivering of the aspen tree leaves is in horror at the memory of the Crucifixion.

Both these superstitions were generally held.

The sealing of nail parings of an ill person in the aspen is part and parcel of one of the most widely held superstitions—that evil and illness could be transferred to objects animate and inanimate. At all times and in all races, Pagan and Christian, this has been rife and constitutes a strange affinity of fear between all peoples. Many more instances will be found in this volume.

It was held in rural Britain that the aspen tree was the more valuable to which to transfer the fever, because of the similarity of the trembling of a person stricken with fever, to the trembling of the leaves of this particular tree. The operation of transferring the fever had to be carried out in the dead of night.

The trembling of the aspen leaves has, itself, a place in superstition. It is held that the Cross of Christ was made from aspen wood and that "from that time the boughs of the aspen have been filled with horror, and have trembled unceasingly."

The fact is that the construction of the foliage of the aspen, with its broad leaf placed upon a long stalk so flexible as scarcely to be able to support the leaf upright, makes it particularly sensitive to even the lightest of breezes.

The aspen tree was used in Cheshire

for the curing of warts. The warts had to be rubbed with a piece of bacon, and the bacon afterwards put into a slit in the bark of the tree. The warts would disappear from your hands, only to reappear in the shape of rough knobs on the bark of the tree.

ASS

Hairs taken from the black cross on the shoulders of an ass will cure the whooping cough.—Common superstition as late as the middle nineteenth century.

Three hairs were deemed essential for the charm to work; and they had to be hung in a muslin bag round the neck of the sufferer. The animal from whom the hairs were taken was declared never to be of any use afterwards, however, and considerable difficulty was, therefore, experienced in obtaining the hairs. Also, it was essential that the sex of the animal should be the opposite to that of the sufferer.

The origin of the superstition lies, of course, in the fact that the ass was regarded as a sacred animal "since it held the honour of bearing our Saviour on its back." The cross is said to be the signal honour accorded to the animal, impressed on it by Jesus.

The ass is popularly supposed to be deaf to music. The origin of this lies in the giving by Apollo of the ears of an ass to Midas because he (Midas) preferred the piping of Pan to the music of Apollo's lute.

See WHOOPING COUGH.

ASTHMA

Collect spiders' webs. Roll them into a ball in the palms of the hand and swallow them. The asthma will be cured.—Cornwall.

A sixteenth century superstition widespread over the country was that asthma could be cured by eating raw cat's meat.

A century later, the belief was held that if a sufferer lived for a fortnight on boiled carrots, his asthma would disappear.

During the Battle of Britain, in the world war, 1939-45, it was almost as widely held that a diet of raw carrots enabled airmen to see in the dark. The dark days of superstitious belief are not by any means ended, yet, in Britain.

BABY

On the birth of a baby a knife should be placed under the door-sill of the house, lest the little newcomer be stricken with the Evil Eye.—Scotland.

To rock a cradle with the baby not in it is to prognosticate its early death.—General.

Spit upon a new-born baby, and you will bring it luck.—Ireland.

Luck will attend a baby's future, if it is rubbed all over with lard.

If a child is born feet first it will be lamed in an accident before manhood, unless bay leaves are rubbed on the legs within a few hours of birth.

If a baby is allowed to see itself in a looking-glass before it is some months old, it will die before the year is out, or develop the childish complaint, rickets.

To cut a baby's nails before it is a year old will make it grow up a thief.—General rural superstition in all parts of Britain even in the present century.

More widespread in Scotland and the Border counties than anywhere else in Britain was the belief in witches, and their power to change babies and people and to present themselves in changed form to the harm of folks who had done anything to annoy them. The knife under the door-sill of a house in which a baby has been born was done in the belief that a witch cannot cross iron or steel, and, therefore, could not get into the house so guarded.

There were, in the Dark Days, many superstitions connected with babies. Mention has been made above of the cutting of a baby's nails, lest it grows up into a thief. The superstition is by no means dead. There are thousands of homes in the rural parts of Britain to-day where the belief still survives, and a baby's nails are bitten off, never cut.

It was the custom of the superstitious in North Argyllshire to open every lock in the house at childbirth. This was supposed to aid the delivery of the child. In the days of Ancient Rome a Roman mother was given a key with the same end in view. The magician, or witch-doctor, of the Hos tribe of Togoland binds a mother about to be delivered with thongs of creeper. He then unties the knots, saying, "I will now open you." This guarantees easy delivery. Thus, in native Paganism, in the older civilization of Rome, and in Christianized Scotland reigned a superstition alike in its beliefs.

It was the custom in East Yorkshire—and still is in some of the more remote parts—to present the baby when it first visits any house, with a box (or bundle) of matches, an egg, some salt in a piece of paper, and a piece of money. By so doing it is ensured that the child throughout its life shall never lack light, food, friendship, or money. Another view of these gifts, current in other parts of the country, is that the egg promises immortality (this must be a survival of the Mundane Egg), the salt salubrity of mind and body, the bread a promise of all things needful through life, and the matches to light its way to Heaven.

Throughout childhood, when the child puts on a new article of outside dress, the Yorkshire custom was to place a small sum of money to "hansel" the dress in one of the pockets. An additional sum was given by friends to whom the dress was shown. Such money was saved in a small "thrift-box" which was stood on the mantelpiece, until enough had accumulated to purchase something useful. Yorkshire folk were not a thrifty race for nothing!

In Plymouth district, it is still believed that if you tickle a baby's feet it will make the child stammer in later years.

To ensure that a baby thrived in Wales, it was the custom and the belief that the water in which the infant was washed for the first three months of its life must be thrown under a green tree.

It was also held if a child in its cradle did not look up at one, it would grow into a deceitful man, or woman.

See BIRTH.

BACHELOR'S BUTTON

If a bachelor's button grows in a man's pocket, he will marry his sweetheart.—General.

The bachelor's button of this love delineation is not the modern press-on button for the trousers, but the little plant and flower so popular in cottage gardens. A small plant is plucked by the doubtful lover, and placed in a pocket of his garments. Should the plant not grow, the searcher after knowledge would soon be looking for another sweetheart.

A like superstition existed among the young women of the day; they carried the bachelor's buttons under their aprons. Reference is made to this custom in *Quip*, by Greve (1502): "Therebye I saw the batchelors butons, whose vertue is to make wanton maidens weepe, when they have worne it forty weekes under their aprons for a favour."

BACK

If you mend your clothes on your back, You will live much money to lack.
—General.

BADGER

To carry a badger's tooth in your pocket will bring you good luck at cards.—Devonshire.

BAKER'S DOZEN

Twelve for the Baker, and one for the Devil.

There is no superstition of the Devil attached to this, so far as the authors can discover. On the other hand the explanation of the thirteen to a dozen, "a baker's dozen," is the hum-drum one resulting from the imposition of a heavy penalty for short weight when bread was sold by the lb. loaf. To avoid such short weight—bread having a habit of shrinking—an extra loaf was given to all baker's roundsmen and shops with each dozen loaves. This was called the unbread and was cut up to add to any loaf which fell short of the 1 lb. or 2 lb.

BAKING

If the "withe" or band of the faggot is burned, the oven will not get hot, and the bread will not bake.—Sussex.

It is necessary to explain, in connection with the above, that the baking ovens of the olden days, and as late as fifty years ago, were generally stone-bottomed, and were heated by burning wood in them. The wood commonly used was a large faggot of sticks, fastened or bound with a twisted branch. This was the "withe" of the Sussex superstition.

When sufficient wood has been burned to make the oven hot enough for baking, the ashes were swept out, and the dough-cakes placed inside; the door was closed, and was not again opened until the bread was well baked.

It may be noted that many country folk still bake their own bread in this way; and no sweeter bread can be tasted.

BALDNESS

Anoint the bald patches on your head with goose dung, and the hair will grow again.

BALLS

To hold three balls in the hand while serving at tennis will bring bad luck to one of the players.

Go out with a golf ball without unwrapping the paper covering, and you will have a bad round.

The tennis ball fetish has the advantage of being a modern superstition. And the authors once saw it cause a moment or two of unpleasantness between two tennis "stars" in a Riviera tournament.

True? . . . Of course it is true! One of the players is bound to lose!

BANNS

Should a bride-to-be attend church and hear her own banns of marriage read out, she will run the risk of having her children born deaf and dumb.— Leeds and the North.

BAPTISM

Children never thrive until they are baptized.—North.

If a child does not cry at its baptism it will be too good to live.—Northumberland, East Yorkshire.

If a boy and a girl are brought to the font together and the girl is first christened, the boy will be condemned to bear through life a smooth and beardless face, while the girl will bear the adornments he lacks.—North and West England.

A child's cry at baptism is the voice of the evil spirit being driven out by the holy water.—North Country.

In contrast to the second of the superstitions quoted above is another North Country version that the cry of a child at baptism is the voice of the Evil Spirit being driven out by the Holy Water!

Custom and superstition connected with baptism were legion. It was generally held that a child should wear a christening cap, and that this cap should afterwards be worn continuously for twelve weeks. The christening water must never be wiped from the face, but allowed to dry.

In Scotland it was held most urgently that the child shoud be baptized as soon as possible after birth, before the fairies carried off or injured it. One method, however, of insuring the safety of the child from the fairies was by placing over the child an article of its father's wearing apparel. In this connection there is a story of a Selkirk shepherd's wife. It tells how she was lying in bed with her newly born babe when she suddenly heard talking and laughing going on in the next room. She recognized at once that it came from the fairies who were even then making a wax substitute for her baby, which they proposed to spirit away. At once, the mother seized her husband's waistcoat from the head of the bed, and flung it over the child. There was a scream from the fairies: "Auld Luckie has cheated us o' our bairnie." Then something fell down the chimney, and the mother, turning towards it, saw a wax figure in the likeness of her baby, and stuck full of pins, lying on the hearth.

It is interesting to note how widespread, and over how many centuries is this belief in the peril to newly born children from evil spirits. Danish mothers of the same time as the above, guarded their unbaptized children by placing in the cradle or over the doors of the house garlic, bread, salt and a piece of steel. (Notice how, in Denmark, the steel to keep away witches ruled.) German mothers placed horehound or snapdragon (Orant is the German name), black cumin, blue marjoram, a right shirt-sleeve and a black, left stocking. Then the fairies (Nickerts in German) could not injure the child.

The Greeks of ancient times took the greatest care never to leave a child alone during the first eight days of its life. Not until the expiry of eight days from birth would the Greek church baptize a child.

Both in Yorkshire and Northumberland baptism was regarded as affecting a child physically; and a sickly or puling babe was looked upon with suspicion as being unbaptized. "Children never thrive until they are baptized" was an old North Country saying; and many are the "authenticated" instances given of children in a weak state of health who have grown strong after baptism. This is probably the origin of the belief. The children would probably have grown out of their infant weakness just as much without the Sacrament.

In Northumberland it was regarded as essential—and it still is—that a child should wear the christening cap for the remainder of the day and night. Mr. W. Henderson, an authority of folk-lore in the northern counties, recalls how a clergyman friend of his, conducting a baptism, was greeted with loud murmurings from the friends and relations of a child because he applied so much water that the cap had to be taken off and dried.

The superstition held sway in East Yorkshire that the baby's face must never be wiped dry of the water, which was left to evaporate. Furthermore it was the custom, on which the prosperity of the child might depend, for the christening party on leaving the church to partake of a feast—the richer the parents and friends of the child, the greater the feast. The feast was followed by an abundance of drink; and in the olden days the baptismal party usually ended up in a drunken orgy. It was, in fact, this baptismal party that is the origin of the popular colloquialism of to-day, "Wetting the baby's head."

A superstition in connection with baptism in the Border Counties, alleged that anyone stepping on the grave of a still-born or unbaptized child subjected himself to the fatal disease of the Grave Merels, or Grave Scab. This complaint came on with trembling of the limbs and hard breathing, until, at last, the skin burned as if touched with a hot iron.

There was, however, a remedy. It lay in wearing a sack prepared thusly: The lint must be grown in a field which shall be manured from a farmyard heap that has not been disturbed for forty years. It must be spun by old Habbitrot, Queen of Spinsters. It must be bleached by an honest bleacher in an honest miller's milldam and sewed by an honest tailor.

See CHRISTENING, COUVADE.

BARNACLE
A barnacle broken off from a ship turns into a Solan goose.—Seamen's belief.

Of this superstition Marston, in "The Malcontents" (1604), wrote:
Like yon Scotch barnacle, now a block.
Instantly a worm, and presently a great goose.
NOTE: A Solan goose is a large marine bird which nests only in a few localities in the British Isles, e.g., on Ailsa Craig, and the Bass Rock. It belongs to the same sub-order as the cormorant.

Geraldus Cambrenis also repeating the superstition—a guide to its antiquity —wrote: "Who can marvel that this can be so? When our first parents were made of mud, can we be surprised that a bird should be born of a tree?" The "tree" is, of course, a reference to the timbers of which ships in his day were built.

BATS
Bats coming out of their holes quickly after sunset, and sporting themselves in the open air, premonstrates fair and calm weather.

An old Scottish superstition stated that if the bat is observed, while flying,

to rise and then descend again earthwards, you may know that the witches' hour is come, the hour in which they have power over every human being under the sun who is not specially shielded from their influence.

This is an unusual superstition, and confined to Scotland, for it is the only instance of bats being associated with humans in Britain. Now, the natives of Tendo, on the Gold Coast, hold that the flocks of bats which, each evening, leave the island for the river mouth are the souls of the dead who retire to the holy isle and are bound to present themselves each evening at the abode of Tano, the good fetish who dwells by the river of that name. And the Wotjobaluk tribe of south-east Australia held that the life of a bat was the life of a man, and if it was killed the life of a man was also shortened. A similar belief obtained in Scotland and the north country in regard to hares. Witches were supposed to transform themselves into hares, and if a hare was shot or wounded, the witch would be found either dead or suffering from a wound. In that way in Britain were many supposed witches traced.

BAY TREE
If bay leaves, thrown into the fire, crack violently, it is a sign of good fortune; if they burn without noise you will be unlucky.

Bay leaves placed under the pillow will give you pleasant dreams.

If bay leaves wither on a tree, it is an omen of death in the family.

Shakespeare refers to the last superstition as rife in his day. In *Richard II*, appears:
'Tis thought the King is dead; we will not stay.
The bay trees in our country are all withered.

From the time of Pliny it has been held that the bay tree was never struck by lightning. The Roman emperor Tiberius always crowned himself with bay leaves during a thunderstorm.

The bay was largely used at funerals in Britain in olden days, in the belief that it was an emblem of the resurrection. This idea was probably brought into being by Sir Thomas Browne who stated that when seemingly dead the bay will revive from the roots and its dry leaves resume their wonted vitality.

BEAM
No one can die comfortably under a cross-beam of a house.—Somersetshire.

It was the practice to remove the bed of the dying person from under the cross-beam.

There are traces of this superstition in other areas, notably in the far north of Scotland and in parts of the north of England.

The same belief was held of a person dying in a bed set crossways to the length of the flooring boards They died hard that way, so it was said, and it was the practice to move the bed so that it ran parallel with the floor boards.

See DEATH.

BEANS

If, in a row of beans, one should come up white instead of green, there will be a death in the family within a year.—Devonshire.

Kidney beans will not grow unless planted on the third of May.—Devon and Somerset borders.

Accidents occur more frequently when the broad bean is in flower.—East Midlands.

Broad bean flowers contain the souls of the departed.—Yorkshire.

Flowers of the broad bean in the north of England have always been associated with death. In other lands they are associated more with the expulsion of devils and demons. On the last night of the year in Japan there was observed in most houses the ceremony of "exorcism of the evil spirit." For this the head of the household, clad in his ceremonial robes, scattered roasted beans on a mat with the remark: "Go forth demons; come in riches."

For very many years in Devonshire and Somerset the superstition of the day for planting beans, mentioned above, was observed. To plant kidney beans on any other day was held to be flying in the face of providence.

There was a fairly general superstition on Midsummer Eve of taking three broad beans. One was left in its skin, one was half-peeled, and the third peeled outright. These were then hidden and searched for. According to which of the three the searchers found was he made cognizant of his future—whether he would be rich, well off or poverty-stricken. Curiously enough, an exactly similar custom was prevalent in the Azores.

See ACCIDENTS.

BEATING THE BOUNDS
(On or about Ascension Day)

This is as much a superstition as a custom of great antiquity. Moreover, it is observed to-day in England with almost the same ceremony as in the ancient days. On Ascension Day, in many parishes, the minister, and accompanied by churchwardens and parishioners "perambulate the boundaries of the parish to keep them in remembrance." Also the custom, and this is the "superstition" part, is to deprecate the vengeance of God, and beg a blessing out of the fruits of the earth.

The process of "remembering the boundaries" varied. In the City of London boys, provided with wands, belaboured the walls and doorways at the edge of the boundary. In country parishes, the boys were taken to the boundaries, and there whipped with wands, thus to impress upon their memory the boundaries. It must be remembered that boundaries were not legally marked out in those days. The boundaries were carried from one generation to another by memory.

In various parts of the country, the beating gives way to "bumping" persons on the boundaries or bounds.

In the Isle of Man it is the custom to pronounce openly the curse set down in Deut. xxvii, 17: "Cursed is he that removeth his neighbour's land mark." It is usual too, when any spot at the boundary over which there is a dispute, or likelihood of dispute, to lay hold of the young lad and wring his ears most unmercifully, so that in after years, when an old man, he should remember the wringing and his wits would be sharpened so that he would remember the parish boundary.

As for the origin, it is claimed by some that it is an imitation of the Pagan feast in Terminalia, dedicated to the God Terminus, the guardian who keeps landmarks, and the keeper of peace among men. The authors of this volume doubt it. We find no incident or any other reference, or custom of Terminus in this country. The possibility is that the custom of going round the boundaries belongs properly to the days when villages and towns in this country were walled, and stockaded, and the visit paid was to ensure that the boundaries were safe.

See ASCENSION DAY.

BED

If three people take part in the making-up of a bed, there is sure to be a death in the house within a year.—Oxfordshire.

To ward off bed-sores, place two buckets of fresh spring water under the bed each day.—Midlands.

If you get out of the bed by the opposite side to that you got in, bad luck will be yours.—General.

To get out of bed on the wrong side means that you will have a bad day.—General.

No mention seems to be made of which is the right or wrong side of the bed for rising; unless the two superstitions quoted are taken in conjunction, in which case the "wrong" side is the opposite to that over which you climbed in on retiring.

It is possible, however, that the wrong side means the side which through many centuries has been regarded as bad, or evil, or unfortunate—the left side; the left having always been associated with the Evil One.

BEDROOM

To place cold boiled water in your bedroom is defying the Devil, and will bring bad luck.

To sweep out a bedroom before a guest has departed an hour will bring bad luck to a friend of the family.

Probably the origin of this is the likelihood, in the days when it was coined, of the guest returning. Travel was an uncertain adventure sixty or more years ago in the rural areas. This superstition ruled mostly among servants of country houses of the gentry.

Curiously enough, it has only one counterpart—in Japan the custom still holds—or did until the World War, 1939-45.

The reason for the cold boiled water "jinn" was told to the authors as:

Boiled water will not freeze, and if the devil wants it to freeze and it won't, he'll get angry.

In point of fact, boiled water freezes as easily as unboiled.

BEES

If a member of the family dies, the bees in their hives must be told, or they will die, or go away.

If a member of a family marries, the bees should be told, or they will leave the hives and not return.

Should the bees swarm on a dead hedge or tree, or on a dead bough of a living tree, a death will occur in the family.

Stolen bees will not thrive, but will pine away and die.

It is unlucky for a stray swarm to alight in your premises.

Before moving bees they should be told by the owner, or he will be stung by the angry insects.

To remove bees on Good Friday will cause them to die.—Cornwall.

When the head of the house dies, the hives should be turned round at the moment the corpse leaves the house for the funeral.

When many bees enter, and none leaves the hive, rain is at hand.—Somersetshire.

Probably no superstition is so widely held in country areas, even to-day, as that of "Telling the bees." In the year of Grace 1945, the *Daily Mirror*, a London picture newspaper, sent a photographer to a country wedding. His best picture was of the bride in her bridal finery bending over the hives and whispering "Little brownies I am married." It was explained to the photographer that this was essential, as should a member of the family owning the bees marry without telling the bees, they would take leave of the hive, and never return.

Thus in 1945 we retained the superstition of centuries concerning bees.

Telling the bees of death was (and, still is, in some remote areas) a most elaborate ceremonial. The procedure was that as soon as the master or mistress had breathed the last, a member of the household visited the hives, and bending over them said, three times, "Little brownies, little brownies, your master (or mistress) is dead." Silence was then observed for a few moments. If the bees then began to hum, it was a sign that they consented to remain under the new owner. A piece of crepe was then put over the hive; and later, sweet drink or part of the funeral cake was put near the hives for the bees to feed upon.

In many places the bees, in addition, were invited to a funeral. The letter to them was written in the same terms as that to relatives of the deceased: "You are invited to the funeral of - - - which is to take place at - - -, etc., etc." This was pinned to the hive.

The authors some fifteen years ago while on a visit to a Cornish farm, alongside some salmon and trout water, noted and commented upon the empty hives in the garden. "Oh," was the reply. "The bees left and never came back, because they had not been informed of the owner's death."

The superstition held similar shape in Devonshire. In a report of the Devonshire Association, 1876, appeared the following conversation:

"All y'en dead, and all's thirteen, what a pity it is."

"What's a pity, Mrs. E——? Who's dead?"

"The bees, to be sure, sir. Mrs. —— when she buried her husband, forgot to give the bees a bit of mourning, and now, Sir, all the bees be dead, tho' the hives be pretty nigh full of honey. What a pity 'tis folks be so forgetful."

An account of the belief in death following the swarming of bees on a dead bough is given by a correspondent in *Notes and Queries,* Vol. IV, p. 396:

"Some time ago the wife of a respectable cottager in the neighbourhood died in childbed. Calling on the widower some time afterwards I found that although deploring his loss, which left him with several motherless children, he spoke calmly of the termination of the poor woman's illness as an inevitable and foregone conclusion. Pressed for an explanation I discovered that both he and his wife had been 'warned' of the coming event by her going into the garden a fortnight before the confinement, and discovering that their bees, in the act of swarming, had made choice of a dead stake for their settling place."

Gay, in *Pastoril,* V. 1714, writes:

"Swarmed on a rotten stick the bees I spied
Which erst I saw when Goody Dibson dyed."

The turning of beehives as a funeral leaves the house is recorded in the *Argus,* 13th September, 1790:

"A superstitious custom prevails at every funeral in Devon of turning round the beehives that belonged to the deceased, if he had any, and that at the moment the corpse is carried out of the house. At a funeral at Cullumpton of a rich old farmer, a laughable incident of this sort occurred: For just as the corpse was placed in the hearse, and the horsemen in a large number were drawn up in order for the procession to the funeral, a person called out "Turn the bees!" Whereupon a servant who had no knowledge of the custom, instead of turning the bees round, lifted them up, and laid them on their sides. The bees thus hastily disturbed, instantly attacked and fastened on the horses and the riders. It was in vain they galloped off, the bees precipitately followed, and left their stings as marks of their indignation. A general confusion took place with loss of hats, wigs, etc., and the corpse during the conflict was left unattended. Nor was it until after a considerable time that the funeral attendants could be rallied in order to proceed with the interment of their deceased friend."

In January, 1941, a reader wrote to a Sussex magazine:

"In a family who kept bees, there was one lady who although not actively looking after them, not infrequently visited them. A short while ago she died. The bees were hastily told of the death by the gardener. None of the bees were seen outside the hives for several days. This is authentic."

It is an ages-old country superstition that bees must not be sold. To barter bees is quite a different matter. If a man wanted a hive of bees, this could be obtained by an exchange of a small pig, or some other equivalent. There may not seem to an ordinary person any difference in principle between a barter and selling, but for the superstitious of those days there is a "host of difference." Then, too, it is held in Wales, still, that a hive of bees *given* to a person will bring good luck.

A common Hampshire saying some years ago was that bees are idle or unfortunate at their work whenever there is a war in prospect; and a chronicler at this time stated in *Notes and Queries* that he had found this to be the case since the time of his movements in France, Prussia and Hungary and down to the time of his writing. Is it purely coincidence that there was a marked scarcity of honey at the time of the breaking out of world war in 1939?

In the possession of the O'Hierlykie family at Ballyrawny, Ireland, is a brass article the shape of a helmet, held by the peasantry in veneration. Water from it, they believe, if given to a dying person will secure admission into Heaven. Cufton Crocker places on record that a priest asked for water for the relic. The story associated with it is as follows:

"About 800 years ago an Irish Chief, about to wage war on another clan, realized how inferior his troops were, and besought St. Gabriel to assist him in his righteous cause. In a field at Ballyrawny, where the battle was to be fought, was a beehive, and the Saint granted the Chief's request by turning the bees into spearmen, whereupon they issued from the hive, fell upon the enemy, and put them to flight. After the battle the Chief revisited the spot to find that the straw hive had changed into the helmet of brass, mentioned above."

Bees are supposed to make a loud humming noise in their hives at midnight on Christmas Eve. When the alteration was made in the style of the calendar, there came into being, and stayed for many years, a practice of watching by the beehives at midnight on the new and old Christmas Eve to determine which was the correct Christmas, by the humming of the bees for the birth of the Saviour.

In Cheshire in the 1900's it was held in many parts that the sting of a bee was a cure for local rheumatism.

Notably in Britain the bee superstition holds sway, but in France, Germany, and as far afield as Lithuania too, they abound in much of the same legendry.

Now what is the origin of these superstitions attached to bees? Sir Charles Igglesden in *Those Superstitions*, confesses that "Try as I will, I cannot trace the origins." Why not? In ancient days in Britain, bees were known as "Birds of God," and were supposed to be in communion with the Holy Spirit. They were then deemed friends and protectors of the house. In Germany they were known as "Mars Birds." Mythology has it that Jupiter was surrounded by bees in his infancy and Pindar is said to have been nourished by bees with honey instead of with milk. The Greeks consecrated bees to the moon.

Come a little nearer. Plato's doctrine of the transmigration of souls holds that the souls of sober, quiet people, untinctured by philosophy come to life as bees. In Cashmere (India) the lives of ogres are bound up with the bees. Later than Plato comes Mahomet, who admitted bees, as souls, to paradise; and Porphyry said of fountains: "They are adapted to the nymphs, or those souls which the Ancients call bees."

There is a strange story told in *My School and Schoolmasters* by Hugh Miller: Two young men lay on a mossy bank on a hot day. Overcome by the heat one fell asleep. His companion, watching drowsily, saw a bee issue from the mouth of his sleeping friend, jump down to the ground and cross along withered grass stubs over a brook cascading over stones, and enter through an interstice into an old ruined castle. Alarmed by what he saw, the watcher

hastily shook his comrade, who awakened a second or two after the bee, hurrying back, had re-entered his mouth. The sleeper protested at his companion waking him. "I dreamt that I had walked through a fine country," he said, "and had come to the banks of a noble river, and just where the clear water went thundering down a precipice, there was a bridge all silver which I crossed and entered a noble palace on the other side. I was about to help myself to gold and jewels when you woke me and robbed me of a delightful dream." Miller adds: "I have little doubt that what he saw was a bee, for this is the form the soul is not infrequently supposed to wear."

There are similar stories from other places; in one the sleeping person was said to have been moved by a companion. A few moments later, the bee returned to the spot and scurried hither and thither in terror looking for the sleeping form, and failed to know it. When the sleeper was nudged in his new resting place, he was found to be dead.

This belief that the bee is a soul of one departed is undoubtedly the origin of the superstition of "Telling the Bees," for souls of the departed, are they not in communion with God?

One last superstition from Wales. If a bee flies to any child in its sleep, the child will have good fortune in life.

BEETLE

To kill a beetle is to court bad luck.

It will bring bad luck if a beetle enters a room in your house or where you are staying.—Scotland.

The remarkable extent to which the otherwise canny Scot held to this beetle ill-luck is related by Sir Charles Igglesden, in one of his books on folklore. In the student days of an eminent present-day doctor, he and a Scottish friend were reading for an examination when a beetle ran across the floor. The Scot threw down his books. "That finishes it," he exclaimed. "No exam. for me." His belief in the bad luck which followed the entry of the beetle was such that he waited another six months to sit for the exam. Even this precaution was unavailing—he still failed!

Now, on the shores of Delagoa Bay, Baranga, the appearance of a beetle is also regarded as bad luck; and a few are collected and placed in a calabash, which is then thrown into a lake. By this it is hoped that as the beetles in the calabash die, so will the other living harbingers of bad luck also die. But then, these beetles are *really* unlucky, since they eat the bean crop.

BELLS

If two bells ring at the same time in a house, it is a sign of parting.

There is curiously little superstition in Britain connected with bells, though on the Continent they are fairly commonly said to drive away evil spirits, especially on Midsummer Night's Eve. But there were a number of country customs associated with bells. One was connected with storms; in Wiltshire during violent thunderstorms, the bell of St. Aldhelm, at Malmesbury Abbey, used to be rung. Now, when the same procedure was enacted at Paris, the great bell of the Abbey of St. Germain was rung. It was explained by Aubrey as: "The ringing of the bells exceedingly disturb spirits." There is no proof, however, that St. Aldhelm's bell was rung with the idea of disturbing the spirit of the storm.

On the eve of the feast of Corpus Christi, the choristers of Durham Cathedral were wont to ascend the tower and in their surplices' sing the Te Deum.

The curfew bell was pretty general throughout Britain in earlier times; it is still rung at one or two places. At Hessle, the day of the month is tolled, following the curfew.

During harvest month a church bell is wont to be tolled at Duffield (Yorkshire) each morning at five o'clock, and each evening at seven o'clock as a signal for beginning and ending work in the fields. In the same town, a bell is rung every Sunday evening at five p.m. It has been said that the purpose is to drive away evil spirits; a more likely reason is a warning to the parishioners to begin dressing for evening service, which followed an hour later!

Behind the ringing at six o'clock every morning (with the exception of Sunday) of a bell in St. Michael's, York, followed by as many tolls as there are days in the month gone, is a story of a traveller lost in the forests which at one time surrounded York. After wandering in terror all night, he discovered his whereabouts by hearing the church of St. Michael's strike six a.m. In gratitude he left to the church a sum of money to ensure that the bell might be rung each day at that hour, as a guide to travellers.

There is one curious reference to bells. In his *Certain Rules for this Time of Pestilential Observances,* 1625, Herne advises that "the bells in cities and towns be rung often, and the great ordnance descharged; thereby the aire is purified."

BETROTHAL

For a girl to hear her own banns read in Church means that her children are in peril of being born deaf and dumb.—North Country.

To break off a courtship a girl should present her no longer wanted lover with a knife.—West Country.

A couple who are betrothed should take from a laurel bush a sprig, break it in two, and each keep half. So long as they each retain their half, so long will love run smoothly.

The cynic with a knowledge of classic lore will doubtless recall, with delight, that laurel was in earlier days the reward for courage in battle!

In Wales, in the late 1700s, it was the custom to signify to one another the betrothal by sending to the lady a bouquet of flowers. The practice was at times a source of embarrassment to strangers, as is instanced in Gunning's *Reminiscences of Cambridge,* where the Dean (of St. Osaph) endeavouring to get to the bottom of a disputed betrothal, asked a young student "Have you ever made her any presents?" He replied that he never had, but recollecting himself, added, "except a very choice bunch of flowers, which I brought from Chirk Castle." "That explains the whole matter," said the Dean. "In Wales a man never sent a lady a gift of flowers, but as a proposal of marriage, and the lady's acceptance of them is considered the ratification."

BIBLE

If you read from an open Bible while a key is supported on the tips of the fingers by a person, and they call out the names of persons suspected of a theft, the key will "turn" at the name of the guilty person.—General.

By "turning" is meant that the key would fall to the ground from the finger tips. This divination by the Bible is a widespread belief, it being held that God, on His Word being read, would not permit the innocent to suffer under suspicion. The key had, as a condition, to be fastened to a Bible by a string.

So confidently maintained was this proof of "Bible and Key," that in an assault charge at the Thames (London)

Police Court in 1832, the "guilt" was described as justification for accusing a woman, at whose name the key had "turned." The accused at once "laid about" the accusers, and was consequently summoned for assault. Alas, it is not recorded what was the judicial decision!

The Bible was in constant use in earlier days as an omen and a divination in all matters of moment. A recorded "infallible method" of solving doubts and perplexities much practised not only in rural Britain, but even by the more sophisticated town dwellers, was to open the Bible at random and, with eyes averted, place a finger on the open page. The verse or verses thus chosen were taken as a Divine indication of the course of action which should be pursued.

Gibbons writes of Clovis, who marching (A.D. 507) for Paris, on reaching the town of Tours, the sanctuary and oracle of Gaul, sent messengers into the church with orders to note the words of the psalm being chanted as they entered. These, as it chanced, expressed the valour and victory of the new champions of Heaven, and the application was easily transferred from Joshua, who went forth to battle against the enemies of the Lord.

Notes and Queries in October, 1861, records the custom of dipping into the Bible on New Year's Day by Oxfordshire people. It must be carried out before noon, and it is held that the tenor of the first passage which caught the eye was a prognostication of the reader's good or bad fortune throughout the year.

The origin, like so many of our religious omens and festivals, lies again in the Pagans, who in their days, similarly dipped into the poems of Homer and Virgil. For these the earlier Christian substituted the Bible, or the Scriptures then in circulation. In the fourth to the fourteenth century these *Surtes Sanctorum*, as they were called, were repeatedly condemned—or repeatedly practised—by Kings, Bishops and Saints.

In *Mount Tabor* (1639) is reported how the then Earl of Berkeley in a dejection of spirit, opened his Bible and casually fixed his eyes "upon the sixth of Hosea," the first three verses. The account goes on in the Earl's own words: "I am willing to decline superstition on all occasions, yet think myself obliged to make use of such a providential piece of Scripture. First, by heartily repenting myself of my sins past; secondly, by

sincere reformation for the time to come."

And William of Gloucester bears witness to the same custom. "As I was to passe thro the rooms where my little grandchilde was set by her grandmother to read her morning's chapter, the 9th of Matthew's gospel, just as I came in she was uttering these words in the second verse: 'Jesus said to the sicke of the palsie, Sonne, be of good comfort, thy sins are forgiven thee,' which was suiting so fitly with my case, whose left side is taken with that disease, and I stood at a stand at the uttering of them, and could not but conceive some joy and comfort in the blessed words, though by the child's reading, as if the Lord had spoken them to myselfe; a paralytick and sinner, as that sicke man was."

In the Isle of Collonsay, in confidence of curing a patient of his illness, the inhabitants had a custom of fanning the face of the sick with the leaves of the Bible.

BIDDING (TO FUNERAL)

After a death, it was the custom in East Yorkshire for one or two women of the household to go round to neighbours, friends and relatives telling of the death, and asking them to attend the funeral. This, called "bidding," was considered as an honour, and the neglect, or oversight, by not "bidding" was known to have been the cause of family feuds which lasted for many years.

There was a strict formula about the bidding. In the North of England, for instance, bidders wore black silk scarves. The knocker of the door was never used; instead, the bidder carried a key, with which she knocked on the door.

At Hesham, the public bellman was wont to parade to invite attendance at the funeral. Ringing his bell, he read out: "Blessed are the dead which die in the Lord. John Jones is departed, son of Richard Jones which was. Company is desired to-morrow at five o'clock, and at six he is to be buried. For him and all faithful people, give God hearty thanks."

BIDDING (TO WEDDING)

Another "bidding" custom was to a wedding. This was not, however, so popular. The bidders to a funeral usually shared in a feast; the bidders who attended a wedding were expected to confer some gift on the couple.

This was particularly prevalent in Wales and the North of England. In

Scotland something on similar lines was known as "A Penny Wedding."

The wedding bidding was resorted to only by those in poor circumstances, who wanted a start in life, so to speak. The couple appointed a Master of the Revels, called (in Westmorland and Cumberland) a "Birler," and it was his job during the dancing to see that all the guests present subscribed to a collection of money to set the wedded pair on their feet.

The usual form of bidding was to send broadcast a bidding invitation. An example is that contained in the *Gentleman's Magazine* for 1789:

"As we intend entering the Nuptial state, we propose to have a bidding on the occasion on Thursday the 20th day of September, instant, where the favour of your good company will be humbly esteemed; and whatever benevolence you are pleased to confer on us shall be gratefully acknowledged and retaliated on a similar occasion by your most humble servants, William Jones, Ann Davies.

"N.B.—The young man's father (Stephen Jones) and the young woman's aunt (Mrs. Williams) will be thankful for all favours conferred on them that day."

As much as £100 has frequently been subscribed at such a bidding. In rural areas, gifts at a bidding might range from a cow, or a horse, down to a calf, half-a-crown, or a shilling.

The authors fear that the custom still prevails: Not so blatantly as recorded above, where guests were expected to contribute, in the words of the fiddler at the party: "Come, my friends, and freely offer, here's to the bride who has no tocher" (dowry), but the modern wedding card of invitation differs very little in expectation of some gift to decorate the nuptial home!

As for the origin, it lies in the word bidding, which, in the Saxon, as *biddan*, meant to pray or supplicate.

BIRDS

For a bird to fly in and out of a room by an open window predicts the death of the inmate of the house.—General.

The flying, or hovering, by birds round a house and their resting on the window sill, or tapping against a pane portends death.—East Riding, Yorkshire.

For a robin to tap the window of a room in which a sick person is lying, portends the death of that person.—General.

To see one magpie is a sign of death.—General.

If jays or crows forsake a wood in flocks, there will be great famine or mortality.

When ravens or crows make a sorrowful, hoarse or hollow noise, it presages foul weather approaching.

The notes of the night-jar are a sure indication of death in a household where they are heard.—Pembrokeshire.

It is unlucky to kill a swallow.—General.

A peacock's harsh clamour foretells rain.—General.

To kill a tom-tit or a wren, or to destroy their nests, means that you will break a bone during the coming year.

Should a bird in a cage die on the morning of a wedding of one of the family, the wedding will be unhappy and the pair will separate.—West of Scotland.

If a crow flies over a house and croaks thrice, someone in the family will die.—General.

Black and grey birds flying round trees in the dark and never settling are souls accomplishing penance.—Irish superstition.

Unbaptized children become birds flying through space until they are baptized by St. John the Baptist before the Day of Judgment, when they go right to Heaven.—Brittany.

(For other superstitions connected with birds, see under individual names of birds.)

From earliest times birds have been regarded as the harbingers of good and evil. Auguries drawn from the flight and actions of birds have formed part of these beliefs from the days when Themistocles was assured of victory at Artemisium by the crowing of a cock, and Romulus claimed to be King of Rome from the appearance of vultures.

The Greeks, of course, made a science of these auguries—the Oracles were adepts at it—and called it ornithomancy. Twelve hundred years ago efforts were made by the church to root them out but they persist, even to this day, in the more rural parts of all countries.

Alcuin, who was born at York about A.D. 735, the friend of Charlemagne and one of the glories of Anglo-Saxon times, writing to a bishop said: "Prognostics, and cries of birds, and sneezings, are altogether to be shunned, because they are of no force except to those who believe in them. . . For it is permitted to the evil spirit for the deceiving of persons who observe these things to cause that, in some degree, prognostics should often foretell the truth"—thereby, you will note, rather giving away the case that they have no foundation.

There is not much record in Ancient Britain of the superstitions attached to birds until the Roman occupation. In Northampton's *Defensative* (1583) is a reference to: "The flight of many crowes over the left side of the camp, made the Romans very much afrayde of somme bad lucke." (The left side was always an evil omen to the Romans.) From the time of the Romans, however, birds became to the rural people of Britain omens of the future, good or ill.

One of the more common of the omens was that if you are about to commence a journey, and see a flock of birds in flight, the direction of their flight will tell you whether you will be lucky or unlucky on the journey. Should they fly to the right of you, things would be propitious; but if to the left, the journey would best be postponed.

In Wales it is considered unlucky to hear the cuckoo before 6th April; and prosperity will attend you should you hear its note first on 28th April. In the South of England it is regarded as unfortunate for anyone to have no money on one's person when the cuckoo is heard for the first time in the season.

A Norfolk superstition was, and still is in many parts, that whatever you are doing when you first hear the cuckoo in any year, you will do most frequently all the year.

It was once a common belief among girls, that if they ran into the fields early in the morning to hear the cuckoo, and as soon as the note was heard, took off the left shoe, a man's hair, the exact colour of that of her future husband, would be found inside the shoe.

In Yorkshire farm circles, it is held that should a robin be killed, one of the cows belonging to the family or the person who killed the bird would give bloody milk.

It was believed in olden times, that during the days when a halcyon (kingfisher) is hatching her eggs, the sea remained so smooth that sailors might venture upon it without incurring risk in storm or tempest.

Dryden refers to this belief in his:

"Amongst our arms as quiet you shall be
As halcyons brooding on a winter's sea."

The belief is also commemorated to-day in our expression "Halcyon days."

Shakespeare in *King Lear* makes the Earl of Kent say:

". . . turn their halcyon beaks
With every gale . . ."

In his days it was a widely held superstition that a dead kingfisher suspended by a cord would always turn its beak in the direction from which the wind blew. Marlowe, in his *Jew of Malta* (1633), mentions by inference the same belief:

"But how now stands the wind?
Into what corner peers my halcyon's bill?"

In many cottages there may still be seen a stuffed kingfisher hanging by a cord for this purpose. The authors, wandering in the New Forest in 1943, came across such a relic of this old superstition.

The raven is another bird which has featured largely in British folk-lore and superstition. In Cornwall, particularly, its croaking over a house is held to bode evil. Hunt, in his *Popular Romances*, quotes an instance of where the superstition (it is alleged) brought its evil fruit.

"One day our family were much annoyed by the continued croaking of a raven over our house. Some of us believed it to be a token, others derided it; but a next-door neighbour said, 'Just mark the day, and see if something does come of it.' The day and hour were accordingly noted. Months passed away and unbelievers were loud in their boastings and inquiries after the omen. The fifth month arrived, and with it a black-edged letter from Australia announcing the death of one of the members of the family in that country. On comparing the dates and the raven's croak they were found to be the same day."

Another Cornish superstition is that King Arthur is alive still in the form of a raven, and it was long held to be a crime to attempt to shoot the bird, lest the mystical warrior should be thus killed.

The owl is another of the "unlucky" birds to see. The Romans held the bird in abhorrence. The legend of the owl is that our Saviour went into a baker's shop where they were baking, and asked for bread to eat. The mistress at once put a lump of dough into the oven to bake for him, but was reprimanded by her daughter who, insisting that the piece was too large, reduced it to a small size. The dough at once began to swell and presently became an enormous size, whereupon the baker's daughter cried out, "Heugh, heugh, heugh," which owl-like noise induced our Saviour to transform her into that bird for her wickedness.

Peacocks are also ill-omen birds. Their shrill noise is said to predict rain. In Derbyshire and the surrounding counties the bringing of a peacock's feather into the house is believed to bring about illness and death to the inhabitants. Stage-people hold the feather still as a portent of ill-luck to the play and the company. All Mohammedans believe that the peacock opened the door of Paradise to admit the Devil.

Strangest of old superstitions is that held on the Lancashire Moors that plovers contain the souls of the Jews who assisted at the crucifixion; and it is believed (says Brand in his *Popular Antiques*) that persons who heard the cries of these "Wandering Jews" were sure to be overtaken by ill-luck.

In the South of Scotland the lapwing is accounted an unlucky bird. But the origin for this believe is very easy of discovery. During the persecution of the Covenanters in the reign of the Charleses, the Covenanters were frequently tracked down by the fact that when they intruded on the usually deserted haunts of the lapwings in the solitary places, they were usually betrayed by the screaming flight of the disturbed lapwings.

When we look into the bird beliefs of savages, we find a similarity with the Irish that black and grey birds are souls. It is the belief of the Boronos of Brazil that the human soul has the shape of a bird, and passes in that shape out of the body in dreams. The soul of Aristeus of Proconnesus was seen to issue from his mouth in the shape of a raven, says Pliny. (Note the stories in Bees of souls issuing from the mouth in dreams.)

The Arunta of Central Australia, in the same belief, hold that the soul of a slain man takes the form of a bird, follows his slayer, and is constantly on the watch to do him a mischief.

See CUCKOO, MAGPIE, ROBIN, etc.

BIRDS' EGGS

Birds' eggs, hung up in a house, will bring bad luck.—General.

BIRTH

Children born during the hour of midnight have the power through life of seeing the spirits of the departed.— Yorkshire.

To bring good luck, a baby should be rubbed with lard immediately after birth and before it is washed.

A baby which sees itself in a looking-glass before it is four months old will suffer from rickets.

At birth an infant should be brushed with a rabbit's foot. This will avert all possibility of an accident to the child.

A new-born child should be laid in the arms of a maiden before being held by anyone else.—Yorkshire.

A new-born child must be carried upstairs to the top of the house for luck before being taken downstairs or out. Even carried up a pair of steps is better than nothing.—General.

> *Monday's child is fair of face;*
> *Tuesday's child is full of grace;*
> *Wednesday's child is full of woe;*
> *Thursday's child has far to go.*
> *Friday's child is loving and giving;*
> *Saturday's child works hard for its living.*
> *But the child that is born on the Sabbath Day,*
> *Is blithe and bonny, good and gay.*

A child born on a Sunday is highly favoured and is secure from the malice of evil spirits.—Scotland.

Although the lines of the verse above are often quoted in the South and West of England, they properly belong to the six northern counties. It was there that they started their tale of superstition. That they spread southwards and westwards is due, probably, to migration by northern people. In Devonshire, however, "Christmas Day" is substituted in the lines for "Sabbath Day," and "fair and wise" for "blithe and bonny."

In Kent it was the practice of the old midwife to prepare, before the birth, a boy's night-shirt and a girl's night-gown. If a child born was a girl she was placed in it the boy's night-shirt; if a boy, it went into the girl's night-gown. This, it is averred, would make the boy, when he grew up, fascinate all women; and the girl would be always surrounded by men from amongst whom she could choose for a happy marriage. Sir Charles Igglesden recalls one midwife's remark to him: "If I didn't do this, I'd never have been able to look my babies in the face when they grew up. Why should they suffer when I can bring them happiness?"

In the northern and border counties, and occasionally in Scotland, cake and new cheese were provided against the birth, and, with them, tea seasoned with brandy or whisky. It was considered unlucky to allow anyone to leave the fortunate household without having shared this fare.

In connection with this custom, there arose the "Shooten" or "groaning cheese," from which the happy father must cut a "Whang o' luck" for all the maidens present at the tea. But he had to take care in the process, for should he cut his finger, the child was ordained to die before reaching adult years. The "Whang" had to be taken from the edge of the new cheese, and divided into portions. One portion went to each unmarried lady, which, placed under her pillow, would serve the same charm as a piece of wedding cake—give her a glimpse during the night of her future husband. That was border county superstition.

But in the North of England it was the practice of the doctor, as soon as the happy event was over, to cut both the cake and cheese. Whereupon all present feasted. Failure to do so meant that the child would grow up without beauty or charm. The Yorkshire cake for this ceremony was known as Pepper-cake, and looked like a thickly made ginger-bread.

They did the thing in better style in Sweden. The cake and cheese was, in fact, placed beside the bridal bed in preparation for the first confinement. They must have been hard eating on the happy event!

In Durham it was customary for the nurse or midwife to claim some of the cake and cheese, which she presented to the first person she met of the opposite sex of the child. A similar custom prevailed in the Dartmoor area; while in Oxford it was the custom to cut the cake in the middle and gradually, with further cuts, shape it in the form of a ring. Through this ring of cake the child was passed on its christening day—for luck.

Further south, the superstition was that a gift of bread and cheese should be given by the woman who carried the baby to church for christening to the first person met. To refuse the gift would, it was held, bring ill-luck to the child.

An old Yorkshire superstition decreed that a part of the father's clothes must be laid over a female child, and the mother's petticoat over a male child. Failure to do so meant, it was augured, that the child would never find favour in after life with the opposite sex. This would appear to be a variant of the Kentish practice recorded above.

The carrying of the child to the top of the house, already mentioned, was general all over the country. It is, indeed, pretty generally practised to-day, and not only by rural dwellers. A nurse in the heart of the West End of London in December, 1945, solemnly took a child to the attic bedroom of the mother's house, and, mounting a chair, held it as near the skylight as she could reach. The hope—or should one say certainty—is that it will ensure that the child will rise in the world. In Oxford on 3rd June, 1912, this was done also to a child of S. L. Wright, one of a very superior family.

On the Border, a little salt or sugar was put into the child's mouth for luck on its first visit to another house. In the North of England, egg, salt and bread were presented to the little visitor; a few matches were added in East Yorkshire, and in the West Riding a small coin.

Now all this was meant to ensure that the child throughout its life would never lack friends (salt), food (bread), light and heat (matches). The egg? Well, the egg has been a sacred emblem from the time of the Mundane Egg.

Much superstition was devoted to the eight days following a child's birth, especially in Scotland. For these days were counted the most dangerous in the child's life; it had not then been christened, and was thus in danger from the fairies. Until christened, it might be spirited away by the fairies, and a "changeling" left in its place. A preventive of this calamity was to place a little salt in the cradle, or sew iron into the child's clothes. The efficacy of iron in barring the way to fairies or witches has been mentioned before. Sweden records the fairy superstition, and to avert it custom demands that fires in the house must not be extinguished until after the christening, nor must any person pass between the baby and the fire. No stranger entering the house must take the child without his hands having touched fire. Germany loaded a newly born's cradle with herbs; the Greeks were careful never to leave the child alone for the first eight days, within which period the modern Greek Church refuses to baptize.

In Scotland the safeguard is held to lie in the nearness of an article of attire belonging to the child's father. Henderson relates the story of a Selkirk shepherd's wife who, lying in bed with her baby at her side, suddenly heard talking and laughter in the room. This she knew was coming from the fairies who were forming a child of wax as a substitute for her baby, which they were planning to steal. She seized her husband's waistcoat, which was hanging at the foot of the bed, and threw it over herself and the child. At once the fairies set up a loud screaming of "Auld Luckie has cheated us o' our bairnie." A minute later the mother heard something fall down the chimney and, looking out, saw a waxen image of her baby, stuck full of pins, lying on the hearth!

In the Orkneys it was usual for a child to be "sained" soon after birth. A large, rich cheese was made before the birth, and after birth was cut in pieces and distributed among the matrons in attendance. The mother and child were then "sained" by lighted fir candles being whirled round the bed three times, by which doing evil influences were held to be averted. Later in the century the "saining" took the form of drawing the bed to the centre of the room, after which the nurse or midwife waved round the bed an open Bible, three-times-three; each three for each person in the Trinity.

Whence was born this welter of superstition on birth? Who can say? Who, or what, could forge the link between the Scottish belief that the first eight days were the vital ones for a child; the Danish belief that fires in the house must not be extinguished until after the christening (seven days) and the belief in the Islands of Saparoca, Harockoe and Noessa Lant, that resin (or a lamp) must be kept burning for seven nights in order that harm may be averted from the child?

In many parts of the country, and especially in Herefordshire, there is a superstition (perhaps belief is a better word) that the father of a child suffers as much at its birth as does the mother. Any aches and pains which a husband feels during the pregnancy of his wife are put down to this belief.

Even as late as the year 1946 the authors were given examples of this by persons whom we know to have no superstitious belief; they aver that there is nothing of superstition about it—that it is solid fact, vouched for at the birth of their three children.

Added to this is a curious belief, still prevalent in parts of the country, that

if a girl gives birth to an illegitimate child and will not disclose the name of the father, he can be found by inquiring which of the men she was known to have consorted with is ill in bed. This opinion was held very strongly in Yorkshire up to quite recently; and the belief was enhanced in one particular case the authors know, by a man who, confronted by the girl's relatives as he lay groaning in bed, admitted the paternity.

"BIT OF MY OWN AGAIN"

It was the practice among horse and cattle dealers in all parts of England, always to give back to the buyer part of the purchase money, to ensure luck.

Old country people, even to-day, will give chapter and verse of instances in which cattle which had been purchased, turned out badly, or died, when the purchasers had not seen "a bit of their own again."

Best, in *Rural Economy* (page 113) relates: "I have knowne 4 lambes sold for 11 pence, and the seller gave the buyer a penny again."

BITTERN

If a bittern flies over your head, make your will.—Somerset.

If you go shooting with a bittern's claw fastened in your buttonhole by a riband, you will have good sport.—Old sporting superstition.

This superstition, put into print by Bishop Hall, gained considerable strength in Porlock Bay, Somerset, when during a severe winter a bittern made an appearance and was promptly shot by a sportsman. Ill-luck befell him within a few days.

BLACKBERRY

To pick blackberries after 11th October is to court calamity. For, on that day, superstition holds that the Devil spits on blackberry, and anyone eating, after that date, a blackberry so insulted, will suffer some grave misfortune.

Why the 11th of October was thus chosen, the authors have failed to discover.

BLACKBIRD

Two blackbirds sitting together on a window sill or a doorstep are an omen of death to someone in the house.

This belief, in parts of Wales, is interesting as being the only example the authors have been able to find of the blackbird as a harbinger of death. It is usually left to a robin, a crow, a magpie or a raven.

BLACK CAT

To see a black cat cross the road is lucky.—General.

If a black cat walks into your house or room, it is a sign of good fortune.—General.

To cure St. Anthony's Fire, draw blood from a black cat's ears, and rub upon the part affected.—Co. Carlow, Ireland.

To cure the shingles, take the blood drawn from a black cat's tail and smear over the affected part.—Cornwall.

Possibly the black cat is among the three most prevailing superstitions of the present day—walking under a ladder, and the number thirteen, are the others. For more years than the authors can remember a black cat has always walked across the path of a bride at one of London's churches for smart Society weddings. We have always suspected that black cat, so beloved of Press photographers!

An instance widely reported at the time, of black cat luck, were the summonses taken out in a London Police Court against two bus conductors. As the first one waited the hearing a black cat jumped on the lap of one of the conductors. When his case was called, he passed the cat over to the other. Both summonses were dismissed!

Charles I owned a favourite black cat, and he had so superstitious a dread of losing it, that the animal was closely guarded. One day it fell ill and died.

"My luck is gone," he said.

It had! Next day he was arrested.

Ranjitsinhji, the Indian Prince cricketer, was convinced that the appearance of a black cat at a shooting gathering would guarantee him a good bag, and twice in succession, he averred in 1905, a black cat had won a county match for Surrey.

Black cats were associated, always in Britain,, with witches. Ben Jonson, in his *Masque of Queens*, writes in the song sung by the witches:

"Yet I went back to the house again.
Killed the black cat, and here's the brain."

Here, again, a superstition rife in Britain is associated in the superstition of Pagan countries. In Sumatra, during a drought, and when rain is urgently needed, a black cat is thrown into a river and made to swim about for a time, and then allowed to escape to the bank, pursued by the scantily clad women of the village, splashing the animal and themselves with water.

The origin may possibly lie in ancient Egypt, with the sacred black cat of the Oagans. Bast—a black cat—was a Goddess in Egypt, and in the reign of Sheshonk, first King of the Libyan Twenty-Second Dynasty, was the official Deity of the Kingdom. Fortune was ever to be had by the wooing of a God or Goddess.

In the Scarborough area of Yorkshire, a black cat in the house of a fisherman was held to ensure the safety of husbands at sea.

This superstition had the not unnatural result of black cats acquiring a very high market value, and they were stolen in large numbers by the racketeers of the day in order that they could be sold to the credulous wives of men in the fishing ports and villages.

The authors came across this peculiar charm in an old book on Herefordshire —by a Mrs. Clarke, a Herefordshire woman: "Bury the head of a black catt with a Jacobus or a piece of gold in it, and putt into the eies two black baenes. Butt it must be donne on a Tuesday night at twelve o'clock at night; and that time nine nights the piece of gold must be taken out and whatever you buy with it (always reserving some part of the money) you will have money brought to your pockets, perhaps the same piece of gold again."

See CAT.

BLACK COCK

To cure the epilepsy bury a black cock alive on the spot where the sufferer fell; and with it bury the parings of the patient's nails and a lock of his hair.—N.W. Highlands of Scotland.

This superstition, again, is an example of the old belief held both in civilized Britain of the eighteenth century and by the heathen tribes of Africa of the transference of evil. The epilepsy was supposed to be buried in the ground with the cock. Curiously, the ancient Hindus believed that epilepsy was caused by a *dog* demon; and after certain ritual had been observed over the afflicted, the demon was exhorted by a prayer: "Doggy, let him loose. Reverence be to thee, barker and bender."

Black cocks were extensively used in Britain in magical incantations. They were the proverbial sacrifice to the Devil. The recipe was as follows. Take a black cock under your left arm and go at midnight to where four roads meet. Then cry three times, "Black Cock," or else just say "Robert" nine times, and the Devil will appear, take the cock, and leave you with a handful of money.

Baring-Gould has described how the great Jewish banker, Samuel Bernard, who died in 1789, leaving an enormous fortune, had a favourite black cock. It was generally regarded as unpleasantly connected with the fortune amassed by its owner. This was strengthened by the fact that Bernard died within a day or two of the black cock dying.

Most "witches" in England were believed to have a black cock familiar—as well as the traditional black cat. The Continent observed the same belief. In Oldenburg when anything was bewitched the innards of a black cock were taken. The heart, or lung, or liver was stuck all over with needles, or marked with a cross-cut, and placed on the fire in a tightly closed vessel. All doors and windows were fastened and strict silence was maintained. When the heart boiled, or was reduced to ashes, the witch would appear, having felt severe burning pains during the operation. She would ask for her release.

The Netheranians, when they wanted rain, used to sacrifice a black cock to the Thunder God in the depths of the woods.

Now, compare the old Scottish epileptic cure with the methods of curing the cholera adopted in Southern Konkan (India). On the appearance of the disease the villagers go in procession from the temple to the outskirts of the village, carrying a basket of cooked rice covered with red powder, and a cock. The head of the cock is cut off at the village boundary and the body thrown away. The cholera thus being transferred to another village is passed on with similar ceremonies *ad infinitum*.

See COCK.

BLACKHEADS

Creep on hands and knees through a bramble three times with the sun—from east to west—and your blackheads will disappear.—Devonshire.

The bramble had to be in the shape of an arch, and one which had taken root at both ends. This was also a cure for rheumatism, rickets, and boils, etc.

See BOILS.

BLACK PENNY

As late as the latter half of the nineteenth century, the Black Penny was the remedy on the Borders for madness in cattle. For generations the Penny, possessed by a family in Hume-buyers, was used thusly. It was slightly larger than a penny and was probably a Roman coin or medal. When cattle were afflicted with madness, the Black Penny was dipped in a well, the waters of which ran towards the South—this was essential. Sufficient water was then drawn from the well and given to the animals affected. In 1870 popular belief still upheld the value of this remedy.

See LOCKERBY PENNY.

BLACK SHEEP

A black lamb foretells good luck to the flock.—Kent.

It is lucky for a shepherd to have one black lamb, or sheep, in his flock.—Sussex.

Bad luck will attend a flock into which a black lamb is born.—Shropshire.

The reader who chances to be a shepherd, or a farmer, will have to decide for himself to which of these varying views he will adhere for his luck!

It should be added here, that while one black lamb was held in Shropshire to signify bad luck, for a ewe to produce twin black lambs marked a forthcoming veritable disaster. However (as is usual!) the calamity might be averted if the shepherd cut the throats of the twins before they had been able to "baa"!

It might be mentioned here that until about 1930 the marshmen of Romney maintained that at dawn on Christmas Day, sheep on the marshes rose, faced the East and bowed. Sir Charles Igglesden relates the story of an old shepherd, gravely ill, who requested his parson to read his favourite hymn, which began: "The roseate hues of early dawn." The old man, who could not read, had always believed the words to be: "The rows of ewes at early dawn."

See SHEEP, SHEPHERDS.

BLACKSMITH

No harm or ill ever comes to a blacksmith.—West of Ireland.

There is nowhere else any reference in superstition or folk-lore to this singularly blessed state of a smithy; and why he should be singled out in this part of Ireland, the divil knows!

BLACK SNAIL

If a black snail is rubbed over your

warts, and afterwards impaled upon a hawthorn, the warts will be cured.—Lancashire, Glamorgan, Gloucester.

The belief behind this was that the warts were transferred to the snail, and as it died while impaled, so, too, did the warts die away. So late as 1945 the authors had evidence of this device being practised in a Surrey village.

Anciently, however, the rubbing had to be accompanied by the chanting of:

"Wart, wart, on the snail's shell back,
Go away soon, and never come back."

In Pembrokeshire, it was essential that, after impaling the snail on the hawthorn, it should be nailed down with as many thorns as you had warts. This impaling of each wart was also prevalent in Gloucestershire.

See SNAILS.

BLEEDING

This was the ancient superstitious remedy to stop bleeding, familiar in the Dartmoor area of Devonshire.

Say "Our Saviour Christ was born in Bethlehem, and was baptized in the river of Jordan. The waters were mild of mood. The child was meek, gentle and good. he struck it with a rod and still it stood. And so shall thy blood stand. In the name of the Father, the Son and the Holy Ghost."

The verse had to be repeated three times, and the Lord's Prayer once; upon which the bleeding, it was confidently held, would cease.

See BLOOD.

BLEEDING NOSE

The eighteenth century cure was to soak a linen rag in sharp vinegar, burn it, and then blow the ashes up the nose through a quill.

BLISTERS

Draw a needle full of worsted thread through the blister. Clip it off at both ends and leave till the dead skin peeled off.—General.

This is one of the old charms behind which lay a sound medical fact; although the superstitious followers did not realize it. For the worsted thread sopped up all the moisture in the blister, which then dried up.

BLOOD

No man can live who has blood let from him on All Hallows Day.—Anglo-Saxon belief.

BLOSSOMS

There are many superstitions in vogue even to-day regarding the blossoming of trees and shrubs out of their season.

For instance, it is unlucky for a household when flowers which normally bloom in the summer, flower in the house in the winter. Of such flowers geraniums are perhaps the most popular.

In Wales the flowering of Christmas roses late in the Spring, and primroses flowering in June, or a summer rose flowering in December are regarded as omens of ill-luck. The untimely flowering of fruit trees is an omen of sickness or of death in the same principality, where it is held that should the trees in an entire district break out into unseasonable bloom, there will be a hard winter with much sickness and death.

One of the proverbs of Wales runs: "Untimely fruit, untimely news."

See APPLE, GERANIUM, PLUM.

BLUE-BOTTLES

A nest of blue-bottles in a man's leg will cure him of gangrene.—Sussex.

You might think this revolting idea to be a superstition of the dark ages. Instead, read the following letter dated from Hythe, 30th May, 1947:

"Dear Sir,—Will you tell my friend that it is true that a nest of blue-bottles in a man's leg is a certain cure for gangrene. My father says it is impossible. Please let me know."

BODY

Disaster will overtake a ship on which a dead person is carried.—Seamen's superstition.

A variation of the superstition is that a ship with a dead person on board cannot make way. Boullaye le Gunz in his *Travels* (1657) refers to the captain of a ship asking him whether he had in his baggage a mummy or other thing which hindered the ship's progress, as he could not make way. Gunz relates how, on that, he secretly threw away the hand of a siren which he was bringing home.

A coffin made of the main-mast of the French ship L'Orient was sent to Nelson by a fellow officer to remind him that amid all his glory he was but mortal. Nelson received the coffin in the proper spirit and had it placed in his own cabin in the Vanguard. But at length in deference to the superstitious feelings of the crew, he had it heaved overboard, and sunk.

BOIL

To put cold, boiled water in a bed-

room is to defy the devil, and bring bad luck.

It seems that this is due to the belief, quite erroneous that water once boiled will not freeze, and the devil gets annoyed if he cannot make it freeze—and consequently visits his anger upon you. We have failed to discover why this should be so in the bedroom, and nowhere else.

BOILING

To boil your dish-cloth is to boil all your lovers—"to boil all her lads own." —Border Counties.

BOILS

To cure boils creep on hands and knees beneath a bramble which has grown into the soil at both ends.—Devonshire and Cornwall.

Poultice the boil for three days and nights and then place the poultices with their cloths in the coffin of anybody lying dead and about to be buried.—Devonshire.

There was still one other Devonshire charm for the cure of boils, not for one-self, but for a friend. The friend had, then, to go into a churchyard on a dark night, and to the grave of a person who had been interred the previous day; walk six times round the grave, and crawl across it three times. If the sufferer from boils was a man the ceremony had to be performed by a woman friend, and vice versa for a female sufferer. The charm would not work, so it was said, unless the night was completely dark.

In a report of the Devonshire Association, of 1867, it is recorded "this remedy was tried by a young woman in Georgeham Churchyard." Unfortunately the record does not say what happened to the sufferer from boils.

BOLTS

If locks and bolts of the house are fastened the soul of a dying person will be hindered in leaving the body.—General.

This is another superstition of the eighteenth and nineteenth centuries, which still lingers here and there in remote rural areas of Britain. The custom was general, in the nineteenth century, of opening all doors in the house when a person was at the point of death, so that the struggle between life and death should be easier and the soul be allowed to accomplish its exit without impediment.

Over the greater part of the country it was held that a person could not die so long as any locks were locked or bolts bolted in the house. Accordingly, it was the custom to undo all the locks and bolts. An extraordinary story of this superstition printed in *The Times*, of 4th September, 1863, is the case of a child at Taunton, who lay sick of scarlatina, and whose death seemed inevitable. The report continued: "A jury of matrons was, as it were, empanelled, and to prevent the child 'dying hard,' all the doors in the house, all the drawers, and all the boxes were thrown wide open, the keys taken out, whereby a sure, certain, and easy passage into eternity could be secured. The child, however, declined to avail itself of the facilities, and recovered."

There is a reference to this belief in *Guy Mannering* (chapter 27): "The popular belief that the protracted struggle between life and death is painfully prolonged by keeping the door of the apartment shut was received as certain by the superstitious elders of Scotland."

This superstition existed also in France. And the Chinese make a hole in the roof of the dwellings in order that the soul may have an easy exit.

The origin is said to be the idea that the minister of purgatorial pains takes the soul as it escapes from the body, and flattening it against some closed door (which alone can serve the purpose) crams it into the hinges and hinge openings. Thus the soul in torment is likely to be miserably pinched and squeezed by the movement, on any casual occasion, of such a door or lid. An opened door, or lid, frustrates this. Up to the early days of the present century the German peasant would never, knowingly, slam a door, lest he pinched a soul in doing so.

Something similar in notion is the abstention of the Congo negro from sweeping the floor of his house for a whole year after death, lest the dust should injure the delicate substance of the departed soul, or ghost.

That the superstition still lives in many parts, or in the minds of those who were brought up in rural parts in remote corners of the country, is evidenced by the inquiry of a child of the authors in the late days of 1945. The child, a girl aged 13, asked why doors were opened and all bolts on doors and cupboards unfastened when her aunt was at the point of death, although it was cold weather. She said that she had asked her mother, who said it always had to be done, but would give no other reason. The girl was writing from a small village in the north of Scotland.

See DEATH, KNOTS, SOUL.

BONES

To cure the dysentery, powder human bones, mix with red wine, and give to the sufferer.

Human skulls, powdered, were recommended, also, for the curing of epilepsy. The *Stamford Mercury* of 8th October, 1858, reported: "A collier's wife recently applied to the sexton at Ruabon Church for ever so small a portion of a human skull for the purpose of grating it similar to ginger, to be afterwards added to some mixture which she intended giving to her daughter as a remedy against fits, to which she was subject." The paper commented that this practice existed more or less all over the country.

BONE-SHAVE

This was an old Devon superstition by means of which sciatica might be cured. It was also prevalent in some parts of Cornwall, adjacent to Devon. The sufferer lay on his back on the bank of a stream with, by his side, and between him and the water, a straight stick or staff. While in this position he made this incantation:

Bone-shave right,
Bone-shave straight,
As the water runs by the stave,
Good for the bone-shave.

Halliwell in his dictionary, dated 1847, refers to this as "a noted charm for the sciatica."

BOOSENING

This was a superstition rife in Cornwall for the cure of madness, consisting of immersing the afflicted person in water until he (or she) is on the point of drowning. Carew refers to it as particularly prevalent in the parish of Altarnum, and describes it as "placing the disordered in mind on the brink of a square pool filled with water from St. Nun's Well. The patient, having no intimation of what was intended, was, by a sudden blow on the breast, tumbled into the pool, where he was tossed up and down by some persons of superior strength till, quite debilitated, his fury forsook him; he was then carried to church and certain Masses were sung over him. The name Boosening or Boossenning, derived from benzi, or bid hyzi,

in the Cornic-British and Armoric, signifying "to dip or drown."

It is almost incredible that as late as 1844, Pettigrew in his *Superstitions Connected with Medicine and Surgery*, says, "Casting mad people into the sea, or immersing them in water until they are well-nigh drowned, have been recommended by high medical authorities as a means of cure."

Reference is also made to the prevalence of the cure in 1808 in *Marmion*:

Thence to St. Fillian's blessed well,
Whose springs can frenzied dreams dispel,
And the crazed brain restore.

In a note, he adds that there were in Perthshire several wells and springs dedicated to St. Fillian, which were places of pilgrimage even among Protestants. "They are held powerful in the case of madness."

In fact, although any kind of water was regarded as efficacious for the complaint, water from any Saint's well was the more certain.

It may not be regarded as strange by some readers that the fury forsook the unfortunate fellow thrown into the water and "tossed up and down by persons of superior strength." By the time they had finished the sufferer was fury-less not from the departure of the disease, but, presumably, from sheer exhaustion.

BOOTS (ON TABLE)

To place a person's boots on a table, or on a chair, means that the owner will meet death by hanging.

Soaked in superstition generally, the Duke of Wellington had a dread of this particular instance. He is credited with having dismissed an old and valued servant who placed his fiancée's boots on a table.

The origin lies in those bad old days when hanging was the most commonly imposed of the law's punishments. Boots placed on a table or chair, could not reach the ground, and superstition saw them as dangling with the body! Such are the absurdities of some of the old superstitions.

There was a second, and less grim, superstition that to put a pair of boots on the table foretold a quarrel. This misfortune, however, could be averted if someone of quick perception and wit at once lifted up the boots and put them underneath the table.

See JOCKEY.

BORROWING

If you borrow a knife to cut an apple, or any other fruit, you must send it back "laughing," or bad luck will attend you.—Yorkshire.

This was a popular school-boy superstition. To send back the knife "laughing" meant that part of the "good thing" to cut which the knife had been used was given back with it.

BORROWING DAYS

The last three days in March, or the first three days in February.

In Devonshire the last three days in March are called Blind Days, and it is regarded as unlucky to sow any kind of seed during these seventy-two hours.

The "Borrowing Days" in the Scottish Highlands are 1st-3rd February inclusive, or Faiolteach by Highland reckoning (that is, old style) between 11-15th February.

Origin? Humboldt in *Cosmos* mentions three cold days in February as confirming his theory respecting the November stream or aerolites.

BOY OR GIRL

To know whether a baby shortly to be born will be a boy or a girl:

Clear a shoulder of mutton of every bit of meat at supper. Hold the blade bone to the fire until it is scorched. Then force the thumbs through the scorched thin part. Through the holes pass a string, knot it, and hang the bone over the back door.

If the first person to enter the door (exclusive of a member of the family) is a male, the baby will be a boy; if a female, it will be a girl.—Denbighshire.

BRAKE (PLANT)

The common brake only flowers once a year—on Michaelmas Eve at midnight —when it puts forth a small blue flower which disappears with the dawn of day. —Shropshire.

The same thing is said of the oak tree and the common fern (q.v.).

BRAMBLE-ARCH

If a person suffering from blackheads creeps on hands and knees under, or through a bramble bush, three times with the sun (i.e., east to west) he will be cured.

The bramble bush, it should be added, must form an *arch*, rooting at both ends. Similar "cures" with the bramble, are joined to whooping cough and bolls (West of England) and rheumatism (Wales) (q.v.).

BRASSES (ON HORSE'S HARNESS)

You must always have brasses on a horse's harness to keep away the Devil. —General.

Few superstitions were more widely held in the rural areas of England than this one—which gave rise to the jingling mass of ornamental and highly polished brasses so common on agricultural horses until the introduction of mechanical farming contrivances sent nearly all horses off the land.

No people have ever been so superstitious as those whose living is wrested from the soil, and is dependent upon the whims of the elements. In olden days the horse was the mainstay of the tiller of the land; if he lost his horse, he was, indeed, helpless. The horse had, therefore, to be protected in every possible way from witches, the Evil Eye, and the other attacks of the Devil.

Whence he derived the idea that shining and tinkling brasses would keep the evil at bay, is lost in the mists of time (mention of theories are made below) but the fact remains that he came to that belief, and thus loaded his horse with brasses. They were always assiduously polished, even if the horse was left unbrushed or un-curried.

The sequel is curious: for the collecting of old horse brasses to-day is a hobby, and a pretty expensive one at that.

The brasses against evil are nearly all attributable to symbols understood by the Saxons, the early British, and still older races. For instance, the Chinese thousands of years ago believed that the sound of brass instruments was particularly terrifying to devils, hence the use they made, and still make, of gongs in their rites of exorcism.

Even to-day, when the death-rate in China rises in the hot days of summer, Chinese people seek with processions of gongs to drive away and banish the evil spirits.

Among the Japs, an undertaker who was to place a corpse in its coffin received from the husband, wife or parent of the dead a brass ring which he wore fastened to his right arm, until the corpse was safely placed in the grave. The ring was held to guard him against any harm the spirit of the dead person might do to him.

BREAD

She who pricks bread with a fork or knife will never be a happy maid or wife.—Shropshire.

This dates back to those happy days when every household baked its own bread in the bake-oven then attached to all houses of any size. In many cases the oven was separate from the ordinary cooking oven, and was heated by firing it inside with wood. When the oven was hot enough the wood was swept out and the bread put on to the hot stone or iron floor, and the oven closed.

The pricking mentioned above was carried out to see whether the loaves were sufficiently baked. The superstition is really meant to say that any girl who stuck a fork or knife in one of the loaves to test the state of the batch bake was so inexperienced a person that she would never be happy as a wife—the pricking should always be done with a skewer.

See BAKING.

BREAD (TO FIND A CORPSE)

A loaf weighted with quicksilver, set on a river, will travel towards, and remain motionless over, the spot where a drowned body is lying on the bottom. —General.

A suspicion widely held in Britain, and still held. As recently as 1945, in the case of a missing person believed to have been drowned in the North of England, this method of locating a body was tried.

What is more, whether from chance, or what, it did, in effect, reveal the approximate position of the drowned person.

It is another instance of the affinity of superstition, that the same belief of bread, quicksilver and a body exists among the North American Indians.

A Biblical reference to quicksilver and life is probably the origin of the superstition.

BREAKFAST

Sing before breakfast and you will cry before night.

The origin of this might well have been a commendable effort to prevent people singing in their bath. It is a pity that this old superstition has died out!

BRIDE

It is ill-luck for a bride to step over the doorstep when she first enters her new home. She should be carried over by her husband.—Rural England.

A bride who leaps over a rope or stool at the church gate, will leave all her pets and humours behind her.—General.

Lucky is the bride who marries in old shoes.—General.

If a bride goes to sleep first on the marriage night, she will be sure to die first.—Yorkshire.

Unlucky will be the bride who marries in green.—General.

The bride should not see the bridegroom on the morning before the marriage, or the marriage will have bad fortune.—General.

Unlucky will be the bride who tries on her completed wedding dress before the wedding day.

For a bride to see herself fully dressed in the mirror before her wedding will make an unlucky marriage.

A stitch added to the bride's dress just before she leaves for the church will bring her good luck.

If a cat sneezes on the day before a wedding, the bride will be lucky in her marriage.

It must be pointed out that the ill-luck of marriage in green does not apply should the bride be Irish; it changes, indeed, to good luck! The bride's leap over a rope or stool at the church gate, to avoid ill-luck is the remnant of an older superstition, and it was meant originally, in some queer manner, as a test of her virginity.

In Devonshire, it was for many generations the custom for an old woman to present a bride with a little bag containing hazel nuts. It seems possible that this was bequeathed to us from the Roman occupation, and continued only in Devonshire, for the ancient Romans bestowed nuts on newly married people. In Germany to go "a nutting" was an euphemism for love-making. Nuts, in fact, signify fruitfulness. Catullus and Virgil both refer to the casting of nuts at weddings. Rice has, of course, the same significance.

The superstition referred to above, of the bride being carried by her bridegroom over the threshold of her new home, is still religiously observed in many rural areas. A year ago the London *Daily Mirror* recorded the ceremony in pictures of a country wedding.

To avoid the ill-luck of a bride looking into the mirror fully dressed, it is still the custom to take a last look at the ensemble—minus one glove!

Another superstition connected with a

country wedding was that unless the bees belonging to the household are told in their hives of the wedding, they will die. This is, of course, on a par with the telling of the bees of the death of the master, or a member of the household.

In Cheshire, it is held that should a bridal couple pass through the lych-gate of a churchyard one of them will die within a year, or the marriage will be an unhappy one. "Lych" was the Anglo-Saxon word for corpse; and the lych-gate of a church is that arched gate on which a coffin is rested as it waits the approach of the clergyman to lead the way into the church.

It was the habit of Nottingham lace-maker girls when they embroidered bridal veils, to take a long hair from a fair-haired girl and work it through the veil with the silk. If the hair went through without breaking it foretold a long and happy marriage; if, however, it broke at the beginning the wife would die early; if at the end, the husband.

Lest it should be thought that modern education and advance has dispelled this kind of superstition, the authors place on record a letter from a lace-maker in 1939, stating that the experiment had twice been tried by herself on veils made for friends. In one case the hair broke towards the end, and the husband had died within three years of the marriage. In the other, the hair went right through, and the marriage is still happy. The writer added that she had not dared try the experiment on her own veil when she married.

In many parts of the North of England, it was the practice after the wedding for the bride to enter her husband's house —her new home—and be handed a poker, shovel and tongs. This, it was said, was to show her authority as the housewife. There was, however, another superstition allied to it; if when a wife poked the fire sparks fell on the upper portion of her apron, then she would have children. The spark had to burn the apron above the knee, and it was at one time a common superstition in Lincolnshire.

Now, in the Slavonian countries a bride was led into her house, taken thrice round the hearth where she stirred the fire with a poker saying: "As many sparks fly up, so many cattle, so many children shall enliven the home."

The ancient Hindus led their brides round the fire and begged the fire god for children. There seems to be a common denominator in these widely separated country superstitions.

Mention is made above of the superstition of carrying a bride over the threshold of her new home as prevalent in Britain; a *bridegroom* of the Iluvand of Malabar is so carried; he must not touch the ground with his feet.

The one-time general superstition—it has been practised in quite recent times, we have a record of it in Dorsetshire in 1944—of a bride leaping over a rope or stool at the church gate after the wedding ceremony, to "leave all her pets and humours behind her" has, the authors think, a much deeper significance.

Older versions of the custom suggest that it was, in some strange way, a test of her virginity. But further back still than this, was the age of the belief in the tree spirits, of which mention is made elsewhere in this volume. The transference, for instance, of diseases to trees by pegging the hair of a sufferer in an ash, or laying parings of his nails in a hollow of the tree, were all a belief in the benevolence of the tree spirits.

In these early times, in Britain and in other countries, a bride after the wedding ceremony at times leaped over either the burnt ashes of wood, or over a tree or bush. At this time also, there was a belief that the blessing of women with offspring was an attribute of the tree spirits. The authors have no doubt whatever that the leaping of the more modern bride over the rope or stool at the church gate is a relic of the bride of the early days who leaped over the wood or the bush to propitiate the tree spirit and assure herself offspring of the marriage.

See BEES, MARRIAGE, SHOES, WEDDING.

BRIDE-ALE

The marriage feast, in Anglo-Saxon times, was called Bredale. It should be noted before details of the custom of bride-ale is given, that the word "ale" in ancient times—earlier than 1060—meant a feast. Thus church-ale was a church feast. Scot-ale a tax feast (Scot being a tax), Whitsun-ale a Whitsuntide feast, and so on.

Reference is made in the Oxford English Dictionary to bride-ale celebrations in 1076. It is from bride-ale that we have derived to-day our marriage word "bridal." It was first used in A.D. 1300.

The feast, in olden days was, in the words of *The Christen State of Matrimony*: "When they came home from the church then beginneth excess of eatyng and drynking—and as much is waisted in one daye as were sufficient for the two new married folkes halfe a yeare to lyve upon."

The Court Rolls of Hales-owen Borough, Salop, in the fifteenth Elizabeth contain the following: "Custom of bride-ale: Item. A payne is made that no person or persons that shall brewe any weddyn ale to sell, shall not brewe above twelve strike of mault at the most, and that the said persons so married shall not keepe nor have above eight messe of persons (Note: A mess was, anciently, four people) at the dinner within the burrowe; and before his brydall day he shall keepe no unlawful games in hys house, nor out of hys house a payne of 20 shillings."

Bride-ales are mentioned by Puttenham in his *Arte of Poesie*. During the course of Queen Elizabeth's entertainments at Kenilworth Castle, in 1575, a bryde-ale was celebrated with a great variety of shews and sports.

Jonson records that at the bride-ales in his time it was the custom to make presents to the pair in proportion to the gay appearance of their wedding.

Newton remarks that "at bride-ales the house and chambers were woont to be strowed with these odoriferous and sweet herbes to signifie that in wedlocke all pensive salennes and towring cheer, all wrangling, strife, jarring, variance and discorde ought to be utterly excluded and abandoned."

It will be noted that the old custom of gifts to the couple at the bride-ale persists even to-day in the display of gifts at our modern bridal reception after the ceremony; and the bride-ale itself in the wedding breakfast.

BRIDE-BED

In Papal times in Britain, it was considered an act of ill-luck for a newly married couple to retire for the night until the bridal bed had been blessed. Blomefield, in his *Norfolk*, cites an earlier statement that "the pride of the clergy and the bigotry of the laity was such that newly married people were made to wait till midnight, after the marriage day, before they would pronounce a benediction, unless they were handsomely paid for it, and the couple durst not undress without it, on pain of excommunication."

BRIDE CAKES

A slice of bride cake thrice drawn through the wedding ring and laid under the head of an unmarried man or woman will make them dream of their future wife or husband.—General.

The superstition is still practised to-day, but without passing the bridal cake through the wedding ring.

It is likely that bride-cake is another legacy to us from the Roman occupation, for it would appear to be a relic of the Roman confarreatio, a mode of marriage practised by the highest classes in ancient Rome. It was performed by the Pontifex Maximus in front of ten witnesses. The contracting parties mutually partook of a cake made of salt water and flour (far).

It came to a curious custom, however. In the North of England, particularly in Yorkshire, the cake was cut into small squares, thrown over the bride and bridegroom's head and then passed through the ring. In certain parts of Yorkshire a cake specially made was broken over the bride's head and then thrown among the wedding guests to be scrambled for. This ceremony was described by Smollett in *Humphry Clinker* (1771): "A cake being broken over the head of Mrs. Tabitha Lismahoge, the fragments were distributed among the bystanders, according to the custom of the ancient Britons, on the supposition that every person who ate of this hallowed cake, should that night have a vision of the man or woman whom Heaven designed should be his or her wedding mate."

An East Riding of Yorkshire custom was for a plate full of small pieces of bride cake to be handed to the bridegroom who threw the plate and its contents over the bride's head into the roadway, where children scrambled for the pieces. If the plate was not broken by the fall, a friend of the newly married pair stamped on it, for the good luck of the couple was held to be in proportion to the number of bits.

A variation of the bride cake placed under the pillow was the Northern custom of the oldest inhabitant of the village, stationed on the threshold of the bridal home, throwing a bride cake over the bride's head as she entered. Those of the guests who succeeded in obtaining a portion of cake in the scramble would dream that night of their sweethearts.

See MARRIAGE, WEDDING.

BRIDE'S CHAIR

A bride who does not sit in bride's chair will never have children.—Northumberland.

Perhaps it should be added that the

superstition is peculiar to that part of Northumberland in the parish of Jarrow. The chair is properly called Bede's chair, and was the chair of the Venerable Bede (673-735).

It is preserved in the vestry of the church, and to it all brides repaired immediately after the marriage service to seat themselves in it.

This act, according to the local superstition, will make them joyful mothers. For very many years no marriage was regarded as complete in the church if the bride had not taken her seat in the chair.

The chair, which is of rude design and very substantial, is made of oak; is 4 ft. 10 in. high with an upright back and sides that shape off for the arms.

There was another superstitious bride's chair in the church at Warton, Lancashire. To it brides were escorted after the marriage ceremony.

See MARRIAGE, WEDDING.

BRIDE DOOR

Run for the bride door.

Even in the North of England, where tradition lasts longer than elsewhere, the custom of running for the bride's door has died, almost beyond memory. Halliwell records it.

To run for the bride's door was to start for a favour given by a bride to be run for by the youth of the neighbourhood, who waited at the church door until the marriage was over, and then ran to the door of the bride's house. The prize was originally one of the bride's garters, but later a riband, which was worn for the day in the hat of the winner.

BRIDE LACES

It was an old superstition in the seventeenth and eighteenth centuries that the bride must be led to church between boys "with bride laces and rosemary tied about their silken sleeves," else the marriage would not be a happy one.

Heywood's *Woman Killed with Kindness* (1607), alludes to the nosegays and bride laces worn by country lasses on these occasions.

The bride laces were a kind of broad ribbon or small streamer. The custom exists to-day in the white ribbons which still ornament the car in which the bride is taken to and from the church ceremony.

BRIDE'S EVE, ST.

(1st February, Eve of Candlemas).

"Briid is come. Briid is welcome."

It was a custom of superstition on St. Bride's (or Bridget's) Eve in the Scottish Western Isles, to prepare a bed of St. Bride for any passing person or homeless stranger. (St. Bride is in legend supposed to have made a bed for the passing of Mary when she brought forth Jesus.) The isles' custom was for each family to make a sheaf of oats, dress it in women's clothes and put it in a large basket. This was called St. Bride's bed. Then the mistress of the house and servants cried, three times, "Briid is come. Briid is welcome."

In the morning, should there appear among the ashes on the hearth the impression of a footstep, it was a presage of a prosperous year of good crops.

In Ireland, particularly in remote parts of Donegal, square crosses of straw or rush were suspended in the house on St. Bride's Eve as a preservative against evil.

Another writer, however (John Ramsay, in *Scotland and Scotsmen in the Eighteenth Century*), has a very different version of the custom for the brides. He relates: "On the night before Candlemas it is usual to make a bed with corn and hay, over which blankets are laid, in a part of the house near the door. When it is ready a person goes out, and repeats three times, "Bridget, Bridget, come in; thy bed be ready." A candle is left burning near it all night.

Still different again, in the Isle of Man, the custom was to gather rushes and, standing with them on the threshold, invite St. Bridget to come and lodge there the night. The rushes were then strewn on the floor by way of a carpet, or bed, for St. Bridget. In some areas of the island a chair, table, and bread and cheese and ale were placed by the bed, in the hope that Breeshey would pay a visit.

The origin is so bound up with legend as to be practically impossible of elucidation satisfactory to the mind. The preparing of a bed for Mary, mentioned above, can be dismissed at once. The St. Bridget of the Isle of Man is held to have gone to the Isle of Man to receive the veil from St. Maughold. Another account says from St. Patrick. She is stated, however, to have received the veil from St. Mel, to have lived in Ireland, and become an abbess in that country. The latter is the more likely. None of these "origins" can in any way justify the St. Bride's bed, the corn or rushes.

There was, however, a Celtic pagan goddess, Brigit, goddess of fertility; and it is probable that by a similarity of sound in pronunciation, this pagan goddess has become, as Fraser describes it, disguised in a threadbare Christian cloak. This would explain the corn sheaves and the straw or rushes. Whether she can be connected with the Kildare (Ireland) St. Brigit, who tended a perpetual holy fire to the time of the suppression of the monasteries under Henry VIII, is a matter for conjecture.

The Roman Martyrology records the death of the Christian St. Bridget, her final repose at Rome, and her day as 7th October.

Valdencey, in his essay on the antiquity of the Irish language, says: "Rollin thinks this Deity was the same Queen of Heaven to whom the Jewish women burnt incense and made wine and cakes." And Leados: "This pagan custom is still preserved in Ireland on the Eve of St. Bridget, and which was probably transposed to St. Bridget's Eve from the festival of a famed poetess of the same name in the time of Paganism. It was another custom in parts of Ireland, that on St. Bridget's Eve, farmers' wives made 'a cake, called Bairin-break, invited neighbours, and spent the night with wine and revelry.

BRIDE'S DAY, ST.

Milk poured on to the ground and porridge thrown into the sea on St. Bride's Day will ensure produce of fish and fertilisation of seaweed.—Ireland and Wales.

BRIDE'S PIE

Another custom which has died. Yet, in the 1800's the bride's pie was so essential a dish on the dining table after the celebration of the marriage that there was believed to be little prospect of happiness without it.

Carr, in *The Dialect of Craven*, describes it as being made always round, and with a very strong crust ornamented with various devices. In the middle it was a representation of a strong laying hen, full of eggs, intended, probably, as an emblem of fecundity. The pie was garnished with minced and sweet meats. It was regarded as an act of neglect and rudeness if any member of the party omitted to partake of it.

BRIDE-WAIN.

The Scottish and Highlands equivalent to the English bride-ale (q.v.).

BRIDGE

If you part from a friend beside a bridge, you part for ever.—Wales.

This, however, did not apply to the most famous bridge meeting and parting in history—that of Dante and Beatrice on the Ponte Vecchio, Florence. After the first meeting they parted beside the bridge, but certainly not for ever.

BROOM

A new broom should sweep something into the house before it sweeps dust out of the house.—General.

If a girl strides over a broom handle, she will be a mother before she is a wife.—Yorkshire.

Buy a broom in May, sweep your friends away.—General in England.

It is unlucky to make brooms during May.—General in Ireland.

The sweeping something into the house before you sweep out was born of the superstition that a new broom used first to sweep *out* a house swept all the luck from the door.

In point of fact, there are many rural housewives to-day—and quite a few town dwellers—who believe that dust should not be swept out of the house but into the fireplace, where it is gathered up in a shovel and carried out. This is prevalent in many parts of Shropshire. It is one instance of the reversal of savage beliefs, because the Dyak people sweep misfortune out of a house with brooms made of the leaves of a certain plant, and sprinkled with rice water and blood. The sweepings are then put into a toy house made of bamboo, and the toy house set adrift on the river, where its cargo of bad luck drifts out to sea. A nice thought.

At Chiaromonte, in Sicily, on Mid-summer Eve the witches are held to acquire extraordinary powers, hence people were wont to put a broom outside their houses, because a broom was regarded as an excellent protective against witchcraft. A curious belief this, because superstitions regarding witches were fairly general throughout Europe, and in Britain a broomstick was popularly supposed to be the "steed" on which witches usually rode.

A word should be mentioned on the Yorkshire belief that if a girl strode over a broomstick she would be a mother before she became a wife. It was not unknown for an ill-wisher to lay a broomstick in the path so that a girl would walk over it by accident—in the hope that the superstition was right.

The authors have found no satisfactory answer why the month of May should be so unfortunate for the making, selling and buying of brooms. It was the rule in Ireland, however, to lay in a stock of brooms (mostly besom brooms) before May Day (1st May) in order that they should outlast the month of May.

The sweep your friends away belief of England attached to a broom bought in May meant, of course, that your friendship would be broken, though in one or two places it was held that the friend would be swept away by death.

BROWNIE
(The Brown Man of the Muirs)

The Brownie is a strange superstition peculiar to the Shetlands, the Highlands and the Western Isles. He is believed in Berwickshire to be the ordained helper of mankind in the drudgery entailed by sin; hence he is forbidden to receive wages. He is, however, says Henderson, allowed his little treats. The chief of these were knuckled cakes of meal warm from the mill, toasted over the embers and spread with honey. The housewife would prepare these and lay them carefully where he might find them by chance.

Pinkerton explains this sprite as an obliging spirit who used to come into houses by night and perform any piece of work that might remain to be done. But if any reward was left for him, he never returned.

The superstitious tales of this little fellow (who is the Pixie of Devonshire) are strange. A woman, prompted by her kindly nature, made a mantle and hood for the Brownie who had cleaned and refreshed her house. Not content with laying the gift in his favourite spot, she called to him that it was there. The Brownie quitted the place for ever, saying:

A new mantle, a new hood,
Poor Brownie, ye'll ne'er do muir gude.

Then there was the Brownie at Cranshaws, Berwickshire, who both saved the corn, and thrashed it on several occasions. At length, after one harvest, someone carelessly remarked that the corn was not well mown or piled up in the barn. The Brownie took offence at this and next night threw the whole of the corn over the Raven Craig, a precipice two miles away.

There are many similar tales of the Highlands.

BUMBLE-BEE

If a bumble-bee enters your house, you will have a visitor.—Buckinghamshire.

Like many superstitions this will probably come true—for there is no time limit set on how many days, weeks, or months after the flight the visitor is to appear; and most houses have a visitor *some time* in the year!

BUN

A bride should be met at the door, after the wedding ceremony, by the mother or nearest female relative, with a currant bun in her hands, which should be broken over the head of the bride before she crosses the threshold.—Scotland.

This, it was held by the curious beliefs of superstition, would bring the marriage good fortune. It was considered most unlucky if the currant bun should break by mistake over the head of any person but that of the bride.

Herrick alludes to the superstition in:
While some repeat
Your praise, and bless you, sprinkling you with wheat.

See BRIDE, MARRIAGE, WEDDING.

BUNIONS

Make a poultice of fresh cow-dung and the bunion will disappear.

An aged villager once told the parents of one of the authors how his bunions were cured. While he was hobbling about the house, using a sweeping-brush as a crutch, a neighbour called, and, on being told of the malady said: "Get some cow-dung, fresh fallen, mix it with fish oil (whale oil), put it on the bunion and let it stay there all night." He complied, but (he said) never slept all the night because of the pain. But the bunion was cured next day; and, "I've never had any trouble with it sin', and that's sixty year agone."

Origin? Probably the fomentation of the preparation. Cow-dung is well known to agriculturists as a "hot" manure; and mixed with oil would retain the heat for a long time.

BURBECK'S BONE.

This was a tablet of ivory, long preserved in the family of Campbell of Burbeck, which was esteemed a sovereign cure for lunacy. When it was borrowed for the purposes of effecting a cure, a deposit of £100 was exacted in order to secure its return.

See LOCKERBY PENNY, STONES.

BURIAL

The corpse last to enter a churchyard or cemetery, must watch the churchyard and guard the graves until the next corpse comes to take his place.—Ireland and the Highlands.

The last person to be buried in a churchyard each year is called the Ankon, who is, in fact, death itself. He is in the form of a skeleton and goes riding through the village in a chariot, warning those who are about to die.—Brittany.

The former of the two superstitions quoted above has, in its time, been the cause of many disgraceful incidents when a funeral approaching the cemetery has come into view of a cortege proceeding to the same cemetery from the opposite direction. The result, in Ireland particularly, has been a wild, helter-skelter race to be in the churchyard first, and thus not be possessed of the corpse left to guard the graves.

Added to this superstition is another in Ireland—that the pace of the cortege on its journey denotes the amount of respect being paid to the corpse. Hence, the predicament when two such corteges are approaching burial at one and the same time.

In East Yorkshire, after a corpse had been laid out, it had to be continually watched until burial, and at night a light was always kept burning in the room. On the night before the funeral a few friends usually assembled for a night watch (wake), and were not expected to leave until a newly lighted candle had burned into the socket.

A further Yorkshire custom, before the coffin lid was screwed down, was to lay the dead person's Sunday School class ticket, his hymn book and Bible with the body, and scatter flowers all over. Bearers of similar age to the dead carried the body to the graveside.

At the funeral of a maiden a pair of white gloves were carried at the head of the procession by a girl of about the same age. The gloves were afterwards hung up in the church near to the place usually occupied by the departed one. The gloves bore the maiden's name, age, and date of death, and the bearers of such were usually dressed in white.

In *Notes on Ancient Britain*, by W. Barnes, it is stated on the authority of Strutt, that "before the time of Christian rites, it was held unlawful to bury the dead within the cities, but they used to carry them out into the fields hardby, and there deposited them." It was St. Cuthbert who obtained leave to have yards made to the churches "proper for the reception of the dead."

There was for many years—and it is still practised in many parts to-day—a superstition that a body must be carried into the churchyard, or cemetery, for burial "with the sun"—that is in the direction of the sun's setting, from east to west.

Many a clergyman unversed in this belief has been staggered when, on waiting at the lych-gate to receive the body coming towards him, he has suddenly seen the cortege whirl round and compass the church before entering the churchyard.

The explanation to the bewildered man that "he wouldn't have the body go agin the sun, would he?" did nothing to disperse his bewilderment.

See CORPSE, DEATH, FUNERAL.

BURIED TREASURE

It was an old Yorkshire superstition, sixty and more years ago, for housewives to bury bottled fruit the better to preserve it. To mark the spot would be, of course, to give away the whereabouts to thieves; and many a hard day's toil has been lost through a housewife forgetting the burial place!

In 1890 there was a treasure trove of twenty bottles of preserved gooseberries buried somewhere near Scarborough Castle Hill, and one of the present authors as a boy, spent much fruitless time searching for them!

BURN (FIRE)

When a fire burns without "blowing." You'll have company without knowing.

It should be explained to the "modern," that blowing in this sense means that the fire, after being lighted, caught on and burned up without the aid of a "blower."

And a blower was a piece of sheet iron placed in front of the grate to make the fire "draw."

BURN (WOUND)

To cure a burn, apply goose-dung mixed with the middle bark of an elder tree and fried in May butter.—Shropshire.

Church linen will heal a burn.—Cheshire.

Lay your right hand very softly over the burn, then repeat these words three times, giving a gentle blast each time from your mouth on the place burned: "Old clod beneath the clay. Burn away. Burn away. In the name of God be thou healed." *After this the pain will go, and*

a deep sleep will fall on the patient.—
Antrim (Ireland).

In the nineteenth century these word charms were accounted the most popular cure for burns and boils, toothache and one or two more of the ills which man and woman are heir to.

The child of a Devonshire labourer died from scalds, and the *Pall Mall Gazette* of 23rd November, 1868, contained this extraordinary account of the inquest (the witness in question was one Ann Manley): "I am the wife of James Manley, a labourer. I met Sarah Sheppard about nine o'clock on Thursday morning on the road with the child in her arms, wrapt in the tail of her frock. She said the child was scalded. Then I charmed it, as I charmed before when a stone hopped out of the fire last Honiton Fair and scalded its eye. I charmed it by saying to myself 'There was two angels come from the north, one of them brought fire and the other frost. Out fire, in frost, in the name of the Father, Son and Holy Ghost.' I repeat this three times. This is good for a scald. I can't say it is good for anything else. Old John Sparway told me this charm many years ago. A man may tell a woman the charm, or a woman may tell a man. But if a woman tells a woman or a man a man, I consider it won't be any good at all." In the Shetlands the words of the charm used are:

Here come I to cure a burnt sore;
If the dead knew what the living
    endure,
The burnt sore would burn no
    more.

The "healer" then blew three times upon the burnt place.

Even as late as 1910, the healing power of church linen (without any doctoring) was held firmly for burns and scalds. Elizabeth Mary Wright in *Rustic Speech and Folklore* relates how in that year a friend of hers, then lodging in Liverpool, had the misfortune to burn a hand. Her landlady, who held a post as charwoman in a church, and who received gifts of church linen, offered to bind up the wound with a piece of chalice lace. She subsequently attributed the healing of the burn to the efficacy of the holy linen.

BURNING THE FAGGOT

Burning the ashen faggot has been a custom in Somerset inns for generations —in fact, since the time of King Alfred, according to tradition.

It was celebrated, in many inns, in that year of grace, nineteen-hundred-and forty-five.

See ASHEN FAGGOT.

BURNING T'OLD WITCH

A widespread North Riding harvest superstition was known as "Burning t'old Witch" (burning the old witch). After the harvest had been gathered in, a fire of stubble was made in the last field to be cleared, and peas were parched therein. These were eaten, with a plentiful allowance of beer. Games and dancing followed the supper.

Why exactly the old witch was burned we do not know. We doubt whether, indeed, the burners of her knew, either.

But a few thousand miles away, in North Western India, at the close of the old year, the Biyars, a mixed tribe, burn the old witch, too. The old year is represented by a stake of the wood of the cotton tree which is planted just outside the village and then burned at the full moon in the month of Pus. Fire is first put to it by the village priest, followed by all the people of the village. Next day the ashes of the wood are thrown into the air, and the festival ends with a saturnalia—exactly as in the North Riding of Yorkshire. Queer, is it not?

BURYING OLD TOM

Old-time superstition of rural Herefordshire labourers on New Year's Eve, when they forgathered in the inns for a few extra glasses, a few sing-songs, and tunes set to special verses. It was known as burying old Tom. Why "Tom" the authors have failed to discover.

BUSH

To prevent smuts or mildew affecting your wheat, cut a large thorn bush, make a fire in the field of wheat, and burn a portion of the thorn. Afterwards hang up the remainder of the thorn in the farmhouse.—Herefordshire.

This ceremony was performed as the wheat showed its sproutings through the ground. But to make the charm successful, superstition ordained that the farm hands had to carry out the ritual before daybreak.

The origin of this lies in the belief that thorn shrubs were anathema to witches and all evil spirits. The Saxons held this superstition, so did the Rumanians, the Czechs, Germans and the Bohemians.

Thorny branches were laid on the thresholds of cow-houses throughout

Europe on Walpurgis Night, to keep evil and disease from the beasts.

The ancient Athenians chewed buckthorn on one morning in the year to banish evil spirits of the dead.

BUTTER

If you do not throw salt into the fire before you begin to churn, butter will not come.—Lincolnshire.

Milk will foam in the churn till the hour of high water is past.—Lincolnshire coastal areas.

If you put a ring of rowan tree on the handle of the churn-dash, when churning, no witch can steal the butter.—Ireland.

A Scottish superstition for use when butter will not form in the churn, was that an evil spirit had affected the cream. There was, however, a remedy— to recite three times the lines:

Come, butter come.
Peter stands at the gate,
Waiting for a buttered cake,
Come, butter come.

At the expiry of the third time of saying, the butter would commence to form.

(If the dairymaid kept the churn turning!)

The Lincolnshire belief that the butter will form when the tide is coming in has its counterpart, only more so, in Brittany, where it is held that the best butter is made when the tide has turned and is just beginning to flow. No Breton farmer's wife would think of churning until this hour.

It was deemed superstitiously essential in the Highlands that the peg of the cow-shackle and the handle of the cross of the churn-staff should be made of rowan wood (mountain ash) to guard against the witches interfering with the buttermaking. Rowan was the principal Highland weapon against witchcraft.

The Estonians on St. John's Eve lighted bonfires, one of the reasons for which was to ensure that throughout the year, the butter will be as yellow as the sun of the fire, and as gold.

See ROWAN.

BUTTERFLY

Kill the first butterfly you see each year, or you will have bad luck all through the year.—Devonshire.

If the first butterfly you see in the year is a white one, you will have bad luck all the year.—Gloucestershire.

A golden butterfly fluttering near a dying person is a good omen.—Scottish Gaelic.

A butterfly hovering near a corpse is a sign of everlasting happiness.—Ireland.

To see three butterflies together is as good as seeing three magpies.—Nottinghamshire.

Butterflies are the souls of the dead waiting to pass through Purgatory.—Ireland.

Butterflies are the souls of unbaptized babies.—Devonshire.

The Gloucestershire white butterfly belief runs, to be exact, this way: "If the first butterfly you see in the year is white you will eat white bread during the remainder of the year." This, in the days when the superstition was coined, meant certain good luck. If the first butterfly was brown, then brown bread, or ill-luck, would be the year's burden.

Hunt, in one of his West of England books, tells a story of an old man, upwards of seventy, as illustrating that the butterfly superstitions of Devonshire were so inborn as not to be discarded by the seasoned judgment of age. The old man was attempting to hobble along with the aid of one stick, instead of his usual two. Asked what was wrong, he explained: "My zin (son) a took away wan a my sticks; won't be abble to kil'n now, though, I b'lieve."

Asked what it was that should be killed, he replied: "Why, 'tis a butterfly, the furst a zeed for the year, and a body'll have cruel bad luck if a ditn'en kill a furst a zeeth."

In the above-listed superstitions, the two from Ireland and the one from Gloucester have, probably, a deeper significance than the others, which have no traceable origin. For they are, undoubtedly, born of the ancient belief that the soul escapes in the form of a butterfly.

Such belief is older, far, than Christianity. The ancient Egyptians' symbol of death was that the soul left the dead as a butterfly emerges from a chrysalis. There have been recorded instances (once in Armagh) of a child being chided for chasing a butterfly which, it was held, was quite likely the soul of a relative who had died recently.

Wander from Armagh for a moment to the Solomon Islands—where a man, on the point of dying, was wont to call his family together and inform them of the kind of creature, popularly a butterfly, into which he proposed to migrate. If, afterwards, they met a butterfly, they would say, "That is Papa," and offer the insect a gift.

Journey across the oceans again, to the Nagus of Assam, where it is held that the spirits of the dead, after undergoing a cycle of changes in a subterranean world, are reborn in the form of butterflies, only in that shape to perish for ever.

How came from Ancient Egypt the butterfly soul idea to Ireland? The authors suggest, probably through the older Gaelic race.

BUTTONS

Put a button or a hook into the wrong hole when dressing, and some misfortune will happen to you during the day.—General.

However, you can avert disaster quite easily—by taking off the garment and putting it on anew!

CAESARIAN OPERATION

A child born from a Caesarian operation has unusual strength, and the ability to see spirits and discover hidden treasure.—Cornwall.

CAKE

If the housewife cuts the first cake from the oven, all the rest will be heavy.—Durham.

The lucky way, so a Durhamite tells us, is to break the cake, not to cut it!

CALF

The tip of a calf's tongue carried in the pocket will protect you from danger; and the pocket will never be without money.—Northumberland.

Calves weaned with the waning moon will never grow fat, but always remain lean.—Wales.

It is unlucky to put your hand on a calf's back. The calf will fall ill, or meet with an accident.—Cheshire.

The latter superstition is still believed in farming districts of Cheshire.

The Northumberland name for the tip of a calf's tongue, mentioned in the superstition above, is the "lucky bit."

See CALF (BURNING).

CALF (BURNING)

Burn a calf to secure luck for the rest of the herd.—Isle of Man.

"Kill a calf to stop the murrain" (*cattle disease*).—General throughout Britain.

The Xmas mistletoe bough, given to the cow first to calve in the New Year, will ensure good luck attending your dairy; if you do not, bad luck will attend you.—Worcestershire.

Bound up with these superstitions of the burning of a calf is the belief in the sacrifice of an animal to stay plague (or murrain) among cattle, which held sway in all parts of Britain from earliest time to as late as the early nineteenth century.

No part of agricultural England was free from the belief, which led to the most vicious of all superstitious rites in Britain, for the calf (or sheep, pig, or lamb) was generally burned alive.

Sir J. G. Frazer, in the *Golden Bough*, states that: "Certainly the practice of burning a single animal alive in order to save all the others would seem to have been not uncommon in England down to the nineteenth century."

Thus Hitchin, in his *History of Cornwall*, records that a farmer in Cornwall, about 1800, having lost many cattle by disease, lighted a large fire, and with fellow farmers, drove a calf, with pitchforks, into the flames whenever it tried to escape, burning the animal alive to save the remainder of the herd.

In Northamptonshire, at the same period, the burning of a calf to stop the murrain ("Sacrifice one for good luck") was a common practice.

As recently as 1928, at Portreath, a calf was recorded as sacrificed for the purpose of removing a disease which had followed a farmer's horses and his cows.

Of Wales, Marie Trevelyan in *Folk Stories of Wales*, records: "I have heard my grandfather and father say that in times gone by the people would throw a calf in the fire when there was disease among the herds."

Writing in 1866, Henderson related how, only twenty years before, a live ox was burned near Haltwhistle, in Northumberland, to stop a murrain.

In the Isle of Man, burning cattle to end a murrain persisted to times within living memory.

In Scotland, Dalyell, in *The Darker Superstitions of Scotland*, written in 1835, states: "Here may be found a solution of that recent expedient so ignorantly practised, where one having lost many of his herd by witchcraft, as he concluded, burnt a living calf to break the spell and preserve the remainder."

It is not so much the origin of the superstition which is strange, as the fact that it persisted for nearly 200 years after the origin had been exploded. In remote districts of Cornwall, it was said by farmers at one time that the sacrifice of a live calf appeased the wrath of God—and they are said to have argued that the Bible gave them reason for that belief. This, presumably, is the Abraham sacrifice on the mountain.

This, however, was probably more of an excuse than an explanation of the sacrifice. There is little doubt that the origin of the burning alive was allied, like other superstitions mentioned in this volume, to the belief in the Evil Eye and in witchcraft.

Nothing was so widely believed in rural areas than that the illness of one of the cattle was due to a spell cast upon them by a witch, or a warlock; and this was, without doubt, the origin of the "burn one to save the herd" superstition.

How did the burning of the one end the evil spell? In one of two ways, according to the lore of witchcraft. First, it was maintained that if one desired to know whom it was that had cast the Evil Eye, it was necessary only to burn one of the sick beasts in the open air, and watch beside it, for the caster of the spell could not help coming to the scene.

Secondly, and this was the more important, it was held that whatever you did to the beast, so would happen to the witch. Hence, if the calf was burned, so would the witch be burned, and the spell she had cast upon the cattle would end with her death.

It is recorded in Lady Gordon's extracts of Suffolk folk-lore, that about the year 1800 everyone in the neighbourhood of Ipswich held strangely the view that a witch had been burned to death in her house in the town by the process of burning alive a sheep she had bewitched. The only parts of her which were not incinerated were her hands and feet; the four feet of the sheep, by which it had been suspended over the fire, were also unconsumed by the flames. The name of the witch is given in history as Grace Pett.

Thus, the origin of the burning of the animal alive was directed as the sole object of burning alive the witch.

NOTE: It is not without interest to note that to-day cattle are killed, and their bodies burned, to end the murrain, which is (and probably was) foot and mouth disease.

See LAMB, NEED-FIRE, PIG, SHEEP.

CALF (HANGING)
To stop death disease among calves, a leg and thigh of one which has died should be hung in the chimney of the farmhouse by a rope.—Durham.

This practice, however, was not confined to Durham. Dead horses and calves were frequently to be seen hung by the legs on farms in the Weald of Sussex.

There used to exist near the Ditchling Beacon a great elm tree which was at times loaded with the dead animals hanging from horizontal branches, all a sacrifice to superstition for the welfare of the remainder of the calves or foals, or of those yet to be born.

The authors can surmise only that the practice is a survival of the sacrifice to Odin, in making offerings to him in hope of his favour towards their herds. It was a custom of the ancient Germanic tribes to hang upon trees the heads of their horses killed in battle as offerings to the god. He was supposed to receive the souls of such as had fallen in war.

Odin, it will be recalled, rode forth on his great hunt across the Heavens and over the "Milky Way" on a horse—Sleepner. And, to lend credence to the suspended animals of Durham and the Weald, he is said himself on one occasion to have hung between Heaven and earth.

It is, perhaps, informative to recall that when in A.D. 15 Calcina visited the scene of Varean's fall, he saw horses' heads hanging on trees round the altars where the Roman centurions and tribunes had been murdered.

CAMPHOR
Camphor carried on the person will ward off any infection.—General.

There is no medical truth in the superstition long held, and often still carried out to-day.

CANCER
Toads have the power of sucking the poison of cancer from the system.—Rural belief in eighteenth century.

It would seem to the authors that something of this wicked belief still exists. A correspondent from the Midlands wrote us some months ago to ask did we know that cancer could be cured, and "had been cured in a definite case I know" by the patient swallowing young frogs.

Presumably, the idea was that the frogs, like the toads of two centuries ago, sucked the poison away.

There is, of course, no vestige of truth in the belief.

CANDLE

A candle should be lighted at the birth of a child in order that evil spirits be kept from the infant.

A candle should be lighted at marriage to prevent the Evil Eye alighting on the bridal couple.

A candle should be lighted at death, so that the demons may not dare to approach near enough to seize the soul of the dying.

A candle showing a bright spark will bring a letter to the person sitting opposite the spark.

Grease congregating round the wick of a candle is a winding sheet, foretelling the death of someone in the family.

Should one desire to know from the spark in the candle the exact date on which one will receive the "promised" letter, knock on the table until the spark in the candle-flame falls. The number of knocks required to achieve this is the number of days to elapse before the arrival of the letter.

The death and spark omens have no possible origin. But not so the superstition which lights a candle at birth and marriage.

Now, why should a candle-flame come to the countryside of Britain as a spell at child-birth? The answer is that it came, in all probability, with the Romans. Most readers will know of the Vestal Virgins, who guarded the sacred fire in the temple of Vesta. Vesta was the goddess of the hearth, a mother goddess, and bestower of offspring on cattle and women.

Thus, in a number of countries, a bride after the marriage ceremony, was led to the hearth, across which she walked three times, in order that she should bear children. When a Slavonian woman desires a child she holds a vessel full of water in front of her, while her husband knocks burning brands together until sparks fly. When sparks have fallen into the vessel the water thus fertilized by the fire is drunk.

Compare this with an old Lincolnshire belief that if a woman's apron is burned above the knee by sparks or cinders flying out of the fire, she will become a mother. Thus is maintained the superstition which gave rise to the story of the conception by fire of a handmaiden who gave birth to the Kings of Rome.

But to return to the candle. The candle is flame, and flame is fire, and Vesta, the mother-goddess, is served by fire. Thus, if a child newly born is guarded by fire, it will be free from attack by evil, being under the protection of Vesta.

In some parts of England, and among the more remote French peasants, it was held that if a girl can blow into flame a spluttering and dying candle-spark, she is a virgin; if she cannot, she is not. The origin, again, lies in the Vestal Virgins. None but those of pure life might blow upon the Holy Fire.

Contrariwise, in Darfus, it was held that should the city catch fire, its only means of safety from destruction would be to bring near the flames a woman, no longer young, who had never been guilty of intrigue. By merely waving her mantle she would put an *end* to the flames. The experiment would probably have been an eye-opener to the men of the city!

In Wales, on Hallowe'en, weirdest of all the tier nos ysbrydion (three spirit nights), women had a custom of gathering in the parish churches and endeavouring to read their fate in the candle each held in her hand.

An Icelandic legend tells how three spae-wives (or Sibyls) visited the infant Gestr, then lying in his cradle. There were only two candles burning, and the younger of the spae-wives, being slighted, prophesied: "I foretell that the child shall live no longer than this candle burns." The elder spae-wife at once extinguished the candle and handed it to Gestr's mother, with the warning that it should not be re-lighted until her son wished to die. Gestr lived 300 years before he relit the candle, whereupon he died.

Candles in Lancashire were used for keeping witches at bay on All Hallows Eve. The witches were wont to gather (says the legend) at the Malkin Tower, a farmhouse in the Pendle forest. Lancashire folk held the belief that you could keep them from working evil by burning a candle. The witches did their utmost to blow it out. If they succeeded, so much the worse for the victim. But let the flame burn till midnight, and the wiles of the witches were defeated. It was the custom for people to go round houses collecting candles with which to "leet" (light) the witches!

Northumberland rural folk as late as the nineteenth century practised the same custom.

In Ireland, on Twelfth Night Eve, it was the custom to set as high as could be done, a sieve of oats with a dozen candles round the edge, and, in the centre, a taller candle in memory of the Saviour and his Apostles, lights of the world.

Other candle omens in olden days were: "If a candle burns blue it is a sign that there is a spirit in the house, or not far from it"—in other words, a death omen.

Contrary Davenport records a belief (1639): "By the burning of the candle blue . . . and by the drippings of the Beadle's nose, I smell a frost."

More to be understood was the saying: "If the flame of a candle does wave or wind itself when there is no sensible or visible cause, expect some wintry weather." When candles were not so readily kindled as at other times, it was a sign of wet weather near at hand.

When candles sparkle and rise up with little fumes, or their wicks swell with things in them like mushrooms, all are signs of wet weather.

The candles offered to St. Blase, on his Saint's Day (3rd February) were claimed to be good for the curing of toothache, or for curing diseased cattle.

Stage candle superstition demands that on no account must three candles be alight at the same time in a theatre dressing room.

Under certain conditions it was held in the sixteenth and seventeenth centuries that a candle could render impotent all attempts to arrest or avert thieves. This thief's candle had to be made of the fat of a malefactor who had died on the gallows, or of the fat of a newly-born or, better still, an unborn child.

The candle was then put into the Hand of Glory, and when lighted had the effect of rendering motionless all people who chanced to be in the house. Once these candles began to burn, said the superstition, nothing but milk could put them out. In the seventeenth century robbers used to murder pregnant women in order to extract the unborn child from their wombs.

The Indians of Mexico had a similar belief. They became possessed of the left forearm of a woman who had died in giving birth to her first child. The arm had to be stolen. With it they beat the ground before entering the house they planned to rob; this caused everyone in the house to lose all power of speech or motion. Robbers of ancient Greece believed that the most ferocious watchdog could be rendered harmless if they

carried with them a brand plucked from a funeral pyre.

A Blackfoot Indian when he went hunting would take a skull with him, holding that it would make him invisible, like the dead person to whom the skull had belonged. The eagles could not then see him, and he would be free from their attack.

Similarly, wives of Bulgaria and Servia used to take the copper coins which were always placed in the eyes of a corpse, wash them in wine and add the liquid to their husband's drink. After they had drunk it, the husbands would be blind to the love affairs of their erring wives—as blind as the dead man from whose eyes the coins had been taken.

See HAND OF GLORY.

CANDLE (CORPSE)

If one corpse candle is seen, there follows the corpse of some infant.

If there be seen two, three or more, of different sizes, some big, some small, then shall so many corpses pass together, and of such ages and degrees.

If two candles come from different places and be seen to meet, the corpses will do the same.

If any candle be seen to turn aside, through some by-path leading to the church, the following corpse will be found to follow exactly the same way.—Wales.

The corpse-candle was the name given in Wales to those lambent flames seen in marshy ground, in a churchyard or over a grave, and superstitiously believed to be an omen of death.

In most parts of Britain they were known as will-of-the-wisps. In Suffolk their name was Sylham Lamp; in the West Country as Joan-in-the-Wad; and in Newcastle, the old name was Weize. Elsewhere it was termed "Friar's Lanthorn." The correct designation is ignis fatuus, which means, simply, "a foolish fire." It is a flame-like phosphorescence, flitting over marshy ground, due to the spontaneous combustion of gases from decaying vegetable matter.

The main reason for the superstition and dread which surrounded it, was that it was frequently to be seen in churchyards and eluded people who attempted to follow it.

In Wales the belief was rampant, and in the wildnesses of the mountain villages it still is, that the flame is the spirit of a relative come from the churchyard to fetch the spirit of a dying man or woman. The tradition is that St. David promised to Welshmen in his territory that none should die without the premonitory sign of a light travelling to his house from the churchyard to summon him. How sincerely this superstition was held is recorded in the following entry in the Cambrian Register (1796):

A very commonly received opinion, that within the diocese of St. David's, a short space of time before death, a light is seen proceeding from the house, and sometimes, as has been asserted, from the very bed where the sick person lies, pursues its way to the church where he or she is to be interred, precisely in the same track in which afterwards the funeral is to follow.

The belief in Devonshire, and in Cornwall, is on much the same lines, except that it is held that no corpse-candle will fetch a soul, unless a relative is already buried in that particular churchyard.

Many stories are told in "proof" of the corpse-candle. There is one from Llangatten, Carmarthenshire, of the room in which slept five domestic maids. The housekeeper going into the chamber saw no fewer than five lights. Soon afterwards the room was replastered and a coal fire was lighted to help in drying the plaster. Next morning the five servants were found dead in bed, having, it was stated, been asphyxiated in their sleep with the fumes of the new-tempered lime and coal.

Another story is "vouched for" by a church dignitary, and is told in *Nightshade of Nature*. A female relative of the dignitary set out on horseback for a visit, accompanied by her manservant. At a spot half-way, where she expected to be met by the servant of her friend, she dismissed her own man.

Shortly afterwards she saw a light approaching, moving some three feet above the earth, and turned her horse out of the bridal path to allow it to pass. It, however, halted opposite⋅her, and remained flickering for half-an-hour, vanishing when there came the sound of the servant's horse.

On reaching her friend she related what she had seen. A few days later the servant died. His body was carried to burial along the road up which the light had moved. Strange to relate, owing to an accident, the coffin halted for half-an-hour at the spot where she had been delayed by the halted light.

Another story relates how a servant of Lady Davis heard feet trampling down the stairs at 3 a.m. and a bump against the clock on the stairs. Opening the door he saw a light, and, terrified, rushed out of the house. There he saw the gleam of light pass out of the door and move towards the churchyard.

Lady Davis was at this time seriously ill in bed, and he took this experience as an omen of her death, so much so that, on his return from market, which had been the reason for his early rising, he inquired whether she was still alive. Told that she was better, he described what he had seen, and expressed his conviction that her death was certain.

Lady Davis did, in fact, recover, but a fortnight later another member of the family died. As the coffin was being taken downstairs for the funeral, the bearers bumped it violently against the clock on the stairs, exactly as the servant had heard.

Now, at the other extreme is Scotland. A Scottish minister, but newly come to his church, while standing near the wall of the churchyard, which adjoined his house, saw a light moving. Supposing that someone was walking with a lantern among the graves he walked through the gate towards it. Before he reached the spot, however, the light moved on. He followed across the road, without being able to see anyone, entered a wood and at last saw the light enter a farmhouse. Puzzled at the fact that he could not see anyone with the light, he was about to make inquiries at the house, when the light reappeared, accompanied this time by a second one. They passed him, and pursued the same road back, finally disappearing where he had first observed the earlier light.

The minister took the precaution of marking the spot; and next day asked the sexton whose vault it was. The reply was that it belonged to a family living up the hill, and the sexton indicated the house—the one at which the minister had seen the light stop and enter. Later in the day the minister was asked to undertake the funeral service of a child who had died in the house the previous evening from scarlet fever.

Another candle superstition, prevalent particularly in the North Country, is of placing a lighted candle in a loaf of bread, which is then set adrift on water, in which it is feared a drowned person is lying. It is held that the loaf will float motionless over the spot where the corpse is resting. The candle flame, here, represents in superstition the soul in quest of its husk.

In many of the remote districts of Wales even to-day the corpse-candle is implicitly believed in.

It is stated that before the explosion at Llanbradach and Glyncorrwg, corpse-candles had been seen at night hovering round the pits. This, in addition to other omens.

See DOVE, ROBIN.

CANDLE-AND-PINS

To bring your lover to you stick two pins through a lighted candle. By the time the candle burns down to the pins, the lover will be certain to present himself.—North of England.

This charm to bring a lover had an enormous vogue even as late as the early nineteenth century in the North of England, and also in remote Buckinghamshire.

With the sticking of the pins had to go the chanting of a verse as follows:

It's not the candle alone I stick,
But A.B.'s heart I mean to prick;
Whether he be asleep or awake,
I'll have him come to me and speak.

It is a rather remarkable commentary (or should we say merely coincidence) that instances abound where disbelievers have vouched that a lover's coming followed the burning of the candle. Henderson records that "he (the named lover) came to one maid because he could not help himself, but came in an ill humour, declaring that he knew she had been up to some devilment or other. No tongue, he added, could tell what she had made him suffer, and he would never have another word to say to her."

In Durham, it was accounted not necessary to burn the candle, but simply to stick pins into it. Here, again, a recorded result is available. Asked by a member of her family why she was sticking pins into a candle, a servant girl replied: "It's to bring my sweetheart. He's slow a' comin', and if I sticks a candle end full of pins, it always fetches him." The member of the family certified that John was thus, and often, fetched from a distance of six miles. The Rev. James Raine, then of Durham, told of the incident.

This is, of course, a later and less harmful copying of the earlier bewitchery, in which a wax image of a person was made and a pin stuck in a part of the body. Wherever the pin point touched, there the person would feel a pain, and should the pin be placed through a vital point, it would cause

the death of the original of the wax image.

Possession of such wax images led to many women being burned in this country as "proved witches."

CANDLEMAS.

(2nd February)

*If Candlemas Day be fair and clear,
There'll be twa winters in the year.*
—Scotland.

*If the sun shine out on Candlemas
Day of all days in the year,
The shepherd had rather see his
wife on the bier.*
—East Norfolk.

NOTE: Meaning the spring would be cold and late.

If all Xmas decoration is not removed out of the church before Candlemas Day, there will be a death during the year in the family occupying a pew where a leaf or a berry is left.

*When the wind's in the east on
Candlemas Day,
There it will stick till the second of
May.*—Shetlands.

The death superstition attached to the removing of all the Christmas decorations by Candlemas Day was so strongly held that Chambers in his *Book of Days* recalls that a woman of his acquaintance was not content to leave the clearing of her pew to the church authorities—who were themselves assiduous in clearing away the decorations—but was in the habit of sending a servant to the church on the Eve of Candlemas to make quite sure that her pew, at any rate, was clear of the threat of death!

In the Highlands of Scotland, it was the custom on the Eve of Candlemas to make a bed for St. Bridget or St. Bride (q.v.).

At the Cornish manor house of Godolphin, it was the custom on Candlemas Day for the reeve of the manor of Lamburne to collect, with time-honoured ceremony, a rent charge upon the estate. He knocked three times upon the door and cried: "I come to demand my Lord's just dues—eight groats and a penny, a loaf, a cheese, a collar of brawn, and a jack of the best beer in the house. God save the King and the Lord of the Manor," afterwards the reeve and guests were entertained to breakfast.

It was at Candlemas that the bacchanalian revels called the King of Misrule came to an end.

In the Roman Catholic Church, on

this day, it has been the custom to consecrate the candles to be used in the churches throughout the coming year.

The secondary name of Candlemas is the Feast of the Purification of the Virgin Mary; and it is commonly stated that the custom of carrying lighted candles in procession is in memory of Simeon's words at the presentation of the Infant Christ: "To be a light to lighten the Gentiles."

This is not, however, quite correct. Felmary is taken from Felma, the Roman goddess *who presided over religious purifications.* Since the Virgin Mary's conception was Immaculate there would seem to be something incompatible in the idea that any purification was necessary.

Now, the purification of Februa was by fire, and the author of *Festival* states that the origin of Candlemas as we know it was as follows:

"Sometyme, when the Romaines by great myght and royal power, conquered all the world, they made so proude that they forgot God, and made them divers gods after their own lust. And so among all they had a god they called Mars, that had been tofore a notable knyte in battaile; and so they prayed to hym for help and for that they would speed the better of this knyte, the people prayed and did great worship to his mother, that was called Februa, after which woman much people have opinion that the moneth February is called. Wherefore the second daye of this moneth is Candlemas Day. The Romaines this night went about the city of Rome with torches and candles brenning in worship of this woman Februa, for hope to have more helpe and succoure of her son Mars.

"Then there was a Pope that was called Sergius, and when he saw Christian people drawe to this false maumetry and untrue belief, he thought to undo this foule use and custom, and turn it into God's worship and Our Lady's, and gave commandment that all Christian people should come to church and offer up a candle brenning in the worship they did to this woman Februa, and do worship to Our Ladye and to her sonne Jesus Christ. So nowe this feast is solemnly hallowed throwe all Christendome."

See KING OF MISRULE.

CANTERBURY BELLS

To pick Canterbury Bells from the garden will toll the death-bell in the village.—The Weald.

If Canterbury Bells will grow in it, a garden will be luchy.—South Country.

Both these superstitions had their birth in the belief that the Canterbury Bell is a "sacred flower." It derived its name from the similarity of the bell-like flowers to the bells carried by the horses of the pilgrims who made the pilgrimage to the tomb of Thomas à Becket at Canterbury. The travelling monk, too, carried a bell, whether he was on foot or on horseback, by which a village knew he was approaching with his blessing and medicine for the sick.

It will be plain, therefore, that in those days, the presence of the "Canterbury Bell" was, indeed, good fortune or luck.

Although this luck superstition was pretty general throughout the South, only in the Weald have the authors been able to find the death threat for the picking of the flower thus given sanctity through Becket. There, however, it has been traced in folk-lore definitely so far back as the year 1700, and probably existed long before that.

Sir Charles Igglesden, in one of his interesting books on folk-lore, relates an old Weald bellringer's aversion to the growing of Canterbury Bells. He referred to some in the garden of a neighbour. "They dunno as 'ow they be sacred flowers," he said. "So long as they don't touch 'em its alright but if anyone picks one it means the tolling of the death-bell in the village. Let 'em grow 'em, but its risky with children about, for the little brats will pick flowers. And we don't want no child burials."

He was asked how long he had known about the superstition.

"Well, it must be many a year," was his reply. "My father told me, and his father told 'im. Both was over eighty, so you can reckon it up. I reckons as 'ow it'd be over two hundred years, for I be ninety."

CARROTS

To cure the asthma boil, eat carrots in quantities at every meal.

This remedy was given by John Wesley, in his *Primitive Physic* (which also advised six middling-size cobwebs for ague!).

Like various others of these old wives' remedies, carrots for asthma had a basis of solid fact. For, many years later, scientists discovered that carrots possess a volatile principle which stimulates the bronchial membranes and promotes expectoration. Hence the relief for asthma.

In the early part of the World War, 1939-1945, carrots were popularly supposed to give R.A.F. fighter pilots the ability to see in the dark.

The authors have failed to secure any reliable evidence to that effect.

CARRYING THE BRIDE

The bride who wishes a lucky marriage should not step first over the threshold of her new home. She must be carried over by her bridegroom.—General.

It is refreshing to find that, in many rural areas, even to-day, this pleasant custom of carrying the bride over the door of her new home is still maintained. Such a ceremony in a small hamlet in the South of England was photographed and reproduced in the London *Daily Mirror* only a few months ago.

There is a custom in some parts of carrying one's bride over a stile.

CAT

To cure illness in a family, wash the patient and throw the water over a cat. Then drive the cat out of doors, and it will take the illness with it.

The mewing of a cat on board a ship foretokens a serious voyage.—Wales.

If a ship's cat stretches so that its paws meet, before the ship reaches Lundy Island from any port in the Bristol Channel, storms will be encountered.—Wales.

For a cat to be frolicsome on board a ship presages a gale of wind in their tails and rain in their faces.—Sailors' superstition.

It is unlucky to let a cat die in the house.—Lancashire.

If a cat sneezes, it is a sign of rain.—General.

Should a cat sneeze thrice, a cold will run through the family.—Northern.

When a cat scratches the leg of a table, it signifies a change in the weather.

Sneezing of a cat near a bride means good luck in her wedded life.

May-cats (born in the month of May) will never catch rats or mice; but, contrary to the wont of cats, will bring into the house snakes and glow-worms.—Devon and Wiltshire.

May cats in Sussex are credited with the same as above, and, in addition, with the misfortune of melancholia.

A cat, sitting with its back to the fire, presages a storm.—Coastal superstition.

When the cat washes her face over her ears, we shall have great store of rain.—Melton Astrogaster.

There is a strange diversity of superstition about a black cat. In the North of England it was considered lucky to own a black cat, but unlucky to meet a strange one.

In the South of England, however, it is regarded as an excellent omen of good fortune should a black cat cross the path of a bride and bridegroom as they leave the church. *En passant*, it is remarkable (to say the least!) how frequently a black cat appears outside a London church famous for its fashionable Society weddings!

Reverting to the Northern belief in the luck of owning a black cat; Yorkshire sailors' wives in the Scarborough area were in the habit of keeping black cats in order to ensure the safety of their husbands at sea.

Should a black cat walk into your room, then your luck is in, indeed. But it is unlucky to open your eyes in the morning and see a cat before your eyes have lighted upon anything else.

Charles I believed in the luck of the black cat. He possessed one which followed him everywhere. When, at last, it fell ill and, despite all efforts, died, Charles exclaimed: "My luck is gone." It had. Next day he was arrested.

Along the Border it is held ominous for a cat to pass over a coffin. Disaster is only prevented by the killing of the cat. Henderson has placed on record one instance of this strange superstition in Northumberland, where, as a coffin was leaving the house a cat jumped over it. None of the bearers would again move the coffin until the cat had been shot and killed. It is difficult to assign any reason for the belief in this superstition.

It is held in Ireland to cause misfortune to take a cat with you on moving from one house to another.

Two final "cat" caterwauls! Should you, while still a young man, throw water over a cat, you are doomed to death before reaching manhood; and:

It is unlucky to hear caterwauling at the start of a journey.

The seamen's theory associating cats with rain has its counterpart so far away as the Malay. There, it is held that if a Malayan woman puts upon her head an inverted earthenware pot and then, setting it upon the ground fills it with water and washes a cat until the animal is nearly drowned, heavy rain will follow. Bathing a cat will also bring rain, so it is believed in Java.

Cats have in this country always been regarded as the familiar of witches. And it has been alleged that a witch could change herself into a cat at will. Glanvil tells a story of an old woman in Cambridgeshire who entered the house of an old man in the form of a cat and sat herself in front of the fire. The man, apparently suspecting the truth, stole a stroke at the back of the animal with a fire-fork and thought that he had broken the back of the animal. It, however, escaped from him and vanished. But the same night an old woman, always believed to be a witch, was found in her home dead with her back broken.

From Lincolnshire comes a story of a man and son who saw a cat in front of them, and at once suspected the animal to be a witch. The man took a stone and hammered it. Next day the witch had her face all bandaged up, and she died within a few days.

Now travel, in superstition, to Swabia. There the story is told of a soldier who was asked by his betrothed not to visit her on a certain night as it would not be convenient. His suspicions aroused, he proceeded to the house. On the way, a white cat ran up to him and tried to turn his steps. Angry at the animal he drew his sword, slashed at the cat and cut off one of its paws. Arriving at the house of his sweetheart he found her in bed, and on asking the reason received a confused reply. Noticing blood on the coverlet, he drew down the clothes and saw that the girl was bleeding from the stump of a leg, the foot having been cut off. "So that's what the matter is, you witch," he said, and left her. She died within a day or two.

CATERPILLAR
If you find a hairy caterpillar, you should throw it over your left shoulder for luck.—East Yorkshire.

CATTLE
To see a woman before a man while driving cattle to market will bring bad luck to the selling.—Ireland.

Hares found in the fields among cattle on May Day are witches with designs on the milk.—Ireland.

Cattle must be tarred behind the ears and at the root of the tail on Beltane Eve (May Day Eve), or witches will suck their milk.—Scotland.

A twig from the Shrew Tree applied

to the back of cattle will cure them of their malady.—Lancashire.

To stay the murrain in cattle, a calf should be burned alive.

An ox or cow breaking into your garden presages a death in the house.—Midlands.

Oxen in their stalls on Xmas Eve go down on their knees in an attitude of devotion.—Cornwall.

A slunk or abortive calf, buried in the highway over which cattle frequently pass, will prevent the staggers occurring to cows.—Suffolk.

For luck in your dairy give your bunch of mistletoe to the first cow to calve in the New Year.—Yorkshire.

To cure the foul (or fellen) in cattle, go at midnight into the orchard, and grave a turf at the foot of the largest apple tree and hang it carefully on the topmost branch of the tree, all in silence and alone. As the turf mudders away, so will the disease leave the animal.—West Riding, Yorkshire.

NOTE: Other accounts say that the turf must be one on which the stricken animal has trodden.

On Beltane Day cattle should be driven through the smoke of a fire of rowan and ash to bring good luck.—Scotland.

So confidently held by the Irish farmer was the fear of first meeting a woman while taking his cattle to market, that it was the custom before setting out with the animals for him to send a farmhand ahead, in order that he might turn after going a few yards, and thus be the first person to be seen by the farmer as the cattle emerged from the farm gate and into the road.

Another Irish superstition was the guarding against cattle being bewitched by scattering primroses on the threshold of the stalls, and placing a piece of red-hot metal on the hearth, and twining rowan or mountain ash about the door.

In the neighbourhood of Pendle, Lancashire, and peculiar to that district—was the method said to be able to stay the hydrocephalus—a disease incidental to adolescent animals. A beast which had died had to be beheaded, and the head conveyed for interment into the nearest point in the adjoining county.

Steperden, a desert plain upon the border of Yorkshire, was the place usually chosen, and became known as "the place of skulls." The origin of this strange belief may be found in the story of Azazel (Numbers xvi, 22) insomuch that as the transgressions of the people were laid on the head of the scapegoat, so might the diseases of the herd be laid upon the head of the deceased animal. But it seems a little out of the teaching of the Scriptures to transfer the disease to a neighbouring county!

On an elevation in the township of Carnforth in the parish of Warton, Lancashire, where the Saxon courts were held, stood the Shrew Tree, mentioned above. According to local superstition this old tree had received so much virtue from plugging up in it a number of living field mice in a cavity prepared for their reception, that a twig cut from it, when freely applied to the backs of disordered cattle was a certain cure for their troubles.

As with other omens, there are a number of examples with which sceptics are presented. Writing in *Notes and Queries*, a correspondent relates how in March, 1843, cattle were driven close to his house, and three trampled through and into the garden. A maidservant showed the utmost consternation and announced that we would hear of three deaths in the family within the next six months. The correspondent adds: "Alas, in April we heard of dear J—— murder; a fortnight after A—— died; and to-morrow (10th August) I am to attend the funeral of my excellent son-in-law."

A further note was added next day: "When I went down to Mrs. ——'s burial, and was mentioning the superstition, they told me that while she was lying ill, a cow got into the front garden and was driven out with difficulty."

On the other hand, the authors can testify to quite a number of cattle having broken, with great regularity, into a Wiltshire country garden they once had, without any tragedy attaching to the event.

Although the cattle bowing in their stalls on Xmas Eve is given above to Cornwall, it existed also in many parts of Devonshire. It is an extraordinary feature of such beliefs as this, that they could, with ease, be proved or confounded, by the simple practice of an organised watch! But nobody ever undertook the organisation.

Brand, however, related how a farmer of St. Stephen's Down, near Launceston, Cornwall, told him that he, with others, kept watch on his oxen, and at twelve midnight on Christmas Eve the two oldest oxen were observed to fall upon their knees. (Note: It may be observed that it is thus that oxen begin their lying down.) It may be mentioned here, *en passant*, that a similar "inquiry" was held by a farmer in the Vosges mountains where, it was believed, cattle on Christmas Eve acquired the gift of speech. The farmer hid in a corner of the byre to hear the talk.

The result did him little good, for one ox said to another ox: "What shall we do to-morrow?" and the other replied: "We shall carry our master to the churchyard." "Sure enough," says Sauve, in *Le Folk Lore des Hautes-Vosges*, "the farmer died that very night, and was buried next day."

The probable origins of the slaying of a calf, and the Christmas Eve bowing of cattle have been already mentioned. There remains, however, that of the passing cattle through the smoke of fires, in order to preserve them from further harm of disease. It is a possible pointer that the ancient Romans purified their flocks by driving them over burning heaps of grass, pinewood, laurel and branches of the male olive tree. The practice of Beltane fires, or New fires, as they are also termed, was pursued throughout Europe for centuries.

Again, in connection with the killing of an animal in the belief that it will save the remainder of the herd, there must be pointed out the practice of the Bahima race of Central Africa. The Bahima are a pastoral people; they could have had no knowledge of the British rural superstition, any more than the British rural people had any knowledge of the Bahimas. Yet, the superstitions of the two merge into the one belief; the Bahimas, when their herds are attacked by disease, kill one animal after tying herbs round its neck, with certain fetishes, to attract the disease away from the others. The animal is driven round the kraal several times, and then despatched by the priest. The herbs from its neck are then fastened upon doorposts of the kraal, to prevent the disease from entering again—in the same way that rowan and mountain ash were placed on the doorposts of houses and cattle stalls in Scotland and the North of England to keep away evil.

It has been stated earlier that the superstition among farmers in Britain was to burn cattle in case of disease among the herds; and that usually a calf was the victim chosen to save the others of the herd. But why should the burning of one animal be supposed to save the others? According to a Cornwall view it was a sacrifice to appease God.

Apparently the authority for this was Abraham's sacrifice of a goat, and the splashing with blood of the doors of the Egyptians. The authors doubt whether any such idea was ever held. They agree that the Cornish farmer who described it thus may have been genuine in thinking it, because he had probably been told the story by his forebears.

The truth of the matter is more likely that the appease the wrath of God business was mere theological gloss to enable a heathen rite, which could not be displaced, to continue. Most things evil which happened to our early forefathers were due to the Evil Eye, to overlooking and to spells. The antidote to spells and the Evil Eye was fire, which is the reason that witches were burnt. And when a calf was burned to save the rest of the herd, it was hoped that the burning would also burn the witch who had cast the evil spell on the cattle.

Some two hundred years ago an Ipswich farmer, stricken with the murrain among his sheep burned one of them alive, according to the custom. Shortly afterwards it was found that a suspected witch had been burned alive in her house in the city of Ipswich. What was the connection? Well, the witch's body was consumed by the flames except for her feet and hands; and so had the sheep's body, except for the four feet by which it had been hung over the flames. Could anything be plainer? There is some ground for believing that the witch in question was the famous Grace Pett, the last of the Ipswich witches.

The burning of cattle alive to stay a murrain seems to have lasted longest in the Isle of Man. Only a few years ago there were people in the island who could distinctly remember seeing the smoking carcase of a sacrifice in the fields.

One place in the island bears the name Cabbal yn Oural Losht, which means the Chapel of the Burnt Sacrifice. Moore in a book on Manx place names says that the name records a circumstance which took place in the nineteenth century. A farmer who had lost a number of his sheep and cattle by murrain burned a calf as a propitiatory offering to the Deity on the spot, where a chapel was afterwards built.

There was at one time in Scotland a cattle disease known as "The Quarter-Ill." This affected a beast only in one limb or quarter. The people of Angus, and probably other places, practised a strange superstition to cure it. A piece was cut out of a thigh of one of the animals which had died of the disease and was hung in the farm chimney in order to preserve the rest of the herd from becoming affected.

It was believed that as long as it hung there it would prevent the disease from approaching the farm. In the case of the family removing from the farm to another, one of the objects most carefully superintended and guarded was this talisman. In addition it has been known for the piece of dried flesh to be handed down from one generation to another to safeguard the cattle of the descendant.

Sometimes instead of a piece of flesh from the thigh, a foreleg of one of the dead animals was used; and some of the people who practised the superstition held that it was sufficient if the foreleg was placed over the door of the cowsheds.

Another variation of the belief was that the severed part could be boiled instead of being hung in the chimney or over the sheds.

See CALF.

CAUL

A child born with a caul will have, in later life, the gift of second sight.

A child born with a caul will be lucky throughout life.—General.

Whoever acquires a caul by purchase will be fortunate and escape dangers.—General.

Nobody possessing a caul can ever be drowned.—General.

If a lawyer buys a caul, he will acquire eloquence.—General.

The owner of a caul is able to know the state of health of the person who was born with it; firmness and crispness denote that the person is alive and well; flaccidity indicating death or sickness.

NOTE: A caul is the name given to a membrane covering the head of some children at birth. Its medical definition is the Amnios, one of the three teguments, or membranaceous films, which cover it in the womb.

This superstition of the caul is world-wide, and of all ages. St. Chrysostom inveighed against it in several of his homilies, being especially severe on one occasion against a clergyman, Proetus, who had bought a caul from a midwife with a view to being fortunate.

From Christian Greece, A.D. 400, come to present Pagan Timor, where when the rice-stalks turn black, and the ears refuse to set, a man takes a caul in its preserving box and runs round the field, in the sure and certain hope that the wind may waft the fortunate influence of the caul over the rice. So has the cult and superstition of the caul progressed. Through Holland, France, Germany, and other countries, the superstition abounded—and to a very large extent still abounds.

It was, however, as a preservative against drowning that the caul was most sought after. In the eighteenth and nineteenth centuries, cauls were advertised pretty frequently for sale. In February, 1813, an advertisement in *The Times* read:

To persons going to sea. A child's caul in a perfect state, to be sold cheap. Apply at 5, Duke Street, Manchester Square, where it may be seen.

A second such advertisement on the same day added, "To prevent trouble, the price is twelve guineas."

The *Morning Post*, Saturday, 21st August, 1779, announced that: "Gentlemen of the Navy, and others, going long voyages to sea, have their attention directed to the fact that a child's caul is to be disposed of."

Even as late as the enlightened 1904, the *Daily Express* had a similar advertisement, and in August, 1915, Mr. E. Lovett, of the Folk-lore Society, wrote to a London newspaper stating that there was at that moment a caul advertised for sale in a shop near London Docks.

The *Athenian Oracle* spoke of this same superstition, extending to the length of believing that those born with a caul were exempt from the miseries and calamities of humanity, their good fortune including even invulnerability, provided they were always careful to carry the membrane with them. Should it be lost or stolen the benefits would be transferred to the new owner.

According to Lemnius the caul must be of reddish colour to bring the good fortune; should it be black, it is an omen of ill-fortune.

Henderson records one story of a caul which came to his own knowledge in a Northern city. A maid was found by her mistress in a state of great dejection for which there seemed at first no assignable reason. After much questioning, the mistress elicited that the girl had been born with a veil over her head which was now presaging evil. The girl explained that she kept the caul locked in her box, and regularly consulted it as her oracle and adviser. If danger threatened her, the caul shrivelled up; if

sickness, it became damp. When good fortune was hers, the caul laid itself smoothly out; and if people at a distance were talking about her, it rustled in its paper.

There was a humorous story of a caul told by Guianerius of a jealous man, who on seeing his child born with a caul over its head, thought it certain that a Franciscan that visited the house was the father—it was so like a friar's cowl—and thereupon attempted to take the life of the friar!

There would seem to the authors to be a slightly more sane explanation of the purchase by advocates of cauls, in the belief that they would, by the possession, be sure to win their cases. One cannot but be struck with the affinity of the large wigs (coifs) worn by judges!

As for the immunity from drowning, the authors, some months ago, through the columns of a widely-read national newspaper, invited authenticated instances of people preserved at sea, who possessed a caul. With the exception of two, all who answered recounted tales of relatives or friends drowned at sea, *with cauls!*

There is one other superstition attached to the caul which the authors have found only in the Horncastle area, though may be it exists elsewhere. It holds that if a caul (known in Horncastle as a "silly hood") is not buried with the person who was born with it, that person will have to walk after death searching for the caul.

An undertaker of that district related how he had been given a caul to place in the coffin of a woman who had carefully preserved it and was most anxious that it should be buried with her because, she said, "my mother and grandmother had been born with silly hoods and had walked dreadfully after death because the hoods had not been buried with them" and she did not want to walk after her death, but to rest in peace.

CHAFF-RIDDLING

If you riddle chaff in a barn at midnight on St. Mark's Eve (24th April) and see a coffin pass the door, you will die before the year is out.—Yorkshire.

This omen was peculiar to Yorkshire. The procedure was as follows:

A riddle and chaff were set down in a barn, the doors of which had to be flung wide open. Those who wished to peer into the future repaired to the barn at midnight, and, in turn, riddled chaff.

If nothing untoward was to befall the riddlers, nothing would be seen. But should one be doomed to die during the year, two persons would become visible passing across the open farm-doors, and carrying a coffin.

There is one "circumstantial" story told in Yorkshire folk-lore, of such an omen coming to fruition. It relates how at Malton, two men and a woman decided to test the omen. The two men each did their riddling without anything happening. But within a few moments of the woman starting, all saw the ominous coffin and bearers.

The men, thinking that a practical joke was being played, ran into the open, but no creature was in sight. The woman died within the year.

See MARK'S EVE.

CHARMS

Cut a withy stick on New Year's Day and put it at once into your pocket. Never let it fall to the ground, or the charm will be broken.—Shropshire.

A cross of whitethorn or birch placed above the house door will keep off witches and their spells.—Monmouthshire.

May-tree or twigs in each seed-bed will make null and void the witches' spells on the crop.—South Wales.

Twigs of rowan tree, witchwood or mountain ash gathered on 2nd May (Eve of Invention of the Cross) wound round with much red thread and placed visibly in the window will protect the house from evil influences.—Denham Tracts, 1895.

Fern seed gathered silently on the Eve of St. John's Day will keep the affections of your sweetheart.—Lancashire and Cheshire.

NOTE: Other charms are given separately under the headings of the ills which they were said to cure; such as hydrophobia, toothache, etc.

If the reader smiles at some of the quaint superstitions of old under this heading, let him, or her, open almost any cheap magazine to-day, and read the advertisements of "Lucky Charms" for sale. "Tiki," elephant's hair in lockets, "Puck" and scores of others. As late as February, 1946, a vendor circulated the authors with a leaflet concerning the remarkable future likely to come from having a piece of lucky cork. Printed on it were the "testimonials" of scores of people who had been "cured" of illnesses, or been prevented from having their usual illnesses(!); or have found good jobs, or been left money since they purchased for 1s. 6d. this lucky cork!

The authors have no doubt whatever that the cork is lucky—a few inquiries showed that the seller of this charm must be making well over £40 a week from its sale!

Another charm greatly in vogue to-day is the "chain letter" entitled "The good luck of London was sent to me." The recipient is requested to copy the letter and send it to twenty-four other people—with the promised prospect of some thousands of pounds reward; and bad luck if the chain is broken by the recipient. In eight months up to December, 1946, the authors received and destroyed 147 of these chain letters.

In olden days these charms were mostly in the form of prayers, written on pieces of paper, and sold in an envelope by old women who were regarded as harmless witches. One such was old Granny Burton of the Kent village of Bethersden. Many old people will no doubt recall her. Sir Charles Igglesden, that great journalist and delver into folk-lore, has recorded that he possesses a piece of paper, browned with age, on which is written a list of her charms.

Following, are three of them:

To cure a burn or a scald: There was two Angels came out of the West. One brought fire and the other brought frost. Say in the Name of the Father, Son and Holy Ghost, "Out fire, in frost."

To cure a blown bullock: Say, "Blessed Virgin Mary, for Thy Son's sake, the blader that is blown, now let it break. Let that bullock that is now blown, cured be."

To cure an ague: Say, "I pray God leave this ague from this man, child or woman, whichever it is, and name its crisoned name."

Sir Charles adds to his account the story of Granny Burton told by a man who went to consult her. While crossing a field he muttered to himself: "I wonder if the old hag's at home?" At that time he was a long way from her house. Yet, when he knocked at the door, she opened it and said, with a smile: "Yes, the old hag is at home." After that there was no doubt in the neighbourhood that Granny was a witch!

In Lancashire, charm rings were worn for the cure of dyspepsia, and charmed belts for the cure of rheumatism. Laughable! May be, but there are still firms who make a handsome profit to-day by selling "electric" or magnetism rings and belts for the cure of rheumatism. Only they have now a scientific explanation, instead of a witchcraft one.

In Blochurch's *Anatomie of the Elder*, the following charm was printed for epilepsy: "If in the month of October, a little before the full moon, you pluck a twig of the elder tree and cut the cane that is betwixt two of its knees, or knots, in nine pieces, and these pieces, being bound in a piece of linen, be in a thread so hung about the neck that they touch the spoon of the heart, or the sword-formed cartilege; and, that they may stay more firmly in that place, they are to be bound thereon with a linen or silk roller wrapt about the body, till the thread break of itself. The thread now being broken and the roller removed, the charm is not at all to be touched with bare hands, but it ought to be taken hold of by some instrument and buried in a place that nobody may touch it."

How that cured epilepsy we would like to know.

A charm for sciatica common in Devon and Cornwall was to carry in a pocket, or round the neck, either the knuckle-bone of a leg of mutton, a raw potato or a piece of lodestone. In September, 1945, the correspondence column of a London daily newspaper contained a number of letters recommending as a "certain preventive for rheumatism" the carrying in the pocket of a raw potato, or a nutmeg!

Now, look for a moment at the heathen races, in their moments of sickness. In India iron rings are worn as an amulet against disease. Masai men wear a ring on the middle finger of the right hand—to protect them from disease of any kind. The Bagobos place brass rings on the wrists and ankles of the sick. There can have been no association between the Masai men and the Bagobos and the British people of the seventeenth century—yet their amulets against sickness are the same. And, as stated above, there are still advertised rings and belts for the prevention of rheumatism.

See LOCKERBY PENNY, STONES.

CHEEKS

If your cheeks burn, it is a sign that someone is talking about you.—General.

CHERRIES

If you visit a cherry orchard, and do not have your shoes rubbed with the leaves of a cherry tree, you will die from cherry-stone suffocation.—Kent.

You will know whether you will wed, and when, if you count the cherry-stones round your plate after a meal, beginning "This year, next year, sometime, never." The last stone gives the answer.—General.

It is passing strange that these are the only two really authentic superstitions attached to cherry trees in Britain; as distinct from a number held abroad. (Usually the same superstitions are found in Britain and in Europe.) In Switzerland it was held that a cherry tree will bear fruit in abundance if its first fruit is eaten by a woman who has just given birth to her first child.

In the Ardennes on the first Sunday in Lent, children ran with lighted torches through the orchards, crying:
"Bear apples, bear pears
And cherries all black
To Scouvion!"
On these words, the torch bearers hurled their blazing torches at the apple trees, the pear trees *and the cherry trees*. Though this wassailing of fruit was common in England, it is devoted only to apple trees.

See APPLE TREE.

CHICKENS

To have a sitting of eggs turn out all cockerels is a sign of good luck.—General rural belief.

Never set a hen on an even number of eggs, or you will have no chickens at all.—General rural belief.

The unlucky "even" number of eggs belief is still rife in country areas to-day, though probably not one person in a hundred realizes that it is the sole reason for the regulation number of eggs sold for a sitting—namely, thirteen.

There is a commercial background for the first of the above two superstitions. A sitting of all cockerels, since cockerels are table birds, the price of which certainly brings good fortune, especially in this year of grace, 1946!

The only reference to chicken superstition abroad the authors have been able to trace is a custom among the Red Karens of Upper Burma, of a maypole ceremony held in May in each village. A new pole is chosen each year. Omens are drawn from chicken bones as to which of the trees in the village shall be felled for the maypole, and to decide which of the days in May is likely to be the luckiest.

In Worcestershire it is considered unlucky in springtime to take less than a handful of violets or primroses into a farmer's house; it would bring destruction on his broods of young ducks and chickens.

A chicken was also used in a superstitious cure for snake bite in Devonshire. The formula was to kill the chicken and at once thrust the wounded part into the stomach of the bird and allow it to stay there until the chicken's flesh was quite cold.

If the flesh, when cold, assumed a dark colour the cure was effected, and the virus had been extracted from the wound. If the flesh retained its natural colour then the poison had been absorbed into the blood of the victim.

And by this time it was too late to do anything to save the unfortunate victim's life.

Much the same superstition for the cure of snake bite was practised by the Hottentots of the Kat River settlement in the eastern area of Cape Colony. A few feathers were plucked from the breast of a chicken and a small incision made in the breast, to which the wound was applied. This process was repeated three times, the fowl, it being held, gradually dying as the poison from the wound operated upon it.

There was not much difference between the mind of the Hottentot and the mind of the Devon rural of the days mentioned, was there?

CHILBLAINS

Thrash your chilblains with holly, keeping your feet, or legs, crossed while doing so, and the chilblains will disappear.

The "crossing" is pure superstition—an ages-old antidote to the menacings of the Evil One who has thus afflicted the sufferer. But there is a sound medical basis for the thrashing, since it must cause blood circulation in the affected part, and lack of proper circulation is the primary cause of chilblains.

There was a superstition rife in certain parts of the south coast area of Britain, and in the Channel Isles, that if the Yule Log was placed on the fire for a short space every day from Xmas Day until Twelfth Night, and was then kept under the bed, it would protect the whole household for the year from chilblains, from damage from thunder and fire; and from all other maladies. If a piece from it was put into water for cows it helped them to calve safely and easily. Furthermore, ashes from the log

sprinkled over the farm fields would prevent mildew from attacking the wheat crop.

The presence of this superstition is rare. It belongs properly to France, whence it is likely it was taken to the Channel Islands, and to the British mainland by emigrants from the Isles. It had little vogue on this side of the channel.

CHILD

If a person steps over a child crawling on the floor, the child will not grow any more.—General.

A child weaned at the time that birds migrate to or from the country will be restless and changeable in after life.—Wales.

If a child is weaned when the trees are in bloom, it will be prematurely grey.

One of the most humorous superstitions the authors have come across is connected with the weaning of a child. It comes, also from Wales, and asserts that if a babe, after being weaned is suckled again, it will become a profane swearer when it grows up.

The association between weaning, suckling and swearing baffles even our conjecture.

CHILDBIRTH

To "turn the bed" occupied by the mother at the birth of a child is unlucky until the child is a month old.—Lancashire.

The child born in the interval between an old moon and the first appearance of the new moon will never reach the age of puberty.—Cornwall.

NOTE: This is the origin of the Cornish saying, "No moon, no man."

If a boy is born in the wane of the moon, the next birth will be a girl, and vice versa.—Cornwall.

When a birth takes place in the "growing of the moon," the next child will be of the same sex.—Cornwall.

Children born during the hour after midnight have the power through life of seeing departed spirits.—General, but particularly in Yorkshire.

Should a woman during pregnancy spin at the spinning wheel, her child will be hanged with a hempen rope.—Wales.

Nails in front of the bed ward off elves from women in child-bed.—Highlands.

NOTE: This is another instance of the power of iron over witches and fairies.

A woman after childbirth is the most dangerous thing on earth. Demons are around her, and if she goes to a river to wash, the fish will go away.

A child born feet first is certain to meet with an accident during its life and become lame, unless laurel leaves are rubbed on its legs within four hours of birth.—Old midwife superstition.

To bring good luck to a child, it should be rubbed with lard as soon as it is born, and before it is washed.—Old midwife superstition.

Spit upon a newly born child to ensure its happiness.—Ireland.

To give a woman easy delivery in childbirth it was the custom in North-Western Argyllshire, Scotland, to open every lock in the house during the birth.

Now regard this in the light of superstition among the Romans; they presented women in pregnancy with a key as a symbol of easy birth. The custom in Argyllshire might, possibly, have been a corrupted survival of the Roman gift, brought here by the occupation; but what is to be said of the practice in the Island of Salsette, near Bombay, where, when a woman is in labour, all doors are opened to ease her?

In parts of Java everything in a house that is shut is opened that the birth may not be impeded. In Chittagong, in the East Indies, the midwife opens all doors and windows, and uncorks all bottles. In ancient India it was the custom to untie all knots in a house at childbirth. So it was, at one time in parts of the Highlands, where girdles, and any tapes on the woman were unfastened. Compare this with the childbirth custom of the Hos of Togoland, West Africa, where the priest ties up with grass the limbs of a woman due to give birth. He then unties the knots saying: "I will now open you." This, it is held, gives easy delivery. How came the same superstitions to exist in Java, in Togoland, among other heathen races—and in Christian Scotland? Is it that superstition has a common belief?

On the other hand, in Southern Celebes, in order to hinder the escape of a woman's soul at childbirth, a band is tied round the body of the expectant mother. A similar custom is observed by the Minang-kabauers of Sumatra.

According to Celes, if a woman with child eats quinces and coriander seed overmuch ("the nature of both which is to repress and stay vapours that ascend to the braine") it will make the child

ingenious. But if the mother eat onions or beans, or such vaporious food, "it endangereth the childe to become lunaticke, or of imperfect memory."

A Scottish superstition (also held by the Swedes) relating to childbirth is that if a child was put from the breast in the moon's wane, it would decay so long as the orb continued to decrease.

But probably the most widespread childbirth custom in the British Isles, in olden days, was the eating and drinking which followed the birth. This was general in town and country, but particularly so in rural areas. In the Border counties the birth of an infant was the signal for plenty of eating and drinking. Tea, generously flavoured with whisky or brandy, and a profusion of shortbread and buns was provided for all visitors, and it was regarded as unlucky to allow anyone to leave the house without partaking of the fare.

In the North of England the celebrations went by the name of "groaning cheese." The custom was for the expectant father to provide before the birth a large cheese and a cake. The father must cut the cake after the birth, taking care not to cut his own fingers, lest the child be doomed by the cut to die before reaching manhood. The first slice of the cheese was given to the spinsters among the company. It was divided into as many pieces as there were spinsters, and the piece received, placed under the pillow that night, would give the spinster a view of her future husband!

In some parts of the North, it was held desirable that the doctor should cut both the cheese and cake, and all had to partake of the fare, under penalty of the babe growing up without personal charm.

In Yorkshire, the cake was called "Pepper Cake," and resembled thick ginger-bread. In Oxfordshire, the cake was usually cut from the middle, and gradually shaped to a ring, and through this the child was passed on its christening day.

In parts of North Lancashire, it was the custom to have a tea-drinking after the recovery from childbirth. Tea and rum were plentifully distributed—and each visitor was expected to pay a shilling towards the expenses of the "birth-feast."

What is the origin of this feasting? It may be observed that there was a feast in the days of ancient Athens, called Amphidromia. It was kept by private families, who, on the fifth day after the birth of a child gave a company of visitors feasting and dancing. The Romans inherited a similar custom. Among the Grecians, too, the custom prevailed of friends sending in gifts or small tokens to the newly born child—the origin, probably, of the later (and present) Christian custom of gifts to the child from godparents at the christening.

A last word on "easy delivery." Following is a charm for easy childbirth much in vogue in the north country. It cost money to buy in a sealed envelope, and was written on a piece of paper inside:

"Thus said Christ: I received 102 blows on the mouth from the Jews in the Court, and 30 times was I struck in the garden. I was beaten on head, arm and breast 40 times, on shoulders and legs 30 times; 30 times was My hair plucked, and I sighed 127 times. My beard was pulled 72 times, and I was scourged with 6,666 strokes. A thousand blows were rained on my head with the reed, smiting the thorny crown. Seventy-three times was I spat in the face, and I had in My body 5,475 wounds. From My body flowed 30,430 blood drops. All who daily say seven Our Fathers and seven Hail Maries, till they have made up the number of My blood drops, shall be relieved of pain in childbirth."

See also EAGLE-STONES.

CHOPPING THE BLOCK

There was at one time a curious Easter superstition at University College, Oxford. A block, in the form of a long wooden pole, decorated with flowers and evergreens, was placed outside the door of the Hall, leaning against the wall of the Buttery, which was opposite. After dinner on Easter Day the cook and his attendant, dressed in white paper caps and white jackets, took their stand on either side of the block, each bearing a pewter dish, one supporting a blunt chopping axe from the kitchen.

As the members of the college came out of Hall, first the masters and then the fellows and so on, each took the axe, struck the block with it and then placed in the proper dish the usual fee for the cook. The tradition among the undergrads was that anyone who could chop the block in two, could lay claim to all the college estates. The custom was, regrettably, discontinued in 1864. But the Easter custom of beating upon the staircase at 7.30 a.m., with a wooden mallet to wake up the undergrads still continues.

CHRISTENING

To call a child by a name before its christening is unlucky.

A baby that does not cry at christening is too good to live long.—General.

When there are boys and girls to be baptized, the boy must come first, or else the girl will grow in after life a beard.—Norfolk.

If a child is christened on any day but Saturday, it will die.—Strange superstition of St. Kilda.

If on the way with the baby to a christening, bread and cheese is not given to the first person met, the child will be unlucky.—North Country.

To ensure that a child shall have health, strength and wealth, a mother should carry with her to its christening a silver coin, an egg and a pinch of salt.—North of England, and other scattered areas.

Children dying unchristened wander in woods and solitudes, lamenting their hard fate, and are often to be seen.—Old Scottish belief.

An unchristened child cannot die.—Cheshire.

The first child christened in a new church is claimed by the devil, and is sure to die.—Yorkshire (and other parts of the country).

The cry of a child at christening is the voice of the Evil One being driven into the baptismal water.

There are two christening superstitions peculiar to Scotland of olden days. One was that spittle should be used by the parson to christen the child. The other that if a child had previously been christened by a layman, the priest, when it was taken to church, had to administer a pinch of salt and moisten the ears with spittle, and then to pronounce exorcisms and to do all the things at the font wont to be done to a child without immersion and the benediction of water.

The origin of this goes back many centuries. The canon law which justified it stated: "Let the nostrils and ears be touched with it (spittle) that the nostrils may be opened to receive the odour of God, and the ears to hear His mandates."

There would seem, too, to be an affinity with the Scottish spittle super-

stition and the Romans. Certain ceremonies, which might correspond to our
baptism, were undergone by children of
the Romans on the eighth or ninth day
after birth, when they were named.
Then, the head of the child was
moistened by spittle to avert magical art.

In the heart of darkest Africa, the
witch doctor spits three times in the face
of a child on bestowing on it its name.

The "averting of magical arts" by
spittle, again, was a practised superstition in Scotland. Cows who fell sick, or
whose milk dried up, were instantly
cured by a "skilful" person spitting on
them. The cows were, of course, regarded
as bewitched. Hence the "magical art."

It was the custom, in Scotland, for a
child, home from its christening, to be
"sained" by fire. The procedure was
for the child to be placed in a basket
having a cloth previously spread over it,
and with bread and cheese in the cloth.
The baby and basket were then moved
three times successively round the iron
crook hanging over the fire for the holding of pots, etc. Either the mother or the
midwife performed this "saining" with
the words: "Let the fire consume thee
now, if ever." This ritual was intended
to counteract the malignant arts of
witches and other evil spirits, so firmly
believed in by Scottish folk.

NOTE: To "sain," old Saxon "Seg-
nom"—to make the sign of the Cross to
ward off evil spirits.

In strange variance to the Scottish
belief that unchristened children which
die haunt woods and solitudes is the
Cheshire superstition that an unbaptized
child *cannot* die. In Liverpool, in June,
1860, a mother charged with attempted
infanticide was said to have placed the
child on the ground on a private
estate, and to have covered it with sods.
She confessed to the act, and said that
she had previously had the child
christened, as otherwise it could not have
died. Shakespeare mentions this superstition. It is, in fact, a very ancient and
widespread one, and this description of
spirit was known as the Latewitch.

The superstition mentioned above that
the first child christened in a new
church is claimed by the devil, is a
variation of the ancient belief that the
first living thing to enter a new church
was claimed by, and allowed to, the
devil. The origin seems to lie in the
medieval ages, when it was deemed
essential to bury a man or a child alive
under the foundations of a church (or

even a castle) in order that the foundations should stand firm and secure.

St. Columba, founder of Iona, buried
one of his monks alive under the foundations of the new Abbey. It is true that
reports state that the monk, Oran, consented to die. That, at least, is how
O'Donnell attempts to gloss over the
story in his *Lives of the Saints*. There is
little doubt, however, that the ambitious
Columba meant the foundations of his
Abbey to stand, and immolated the
monk.

Baring-Gould finds an origin in the
period, in heathen times, when every
house, castle and bridge had provision
made to give each its presiding, protective spirit. This may, and possibly
did, grow out of the earlier pagan idea
of a sacrifice associated with the
beginning of every work of importance.
Thus the sacrifice was buried under the
foundations.

It may be that this explains ghost-
haunted houses—the protective spirit of
the sacrifice on its patrols.

Grimm, in *German Mythology*, says:
"It was considered necessary to build
living animals—even human beings—
into the foundations on which any
edifice was reared as an oblation to the
earth to induce her to bear the super-
incumbrance of weight it was proposed
to lay on her.

When, in 1885, Helsworthy parish
church was restored the south-west angle
wall was taken down. In it, embedded in
mortar and stone was the skeleton of a
man who had obviously been buried,
hurriedly, alive. There was no sign of
an orthodox tomb.

Probably associated with the same idea
of sacrifice to mother earth is the superstition still widely held in country areas
that unless the carcase of an animal is
buried under the roots of a newly
planted fruit tree, it will not bear fruit.

In Wales it was a widely held superstition that a christening following after
a funeral was an omen of death. The
belief was that the child, as a member
of the household, would "follow the
dead." If the christening followed a
wedding, however, the child would
become rich and happy.

A Herefordshire belief was that if the
initials of a child's name themselves
spelt a full name, then it was lucky for
the child. This, by the way, doubtless
explains the many Christian names
which the elder generation of Herefordshire people bore.

The same county people held that it was dangerous to christen a child with a name of a favourite animal pet. In her *Herefordshire Folk Lore*, Mrs. Leather records an instance of a child being named after its father's favourite mare. The child was burned to death at the age of three, and the mare sustained a fatal accident shortly afterwards. The family without hesitation put the double calamity down to the name given to the child.

Widely held in all parts of the country at one time was the superstition that ill fate would attend any child whose name-to-be was told to anyone before the christening.

There seems to be in this an affinity with many native races in various and widely scattered parts of the world, who have not only the greatest repugnance, but also the greatest fear of their real name being known.

Among the Indian tribes, from the Atlantic to the Pacific, for instance, the North American Indian conceals where-ever possible his real name. He believes that his name is not merely a label, as it were, but a distinct part of his personality, and he holds that evil may befall him from the machinations of anyone who knows his "personality." The same belief is held in many countries concerning a person's hair clippings and nail parings, which, in the hands of a witch, or an evil spirit, can be used to make magic against their former owner.

Thus it may be on account of this repugnance to giving names by the American Indians that both Powhatan and Pocahontas are known to history under assumed names, their true names having been concealed from the white man until the pseudonyms had become too firmly established to be sup-planted.

The Tolampoos, of Central Celebes, believe that if you write down a man's name you can carry his soul off with it. But they have no objection to their "second name" being mentioned or written. An Australian black, the authors are told, is most unwilling to give his real name; the reason being that there is peril that through his name he may be injured by sorcerers.

Amongst the tribes of Central Australia every man, woman and child has not only a personal name, but a secret or sacred name which is given to him by the elders of the tribe upon birth and is known to none except the fully initiated members of his tribe. This name is never

mentioned save on the most solemn occasions, and never in the presence of any woman. Even when mentioned among the men, it is spoken only in a whisper. Spencer and Gillen, in their *Native Tribes of Central Australia*, give the reason for this: "The native thinks that a stranger knowing his secret name would have special powers to work him ill by means of magic."

Thus, somewhere there is an undoubted link between all these beliefs and the Herefordshire belief that ill luck will attend the child should its name be mentioned before it is actually given to him at his christening.

It is intersting to note in passing that our "nickname" was, originally, spelt eke-name, which in the Anglo-Saxon meant "other name."

See BAPTISM, CHURCH.

CHRISTMAS

All cattle low and kneel on Christmas Eve.—General.

A person born on Christmas Day will never be hanged.

Bees hum the Hundredth Psalm on Christmas Eve.—General.

If the sun shine through an apple tree on Christmas Day there will be an abundant crop the following summer.—General.

A green Christmas brings a heavy harvest.—Rutland.

Light Christmas, light wheatsheaf; dark Christmas, heavy wheatsheaf.—Rutlandshire superstition about a full moon at Christmas. Current also in Huntingdonshire.

When the Christmas log is burning you should notice the shadows of people on the wall. Those shadows which appear without heads belong to the persons who are to die within the year.—Wales.

A nice, cheerful recreation for the Christmas party.

In Devonshire, it was the custom for young women on Christmas Day to look at a rose which they had put away, it having been plucked on Midsummer Day. Should the rose be fresh (as it was superstitiously held it would be) it was worn to church in the morning, where-upon the girl's intended husband would come along and take it. Since the lady had invariably begun "walking out," the intended partner was usually on the spot in readiness!

The supposition that cows low and kneel to the Saviour on Christmas Eve, also held sway in parts of Lincolnshire, and the south country, and also on the Romney Marshes. It was contemporary with the belief that ewes knelt to the Saviour on Easter Sunday morning. In Devonshire and parts of Cornwall, it is believed that all animals thus bowed.

The authors, when living in Lincolnshire, were assured by an old cowman that he had, on many occasions, gone to the cow-byre to test for himself the belief, and had always found the cows on their knees at midnight. We do not doubt it. Yet, the origin would seem to be fairly simple. Cows, on rising, get up on their knees first, and any person going to the byre at midnight would disturb the occupants. The first, and automatic, action of a cow thus disturbed is to rise to its knees preparatory to moving away from the disturber.

As for bees humming the Hundredth Psalm, is there anything more easy than to fit the buzzing of bees to any tune we might have in mind?

The reader should bear in mind that the majority of these Christmas superstitions refer not to the present 25th December, but to the *old-time* Christmas Day, which corresponded to our present 6th January. It was on this day that the Glastonbury Thorn is said to bloom.

There is recorded in the *Gentleman's Magazine* for 1753, the story of the visit of 2,000 people with lanterns and candles on the night of 24th December that year to Quainton (Bucks) to see a blackthorn, said to have been a slip from the Glastonbury Thorn. As there was no sign of a bud, the 2,000 concluded that 25th December, new style (which had been introduced the previous day) could not be the actual anniversary of Christ's birth, and they accordingly refused to attend church on the following day.

See GLASTONBURY THORN.

CHRISTMAS BOX

The origin of the Christmas Box had its start as a church charity. Boxes were accustomed to be placed in the churches for casual contributions, for opening on Christmas Day after the morning service. The contents, called "The Dole of the Christmas Box," or the Box Money, was distributed next day (Boxing Day) by the priests to the poor of the parish. The present general custom of gifts to tradesmen's assistants, dustmen, postmen, etc., developed from the custom of apprentices who carried a box round to their master's customers for small gratuities.

There is extant a fanciful origin that the Christmas Box originated from the term Christ's Mass. Romish priests, it states, had Masses said for pretty nearly everything. If a ship went out on a journey the priests had a box on her under protection of some saint, and for Masses to be said for them to that saint. Money for each Mass had to be put into the box by each person, which was not opened until the ship's return, and was given to the priest to pay for Masses to the saint, to forgive the people the debaucheries of those times!

CHRISTMAS CARDS

The sending of Christmas cards is a comparatively modern practice, though it has grown enormously since the first one was designed by J. C. Horsley, R.A., in the year 1843. It depicted, in colours, a party of grown-ups and children with glasses of wine raised in greeting over the words: "A Merry Christmas and a Happy New Year to you." Still preserved, it bears the inscription: James Peters, wife and family, from John Washbourn and his wife, of 22, Theberton Street, Islington" (London). It is dated 23rd December, 1843. In the year before the World War, 400,000,000 Christmas cards were sold in Great Britain.

CHRISTMAS DAY

A dark-haired man should be the first to enter a house on Christmas morning. —North country.

It would be unlucky to allow any person to go out of the house till the threshold had been consecrated by the entrance of a male; a female entering would presage disaster.—Filey (Yorkshire) fishermen.

Should a woman or girl be the first to enter a house on Christmas morning, ill-luck will result.—Yorkshire.

If every remnant of Christmas Day decorations is not removed from the church before Candlemas Day (2nd February) there will be a death in the family occupying a pew in which a berry or leaf is left.

This custom of "First-Footing" Christmas Day—a custom more general throughout the country on New Year's Day—was peculiar, and lasted until well into the 1900's in Yorkshire, Derbyshire, Nottinghamshire, Lincolnshire, Shropshire, Herefordshire, Staffordshire and Worcestershire. The first-footer had, necessarily, to be a dark man. There was one exception—in the East Riding a *fair* man was chosen. Why this particular

Riding of Yorkshire should thus have been different from the rest of the North of England it is difficult to understand.

The first-footer throughout Yorkshire was usually designated the "Lucky Bird." One colour of hair he must never have—and that was red, for tradition associated red hair with Judas Iscariot. The "Lucky Bird" in the East Riding of Yorkshire brought into the house with him a sprig of evergreen. He walked in at the front door and out of the back door, and was usually given sixpence for his "footing." After he had left, all members of the household, and any guests, went out of the house unwashed (it was not permissible, even to wash the hands), and together they carried a bough, or sprig of evergreen into the living room. In other cases, the "Lucky Bird" was given bread, salt and a groat.

As recently as 1915 the custom was still maintained in the small villages, and the first boy to reach any house on Christmas morning, whether he entered or not, was given a coin lest misfortune should overtake the household.

In pursuance of this custom of first-footing, it should be said that many families to make sure that no ill-luck should attend them by a chance visitor, were accustomed to arrange with a dark man (light man in East Riding) to visit the house immediately after midnight.

In Herefordshire—in the Blakemere and Weobley areas—no woman was allowed to enter a house on Christmas Day. Helps who were to assist at the Christmas Day parties had to sleep in the house on Christmas Eve. They could go home on Christmas morning if they so desired and then re-enter, but that applied only to those who had slept in the house during the previous night.

A Christmas superstition at Newbury (Berkshire) was for carols to be sung at the top of the church tower early in the morning; at Crondall (Hampshire) a similar custom prevailed until 1870. At the Collegiate Church, Ripon, the choir boys were accustomed to carry into the church large baskets of apples, each with a sprig of rosemary, and to present them to the members of the congregation, receiving, in return, small sums of money.

A superstition common in apple-growing counties was the Christmas Day wassailing of the apple trees. (It should be noted that this relates to the old-time Christmas Day, 6th January, now Twelfth Day.) In Cornwall and Devon-shire, parishioners of the village church walked in procession, visiting the principal orchards in the parish. There, a principal tree was singled out, a verse of wassail was chanted, and cider thrown over it. Then, the remainder of the cider was drunk by the wassailers. The ceremony was varied in some places by placing cakes, soaked in cider, in ox-forks of the principal trees.

Farm labourers in Sussex also wassailed the trees. In this county the wassail party was led by a man carrying a bullock's horn. Having wassailed an orchard a visit was paid to the house of the owner where ale was given them, usually in the kitchen.

In Herefordshire the wassailers were usually accompanied by mummers and Morris dancers. The wassail bowl here held as much as two gallons, and was made of beech wood.

Another wassail superstition, unconnected with trees, was the carrying of a wassail bowl or cup from door to door. The household being wassailed, the bowl was filled by the master of the house. The custom prevailed from Cornwall as far north as Cumberland. The wassail teams were, usually, "organized" and the captain himself kept the wassail bowl, usually made of maple, during the remainder of the year.

Later, the "wassail cup" took its place. Cup was hardly the correct designation: it was, in fact, a box in which usually lay two wax dolls, representing the Virgin Mary and the Babe Jesus. The interior was decorated, and the whole covered with a white cloth which was removed at the request of anyone to be allowed to see the "wassail." To send away any wassailer without a donation was considered to presage the worst of luck for the household.

Later still, the tradition was kept alive only by children who carried a box in which was a waxen image of Jesus. In Yorkshire it was held as a superstition that whatever you might do to successive visitors, it was the height of bad luck to turn away the first company of children who came with their box and doll and sang carols.

It is a curious circumstance that, alone of all the northern counties, we have found no record of wassailers, in any shape or form, in Shropshire.

The last corn cut in the Highlands of Scotland during the harvest was called the Maiden. It was dressed with ribbons to the shape of a doll, and was carefully preserved in the farmhouse until Christmas morning. On that day it was divided among the cattle "to make them thrive all the year round."

There was in Britain and the Isle of Man one particularly vicious custom—that of hunting and killing the wren. The birds were killed with stones or sticks. One bird thus killed was fastened by the legs to a hoop, or amid holly and ivy on a broomstick. The hunters then went from house to house singing a verse of doggerel, and asking a reward. In return they plucked a feather from the dead bird and handed it to the donor "for luck."

See CANDLEMAS DAY.

CHRISTMAS DECORATIONS

Evergreens should be taken down on Old Christmas Day (6th January) or illluck will follow.—General.

To take holly into the house before Christmas Eve is to invite bad luck.—General.

Christmas evergreens must not be burnt but carefully thrown away.—Cheshire and parts of Shropshire.

It will bring bad luck to hang up mistletoe in the house before Christmas Eve.—Wales and Border counties.

If Christmas evergreen decorations are thrown out of doors, a death will occur in the house before next Christmas. They should be burnt on Candlemas Eve.—Shropshire (parts of).

Holly and ivy must not be burnt, but must be kept till next year to save the house from lightning.—Staffordshire.

There is a curious disagreement over the disposal of evergreen decorations, particularly in Shropshire, where, in the Burford, Church Stretton and neighbouring areas, to burn them is regarded as lucky, and to throw them away as unlucky, whereas in the Shrewsbury, Ford, Wothern and Rugton localities, to burn the evergreen is to lay oneself open to ill-luck. The same belief applies to Staffordshire.

It was regarded as essential in Derbyshire, that had a cottage or house leaded panes care must be taken that one pane of each window should have a sprig each of yew (which must not have been taken from a churchyard tree), of box, and of variegated holly.

In every part of Britain it is held unlucky to keep evergreen decorations after Twelfth Day (6th January).

CHRISTMAS EVE

If a girl walks backwards to a pear tree on Christmas Eve, and walks round the tree three times three times, she will see an image of her future husband.—General.

On Christmas Eve at midnight, the rosemary bursts into flower.—Gloucestershire and Berkshire.

Fairies meet at the bottom of mines on Christmas Eve and perform a Mass in celebration of the birth of Christ.—Cornwall and the Black Country.

It is unlucky to give out fire or a light from a house on Christmas Eve.—Malvern and Sheffield areas of Yorkshire. NOTE: This is also a superstition widely associated with New Year's Eve.

It is unlucky to cut the Yule Cake before Christmas Eve.—Yorkshire.

Ghosts never appear on Christmas Eve.—Northern Counties.

When the clock strikes midnight on Christmas Eve, all doors should be opened to let out bad spirits.—Midlands.

If an unmarried girl goes over to the door of the fowl-house on Christmas Eve and taps it sharply she will know if she will wed before the end of the year. If a hen cackles, she will not be wed; if a cock crows first, she will.—Devonshire.

The maiden who, on Christmas Eve, goes into the garden at midnight and plucks twelve sage leaves, will see the shadowy form of her husband-to-be approaching her.—Northamptonshire.

If you tie wet straw or haybands round your fruit trees on Christmas Eve, they will yield plentifully during the next year.—Wales.

There are other marriage divinations connected with the burning of the Yule Log (q.v.). In Devonshire the log was referred to as the Ashen Faggot. It was hauled into the house on Christmas Eve and lighted. Each of the younger members of the family chose one of the bands round the faggot. During the burning the bands were burnt through in succession. It was believed that the one who chose the band first to be burnt through would be the first to be wed.

An Oxfordshire superstition was for a maiden to make a dough cake in silence. Placing it on the hearth, still in silence, she pricked her initials on the dough. At midnight, while she waited with the door open, her future husband (or his spirit) would walk in, prick his initials besides hers and walk out again.

NOTE: Oxen kneeling at midnight, and bees buzzing are dealt with under Christmas Day, to which they properly belong.

A Christmas Eve superstition prevalent in the Border counties, Lancashire, Cheshire, and Nottinghamshire, is that the bells of churches buried in earthquakes, floods, or cavings in, may be heard below the ground ringing at midnight. Pilgrimages were made in the older days to these sites at Preston, and Kilgrimole, near Blackpool.

A Midlands superstition was that a piece of Christmas mistletoe, tied in a bag and worn round the neck, would protect the wearer against witchcraft.

Wassailing the apple trees, already referred to under "Christmas Day" was also carried out in many parts on Christmas Eve. At Warleggan (Cornwall) a jar of cider, a bottle and a gun were taken into the orchards. A small bough of the principal tree was placed in the bottle, and the household chanted:

Here's to thee, old apple tree.
Hats full, sacks full,
Great bushel-bags full,
    Hurrah.

The gun was then fired off.

In Devonshire, in the Tavistock area, cider was taken to the orchard in a bowl, with toast floating in the liquid. Pieces of the toast were placed in the forks of the tree; cider was thrown round the roots, while the family forming a ring, chanted:

Health to thee, good apple tree.
Well to bear, pockets full, hats full,
Pecks full, bushel-bags full.

This (Christmas Eve) pilgrimage to trees has indeed, a world-wide application. On this Eve, South Slavonian and Bulgarian peasants whose trees did not fruit well the previous summer, visit the tree with an axe swung threateningly, while his neighbour intercedes for the tree. After this the frightened tree will give a good crop at the next harvest!

German peasants, on Christmas Eve, were wont to tie fruit trees together with ropes of straw. Being thus married, they would, in the following summer, bear fruit.

The origin? It lies in the world-wide belief, from earliest times in the beneficent powers of the Tree Spirits. This rules alike among native tribes as it did in Christianized and civilized Europe.

As the people of the apple-growing counties in England made libations to the trees for fruit, so did (and still do) the peoples of Upper Burma offer gifts to the trees to give rain; as in the six-teenth and seventeenth centuries English country people believed that you could, by means of the Tree Spirit, transfer one's sickness by nailing it to a tree; so, too, do the hill tribes of South Mirazapar, and many other native races.

Here, as before emphasized, there could have been no collusion, no connection between the countries, yet exactly the same superstitions prevail.

Apropos this, was the similarity between the country belief here that cows and other animals kneel and low on Christmas midnight, with the Vosges superstition that at midnight on 24th December, cattle acquired the gift of speech and conversed with each other in the language of Christians. A story is told by one farmer, who hid in a corner of the stalls to hear this conversation: One ox said to another: "What shall we do to-morrow?" "We shall carry the master to the churchyard," replied the other. It is recorded that the farmer died that night, and was, in fact, buried on Christmas Day.

The mummers played a considerable part in the old-time customs of Christmas Eve. Performances were given at Stourton (Wilts) and at Wootton Bassett (Wilts), at both of which places the performances were in costume. At Stourton, also, there was performed *The Christmas Bull*. This was the head of a bull, with large eyes and horns, and a lolling tongue, manipulated by a man astride a broomstick, and hidden by sacking or some other cloth. Thus arrayed, he paraded the streets.

The bull was made to knock at doors of houses, and, if admittance was permitted, he chased the youngsters in the family. This custom was peculiar in that it was practised only in this Wiltshire village. *Antiquary*, vol. 44 (1908), stated that the component parts of the bull had been in the possession of one family for more than 100 years.

It is interesting to note, *en passant*, that in parts of Lancashire, all the Christmas evergreen decorations when taken down were kept and used as fuel for the frying of Shrove Tuesday's pancakes.

Another practice, peculiar to one part of the country was that in certain Midland rural areas men paraded round with a white horse's head and spin (real, if possible, but if not, an imitation). In the earlier days of the custom one of the men was dressed as a sailor, the remainder dressed as women. The practice was to enter a house, sweep up and tidy the hearth, and then ask for

Christmas boxes. The origin for this strange performance has not been preserved; but it is significant to note that the god Wodin, or Odin, was accounted a great hunter, and rode Gleiper, a white steed. Many of the customs and superstitions of the Northern and Midland areas of England show signs of the Scandinavian influence in those parts of the country.

CHRISTMAS MUMMERS

Apropos Stourton and Wootton Bassett mummers mentioned above, similar performances were common in other areas. Tenby, for instance; and in London had become, by 1334, such a nuisance that by a proclamation of Edward III it was ordained: "We do forbid, on pain of punishment, that any man shall go about at this feast of Christmas with companions disguised with false faces, or in other manner, to the houses of the good folks of this city."

CHRISTMAS STOCKINGS

The superstition of the stocking filled by Santa Claus is well-known to-day, though it is, alas, like so many of those mentioned in this work, slowly dying out. Its reputed origin, however, has its only connection with Christmas in the name of Santa Claus—St. Nicholas, the patron saint of Christmas Day.

The saint, who liked to do good by stealth, hearing that three lovely sisters, who lived in a poor cottage on the outskirts of a town, were so destitute that if they desired to continue living at all, a life of shame was their only alternative. Accordingly, the good saint made his way to their home one night, and tossed three pieces of gold through the smoke hole in the roof. (There were, of course, no chimneys, as we know them, in those days. The smoke went out from a hole cut in the roof.)

Instead of the gold pieces falling on to the hearth, as the saint had intended, they fell into the stockings of the girls, which had been hung over the fire to dry. The tale became known, since when has existed the custom of hanging stockings in the chimneys, or over the hearth, in hopes.

Christmas Eve was chosen for this custom because of Santa Claus. It is, also, easy to perceive from the story, the origin of Santa Claus coming down the chimney!

CHRISTMAS TREE

Queen Victoria, and Prince Albert, erected the first Christmas tree in England, at Windsor Castle, in 1844, as a surprise for the Prince of Wales (later Edward VII) and the Princess Royal. It was introduced by Prince Albert from Germany, where it had long been popular.

It is not true, however, that the Christmas tree originated in Germany. Its probable beginning for Christmas was from Egypt, and its origin from a period long antecedent to the Christian era. The palm tree is known to put forth a shoot every month, and a spray of this tree, with twelve shoots on it, was used in Egypt, at the time of the winter solstice (25th December) as a symbol of the year completed.

CHRISTMAS YULE LOG

See YULE LOG.

CHURCH

Should you turn over a hassock in a pew (even though the hassock may be already upside down) you will have a sequence of twenty unlucky Sundays.

Church dust, brought to the bed of a dying person, shortens and eases a lingering and painful death.

Whoever pulls the first stone out of a church, although it is for a good purpose, to make way for a new one, will come to a violent end.—Scotland.

Whoever watches at the porch of a church on St. Mark's Eve at midnight, will see the forms of those who are to die within the next twelve months.—Yorkshire.

If a church door rattles without any seeming reason, it is a sign that it will shortly open to admit a coffin.—General rural belief.

*A bird perching on the weather vane of a church is a sign that a death will occur in the village within a week—*Suffolk rural belief.

Should a bird fly into a church during a service it will bring good luck to all those present at the service.

A robin flying into a church and singing, means a death among the parishioners.—Widespread rural belief.

The first living thing to enter a new church becomes the property of the Devil.

The first child christened in a new church is claimed by the Devil, and is sure to die.—Yorkshire and other parts.

We will enlarge, first, on the ill-luck of pulling out of the first stone in a church, which was for many generations widely held in Scotland. The superstition led to a curious deadlock some eighty years ago in Aberdeenshire. A new place of worship had been built, and the old one was sold for demolition. But no workman would begin the task. Eventually after a hold-up of several days the agent to the estate pulled out the first stone, and the men thereafter raised no objection to pulling down the building.

Very widespread was the superstition quoted above that a person who kept watch at midnight on St. Mark's Eve would see entering the church the forms of those parishioners who were to die during the coming twelve months. The custom was, however, more widespread on All Hallowe'en, extending throughout the country from Scotland into Wales.

In Scotland the procedure was to sit on a three-legged stool at three crossroads, while the church clock was striking midnight, when there would be called out the names of parishioners thus doomed to die. It was, however, in the person's power to save the victims by taking articles of wearing apparel and throwing them away, one by one, as each name was called out by the mysterious voice.

It was Yorkshire which chiefly kept the vigil on St. Mark's Eve. Churchgoers thus to peer into the future had to keep watch from an hour before midnight to an hour after midnight on three successive years. On the third occasion they would see the forms. The doomed, it was said, would pass into the church one by one. Should the watcher, however, fall asleep during the two hours, then he (or she) would die during the year.

A number of remarkable stories are told in connection with this superstition. A humorous one. is of a sexton in a North country parish who kept vigil in order that he might gain some idea of his likely income from grave-digging during the next twelve months!

Another, more grim, relates to a woman who watched at the porch of St. Mary's Church, Scarborough, some 150 years ago. As the figures glided into the church she recognized one after another, the familiar faces of her friends. The last figure was hidden from her until the last moment. It turned and gazed at her, and she recognized herself. Neighbours found her senseless in the porch next morning, and she died shortly afterwards.

That the Devil claimed the first living thing to enter a new church was widely held, not only here, but in Germany. It was the custom to drive a dog into the doorway after the consecration of the outside.

There is at Aix-la-Chapelle (or, at least, there was before the World War 1939-45) a church, the door of which had a large rent. The story attached to the rent, and told to the authors, was that when the church was ready for consecration, a dog was driven in. The Devil, in a rage at being cheated of his human prey, flew away with the dog through the door, shivering the wood as he passed through it.

One of the most curious practices associated with churches was that at Kingston-on-Thames (Surrey) as late as 1850. Here, in the church of All Saints, on Michaelmas Eve, the entire congregation cracked nuts in their pews. The origin or meaning of the absurd practice is unknown.

At Great Yarmouth (Norfolk) on the first Sunday in October, it was the custom to place fishermen's nets before the altar of St. Nicholas's Church, where the service of the "Blessing of the Nets" was held.

Another curious custom was "clipping" St. Mary's Church, Painswick, on the first Sunday after the Nativity of the Virgin Mary (old style, 19th September). The authors have a record of the performance as recently as 1912, when a procession was formed at 3 p.m. and marched into the churchyard, headed by the church banner. Including children, it marched to the steps leading to the belfry, where the clipping began. Children clasped hands and formed a ring round the church, swaying backwards and forwards. They then reformed in procession to the church tower, where a service was conducted.

In Norfolk, at one time, lights called plow (plough) lights were maintained before certain images by husbandmen, as a means of ensuring success in their crops.

The decorating of church doorways, porches, and even the interiors with lanthorns, on May Day, was at one time a universal custom.

Reference has been made under "Christening" to the practice of burying an animal, or a human being, under the foundations of a church. (See CHRISTENING). The authors have, on many occasions, been asked whether the modern custom of burying newspapers and coins under buildings erected in present times is a survival of the custom. The answer is that it is not. The newspapers and coins are thus buried with the sole idea of leaving some concrete evidence for posterity of the customs, habits and coinage of our day; the origin of the immolated man, child or animal, was a sacrifice to the earth to bear safely the added burden the edifice imposed upon it. The Rev. S. Baring-Gould, so vast an authority on folklore, held this view for many years, but later recanted. The present authors hold it still.

The robin superstition referred to above had a fairly wide vogue. It was held, some 70 years ago, by the students at St. John's College, Hurstpierpoint, that when a death takes place in the school, a robin will enter the chapel, alight on the altar and sing.

In connection with this, the Rev. S. Baring-Gould has related how he chanced, on one occasion, to be in the chapel in the evening when a robin entered at an open circular window, perched on the altar and began to sing. "A few minutes later," he wrote, "the passing bell began to toll for a boy who had just died."

CHURCH BELLS

To drive away fiends and wicked spirits during a thunderstorm, the church bells should be rung.—Widespread belief in olden days.

For this purpose Aubrey states in his *Miscellanies* that it was the custom, when it thundered and lightened, to ring St. Adhelm's Bell at Malmesbury Abbey; and Bacon, in his *Natural History,* states: "It is believed by some that great ringing of bells in populous cities charms away thunder and also dissipates pestilent airs." He adds, wisely, "All of which may be from the concussion of the air, and not from the sound."

A certain amount of this latter belief exists to-day, for during the World War, 1939-45, there was considerable support in newspaper correspondence columns for the theory that the disturbance of the air by gunfire was responsible for much rain: and attempts have on many occasions been made in countries visited by drought to induce rain by firing guns into the air.

A popular bell custom and a widespread one in olden days was the Sunday "Pudding Bell." It consisted of the tolling of a church bell at the conclusion of the sermon. The idea was to announce to the cooks at home that their folk would soon be on the way back, and the dinner should now be prepared for the table. "Pudding Bell" is of Yorkshire origin. The story is that in Yorkshire it was the custom to begin the midday Sunday meal with Yorkshire pudding, swimming in gravy.

At Ravenstonedale, Westmorland, it was customary to ring "The Saint's Bell" after the Creed, to call in dissenters to the sermon.

For very many years, on the Eve of the Feast of Corpus Christi, choristers ascended the tower of Durham Cathedral and, in their white robes, sang the Te Deum. The ceremony was in commemoration of the miraculous extinguishing of a fire on that night in 1429. The monks were at midnight Mass when the belfry was struck by lightning. The fire raged for 48 hours, but the tower escaped serious damage and the bells remained uninjured. The miracle was ascribed to the special influence of St. Cuthbert, enshrined in the cathedral.

For other superstitions associated with bells, see PANCAKE BELL, PASSING BELL, CURFEW BELL, and the seasons such as NEW YEAR'S DAY, MIDSUMMER DAY, etc.

CHURCHING (OF WOMEN)

A mother must not cross the doorstep till she goes to be churched, after a child's birth.

A mother who, before she is churched after the birth of a child, enters any house other than her own will bring ill-luck on the house.

The origin of these superstitions associated with child-birth was the ancient belief that a woman after child-birth was open to fairy influences. (See BIRTH, and BABIES.) Such influences might, in certain circumstances, be evaded, for instance, by the placing over her of part of her husband's clothing, thus deceiving the fairies into thinking her to be a man. Which does not say much for the perspicuity of fairies!

It is believed, also, that should a mother venture out from under her roof before churching, and be insulted or injured by neighbours, she had no remedy at law. Nonsense, of course, but it was widely held.

However, in Ireland, the ill-luck of venturing out before churching could be evaded if a piece of thatch, or a slate, was pulled from the roof and worn on the top of a new hat. With such a decoration the mother could wander where she listed. The origin? Quite simple. She was still under her own roof!

CHURNING

Whenever churning is going on, a small piece of burning turf should be put under the churn to prevent the abstraction of butter by the "good people" (fairies).—Ireland.

The handle and cross of the churn-staff should always be made of rowan wood, because that is the most potent charm against witchcraft.—Highlands of Scotland.

In her *Superstitions of Ireland*, Lady Wilde records the widespread practice of putting a ring of rowan wood, or quickenmas as it is called, on the handle of the churn-dash when she is churning, so that no witch can steal her butter.

CIDER

Cider should be made when the moon is on the wane, else the apples, when gathered, will "shrump-up," and the cider will turn sour.—Hereford and Devon.

For other superstitions concerning the cider crop for apples, see APPLE TREES; WASSAILING.

CIGARETTE

To light three cigarettes from a single match will mean bad luck.—General.

The superstition in Britain is said to date from the Boer war. It has, like so many superstitions, a practical value. Kruger's men were perfect snipers, and our soldiers from experience worked out that a soldier shot while lighting his cigarette on the veldt was invariably the third to use the same match. It was argued that the sniper saw the flame as the first cigarette was lighted, took aim at the illumination for the second cigarette, and fired when the third light was being given.

This origin may be correct, but in the Crimean War, Russian prisoners had a reluctance to lighting three articles with the same match, and explained it as being due to the Russian Orthodox Church ruling that only a priest could light the three candles on the altar with a single taper. No layman would dare do such a thing.

CINDERS

"Coffins" coming out of the fire are a sign of death in the family.

"Cradles" coming out of the fire betoken that a baby will be born in the house very soon.

A "coffin" is an oblong cinder shooting out of the fire. A "cradle" is an oval shaped cinder similarly shooting out. However, it was provided in the ancient superstition that should the cinder give a clinking noise as it shot out, good fortune would follow. If, however, it shot out silently, a funeral would start from the house.

CLOCK

If the town clock strikes while the church bells are ringing there will soon be a fire in the parish.—Wales.

If a clock strikes in the church while the text is being given, a death may be expected in the parish.—Somerset.

Should a clock which has not been going suddenly strike the hour, or a number of chimes, a death will occur in the family.—General.

The authors have been presented with a remarkable number of instances in connection with the latter superstition.

As recently as January, 1946, a family related to them an extraordinary circumstance. For more than twenty years a clock had stood in the hall of their residence. It had never worked, but, being a handsome piece of furniture, had been kept as an ornament to the hall. To the amazement of the family one evening it commenced to strike, and continued for no fewer than sixty chimes. A week later a member of the household died. Although the clock was examined, no reason for the sudden chiming could be found.

Twelve months later the clock began once more to chime in similar fashion, and again a member of the family died, this time in distant Australia. Once again, the clock was examined, without any reason for the chiming being discovered.

On the other hand, the authors have investigated a number of cases in which a clock chimed, though unwound and unused—and no untoward effect followed.

A queer superstitious story attaches to a clock in Reading. A new clock was installed in the spire of St. Mary's Church in that town because the old one was pronounced, after long investigation and deliberation, as being not dependable.

The story goes that the old church clock had been cursed by a man condemned to death for a crime of which he was innocent. That, in the general belief was the reason that the clock never kept dependable time.

The new clock functioned well.

CLOTHES

If you have clothes mended on your back, you will come to want.—General.

If, on putting on a new coat or dress you do not at once put money in the right-hand pocket, you will want for money so long as you wear the coat. But with money in the pocket you will ensure your pocket always being full.

To hook an eye into the wrong eyelet, or place a button in the wrong button-hole will bring you an unlucky day. This may be evaded, however, if the garment is at once taken off, and then put on anew.

There was in East Yorkshire, a custom whereby if a youth went to school in new clothes he had to endure the penalty of pinching from his companions, who repeated the doggerel: "Nip for new, two for blue, and three for corduroy."

There existed the custom in many parts of the country of undoing all buttons on clothes in the house in which a person was dying, the superstition being that anything fastened helped to hinder the soul from leaving the body easily. This applied to locked or bolted doors, etc.

A custom, or shall we say superstition, on clothes which remains down to the present time, is that something new should be worn on Easter Sunday. The ill-luck of wearing green for a bridal gown, or white, if the bride is not a spinster, is also held to-day to obtain.

The origin of these beliefs associated with clothes lies probably in the sympathetic connection which men of all races have held to exist between a person and his clothes. It is less prevalent in Britain than almost anywhere else.

Because of it, the Papuans of Tumleo search for even the tiniest piece of their garments which may have been lost. In Prussia of old it was held that if you could not catch a thief, then if you obtained a piece of garment that he might have discarded in his flight, and if you beat the garment, the thief would fall sick, and thus be quite easily recognized. The stick, however, had to be one-year-old hazel sapling and cut with three strokes, in the names of the Father, Son and Holy Ghost.

A curious Act concerning death clothes was enacted in 1678, whereby the curate of every parish had to keep a register in which to enter all burials of persons being buried in woollen. The Act was entitled "An Act for lessening the importation of linen, and the encouragement of the woollen and paper manufacture of the kingdom."

CLUB-MOSS

Club-moss, if properly gathered, is good against all diseases of the eyes.—Cornwall.

The operative clause seemed to be the phrase "if properly gathered," and it took the authors two months of inquiry to discover an old Cornishman who could tell the proper way to gather the club-moss. Here is the correct method for gathering:

On the third day of the moon, when the crescent is seen for the first time, show it the knife with which the moss is to be cut, and repeat this sentence: "As Christ healed the issue of blood, do thou cut what thou cuttest for good." At sundown, having washed the hands, cut the moss, kneeling, wrap it in a white cloth and boil it in water taken from a spring nearest to its point of growth."

CLUBS (PLAYING CARDS)

There is never a good hand at cards with the four of clubs in it.

The reason given for this is that the four of clubs is the Devil's own card, because it is the Devil's four-poster bedstead.

Since cards are referred to as "the Devil's playthings," we should have thought that the Devil's own card would have brought good luck to a hand.

COAL

If a burglar carries in his pocket a piece of charmed coal, he will be able to defy authority.

Scotland Yard detectives in the 1880's vouched for the prevalence of this strange superstition among burglars. But why coal as an amulet, and how it was "charmed," the authors have been unable to discover.

See HAND OF GLORY.

COBBLERS

Shoe-makers (cobblers) of Devonshire long ago held the curious superstition that they were a poor slobbering race, and have been since the curse was placed on them by Christ.

This curse, it was explained, was laid when Christ, passing a shoe-maker's bench on the way to Calvary, was spat on by the cobbler, and was told by Christ: "A poor, slobbering fellow shalt thou be, and all shoe-makers after thee for what thou hast done to Me."

The origin lies, of course, in the story of Ahasuerus, who cursed Christ, and refused to allow Him to rest in the doorway of his shop. Ahasuerus, the Jew, is the man around whom has been wound the legend of the Wandering Jew.

COBWEB

Bleeding of a wound can be stopped instantly by laying a cobweb over the wound.—General.

It is unlucky to destroy a cobweb.—Old-time belief.

To take the latter first: this belief, once held very extensively among ultra-good people, was derived from a belief that a cobweb concealed the infant Jesus as He lay in the manger, against the messengers of Herod.

The superstition is one that has completely died out to-day, but it may serve as an excellent excuse for the dirty, or lazy, housewife still.

But the belief in the cobweb to stop bleeding is by no means extinct; on the contrary it is still widely held in many rural parts of the country; the authors have come across it on scores of occasions.

COCK

If a cock crows near the door with his face towards it, it is a sure prediction of the arrival of a stranger.—Lancashire and Yorkshire.

At cock-crow midnight spirits forsake this world and go to their proper places.—General.

If the cock crows on going to bed, he's sure to rise with a watery head.—Shropshire and Montgomery weather superstition.

If the cock moults before the hen, we shall have the weather thick and thin. If the hen moults before the cock, we shall have the weather as hard as a block.—Midland counties.

If a cock crows at midnight, the angel of death is passing over the house.—Cornwall.

For a cock to crow late at night means a death in the family.—East Riding of Yorkshire.

If a cock stays on the perch longer than usual in the morning, it is a sign of wet.—Derbyshire.

If a cock near the door crows with his face towards it, it is a sure prediction of the coming of a stranger.—Lancashire.

If a cock crows much more than usually, it is a sign that a stranger is coming.—Devon and Cornwall.

To cure the epilepsy you must bury a black cock alive, along with a lock of the patient's hair and some parings of his nails.—Highlands of Scotland.

The latter superstition is still another example of a world-wide belief for which there seems to be little explanation. Doctor Mitchell, referring to the Scottish cure for epilepsy, states that it dates from remote antiquity and is very widely spread. But then he proceeds to explain that the cock was a creature consecrated to Apollo, who, in classic mythology, was in some measure connected with the healing art.

This is all very well, but it can hardly be said that the people of Timor-laut, in the East Indian Islands, would have any knowledge of Apollo. Yet, if one of them falls sick the whole body of the patient is rubbed with a live cock, which is then committed to a little proa (a tiny ship), and allowed to go out to sea, taking, of course, the illness with it. Nor are the people of Konkan, in India, likely to have been acquainted with Apollo. Yet, when sickness seizes upon a village the inhabitants go in procession from their temple to the boundary line of the village and there they cut off the head of a cock and throw the body over the boundary line. So does the pestilence leave them.

Thus, the authors feel that there is something much deeper behind this superstition of the cock than the theory of Apollo and his worship. Again, in the Uganda Protectorate, if a person has been struck and injured by lightning, a cock is sacrificed over a running stream while the patient kneels.

In Oldenburg a black cock was the witch diviner. The heart, lung and liver was stuck all over with needles and placed on a fire in a tightly closed vessel. All present had to keep silence. When the heart boiled or was reduced to ashes, the witch, it was said, must appear, for she would have felt the burning pain and would come to be released.

Something much on the same lines was practised in Britain, with the object of causing the witch to betray herself either by coming forward, or being marked in the same way that the sacrificed article was marked.

The authors were once taken seriously to task by an old Yorkshireman for doubting that a cock which had crowed during the night in his farmyard had given him notice of a death coming in his family. "Dis tha meean t'tell me at our old cock dizzn't knaw when theer's boon t'be death i' our family?" he demanded. The point was that there obviously HAD to be a death some time or other, so what was the use arguing the matter?

To cure a person of insanity in Scotland in olden days, a cock was buried alive. A rite to effect a cure of an invalid, also in Scotland, was to administer to the patient the blood of a red cock mixed in a flour cake; and the female of the cock burnt alive was a remedy for distemper.

In any case it became a supreme superstition that all medicine to be of any effect must be administered only at cockcrow. This, by the way, became an accepted principle of healing all over Europe.

See BLACK COCK.

COFFIN RINGS

Coffin rings, when dug out of a grave will protect from the cramp.—Somerset, Lancashire and elsewhere.

The rings also prevented, or cured, rheumatism. Anciently, the rings were made of silver, the silver being obtained from the hinges of coffins, that metal being extensively used at one time for this purpose.

The superstition still holds in parts of Lancashire to-day, principally, of course, among the old people. The rings, however, are no longer of silver, but of other metal. If you see a Lancashire, or Somerset, old woman wearing a plain metal ring, or galvanized one, you can know that she is wearing a coffin ring against cramp or rheumatism.

There are many country folk to-day, also, wearing galvanized rings made of two hoops, one of zinc and the other of copper, and soldered together. These, too, are coffin rings.

Silly? Perhaps so, but the superstition of rings for cramp and rheumatism is pretty nearly as much alive now as it was in those old days of the coffin rings of silver. The rings were cheap then; the modern ring is not so cheap. It is made of an alloy of gold and copper; it is a "magnetic" ring, and costs a few guineas. You can hardly open a magazine without seeing the picture of a man wearing either a ring or a belt from which magnetic lines were radiating, as a cure for rheumatism. They are probably as much good, or as little good as the coffin rings of silver, or zinc and copper.

If you took a nail which had been in a coffin and drove it into the footstep left by a man, it was believed in Mecklenburg (Germany) that the man would become lame and remain lame so long as the nail remained in the footprint. A German huntsman long held that a coffin nail stuck into the spoor of his game quarry would hinder the animal from escaping.

See CRAMP.

COINS

To dig up an ancient coin while ploughing a field is a curse of the Devil, unless you at once spit on each side of it.—Kent and elsewhere.

To receive, as change, a coin with a hole in it will bring you good luck.—General.

The extent to which coins found were "cursed" is seen in the old Kentish name for them—"hegs," the word coming from hag, by which name a witch was more generally known.

No Kentish labourer ever found a heg-penny without doing the necessary spitting. Which reminds the authors that there seems to be no feasible explanation why spitting should negative bad luck. It is used in all kinds of charms—when meeting a cross-eyed man, or a load of hay, when two people wash their hands at the same time in the same water, and so on. We have been able to find no confirmation of its efficacy.

But to return to coins: It was the practice—and we believe it is still in many parts—to place a penny in each of the eyes of a person on death to prevent the eyes reopening. You will remember that in *Martin Chuzzlewit*, Mrs. Gamp saw Gamp in Guy's Hospital with a penny piece on each eye and his wooden leg tucked under his left arm.

There was a superstition current to a very slight extent in Britain, but to a far greater extent in Servia and Bulgaria, that if these penny pieces were taken from a corpse's eyes and washed in wine, and the wine afterwards given to a husband, he would henceforth be blind to any little peccadilloes of an unfaithful wife.

COLD (IN HEAD)

Pare very thinly the rind of an orange. Roll it up inside out and thrust a roll into each nostril. The cold will disappear.

The above was an eighteenth century cure.

But a few months ago the authors came across a modern one. They were attracted to the strange conduct of two elderly people—a man and a woman—in Hyde Park, London. They were looking up at an oak tree and endeavouring to catch in their hands leaves that were falling under the autumnal wind.

Having at last caught one each, they ceased their quest and walked away apparently satisfied with their achievement.

A question to them elicited the fact that they expected to be free of colds in the head by reason of their performance. They explained that they were country bred and had from childhood caught leaves like that to prevent a cold in the head and "We've never had a cold yet," they concluded.

COLIC

To cure the colic, stand on one's head for a quarter of an hour.—Cornwall.

Jumping through the Midsummer Bonfire is a good guard against the colic. —General.

The bonfires mentioned are treated elsewhere in this volume, mostly under the heading "Need-fires." Jumping through the smoke and flames of the fires to prevent colic was not confined by any means to Britain; in the Ardennes of Belgium it was also a recognized preventive.

Pliny has left on record another superstition for the cure of colic—the pastern bone of a hare, provided that it has not touched the earth and has not been touched by a woman.

The superstition attaching to colic in Cochin-China and China proper is that it is due to the sufferer having in some way pierced the stomach of a god who lives like a mole, in the ground. The injured deity has punished the offender by abstracting his soul and burying it under a plant. The remedy is to find the plant, tear it up by the roots, and pour into the hole a quantity of millet wine and the blood of a fowl, goat or pig.

COLLIERS

If a collier meets a woman, or even catches a glance of her draperies, on his way in the middle of the night to the pit, he must return home, lest misfortune befall him.—General.

If a collier washes his back, he will suffer from weakness in the back.—General.

The same ill-luck was held to attend a fisherman going to his ship who saw a woman while on his way there. In the childhood days of the authors, a few old miners still held to the superstition.

Illustrating the strength of the feeling of miners of the old days against seeing a woman while on their way to work is the report in the *Oswestry Advertiser* of May, 1874. It reports how a woman was employed as a messenger at one of the local collieries, and how, going about her duties, she met large numbers of miners coming to the pit in the early hours. Some of them, considering the meeting to be a bad omen, and unable to deter her from her work by any other means, visited the pit manager and announced that they would stay away from the pit unless she was dismissed.

See MINERS, FISHING.

COMMUNION, HOLY

The Sacrament of Holy Communion cannot, perhaps, be regarded as a superstition in the meaning of this volume. It is mentioned, however, because of the superstition and rite of the Aztecs of Mexico in ancient days, in connection with the present Christian belief of "Take, eat, this is my body," in the Sacrament.

The Aztecs, in the days before the conquest by the Spaniards, ate bread, sacramentally, as the body of a god. Twice a year, an image of the great Mexican god Vitzilipuztli was made in dough, broken in pieces, and solemnly eaten by his worshippers. They could, in those days, have had no knowledge of the sacrament associated with the Christian church.

CONFIRMATION

The authors can discover only one superstition connected with the confirmation service of the Church of England, and that is connected with the hands of the Bishop. The preference is for touching with the right hand.

Henderson, in this connection, recalls the story of a poor woman who presented herself to a clergyman as a candidate for confirmation, but was recognized by him as having been confirmed some years previously. She admitted the impeachment, but pleaded that she "had had the Bishop's left hand," had been uneasy ever since, and was "trying her luck again."

In the Northern counties of England to be touched by the left hand of the Bishop during confirmation was accounted a sure sign that the person confirmed would never marry.

CONSUMPTION

Swallow baby frogs before breakfast, and the consumption will go.—Midlands.

To cure consumption the person affected should be carried or led through a flock of sheep as they are led out of the fold in the morning.—Surrey.

Pare the nails of the fingers and toes of a consumptive, put them in a bag made from his clothes, wave the bag thrice in the air round his head, crying "Deas Soil," after which the bag should be buried.—Moray Province of Scotland.

NOTE: Pliny records a similar practice as being used by the magicians of the Druids.

These superstitions are, of course, connected with the belief that illness could be transferred to earth, or to another creature. This transference of evil is among the oldest beliefs of the human race. In the case of the Surrey superstition, the belief was that the consumption would be passed to the sheep, leaving the human patient free. The parings of the nails transferred the evil to the earth with the burying of the parings.

It must be remembered that the belief in olden days was that the disease was a harmful thing, or a demon, clinging to the sufferer. Where it was held that the illness was caused by a demon, a different approach was made to rid the patient.

On the coasts of Morven and Mull are ledges of rock pierced with holes. Consumptive patients used to be brought to the stones and, when certain conditions of wave and sea were propitious, were passed through the holes. It was held that the demon clinging to the sufferer could not himself be passed through with the patient, and was, accordingly, displaced.

There stood on a farm in Coll a stone called Clach Thuill (Hole Stone), through which persons suffering from consumption were passed as lately as the eighteenth century. Three times the sufferer was passed through in the name of the Father, Son and Holy Ghost. Meat and bread was taken by the patient and placed on the stone; the birds which later came for the bread and meat took the consumption away with them.

In Oldenburg, the practice was to hang a goldfinch or a turtle dove in the room with a consumptive patient in order that the bird might draw the malady to itself.

An Arab cure was to put a dish of water on the patient's head, drop melted lead into it, and then bury the lead in a field. Thus was the malady buried in the same belief that were the parings of nails of the Surrey folk.

Mention is made above of the swallowing of baby frogs before breakfast as a cure for consumption. Incredible though it may seem, the authors as recently as 1946 received a letter from a person living in Derbyshire who sent a cure for consumption, and sent it in all seriousness, stating that he had known a person thus cured. The cure was to eat young frogs every morning.

CORNS

To cure corns steal a small piece of beef and bury it in the ground. As it rots away, the corn will go away.

This is, of course, another instance in the belief of the transfer of evil to inanimate objects. Incidentally, at the time the superstition became rife in Britain, the stealing of meat was punished by the treadmill. So the "cure" was a bit of a risk. If the corn vanished, the cured sufferer stood a good chance of being indicted for stealing beef. The pain of the corn might have been the more desirable.

CORPSE

If a corpse remains warm longer than usual, it is a sign that there will be another death in the family before long.—Northumberland and parts of Dorset.

For any animal to jump over a corpse or a coffin is so ominous that only the death of the animal can avert tragedy in the family.—Scotland and the Border and Northern counties.

Every string in the shroud of a corpse must be cut before coffining, otherwise the dead will get no rest.—Gaelic.

Should a corpse remain unburied on a Sunday it will mean the death of another resident in the village before the week is out.—Sussex rural areas.

The last corpse to be buried in a cemetery must stay and keep guard over the graves until the next corpse comes in to take his place.—Irish.

If a corpse is carried over private ground the ground becomes a right of way.—Widely held belief, which is, legally, sheer nonsense. It is still widely held and the authors were called upon to testify to it only a few months ago.

On visiting a house in which a dead body is lying a person must touch the corpse in token that they wished no ill to the departed and were in peace and amity with him.—Durham. The origin of this belief was probably the old theory that a corpse would bleed at the touch of a murderer. This was one of the old trials of murder procedure.

If a corpse is taken across a field, that field will become barren, no matter how fruitful it may have been before.—Widespread rural belief.

A gun fired over a corpse thought to be lying at the bottom of the sea, or a river, will by concussion break the gall bladder, and thus cause the body to float.—Widespread belief.

If a loaf, weighted with quicksilver is allowed to float on the water it will swim towards, and stand over, the place where the body is lying.—Very widespread belief. It was actually practised with success in the month of May, 1945, in the south country, in the case of a missing child.

Blessed is the corpse the rain drops on.—Hull.

The removal, or exhumation, of a body bodes death or calamity to members of the deceased's family.—Norfolk, Leicester and Northampton.

Never carry a corpse to church by a new road.—Cornwall.

An illustration of the first-named of the above superstitions appeared in *Notes and Queries,* 5th series. The account runs as follows: "T—— of P—— was on his deathbed. After he had breathed his last, he was measured for his coffin. When two days later the undertaker came to put him in the coffin he was not at all stiff, but 'as soople as a wulie.'"

The old women of the village stated, quite emphatically, that someone who attended the funeral would die soon, owing to the body not getting stiff as it should have done. In less than three weeks the prophetesses of ill were triumphant; a man named R—— S——, one of the bearers at the funeral, a "muckle strong sober fellow who went wi' the cairts to the mill" took ill and, after lingering for a few weeks, died.

Another correspondent of *Notes and Queries* stated that he had been told by an old woman that if a corpse remained warm and "limmack" (flexible) it was a sign that there would be another death in the family.

In his *Vulgar Errors,* Sir Thomas Browne refers to the widely held superstition that "If a child dieth, and the neck becometh not stiff, but for many hours remaineth lithe and flaccid, some other in the house will die soon after."

In Dorsetshire it was held that if one of twins die, and the limbs do not soon stiffen, the funeral should be delayed because the dead one was waiting for the other twin. In the same county, another belief is that if the eyes of a dead person are difficult to close, they are "looking after followers." Thus, great care is taken to have someone at the deathbed who shall close at once the eyes of the deceased person.

The belief that calamity will overtake the family of a man whose body is exhumed was widely held, and on one occasion led to a riot in a Norfolk village. The body of a woman was exhumed owing to a suspicion that she had died of poison. The police were attacked and severely handled by the villagers before they were able to carry out their duty. For many years the villagers refused to pass the grave of the exhumed woman, though she was reburied, death having been found to be due to natural causes.

The grave was beside a footpath leading to the church door, but when the authors were shown the spot, the villagers had diverted their steps in a semi-circle over the grass, in order to avoid the grave. The semi-circle was a diversion of twelve feet. In the end the vicar of the parish was compelled to construct a new permanent footpath. The objection of the villagers to passing the spot was that it would bring bad luck. The twelve feet diversion was held to have some connection with the twelve Apostles.

The superstition relating to a cat or dog jumping over a corpse in a coffin is widely held in Northumberland. One clergyman in particular, the Rev. J. F. Bigge, has recorded his own experience. A cat jumped over the coffin as a funeral was about to leave the house for the church, he stated. As a result nobody would leave the house until they were assured that the cat had been shot by one of the men of the family. The superstition also had a strong hold in the Shetland Isles.

In some parts of Ireland, in addition to all the strings in the shroud of a corpse being removed before coffining, it was the custom to deposit in the coffin a piece of candle, a coin and a small quantity of wine—to give light to the deceased's journey to the other world, to pay his fare over the river of death, and to sustain him on the passage.

In the West Highlands a wax candle, a gold coin and a hammer and pair of scales were deposited—the hammer to knock for admittance to the other world, and the scales to weigh the soul. The latter is obviously origined in the ancient Egyptian rite described in the *Book of the Dead*. The Egyptians, too, it will be recalled, deposited articles of food and drink, and money, in the tombs of their dead pharaohs.

Reference is made above to the custom of touching a corpse to show that there was no ill-feeling against the dead, and to the fact that this may have been a relic of the old trial by ordeal. The trial ordained that a man accused of the murder of an individual should be taken to the body and made to touch it with his hands. Should blood ooze from the wound, he was adjudged guilty. Or should a change take place in the colouring of the face, or hands and feet, of the corpse, then the accused, in the absence of any wound on the deceased, was adjudged guilty of poisoning.

Is the superstition dead? We wonder. On Tuesday, 3rd September, 1946, the authors received the following letter from a correspondent in Newcastle-on-Tyne: When any person up here dies, nearly all the neighbours visit to have a last look at the dead person, and all touch his or her brow before leaving. If this is readable, I should be happy to know the reason.

Well, if our correspondent see this, he knows now the reason, or at least what was the reason when the superstition first started.

The authors believe that the test was not so farcical as at first seems. It may be that its instigators depended more upon psychology than any actual manifestation; the accused might well lose his nerve and admit his guilt by his demeanour, if not by actual confession.

Reference to the untying of all the knots in the shroud of a corpse among the Gaelic people has a curious counterpart among the Pidhireanes, a Ruthenian people on the hem of the Carpathians. There, if a widow has any intention of marrying again, she unties the knots on her dead husband's grave-clothes before the coffin is shut down on him. This removes all impediments to her future marriage.

See DEATH, FUNERAL, SIN-EATERS.

COUGHS

To cure a cough here is an excellent mixture: Boil two or three snails in barley water, but do not let the patient know it. This is known to have effected great cures.—General.

If a person has a bad cough, take a hair from the patient's head, put it between two slices of buttered bread, and give the sandwich to a dog, saying, "Good luck, you hound. May you be sick and I be sound." The patient will then lose the cough and the dog go away with it.—Wales, Northants and Devonshire.

A prescription for a cough which was practised in Sunderland was to shave the patient's head and hang the hair on a bush. When the birds carried the hair away to line their nests at nesting time, they carried the cough with it.

This, if the cold was contracted on a cold November day, seems to suggest a miserable winter for the patient, what with his head shaved, and no chance of any bird starting nesting until at least next Valentine's Day!

See WHOOPING COUGH.

COUVADE, THE

At a child's birth, the father of the child will experience pains at the same time as the mother, during her pregnancy.

If a husband has the toothache, or is taken sick, it means that his wife is going to have a baby.

NOTE: Couvade, from the French "couver," to hatch.

In great Britain, even to-day, this is a widely held belief. More than a dozen times within the past few months the question has been asked of the authors whether this birth pain of the husband is legend or fact. The answer is that we do not know. There are instances without number of husbands being afflicted with pains, to which they are not normally accustomed, during the pregnancy of their wives.

In the 1914 war, and also in the 1939 war, the appearance of a man in the front line with a badly swollen jaw, the result of toothache, usually met with the question from a sympathetic sergeant-major: "Is your missus THAT way?" and the answer invariably was yes.

It is argued that the man's anxiety for his wife in the dangerous occupation of child-bearing may have the psychological effect of causing him worry over the pain which he knows is being undergone by his wife, and thus due to his anxiety his own physical and mental condition is lowered, rendering him less resistful to the ailments which attack his lowered vitality.

But the origin goes deeper than that — into the age-old couvade, of which the beliefs tabulated above are but a small part.

The subject of the couvade is one of the most curious in the history of sex psyc' ology. Briefly, its earliest origin lies in ʾ ːc belief of primitive people that it wɑs essential for the father to pretend to pɪay the maternal part at childbirth because he is the better fitted in strength and guile than the mother to combat the influences of evil spirits at such a critical time. (The reader will note how, once again, evil spirits are the background of fear.)

In its perfect form, in couvade, the husband behaves as if he had been confined and was "lying in," while the wife goes about her household duties as soon as possible after delivery. Thus, the evil spirits coming to beset the mother and child, find a man in combat with them, and retire.

This form of the couvade has been identified so far apart as among the Californian Indians, and of South America, in Southern India, in the Nicobars, in Malabar, in Celebes, in Borneo; and, according to Diodorus Siculus, it also prevailed among the ancient Corsicans, and in Spain.

The most elaborate example of the couvade known is that to be found among the Indians of Guiana. There, the mother pursues her daily tasks until within a few hours of delivery, when she goes into the forest accompanied by other women of the tribe, and there the child is born. She rises in an hour or two and resumes her work. But the father takes to his hammock in the hut, and is refused his ordinary nourishment, being allowed only a little gruel. Nor may he smoke or wash himself. He is nursed ceremoniously by the women of the tribe for several weeks.

In South India, after the birth, the husband dresses himself in some of the garments of his wife, and retires to bed in a darkened room. The infant is laid beside him, and he is dosed with drugs appropriate to female recovery. The foods which it is held must be avoided by a prospective mother, or by the mother after the birth, are equally taboo with the husband, lest the spiritual bond between both parents and the child should, by partaking of the banned foods, result in evil attending on the infant.

The other side of the couvade is that already referred to—the actual substitution of the man for the woman. This simulation by the father of the mother's part is really the essence of the superstition. It has always been held by the civilized and the savage that the period of birth is one of peril, especially from evil spirits which lie in wait to harm the child, and since savage man was the natural protector of his women and children he took upon himself (and still takes in many savage races to-day) the task of guarding them. To do so, he pretends to be the mother. Thus, when the evil spirits appear, instead of a weak woman prone to magical influences, they have to deal with a hale and strong man.

It is this part of the couvade that is beyond question the reason for the belief in the Highlands of Scotland that the Little Folk can do no harm to a newly-born child, and cannot effect a changeling, if part of the father's attire is laid across the bed in which mother and child are lying.

Indeed, in the Watabella Islands, when a wife's delivery is retarded, some of her husband's garments are placed beneath her to render birth more easy. It is believed that the man's vigour will thus be transferred to the woman from his clothes.

The "saining" of a child immediately after birth in Scotland, and in parts of the North country, as a protection against evil spirits is, again, from the couvade.

Some months after the above account of the couvade beliefs had been penned, and while the authors were reading the proofs of this volume they contributed an article to a newspaper ' on the couvade. The result was a remarkable number of letters on the suggestion that the father feels the labour pains of his wife. Following are a selection:

"I was married in December, 1945, and in the last week of 1946 I was ill with sciatica. I had to use two sticks to walk at all, although I was only 26 years of age. One day the doctor asked me how my wife was. I told him 'Very well.' 'Is she expecting a baby?' was his next question. 'Yes,' I replied, 'in September.' 'Ah!' he said, 'you are carrying it for her.' I laughed, but he said I should be all right by the end of September. His words were true."

Another: "I have a bonny wife and four very lovely kids. But no more for me. On each occasion of the wife being 'that way' I have suffered agonies, and it hasn't stopped at toothache. In 1944 it took several hospital doctors and a fortnight in bed, with numerous X-rays and duodenal tests to find out the cause of the pother. It subsequently transpired that had I thought to tell them that a baby was on the way, it would all have been unnecessary."

A third, this time from Norfolk: "A relative of mine, while on a fishing trip, was suddenly afflicted with the most violent toothache, although he hadn't a tooth in his head. His mates told him to write home and ask a few questions of his wife. To his surprise, she WAS!"

We could quote a score of others, but these few will, perhaps, suffice.

See BIRTH.

COWS

If a cow lows three times in your face, it is a sign of death.

If a cow breaks into an enclosed garden, a death will occur in the family of the person owning the garden; should three cows break in, there will be three deaths.—Midlands.

To preserve your cows against harm, pour holy water down their throats on Midsummer Day, and sing the Athanasian Creed to them in Latin.—Somerset.

If a milkmaid does not wash her hands after milking, her cows will go dry.—General.

NOTE: The authors suspect that this was a very excellent superstition invented by a farmer to ensure that his dairy-maids did, indeed, hygienically wash their hands.

Cows in their stalls rise to their knees and bow on Christmas and Easter mornings.—General.

Cows eat buttercups to help them make better butter.

Curst cows have curb horns.

Shakespeare refers to the last superstition in *Much Ado About Nothing,* act ii, sc. 1: "God sends a curst cow short horns."

The buttercup superstition is pure nonsense. In fact, the cow in every possible way, does its best to avoid eating the buttercup, which is a nauseous, bitter herb. The authors have many times watched cows tearing the grass from around buttercups and leave the plants untouched. Farmers like to see their grazing pastures with plenty of buttercups, because the flowers prefer good sound dry old pastures, and the remainder of the herbage is, therefore, generally good.

One more superstition attached to the cow is that prevalent in the North of England, and in Wales, which holds that if you wish your dairy to thrive, you should give your Christmas bunch of mistletoe to the first cow that calves after New Year's Day, for, it is said, it is well-known that nothing is so fatal to milk and butter as witchcraft.

In Wales, to ensure good luck to the dairy, people used to give a branch of mistletoe to the first cow to calve after the first hour of the new year. In rural districts of Wales a good supply of mistletoe was kept handy after the Christmas season for this purpose.

In Ireland, should a cow fall sick without apparent cause, it was believed that she had swallowed an insect of the beetle class, called the derib. The insect lives in ditches and stagnant pools. The old remedy was to strike the animal three times across the loins with a garment belonging to a person named Cassidy. But—why on earth CASSIDY?

Superstition had a remarkable cure for the disease of foul or fellen in a horse or cow, or any other animal. The owner of the animal had to go at midnight into his orchard or a field and "grave" a turf at the foot of the largest apple tree (or the largest tree), and hang it carefully on the topmost bough of the tree—all this being done alone and in silence.

As the turf "muddered" away, so would the disease leave the animal. The cure was known in many places in the North of England; but in some of them it was held that to be effective the turf graved must be one on which the stricken animal had trodden with its diseased foot.

As a commentary on superstition the authors cannot forbear giving a story told by Henderson in his *Folklore of the Northern Counties* concerning the cow of a poor woman which had been taken ill. The woman, who lived in Northumberland, described the recovery of the cow as follows: "I was advised to gan to the Minister, and I thought he might do something for her; so a gaes to the minister and I says, 'The cooo's bad; cuddn't ye cum and make a prayer o'er her like?' 'Well, Janet,' says he, 'I'll come.' And come he did, and he laid his hand on her shoulder and said, 'If ye live, ye live, and if ye dee, ye dee.' Well, she mended from that hour. Next year who but the minister should be ta'en ill, and I thought I wud just gan and see the auld minister—it was but friendly, ye ken. I fund him in bed, and I gans up to him, and lays my hand on his shoulder, and I says, 'If ye live ye live, and if ye dee ye dee.' So he burst out a'laughing and his throat got better fra that moment.''

The minister, it should be stated, was suffering from a quinsy, and the sudden burst of laughing burst the quinsy.

A peculiar superstition in Scotland of olden times was the prejudice against white cows. It was held that the milk was inferior to that of the red cow, for which Scottish peasants at the time had a liking. It is possible, however, that the reason may have been a deeper superstition regarding the lawfulness of consuming the product of a consecrated animal; for the veneration of white cattle in the East even to-day is widespread. A white elephant is still venerated in Siam. A white ox was a gift of special favour in Africa. A sacred white ox was kept anciently at Aphroditopolis, a town in Arabia. Earlier still, a single white hair disqualified cattle for a sacrifice to the God Isis in ancient Egypt. In China a white horse was the most esteemed.

See LOCKERBY PENNY, STONES.

COW DUNG

To heal a wound, it should be plastered with cow dung for several days. —Sleaford area of Lincolnshire and, earlier, many other places.

This was held to be particularly so of ulcerated legs or arms, and it was extensively practised. In other parts of the country it was used as a cure for pneumonia. Only a few years ago, in this twentieth century, a doctor, called to a man seriously ill with a chill, found him covered all over with cow dung.

In point of fact there is some foundation for the belief in the dung as a remedy for a chill, for cow dung, as every gardener knows, is an exceedingly hot manure, and heat is engendered when it is thus applied. It is still used very widely in many rural parts of Britain for the treatment of animals on farms.

CRADLE

To rock an empty cradle means that it will be filled again within a year.— General.

Exceptions to this belief are Durham and Yorkshire and certain other northern areas. There the rocking of the toom (empty) cradle is said to presage the death of the infant. The same belief exists all through Holland.

An old cradle custom in Nottinghamshire, existed at the parish church of Blidworth, where the vicar rocked the last-baptized infant in an ancient cradle bedecked with flowers and surrounded with candles. After the custom had lapsed for a century the vicar, the Rev. J. Lowndes, on 3rd February, 1930, revived the practice in front of the altar of Blidworth church on Candlemas Day.

A kindly Northern England custom held that in all sales, either under distraint for rent or common debt, the cradle must be left unsold, and remain the property of its original owner. Superstition had it that to seize the cradle would bring bad luck upon the seller.

CRAMP

To cure the cramp, place cork between the bed and the mattresses, or between the sheets.—Lincolnshire.

A cure for cramp is to make cork garters by sewing thin discs of cork between silk ribbons.—Southern Lincolnshire.

Wear an eel's skin on the naked leg, and you will never have the cramp.— Durham and Northumberland.

Lay your shoes across the cramp.— General.

Keep a piece of brimstone in your bed, and the cramp will never attack you.— General.

Rings made from the screws, nails or hinges of coffins are a preventive of the cramp.—Yorkshire.

Go to bed with the skin of a mole round yourl eft thigh.—Durham, Northampton, East Anglia, Somerset.

Wear eel skin garters.—Yorkshire.

The most remarkable cramp superstition in the country, however, was that practised at Christ's Hospital, from its foundation until, at least, the time of Coleridge. It was as follows: If a boy was seized with cramp, he should get out of bed, stand on the leg affected, make the sign of the Cross over it three times, saying:

The Devil is tying a knot in my leg.
Matthew, Mark, Luke and John
  unloose it, I beg.
Crosses three we make to ease us,
Two for the thieves, and one for
  Christ Jesus.

Archbishop Whateley recalls in his *Miscellaneous Remains* that the cramp bone of a leg of mutton (the kneecap) had long been in repute as a preventive of cramp.

Another "cure" prevalent in Sussex was to say aloud:

Foot, foot, foot, is fast asleep.
Thumb, thumb, thumb, in spittle we steep.
Crosses three we make to ease us.
Two for the thieves, and one for Christ Jesus.

The more interesting of all these superstitions for the cure of cramp, however, are those referring to the properties of rings from appointments of a coffin. They existed from very early times. Pliny refers to them. Bacon wrote: "There are two things in use to prevent the cramp, viz., ring of seahorse teeth, worn upon the fingers." He then refers to rings.

Andrew Boorde, who lived in the time of Henry VIII, alluding to the cramp, states: "The Kynge's Majeste hathe a great help in this matter in hallowynge crampe ryngs, and so given without money or petition." Elsewhere he wrote: "The Kynges of Englands doth halowe every yere crampe ryngs, ye which ryngs worne on one's fynger doth helpe them whyche hath the crampe."

The ceremonial seems to have been practised by previous Sovereigns, but was discontinued by Edward VI. Documents in the Archæological Institute include a Manuscript of Ceremonies, one of which is described as: "Certain prayers to be used by the Queen's Heighnes in the consecration of ye Crampe-rynges."

In Pegge's *Curalia Miscellanea* is the following form of prayer for the blessing of cramp rings: "O God, the Maker of heavenly and earthly creatures . . . send down from Heaven the Holy Spirit the Comforter upon these rings artificially framed by the workmen, and by thy great power purify them so that all the malice of the fowle and venomous serpent be driven out; and so the metal, which by Thee was created, may remain pure and free from the dregs of the enemy."

And, of course, there is the remedy of rings made from the hinges of coffins, to which reference has already been made under the heading of COFFIN RINGS.

CRAWLING

One of the most rife of all superstitions in Britain for generations was that which entailed crawling through or between something.

A patient with whooping cough, for instance, could obtain relief from the complaint, so it was believed, by crawling underneath a bramble arch made by a spray of bramble reaching the ground and taking root.

On the coast of Morven and Mull are rock wedges through which the sea has pierced holes. It was held that a person taken thither and made to pass through one of the rifts three times in the direction of the sun would be cured of consumption, provided always that the tops of nine waves had been caught in some utensil and thrown over his head before he essayed the passage.

In Crossapol, in Coll, the crawling cure for consumption was through a stone called Clach Thuill (Hole Stone). There was the addition here that the patient had to take meat with him which he left on the stone. The bird that took away the meat took also the consumption.

In the River Dee near Ballater is a rock with a hole through which childless women used to squeeze themselves in order that they might bear a child. In the village of Madern, Cornwall, people formerly crept through the Menen-Tol, or "holed stone" to cure weakness of the back and limbs, and children to get rid of rickets.

Similarly throughout France, Germany, Austria and Greece, and in Asia Minor and India crawling through a narrow orifice was accounted a sure and certain remedy for disease.

The origin lies of course in an intention of ridding the patient of some incubus. The supposition was in the earliest days that a ghost or demon was clinging to the sufferer, and the remedy was to drag it away by the crawl through some opening in which only the person's body could pass, and that only with difficulty. The belief was held by the simple native races that the evil spirit was left behind the entrance obstacle through which the crawl was made.

Further details of these superstitious cures are given under the heads of the individual diseases for which the cure was practised.

CRICKET

If a batsman takes guard twice, he will be soon bowled.

A batsman whose pads are on the wrong legs (i.e., reversed) will score no runs.

If two members of the team wash their hands at the same time, it means a duck for both of them.

George Ullyet, the Yorkshire bowler, had a superstition all his own—that if he missed his stride, and had to return for another start, he would do no good in that spell of bowling. He invariably asked to be taken off for a time. Tom Richardson, at a later stage in his career, arrived at the same conclusion—and decision.

The belief that reversed pads presaged misfortune was held by A. N. Hornby (Lancashire). He usually went in first, but on one occasion, noticing on the way to the pitch that his pads were on the wrong legs, returned at once to the pavilion, where he said, "I'm going in last instead of first. If I went in now, I should have the bad luck to get somebody else or myself out without scoring!"

The great W. G. Grace held the belief that if he went in the batting list with an even number he would make no runs. So he always went in first!

CRICKET (IN THE HOUSE)

The cricket brings good luck to the house. Its departure from the house is a sign of coming misfortune.—Yorkshire and Norfolk.

To kill a cricket is unlucky.—Norfolk.

A cricket eats holes in the worsted stockings of the members of a family who kill it.—Lancashire.

If a cricket forsakes a house a death in the family will soon follow.—General.

The utter foolishness of superstition is best illustrated in these "omens" derived from the sound of crickets "chirping" in a house. In one part of the country, it will be seen the chirping of the cricket presages a death in the family; in another part of the country, it means good luck.

To kill a cricket is regarded in one instance as saving the ill-luck; in the other the killing will bring misfortune on the family—or cause them to have trouble with their worsted stockings. Could folly be more proved?

The fact is that the cricket is an insect that revels in warmth, and will travel along the timbers to the fireside in winter time. And there he chirps, like the cuckoo, monotonously. The sound is made not by the mouth, but by rubbing his wings against the rasp-like serrations on its hind legs.

Grose puts down the superstition of misfortune from killing a cricket to the fact that such an act is a breach of hospitality, the little insect invariably taking refuge in houses.

In East India the superstition of the cricket lies in the story of the peril of the soul which, it is held, can leave the body during sleep. The soul, says this Indian fable, leaves the sleeping person in the form of a cricket emerging from the nose.

Some Cherokee Indians drink tea made of crickets, in order to become good singers like the crickets. That is, again, an instance of the folly of this particular superstition, since the cricket does not sing—as explained above.

CROPS

Crops sown with the full moon will be ready a month earlier than crops sown with the waxing moon.—General.

Crops should be sown from North to South, rather than from East to West.—General.

To get a good crop of cereals, fetch some mould from three adjoining fields inherited by one person, and mix it with the seed at sowing.—Wales.

The first superstition still lingers, especially among gardeners. In a gardening paper, in the spring of 1944, a long correspondence was printed on the effect of the moon on certain crops. It was held that root crops should be sown when the moon was rising, and above-ground crops when the moon was waning.

There seems good ground for holding that the North to South direction of the rows has sound commonsense behind it. The origin would seem to be that such crops get a longer period of sunshine between the rows than if they are sown from East to West.

In connection with crop superstition, mention should be made briefly here of the need-fires, with the ashes of which fields were believed to be fertilized, and in which offerings to crops were made; and also of the wassailing of crops both field and fruit. They are treated with at greater length in their respective sections. Throughout Europe and among the Matabele and the Zulus this fire worship was common. In France, Austria and Germany sowers of seed used to leap high in order to ensure that the crops would grow tall.

See NEED-FIRE, WASSAILING.

CROSSED EYES

It is unlucky to meet a cross-eyed woman, but lucky to meet a cross-eyed man.—General.

If a cross-eyed man marries a cross-eyed woman, it presages happiness for both of them.

Not only was it unlucky to see a cross-eyed person, but the ill-luck was also associated with a person with a squint. The origin lies probably in the fear of the Evil Eye (q.v.). It was held that the first glance of a cross-eyed or a squinting person was the more dangerous than a second or subsequent glance; and it is said of a cross-eyed man in the Craven district of Yorkshire, that he used on rising in the morning to glance first at a tree in his garden in order to spare his neighbours the baleful influence of his first glance. It is added that the tree, in time, withered and died.

CROSSED THINGS

Unlucky is the person who crosses knives at table.

To place one's slippers or shoes in a crossed position is to bring bad luck.

Fortunately, the ill-luck is easy to avert; you get some other person to uncross the knives or the slippers or the shoes.

The origin of the superstition lies in the medieval ages, when such crossing was regarded as a flouting of the Cross of Christ.

CROW

If a crow flutters about a window and caws, it portends death in the house.—General.

If a crow flies thrice over a house and croaks thrice, it is a bad omen.—General.

To see a crow flying alone, is a token of bad luck.—Northamptonshire.

An odd crow, perched in the path of an observer, is a sign of wrath.—Northamptonshire.

If crows flock together early in the morning and gape at the sun, the weather will be hot and dry; if they stalk at nightfall into water and croak, rain is at hand.—General.

When crows forsake a wood in a flock, it forbodes a famine.—General in olden days.

If a crow croaks an odd number of times, look out for foul weather. If an even number, it will be fine.—General.

In regard tot he last-named weather superstition, Dr. Hall, in *Character of Virtues and Vices,* wrote: "The superstitious listen in the mornings whether the crow crieth even or odd and by that token presage the weather."

Throughout the ages the crow has been regarded as a messenger of death or misfortune. A number of crows are said to have fluttered round Cicero's head on the day that he was murdered. Pliny wrote: "These birds, crows and rooks, all of them keep prattling and are full of chat, which most men take for an unlucky signe, and presage of ill-fortune." And Pliny died in A.D. 79.

The power of magic and prophecy is ascribed to the birds in East and West. Reference has already been made to the British belief in their weather prognostications and death portents. The ancients believed that by eating the vital parts of a crow they acquired the prophetic soul of the bird.

In Russia the witch's spirit is supposed to assume the form of a crow.

A Brahmin who converts money given to him for sacrifice will hereafter, it is held, be doomed to be a crow, or a vulture, for a hundred years thereafter.

Scholars will recall that to restore the aged Aeson to youth, the witch Medea infused into his veins a decoction of the liver of a long-lived deer, and the head of a crow that had outlived nine generations of men.

An ancient Indian book of magic, entitled *Kausika Sutra,* describes a way of getting rid of ill-fortune by fastening a hook to the left leg of a crow, attaching a sacrificial cake to the hook, and letting the bird fly away in a south-westerly direction while the priest, or magician, recites the customary formula.

CROWING HEN

A whistling woman and a crowing hen, Are neither fit for God nor men.

—General.

In Normandy they say: "Une poule qui chante le coq et une fille qui siffle, portent malheur dans le maison;" and in Cornwall: "A whistling woman and a crowing hen are the two unluckiest things under the sun."

The former miscreant (!) is greatly dreaded on the coast of Yorkshire. When a party of friends were going on board a vessel at Scarborough the captain astonished the company by refusing to allow one of them on board. "Not that lady," he said. "She whistles." Strange to relate the vessel was lost on the voyage.

In Devon and Cornwall no miner ever whistles underground.

In the Border counties a crowing hen is a portent of death. There is recorded in the parish of East Kilbride a remarkable happening which gave great support to this superstition. An old woman heard one of her hens crowing loudly on the top of a ditch near her house. She told the story to her neighbour saying that no good would come of it. Within a few weeks her husband died. A month later the hen crowed again, and a few days later tidings reached her that her son had been killed. A third time the hen crowed and the woman's daughter died. At that she herself wringed the neck of the hen. And no other member of the family departed this life suddenly.

CRYING BACK THE DYING

The dying are held back from their repose by the love that will not give them up.—Still believed in rural Fife.

If a person is withheld from dying by being cried back, the person called back will be deprived of one or more of the faculties as a punishment to the parent, or other relation who would not acquiesce in the Divine will.

There was a time when these strange superstitions were very prevalent in the rural areas of the country. A record of it is contained in *Notes and Queries* as follows:

"I said to Mrs. B——, 'Poor little H—— lingered a long time. I thought when I saw him that he must have died the same day, but he lingered on.' 'Yes,' said Mrs. B——. 'It was a great shame of his mother. He wanted to die and she would not let him die; she couldn't part with him. There she stood, fretting over him, and couldn't give him up; and so we said to her he'll never die till you give him up, and then she gave him up and he died quite peacefully.' "

In many rural parts, and again especially in Scotland, it is held that the departure of life is delayed, if any locks or bolts in the house are fastened. It is a common practice still, in these parts, when a person is on the point of death, to open every door in the house, in order that the struggle between life and death shall not be painfully prolonged.

See BOLTS, CORPSE, DEATH.

CUCKOO

It is unlucky to have no money in your pocket when you hear the cuckoo for the first time in the season.—General.

If, when you hear the cuckoo for the first time in the season, the sound comes from the right, good luck will attend you; if from the left, ill-luck will be your portion for the rest of the year.—General.

If the cuckoo's song comes from the right, then you should wish, and, if reasonable, the wish will come true.

Whatever you are doing when you first hear the cuckoo in the spring, you will do most frequently all the year.—Norfolk.

If you turn over the money in your pocket and wish the first time you hear the cuckoo each year, the wish will come true.

If you turn the money over in your pocket on hearing the cuckoo for the first time, you will have money in your pocket till the cuckoo comes again.

According to the number of the cuckoo's notes the first time you hear it in the spring, will be the years an unmarried girl must wait for a husband.

Say "Cuckoo, cherry tree come down, tell me how many years I have to live," and count the number of times the cuckoo croaks before going out of hearing, that will be the answer.

It is unlucky to hear the cuckoo before 6th April; but you will have prosperity for the whole year if you hear it first on 28th April.—Wales.

If you hear the cuckoo after Midsummer Day it is a sign of evil portent, and your call too, for you will never hear it again.—Somerset.

NOTE: This referred to old Midsummer Day, which was 6th July.

If an unmarried woman runs into the fields early in the morning to hear the cuckoo, and, as soon as she hears it, takes off her left shoe and looks into it, she will find there a hair exactly the same colour as that of her future husband.

NOTE: Gay, in his *Shepherd's Week*, speaks of this; and an allusion has also been contained in the *Connoisseur*.

Cuckoo oats and woodcock hay, make the farmer run away. NOTE: The meaning of this is that if the spring is so backward that oats cannot be sown until the cuckoo is heard, or the autumn so wet that the lattermath crop of hay cannot be gathered in till the woodcocks come over, the farmer is sure to suffer bad loss.

When the cuckoo purls its feathers, the housewife should become chary of her eggs.—Rural belief. The housewife in this case means a farmer's wife.

With reference to the sowing of crops, the Norfolk labourer has a saying, "When the weirling shrieks at night, sow the seed with the morning light. But 'ware when the cuckoo swells its throat. Harvest flies from the mooncall's* note.

It is a peculiar coincidence that lore for generations has been associated with the cuckoo's note, not only in this country, but in Germany, Denmark and Sweden.

Swedish girls have the same superstition as to the number of years they have to wait for a husband from the cuckoo's note; and also as to the number of years they have to live. In each case the method of divination is the same as those quoted above.

In Shropshire, it was at one time the custom for the farm-labouring folk as soon as they heard the cuckoo for the first time in the spring, to leave off work and devote the rest of the day to merry-making, which went by the name of cuckoo-ale.

* The nightingale.

CURES, IN SEASON

One of the oldest superstitions in Britain was that connected with healing, and which lasted for centuries. Times were appointed when such healing was the more likely to be effective.

Old almanacks of "Leech-craft," as they were called, printed a column in which parts of the body (head, arms, loins, etc.), were placed opposite the days of the month; and no operation was performed on any part of the body except on the day specially appointed as being favourable.

For instance, no old countryman of that day would have his hair cut except on a day which had the word "head" opposite it in the almanack. Even so, should Friday be the appropriate day he still would not visit the barber, because:

Friday hair,
Sunday born.
You'll go to the Devil
Afore Monday morn.

The same procedure was followed in farming. Farmers would not geld their lambs except on the day on which that part of the body was given. "What's almanack say?" was the catch phrase for all operations, whether on humans or animals.

CURFEW

When the curfew sounds it is the signal to ghosts for their walking. Their furlough lasts till the first cock-crow.
See COCK.

CURLEW

If the curlews fly and call, a storm is brewing.—General along the English Channel coast.

The calling curlew is the sailor's pet aversion in his navigation of the Channel. A sailor's name for curlews is "The Seven Whistlers," the whistling having the meaning of calling up wind.

Sir Charles Igglesden, in *Those Superstitions*, quotes an extract from a letter written by a fisherman many years ago. "I knew we were to be in trouble when the Seven Whistlers flew over us with their 'ewe-ewe' cry. Our men wanted to turn back. The night came on with wind and rain, and sure enough before morning a boat was capsized and seven poor fellows drowned. I never did like those birds."

See CROWING HEN.

CUTS

To heal a cut or a wound made by an instrument, clean and polish the instrument, and the wound will heal cleanly.—Border counties, and elsewhere.

This belief is one of the oddest of all British superstitions. For decades, a rural worker who wounded himself with any implement or piece of metal, made no attempt to treat the wound itself. Instead, he treated the instrument that had caused his injury, in the belief that as he kept clean the instrument so would the wound itself remain clean and unpoisoned.

Moreover, the practice was still in vogue in the Eastern Counties of England as late as the 1930's. The authors place on record a reaper in Lincolnshire in 1931 who, having cut himself with a scythe, explained with earnestness that no attention was necessary, as he was taking care to keep the weapon bright, and was oiling it regularly, so that his wound would not fester.

The belief was widely prevalent in the time of Francis Bacon. He wrote in *Natural History*: "It is constantly received and vouched that the anointing of the weapon that maketh a wound will heal the wound itself." The anointing was done with fats.

Innumerable instances of this belief in contagious magic have been placed on record. Frazer recalls that a man who visited the doctor with an inflamed hand, on being told that the wound was festering, replied: "That didn't ought to, for I greased the bush well arter I pulled it out."

At Norwich in 1902, a woman named Matilda Henry accidentally ran a nail into her foot. Without making any examination of the wound she ordered her daughter to grease the nail, saying that if this was done no harm would follow. Within a few days she died of lockjaw.

A Suffolk woman who had burnt her face with a flat iron remarked that the burn would not heal until the iron had been put out of the way. Furthermore, it was her firm belief that every time the iron was used, or even heated, the face burn would break out again.

In Cambridgeshire it was held by farm labourers that if a horse ran a nail into its foot, all that was necessary was to grease the nail with lard and put it away in a safe place. If this were not done the horse would not recover.

Frazer reports a case of a veterinary surgeon called to a horse which had ripped its side open on a hinge of a gate. He found that no attempt had been made to attend the wound, but that the farmer and his men were endeavouring to prise the gate from its setting, in order that the hinge might be taken away and greased.

It is of passing strangeness to consider that this same healing magic exists in countries which could have had no association with the people of Britain at that time. For instance, in Melanesia a man's friends if they can obtain possession of the arrow which has wounded one of their number will keep it in a damp, cool place, by which means it is held that the inflammation of the wound will be kept down, and thus do little harm. On the other hand, if the attackers can get possession of the arrow, they heat it in order to ensure that the inflammation shall grow hotter and hotter.

Pliny expressed the belief that should you wound a person, and feel regret for it, you had only to spit on the hand that had caused the wound and the pain of the injured one was at once alleviated.

It is this theory of contagious magic that led to the practice of moulding in wax an image of a person to whom it was desired to do harm, and then to stick pins in such parts of it as you wanted the original to feel pain. This was the popular operation of witches in England.

The origin? It is probably founded on the belief that any blood on a weapon continues to feel pain with the blood in the body of the person to whom the hurt has been done. It is in this belief that natives of Tumlea, in part of New Guinea, throw into the sea bandages with which their wounds have been dressed, lest they fall into the hands of one with a grudge against them who could by such contagious magic effect new injuries upon them.

Finally, we may quote Sir Walter Scott for authority on the prevalence of the superstition on the Border. In the *Last Minstrel*, he records the pursuit of the Ladye of Buccleugh towards the wounded mosstrooper, William of Deloraine:

She drew the splinter from the wound,

*   *   *   *

No longer by his couch she stood,
But she hath ta'en the broken lance,
And washed it from the clotted gore,
And salved the splinter o'er and o'er.
William of Deloraine, in trance,
Whene'er she turned it round and
    round,
Twisted, as if she galled the wound.

*   *   *   *

Full long she toiled, for she did rue
Mishap to friend so stout and true.

DADDY-LONGLEGS

During harvest time in parts of England, the greatest care was taken by reapers not to injure a large kind of daddy-longlegs (popularly known as "The Harvestman") under the superstitious belief that harm would come to the crop or the reapers of it.

DAFFODIL

If you find the first daffodil of the Spring, you will have more gold than silver that year.—Wales.

It is unlucky to bring daffodils into the house before the goslings are hatched.—Manx farm superstition.

The reason for the latter of the superstitions given above lies in the fact that the old Manx name for the daffodil is las-ny guiy, which means the goose-leak.

DAIRY

If you want your dairy cattle to thrive, you must give your Christmas bunch of mistletoe to the first cow that calves after New Year's Day.—Wales.

The explanation of this old superstition, which is still practised in parts of Wales, albeit the cowmen do not know the reason for their giving it, is the belief that the mistletoe was a powerful weapon against witches. This is probably the reason that in Austria a piece of mistletoe laid on the threshold of the house is regarded as a certain way of preventing the inhabitants of the house from experiencing nightmares.

Mistletoe was, with the oak, the great sacred plant of the Druids.

In Scotland on days and nights when witches were supposed to be abroad, dairy cattle were "preserved" with rowan wood laid at the doors of the byres, and with red thread tied round their tails.

See MISTLETOE.

DEAD EMBERS

Bad luck will come into the house if you fail to clean the dead embers out of the fire before retiring.—General

Like many other superstitions this has a sound practical origin behind it. Embers that are apparently dead may burst into flames at any minute.

DEAD MAN'S HAND

To cure a wen, rub it with the hand of a man newly executed.—General.

Arthur Beckett describes this goulish superstition in *The Tragedy of Donkey Row*. He wrote:

Hardly had the crowd which had witnessed the execution dispersed than a countryman of Cowfield, with a huge wen on his forehead, sought the executioner and bargained with him to have his wen rubbed with the hand of the dead man.

The countryman mounted the scaffold, and the executioner untying the cords which had bound the wrists of Holloway, placed the hands of the deceased on the countryman's forehead, who sat trembling for five minutes in the hope of a miracle.

Then, taking the handkerchief from the dead man's neck, the executioner thrust it into the dead man's bosom until it was warmed by the declining heat of the dead body. Taking the handkerchief the countryman pressed it to his wen and left the scaffold, proclaiming his faith in the remedy.

See HAND OF GLORY.

DEAFNESS

To cure deafness, anoint the ears constantly with the oil of eels, used perfectly fresh.—Ireland.

It is difficult to conjecture by what process of reasoning the oil of eels can restore hearing. In most such cases the origin of these charms lies in the belief in homœopathic magic. For instance, the Tarahumares of Mexico when they run races tie deer hooves to their backs in the belief that by this they will become as swift-footed as the deer. Cherokee ball players rub their bodies with eel-skins so that they will become as slippery and as hard to hold as eels.

But the authors can find nothing to support this homœopathic evil theory in the oil of eels for deafness; they have never seen it stated, or even suggested, that eels have keen ears.

DEATH

Three loud and distinct knocks at the head of the bed of a sick person, or at the bed's head of one of his relations, is an omen of death.

Tears must not be allowed to fall on the dead, for the dropping of the tears of mourners are felt like heavy weights, hindering the dead from the rest he needs.—General.

A person cannot die so long as any locks are locked or bolts shot in the house.

After death all the windows and doors in the house must be opened in order that the soul of the dead may be released and fly away.

To turn one's back on the dead while in or leaving the death chamber will harm the dead one.

If a person dying is lying on a bed of pigeons' feathers, he should be lifted in his sheet and laid on the floor, else he will have a hard death.—General rural belief.

No one can die on pigeons' feathers.—Kent and Northampton.

The appearance of a white-breasted bird is a sure omen of death.—Devonshire.

If a pall is placed on a coffin wrong side out, there will be another death in the family.—Wales.

If the wind blows out a candle on the altar of a church, the minister will soon die.—Wales.

The first of the superstitions quoted above—of warning knocks—is in all probability a relic of the Roman occupation, for the Romans held the belief that the genius of death announced his coming by some mysterious and supernatural noise.

The lamenting at death had its counterpart in the islands off the west coast of Ireland, where no funeral wail was permitted to be made until three hours after death, lest the sound of lamenting might hinder the soul from leaving the body, and thus place the demons, lying in wait, on the alert.

Reference has already been made to the number of superstitions prevalent in these islands which have their counterpart in remote races, who could have had no contact with our beliefs. Another such is associated with the legend that a person cannot die while on his body, or around it, are knots. A tied knot was held to be a protective amulet.

When, at St. Andrew's, Scotland, in 1572, a woman was led to the stake to be burned as a witch, there was taken away from her a white cloth on the strings of which were many knots. As it was removed she said, "Now I have no hope of myself."

In Masai, East Africa, a man whose sons have gone to war will take a hair of each son and tie a knot in it, secure in the belief that in this way he has protected them from death.

The Times reported on 4th September, 1863, the case of a child lying, it was said, on her deathbed. In accordance with the belief, strongly held in Devonshire, that death would be "hard" without aid, all the doors in the house, and all drawers and cupboards, were unlocked and thrown open, thus securing for her an easy passage to Eternity. The child, however, refused to avail herself of the advantages; she recovered.

Testimony to the belief in the death omen of a white bird is contained in Howell's *Familiar Epistles*, in the form of a death history of the Oxenham family of the county. In a stonemason's shop in Fleet Street, he saw a large marble with the following inscriptions:

"Here lies John Oxenham . . . in whose chamber as he was struggling with death, a bird with a white breast was seen fluttering about his bed, and vanished.

"Here lies also Mary Oxenham, sister of the said John, who died the next day, and the same apparition was seen in the room.

"Here lies, hard by, James Oxenham, son of the said John, who died a child in his cradle a little after. And such bird was seen fluttering over his head a little before he expired, and vanished."

At the bottom of the stone there was:

"Here lies Elizabeth Oxenham, the mother of the said John, who died sixteen years since, when such a bird with a white breast was seen about her bed before death."

Howell ends his account by stating there were divers witnesses to the deaths, both squires and ladies whose names as witnesses were engraved on the stone.

In Cornwall the superstition was strenuously held—and still is in some parts—that should an old burial ground be ploughed or dug, the eldest son of the family thus ploughing will die. As recently as 1925, a field known as "Vounder" in Predannack, near Mullion, Cornwall, England, had never been ploughed or broken because of this superstition. The reason given the authors by the owner of the land was that the field had once been a burying ground; which, in fact, it had been. In Wisbech (Cambs.) is a piece of land which up to now is not dug or ploughed, because it was at one time a burying ground for Quakers.

In Wales, it was held that if a dead person's linen was not washed immediately after death, the dead would not rest in the grave. The authors have also found traces of this superstition in parts of the North of England.

From Wales, too, comes the superstition that if a mole is found to have burrowed under the wash-house or the dairy, the death of the mistress of the house can be looked for during the year.

Cornish death legend held that if cage birds and flowers were not draped with black on the death of their owner, they will "quail" away with grief. This is, of course, on all fours with legend of telling the bees of the death of their master or mistress. (See BEES.) Courtney, in his *Cornish Feasts and Folk Lore*, recalls a visitor inquiring after a fine maidenhead fern he had seen on a previous visit to a cottage. He was told that it had died through being neglected, in not being told of the death of the owner.

In North-East Scotland on a death taking place a piece of iron, such as a nail or a knitting needle, used to be stuck into all the meal, butter, cheese, flesh and whisky in the house. The reason was "to prevent death entering them." Neglect of the precaution was held to be certain to be followed by corruption of the food and drink. The whisky, it was added, had been known to turn white—a sad blow, of course, to any Scot.

Finally, there is the widely held superstition at one time that a soul cannot pass easily if the body of the dying person is "athurt the planshun"—that is, across the direction of the floorboards.

It was the custom to move the bed round if a person was lingering and the bed was found to be across the floorboard lengths. Jenkin in *Cornwall and the Cornish* quotes a conversation over a woman who, it was thought, would have died, but still lingered on. It went thusly:

" 'Tis my belief she wean't never pass on, as she is, for her body be lyin' athurt planshun."

"Why, ais that's so (from the daughter of the house). I never thoft upon it before. Just help me move her round, will ee?"

Some hours later, when the doctor called, he was greeted with: "She's gone, doctor. We just shifted her round and she went off like a lamb."

See CORPSE, FUNERAL, MAGPIE, ROBIN.

DEATH AT LOW TIDE

Deaths mostly occur at the falling of the tide.—Widely held, especially among seamen.

This, one of the most ancient of beliefs in death, is still widely believed in many coastal areas, particularly along the East coast, as far down as Kent.

Alike in all countries it has been held at some age or other. Aristotle averred that no creature can die except at low tide. Frazer, in that mighty work, *The Golden Bough*, relates how a Haida (Queen Charlotte Islands) man when he is about to die sees a canoe manned by his dead friends who come in with the tide to bid him welcome to the spirit land. "Come with us," they say, "for the tide is about to ebb and we must depart."

A Chilote Indian, in the last stages of consumption, after preparing to die like a good Catholic, was heard to ask his sister how the tide was running. Told that it was still coming in, he smiled and said that he had yet a little time to live.

At Port Stephen, New South Wales, it was the custom all along the coast always to bury their dead at flood time, never at ebb, lest the retiring water should bear the souls of the departed to some other country.

The belief was obviously rife in the days of Shakespeare, for he makes Falstaff die "even just between twelve and one, even at the turning o' the tide" (*Henry V*, act ii, sc. 3).

Dickens, too, confirms the prevalence of the belief. Recall Peggotty's words to David Copperfield of Barkis: "People can't die along the coast except when the tide's pretty near out. They can't be born unless it's pretty nigh in."

Death records in coastal parishes confirm this belief. A record in the register at Heslidon (Hartlepool) states: "The XVII daye of Maye, at XII of ye clocke at noon, Mrs. Barbara Mitford died, it being low water."

As in the case of so many of these old superstitions, there may be some physical cause for the hour. A change of temperature not infrequently takes place with the turn of the tide, and may indeed have some reaction on a dying person.

DEATH-COME-QUICKLY

If children pick the herb Robert, it means death to one or other of their parents.—Cumberland.

This was the stupid origin of the name "Death-Come-Quickly" for the little herb. Incidentally, for a similar reason, the red and white campion is called "Mother Dee" in Cumberland. Should the child pick the red species it is held that the father would die; if the white species, the mother was doomed to be the victim.

DEATH DIVINATION

To know who next will die in a family where a death has occurred—

The straw or chaff from the bed of the dead person should be taken to an open space and burned. The family survivors should look among the ash for a footprint. That member of the family whose foot fits the print exactly will be the next to die.—Northumberland old superstition.

Presumably, should no member of the family have a foot to fit the print exactly, they would all be immortal.

DEATH PORTENTS

The sound of bells at night.
Chirping of crickets.
Circular lights seen in the air.
Death watch beetle.
Call by some absent person.
Howling of dogs at the house door.
Hens bringing off a sitting of all hen chicks.
Hens laying eggs with double yolks.
Chirping of fish after they have been taken from the water.

Further and augmented details of these superstitions will be found under their separate headings.

See COCK, CROWING HEN, MAGPIES, ROBINS.

DEATH WATCH

If a churchgoer desires to know who in the congregation will die during the year he or she should keep watch in the church porch on St. Mark's Eve for three successive years. On the third occasion he will see the doomed pass into the church one by one.

This ghoulish belief was at one time pretty widely held from Yorkshire down to Devon. There is little evidence of it elsewhere, however.

The time for the death watch was from one hour before midnight to one hour after midnight. Should the watcher fall asleep during the hours, then he himself would die before the year was out.

Henderson tells a grim story of this watch by a Scarborough woman who kept vigil in the porch of St. Mary's Church in that town. Figure after figure glided into the church and among them she recognized many familiar faces. At last came one she could not identify, the face being turned away from her. As the figure entered the porch (so the narrative goes) it turned, and gazed at her. The watcher, recognizing her own features, fell senseless in the porch. She was found, still senseless, next morning by neighbours, and carried home, but did not long survive the shock.

Montgomery has an allusion to the superstition in a poem, one verse of which goes:

How, when the midnight signal tolls,
Along the churchyard green,
A mournful train of sentenced souls
In winding sheets are seen.

To impart a little humour into the grim tale, there may be quoted the story of a North Country sexton who kept the vigil in order that he might gain some idea of the extent of his income for the ensuing year.

In the Woodhall Spa and Horncastle areas, however, the order of the superstition was reversed. There the watchers were reported to see all the parishioners go into the church on St. Mark's Eve, and those who were not seen to *COME OUT* again were the ones doomed to die.

There is a dramatic story of a parish clerk at Martin, four miles from Wood-

hall Spa, who was angered at a farmer's criticism of the amount of the rate which he, the clerk, had levied on him. "You needn't worry," he said. "You won't have to pay them. I never saw you come out of the church last Mark's Eve." Sure enough, the farmer was thrown from his horse and killed before the time came for the payment of the rates he had criticized.

A pleasant variation of this grim death watch superstition was that associated with it in the Horncastle district. There it was held that any couples in the parish who were to wed during the year would walk out of the church on St. Mark's Eve, side by side, as though they had actually been already married. This is the only instance of which we have found the wedding portent walking side by side with the death portent.

Finally, a warning to any of the superstitious who feel inclined to try the experiment. Anyone who begins a watch on St. Mark's Eve will not be able to stop doing so until the last St. Mark's Eve which they are to see. On that last occasion they will be overcome by sleep and when they awake at the end of the march, they will know that they must die within the year.

DEATH WATCH BEETLE

The tapping in a house of the death watch beetle is an omen of death in the family.—General.

So rife has been this belief that the little insect of the timber-boring genus Andbium has come to be called "the death watch beetle." The superstition is held even to the present day.

In October, 1945, the authors received a terrified letter from a woman who had heard the tapping and was told by neighbours that nothing could prevent a death in her household. The woman's husband was then abroad with the British Army. He subsequently returned, and is still alive and well.

The explanation of the tapping is simple. The sound is not that of its boring into timber, but a call from one beetle to another. Raising itself upon its hind legs, with the body forward inclined, it beats its head with force upon the plane of the position. The general number of distinct strokes is from seven to nine or eleven, following each other quickly at regular intervals.

DEER

There are only two superstitions connected with deer that the authors have been able to trace; and both are bound up with families.

In the island of Rum, between Oban and Skye, it was held that if one of the family of Lachlin shot a deer on the mountain of Finchra, he would either die suddenly or contract a distemper which would prove fatal.

The second of the stories relates to a well-known family in the Lakeland District. For more than 200 years a legend had persisted that no heir would be born to the estate until a white doe should be born in the park, and the river in the same park ceased to flow. In 1895, the river did actually cease to flow, being frozen completely over, and a white doe suddenly appeared among the deer in the park. Within a few months an heir was born to the house—the first son for nearly 300 years.

DEW

Dew collected from plants on St. Bride's Day (1st February) and applied to the face rejuvenates and improves the features.—Midland Counties.

If you wash your face in May dew at daybreak on May the first, you will have a good complexion through all the year. —One of the most widely spread beliefs in England for very many years.

A maiden washing herself with dew from the hawthorn on the first day of May, at daybreak, will preserve her beauty for ever.—General.

To cure a goitre, go before sunrise on the first of May to the grave of the last young man buried in a churchyard and apply the dew collected by passing a hand three times from head to foot of the grave to the part affected.—Cornwall and Plymouth.

Very widespread was the dew complexion superstition, from the rural girl to the ladies of the Court.

In 1515 we read of Catherine of Aragon, accompanied by twenty-five of her ladies-in-waiting, going out on May Day to gather the dew for the purpose of preserving her complexion.

The *Morning Post* of 2nd May, 1791, reported that: "Yesterday being the first of May, according to annual and superstitious custom, a number of persons went into the fields and bathed their faces with the dew on the grass, under the idea that it would render them beautiful."

Pepys notes in his diary, in 1667: "My wife away with Jane and W. Hewer to Woolwich . . . to lye there to-morrow

and so gather May-dew to-morrow morning." In Spain and in Italy the same belief in the properties of May dew was held.

Dew was used also by the Slavs, not only for their complexions, but because it saved their milk from the charms of the witches.

DISH

Should the bride at her wedding breakfast break a dish, it bodes ill for the marriage.—West of Scotland.

DISHCLOTH

To boil a dishcloth is to boil all your lovers; to turn all the lads awa'.—Border Counties.

This is still a widely held superstition in many rural parts of Britain. The authors have come across it in the last few years time and again.

DOG

If a dog passes between a couple who are going to be married, much ill-luck will result to them.—Highlands.

If a dog digs a big hole in your garden, there will be a death in the family.—Gipsy belief.

A strange dog following you is a sign of good luck.

A dog howling is a sure sign of death. —General, except that in Lancashire it is held that the dog must be howling up at the windows of a house.

It is unlucky to meet a barking dog early in the morning.—Irish.

To cure a cough, or the measles, place a hair of the patient's head between two pieces of buttered bread and give it to a dog. The dog will catch the cold (or the measles) and the patient will lose it. —Northants, Devon, Wilts, and Gloucester.

It is sacrilege for a dog to enter a church.—General, but especially in Yorkshire.

Dogs will go mad if given a bone of lamb at Eastertide.—Wales.

Let us take, first, the howling for death portent, which is the most widespread of all the dog superstitions. It exists in strength not only in this country but throughout Europe and even in parts of Turkey.

The origin? The belief that dogs and other animals can scent death and are able to see the ghosts of departed, or departing, persons. Horses, for instance, have been known to tremble and stop dead when they have come near a dead body, even though the body has been invisible to them. The authors have trustworthy accounts of a horse that refused on every occasion to pass the spot where a gibbet had once stood, and no power could make him pass. In the *Odyssey*, Book XV, the dogs of Eumæus are described as terrified at the sight of Minerva, although she was invisible to Telemachus. Capitolinus states that dogs by their howling presaged the death of Maximus.

The superstition of a dog digging a grave in one's garden came to the authors in a peculiar way. On 6th February, 1945, the authors received a letter from a Mr. P. J. Mitchell, then living in Brownhills, Staffordshire. "About 40 years ago," he wrote, "I was told by a gipsy that when a dog digs a big hole in your garden, there will be a death in the family. Last week a dog came in my garden and dug a big hole. I filled it in, but he came again and dug it out. Next day, my brother-in-law's father died. I have not seen the dog since."

A footnote added that the father-in-law was aged ninety-one.

Brand describes how, in Gloucester, whooping cough was cured by the hair sandwich described above; and the following description appeared in *Notes and Queries* of the "certain cure" for the measles. "My nurse (says the correspondent) declared that I and my brother were cured of the measles by having hair cut from the napes of our necks and then separately placed between two slices of bread and butter. She says that she watched anxiously for a stray dog to pass. She gave him the bread and butter, and as he ate it without loathing she was sure that we had been cured. He never came back, because, naturally, he died of the measles."

The superstition is, of course, a version of the widespread belief in the transference of evil. It existed in many countries, civilized and savage. For instance, in Oldenburg a person with a fever set a bowl of milk before a dog and said, "Good luck dog, may you be sick and I be sound." When the dog had lapped some of the milk the person ill of the fever had a drink from the bowl. When this had been carried out three times, the dog had the fever and the human was cured.

On the same theory, the Hindus of old sent consumption away with a blue jay. On one day of the year the Bhotiyas of Juhar, in the Himalayas, intoxicate a

dog with spirits, then chase him round the village and kill him. Thus is ensured the freedom of the village from disease or misfortune.

In parts of Breadalbane, Scotland, it was formerly the custom on New Year's Day to give a dog a piece of bread and drive him away from the door with the curse, "Get away, you dog. Whatever death of men or loss of cattle happens in this house to the end of the year be on your head."

The Iroquois on their New Year Festival take two white dogs, decorate them with red paint, feathers and ribbons, lead them out and then hang them on a ladder. Afterwards the animals are taken into a house, "where the people's sins are transferred to them."

Thus is the dog a scapegoat for illness and evil—which in early days meant the same thing—in widely scattered countries.

In the Miracle Play in Longfellow's *Golden Legend*, where the Rabbi asks Judas Iscariot why howl the dogs at night, the answer given is:

In the Rabbinical Book it sayeth
The dogs howl, with icy breath,
Great Samael, the Angel of Death
Takes through the town his flight.

There existed in Berkshire a strange superstition to explain why a dog's nose and a woman's elbow are always cold, when they are in good health. According to this, in the days of the Flood the Ark sprang a small leak, and Noah, who had forgotten to bring his carpenters' tools on board, was at his wits' end how to act. In his trouble he seized his favourite dog and crammed its nose into the place where the water was leaking through.

That stopped it, but Noah realized that the dog must die if left in that position. Noah's wife was looking on, and Noah, taking her arm, stuffed her elbow into the leak. The danger was thus averted, but a dog's nose and a woman's elbow will remain cold as long as the world lasts.

It would be interesting to know whether Mrs. Noah's elbow remained in the crack until the Ark touched land again, or whether Noah found his tools after all.

It would be interesting to know, too, how this story came to be the exclusive superstition of Berkshire.

DOG WHIPPING

Mentioned above is the superstition that it was sacrilege for a dog to enter a church. There was one exception to the rule—when, in olden days, a church newly built was to be consecrated, a dog was driven into the building before any human foot entered.

The practice arose from the belief that the first living thing to enter a church after completion belonged to the Devil, and was claimed by him.

Apart from this dogs were not only prohibited from entering a church, but in those days most parishes in Britain employed a "Dog-Whipper." His duties consisted in expelling any dog or dogs which might intrude into the church during service. He was provided with a stout short dogwhip for that purpose.

The origin has been placed with the Romans. This, however, the authors doubt, being unable to find any evidence of such practice in Rome. The most probable origin is the story that when Roman Catholicism was the religion in this country, a priest celebrating Mass in the church at York, dropped the Pax after consecration. It was snatched up suddenly and swallowed by a dog which had been lying underneath the altar.

The profanity of this High Mystery caused the death of the dog by the congregation, and the persecution continued in York every St. Luke's Day, when boys whipped any stray dogs which might be in the streets of the city. There was a similar practice in Hull.

DOLPHIN

Dolphins and porpoises, when they play about, foretell a storm.—Seamen's belief.

The authors in their many journeyings throughout the world have never found any truth in this belief; on the contrary, when dolphins and porpoises have played round the bows of the ship, the weather has been uniformly good.

We hold the view that in some extraordinary manner the superstition has been reversed, perpetuated by word of mouth through successive generations, for the ancients regarded the appearance of the dolphin as a mark of fair weather.

According to their fables dolphins and porpoises offered themselves in time of storm to convey shipwrecked mariners to shore.

DONKEY

To cure a child of whooping cough, pass it under the belly of a donkey nine times—three times three.

Another method practised in various parts was to place the child on the cross of a donkey's back and ride it round the grounds nine times.

See WHOOPING COUGH.

DOOR

It means ill-luck to depart from a house leaving doors open throughout the house. The back door must be closed before the front door is opened.—General.

All doors of a house should be opened at the time of death, so that nothing shall hinder the passing of the soul, and the dying person's end shall be an easy one.—General, but especially in Scotland and the Northern Counties.

Doors should be opened at childbirth in a house, else the mother will have a hard delivery.

Several authorities have stated that the origin of the opening of doors to give easy travail to a woman came from the Roman custom of presenting women with a key as a symbol of easy deliverance. The authors doubt it.

The people of Chittagong, in the East Indies, could hardly have heard of the Roman custom; yet a midwife there will order all doors and windows to be thrown open when the hour of birth arrives.

In Java, the same practice prevails. The Sinhalese, a few hours before birth is expected, open all doors, cupboards, boxes, and everything else in the house that is shut. So, too, do the Battas of Sumatra, and the natives of islands near Ceylon. They could not all be aware of the Roman custom.

Similar superstition exists throughout Europe.

The explanation seems to lie in the strange streak in human nature, already referred to, whereby across the face of the earth, among all peoples, there have been given the same fears, the same charms, and the same beliefs to overcome them.

See BIRTH, DEATH.

DOORSTEP

When a bride has left her parents' house for the honeymoon, or her husband's house, the step should be well scrubbed with soap and water to wash away the impress of her feet, else her marriage will not be a happy one.—Devonshire.

NOTE: Another, and not a superstitious, reason is to show to friends and neighbours that the old home was to be no more her home, she having chosen another.

If a kettle of boiling water is poured over the doorstep just after the bride has left her old home, another marriage is sure to be agreed upon before the water dries up.—Yorkshire and the North.

A bride should never step over the doorstep of her new home; she should be carried over it by her bridegroom.—General.

The latter custom, supposed to show the husband's authority, is still widely practised in the southern counties. Pictures of the ceremony of carrying not infrequently appear in the picture papers.

DOVE

If a dove hovers round a pithead of a colliery, there will be a disaster in the mine.—Welsh coalfields.

This superstition is by no means dead in the principality. In the year 1902 there was something of a panic in the colliery town of Glyncorryg after a dove had been seen round the pithead. Three hundred miners refused to enter the pit that day.

It was stated that doves were seen in the vicinity before earlier accidents at Senghenydd and Llanbradach pits.

See MAGPIE, ROBIN.

DRAKE'S DRUM

When Britain's need is direst Drake's Drum should be beaten, and he will return to aid her.—Devon.

There is another version, however, which says that when Britain is in danger the drum sounds itself.

It is claimed that the superstitious promise has been thrice fulfilled. First, when he came back as Blake, and played the whip to van Tromp's broom. Secondly, that he came back as Nelson at Copenhagen and Trafalgar. Thirdly, that in 1914 Drake's Drum was heard in the English Channel calling Drake again. And Jellicoe later won his naval victory over the German fleet.

DREAMS

To dream of your sweetheart, take the blade bone of a rabbit and stick nine pins into it. Then put it under your pillow and you will be sure to see the object of your affections.—Yorkshire.

To see a lover in a dream pluck yarrow from a young man's grave, saying as you do so: "Yarrow, sweet yarrow, the first I have found, and in the name of Jesus I pluck it from the ground. As Joseph loved sweet Mary and took her for his dear, so in a dream this night I hope my true love will appear."—Devonshire.

A maiden who wishes to know her lot in marriage should spread a white cloth under an oak tree on Midsummer Eve. In the morning she will find a little dust which is all that remains of the fallen blossoms. She should place a pinch of this dust under her pillow, and then her future husband will appear to her in her dreams.—Pulverbatch in Shropshire.

NOTE: The point of this superstition lies in the fact that in Pulverbatch it was believed that the oak tree blooms on Midsummer Eve and the blossom withers before daybreak.

A sprig of mistletoe gathered on Midsummer Eve and placed under the pillow will give prophetic dreams.—Wales.

To dream of lizards is a sure sign of treachery. It means that you have a secret enemy.—General.

The above are but a few of the amazing number of dream superstitions. Among the others, most generally believed at one time or another were:

To dream of sickness betokens marriage to young people; of being before an altar indicates sorrow and misfortune; to see angels is a sign of happiness soon to come; if you dream of being angry with a person, it means that the person is one of your best friends.

In a dream of catching fish, every fish you land betokens the death of a personal friend; of dances that you will shortly have good fortune; to lose your hair is a sign of the loss of valued friends or property.

To dream that you have lost one or two teeth is evidence, according to superstition, that you will lose the same number of lawsuits. If bees sting you, it is a sign of bad fortune. To dream of marriage and brides betokened death or sickness. To dream of falling indicated losses. So does dreaming of being drowned. To dream of being naked means shame and misfortune. To dream of a wedding means death.

There are a flood of other dream interpretations, but they are mostly confined to certain areas and are not of general application.

As for the origin—who can say? The ancient Greeks and Romans regarded dreams as so many warnings. They prayed to Mercury to vouchsafe to them each night good dreams. So, too, in the less civilized countries do dreams control beliefs and habits.

George du Maurier wrote that the whole cosmos is in a man's brain, or so much as a man's brain will hold. And when sleep relaxes the will, and there are no earthly surroundings to distract attention, riderless fancy takes the bit in its teeth and the whole cosmos goes mad and has its will with us. We cannot think of a better explanation of dreams.

DRESS

Anyone appearing for the first time in a new dress should be pinched by a friend for good luck.—North Country.

This superstition, which seems to have become a pleasant custom, is still held in the North Country. Most schoolchildren, for instance, appearing in a new suit or new dress at school are pinched by their fellows. The authors know of a famous artist friend who was pinched by a colleague when he appeared in his club in a new summer suit.

In Northumberland, even to-day, the pinching is accompanied by the formula: " Health to wear it, strength to tear it, and money to buy another."

At the time of writing, clothing coupons to buy another should have been interpolated.

DRESSING

If when dressing you place a button in the wrong buttonhole, or the wrong hook in the eye, it will bring you bad luck all the day.—General.

If you have your dress or any clothes mended on your back, you will be ill-spoken of.—General.

Bad luck will attend you if in donning a garment you put the left arm in first.

The last-named is, of course, another instance of the belief that the left side is associated with the Devil. It was so strongly held a belief by the Romans that houses of the elite employed a man to wait at the door in order to ensure that no visitor should step over the threshold with his left foot first. That is the origin of the modern footman.

Another instance is the phrase "He got out of bed on the wrong side"—i.e., the left side.

DROPPING OF FORK (KNIFE, etc.)

Should a maid drop a fork when laying table, it means the breaking of her engagement.

Here is another old superstition of the servants' hall: Knife falls, gentleman calls; fork falls, lady calls; spoon falls, baby calls.

DROPSY

To cure the dropsy: Take several fully grown toads and place them in a vessel in which they can be burned without the ashes being mixed with any other matter. When reduced to ashes pound them in a mortar. Place the ashes in a wide-mouthed jar, cork tightly and keep in a dry place. One teaspoonful of the ashes to be taken at the growing of the moon for three mornings.—Devonshire.

Here is an old wives' remedy for dropsy prevalent in the sixteenth century in most parts of Britain:

"Take three earthworms, cut off their heads and immerse them in Holy Water, to which has been added a pinch of sugar and a pinch of liquorice. Put in a jar, leave for nine days and then drink from the mixture on each of nine consecutive days. The dropsy will disappear.

Could cold superstition go further? We should think that the patient, too, would disappear—into his grave.

DROWNING

The sea (or river) will have its victim.—West Ireland and Scotland.

The sea will search the four divisions of the universe to find the graves of her children.—The Hebrides.

To find the body of a drowned person a loaf of bread with a quantity of quicksilver in a hole in the middle of it should be allowed to float on the water. It will stand still over the spot where the body lies.—General.

Drowned bodies float on the ninth day.—Durham.

NOTE: Elsewhere the third day is usually quoted.

If a gun be fired over a dead body lying on the bed of the sea or river it will float.—Durham.

NOTE: The explanation given is that the concussion will break the gall bladder, thus floating the body.

A drowning person cannot drown until he has gone under the water for the third time.—General.

To see a drowned dog or a cat while going to one's fishing coble means bad luck—unless the fisherman turns back and stays at home.—Whitby (Yorks).

It is a lamentable fact that as late as 1928 people in the West of Ireland allowed a man to drown because of their firm belief that the sea or river must claim a victim a year, and would revenge itself upon a rescuer by drowning him in the place of the man of whom he tried to cheat it.

The superstition existed in Scotland, where some years ago when a boy was drowning in the River Ross his brothers were warned to keep away from the bank. The voice of the crowd was given by an old man who ordered: "Let him go. No one else will be drowned this year. The river has had its dree."

In the Orkneys within the last fifty years not only would boatmen not put off a boat to save a drowning person, but would take the oars out of their boats so that nobody else would use it for rescue purposes.

The Hebrides superstition quoted above resulted in all bodies washed ashore being buried as near as possible to the waterline, so that the sea could recover its own. One of the rivers said thus to demand a life is the Spey. One victim a year is the superstition.

The River Ribble was said to have a spirit called Peg O'Nell, and at the end of every seven years, on Peg's Night, she claimed the sacrifice of a life unless she was placated by the drowning of an animal or a bird.

The River Tees had a sprite to whom was given the name Peg Powler. The name given, superstitiously, to the River Forth was the Deaf and Soundless One, because the Forth is a quietly flowing river.

There was supposed to be a rivalry between the rivers of Scotland for the life of man. It is expressed in the following verses:

Bloodthirsty Dee,
Each year needs three.
But bonny Don,
She needs none.

Tweed said to Till,
What gars ye rin sae still?
Till said to Tweed:
Though ye rin wi speed,
An' I rin slaw,
Yet, whar ye droon ae man,
I droon twa.

It is said that salt thrown over the water and nets propitiates the greedy spirit of the Tweed, and that many a plaid has been made an offering to the Dee in place of a human life.

Along the Norfolk coast it was held that when any person is drowned in the sea, a voice is heard from the water, ominous of a squall. The same belief is held in the Norwegian fiords.

It may be noted in passing that, apropos the reluctance to rescue drowning people, China, Russia and the Shetlands are equally superstitious on the point.

The bread and quicksilver clue to the whereabouts on the water bottom of a body is still believed in implicitly to the present day by many people. Its efficacy gained some ground in 1944 by its being used to locate the body of a drowned child in a river in the South of England —and in some extraordinary fashion the loaf did, indeed, stop almost over the spot at which the body was recovered.

There is no truth whatever in the belief that a person must go under the water three times before drowning.

Before leaving the belief that water must have its victim, we will mention the fact that when the Arabs conquered Egypt, they discovered that at the annual rising of the Nile the Egyptians had a custom of throwing a young virgin decked in gay apparel into the river as a sacrifice. She was the victim for the river to claim.

At the mouth of the Bonny river, in Nigeria, there existed a dangerous sandbank. Many vessels were lost there annually. Accordingly, the natives each chose the handsomest of their young men. On an appointed day he was rowed out to the sandbar, and induced to jump. Then the boat was rowed rapidly away from him and he was left to drown—as were the drowning people off the Irish and Scottish waters.

DRUNKENNESS

To prevent drunkenness, take the lungs of a hog and roast them. If a man eats these, after fasting all day, he will not get drunk next day no matter how much he drinks.—Wales.

To cure a husband of drinking to excess put a live eel in his drink.

We feel impelled to comment that the efficacy of this latter superstition in all probability lay in the shock that the husband would receive on first catching sight of the eel. The shock would, we should say, be greater than any pink elephant!

However, the suspecting husband could, perhaps, overcome the "charm" by eating the roasted hog lungs, thereby showing no sign of drunkenness to induce the wife to go searching for a live eel.

Swan, in his *Speculum Mundi*, relates that "the eggs of an owle, broken and put into the cup of a drunkard, will so work with him that he will suddenly loathe his good liquor, and be displeased with drinking."

DUCK

A dead duck should always be hung up with head down in order that the evil spirit shall depart from it.

To give a farmer's wife less than a handful of violets or primroses in her house will bring destruction on her broods of young ducks or chickens.—Worcestershire.

Ducks' eggs taken into a house after sunset will do no good and will not hatch out.—Rutland, and many other rural areas.

For a duck to lay eggs of a dun colour is a bad omen for the household and it can be averted only by the duck being destroyed.—General, especially in Kent.

There is a record in the *County Annual Register of Kent* of the last-named superstition. A farmer at Hoo having a duck in his possession which laid eggs of the dun colour was considered unlucky, and the decision was taken to destroy it. As ill-fortune had it, distemper broke out almost at once among the farmer's cattle. This was, of course, attributed to the bird. Accordingly, a servant in the family heated the oven, and put the bird into it alive.

To answer the natural query as to how the burning of the bird can break a spell, one can only turn to a similar instance recorded in Suffolk by Lady Gurdon in her *County Folk Lore (Suffolk)*. She refers to a bedridden toothless old crone who had for years given the impression that she had some power of charming away disaster. It happened that a number of ducks of which she had charge suddenly failed to lay eggs. Notwithstanding the fact that all laying birds at some time or other go off producing eggs, the old hag took it for granted that the ducks had been bewitched. The method of combating witchcraft was fire. And the belief in those days, too, was that the whole could be saved by the sacrifice of one. Accordingly, she placed one of the ducks in the oven alive, and roasted it to death.

Elsewhere in this volume is given a similar story concerning the roasting alive of a sheep tethered by its four feet in order to avert witchcraft. It was held that the burning of the sheep would be followed by the burning of the witch. After the death of the sheep and its burning, with the exception of the tethered feet, a suspected witch is said to have been found burned to a cinder in Ipswich with the exception of her hands and feet—corresponding to the parts of the sheep which had remained unburned. The suspected witch was a woman well known under the name of Grace Pett.

It is a fact that she was found burned; her fate is officially recorded in the *Philosophical Transactions* as a case of spontaneous combustion.

DUST

Church dust brought to the bed of a dying man will shorten and ease a painful and lingering death.—General.

DYKE

To fall into a dyke is to postpone one's death for only a short time.—The Fenland country.

To fall into a dyke means that you will meet death by drowning.—Fenland country.

In the Fenland country, particularly in the Spalding area of Lincolnshire, dykes most frequently take the place of hedges between fields and between the roadway and the farmlands on either side.

One of the authors suffered the misfortune of falling into the dyke on dark nights on numerous occasions. He still remains alive nearly forty years after leaving the dyke-ridden areas of Sutton St. James, Lincolnshire, and can tell the tale.

See DROWNING.

DYSPEPSIA, TO CURE

This was the superstition by means of which the people in all parts of Ireland cured dyspepsia:

Fix a small candle on a penny-piece, place the penny on the region of the stomach where is the suffering. Light the candle, and over all place a well-dried tumbler, when the skin will be drawn up as in "cupping." This is "lifting the evil" from the body, and will rid you of the dyspepsia.

EAGLE

If you rob an eagle's nest of its eggs, repose will never again come to you.—Wales.

One eagle's egg boiled and eaten by two persons will keep witches away.

It was held in Wales that if the eagles of Snowden hovered over the plains their visit would be followed by disease and death.

It is interesting to remark, in passing, that the eagle is viewed with superstitious terror by most of the uncivilized races where the bird is known.

The sanctity of its eggs, illustrated in the Welsh superstition given above, has a counterpart among the Ostyaks of the Finnish-Ukraine stock of Siberia. They regard as holy any tree in which an eagle has built its nest for several years, and they spare both such a bird and the tree.

EAR

If your right ear tingles somebody is speaking well of you.

If your left ear tingles somebody is speaking ill of you.

The belief is very old indeed. Pliny knew of it. He supposed it to have proceeded from the notion of a signifying genius or universal mercury that conducted sounds to their distant subjects and taught to hear by touch.

Herrick refers to the superstition in the following verse:

One eare tingles; some there be,
That are snarling now at me.
Be they those that Homer bit,
I will give them thanks for it.

Shakespeare knew of it, and in *Much Ado About Nothing* makes Beatrice say, "What fire is in mine ears."

In Holland tingling in the ear is taken as an indication that somebody is speaking of you behind your back. If the tingling is in the right ear he is praising you; if in the left he is calling you a scoundrel or something of the sort.

Notice how, once again, it is the left side from which the evil is coming. There is, however, in Holland a way of revenging his slanderous statements. If you bite your little finger on getting the tingling in the left ear, the evil speaker's tongue will be in the same predicament; he'll bite his tongue, and bring to an end his vilification of you. That, at least, is how the Dutch have it.

EARACHE

To cure the earache, procure a snail, prick it, and let the exuded froth drop into the ear.—Gloucestershire.

Another "charm" for the earache known in Cambridge was the skin of an eel. Within the authors' lifetime there was in Cambridge a man known locally as "The Duke of York," who earned a living by sitting on the steps of King's College Chapel, and exhibiting to visitors live specimens of the common English snake. He added to his earnings by selling the cast off skins of the reptiles (the sloughs) as being unfailing remedies for the cure of all pains in the head if they were worn bound round the forehead and temples.

EARRINGS

To cure bad eyesight, wear earrings through a hole pierced in the ear lobes. —General.

Wearing earrings will guarantee a sailor against drowning.

There are few superstitions more common to-day than this one of pierced ears assisting the eyesight. It is complete nonsense. Yet it has persisted for several centuries.

The *Exeter and Plymouth Gazette* on 15th March, 1877, recorded: "A woman residing at Braunton, Devonshire, recently made a house-to-house visit begging penny pieces, her idea being when she had reached four shillings and sixpence she would purchase a pair of earrings, the wearing of which was supposed to cure her bad eyesight."

The report added that to make the cure effective she was only to beg from males and not to say please or thank you, lest the spell be broken.

The earring guard against drowning, mentioned above, is so old that its origin is now forgotten. But seamen of generations ago so firmly believed in it that hardly one could be found on board ship who was not wearing the decorations in his ears. A glance at any of the old paintings of seamen and pirates will prove that fact beyond doubt.

EASTER

The sun dances at its rising on Easter Sunday morning.—General.

On Easter Sunday morning at sunrise a lamb and a flag appear in the centre of the sun's disc.—Devon.

If the sun shines on Easter Day it shines on Whitsun also.

A good deal of rain on Easter Day gives a good crop of grass but little good hay.—Herts.

The dancing sun at Easter morning was fully believed in in the young days of the authors. And in country villages pilgrimages were frequently made to the crest of a hill before dawn in order that the dancing sun might be seen.

Devonshire maidens were wont to rise at the same hour in order to see the lamb and flag in the sun's disc. It had to be looked for through a smoked glass.

In the island of Corfu, Italy, it was the custom on Good Friday to climb up one or other of the steep precipices and fling potherbs, at the same time mouthing curses on the traitor Judas.

It is, so far, unexplained how this custom, or superstition, came to be practised some hundred years ago in a small village in Devonshire—the only piece of Easter lore of its kind in Britain.

EASTER EGGS

Gebelin, in his *Religious History of the Calendar*, says that the superstition of giving eggs at Easter is to be traced to the theology and philosophy of the Egyptians, Persians, Gauls, Greeks, Romans, etc., among all of whom an egg was an emblem of the universe, the work of the supreme Divinity.

Eggs were held by the Egyptians as a sacred emblem of renovation of mankind after the deluge. The Jews adopted it to suit the circumstances of their history as a type of their departure from the land of Egypt, and it was used in the Feast of the Passover as part of the furniture of the table with the Paschal Lamb.

The Christians adopted it, as retaining the elements of future life, for an emblem of the Resurrection. The reason, of course, the extrusion of a living creature by incubation after the vital principal had lain a long time dormant, or seemingly extinct.

A writer in *The Gentleman's Magazine:* An egg at Easter . . . an emblem of the rising up out of the grave, as a chick entombed in the egg.

EBB TIDE

Death is delayed until the ebb of the tide.—General, especially in coastal and fishing districts.

This was for many generations a widely held belief, not only in this country, but among native races who lived on the coastline.

There would seem to exist between people who live in sight of the sea, and in most cases get their living from the sea, a kind of secret harmony between their lives and the tide.

Not only does this have an affinity with the ebb and flow of actual life, but is also apparent in the ordinary things of life. For instance, the Breton peasant's wife has always held that the best butter is made when the tide has just turned and is beginning to flow. The Galelareese hold that if oil is made while the tide is yet high, there will be a plentiful supply of oil, but little if it is made when the tide is low.

Pliny stated, and there is no reason to distrust his observations, that nearly all creatures on the coast of France die when the tide is running out.

On the Cantabrian coast of Spain it is held that people who die of chronic or acute disease expire at the moment when the tide starts its ebb. And Charles Dickens, you will remember, makes Mr. Peggotty say: "People can't die along the coast, except when the tide's pretty nigh out. They can't be born unless it's pretty nigh in—not properly born till flood."

See DEATH, TIDE.

EDGEWELL OAK

This venerable tree near the castle of Dalhousie, near Edinburgh, has long been linked in superstition with the fate of the family. On seeing a branch fall from the tree on a still day in July, 1874, an old forester ejaculated: "The laird's deid noo." A few minutes later came the news that the eleventh Earl of Dalhousie had died.

There is a similar story told of the family of the Earls of Howth. At the family castle in Howth, Ireland, the branches of an ancient tree are propped on supports. Tradition maintains that when the tree falls the direct line of the earldom will become extinct.

A similar tree legend was connected with the House of Hanover, Germany. And in the Forbidden City, at Peking, in a tiny private garden, in which the emperors of the now vanished and fallen Manchus used to take the air, stood in 1901, under so many props that it was hardly distinguishable, the "Life Tree" of the Dynasty." According to Chinese legend the prosperity or fall of the Manchu dynasty went hand-in-hand with the life of the tree. In 1901 the tree was virtually dead; if a prop had been removed from it, it would have fallen down. Twelve years later the dynasty fell. But see how kindred are the tree superstitions in Britain, Ireland, Germany, and China.

EELS

A horse-hair kept in water will in due time turn into an eel.—General application, but credited more strongly in Yorkshire.

Eel skin worn on the naked leg is a sure preventive of cramp in swimming. —North Country.

To cure a man of drunkenness put a live eel in his drink.

It is suggested that the stupid superstition of the horse-hair is traceable to the appearance after rain of long hair-like worms in the deep marks left in the ground by horse's hoofs.

They were not seen before the rain, or before the marks of the hoofs were made; so the superstitious people long ago said they must be the hairs dropped from the horse's mane and tail, and in the course of transition into eels. And there are a large number of people who still believe it to-day.

In February, 1946, the authors received a letter from a company of soldiers in Germany. They were, they said, arguing on a topic which they asked us to decide —and also settle a bet. The topic was "Do eels come to life from horse-hairs?"

The eel, among the native Mexican races, shares with other reptiles, birds and animals in homœopathic or imitative magic. Cherokee ball-players, for instance, rub their bodies with eel-skins in the belief that it will make themselves as slippery, and as hard to hold, as eels. In the same way they will not eat rabbits in case they themselves should be confused in their running, as is a rabbit. Nor would any Cherokee woman eat the flesh of the ruffed goose, because that bird hatches a large brood of young, but loses most of them before they reach maturity.

EGGS

If, after eating a boiled egg, you throw the eggshell into the fire, the hen that laid that particular egg will cease laying. —N. Lincolnshire.

If, after eating a boiled egg, you do not knock your spoon through the bottom of the shell, no luck will attend you. —General.

Ducks' eggs should never be brought into the house after sunset if they are required for "setting." If they are so brought, they will never hatch into ducklings. —Rutland, and many other rural areas.

It is a bad omen to gather eggs and bring them into the house after dark. —Derbyshire, Lincolnshire, and Nottinghamshire.

Eggs should not be brought into the house on a Sunday, nor set under a hen on that day. —Derbyshire.

If eggs are brought over running water, they will have no chicks in them.

If a hen hatches a brood of all hen birds from a sitting of eggs, it presages a death in the family of the owner. —Scottish Border.

If the owners of horses eat eggs, they must take care to eat an even number, otherwise mischief will befall the horses. —Irish.

If a less number of primroses than thirteen are brought into a house on the first occasion of bringing any in, so many eggs only will each hen or goose owned by the house hatch in that season. —Norfolk.

To cure the ague, pay a visit at the dead of night to the nearest cross-roads, and there bury an egg. Five visits must be paid, and five eggs buried. The ague will be buried with the eggs. —Devonshire, and elsewhere.

Prick an egg with a pin, and let the white drop into a wine glass three parts full of water. Take some of this in your mouth and go for a walk. The first name you hear mentioned aloud will be the name of your future wife, or husband. —General.

NOTE: One lady known to the authors trying this heard the name Lancelot. However, disliking this name, she tried again with another egg and married a George!

Eggshells should be broken after boiled eggs have been eaten or the witches will go to sea in them, and sink good ships. —Cornwall and Devonshire.

The last-named superstition was very rife in Cornish and Devonshire fishing ports at one time, and is widely practised to-day, not always with a knowledge that it is superstition.

The belief was that the witches, journeying in the shells out to sea, would thus cause the deaths of many sailors and fishermen by sinking the ships; and the authors well remember the desperate alarm of one Devonshire fisherman's wife at their failing to carry out the crushing up of eggshells after a meal.

Number 9 of *The Connoisseur* stated: "It is a common notion that a witch can make a journey to the East Indies in an eggshell." And Sir Thomas Browne remarks in one of his many works that witches can draw or prick the name of a person on unbroken eggshells and thus "mischief the person."

The origin? It is difficult to say. In antiquity the Romans used to break the shells of eggs which they had eaten in order to prevent enemies from making magic with them. There may be some connection between the Romans' belief and ours, following the Roman invasion. Many such beliefs, practised by the

Romans, can be traced here to their presence.

To the superstition, given above, that eggs should not be brought into a house after sunset, under penalty of their not hatching out, is a further one, rife in Nottinghamshire and Lincolnshire for very many years, that eggs should *not be sent out* of a house after sunset.

The *Stamford Mercury* of 29th October, 1852, records a letter from a reader of a person in need of eggs who called at a farmhouse in East Markham and inquired whether the farmer's wife had any to dispose of. Told that she had, the reply was made: "Then I'll take them home with me in the cart."

"That you'll not," was the retort. "Don't you know that the sun has gone down."

Writing in *Notes and Queries* of the primrose stories, a clergyman explained how, when he was called in to settle a dispute between two women, he found that the trouble arose over one of them giving to the child of the other a single primrose, with the idea, said Number Two, of making her hens hatch out only one chicken from each clutch of eggs. Only one chick DID come out of the first clutch, hence the quarrel between the two women.

The authors have come across one or two instances in this country of a custom greatly prevalent in Denmark. There, on New Year's Eve, members of both sexes take a newly laid egg, perforate with a pin the smaller end and let three drops of the white of the egg fall into a basin or bowl of water. The drops diffuse themselves over the water in fantastic shapes of what look like trees. From these, so it is averred, the fortune of the egg-dropper, the character of his wife-to-be (or husband-to-be) and the number of children from the marriage can be told!

Just one more egg superstition. Swan, in his *Speculum Mundi*, relates that "the eggs of an owle, broken and put into the cup of a drunkard, or one desirous to follow drinking, will so work with him that he will suddenly loathe his good liquor and be displeased with drinking."

In Spain, by the way, the same belief is held about the eggs of the stork.

Sir Charles Igglesden tells a personal story of the superstition relating to throwing eggshells into the fire. He was staying at a hostelry at Rye and the superstition, with others, was mentioned. Whereupon the hostess related:

"Two years ago I had four hens laying at Christmas time, when eggs are worth having. And two gentlemen, who were snipe shooting, came in for breakfast. I boiled four eggs for them, two apiece. When they'd finished, what do you think they did? Threw the eggshells in the fire. They wanted their plates for jam. I didn't think anything of it at the time, but the next morning there wasn't a single egg laid—nor on the next day, nor the next week. The four laying hens moped. I gave them hot food, but all they did was to mope. And now, I'd like to ask you, didn't that prove that the superstition was right—never throw an eggshell in the fire?"

It did not occur to the lady that the hens had to go off laying at some time, and since they all started to lay about the same time, they would all stop about the same time.

There is, of course, a love divination associated with eggs. It goes that if you take an egg and roast it hard, take out the yolk and put salt in its place and eat it fasting for your supper when you go to bed, you will dream of your future husband.

In the *Index Villarum* (Baynes) it is recorded that "Mrs. Fines, of Albery, Oxon (? Surrey) did this and dreamt of an ancient grey or white-headed man of such a shape which was her husband. This I had from her own mouth."

ELDER WOOD

If boys are beaten with an elder stick, their growth will be checked.—General belief in seventeenth century.

An elder tree is safe from lightning.— Lincolnshire and other parts. It is still held to in many places.

To cure a wart, rub it with a green elder stick, and bury the stick in muck to rot.

If elder wood is burnt in the fire in a house, there will shortly be a death in the family.—Sussex.

If one rides a horse with two little elder twigs IN ONE'S pockets, he shall not fret or gall, let the horse go ever so hard.

NOTE: This was advice given in Culpepper's *English Physician*; and the authors know indifferent horsemen who still carry the elder sticks.

If you gather the leaves of the elder on the last day of April, and apply them to wounds, the wounds will take no harm.

To cure the erysipelas, cut a piece of elder between two knots on which the "sun hath never shined," and hang it about the patient's neck.—Widespread in the seventeenth century.

Now, all this superstition about the elder tree has its origin in the belief that it was of elder wood from which the Cross was made; and on an elder tree that Judas hanged himself after the Betrayal.

And in all Christian countries its charm against evil was for centuries held strongly. In Scotland, in the darker ages, houses and gardens were protected from witches by having elder leaves over the doors and windows.

In the cemetery of an ancient church-yard in the Isle of Sanda there laid for a great many years the remains of an elder tree over which, should anyone walk, it was held as certain that he was doomed to die before the expiry of the year.

In Germany clippings of hair and the parings of nails were religiously buried secretly under an elder bush, lest a witch should get hold of them, and by con-tagious magic bring harm to the person from whom the clippings had been taken.

Slav people to cure the fever, pull down three shoots of an elder bush to the ground and there pin them with stones. The feverish one crawls three times through the arch thus formed, and then cuts off the three shoots with the words "In three shoots I cut the sickness out."

Curiously enough, in England, this transference of evil was performed with the oak or the ash.

Bavarian folk cured the fever by stick-ing a twig of elder in the ground without speaking. The fever was thus transferred to the twig, and whoever pulled the twig out of the ground caught the disease.

Elder wood was also regarded as a cure for the falling sickness (epilepsy) or at least as a preventive. An Irish super-stition says: "Cut a twig of elder into nine parts, and string the pieces as a necklace tied round the neck of a sufferer from epilepsy, and the disease will be cured."

But it is added that should the neck-lace at any time fall to the ground, the charm is lost and the wood should at once be burned, and a new one made.

ELM TREE

The falling of the leaves of an elm tree predicts a murrain among cattle.—General.

At Lichfield, on Ascension Day, choristers of the cathedral decked (at any rate up to 1900) the house and street lamps in the parish of the Close with elm boughs, and after a service went round the Bounds carrying small pieces of elm.

This is the only instance the authors can discover of the elm being used in such a way; and the reason for the carry-ing of the elm, instead of, for instance, the elder (see ELDER) has apparently been forgotten. There is no superstition, apart from the cattle murrain, about the elm.

It was the rule, however, according to *The Field* of 28th April, 1866, to regulate operations in the field and the garden by the leafing of the elm. The tag was:

When the elmen leaf is as big as
    a mouse's ear,
Then to sow barley never fear.

The elm, too, was one of the woods always used to start a "Need Fire" (q.v.).

ENEMIES

To rid yourself of an enemy, make a rude clay image of him, or her, stick it full of pins, nails and broken glass, and then place it in a running stream with its head to the current.—General.

The general idea was that as the puppet crumbled away in the running water, so the body of the enemy would waste away until he died, and you were free of him.

But the charm worked the other way round. The enemy would make a figure of his intended victim, and follow the same rule. It was held that as a pin was stuck into the clay figure to the accom-paniment of an incantation, so the bewitched person would feel a pain in the corresponding part of his actual body.

If it was the intention to cause a lingering death, the operator was careful to stick no pins in the region of the heart, until such time as he desired the death of his victim.

If the clay image was toasted in front of a fire, the victim in his home would writhe in agony.

It was the favourite device of the witches in England, and many hundreds were burned after such images had been found in their possession.

As late as the 1900's the rite was practised in the remote parts of Scotland; and in England, in the summer of 1944, a police court hearing made mention of the image of a person in clay found in the possession of a woman, for, it was suggested, the object of the old superstition.

The cult of the image was widespread throughout the world, and its origin is lost in antiquity. Both in Babylon and in Egypt this ancient tool was pressed into service of religion to confine and overthrow demons.

The wizards of Egypt took a drop of a man's blood, clippings of his hair or of his nails and a rag of a garment he had worn. These were dressed round a kneaded lump of clay and the man was then at the mercy of the magician. If the image was exposed to a fire, the victim fell into a burning fever; if it was stabbed with a knife, he felt the pain of the wound.

Ancient books of the Hindus tell how, to destroy a foe, a man would fashion a figure of him in clay and transfix it with an arrow which had been barbed with a thorn and winged with an owl's feather. Or he would melt the wax figure in fire.

So, throughout Japan, Burma, the Torres Straits, Borneo, Mexico the magic was enacted that was known thousands of years ago to the sorcerers of ancient Egypt and Babylon, as well as to those of Greece and Rome.

And by some unexplained magic it was born, too, in the minds of the people of this country in the Dark Ages.

EPILEPSY

*To cure the epilepsy a ring must be worn that was made from a half-crown given in a church collection after a celebration of Holy Communion.—*General.

*Bury a black cock alive at the spot where the epileptic fell. And with the cock a lock of the victim's hair and some parings of his nails.—*General, especially in Scotland.

*To cure the epilepsy make a decoction of mistletoe. The patient if he drinks it will be cured.—*Lincolnshire.

*Cut a twig of elder into nine parts and string the pieces as a necklace tied round the neck of the patient. The epilepsy will be cured.—*Ireland.

Drive a nail into the ground at the spot where the patient fell.

The heart of a crow beaten up with his blood and drunk for nine days will relieve the disease.

*Burn the patient with a red-hot church key along the head, and he will be cured.—*Ireland.

Tie three hairs of a milk-white greyhound and place them round the neck of the patient as an amulet. This keeps the fit away.

Taking the mistletoe first, it should be remembered that in the time of the Druids, the mistletoe was regarded as "The All Healer;" and All Healer is still the name for mistletoe in the modern Celtic speech of Brittany, Wales, Ireland, and Scotland.

Also, its efficacy as a cure for epilepsy, or "the falling sickness," prevailed in many other countries. Thus in Sweden, persons so afflicted hold that they can ward off attacks by carrying about with them a knife which has a handle made from mistletoe wood; in Germany pieces of mistletoe are hung round the necks of sufferers.

Indeed, mistletoe was recommended for the falling sickness, not only among the illiterate peasantry, but by high medical authorities in England and Holland down to the eighteenth century.

The origin of its powers over the falling sickness is obviously from the fact that the plant, rooted as it is on a branch of a tree above the earth, cannot fall to the ground. Hence, a person could not fall in the falling sickness so long as he carried in some shape or form a piece of mistletoe.

That was one superstition which is associated, of course, with the classical legend of the death of Balder. The alternative cure is the transference of the epilepsy to some other living creature, or even dead thing. In this respect comes the black cock buried alive. The black cock has figured in many countries as a source of magic. Classical scholars will recall that the cock was a creature dedicated to Apollo, who was in classical mythology connected with the healing art.

The dead thing that was also associated with the cure of epilepsy was a nail. This, according to Pliny, had to be driven into the ground at the spot where the afflicted person fell. Curiously enough, it was not prevalent in Britain.

The superstitious cure by a half-crown from the Holy Communion collection plate was rife more in the North of England than elsewhere. So recently as 1890 clergymen were the frequent recipients of requests to be allowed to exchange thirty pennies for a half-crown from the plate for the purpose of having the coin made into a falling sickness ring.

In 1870 the Vicar of Danby, near Whitby, was thus asked by a prosperous farmer whom, he would have thought, would have known better.

Silver rings made from offertory money are still treasured in many cottages in the Forest of Dean. In a curious old account book which the authors saw some years ago appeared the following: A poor woman at Barton, who had fits, towards buying a silver ring, one penny. The donor was a man of education and a county family. The Barton in question was the Lincolnshire village of that name.

Here is an Irish cure for epilepsy. It dates from the fifteenth century, and is preserved in the Royal Irish Academy.

"None should touch the person in the fit, only one man who has the charm. He takes a bundle of unbleached linen yarn, and ties it round the patient, then cuts the patient's hair, finger and toe nails. These clippings he gathers together and burns with the linen yarn. The ashes are divided into two parts, after which the patient is lain flat on the earth and two holes made, one at the head and the other at his feet. Into these are poured the divided ashes while a harrow-pin is placed over all. So they leave him for a day and a night. And thus the falling sickness is buried for ever in the spot never to rise up again while the ashes and iron remain untouched."

There were a number of Irish recipes containing herbs and plasters. Though they may be called superstitions they are actually herbal treatment which might well have medicinal value. For that reason they are not given here.

See BLACK COCK, NAIL.

ERYSIPELAS

To cure the erysipelas apply sheep's dung as a poultice.—Old wives' remedy.

Cut off half of one ear of a cat, and let the blood drop on the part affected and the erysipelas will be cured.—Northwest Scotland.

Cut a piece of elder wood between two knots, on which the sun "has never shined" and sling it about the patient's neck.—Widespread belief in seventeenth century.

Sparks struck from stone and steel against the face will cure the erysipelas.—Wales.

The sheep's dung rather puzzles us and others who study country lore. Had it been cow's dung, it would have been more understandable, for cow's dung emits more heat than any other and is a good fomentation not only on humans but on animals, for which latter purpose it is still often used in the rural districts.

The Irish used a black cat's blood to cure erysipelas. They called the disease "the wildfire" and believed that it originated in fairy malice. Therefore, they said, blood must be spilt. The blood of a black cat was regarded as the most suitable, and the usual plan was to cut off a piece of the cat's tail (not the ear, as in Scotland) and with the blood anoint the sufferer.

Lady Wilde, in her *Ancient Cures, Charms and Usages of Ireland*, states that in Ireland the black cat was regarded as a weird and mystical creature. If you managed to possess one particular bone of such a cat you could at will render yourself invisible. To obtain this gift, the cat had to be boiled alive. The bones were then taken, one by one, and held singly in the mouth in front of a mirror. Each time observance had to be made to see if the bone thus held was reflected in the mirror, for should the looker happen to hold one bone that was not reflected, that was the mystic bone which made him invisible at will.

EVERGREENS

It is defying God to burn the evergreens which have been used in the Christmas decorations. They should be thrown out to decay.—General.

If evergreens are not removed from the house before Twelfth Night, bad luck will attend the house for the remainder of the year.—Widespread.

The latter belief is still widely held in all parts of the country. One of the co-authors of this work, to whom superstition is practically anathema, yet insists on this removal!

We were once taken to task by a young woman to whom we deplored the superstition. She said she had proof of it. A demand to produce it, brought the information that on one occasion her family did not so remove the decoration until February, and in April her mother had a stroke and from that day did not leave her bedroom.

EVIL EYE

Of all the superstitions which darkened the intellect of Britain in the sixteenth and seventeenth centuries, none can compare in strength with that of the power of the "Evil Eye," of being what was termed "overlooked." The same might be said of all parts of the world, civilized and uncivilized.

Did a man or woman fall ill of some complaint not easily recognized, it was taken for granted that someone had put the Evil Eye on him. If his cattle died, or his hens refused to lay, it was the Evil Eye. If his house caught fire, the power of a witch's Evil Eye was the incendiary power.

During the witch-hunting period of our history, the Evil Eye flourished as nowhere else in the world, and hundreds of women were burnt for no reason at all except that an accusation of putting the Evil Eye was made against them by somebody.

Ways and means wonderful to review were invented to combat this Eye. Here are some of them.

Draw blood from the mouth of the person suspected.—Craven, Yorks.

Spit three times in the person's face.—General.

Turn a live coal in the fire and say "The Lord be with us."—General.

To turn away the Evil Eye in a child: Put a shilling and a sovereign in some water and sprinkle the water over the child in the name of the Trinity.—North-west Scotland.

NOTE: This was called the gold and silver water cure.

Most popular of all "cures" was to identify the person casting the Evil Eye, and confront her.

The usual way was to make an image of the person believed to be the culprit, and then stick pins in its heart. It was held that the witch feeling the pain would appear at the house of the victim, and beg to be relieved of the pain. It would be granted on condition that the Evil Eye was removed.

Failing this working, it was possible to obtain the relief by going out at night until you had collected nine toads. The toads should then be strung together with string, a hole made somewhere and the toads buried in it. As the toads pined away, so the person who had looked at you with the Evil Eye would pine away and die. This was a remedy very rife in Derbyshire.

If the Evil Eye had fallen on cattle, a cure was to burn alive a pig and sprinkle the ashes over the byre and other farm buildings. Banffshire viewed this with great popularity; and so also did the people in the Carpathians.

In Egypt, in India, in East Africa, and throughout Europe, and in Madagascar this power of the Evil Eye was feared and fought against. It is not possible in the confines of this volume to recount all the superstitions concerning it; they would take a volume on their own. An excellent book of this kind for those who wish to delve deeper into the subject is *The Evil Eye,* by F. T. Elworthy.

It was once believed throughout England that the power of fire was so great that it could draw a person towards itself, and make him helpless to resist.

Thus, when an animal died on a farm and the death was suspected to be due to the Evil Eye or influence, it was the practice to burn the carcase in the open air and set a watch on the spot to see the person who came to the fire, drawn by its power.

Sir John Rhys tells of four men who were fishing with considerable success when one insisted on being landed, and would have leaped into the sea had the boat from which they were fishing not been beached. When the insistent fisherman was put ashore he was seen to hurry towards a field in which a beast was burning.

EXHUMATION

The removal or exhumation of a body after interment bodes death or calamity to the surviving members of the deceased's family.—General.

It does. It generally means a hanging. But the superstition was so firmly held that a free fight occurred in a Norfolk village when the body of a woman was exhumed owing to a suspicion that she had died of poison. The police were badly handled before they could carry out their duty.

A sequel to the incident was that, twenty years after, no villager would pass near the grave of the woman who, after the exhumation, was found to have died a natural death. The grave lay near a footpath leading to the church door, but the villagers so diverted their steps in a semi-circle over the grass to avoid passing the grave that the vicar had to construct a new permanent footpath. It was held that to pass within twelve feet of the grave would bring bad luck. Why the twelve feet none could explain.

Turner, in his *History of Remarkable Providences,* published in 1677, alludes to the exhumation superstition in a reference made to James I that he should not remove the Queen of Scots' body from Northamptonshire, where she was beheaded and buried. The reason given to the King by Thomas Fludd, of Kent, was that "it always bodes ill to the family when bodies are removed from their graves. For some of the family will die shortly afterwards, as did Prince Henry, and I think, Queen Anne."

EYEBROWS

Persons whose eyebrows meet will be lucky in all their undertakings.—North Country.

There seems, however, to be a divergence of opinion on this between the north and south, for in the south country a couplet runs:

Trust not those whose eyebrows meet,
For in their heart they carry deceit.

But perhaps on second thoughts north and south are not so variant as they at first appear, for deceit may possibly be an attribute to being lucky in one's financial undertakings.

Curiously enough, another southern superstition on eyebrows suggests that, should they meet, the person thus adorned will be unlucky, for it is held that

If your eyebrows meet across your nose,
You'll never live to wear wedding clothes.

EYES

If your right eye itches, it denotes good luck; but bad luck will attend you if your left eye should itch.

If the eyes of a person who has just died do not close they are looking after followers.—General.

To cure the little gatherings that occur on the eyebrows of children, pass a black cat's tail nine times over the place. If a tom cat the cure is more certain.—Cornwall.

For sore eyes bathe with rain water gathered on Ascension Day.—Shropshire and Worcestershire.

Rural people had so much faith in the second of the above superstitions that the greatest care was taken to have someone at the deathbed who would undertake securely to close the eyes of the deceased, so soon as the breath had gone from his body.

A popular superstition in many country areas was that sore eyes could be cured by bathing them in the water found in the hollow cup formed by the teazel's leaves. There may be something more than superstition in this, for the water is derived not from dew or rain, but from the teazel plant itself.

In Cornwall the same belief of a cure for sore eyes is attached to club-moss.

More superstitious still, however, was the method used in the nineteenth century in Devonshire, where it was necessary to make a house-to-house search begging penny pieces. When the sum of 4s. 6d. had been obtained in this way a pair of ear-rings could be purchased, the wearing of which could cure the eye complaint. There were, however, certain rules; a woman had to beg the pence only from males and a man only from females, and the words "please" and "thank you" had not to be spoken, else the charm would not work.

If the reader is inclined to smile at the foolishness of this charm superstition, let him remember that it still exists to-day in the very widespread belief that the piercing of ears and the wearing of ear-rings in the pierced holes will help poor eyesight.

In the neighbourhood of Banbury, Oxford, rain which falls on Holy Thursday was carefully preserved and bottled. It was held to be an unfailing remedy for sore eyes.

On Tweedside there was owned by a family a talisman which had a great reputation as a healer of eyes. It was known as a lammerhead, lammer being Scots for amber (from the French l'ambre). The stone, said to have been dug out of an ancient British grave (barrow), was drawn across the ailing eyes, and was said to give instant relief. It performed the same service if drawn across a sprained limb. It was still being used in 1880.

FAIRING PARTIES

A great feature of Yorkshire country life were the feasts of the sick and benefit societies. Fairing parties were a feature of these celebrations.

A large round cake, called matrimony cake, was baked for the fairing. It contained a layer of currants between two layers of pastry and was covered with sugar. This cake was cut into as many pieces as there were people present. Into one piece was placed a silver coin, in another a wedding ring borrowed from the hostess, in a third a button.

Those to whom the money fell were superstitiously held to be destined to be rich, the receiver of the ring would be married before the next "fairing;" while the luckless recipient of the button was destined to live in single blessedness for life.

FALLING BLIND

A falling blind is an augury of death in the house.—General.

This is a variation of a falling picture which also, it was held, presages death. We said "was" held; it is even now regarded with terror by many people.

The authors were regaled only a few months ago (1946) with the story of how after a picture of a husband had fallen, he was reported killed in an accident in Germany within a few hours. And, it was added, the time of his death was the exact time that the picture had fallen off the wall.

FALLING STAR

Falling, or shooting, stars are souls coming down from Heaven to animate new-born children.—Yorks.

When death occurs the flame of life lights up a new star.—Yorks.

This association of a star with the human soul extends in widespread belief throughout Europe to America and round the world to China and Australia. In the legends of the Irish saints the mother of one dreams that a spark has fallen into her mouth from a star. It is the soul come to her unborn child.

The Mandans of North America fancied that the stars are dead persons, and that when a woman was brought to bed, a star fell from Heaven, and entering her was born as a child.

The Maoris hold the view that at death the soul leaves the body and goes to the nether world in the form of a shooting star. The Lolos, an aboriginal tribe of Western China, hold that for each person on earth there is a corresponding star in the sky.

In Belgium and parts of France the people suppose that a meteor is a soul which has just left the body. Parallel with this belief is another that it is specially the soul of an unbaptized infant, or of a person who has died without absolution of sins.

FEATHER BED

To sleep on a feather bed which has been turned on a Sunday will give the sleeper fearful dreams for a week.

To turn a feather bed on a Sunday will bring death into the house.—Devonshire.

Nobody can die happy, or painlessly, on a feather bed, if the feathers come from pigeons or game birds.—North of England.

It was the practice in the North of England if a sick man was resting in a bed of pigeon, game or cocks' feathers, and his end was approaching, to remove him from the bed in the sheet and lay him on the floor, in order that he might die easily and without pain. The superstition behind the action was that a bed of pigeons' feathers hindered the soul from passing.

Whence came this superstition linking feathers with a hard death the authors cannot say. Diligent search has revealed no credible origin.

See FEATHERS.

FEATHERS

The feather of a wren is a preservative from shipwreck for a year.—Isle of Man fishing villages.

There had, however, to be a certain ritual to make the feathers effective. The wren had to be chased, caught and killed on Christmas Eve, and carried aloft on a pole with its wings outstretched.

In return for a coin a feather was given from the bird, so that at the end of the day it was pretty near featherless. The bird was then buried on the seashore or in some waste place. After that the feathers, it was supposed, became a potent charm against shipwreck. Any fisherman who refused a feather was regarded as most foolhardy.

It is a matter of regret that in 1933 this hunting of the wren was still followed in the Isle of Man.

FEET

It is unlucky to meet a man with flat feet on a Monday morning.

If a flat-footed person is the first to enter a house on New Year's Day, he will bring ill-luck.—Northumberland.

Good luck for a year will accrue to a house entered on New Year's morning by a person with a high instep.—Northumberland.

Those born feet first have power to heal all kinds of sprains, lumbago, and rheumatism by trampling on the affected part.—North-east Scotland.

It is unlucky to enter a house with the left foot first.

In passing it is not without interest to note, in connection with the feet first Scottish superstition, that in the Punjab of India it is held that a first child born feet first can cure backache by kicking the patient in the back on a crossing.

It may be as well to mention in connection with the first of the beliefs quoted above, that the misfortune of meeting a flat-footed man on a Monday morning can be safely averted by returning home, eating and drinking, and setting out afresh on the journey as originally intended.

The left foot omen of ill-luck probably came to us from the Romans. So strongly did they hold the omen that most noble houses employed a man to be stationed at the door of their houses whose duty it was to ensure that visitors should step over the threshold right foot first. He was designated for this reason "footman." And that is the origin of the footmen employed in mansions, and by the wealthy in this country to-day; they may be interested to hear of it.

See FIRST FOOTING.

FERN

Cut a fern root slant-wise and you will see a picture of an oak tree. The more perfect is the picture, the luckier chance it is for you.—Surrey and elsewhere.

A person who can wear fern seed about him will become invisible.—Once widely held.

Fern found growing on a tree will relieve the stomach-ache.

Whoever ascends a mountain holding fern seed in his hand on Midsummer Eve will discover a vein of gold or will see the treasures of the earth shining with a bluish flame.

If you wear a fern, you will lose your way, and adders will follow you.—Wales.

The superstition attached to fern seed was probably the most extraordinary in Britain. The ancients believed that the fern had no seed. But later generations discarded the theory, adding that it had seed which was invisible.

Hence, by some remarkable method of reasoning, somebody concluded that if a person could secrete this invisible seed on his person he, too, would become invisible. So the superstition passed down as a statement of fact in this country, and was widely held, even so late as Addison's time.

Shakespeare refers to it in *Henry IV*, part one, act ii, sc. 1: "We have the receipt of the fern seed, we walk invisible," spoken by Gadshill. Ben Jonson, and Beaumont and Fletcher also have reference to the "herb which makes men invisible."

Extraordinary precautions had to be taken in the collecting of the fern seed. The fern was supposed to bloom at midnight on Midsummer Eve, and to seed shortly afterwards. The seeker must neither touch it with his hand nor let it touch the ground. The practice was to place a white cloth under the plant or the blossom, and the seed fell upon it.

Not only throughout Britain, but in Germany, Bohemia, Brittany, and Styria was this superstition rampant.

FEVER

To cure a person of fever place an agate stone on the forehead of the sufferer.

To cure the fever take a thread with three knots, rub the sick person with the united threads, throw two of the knots in the fire saying, "I put the fever and the sickness on top of the fire," and then tie the third knot round the patient's neck, but so as not to be seen.—Argyllshire.

This is, of course, another belief that evil and disease can be transferred. Its origin here was probably the Roman occupation, for a Roman cure for the fever was to pare the patient's nails and stick the parings with wax on a neighbour's doorway before dawn. The fever was thus transferred to the neighbour.

The Romans seem to have acquired the superstition from the Greeks of early times. Even after Christianity the Greeks maintained their belief in transferring disease. In Athens there is a chapel dedicated to St. John the Baptist. Fever patients up to a few years ago attended the chapel and attached from themselves a wax thread to the pillar of the chapel, believing that by so doing they transferred the fever to the pillar.

In Co. Leitrim, Ireland, in order to prevent fever from spreading, all fires in the town were put out. Then men would go to one house carrying two large blocks of wood. One of these was placed on the floor, and the other, fitted with handles, was drawn backwards and forwards across it until the friction caused a fire. From this the fires of the town were relit. This, it was held, prevented the fever from spreading.

This transference of fever, and indeed other diseases, to animate and inanimate objects was widely held throughout Europe. In some places it was transferred to animals; in Italy to a tree, in France to a tree, and in Bohemia to a bush.

FINGERS

To defeat the machinations of the Devil, point two fingers downwards.

Mr. Winston Churchill, during his war-time Premiership, seems to have come to the conclusion that a more potent charm was to point two fingers UPWARDS, in a "V" form.

About the time that Mr. Churchill was thus delivering himself of his confidence in victory, the authors received a letter from a woman in Cornwall, who pointed out that the sign given by the then Prime Minister was one invoking the Devil, not victory. The letter was communicated to the Prime Minister, but had no effect—and the sign, seemingly, had no ill-luck.

FINGER NAILS

To cut or pare the finger nails on a Friday or a Sunday will bring bad luck. —General.

If a baby's nails are cut before it is a year old, the child will grow up a thief. —General.

A baby's right hand should be left unwashed in order that it may acquire riches.—West and North.

If the first parings of a child are buried under an ash tree the child will turn out a "top singer."—Northumberland.

White specks on the nails presage good fortune; black specks, misfortune.

NOTE: There is a variation in Kent, where white specks are known as "gifts."

To have yellow specks on the nails is a great sign of death.

NOTE: This was a belief in the days of Burton, and is referred to in his *Astrologaster*.

To cure epilepsy, the nail parings of the patient should be buried with a black cock at midnight on the spot where the epileptic fell.—General.

It is strange to relate that there still exists in many rural areas of England a disinclination to cut the nails of a baby before it is a year old; and mothers, as did those of old, bite them short. Whether or not this is still due to the superstition that the child whose nails are cut before twelve months will turn out to be a thief, the authors have not been able to verify. There is on record a number of instances whereby, to add assurance to assurance, mothers in those days pared the children's nails (after the twelve months) over the Bible, thereby guaranteeing that the child would grow up honest, and not "light-fingered." The Hindus, too, do not cut their babies' nails for twelve months; and the North American Indians for four years.

But perhaps one of the most remarkable superstitions of finger nails held in this country in olden times was that with the parings of a person's finger nails in her possession a witch could work havoc with the late owner. For this reason, the parings were generally buried in a safe and secret place, along with hair clippings.

Now, note the fact that in Siam nail parings are buried under a lucky tree; in Germany under the threshold of the house; in Ugi, in the Solomons, the nail parings and hair clippings were buried lest someone should work magic with them; in West Africa and in Tahiti, the same.

What explanation can be advanced for this custom, simultaneously, among the natives of the Solomons and the civilized people of these islands? What explanation other than a world-wide, instinctive fear and antidote?

Parings of finger nails were used, too, in superstitious ritual for the cure of various diseases. For instance, they were buried with a black cock and hair cuttings at a cross-roads at midnight in order to rid a sufferer of epilepsy. Also, if they were lodged in a hole in an elder tree or an aspen tree, also with hair clippings, they could take with them the ague troubling a sufferer.

See AGUE, COCK, EPILEPSY.

FIR TREE

If a fir tree be touched, withered or burned with lightning, it signifies that the master or mistress of the house will surely die.

With the exception that wood of the fir tree was, in some places, regarded as the best for the lighting of the Need-fires (q.v.), the above is the only superstition associated with the fir tree in England.

This is passing strange, for in other parts of Europe it was held to possess healing qualities. In Germany, for instance, a sufferer from the gout believed that he could rid himself of the painful attack by going to a young fir tree, tying a knot in one of the twigs of it, and then addressing it with: "God guard thee, noble fir tree. I bring thee my gout."

In Bohemia, poachers were under the belief that they could render themselves invulnerable by swallowing seeds from a fir cone found growing upwards before sunrise on the morning of St. John's Day.

Probably the best-known (to folk-lore) superstition attached to a fir tree concerns one which stood for ages on a promontory in Lake Keitele, Finland. The tradition attached to it was that it had been planted there by the first colonists, as an emblem and symbol of their fortune. Generation after generation of the colonists placed before the tree the first-fruits of their harvest before any of the new crop was tasted.

As the tree aged and branches of it died, so did the descendants of the colonists die; until, at last, only one of the people whose ancestors had planted the tree remained. Then, one day, the aged tree fell. A few days later the remaining old woman died—and the last of the colony and its tree disappeared.

FIRE

Hang an adder's skin in the rafters and your house will never catch fire.— New Forest.

To hang an egg laid on Ascension Day in the roof of the house preserves the premises from all harm.—General

Take some branches of seaweed, dry them, fasten them in turned wooden frames and stand them on the mantelpiece, and your house will be preserved from fire.—Cornwall.

If the fire burns brightly after it has been poked, it is a sign that an absent lover, wife or husband (as the case may be) is in good spirits and humour.—Midlands.

If the fire draws badly, evil influences are at work. They must be counteracted by placing the poker upright against the bars, thus making the sign of the Cross.—General.

When there is a hollow in the fire, a grave will soon be dug for a member of the family.—Wales.

Coffins flying out of the fire are a sign of a death in the family.—General.

Cradles flying out of the fire are a sign that there will be a birth in the house. —General.

NOTE: A coffin is an oblong hollow cinder; a cradle an oval cinder.

If the fire roars up the chimney, there will be a row in the house.

If the embers of a fire break in two, the housemaid will lose her situation.

Bad luck will attend the household where dead embers are not taken out of the fire before the family retires.—General.

There would seem to be sound reasoning in the last superstition. There have been numerous occasions on which a fire, seemingly extinguished, has suddenly burst into flame, and sparks flying from the falling embers have

ignited paper left in the hearth, or clothes left to air hanging from the mantelpiece. A fire in the dead of night would most certainly be bad luck, just as would a blob of paint falling on a person so unwise as to walk under a ladder set against a wall of a house for a painter!

Another fire-superstition relates to New Year's Eve. It was widely held in Scotland and parts of Northern England. According to it, if a fire did not burn *throughout* the night of New Year's Eve, it betokened bad luck during the coming year. In addition, the ill-fortune was passed to anyone who accommodated his thus unfortunate neighbour by giving him a live coal or any kind of a light with which to start up the extinguished fire.

/With reference to the placing of a poker upright against the bars when a fire will not draw: this is still a widely held belief, not as it was, originally, as a superstition, but as an old wives' tale. It has, of course, no effect whatever, though there is sound scientific reasoning in the idea *should the poker be red-hot*, for the heat would quite possibly attract a draught which would have the effect of drawing up the fire.

See NEED-FIRE, HALLOWE'EN, MIDSUMMER FIRES.

FIRST FOOTING

NOTE: It should perhaps be explained for those readers not conversant with British customs that "first footing" is, or was, a common custom practised on New Year's morning, immediately after the the clock had struck midnight. A pilgrimage of "wishing well" was made to the houses of neighbours and friends. The superstitions given below will now explain themselves.

It will bring bad luck to the house for a year if the first person to cross the threshold on New Year's Day is a woman. —General.

A fair man to be the first to cross the threshold will bring ill-fortune.— General.

These are superstitions still held in many parts of the country, especially, of course, in rural areas. The status of the "first footer" varies in parts of the country; in Co. Durham, for instance, he could be either a married or a single man. In Northumberland it was regarded as important that he should be a bachelor. But it was held firmly and generally that he must be a dark-haired man.

In an earlier generation the first footer brought with him a shovelful of coal, additional luck to keep the home fires burning. The practice, however, degenerated (!) in Scotland to the first footer arriving with a bottle of Scotch. And he still does—or at least he did up to the 1939-45 war.

Many Yorkshire villages indulged in a first footer "retainer." He was picked because of his "lucky" atmosphere. He made a round of the village visiting each house in turn.

The ill-luck of a woman first entering the house was widely held. In most parts of the country up to the beginning of this century, doors were barred until the first footer had paid a visit, lest a woman caller should gain entrance. This was the practice in Yorkshire.

One village of the authors' acquaintance, containing only a few hundred souls, was the more convinced of the value of this barring by reason of the fact that at the house of one of the residents, when a knock came to the door, and it was opened to admit the first footer, a woman friend instead stepped over the threshold. The dismayed family accepted the visit as an undoubted harbinger of ill-luck. The following night, returning home from a party they found that the house had been entered and all their valuables purloined!

See NEW YEAR.

FISHING (COASTAL)

To meet a woman with a white apron when going to a boat on a fishing trip is unlucky.—Yorkshire fishing villages.

NOTE: A fisherman so doing in older days would at once turn back and wait for the next tide, thus averting the ill-luck.

To meet a parson while going on board a fishing boat means bad luck for the trip.—Manx.

If the words pig, sow or swine be uttered while a line is being baited, that line will be surely lost.—Scottish.

If while at sea the word pig is mentioned, a fisherman must feel for the nails in his boots and say "cauld airn," else misfortune will overtake the fishing.—Scottish fishing villages.

NOTE: The same magic words were uttered in church by Scottish fisherfolk when the lesson for the day chanced to be the account of the Gadarene swine.

If a fisherman loses the first fish he is hauling in on a line, the trip will be unlucky.—Manx.

To take the name of God in vain while at sea is unlucky unless every man of the crew at once grasps the nearest piece of iron and holds it for a time.—Scottish.

If the first fish is caught by the sternmost man it means bad fortune.—Manx.

If blood be drawn in a quarrel on the coast while herring are being caught at sea the shoal will depart and not return that season.—Scottish.

The last-named superstition was widely believed as an explanation for the disappearance of herring from the Moray Firth in the reign of Queen Anne. There had been, it was stated, a violent quarrel and blood had been spilt in the sea.

Scottish superstition also held that herring will forsake a coast on which suicide has been committed. At Loch Carron when the herring deserted the coast it was held that two men, who had drowned themselves, were the cause. After several years without herring the local fishermen lighted bonfires on the spot where the bodies had been found as sacrifice to appease the herring. It is rather an odd fact that within twelve months herring were back round the coast.

Apropos the ill-luck of meeting a woman with a white apron, at Cockenzie, in the Scottish lowlands, a stranger's well-intentioned "good morning" to a fisherman on the way to a boat would result, at one time, in his turning round and going back home. Such a greeting was one of the worst of omens.

In the same area it was held that anyone at all who crossed a fisherman's path while he was on his way to the boat intended to "scathe" him. So when any fisherman reached the spot where his way had been "crossed," he took out his knife and scratched a cross on the ground uttering, at the same time, the words: "twel oto-see-die," afterwards spitting on the spot. The sign of the cross was an antidote to the intended evil, and the spittle was just contempt for the ill-wisher.

A further superstition current both in all Scottish fishing villages and those in the Isle of Man was that it was unlucky to call things at sea by the names they were known on land. This was particularly so in the case of the Scottish Highlanders.

For instance, a church, known ashore as a kirk, was at sea referred to always as "the bell hoose," and the clergyman or preacher as "the man wi the black quyte."

Far away on the east coast of Malay the natives never refer at sea to things by their shore names. Curious, is it not?

'A very strong Manx superstition was that a fishing boat should always go out with the sun on going to sea. It was the custom, if a boat was lying in harbour with her bows up, to turn her to the sun. It was held unlucky to go to sea any other way.

The Manx fishermen also held that to go out third boat to sea on the first day of the season spelt disaster to that boat throughout the season. To counteract this, after two boats had left a number of boats in line followed so that no boat could be called the third. We believe this practice is still followed.

Probably the most superstitious of all sea fishermen are those of the Yorkshire coast. Some of their old beliefs are given above; they do not complete the "charms" by any means. For instance, it is still held in many parts that when a fishing boat is launched a coin must be put, and kept permanently, under the mast in order to ensure good luck.

Another of their superstitions made it obligatory, when the nets were being paid out, to cut a slice in one of the pieces of cork attached to the nets and to insert therein a piece of money; otherwise the catch would be a poor one. The origin of this seems to be the idea of informing Father Neptune, proprietor of the deep, that they were prepared to pay for all the fish they took out of his domain.

Further, if no fish were caught for several nights, the first fish that subsequently came into the boat had to be preserved, and, when the vessel arrived back home, burnt as a sacrifice to the Fates. This, like the one above, was a Yorkshire belief.

One of the best charms to take to sea was the fact that one or more of the crew while on the way to the boat had met a deformed person. This, it was held, would mean the best of luck.

The reason? Because the deformed are "God's Poor." Although it is not recorded in the superstition, the authors incline to the opinion that the luck worked if to God's Poor was given by the fisherman a little offering of good-will and sympathy.

Mention has been made above of the ill-luck attaching to the fishing if a minister, or a church, or a pig are alluded to at sea by their correct names. This taboo applies with equal determination to a number of surnames of people.

In the village of Buckie, no fisherman would at one time pronounce the names Ross and Coull. A fisherman hearing either of these names in any place, immediately spat to disperse the bad luck. If reference has to be made to one of the Ross's, it is done in a roundabout way such as "the lad it lives at so-and-so a place," mentioning the street or the house. During the herring season, anyone bearing one of these names has little chance of a place in a crew, however hard put to it the ship might be for a crew.

Why the names Ross and Coull should have been so unlucky the authors have been unable to discover.

FISHING (INLAND)

If you count the number of fish you have caught, you will catch no more that day.—General.

If you are right-handed you should never cast a line with the left hand, or you will have no fish to creel.

If you should see an earwig while on the way to the water, you will be lucky indeed.

If the fish will not bite, one of the company of fishermen should be thrown into the water and quickly hauled out again as if he were a fish. The fish will then begin to nibble.—Scottish, especially Loch Aline.

Whence the origin of this the authors do not know; any more than they can explain how it comes about that in far away Cambodia the fisherman with no bites walks into the sea and as though he did not see his trap lets himself be caught in it. After that he is certain to catch fish!

En passant, the best day's trout fishing the authors ever had was when, with dry fly, they had to fish four miles of water with the left hand, because of the run of the stream, they being both right-handed.

FITS

To be cured of fits go to the parish church at midnight on 23rd June, and walk three times through each aisle. Then crawl three times from north to south under the Communion table as the clock strikes twelve.—Devonshire.

To cure fits secure a small portion of a human skull, grate it similar to ginger, mix it with food, and give to the patient to eat.—General.

If a female be afflicted with fits, nine pieces of silver and nine three-half-

pennies must be collected from nine bachelors. The silver must be converted into a ring to be worn by the afflicted female, and the nine three-halfpennies should be paid to the maker of the ring, which he good-naturedly accepts.— General.

NOTE: Should the affected person be a male, the money had to be collected from females. The number of coins to be collected differs in various parts of the country.

In *The Times* of 7th March, 1854, appeared the following account of the working of this superstition:

"A young woman living in the neighbourhood of Holsworthy, having for some time past been subject to periodical fits, endeavoured to effect a cure by attendance at the parish church accompanied by thirty young men, her immediate neighbours. The service over, she sat in the porch of the church, and each of the young men, as they passed out in succession, dropped a penny into her lap; but the last, instead of a penny, gave her a half-crown, taking from her the twenty-nine pennies she had already received. With this half-crown in her hand she walked three times round the Communion table, and afterwards had the half-crown made into a ring, the wearing of which she believes will recover her health."

The *Staffordshire Advertiser*, in 1874, reported that on Christmas Day in a Wiltshire village a labourer's wife asked for a sacrament shilling in exchange for one she tendered. On inquiry she stated that the only way to cure her son's fits was to hang a sacrament shilling round his neck. This had first to be obtained by collecting a penny piece from each of twelve maidens, then exchanging the pieces for an ordinary shilling, and the shilling for a sacrament shilling.

In the *Stamford Mercury* of 8th October, 1858, appeared the account of a Ruabon miner's wife who went to the sexton of the local church for an "ever so small" portion of a human skull from the graveyard for the purpose described above.

FIVE-SHILLING PIECE

An exceedingly curious modern superstition sprang into being in London in 1945.

It was held by barmaids and other employees in the bars of public-houses, that should they change a five-shilling piece into separate shillings for a customer, somebody in the bar would receive dismissal notice before the week was up.

The authors, who tested the superstition in dozens of London bars, are totally unable to track it down to any origin.

FLEAS

The little sable beast (the flea) if thirsting for blood, it augurs rain.

Windows of a house should be kept shut on the first day of March to prevent the annual effort of fleas to gain entrance.

NOTE: If this were done, it was held that the house would be free of fleas for the remainder of the year.

Fleas and other parasitic insects never infest a person who is near death.— General.

The origin of the latter superstition may have a medical origin in the state of fluids immediately under the skin, either in quality or quantity.

The explanation of the shutting of the windows on the first day of March is due to the belief which existed that fleas arrived (whence we do not know!) on that date.

However, if the careful housewife took the precaution of sweeping the step on that day, as well as keeping the windows closed, she would be free of fleas for the rest of the year, for sweeping the step on 1st March was another way of ensuring freedom from fleas.

FLOWERS

It is unlucky to bring flowers into the house outside their season.—General.

If flowers that bloom in the summer flower in the house during the winter, the house will be unlucky.—Wales.

Geraniums are, of course, an example of the latter superstition. It is recorded of an old Welsh woman that on her geraniums coming into flower in November she announced her fear that death would visit her family.

In point of fact, three relatives did die between that time and the following March.

On the other hand there seems hardly a country cottage in which geraniums are not flowering in windows throughout the winter; and the authors have such plants in their own conservatory.

In the eighteenth century it was believed that the flower agrimony, placed in a house, produced sleep. Lily and antirrhinums procured wakefulness, the rose checked fertility, schambrune and verbena together excited love, but that verbena alone created discord.

For superstitions relating to other flowers see under separate flower names.

FLY

If a fly falls into the glass from which you are drinking, or about to drink, it is an omen of prosperity.—General.

It is also an omen that any hygienically minded person is going to call for another drink!

FOOTBALL

It will be an unlucky match if, before the team leave the dressing room, the ball is not bounced between the oldest and youngest player, and caught on the bounce by the youngest.

This belief was held by at least a dozen teams of which the authors have knowledge, and was, at any rate at one time, regularly indulged in by Leeds City F.C.

It is possible that the game of football itself was born of superstition. The suggestion is worth following up. It was made, if we remember correctly, by Sir James Frazer, somewhere in his *The Scapegoat.*

There was at one time in the Bocage of Normandy on Shrove Tuesday a fight for the possession of a large leather ball stuffed with bran. This, thrown on to the village green of one of the hamlets, was fought for by rival players of the surrounding hamlets, the aim being to obtain the ball and house it in one particular hamlet.

Now, the object of this was the belief that the victorious parish would have better crops than its rivals. This belief is the basis of the suggestion that football came to Scotland by way of Normandy, and was first played with the same object. There is nothing strange in the idea. For generations previously people in neighbouring villages in many parts had engaged in tug-of-war. For what?

Some of the Khasis of Assam place a bamboo pole athwart a stream and from opposite sides. The party which succeeded in dragging the pole across to their side of the stream gained health and prosperity during the year. The Chittagong hill people engaged in a tug-of-war at funerals; one side represented good and the other evil. So too is the same mystery behind a similar performance in Burma. There also a tug-of-war is staged between drought and rain, when rain is needed. And again in the

East Indies. In Assam, a month after the rice has been sown, the Tangkhuls hold a tug-of-war in order to take the omens of the crops. In Korea in the middle of the first month of the year the village which wins a "tug" is thought to ensure a good harvest. In Morocco the tug-of-war is resorted to as a means of influencing the weather.

Among the Sinhalese the tug-of-war is designed to propitiate the goddess Patine, thus ensuring fertility of the crops.

Now, amid all this welter of tug-of-war through many countries we come to the first-mentioned ball game at Bocage and neighbourhood. The fight was not for the bran-filled leather ball, but for what it represented, for it was believed that the side which gained possession of the ball won for the parish a better crop of apples than that which would accrue to any of the other contestants. Thus the origin of the game was undoubtedly a magical rite to ensure fertility.

It is not, therefore, unreasonable to assume that the older British game of tug-of-war, which later was almost entirely abolished in favour of some kind of ball game, yet having the same object of getting the prize into the possession of one side, was in the days of superstition a charm to ensure fertility of crops and cattle.

FOOTLING

A child born feet first has magical gifts.—Cornwall.

A child born feet first can cure the backache by kicking the patient in the back on a crossing.

In the North-East of Scotland it was firmly believed—and there are still traces of belief in the more remote parts—that those who were born feet first possessed great powers of healing all kinds of sprains, lumbago, and rheumatism.

The cure consisted in either rubbing the affected part with the feet or trampling upon it. The chief virtue lay in the feet of the "lucky" persons.

Very much similar beliefs were attributed to the seventh son and the seventh son of the seventh son.

Among the Indians of Peru a child born feet first is regarded as rather a liability. Should it survive the ritual demanded of it, blame will still be attached to the child for any ill-luck. For instance, if an unexpected frost sets in the priests send for any people who were known to have been born feet first and soundly rated them—together with any twins—as being the cause of the damage done by the frost.

FOWL

In the church of St. Tecla, in the village of Llandegla, Wales, the falling sickness (epilepsy) was wont to be cured with the aid of a fowl. It was, in fact, transferred to the fowl. The patient had first to wash his limbs in the sacred well close to the church, drop fourpence into the well as an offering, and repeat the Lord's Prayer three times. Then a fowl —a cock or hen according to the sex of the sufferer—was placed in a basket and carried first round the well and afterwards round the church. Next, the patient entered the church and laid at full length under the Communion table until break of day. He was then free to depart after he had offered sixpence. The fowl was left in the church. If it died the epilepsy was supposed to have been transferred to it from the patient, who was now rid of his, or her, disorder.

If you doubt the efficacy of the "cure" you have the word of the parish clerk, as late as the year 1855, that he had seen birds in the church staggering from the effects of the fits transferred to them.

On the other hand, since they had had no food and had been confined in a small basket, they may well have been staggering from hunger and confinement.

See BLACK COCK, COCK,
CHICKENS, EPILEPSY

FOX

To see several foxes together is unlucky; but to see a lone one means that good luck will attend you.—Wales.

If foxes enter a courtyard, disaster and death will follow.

A correspondent of *Notes and Queries* relates that when staying in an Oxfordshire village he was told by an old woman that she and her brothers were cured of the whooping cough by going to a house near their home where a fox was kept, carrying with them (in the early morning) a can of milk. This they placed down in front of the fox and when he had taken as much as he cared to drink, the children shared what was left—and the whooping cough vanished.

It was believed in parts of Wales that witches transformed themselves into foxes, and at the Need-fires (q.v.) a fox was burned in the fire as a warning to all witches having the intention of assuming the shape of a fox. It must be remembered that at this time fire was held as the most certain way of getting rid of witchcraft. Similar practices were held in France.

It is of passing interest that in Bohemia a fox's tongue was worn as an amulet to make the shy wearer bold.

FRIDAY

Unlucky will be the child born on a Friday, for it is a day of ill omen.

It is unlucky for a servant to enter a new situation on a Friday.—General.

Bad luck will attend a wedding solemnized on a Friday.—General.

A bed must never be turned on a Friday, or sleeplessness will be your fate.—General.

If you dream on a Friday night and tell the dream on the following day, it will come true.

If you wash blankets on a Friday, they will dry too quickly. The authors do not know what the result of this is, but doubtless it is disastrous for the housewife.

Rain on Friday, fine on Sunday.—A general weather superstition.

Friday's moon come when it will it comes too soon.

It is unlucky to pare one's nails on a Friday.

It is unlucky to go courting on a Friday.—Lancashire.

Good Friday is the best day on which to wean children.—Lancashire.

To dibble potatoes on a Friday will mean the crop will fail.

Eggs laid on Good Friday will go stale.—General.

In 1931 the sailings of two Atlantic liners were postponed from Friday night until one minute after midnight, following protests at the Friday sailing from a large number of superstitious passengers.

Criminals have long regarded themselves as distinctly unfortunate if brought before a judge on a Friday. Apropos of this it is a curious fact that very few crimes such as burglary take place on a Friday.

The extraordinary extent to which the Friday bad luck goes, even in these days, is instanced by a report in the *Scotsman* of 6th September, 1900. The report referred to a row of almshouses which had been built for ten women, who all occupied hovels in a bad state of repair. The new houses were in Abaracle, and the hovels in Aberbade.

When, on the day appointed, Mr. H. M'Pherson, Inspector of Poor, visited Aberbade to superintend the removal of the women he found them in a state of rebellion. They refused to move in spite of all his pleas and description of the new and comfortable homes. Threats of a sheriff's warrant to evict them had no effect.

It was then discovered that the reason for their rebellion was that the day was Friday, and that to move on a Friday meant, in Highland superstition, the worst of bad luck. On the inspector promising that the removal would be postponed until the Saturday, the women became instantly amenable.

Throughout the centuries in all countries this Bad Friday superstition has continued to this day. The origin is, of course, the Crucifixion, though why this superstition should not have been confined to Good Friday, no one can say.

FROG

To cure the "thrush" a young frog should be held with its head for a few moments inside the mouth of the sufferer, when it will take the malady to itself.—Cheshire.

To cure warts, impale a frog on a stick and rub the warts on the frog. They will disappear as the frog dies.—Wales.

To cure the cancer swallow young frogs.—Midlands.

A frog brings good luck to the house in which it enters.—General.

The origin of the last superstition, which was pretty general at one time, is the belief that the frog possesses the soul of a dead child. And the origin of this belief is the cry which it gives when injured—resembling the cry of a child.

The "thrush" mentioned above is an ailment which affects the throat of children. The efficacy of the frog treatment was described to Sir James Frazer by an old woman who had often superintended the "cure." "I assure you," she said, "we used to hear the poor frog whooping and coughing mortal bad for days; it would have made your heart ache to hear the poor creature coughing as it did in the garden."

Incredible though it may seem the superstition is still held in at least one part of the Midlands that the swallowing of young frogs will cure cancer. A correspondent in that part of the country wrote us a few months ago to inquire did we know that cancer could be cured, and "had been cured in a definite case I know" by that means.

Presumably the belief is the same as that which held that toads have the power of sucking the poison of cancer.

In some parts of the country a frog was supposed to possess the soul of a dead child, and it was very unlucky therefore to kill one. The origin, again, probably lies in the cry of the frog if injured, which is almost human in its note.

Mention is made above of the superstition for curing cancer by means of young frogs. If you are tempted to smile at its absurdity, and to refer to silly superstition of past days, read this letter, addressed to the authors.

> New King's Road, Fulham,
> London, S.W.6.

Dear Sirs,—There is no superstition about swallowing small live frogs as a cure for cancer and for T.B. The frogs assimilate the disease and cleanse the system. It is as scientific as penicillin. —Yours faithfully, ——.

There seems no age or end to superstition.

See CANCER.

FRUIT TREES

If a fruit tree blooms and fruits twice in a season a member of the family owning the tree will die before the year is out.—Suffolk.

If a dead animal—dog, cat, or rabbit, etc.—is not buried under the roots of a fruit tree when it is planted, it will not bear fruit.—Yorkshire.

If you tie wet straw bands or hay bands round your trees on Christmas Eve, they will yield plentifully next year.—Wales.

Strange to relate, the second of the above superstitions still remains. On 8th January, 1945, the authors received the following letter from Sheffield:

> "My husband bought two apple trees and three pear trees, and set them according to a gardening book. But four different people have told him that they will not bear fruit because he did not plant a dead animal under the roots."

This is, the authors think, an example of how a perfectly natural practice can be so distorted as to be unrecognizable. Many years ago it was the custom when planting out grape vines to do so at a time when it was possible to obtain the carcase of a horse. Many vines are thriving to-day on this burial.

The reason is obvious—the manurial value. It is to this custom that the stupid Yorkshire superstition refers. There is no doubt that such a carcase would have beneficial effects on the trees. It is not necessary, of course. In point of fact, a good deal remains to-day of the old horse in the way of manure such as hoof and horn meal, superphosphates, dried blood, etc.

See APPLE TREES and WASSAIL-ING for superstitions for the increase of crops of fruit trees.

FRYING PAN

If a frying pan is left on the fire with nothing in it, the wife of the house will have puckers in her face.—Wales. ·

And not without reason, since if the pan was thus left she would probably want a new frying pan. This seems not so much superstition as just plain commonsense.

FUNERAL

He who meets a funeral is certain soon to die unless he bares his head, turns and accompanies the procession some way. If the coffin is carried by bearers he must take a "lift." That done, he should bow to the company, turn and go on his way without fear.—Border Counties.

If the sun shines brightly on the face of one of the attendants at a funeral, it marks him as the next to be laid in that churchyard.—Border Counties.

Three funerals always follow one another in quick succession.—Northumberland.

If the clock strikes an hour while the church bell is tolling for a funeral there will be another death within the week.—Bucks.

If the cathedral funeral bell tolls once, it will toll three times.—Durham

If the door of a house is closed after the coffin has been placed in the hearse, and before the mourners have taken their places in the coaches, it has been "shut on the corpse" and another death will occur before many days are passed.—Yorkshire.

A coffin must be carried three times round the "Funeral Stone."

If the doors of a house are closed during a funeral, and before all the mourners have returned, family quarrels will take place.

If a corpse is carried over private ground it establishes a right of way.—General, and widely held to-day.

NOTE: This is legal nonsense, but is still firmly believed.

The south side of the churchyard is holiest, the north side being really unhallowed ground, fit only for the last resting-place of stillborn infants and suicides.

NOTE: The origin for this belief is that the south wind is thought to bring corruption with it.

The last corpse to be buried in a graveyard or cemetery must stay and guard the graves until the next corpse comes to take its place.—Ireland and Highlands.

The first corpse laid in a new churchyard is claimed by the Devil.—Aberdeen and Devon.

In Scotland the last superstition was so strongly held that in one new area it was found impossible to bring the churchyard into use. At last, a tramp who had been found dead by the roadside was buried there, and after this no more difficulty was experienced with parishioners.

In Bovey Tracey, Devon, the churchyard at the Church of St. John's was long unused, the country people holding that the Devil would claim the first body interred in it. Not until a stranger was buried there, the servant to one of the residents, would any of the parishioners allow their dead to rest in the plot.

With reference to the coffin being carried three times round the funeral stone quoted above: This superstition was enacted at Brilley, in Herefordshire. The stone stood in an open space outside the churchyard. The body had to be carried "sunwise"—that is with the sun—and was believed to have the effect of preventing the Devil from obtaining the soul of the dead.

It was a belief in Northampton district that if, at a funeral, a hearse has to be turned after the coffin has been placed in it, another death in the family will quickly follow.

It is a fact that a hearse is never so turned, because the undertaker, if the direction is likely to need a turn, will drive along the street and turn, thus coming back in the starting direction before he has the body placed in the hearse. It is probably this action that has been corrupted into the superstition mentioned.

In the Hebrides it was held strongly—and actually still is in certain parts—that the bier on which a corpse has been carried must be broken after the funeral to prevent the "sluagh" using it to carry the newly dead through the air.

It should be mentioned in explanation of the belief, that the sluagh (fairy hosts) are held to be the spirits of mortals who have died.

See ARVAL, BURIAL, CORPSE, DEATH, SUNWISE.

FURNITURE

If furniture in a house cracks and creaks, it is a sign of a break in the weather.—Shetlands fishing villages.

The origin of this belief lies in the fact that in olden days in the Shetlands various articles of furniture in a fisherman's dwelling were generally made of raaga trees—driftwood.

GALL STONES

Sheep's dung boiled with new milk until dissolved, and then taken internally, is a sure cure for the removal of gall stones.

GAMBLING

If you have bad luck at cards, and rise and turn three times with your chair, your ill-luck will change.—General.

If a player places a matchstick across one which you have previously placed in the ashtray, bad luck will attend you.—General.

If in a game of chance a woman touches your shoulders, or should you meet a woman while on the way to the gambling rooms, you will have no luck.

If you show passion at losses, the demon of bad luck will follow you.

NOTE: It will be more likely the demon of bad judgment.

There was never a good hand with the four of clubs in it.

NOTE: The four of clubs is nicknamed the Devil's four-poster bedstead.

Borrowed money cannot lose.—Gamblers generally.

The "luck" of borrowed money, together with the belief that a newcomer to gambling cannot lose are two of the strongest superstitions prevalent among the gambling fraternity who visit Monte Carlo. The authors have seen time and again seasoned gamblers, who strive hard to make a permanent living out of the Casino, meet trains from Britain and the coast, and after picking out with unerring eye those paying their first visit to the Principality will offer them money with which to gamble, allowing them to take a percentage on their first day's play.

It is, indeed, remarkable how frequently a newcomer will on his, or her, first visit to the tables, win handsomely, and afterwards have little fortune.

The belief that borrowed money cannot lose is or was in earlier years almost a fetish. The authors, who spent many winter seasons in Monte Carlo prior to 1939, have known many scores of people who would on no account go to the tables with money in their pockets, especially in the Sporting Club.

Their practice was to go to the barman in the club—he was, by the way, a man of considerable wealth—and request the loan of two or three or more thousand francs, and having received it, start playing. We place on record that the recipient of the greatest luck in this borrowed money was the barman; he expected 10 per cent. interest on his money!

One of the authors was nearly converted to this superstition after a night's very ill-luck on the roulette wheel in the Sporting Club large salon. After nothing would come right, no matter what system was played, and after losing some 5,000 francs, all he had on him, he approached the barman and received a loan of 2,000 francs. Returning to the same table he steadily won, until at 3 a.m. he had won back not only the 5,000 francs previously lost but another 3,000 as well.

Perhaps the most disastrous ill-luck in gambling is the belief that after one card or colour or combination has come up continuously a certain number of times, say ten or twelve, the other colour or another card MUST come up. The law of averages is quoted for this. One of the present writers once saw an American lose £10,000 in four hours at Trente et Quarante by systematically backing black, starting after red had turned up some thirteen times. Throughout four "slippers" of cards, black did not once turn up. It is true that the law of averages operates in all things; what those who quote it forget is that the law of averages doesn't work just for a Monday night—its averages average between creation and eternity!

GAME FEATHERS

A person cannot die if his bed is stuffed with game feathers.—Sussex, Surrey, Cheshire, and other parts.

In *Notes and Queries*, Mr. A. Way relates how, in a Surrey village, he inquired if a man whom he had left very ill the previous day was still alive.

"Yes," was the reply. "We must change his bed."

"Change his bed?" echoed Mr. Way. "What do you mean?"

"Why, sir, we think he can't pass away while he is in that bed. The neighbours think there must be game feathers in the bed."

A similar story, told of a Sussex man, ended: "So we took'n out o' bed and laid'n on the floor and he pretty soon died then."

From pneumonia, the authors should surmise!

See PIGEON FEATHERS.

GARDEN

If cabbages grow double—with two shoots from the root instead of one—or lucker (with leaves open instead of closing in to form a heart) it is a sign of good luck.—General.

A pod containing only one pea is an auspicious circumstance.

The authors would have thought that either of these two superstitions was definitely unauspicious to a gardener.

Above-ground crops should be sown in the wane of the moon; under-ground crops—carrots, parsnips, etc.—at the change of the moon.—General.

In 1944 the columns of the London *Daily Mirror* contained much correspondence on this subject, and so did the columns of a popular gardening paper. It was held by gardeners that all top crops should be sown on the wane of the moon and all root crops at the rise. The authors carried out experiments in their Surrey garden on one plot. They found no difference whatever in the crops sown at the given times with those sown at the opposite times.

The rhyming couplet which memorises the superstition is:

Sow beans when the moon is round.
They'll pod down to the ground.

Another good "omen" in gardening is to have among one's crop gooseberries, potatoes and other vegetables of unusual shape.

Still another, that crops should be sown in rows running from north to south and not from east to west.

GARLIC

Garlic, hung about the house on All Hallows Eve, will keep away evil spirits. —Scotland.

Great reliance was placed by the Scots on the use of garlic as warding off evil at all times, but especially on All Hallows Eve.

In many of the more remote parts the belief is still held. In this connection it is interesting to recall that in a play broadcast by the British Broadcasting Corporation on the afternoon of Saturday, 6th January, 1945, the theme of which was the Black Art, garlic was described as being hung over the doorways of an old house by the housekeeper on the eve of All Hallows.

At the Midsummer fires in Provence, in the Department of Var, pods of garlic were roasted, and afterwards distributed to all the families.

In Sumatra garlic was supposed by the Battas to possess soul-compelling virtues, and was made use of in rites for the recovery of lost souls.

GEMS

If you wear a ruby, it will prevent all evil and impure thoughts.

Jaspar will cure madness.

Agate is an antidote to the poison of scorpions and spiders as well as being beneficial to the eyes.

An engagement ring containing pearls will bring tears to the marriage.

Opals are unlucky, except if it is the stone corresponding to the birth of the wearer (October) when it is lucky.— General.

Most of the foregoing beliefs were strongly held in the Middle Ages, especially that of power of the ruby to prevent evil. It was worn by priests of the day on account of its presumed power to preserve the chastity of the wearer. Another power ascribed to it was that it could kill any venomous reptile that was put into the same vessel with it.

The correct list of birthday stones supposed to bring luck as presents are: Garnet, January; Amethyst, February; Bloodstone, March; Diamond, April; Emerald, May; Agate (or Pearl), June; Ruby, July; Sardonyx, August; Sapphire, September; Opal, October; Topaz, November; Turquoise, December.

The ill-luck of the opal as a stone of tears has many stories attached to it. But perhaps the most curious is that told of an opal which belonged to Alphonso XII of Spain (1874-1885). On his wedding day he presented it set in a ring to his wife. Her death occurred shortly afterwards. Before the funeral of his wife he gave the ring to his sister. She died a few days later. The ring was then presented by the king to his sister-in-law, who died within three months.

But more was to follow. Alphonso, distracted at these tragic ends to the gift of the ring, decided to wear it himself. He did so, and within a short time was dead. By this time the ring's evil possession was generally recognized. It came into the hands of the Queen Regent, who hung it round the neck of the statue of the Virgin of Almudena of Madrid.

During the fifteenth and sixteenth centuries in England, a toad stone ring was regarded as a charm of great power. The ring was of silver with the toad stone set in it. This stone was supposed to have been found in the head of an old toad and was believed to warn the wearer of poison by its perspiring and changing colour.

In the early part of the present century there began an American craze for lucky stones set in the front teeth of women. Its originator was an American dentist who claimed that he had the gift of being able to discover which stones would impart good luck to women who had them set in one of their front teeth. The craze lasted but a brief while; even American women could not be long deluded by the idea.

See TOAD STONE.

GEORGE

No man with the Christian name George has ever been hanged.—General.

This absurd idea, which proves nothing anyway, is still held to-day; and once or twice every few weeks the authors are asked by correspondents if this is indeed a fact.

For the benefit of those thinking of committing murder and getting away with it because their baptismal name is George, we state here and now that quite a number of Georges have been well and truly hanged. Possibly the best remembered of them is George Smith, the "Brides in the Bath" murderer.

GETTING OUT OF BED

It is unlucky to get out of bed in the morning on the side other than the one by which you got in.—General.

An irritable man has got out of bed on the wrong side.—General.

At first glance it might seem that these two beliefs are associated. In point of fact they are not. The latter is of much older vintage than the former. Getting out of bed on the wrong side dates back to the Romans. The "wrong side" was the left side, so much dreaded by the Romans of old—and by the Greeks for that matter.

GHOST

Make two pieces of rowan wood into the form of a cross, tied with red thread. Insert the cross betwen the lining and the cloth of your garment, and neither ghost nor witch can interfere with you. —Scotland.

Rowan wood, known as mountain ash, was for centuries the Scottish protection against ghosts and witches, and red thread tied round the tails of cows on May Day kept away the witches who would otherwise abstract the milk from the cows.

GIPSIES

Many stories have been told of the power of gipsies to place a curse on all kinds of people who have offended them; or to give warning of tall dark men who seek to encompass a girl's ruin.

There is one classic tale of a gipsy whom a rich man turned away from his mansion. The woman (so the story goes) looked him in the face and said that by the end of the year he would have lost wife, son and daughter. And his wife and children sickened one by one, and all were dead by the end of the year.

Another story concerns a Welsh football team, who finding gipsies camped on their playing pitch at once bundled them off. In return the gipsies placed a curse on the team that they would not win a game on the ground for seven years; and sure enough the opposing team were a "banker" certainty for an away win.

Lest it should be supposed that such nonsense is no longer believed in, let us quote a letter received by us from the Rhondda Valley in January, 1946. Here it is:

Gordon Richards has not won the Derby because he insulted a gipsy, and she has put a curse on him that he will not win a Derby so long as he is in the racing profession. Since he can't win one without being in the racing profession, it sounds rather a good tip to save stake money.

GIRL SITTING ON A TABLE

A courtship superstition very prominent in many country places is that should a girl sit on a table while talking to her sweetheart, she will never marry.

The origin of this belief is a mystery.

GLASS ROD OF HEALTH

A curious Devonshire superstition, the remnant of which still remains in the more remote parts, concerns the healing propensities of a glass rod.

This was a twisted rod in the form of a walking stick, usually from four to eight feet long. It was set up somewhere in the house and wiped clean every morning, in the belief that by this means all the diseases and contagious maladies would gather round the rod, and thus be wiped away daily.

Should the rod be broken, illness and misfortune was expected to fall upon the household.

The belief was somewhat akin to that of the onion, the hanging of which, it was held, and is still largely held, will keep away disease. But for this there is some good ground, for the onion does, in point of fact, attract germs to itself. No onion should be eaten which has been cut and left exposed for a few hours in the kitchen if it is to be eaten.

GLOVES

If gloves are left at a house after a visit, the visitor must return and sit down before picking them up. They must then be put on standing, or the visitor will never again visit the house. —General.

GLOW-WORM

If a man should kill a glow-worm, it will endanger his love affair, and may cause the death of his beloved.

The origin of this is the belief that only the female glow-worm has the luminous tail, which she uses for the purpose of attracting the male. Thus the tradition that any male who should put out her light will have his own love affair go awry, and his woman killed.

GNAT

When gnats dance in February the husbandman becomes a beggar.— General.

The surest way to prevent infection from disease is to open the windows of the sick room at sunset in order to admit the gnats, who will load themselves with the infection and then fly forth and die. —Huntingdonshire.

"Smoking and tar water and white-wash are fools to them there gnats," was the verdict of an old woman, said to be a "wise woman" in treating illness.

Those who find themselves troubled by gnats might take a page out of the superstitious notebook of the ancients.

The belief was that one way of getting rid of noxious insects without hurting their feelings or showing disrespect (either of which might bring misfortune) was to make images of them.

Thus, Apollonius of Tyana is said to have cleared Antioch of scorpions by making a bronze image of a scorpion and burying it under a pillar in the middle of the city; and to have freed Constantinople of gnats by means of a bronze gnat.

A curious commentary on this is the story of Gregory of Tours who related how Paris never knew the presence of dormice and serpents until, in his life-time, workmen cleaning one of the city's sewers found and removed a bronze dormouse and a bronze snake. After that mice and serpents abounded in the city.

GOAT

Goats are never seen for twenty-four hours together. Once in that space they pay a visit to the Devil to have their beards combed.—England and Scotland.

A he-goat hanged to the boat's mast will assure a favourable wind.—Western Isles.

Black goats on lonely bridle paths mean that treasure is hidden there.— Wales.

Whence sprang the extraordinary idea in the first of the above the authors cannot trace; unless it is in the old association of a goat with Pan, who is regarded as one aspect of Satan.

There is or was a goat superstition in old Prussia that had a counterpart in parts of Britain. The Prussians when sowing their winter corn, killed a goat, ate the flesh with superstitious ceremonial, and hanged the skin on a tall pole near an oak. There it remained until the harvest, when a great bunch of the corn was fastened to the pole above the skin. Dancing then took place and there was a feast.

The part that seems to have come to Britain was the latter belief that the corn spirit is a goat. The idea was that when the corn on one farm was cut, the goat fled to another where the corn was still standing.

In the Island of Skye the farmer who had first finished reaping sent to another farm where reaping was still in progress a sheaf of wheat. The sheaf was known as the goabbir bhacagh, translated the cripple goat. In like manner the sheaf was passed on from farmer to farmer until all the corn had been cut.

Then followed the harvest supper for the men. It was still carried out in some parts, by the way, as late as 1930.

Crofters in Scotland also celebrated the harvest this way; but in their case the sheaf was known as the lame goat. The lame and crippled description seems to have been due to a belief that the goat spirit of the corn was crippled at the first cutting of the first crop in the district.

In England, the sheaf was treated in the same way, but not as a spirit of the corn, but as an emblem of pleasant rivalry. It was known as the baby. "Left holding the baby" comes from this.

In parts of Wales black goats have from time immemorial been regarded as keepers of treasure and as being on good terms with both the devil and the fairies. Hence the belief that to meet a black goat on a lonely bridle path was to know that somewhere near there was hidden treasure.

Goats have been little used in Britain in the making of magic. Elsewhere, they are better known in this connection. In India, and particularly in Saga, the goat was a scapegoat to bear away the disease which may have attacked a town.

The animal was gathered and garlanded, and then driven from the town boundaries. As it went the disease went with it. But should the goat return, then the disease came back to the town. However, the animal was generally despatched before it had a chance to get back with its burden of sickness.

This method of transferring illness by means of a goat was prevalent in many parts of the world, including the lands of some of the native tribes of America.

GODPARENTS

If an engaged couple have undertaken to be godparents to a child, it is unlucky for both to stand at the font together; it presages a parting within three months.

In one case, recorded by Wright in *Rustic Speech and Lore*, the problem was solved after much argument in a church by the godmother taking her place and making her vows in a pew a little distance away from the remainder of the christening party.

In pre-Reformation days godparents were not allowed by church law to marry each other.

GOITRE

To cure the goitre (a large swelling in the neck) form the Sign of the Cross on the neck with the hand of a corpse.—Surrey.

Go before sunrise on the first day of May to the grave of the last young man buried in a churchyard, and apply the dew collected by passing a hand three times from the head to the foot of the grave to the part affected.—Cornwall and Plymouth.

The superstition was prevalent especially in the nineteenth century in the neighbourhood of Launceston.

The Times of 9th May, 1855, reported from the city of Plymouth, the following: At an early hour on the morning of 1st May, a woman respectably attired, and accompanied by an elderly gentleman, applied for admittance to the cemetery at Plymouth. On being allowed to enter they proceeded to the grave of the last man interred; and the woman, who had a large wen in her throat, rubbed her neck three times each way on each side of the grave, departing before sunrise. By this process it was hoped that her malady would be cured."

A Sussex cure for the goitre, or any swelling of the neck, was to catch a common snake, hold it by its head and tail, and draw it slowly nine times (three times three) across the front of the neck of the person affected. After every third time, the snake was allowed to crawl a short distance, and at the end of the "charm" it was put alive into a bottle, which was then corked and buried in the ground. The belief was that as the snake decayed, the swelling of the neck would also decay.

GOLD

To cure a stye in the eye, rub the part affected nine times with a golden wedding ring, or any other piece of gold. —General.

Beaumont and Fletcher refer to this superstition in several of their early English comedies.

The present name of "Golden Ointment" for eye troubles undoubtedly is borrowed from the superstition which not only had a great vogue as recently as the late nineteenth century, but is still believed in in many rural areas to-day.

In some parts of the country, notably Lincolnshire, it was held that the wedding ring cure for a stye in the eye only worked with the wedding ring of one's mother. Elsewhere there was no such condition.

We might perhaps recall the superstition that if you go to the spot where the rainbow ends, you will find in the ground at that spot a bag of gold.

GOLDEN BROOM (FLOWER)

If you wave a spray of golden broom over a sleepless person, he will at once sleep peacefully.—Wales.

GOLF

To take the paper off a new ball before reaching the first tee means that you will have a bad round.

If you change your club for a shot after taking one from the bag, you will muff the stroke.

It is unlucky to start a game at 1 p.m.

Since there are at least two, and sometimes three or four in a match, the ill-luck would seem to level itself out after a start at 1 p.m.—the thirteenth hour.

The origin, and the holding of these superstitions in golf is, the authors think, purely a matter of psychology. In golf, perhaps more than any other game, to start out with the thought that because you have taken the paper off your ball before the first tee you will have a bad round, is almost certain to affect one's nerves and confidence. Once confidence has gone in golf the game goes.

One of the great golfers who held strongly to the belief that it was unlucky to change your club was Tom Morris and another Alexander, the Littlestone professional; and Ivo Bligh, who became Earl of Darnley, held strongly to the superstition that bad luck would attend him on the round at the start of which he had taken the paper off his ball before actually ready to start from the tee.

GOOD FRIDAY

A hot cross bun preserved from one Good Friday to another will prevent the whooping cough.—Lancashire.

A loaf baked on Good Friday will never go mouldy.—Suffolk.

To eat of a loaf baked on Good Friday will cure all illness.—General.

If parsley seed be sown on any day other than Good Friday, it will not come up double.—Suffolk.

To remove bees on any other day than Good Friday will certainly ensure their deaths.—Cornwall.

Rings hallowed on Good Friday will, if worn, prevent illness.—General.

Clothes washed and hung out to dry on Good Friday will be spotted with blood.—Cleveland and Yorkshire generally.

No blacksmith in Durham would in olden days drive a nail on this day—a remembrance of the purpose to which hammer and nails were used on the first Good Friday.

Iron should on no account be put into the ground on Good Friday, or disaster will overtake the user.—The Highlands.

If you endure thirst on Good Friday, whatever you drink during the rest of the year will not hurt you.—Wales.

The effect in the Scottish Highlands of the belief that no iron should touch the ground was that no grave was dug, and no fields were ploughed on that day; nor were any repairs involving iron carried out on any house or establishment.

It existed throughout some of the northern counties of England, too, especially in the North Riding of Yorkshire where the greatest concern was taken not to disturb the earth in any way on that sacred day. To emphasise the disastrous effect of digging on the day to any of the younger generation who were inclined to run wild, the example of Charlie Marston was quoted. He shocked his neighbours by planting out a plot of land with potatoes—and not one came up!

On the other hand no such superstition ruled in the south. In Devonshire Good Friday was accounted a very handy day on which to plant crops, particularly beans and peas which, it was maintained, would sure to come up "goody." It was also held to be an auspicious day for grafting trees.

Back in Yorkshire again, the people of Tenby at one time were so concerned that no iron should penetrate the earth that they were wont to go barefoot to church, lest the iron nails in their boots should leave a mark on the soil. The custom was kept up till the close of the eighteenth century.

All traces of this ancient iron superstition have now vanished, for Good Friday is perhaps the most popular and recognized day in England to start work in the garden for the summer harvest.

A word or two on the Good Friday loaves and cakes may not be out of place. During Easter week of 1946 the authors received considerable correspondence from many parts of the country, stating that the writers possessed bread, or buns, baked on Good Friday which had kept unmouldy for years. One such correspondent said that her grandmother had baked it twenty-five years before. Why the bun had been kept was not mentioned except by a single writer who had some vague idea that it would bring good luck—or at least bad luck if she threw it away.

Brighton fishwives had a superstition that buns baked on Good Friday would keep their men from shipwreck. Many buns were baked and the husbands had to take one on their fishing trips so long as the supply lasted.

The legend behind the superstition that clothes should not be washed on Good Friday was anciently told as follows: While Jesus was being led to Calvary they took him past a woman who was washing and the woman waved a garment in his face. On which Jesus said, "Cursed be everyone who hereafter shall wash on this day."

The hallowing of rings on Good Friday was a custom of the kings of England. It took its rise from a ring long preserved in Westminster Abbey which was reported to have been given to Edward the Confessor by some returned pilgrims from Jerusalem. The rings consecrated were, as stated above, believed to prevent illness.

Good Friday was accounted as the best of all days on which to begin weaning a baby. All babies the weaning of whom began on this day were bound to prosper in health.

There is a Good Friday superstition which exists only in Devonshire, so far as the authors have been able to trace in this country. It holds that if you break pottery on the sacred Good Friday, every shred of the broken pieces will pierce the body of Judas Iscariot.

Finally, a curious superstition still maintained in an East End public-house of London. There is a clause in the lease of this house which entails upon the holder that he must bake a hot cross bun on Good Friday and add it to a collection of buns kept in the house in a basket.

The story goes that a former licensee, a widow, put a hot cross bun away each Good Friday for her son, a sailor. One year he did not return. After her death her successors kept up the custom of getting a sailor to put a bun in the basket on Good Friday, for which he received free beer and a bun for himself. In 1947 the 178th bun was put away.

Incidentally, it says something for the superstition that buns baked on Good Friday never go mouldy, that the buns in this basket are still in a good state of preservation.

GOOSE

If you eat goose on Michaelmas Day, you will never want money all the year round.—General.

The shearing of the last portion of grain on the farm is called "cutting the gander's neck," and betokens plenty.—Shropshire.

If geese wander away from their homes, it is an omen of fire at the farm.—Wales.

When all the corn was gathered into the stackyard in Yorkshire an entertainment and feast was given the farmhands called "The Inning Goose." During the reign of Henry IV the French subjects of the English king called the harvest festival the "Harvest Gosling." The Danes had also a goose for supper after harvest.

The origin no doubt lies in the belief of the early Egyptians that Ra, the Sun god, was hatched from an egg which rose from the primordial deep.

Another Welsh superstition holds that should a goose lay one soft egg and one hard egg or two eggs in one day misfortune will overtake the family.

GOOSEBERRY

Prick a wart with a gooseberry thorn passed through a golden wedding ring, and the wart will disappear.

See WARTS.

GORSE

To bring the blooms of gorse, whin or broom into the house is to invite the death of a member of the family.—General.

The same is said of the white lilac, and the hawthorn, with the exception that the latter brings not death but just bad luck.

This branding of gorse as unlucky is not sustained in the Isle of Man, where on May morning it was general practice to set the gorse, or ling, on fire for the sake of burning out the witches who were wont to take the shape of hares and lie in among the gorse.

It has always been a matter of speculation to the authors why witches, who knew all that was working against them, should not have taken some other form on May Day rather than risk burning in the time-honoured and popular shape of a hare.

GOUT

To cure the gout, you should catch

*a spider, remove its legs and apply it
to the foot wrapped in deer skin.*

*If you would be free of the gout, pare
the nails and clip some hairs off the
stricken leg. Bore a hole in an oak tree,
stuff the hair and nails in the hole and
smear it with cow dung. If for three
months afterwards the gout has not
returned you may be sure that the tree
has it in your stead.*

This is, of course, still another example
of the belief in the transference of evil.
In many parts of Europe, but especially
in Germany, there existed a strong belief
that gout, which Topsel called "the
knotty whip of God," could be transferred to trees, and was shown to have
been thus transferred by the knots which
appeared on the stem and branches!

In Sonnenburg, a fir tree was chosen
as the victim. The sufferer went to the
tree and tied a knot in one of its twigs,
saying: "God greet thee, noble fir. I
bring thee my gout. Here I will tie a
knot and bind my gout into it. In the
name of the Father, etc."

Not far from Marburg there is a wood
of birches. Frazer records that thither on
a morning before sunrise, in the last
quarter of the moon, a procession of
gouty hobblers each took a stand before
a separate tree and intoned: "Here I
stand before the Judgment Bar of God
and tie up all my gout. All the disease
in my body shall remain tied up in this
tree."

GO WITH THE SUN

The dead must go with the sun.—
North of England.

By "with the sun" it was meant that
the body must be carried to the church
for the funeral service with the sun
behind it, even though it meant making
a detour from the nearest and straight
route. The ritual was especially held in
Durham.

The authors have cognizance of a
clergyman newly arrived in the Hartlepool district who was awaiting at the
lych-gate the arrival of the body he was
to bury. He was astounded when the
cortege, having arrived within a few
yards of him, suddenly wheeled and
made a complete circuit of the churchyard, traversing its west, north and east
boundaries. He inquired of the sexton,
standing beside him, the reason for the
peculiar proceeding; and received the
reply: "Why, ye wad no hae them carry
the dead agen the sun, wad ye? The
dead maun aye go wi' the sun."

Something of the same meaning is

practised in the Highlands of Scotland
under the name of "Making the Deazil."
It consists of walking round a person
three times according to the course of
the sun. In the fastnesses of the lonely
Highlands, the authors are informed,
the "Deazil" is still performed to those
whom the walkers wish well.

On the other hand, to walk round a
person in the opposite direction is to
bring the person ill-fortune.

The origin lies, probably, in the spells
of ancient witchcraft. Earliest references
to it in print appear in the old Icelandic
Vatnsdœla Saga, which describes how
a woman by walking against the sun
round a house and waving a cloth
brought down a landslide against the
house. The date is given as about A.D.
900.

A fuller description appears in
Thorfinn's *Karlefris*: "The hag did not
lie down to sleep that night, she was so
restless. The weather was cold without
a keen frost, and the sky clear. She went
several times against the sun round the
house, her face set in all directions, and
turned her nose up. And as she thus
went about, the weather began to
change. There arose a dense fog, and
after that an icy blast; and an avalanche
broke off the mountainside and the snow
shot down on the farm of Berf, and
twelve men died in it.

See DEATH WITH THE TIDE.

GRAHAM

The writers received on 19th January,
1945, the following letter from Fenham,
Newcastle-on-Tyne:

"A few years ago my father, mother
and I went to stay in a small fishing
village in Northumberland for a
holiday. We stayed at the house of a
fisherman and his wife. When they
heard our name was Graham they
were in a dreadful state. Apparently,
the name brings bad luck to the fishermen in this particular village and we
were told that if our name was mentioned in the house it would be useless
for their menfolk to go fishing as they
would have no catch. They insisted on
calling us Mr., Mrs., and Miss Puff.
Silly, isn't it, but it's true."

We have been unable to find the name
Graham as a harbinger of ill-luck anywhere else.

See NAMES.

GRAVE, GRAVEYARD

*If every string is not untied or cut in
the shroud before a body is committed*

to the grave, the spirit of the dead will not rest.—Highlands of Scotland.

Graves on the south side of the church are the holiest.—North of England.

The dead will be lucky that has had a stillborn child put into its grave when it was open. It is a sure passport to Heaven.—Old belief in Devonport area.

The body in the first grave to be dug in any churchyard or cemetery is claimed by the Devil.—General.

It is unlucky to dig or plough any land in which a body has been buried.—General.

The belief in the Devil's claim to the first body was at one time so firmly believed that it was only with the utmost difficulty that new resting places for the dead could be opened up.

Henderson in his *Folk Lore of the Northern Counties* relates how in one parish not one parishioner would allow the body of a loved one to be buried in a new churchyard. When things began to look serious a tramp chanced to be found dead on the borders of the parish. He was buried in the new churchyard, and thereafter no objection was raised by the parishioners to their dead being buried there.

The same thing happened at Bovey Tracey, Devonshire, where, for a long time, the parishioners of St. John's Church would not use the church burial ground. Not till the burial there of a servant of a visitor to the town was the Devil's spell regarded as broken.

In Germany it was the custom to bury a dog or a pig in the churchyard as an offering to the Devil.

The superstition that the south side of the church is the holiest and most consecrated ground for a grave is due to the belief that the south wind brings corruption—a very old belief prevalent in many countries of Europe. The north side of churchyards in olden days was regarded as really unhallowed ground, fit only for the burial of still-born infants and suicides.

The visitor to the hundreds of old churches in this country can with interest satisfy himself of the extent of this superstition by noting the age of the graves on the north side of the church. He will find that the south side contains most of the stones recording dates of two or three hundred years ago; the north side will hallow those of more modern years, when the superstition had died out.

Graves, it will be noticed, are in churchyards dug east to west.

In many parts of the country there existed—and it still exists to-day—a belief that to plough or dig an old burial ground will result in the death of the eldest son of the family doing the ploughing.

As recently as 1925 a field in Pradannach, Cornwall, had never been ploughed because of this superstition. The field had once been a burying ground.

In the town of Wisbech, in Cambridgeshire, there is to this day a rood of land that must on no account be "dug, delved or ploughed." It is a piece of ground at the corner of Quaker Lane and Silk Lane, part of a plot rented in 1946 by a Mr. Charles Beakley. Quakers were buried there many years ago and the deeds ensure that it must remain sacred.

See CHURCHES, CORPSE, DEATH.

GREEN

For a bride to include the colour green in her wedding ensemble will bring her bad luck.—General.

The green bough of a tree, fastened on May Day against the wall of a house, will produce plenty of milk in the summer.—Irish farm belief.

For any green (a dress, etc.) to be worn on the stage will be unlucky for the play and the actors.

The colour green is so allied throughout Europe with luck and protection from the tree spirits, that it is at first thoughts passing strange to find it regarded at all as an unlucky colour.

Branches of rowan, for instance, put over a house door on May Day, or All Hallows Eve, were an accepted protection from witches and the Evil Eye. The beneficent oak tree was another instance of the goodwill of green in the form of protection by the tree spirits.

The ill-luck of a bride's choice of green, however, originated in the Little People. Green is the proverbial colour of the fairies, elves, and pixies, and was held to give them power over anyone who wore green. Thus, a bride in green, it was anciently believed, was liable to be carried off by them to their underground abode. The fairies would resent their colour being appropriated by a human.

The Rev. S. Baring-Gould, that distinguished authority on folk-lore, wrote that, apropos the ill-luck of green, he once heard a cultured man in Yorkshire explain quite seriously that the disturbed conditions in England (prior to 1914), including strike, labour unrest and Suffragist outrages, were all due to the introduction of GREEN halfpenny stamps.

GREEN CHRISTMAS

A green Yule makes a fat churchyard. —General.

There is, of course, a certain amount of possible truth in the churchyard superstition, since it is generally followed by a hard and cold early spring, the unpreparedness for which is too much for many old people.

GREYHOUND

A greyhound with a white spot on its forehead will bring luck to the people of Gower.—Wales.

Why only to the people of one particular place, the authors have been unable to ascertain. But they hope that the good people of Gower will not take this as a greyhound racing "tip" and start backing any greyhound with a white-spotted forehead.

GROANING CHEESE (OR CAKE)

To ensure that a newly born baby shall be lucky in life, it should be passed through the groaning cheese.— Oxfordshire.

The maiden who takes a piece of groaning cheese, places it in the foot of her left stocking and throws it over the right shoulder, afterwards retiring to bed backwards without speaking, will see her future husband in her dreams.—Lancashire.

Some explanation of these odd beliefs is necessary. It was customary, as late as 1900, in various parts of the country, to make a large cake (sometimes a cheese) against the birth of a child, and to cut the cake for the company which gathered for the child's christening. This cake was known as the "Groaning Cake." Why groaning, the authors have never been able to discover.

In Oxon it was the custom to cut this cake from the middle and by degrees form it into a large kind of ring through which the baby was passed after its christening, for the reason stated above.

In Lancashire and Yorkshire the cake was then distributed to the unmarried women present, as described above. It was regarded as necessary that the groaning cake should be cut by the doctor who had brought the child into the world.

GUESTS

A bedroom should never be swept and garnished until the guest has been an hour on his (or her) journey.

The origin possibly lies in the possibility that the guest might return unexpectedly, travel being an uncertain undertaking in the days when the saying was an *obiter dictum.*

GULL

To kill a seagull is unlucky, for gulls are the souls of the dead.—Sutherland.

Three seagulls flying overhead together are a death warning.—Seamen's belief.

Sir Charles Igglesden records in *Those Superstitions* a remarkable instance of the belief on the three seagulls.

As a ship was to leave Gibraltar, the ship's doctor approached Sir Charles. "These natives are the limit," he said. "I've got a native who is going to die for no apparent reason whatever." He then explained that the man had seen three seagulls flying close together overhead and had taken it as a death warning. He had gone straight to a cabin and said he would be dead by noon next day.

"And he *will* die," said the doctor. "I have had similar cases. I've examined him and there is nothing wrong with him. But he will die. Come and look at him."

"There he was," writes Sir Charles, "his eyes rolling and his face the ghastly hue that only a coloured shows when he is ill. We left him and as we passed along the alley way the tapping of a hammer could be heard. 'His pals are making the coffin out of an orange box,' explained the doctor. 'He will be ready for them.' At noon the next day the orange box with the Afghan stoker inside was thrown over the side of the ship."

GUNFIRE

Fire a gun over a body supposed to be lying at the bottom of the sea or a river, and the body will come to the surface. —General.

It was held that the concussion from the explosion of the discharge would break the gall bladder of the body, which would then, of course, float, and could be recovered.

HADDOCK

The two black marks behind the head of the haddock are the marks of a thumb and finger of St. Peter.—General.

The legend is that the haddock is the fish which furnished St. Peter with the tribute money mentioned in the Bible.

The claim is disputed in some circles; the fish supplying the tribute being, it is said, actually the dory. Some weight can be attached to this, since the haddock does not inhabit inland seas.

The Yorkshire town of Filey, however, dismisses both the above legends. Filey fishermen have an altogether different story. They claim that the Evil Spirit determined to build Filey Bridge for the destruction of ships and sailors and the annoyance of fishermen. In the progress of the work, he accidentally let his hammer fall into the sea, and being in a hurry to get it back caught a haddock instead, and thereby made the marks retained by the fish to this day.

In view of the popularity of the haddock as a fish diet to-day, it is interesting to note that a comparatively short time ago it was regarded as a sacred fish not to be eaten under threat of dire calamity.

The story of the change, and the collapse of this long-held sea lore is interesting. The popular smoked haddock is known as a Finnon haddock; and it was an old Scotsman named Finnon who discovered the special way of smoking the fish and made the haddock a popular dish.

HAIR

If birds find your hair cuttings and build nests with them, you will have an eruption of the head.—Sussex.

If cut hair is allowed to blow away with the wind and it passes over an empty nest, or a bird takes it to its nest, the head from which it came will ache. —Scottish Highlands.

If a magpie should use your hair cuttings in its nest, you will die within a year and a day.

No sister should cut her hair at night if she has a brother at sea.—Scottish Highlands.

Hair should only be cut while the moon is on the increase.—General.

Clip hairs from a sufferer with epilepsy, pare his nails and bury both with a black cock at the spot where the epileptic fell down, and the patient will be cured.—General, and the Highlands.

Clip hairs from the legs of a sufferer with the gout, and with the parings of his nails put them in a hole bored in an oak tree. Stop up the hole and smear it with cow dung. If for three months the patient is free of the gout, the oak tree will have had it in his stead.—General.

If a person's hair burns brightly when thrown into the fire, it is a sign of long life. The brighter the flame the longer the life.—Durham.

If hair smoulders and refuses to burn in the fire, it is a sign of approaching death.—Durham.

If hair grows down on the forehead, and retreats up the head above the temples, it is a sign of long life.—Devon.

People with much hair on their arms and hands will at some future time gain wealth. They are "born to be rich."— Midlands.

Hairy chests are a sign of strength.— General.

To cure the ague, cut a few hairs from the cross marked on a donkey's back. Enclose these hairs in a small bag, and wear it on your breast next to the skin. If you keep your purpose secret, a speedy cure will result.

NOTE: The cross on the ass's back is said to have been placed there by Jesus after his ride into Jerusalem.

A hair from the dog that bit him is a much used cliche. It may not be generally known that this, too, is born of superstition.

In *Notes and Queries*, volume v, page 581, appeared the following letter from Salop:

"A few days ago I observed my old servant thrusting something in the ears of one of my cows. Upon inquiry I was informed that it was hair cut off a calf's tail, the said calf having been taken away from the mother the previous morning. The butcher had been asked to cut off the hairs 'to make the cow forget her calf.' I half resolved to send this account to *Notes and Queries*, but hesitated under the idea that it would hardly be worth while. But this afternoon my eye caught the following scrap in a newspaper just published, 'At Oldham last week, a woman summoned the owner of a dog that had bitten her. She said she would not have adopted this course had the owner of the animal given her some of its hair, to ensure her against evil consequences following the bite.'"

Outside Berkhamsted, in Hertfordshire, there stood on a spot where two roads crossed each other, a few oak trees called Cross Oaks. Here persons suffering from ague used to resort to be cured. A lock of the hair of each of them was pegged into a tree, and then the sufferer, by a sudden wrench, transferred the lock to the tree. In this way, they were assured that they had transferred the ague to the tree.

But perhaps the most extraordinary superstition attached to hair—if not the most remarkable of all British superstitions—was that of a number of old women in Drumconrath, Ireland. Believing that the Scriptures were definitely truthful when they state that the hairs of our heads are numbered, they stored all the cuttings of their hair, and all the combings, and stored them in the thatch of their cottage, in the belief that they would be called upon to account for them on the Day of Judgment.

Now journey backwards for a few moments to the ancient Incas of Peru. They took the greatest care to preserve their nail parings and hair clippings, placing them with solicitude in niches in a wall. Garcilasso de la Vega wrote that in answer to his inquiries for the reason for this practice, the Indians said: "Know that all persons who are born must return to life, and their souls must rise out of their tombs with all that had belonged to their bodies. We, therefore, in order that we may not have to search for our hair and nails at a time when there will be much hurry and confusion, place them in one place."

The old ladies in Drumconrath, albeit unknowingly, were in good company.

In point of fact the custom, too, is followed by Armenians, Esthonian peasants, and the Arabs of Moab.

Still another superstition widely held in the sixteenth and seventeenth centuries was to bury secretly hair cuttings and nail clippings. It was held that should they come into the hands of a witch, she could with the aid of them bring harm to their late owner.

For instance, the hair put on a wax image of the person could be used by the witch's plucking of them out of the image, to cause head pains to the original owner. In this connection it is interesting to note that in the days of ancient Egypt, a drop of a man's blood, the clippings of his hair and the parings of his nails sufficed to give a sorcerer complete power over him.

Apropos the taking of hair by birds to their nests, and the direful fate of the hair's owner: not only was this a prevalent belief here and in other parts of Europe, but also with the Todas of South India. They hid, and still hide, their hair clippings in bushes and hollows in the rocks in order that the hair may not be found by crows, and taken to nests. Thus, once again, we find

a British superstition practised at the same time by native tribes without any connection or intercourse.

The suggestion that hair should be cut while the moon is on the increase is due to the belief that hair, nails and corn crops grow fast on the moon's increase, but will be menaced by sowing during the moon's decrease. Hair cut on the moon's decrease is legendly likely to fade away and vanish. The Highlanders of Scotland used to expect better crops by sowing the seed during the moon's waxing.

In Cornwall it was held that red-haired people can never make good butter. The butter always has a slight tang about it.

In ancient Scotland "shaking the hair loose" was regarded as a superstitious act to render a person ill, or to extend the illness. It was supposed to be the act of a witch casting a spell. Thus it became ominous to meet a woman with her head uncovered.

There is a record of one Bessie Skebister thus acting towards Margaret Mudie, whose cow had trespassed among her corn. Margaret complained that Bessie had "sat down and taking off her curtch, sheuk your hair lous and ever since I have bein so vehementlie pained, and have nevir beil weill since ye curst me." The account of the trial (on 21st March, 1633) says that the jury convicted the delinquent of "taking of hir curtch, shaking of hir hair (lous) and Margaret Mudie's diseas."

HALLOWE'EN

All souls in Purgatory are released for forty-eight hours from All Hallows Eve. On these nights they are free.—Gaelic.

On Hallowe'en, the wind, blowing over the feet of the corpses, bears sighs to the houses of those about to die within the year.—Wales.

If you go to a crossroads at Hallowe'en and listen to the wind, you will learn all the most important things that will befall you during the next twelve months.—Wales.

Take a three-legged footstool and sit at a crossroads while the church clock is striking twelve on Hallowe'en. You will hear proclaimed aloud the names of the church parishioners doomed to die within the next twelve months.—Highlands of Scotland.

NOTE: It was regarded as in the power of the watcher to save the destined victims by taking with him articles of apparel, and throwing them away one by one as each name was called out by the mysterious voice.

To ensure fertility of crops during the coming year, make a circuit of fields with lighted torches on Hallowe'en.—Braemar.

A maiden who washed her chemise and without saying anything about it hangs it over a chair to dry will, if she lies awake long enough, see the form of her future spouse enter the room and turn the chemise.—Border counties.

Let a maiden take a willow branch in her right hand, and without being observed slip out of the house and run three times round it, saying, "He that is to be my gude man come and grip." During the third run the likeness of her future husband will appear and grasp the other end of the stick.—Scotland.

On Hallowe'en force all the sheep and lambs to pass through a hoop of rowan tree to ward off witches and fairies.—Strathspey.

A Border story is told apropos the washing of the chemise superstition quoted above. It tells that a girl tried out the formula and saw a coffin behind her chemise on the chair. Terrified, she woke her family and related the circumstance. Next morning she learned of her lover's death.

Another Scottish superstition of Hallowe'en demands that a maid shall take three pails of water and stand them in her bedroom. Then pin to her nightdress, opposite the heart, three leaves of green holly and go to sleep. She will be aroused from her deep sleep by three yells, as if from the throats of three bears. As these sounds die away they will be succeeded by many hoarse laughs, after which the form of her future husband will appear. If he is deeply attached to her he will change the position of the pails. If he is not, he will pass from the room without touching them.

There are, in addition, many minor superstitions performed during the course of the Hallowe'en Fires, which are more games and customs than accredited superstitions. They, however, were practised throughout Europe in identical form. Bobbing apples in a bowl of water, the heating of stones in a fire, dropping the white of eggs into a bowl of water to ascertain how many children each member of the company would have in the future, were some of them.

The Hallowe'en Fires, together with Beltane Fires, were the great fire festivals of Europe.

To know the name of their future husbands, Ayrshire girls went to the kailyard of a neighbour and stole the first kail that came to hand. This, taken home and examined, told by its height, shape and features what would be the height, shape and features of the husband to be. The taste of the heart of the stem was an indication of his temper and the clod of earth adhering to the root was an indication of the amount of money he would bring to the common stock. If the superstition was practised by a bachelor the same characteristics would apply to his future wife.

In the north-east of Scotland, girls sowed hemp seed over nine ridges of ploughed land saying, "I sow hemp seed and he who is to be my husband, let him come and harrow it." On looking back over her left shoulder, she would see the figure of her future partner in the darkness behind her. There were other ways, but they are too numerous to be enumerated.

In the Orkneys a young girl takes a clew of worsted at midnight and mounts the kiln which is attached to every farm. There she calls out: "Wha holds on to ma clew's end?" Her future husband will, she believes, be the answer.

Ireland has its own superstitions for Hallowe'en. One insisted that should you hear footsteps following you, you must not look round, for it is the dead who are following, and should you meet their glance, you would die.

Another held that a man who on this night crawls under the large trailing branches of the blackberry bush will see the shadow of the girl he is to marry.

A third maintained that a gambler who hides under the tendrils of the blackberry bush and invokes the aid of the Prince of Darkness would always have good luck at cards.

It should be mentioned that all these Irish superstitions of Hallowe'en to be successful had to be accompanied by an appeal to the Evil One in "words too diabolical to repeat," according to an old Irish book. In this the Irish superstitions differ from those in England and Scotland, for Ireland holds, or rather held, that Hallowe'en is an evil night.

HALTER
A halter with which anyone has been hanged if bound round the forehead will cure headache.
See **HEAD, HEADACHE.**

HAND

Rub your warts with a dead man's hand; they will soon disappear.—General.

A moist hand is the sign of an amorous disposition.—General.

If the palms of a baby's hands are washed before it is a year old, the child will never have money.—Devon.

If two people wash their hands together in the same bowl, they will quarrel before nightfall.—General.

NOTE: Fortunately, there are two antidotes. If one of them makes the sign of the cross, or spits into the water, the ill-luck is prevented.

To cure the goitre, form the sign of the cross on the neck with the hand of a corpse.

Go before sunrise on the morning of the first of May to the grave of the last young man to be buried in a churchyard, and pass a hand three times from head to foot of the grave. Apply the dew thus collected on the hand to the goitre, and it will be cured.—Cornwall and Devon.

Most people know, of course, and still use the expression, that an itching right palm of the hand means that you will shortly receive money; while the itch in the left palm is an intimation that you will shortly be paying out money.

The palm of the right hand of any income tax collector to-day, must be an affliction to him!

HAND OF GLORY

If a candle made of the fat of a malefactor who has also died on the scaffold is lighted and placed in the Hand of Glory as in a candlestick, it renders motionless all persons at whom it is presented, and they cannot stir a finger.

The Hand of Glory holding a lighted candle renders the holder of it invisible.

When the Hand of Glory is lighted with a candle, all in the house will fall into a deep sleep from which nothing can awake them until the candle is extinguished.

The Hand of Glory, so-called, was the hand of a man who had been hanged. It was prepared in the following manner:

Wrap the hand in a piece of winding sheet, drawing it tight so as to squeeze out the little blood that might remain. Then place it in an earthenware vessel with saltpetre, salt and long pepper, all carefully and thoroughly powdered. Let it remain a fortnight in this pickle till it is well dried then expose it to the sun in the dog-days till it is completely parched. If the sun be not powerful enough, dry it in an oven heated with vervain and fern. Next, make a candle with the fat of a hanged man, virgin wax and Lapland sesame. The Hand of Glory is used to hold this candle when it is lighted.

Numerous stories are told of the use of this hand by thieves enabling them to work either unseen or in the view of victims unable to prevent their depredations.

In the only one instance of which authenticity can be assured, however, the charm seems to have failed. On 3rd January, 1831, thieves attempted to rob the house of a Mr. Napier, Loughcrew, Co. Meath. They entered the house armed with the Hand of Glory and candle, believing, of course, that it would ensure the occupants sleeping. The inmates, however, were alarmed and the robbers fled, leaving the hand behind them.

A story is, however, told of an happening at Stainmore. According to this, one evening in 1790, a traveller dressed in woman's clothes arrived at the Old Spital Inn, where the mailcoach of that day changed horses, in High Spital, on Bowes Moor. The visitor asked that she might be allowed to stay all night, as she had to leave early in the morning. If a mouthful of food was spread on the table for breakfast, she said, the household, need not be disturbed by her leaving. The host, however, arranged that a housemaid should sit up all night till the stranger was off the premises.

The girl lay down for a nap on a settle by the fireside, but before she shut her eyes had a good look at the traveller. Espying a pair of man's trousers peeping from underneath the dress, she at once lost all desire for sleep, but feigned to be sleeping, and even began to snore.

On hearing this, she said afterwards, the traveller rose, pulled out of his pocket a man's hand, fitted to it a candle which he lighted. He passed hand and candle several times across the girl's face, saying: "Let those who are asleep be asleep."

This done, he placed the light on the table, opened the outer door and began to whistle for his companions. The girl now arose from the settle, ran up to the man and pushed him down the steps, then locking the door. She then tried to rouse the family but failed. In despair, for she heard the traveller and his companions trying to force the door, she ran into the dairy, picked up a bowl of milk and threw it over the hand and candle. After this she found no difficulty in waking the family.

Milk, thrown over the Hand of Glory, was held to be the only antidote to its charm.

HANDKERCHIEF

To give your lover a gift of handkerchiefs will cause a parting between you. You will never marry.—General.

This superstition was not only widespread, but exists to a great degree even at the present time.

A few months ago the authors' advice was sought by a correspondent who desired to know whether she should accept a gift of six handkerchiefs from her fiancé, as she was assured it was a sign of parting.

Whence started the superstition, or the reason for it, the authors have been totally unable to trace.

Incidentally, they for years before their marriage were in the habit of presenting each other with handkerchiefs on the occasions of birthdays. They had no parting of their friendship or courtship.

HANDSEL

Take the first money you receive for a purchase each day, kiss it, spit on it, and put it in a pocket by itself, that it may draw more money to it.—Market superstition.

Leman, the chronologer, explains: Handsel is the first money received at the market, which many superstitious people will spit on either to render it tenacious, that it may remain with them and not vanish away like a fairy gift or else to render it propitious and lucky.

It was originally tenaciously clung to by London's "butcher women"—those women who sold fowls, butter and eggs in the open markets.

Later, handsel money came to mean, also, that part of the purchase money for any article which was returned to the seller "for luck."

"Handsel money," given to children on various days of the year, and to babes at a christening, and also put into the pockets of a new suit when it is first worn, are customs and not properly superstitions.

HARE

If a hare runs along a road or a main-way, a house will catch fire during the day.—Northants.

It is unlucky to meet hare.—Lancs. and the North.

NOTE: Possibly not so unlucky if you chance to have a loaded gun.

Bad luck will attend a wedding if a hare crosses the path of a bride and groom—even at a distance.—The North.

Hares yearly change their sex.—Old belief (absurd, of course).

The hare is so timid that it never— even in sleep—closes its eyes.

The bone of a hare's foot, carried on the person, will prevent cramp.— General.

If a hare crosses your path, it is an ominous sign.—General.

NOTE: In Somerset it was regarded as a death omen.

Possibly the oldest and most widely held belief regarding hares was that they were the form most usually chosen by witches into which to transform themselves.

In his *Topography of Ireland* (chapter 19), completed in 1187, Cambrenis records that: "It has been a frequent complaint from old times as well as at the present, that certain hags in Wales, as well as in Scotland and Ireland, changed themselves into the shape of hares that, sucking teats of cattle under this counterfeit form, they may stealthily rob other people's milk."

Thus the Irish people on the morning of May Day killed all the hares they found among their cattle, supposing them to be old women who had designs on their butter.

In the Isle of Man, daybreak on May Day was the signal for the firing of the ling or gorse to burn out the witches supposed to have taken the form of hares. A similar course was taken in Ireland.

There is a story told by Mr. J. G. Campbell of a young man who, while shooting in the island of Lismore, near Balnagown Loch, saw a hare and fired at it. The animal gave an unearthly scream, and then for the first time it occurred to the sportsman that there were no real hares in Lismore.

He threw away his gun in terror and turned home. Next day he heard that a notorious witch was laid up with a broken leg.

This is, of course, a variation of the general superstition of that time, and of the time when witch-hunting was a popular British sport, that if you killed a hare, or wounded it in any part of its body, a witch would be found dead next day, or with a wound corresponding exactly to the wound inflicted in the hare. Many an old woman was hanged or burnt as a witch on this evidence.

Now take a momentary journey from Ireland, Lismore and England to the Aino people of West Africa. They believe that hares are bewitched people. Hare tracks, seen in the snow, are dug up, turned over and buried in the hope that the witch will be suffocated by the burying.

The hare was used in Britain in divination from the earliest times, and for that reason the Ancient Britons never killed it for the table.

Borlase, in his *Antiquities of Cornwall*, relates an example of this divination by Boadicea. "When she had harangued her soldiers to spirit them against the Romans, she opened her bosom and let go a hare, which she had there concealed, that the augurs might then proceed to divine. The frightened animal made such twistings and turnings in her course, that as according to the then rules of judging, prognosticated happy success. The joyful multitude made loud huzzas; Boadicea seized the opportunity, led them straight to their enemies, and gained a victory."

Cornish superstition held that when a maiden who had loved not wisely but too well, died forsaken, and broken-hearted, she came back to haunt her deceiver in the shape of a white hare. The vision was said to haunt the deceiver everywhere, but was invisible to all but him. This is one of the oldest of Cornish superstitions, and many stories are told of men said to have been driven to suicide by the sight of the white hare.

It was regarded by seamen, especially in Scotland, very unlucky to see a hare when going to a ship. If a hare was found on board a ship, the luck was even worse; the ship was regarded as witch-ridden. The *Scotsman* in the present century recorded a case of youths who placed a hare on a fisherman's boat and were hailed in front of the Sheriff for "conspiracy."

HARVEST BUG
It is most unlucky for a reaper to kill a harvest bug on purpose.—Essex.

The apparent reason for this is that the harvest bug, called the harvest-man, has three things on its back: the scythe, the rake, and the sickle.

HARVEST MOON
Brand, in his *Popular Antiquities*, gives this superstition which was extensively practised by girls at the time of the harvest moon:

"When you go to bed place under your pillow a prayerbook open at that part of the Matrimonial Service which says 'With this ring I thee wed'; place on it a key, ring, a flower and a sprig of willow, a small heart cake, a crust of bread and the following cards—ten of clubs, nine of hearts, ace of spades and the ace of diamonds. Wrap all these in a thin handkerchief of gauze or muslin, and on getting into bed cross your hands and say:

'Luna, every woman's friend,
To me thy goodness condescend;
Let me this night in visions see
Emblems of my destiny.'

"If you then dream of storms, trouble will betide you; if the storms end in a fine calm, so will your fate; if of a ring or the ace of diamonds, marriage; bread, an industrious life; cake, a prosperous life; flowers, joy; willow, treachery in love; spades, death; clubs, a foreign land; diamonds, money; keys, that you will rise to great trust and power; birds, that you will have many children; and geese, that you will marry more than once."

HAT
To put on one's hat the wrong way round is to invite all the bad luck there is going.—General.

Curiously enough, the people most prone to this superstition are those hard-headed business people known as "City men."

As an antidote, one may purchase at once a new hat to take the place of the misused article of headgear, provided that one ensures that the original hat is not used again on that day.

This is obviously a man's superstition; no woman nowadays could don her "hat" the wrong way round, supposing that she wore a hat at all!

HAWTHORN
To cut down a hawthorn tree is to risk great peril.—Irish.

Hawthorn boughs, fastened on May Day against the walls and windows of houses will produce plenty of milk that summer.—Irish farm superstition.

Branches of hawthorn fastened to doors and windows keep out witches.—General throughout Britain.

NOTE: A similar virtue was attributed to the hawthorn by the ancient Romans.

From earliest times great virtues have been attributed to the hawthorn in Britain, particularly in association with the superstitions of May Day.

Thus, on this day, Cornish folk from time immemorial, decked their doors with the green hawthorn. In the North of England young people rose early, went into the woods and returned with branches broken off the trees, with which they held revel. At Abingdon, Berkshire, the same procedure was followed.

In Suffolk there was an old custom, observed in most farmhouses, that any servant who could bring in a branch of hawthorn in blossom in time for breakfast was entitled to a dish of cream. In Cornwall, up to at least 1924, whoever brought to a dairy a piece of hawthorn in bloom long enough to surround the earthenware bowl in which cream was kept, was given a bowl of cream.

The tradition is part of the European survival of the worship of trees, and the belief in the power of the tree spirits. The pegging of illnesses in trees, before referred to, was another example of the cult.

With reference to the Irish tradition against cutting down a hawthorn tree, the story is told of two brothers named Bergin on a farm at Ballyroan who cut down all the hawthorns on their land. One of the brothers became "fairy stricken," and could not be cured.

At Garryglass a farmer who cut down a hawthorn tree lost all his cattle, his children died, his money went and he was evicted from his farm. Two generations of successors at the farm are said never to have prospered.

How far back in the ages this "charm" of the hawthorn goes, it is not possible accurately to say. But the Greeks believed that branches of buckthorn (rhamnus) fastened to doors or windows kept out witches, and a similar virtue was held to lie in the buckthorn and hawthorn by the ancient Romans.

In parts of Bosnia, when peasant women pay a visit to a house which death has visited, they place first a little hawthorn behind their headcloth, and on returning from the house of death throw it away in the street before entering their own homes. This is deemed to be necessary lest the dead turn into a vampire. In such a case he would be so busy picking up the hawthorn that he would not be able to follow them into their home.

HAYCART

To meet a load of hay in an English country lane will bring you bad luck.

However, you can avert the ill-fortune by spitting at it as it passes; and if you remember to wish as you spit, the wish will come true.

Curiously enough, in Wales the appearance of a load of hay in front of you, means that good luck will attend you throughout the day.

HAYSTACKS

One of the most common forms of fires on a farm is internal combustion in hay stacks.

This can be averted, superstitiously, by placing a scythe crossways on top of the rick, and leaving it there until it shows signs of rust.

The paternal families of the authors made sure that stacks were properly pitched and laid at the time, and also properly thatched. They thus averted internal combustion, and saved a good scythe at the same time!

HAZEL

If you make a cap of hazel leaves and twigs, and wear it, it is possible to obtain any wish.—Wales.

In other parts of the country much the same power is held to be placed in a cap of juniper sprigs and berries. These caps were known by the old Welsh people as "Wishing Caps."

If the captain of a ship wore such a cap it was believed that the ship would weather any storm. Fortunately for his authority, the captain could wear the confection under his sailor's cap.

In Ireland, too, the power of the hazel was a rife superstition. After the Midsummer Fires were nearly burnt out, the ashes were trampled down, and the cattle driven through the smouldering fragments, their backs singed with lighted rods of hazel. The rods were afterwards safely kept, for they were regarded as possessing immense power to drive the cattle to and from watering places.

The wood figured in a curious Prussian belief—that if you cannot catch a thief who has robbed you, the next best thing to do is to get hold of a garment that he had worn and dropped, and beat it with a stick. If you did so, the thief would fall sick. But the stick had to be of hazel wood in order to take effect.

HEAD, HEADACHE

The slough (or cast skin of a snake) bound round the forehead or temple will cure all pains in the head.—Cambridgeshire.

A halter with which a man has been hanged, if tied about the head will cure the headache.—General.

Grasp tightly in the hand some scraped horse-radish; your headache will go.

Moss growing upon a human skull, if dried and powdered and taken as snuff, will cure the headache.

The good people of Sunderland had their own superstition for a bad head, including a severe cold. The patient's head was shaved and the hair hung on a bush. When the birds carried the hair to their nests, they carried the cough or cold with them.

The authors can only comment that it seemed a dreary wait for the patient if he, or she, contracted the cold about the end of November! Anyway, this superstition is at direct variance with the usual run of superstition about hair.

In one or two parts of the country traces existed of the use of the superstition of "nailing the headache." This consisted in taking a lock of the patient's hair, and nailing it to an aspen or ash tree. By this means the headache was transferred to the tree.

The practice was more common in Germany and in Islay; and the Egyptians, afflicted with headache, knocked a nail into the great wooden door of the old south gate of Cairo.

In Germany the same transference of evil was done, but not by nailing. Instead, some of the sufferer's hair clippings and nail parings were wrapped in paper, and the parcel stuffed into a hole made in the trunk of a tree. The hole was then plugged up with a spit of wood taken from a tree that had been struck by lightning. This was to prevent the headache getting out of the hole and back into the sufferer's head.

There was at one time an old man who made a good livelihood by sitting near Trinity College Chapel, Cambridge, with a collection of snakes, and selling cast skins (slough), which, he said, wrapped round the head would cure all head pains.

See HAIR.

HEARTBURN

Letter to the authors by a "Bevin Boy"—that is a youth who, called to national service in Britain during the 1939-45 war, was directed to work in the pits:

"Can you tell me whether it is right that a cure for the heartburn is to suck a piece of coal, as some of the miners here say it is? Is there any truth in it?"

The letter was written from the miners' hostel at Ferryhill, Co. Durham.

The only truth in it is that it was a Co. Durham superstition for many years —and appears still to be one.

HEARTH

To let the fire on the hearth go out, is to court ill-luck.—Highlands and Gaelic.

If a woman's apron is burned above the knee by a spark or red-hot cinder flying out of the fire on to the hearth, she will have a child.—General.

Thus the superstition of the birth of the old Roman kings holds ground even in England to-day. There is little doubt that the old English custom of leading a bride formally to the hearth of her new home was the outcome of the same superstition—a hope that she would be made fruitful by the virtue ascribed to the fire.

It may be of interest to note, in passing, that in the Slav countries when a woman wished to have a child, she held a vessel full of water in front of the fire, while her husband knocked burning brands together so that sparks flew from them. When some of the sparks had fallen in the water the woman drank the water which was regarded as having been fertilized by the fire.

With reference to the fire ever burning on the hearth, the Gaelic people never allowed their fire to go out. At night it was raked together and a coal or two was covered by the embers so that it might be alive in the morning. In Co. Cork, the action was accompanied by the reciting of the following lines: "I save this fire as Christ saves Mary, at the two ends of the house and Brigit in the middle." (NOTE: St. Brigit, keeper of fires.)

Throughout the ages and in many lands the hearth has been regarded as the home spirit, the ancestral spirit of the home, and the community.

The Romans maintained the sacred fires of Vesta. Far away in Damaraland, the Hereros maintained sacred fires in their villages, and the customs of these native people bear a close resemblance to those of the civilized Romans and their Vesta goddess.

At the firesides of the Hereros sits the head of the family, silently communing with his ancestors. To the fireside the new-born baby of the house is brought with its mother to be introduced to the spirits of those ancestors and to receive its name.

Taking the child, the chief addresses his ancestors through the sacred fire of the hearth: "To you" (he announces) "a child is born in your village. May this village never come to an end." To the fire the sick are brought that the spirit of the ancestors might heal them; and the bride is taken to the fire also.

The fire is never let out; as the fires of the Temple of Vesta were never allowed to go out. There seems little doubt that the Highlands belief in the ill-luck of allowing a fire to go right out came from the Roman belief; but how that same belief got to the people of Damara-land—who can say?

HEDGEHOG

Hedgehogs bring bad luck. But the spell can be broken if the animal is killed.—General.

And a delicious dish had into the bargain!

Hedgehogs at night suck the milk of the cows lying in the pastures, and thus lessen the milk supply.—General.

NOTE: For this reason farmers have for many years killed all hedgehogs they came across.

Observe which way the hedgehog builds her nest. To front the north, the south, the east or west. For if 'tis true that common people say. The wind will blow the quite contrary way.

The above is an extract from *Poor Robin's Almanack* of the year 1733.

In Madagascar soldiers were forbidden to eat hedgehog, as it was felt that the propensity of the animal to coil himself up when alarmed, would render timid a soldier who ate its flesh!

HEN

If hens gather on rising ground and trim their feathers, it is a sure sign of rain.—Derbyshire.

If a person takes into the house of a newly married couple a hen, and makes the bird crow, good luck will attend the marriage.—Yorkshire.

There is, finally, of course, the old tag which held that "A whistling woman and a crowing hen, is good for neither beast nor men."

The Welsh had a superstition that if hens were fed on New Year's Day with some of all the fruits of the house they would lay whether they wanted to or not. The fruits had to be chopped up small and mixed together.

HENBANE

If a child lies down and falls asleep near henbane, it will sleep for ever.—Wales.

HERBS

Mugwort, gathered on Midsummer Eve, is a preventive against the influence of witches.—Isle of Man.

If two people gather orpine (a plant) on Midsummer Eve, and plant slips of it, they will be sure to learn their fate.—General.

The fate was learned by the growing, or otherwise, of the planted slips. If in growing they leaned towards each other, the couple would eventually marry. If one withered, then the person it represented was doomed to die.

Perhaps the most curious superstition connected with herbs was that a rare coal was to be found under the root of the mugwort at a single hour of a single day in the year, i.e., at noon or midnight on Midsummer Eve. This coal, worn on the person, would protect the wearer from the plague, carbuncles, fever and ague.

HERRING

If the first herring caught on the first day of the season has a roe, the season will be a good one. If the first herring is a melt one, the season will be unlucky.—Isle of Man.

The first herring pulled aboard must be boiled whole, the others being put into the pot with their heads and tails cut off.—Isle of Man.

To catch the first bee seen in April is a good sign for the herring season.—Isle of Man.

NOTE: It is recorded in Manx *Notes and Queries* that fishermen have been known to chase the first bee they see in that month for quite a considerable way, and when they have caught it, to put the bee in their purse. If the bee was not caught, it was a sign that their fishing earnings would be small.

If the herring season is bad a cooper should be dressed in a flannel shirt with burrs stuck all over it, and in this condition carried through the town in a hand-

barrow. *This will bring good luck to the fishing.*—Buckie (Scotland).

NOTE: An account of such a procession appeared in the *Banff Journal* in 1880.

To have a dream that will reveal the future, eat a salt herring, bones and all, in three bites, and without speaking a word, even in prayer, go to bed making sure to drink no water.—Outer Hebrides.

If blood is spilt in the sea in a quarrel on the coast where herring are being caught, the shoal will depart and not return that season.—Scotland.

To destroy the Royal Herring will bring bad fortune to the fishing; it should be put back into the sea.—West Highlands.

NOTE: The origin of this, is the belief in the West Highlands that every shoal has its leader which is twice as big as an ordinary herring, and which is followed by the shoal wherever it goes. It is called the King of Herring, or the Royal Herring.

In the time of Queen Anne, herring mysteriously disappeared from the Moray Firth, a great fishing water. It was held that the reason for this was a quarrel in which blood had been spilt in the sea.

The disappearance of herring from the sea around Heligoland, in 1530, was blamed on boys who had caught a King Herring, whipped it and thrown it back into the sea.

Possibly, the most curious of all herring superstitions was that related by Doctor Johnson, who was told it in Skye. It was held that the return of the Laird (chief of the clan of the Macleods) to Dunvegan, after a long absence, had produced a plentiful supply of the fish, after they had been scarce.

En passant, the family still owns a banner called "Macleods' Fairy Banner" because of the supernatural powers ascribed to it. When it is unfurled, victory in war is certain, and all its followers are protected from hurt. Every woman who sees it is taken with premature child and every cow drops a calf. When, many years ago, the potato crop failed, it was asked that the magic banner should be shown and thus produce a good crop.

At Flamborough, it was held that a good herring season could only be assured if young married women, dressed in various disguises, paraded the town with music and merriment and called at various houses soliciting money and good wishes.

It was religiously held in many fishing ports that if a female herring is first drawn on board at the opening of the season, the season will be a good one; but should the first herring be a male fish, the season will be bad.

When herring were recorded as near the coast of Monance, the bells of the church were never rung. It was held that the silvery harvest of the sea was frightened by the jangling bells.

HERON

To shoot a heron will bring bad luck.—General.

Whenever a Bishop of Chichester diocese is to die, a heron sits on the pinnacle of the spire of the cathedral.—Sussex.

If herons drive rooks away from a rookery, bad luck will attend the family owning the rookery.—Kent.

Two stories will illustrate these superstitions. Daniel Defoe, in his *Tour Through England and Wales*, records the Chichester superstition and adds that it "accordingly happened when Dr. Williams was bishop. A butcher standing at his shop door in South Street, saw the bird, ran in for his gun and shot the heron. At which his mother was very angry with him, and said he had killed the bishop, and the next day news came to the town that Dr. Williams, the bishop, was dead."

The second concerns the purchase many years ago by a man named Heron, of Chilham Castle, in Kent. When he came into possession, so runs the story, several herons appeared and drove a colony of rooks from their nests.

The village took the view that no family would succeed to the same property for two generations. Added to this was the fact that birds named heron had settled on the land of Mr. Heron. Curiously enough, none of the family did succeed to the estate.

HERNIA

If a child has a hernia, pass him three times through a slit cut in an ash sapling before sunrise, fasting. After which the slit in the sapling should be bound up. As the portions united, so would the malady be cured.—General.

This is, again, a belief in the transference of evil, and also of the belief in the passing *under* something and leaving the evil behind.

There was, however, a vicious side to this charm for hernia. It was believed that once the child had been passed through the ash sapling its life was bound up with the tree. If the split when bound together did not heal and the tree accordingly died, then the hernia would not heal in the child, and the child, too, would die. Not only was it believed that this was the immediate result, but that should the tree in the years to come wither or die, the hernia which he had as a child would return to the grown man, and it would then mortify and cause his death.

For this reason the utmost care was taken to see that the tree flourished.

There is on record a tree in the neighbourhood of Birmingham through which the son of a farmer was passed in childhood. Even when he had grown to man's estate he would not have a limb of the tree cut off nor a branch lopped, believing that to do so would be visited on his own body in the form of an amputated limb; and by his own death should such lopping cause the death of the tree.

In a Sussex village when a piece of land was purchased by a stranger, and he announced that he was cutting down a row of ash saplings, there was consternation among the villagers who pointed out that for many years their children had been passed through the trees, and to cut them down would spell disaster to the children now grown up healthy.

See HOLES (PASSING THROUGH), RICKETS.

HICCOUGH

To cure the hiccough, wet the forefinger of the right hand with spittle, and cross the front of the left shoe three times, saying the Lord's Prayer backwards.—Cornwall.

HOLES (PASSING THROUGH)

To cure a child of the rickets draw it through the perforated stone called Men-an-tol (holed stone).—Parish of Madern, Cornwall.

Few superstitions had a wider play on the minds of British people than that of curing disease by passing the sufferers through some hole, ring or hoop.

The belief was that, subject to certain ceremonies being performed, the patient on passing underneath and through the hoop, arch, ring or hole left his disease behind him and emerged clean and healthy.

In almost every country of the world the same superstition prevailed, though there could have been no collusion of the peoples, and no knowledge the one of the other of the superstition. It is, again, an instance of some curious instinct and fear of men of all colours and races leading them to one general belief or trust in an unseen power.

It did not seem to matter of what the arch, hoop, or hole was formed. For instance, children who had the whooping cough were passed three times *under* the belly of an ass; the Highlanders of Strathspey, Scotland, used to pass their sheep and cattle through a hoop of rowan tree on All Saints' Day and Beltane.

On the Morven and Mull coast thin ledges of rock pierced with holes may be seen. Consumptives used to be brought there and after the tops of nine waves had been caught in some vessel and thrown over their heads, the consumptives were made to pass through one of the holes in the direction of the sea. By so doing, it was believed that the evil pursuer (consumption) had been left behind.

In Coll, on a farm, there was a stone called Clach Thuill (Hole Stone), and through this, consumptives passed "in the name of the Father, the Son, and the Holy Ghost," and were, it was held, certain to be cured.

Through a rock with a hole in it in the River Dee, near Ballater, childless women used to pass after wading out into the sea to reach it; they believed that the act would make them fruitful in the womb. The stone at Madern, mentioned above, people crept through who suffered with pains in the back; to-day they would take backache pills.

To get rid of boils it was deemed necessary to crawl under a natural arch —for instance, a bramble which had formed an arch by sending down a second root into the ground. In the West of England the passage had to be negotiated nine times against the sun, but in Devonshire the direction was three times with the sun—i.e., from east to west.

In all parts of England ruptured children or those with rickets were passed through a cleft made in an ash, oak, and in some cases a holly tree (the latter in Surrey). The tree, to ensure success, had to be a maiden—that is, it should never have been topped or cut. The split had to be made from east to west. The child had to be passed through by a maiden and received on the other side by a boy. And it had to be passed through head foremost (in some parts feet foremost).

The ceremony over, the cleft, which had been kept open by a wedge, was allowed to spring together again. It was then tightly bound, and the fissure plastered up with mud or clay. As the cleft healed and grew together again, so it was believed did the child's rupture heal in a like manner. As late as the nineteenth century this was a recognized "cure" in Surrey.

Down to the second half of the nineteenth century the practice was common at Fittleworth and other areas of Sussex, and in other parts of the south.

There was, however, a risk in the "cure." A child, once passed through a tree in the way described, was held to have an affinity with the tree. If the cleft failed to heal, then the disease, or the rupture of the child failed to heal; if the tree withered and died, the child would wither and die, even though the withering might not ensue until the child had grown to manhood.

Take the story of Thomas Chillingworth, who at the age of twelve months was passed through an ash tree near Birmingham. He preserved the tree with scrupulous care, not allowing it to be trimmed or a branch cut, for, he maintained, his life depended upon the life of the tree.

At Petworth, Sussex, a builder purchased an ash tree intending to cut it down for timber. As it happened, it was one of a row of ashes which had been used for "passing." The father of a child who had been passed through the tree appealed to the builder that should the tree be cut down, the rupture, and even worse, would return to his son. The builder agreed that such would be the case. He said he would leave the tree undisturbed—and did.

In Germany, the same belief was held; in the Greek island of Ceos when a child is sickly, it is passed through a cleft in an oak tree; so in France, Denmark and Sweden.

Among the villages on Lake Nyassa sick natives form an arch by bending two saplings to the ground and pegging them. Through this they creep—and leave the disease behind. In Uganda, a medicine man splits a plantain tree—and the sick pass through it.

These instances could be multiplied a thousand times, but enough has been given to point the universal belief in the superstition.

HOLLY

To stamp on a holly berry will bring you bad luck.—General.

If holly is used in the house as a Christmas decoration, it should be removed on Twelfth Night, and burned. —General.

NOTE: If it is merely thrown away, the ill-luck will continue as though it had not been taken down.

To cure a child of the rickets or a rupture, pass it through a cleft holly bush.—Surrey.

To take holly into a house before Christmas Eve will lead to family quarrels.—Wales.

A "future" superstition attached to holly concerned "she" holly—that is holly without prickles.

Leaves had to be gathered late on Friday night, and brought home in a three-cornered handkerchief, silence being observed by the picker. On reaching home nine of the leaves had to be selected and tied with nine knots into the handkerchief, and placed under the pillow. Whatever was dreamed that night would come true.

The origin for the ill-luck from stamping on a holly berry was that during the winter the robin fed on holly berries, and the robin is a sacred bird.

It was held in Wales, and is still held by some of the older country people, that to pluck a sprig of holly in flower will cause a death in the family of the picker. Another version, we believe in North Wales, is that to take holly into a friend's house, will lead to a death.
See HOLES (PASSING THROUGH).

HOPFIELDS

If a person paying a first visit to the hopfields does not contribute foot money, luck will go from the fields.—Kent.

Some years ago the authors visited a Kentish hopfield for the purpose of gaining local colour for a book then in preparation. Mentioning by chance that this was our first view of hop-picking, we were told that unless we paid shoe money, luck would go from the field and from the pickers. Accordingly our shoes were rubbed with a bundle of hops and we handed over a few shillings to propitiate the gods!

We tremble to think what might have been the fate of the pickers and the hops had we not mentioned that it *was* our first visit.
See CHERRY.

HOOP

See HOLES (PASSING THROUGH).

HORSE

It is unlucky to meet a white horse on leaving home—unless you spit on the ground.—Yorkshire.

The plant moonwart will draw the shoes from the feet of horses.—General.

A hogstone with a hole through, tied to the stable door will protect horses from witchcraft.—General.

It is lucky to own a horse whose fore-legs are both equally white-stockinged; but if one fore and one hind leg are the same it is unlucky.

It is unlucky when only one leg of a horse is white-stockinged, but if opposite legs (as off fore and near hind) are white, it is very fortunate.

If horses are lost from disease or illness, the disease can be ended by burying one of the dead horses entire.—West Riding, Yorkshire.

When horses stand with their backs to a hedge, a storm can be expected.—General.

Wash a dish-towel on New Year's Day and put it to dry on a hedge. If you then rub your horses with it, they will grow fat and well.—Wales.

Following is a cure which had quite a vogue in the Yorkshire Ridings some 80 years, and more, ago. It was intended for the foul, or fellen (a disease of the feet). The superstition is vouched for by the Rev. G. Ormsby.

The owner of the horse must go at midnight into his orchard and "grave" a turf at the foot of the largest apple tree, and then hang it carefully on the topmost branch of the tree, all in silence and alone. As the turf "maddered" away so would the disease leave the animal.

This cure was known in many other places in the North, but had the additional condition that the turf thus graved must be one on which the stricken beast had trod.

Denham, in his *Folk Lore of the North of England,* states that many people had no use for any other remedy for the foul, and ignored any veterinary advice, regarding the graved turf as infallible.

At Alcombe the village blacksmith has possessed for generations a charm with which he has the power to draw out nails from the frog of a horse's foot, and at once heal the wound. The superstition attached to the charm states that it can be handed down to only one person at a time.

In 1940 the daughter of the late smithy was using the charm; and whether superstition or not—which nobody but she knows—it was invariably a success.

See LOCKERBY PENNY.

HORSE BRASSES

See BRASSES (ON HORSES' HARNESS).

HORSESHOE

A horseshoe nailed over the door lintel of a house will bring good luck to all inside.—General.

If a horseshoe over the threshold was cast from the near hind leg of a grey mare luck will be of the greatest.

A horseshoe nailed to the mast of a fishing smack will protect it from storms.—Scottish fishing coast.

If you see a horseshoe in your path, pick it up, and spit on it, and throw it over your left shoulder, at the same time framing a wish, the wish will come true.—North country.

It is lucky to find a horseshoe in the road.—General.

If a horseman places a coin on one of the stones of Wayland Smithy (Berks) and then withdraws out of sight, his horse will be magically shod by Wayland.

NOTE: Wayland was once a god of the Scandinavians; Wayland Smithy is a collection of ancient stones under the White Horse in Berkshire.

This belief in the luck of the horseshoe is still one of the most prevalent in the country to-day. Even those people who will deny, emphatically, that they are superstitious, will nevertheless nail up any horseshoe they chance to find.

But, the superstition demands—a point that from the observation of the authors of the many decorations they have seen—that the shoe must be in a certain direction. It must be nailed with the points upwards.

The origin of this was the belief that the Devil, against whom the "charm" is directed, always travels in circles, and is consequently interrupted when he arrives at either of the heels of the shoe, and is obliged, thereby, to take a retrograde course.

In Devon and Cornwall, that pixie and fairy ridden countryside, the horseshoe is particularly rife at the present time.

To keep away the Devil there was at one time a horseshoe graved on a tile under the porch of Staninfield Church, Suffolk. The congregation seemed to place little faith in the power of the Holy Water which, elsewhere, was accounted sufficient for such a purpose.

Great men have had this failing for horseshoes. Nelson had a horseshoe firmly nailed to the mast of the *Victory*.

Mr. Cary Hazlitt has recorded how, driving one day with a distinguished friend in a hansom cab in London, the horse cast a shoe, whereupon his friend at once jumped from the cab and secured the shoe to nail over his house.

When Dr. James, then a poor chemist, had invented the fever-powder, he was introduced to Newbery, of St. Paul's Churchyard, to sell the medicine for him. As he was making his way to Newbery's house at Vauxhall he saw a horseshoe lying in the road, and picked it up, putting it in his pocket. Dr. James ascribed all his success with the powder to this shoe, so much so that he adopted a horseshoe as a crest for his carriage.

Now, the origin of all this is ascribed to the legend of St. Dunstan and the Devil. The saint was noted as a blacksmith, and, so the legend goes, one day the Devil presented himself and asked to have his hoof shod. St. Dunstan recognized him, and after fastening his visitor to a wall went to work upon the hoof with such roughness that the Devil roared for mercy. Before releasing him, St. Dunstan exacted a promise that he would never enter a place where he saw a horseshoe displayed.

The authors prefer to believe, however, that the horseshoe protection against evil had its origin in these islands from the Roman invaders. One of the principal beliefs of the Romans was that evil could be nailed, and the hammering of nails on the doors and over buildings was a well-recognized means of curing, or diverting ill-luck and plagues and disease.

How great was the belief in the charm of the horseshoe at one time is illustrated by the fact that one of the "good wishes" of the early part of the last century was: "That the horseshoe may never be pulled from your threshold."

This horseshoe luck, incidentally, is held by the Jews, the Turks and heretics and infidels the world over.

See HORSE.

HOSPITAL
Should a nurse in hospital twist her apron strings when dressing, it means that she will soon be taking over new work.

If a nurse knocks over a chair in the ward, a new patient will soon be arriving.

HOT WATER
If hot water is poured over the doorstep of the hall door as bride and bridegroom drive away after their wedding, another marriage is sure to be agreed upon before it dries up.—Yorkshire.

A writer in *The Athenæum* of 16th November, 1867, describes the custom thusly:

"At a wedding in ·Holderness the other day, at which my granddaughter assisted, a ceremony was performed there I had not observed before. As soon as the bride and bridegroom had left the house, and had the usual number of old shoes thrown at them, the young people rushed forward, each bearing a tea-kettle of boiling water, which they poured down the front steps, that other marriages might soon flow, or as one said flow on. This piece of folklore goes by the appellation of 'keeping the threshold warm for another bride.' "

HOUSE
To bring luck to your new house, you should go into every room bearing in your hands a loaf and a plate of salt.— N. Yorkshire.

This is known, locally, as "house-handsel."

There is surprisingly little superstition in this country regarding the house. Germany has more. There, it was held that a brand taken from the festival bonfires, such as the Midsummer Fires or the Need Fires, if kept in the house will preserve the home from fire—apparently on the principle that one fire will keep off another—a closed shop in superstition, so to speak!

The Sudanese of the Indian Archipelago regard it as unlucky to build a house with certain kinds of wood, or use the wood in the building. One such was any wood with prickles or thorns. The belief was that it would result in prickles and a thorny path for the people who lived in it.

HOUSE LEEK
If the house leek grows on your roof, the house will be struck by lightning.— England.

As showing the farce of these superstitions, it may be mentioned that in Wales it is considered lucky for the peasantry to have the roofs of their houses covered with the house leek, as it preserves and protects them from disease and insures prosperity.

HUNCHBACK

To meet a hunchback is lucky; to touch his hump is still more fortunate. —General.

A variation of this is the luck which is held by fishermen of the sea, to follow the seeing of a deformed person as they are on their way to their ship. Such a deformed person is held to be one of "God's Poor."

HUSBAND'S TEMPER (FUTURE)

A maiden should go at night and draw a single stick from the woodstack without attempting to pick and choose. If the stick be straight and even, without knots, her future husband will be gentle; if crooked and knotty, he will be a churl.

HYDROPHOBIA

An inquest at Bradwell, Buckinghamshire, on 5th October, 1866, reported in the *Pall Mall Gazette*:

"At an inquest held on the body of a child of five years of age, which had died of hydrophobia, evidence was given by Sarah Mackess who stated that at the request of the mother of the deceased, she had fished the body of the dog, by which the child had been bitten, out of the river, had extracted its liver, a slice of which she had frizzled before the fire, and had then given to the child to be eaten with some bread. The dog had been drowned nine days previously. The child ate the liver greedily, drank some tea afterwards."

Twenty years before, the *Maidstone Gazette* had reported a peasant of South Wales, bitten by a mad donkey, who had been sent to eat grass in the churchyard of St. Edrins. The grass was reputed, together with the custom, of being an antidote to hydrophobia.

Another cure for hydrophobia was quoted in *Notes and Queries*, in the form of an old recipe in a cookery book. According to this, "Against a bite of a mad dog, write upon apple, or on fine white bread, 'O King of Glory come in Peace.'"

Should this fail, then a Dorsetshire remedy might serve. Here it is: "Write these words, *Relus rubus Epilepscum* on a piece of paper and give it direct to the party bitten to eat with bread." Aubrey describes this remedy and adds:

"Mr. Denys, of Poole, in Dorsetshire, sayeth this receipt never fails."

HYMNS

If a clock strikes twelve while a hymn is being sung at the morning service, a death will occur in less than a week.— Sussex.

IMBECILE

It is good luck to meet an imbecile, or a person deformed from birth, when going to join a fishing boat.—Shetlands.

Such afflicted people were regarded as "God's Poor," and being of God's making were not to be despised.

After such a meeting when setting sail, should the voyage prove prosperous, a dole was given on the boat's return, to "God's Poor."

See FISHING.

INFLUENZA

To cure the influenza take some clay scraped off the threshold, make it into a paste and apply as a plaster to the chest. —Ireland.

But to be effective the clay had to be taken from the very spot where a person first set foot on entering a house, where it was the custom to say, "God save all here;" for these numerous blessings, it was held by the very superstitious Irish people had given the clay a peculiar power to cure the chest and to help the voice when it was affected.

There was a curious mode of curing an influenza epidemic in the Sagar district of India. It is recorded in *Rambles and Recollections of an Indian Official* by Major-General Sir W. H. Sleeman. Sir James tells how the Queen Dowager of Sagar asked his permission "to allow of a noisy religious procession for imploring deliverance from this great calamity" (the influenza).

The result was a crowd of men, women and children singing at the tops of their voices and banging upon brass pots and pans.

A goat was purchased by public subscription and driven out of the town. The crowd followed it for eight miles, when it was turned loose for any man to take it. But if the animal returned to the village, the influenza would start again.

The use of a goat as a scapegoat was by no means uncommon in India.

See GOAT.

INVALID

When an invalid goes out for the first

time, convalescent, he must make a circuit of the house with the sun.—Cornwall.

If he moved round the house against the sun, he was certain, so it was believed, to have a relapse.

See RIGHT-HAND TURN, SUN-WISE.

IRISH STONES

These were accepted as powerful charms in many parts of the country, but in none more so than round the Stamfordham area.

There were three in the neighbourhood of great repute both for healing the ills of humans and of cattle.

The Rev. J. F. Bigge has stated how it was related to him by a villager that he had on one occasion been sent to the house of a neighbouring lady to borrow such a stone. It had been brought from Ireland and had never been permitted to touch English soil. The stone, he says, was placed in a basket, carried to the patient with a sore leg, the leg was rubbed with it, and the sore healed.

People were wont to walk miles to be touched by these Irish stones, but they were considered more efficacious if they were used on the wounds by the hands of an Irish man or woman.

At one time they were in high repute in the Northumbrian dales as a charm to keep away snakes, frogs and other vermin.

One such stone was owned by a Mr. Thomas Hedley at Woolaw, Redesdale. It was coloured pale-blue, was three-and-a-quarter inches in diameter, and nearly an inch thick. Strangely enough it was not perforated. Self-bored stones were regarded as the more potent in healing.

IRON

To bring old iron into the house will bring bad luck.—General.

NOTE: Even a nail picked up in the road was included in iron, in this sense of ill-luck.

A hot iron put into the cream during the process of churning, expels the witch from the churn.—Lancashire.

This magic of iron has existed for a very considerable time in Britain. In England, iron was considered as one of the charms which could keep witches away. In Scotland a piece of iron laid on the threshold, or under the window ledge, would be sufficient to save a child from being changed by the fairies. The iron of the horseshoe has been mentioned already.

Now, all this is in strange variation to earlier superstition, where iron was almost entirely banned. It had been for generations—in fact since Pliny's days—a rule of superstition, for instance, that plants to which magical virtues were attributed should not be cut, or dug, with iron.

Mistletoe, the sacred plant of the Druids, was gathered on the first day of the moon without the use of iron—in point of fact, the Druid high priest generally used a silver knife to cut the plant. Mistletoe thus obtained was deemed a certain cure for the epilepsy. It was also carried by women to assist them to conceive.

The same disinclination to use iron was prevalent in other countries. For countless generations the only plough used in eastern countries was a wooden one. The first introduction of iron plough-shares into Poland was, unfortunately, followed by a succession of bad harvests. This was at once attributed to the use of the iron plough-shares, whereupon the farmers reverted to their old wooden ploughs.

Many other instances could be given. The belief remains in one or two northern parts of Britain, but only in relation to Good Friday, when it is considered that ill-fortune will attend anyone who puts iron to ground on that day.

See HORSESHOE, MISTLETOE.

ITCHING

If your nose itches, you will shortly be crossed, or vexed, by a fool.

If your feet itch—or one of them—you will soon be treading strange ground.

If your right hand itches, you will be receiving money; if your left, you will be paying away money.

If the right ear itches, you are being well spoken of; if the left, someone is speaking ill of you.

If a knee itches, you will very shortly be kneeling in a strange church.

If an elbow itches, you will be sleeping with a strange bedfellow.

IVY

Ivy leaves, steeped in water for a day and night help sore and smarting eyes if the eyes be washed with the water wherein they have been steeped.

If children with the whooping cough are allowed to drink all they require from cups made of the wood of the common ivy, they will be cured.—Salop.

If boys gather ten leaves of ivy at Hallowe'en without speaking, throw away one, and put the other nine under their pillow, they will dream of love and marriage.—Co. Leitrim.

The latter is a curious superstition, for it is the only one giving love divination exclusively to the male sex.

In the days when the enlightened(!) opinion of old wives cured whooping cough with ivy cups, there was quite an industry in the making of them. But the authors doubt very much whether any of the cups were any use as a charm, for, to be efficacious the ivy wood had to be cut at a certain change of the moon, and at a certain hour of the day or night.

Old Welsh people held another superstition connected with ivy. If ivy which has grown old on a house falls away, they said, the owner of the house will have financial misfortune and the house will pass out of his hands.

JACKDAW

To see a single jackdaw is a presage of ill-luck.—General.

In some parts of the country, the jackdaw is bracketed with the magpie in a similar superstition.

There was related in *Notes and Queries* an account of a stonemason relating an accident that occurred to a workman during the building of the suspension bridge at Bristol, at the time that the Avon was spanned by a single chain.

Shortly before the accident, he said, a single jackdaw was seen perched on the centre of the chain. It was noted by the workmen as a precursor of bad luck.

See CROW, MAGPIE, ROBIN, ROOK.

JANUARY

If the calends on January be smiling and gay; You'll have wintry weather till the calends of May.—Bucks.

NOTE: There is much more lore in the same strain concerning January; they all have the same belief that a mild January is bad for humans and for the crops.

January is an unlucky month for monarchs.

Charles I was beheaded in January. Napoleon III died in January, 1873, and King Victor Emmanuel in 1878.

JAPONICA

There existed some years ago a remarkable superstition in parts of Kent concerning the japonica flower, which comes in the early spring.

After flowering the japonica seeds in the form of large green berries, which grow as large as an apple.

The Kentish superstition held that these were the "Forbidden Fruit" of the Garden of Eden, and that something dreadful would happen to anyone who plucked the fruit.

To-day, the fruits are extensively made into a fruit jelly, or into jam.

JAUNDICE

To cure the jaundice, eat nine lice on a piece of bread and butter.—Dorset.

This is probably the most revolting of all the British superstitions. But it was believed in even to the middle of the nineteenth century.

South and West Ireland had a common cure for jaundice. This was it: Take twelve large earthworms, bake them on a shovel, then reduce to powder and make a philter to be drunk every morning. "This," says the old recipe, "is an unfailing cure for the jaundice."

In Wales, the cure was to put a gold coin in a pewter mug, fill the jug with mead and ask the patient to look into it without drinking any—surely a test of endurance! The Lord's Prayer had then to be repeated over him nine times and he would be cured.

It will be noticed that the golden coin was the beginning of the charm. This illustrates what became known as "Sympathetic Magic"—that is, that the curing medium was in sympathy with the disease in some way.

Jaundice gives to the patient a yellow appearance; therefore, the cure was to be effected with a golden object. The greatest importance was paid to this. For instance, the disease of ague was transferred to only one tree, the aspen, because the leaves of the tree shook in horror, it is said, at the wood of the tree being used for the Cross of Christ.

From this "sympathy" of cure we derive our names for the liverwort plant, and many other herbs.

The tench has a golden tint. Therefore if you take a living tench, and tie it to your bare back for a whole day, the fish will turn its yellow colour and die. If then, it is thrown back into the river, it will take with it your jaundice. This was the belief of the Danes.

The ancient Hindus knew of this "Sympathetic Magic." For jaundice, they performed elaborate ceremonies with which to banish the yellow colour to yellow creatures or yellow things, and to procure for the patient a healthy red colour from some living source, say a bull.

Accordingly a priest recited over the victim of the jaundice this spell: "Up to the sun (yellow) shall go thy heartache and thy jaundice; in the colour of the red bull do we envelop thee. We envelop thee in red tints, unto long life," and much more in the same strain. The patient then drank water which had been poured over the hair of a red bull, and as a final to a long drawn out daubing with yellow and red, a few hairs of the red bull were glued to his skin.

Thus, from ancient India, through Denmark and into Britain "Sympathetic Magic" followed the same lines.

JOCKEYS
See RACING.

JOHN'S EVE, ST.

On St. John's Eve spirits warm themselves by sitting on the hot pebbles that have been thrown into the bonfires. If a tripod is left on the hearth, a firebrand should be placed underneath it to warn the souls that it is still too hot.

On this eve beasts in the field go down on their knees at the hour of midnight. —Sussex.

The ghosts of dogs walk abroad on St. John's Eve, but are seen only by dogs. —Sussex.

Mugwort gathered on St. John's Eve (Midsummer Eve) will be a preventive against the influence of witches.—Isle of Man.

Mistletoe gathered from an oak tree on St. John's Day is a palliative for the epilepsy.—Lincolnshire.

NOTE: The mistletoe had to be decocted.

A real sprig of mistletoe gathered on St. John's Eve, and placed under the pillow will induce prophetic dreams.— Wales.

A Shropshire superstition was that the oak tree blooms on St. John's Eve, and the blossom fades before daylight. If a maiden spread a white cloth under the tree at night, and in the morning found a little dust, then that was all that there was left of the blossom. Should she find the dust and place it under her pillow, she will see the form of her future husband in her dreams.

It will be recalled that a similar superstition prevailed about fern seed (q.v.). There were other superstitions which belong to this eve and day, but they belong more to the heading of custom.

See MIDSUMMER EVE, NEED FIRES.

JOURNEY

To turn back after starting a journey will mean bad luck for the rest of the day.—General.

Quite a lot of people to-day faithfully observe this old superstition. Especially, it may be observed, City men.

They appear not to have heard of the antidote, which will prevent any of the ill-luck. If you ask for meat and drink, and partake of them, and then set out on the journey again, you may do so in comfort.

JUNIPER

If you cut down a juniper tree, you will die within a year.—Wales.

The origin of this fate from a juniper tree the authors have been unable to trace. There seems no reason why fate should rest in the cutting down of this particular tree; but from Glamorgan and Carmarthenshire have come many stories and superstitions of family tragedies after a juniper tree has been cut down by a member of the families.

The juniper, however, was a necessary adjunct to the Need Fires for cattle disease (q.v.). After the fire had been kindled by the rubbing together of two pieces of wood, juniper was thrown into the flames and the stricken, and also the healthy, cattle were driven through the smoke. This had the effect, according to the belief of that day, of staying the disease and curing such cattle as already had it.

This may be the reason for the curse on cutting down the juniper.

KETTLE

If you turn the spout of a kettle towards the chimney or the wall, you will be an old maid.

KEY

If a wife's keys persist in getting rusty, some friend is laying up money for her. —Co. Durham.

If a maiden on St. Valentine's morning looks through the keyhole of the door and sees a cock and hen in company it is a certain omen that she will be married before the year is out.—Derbyshire.

All keys should be turned and the doors thrown open when a person is near death, to give the soul no hindrance in leaving the body.—General.

Key and Bible Turning. If you would know the name of a thief, or offender of any kind, let one of a company hold a key upon a finger. Open the Bible and read a passage. If the name of the person suspected is then mentioned, and the person is guilty, the key will turn on the finger of the person holding it.—General.

The belief in this strange form of assessing the innocence or guilt of a person was placed chiefly in the reading of the Scripture from the open Bible.

It was maintained that God would never let the innocent suffer after His Holy Word had been evoked. It was the custom for several names to be called out before that of the suspected person.

The superstition was implicity believed in, and there is on record a case of assault in a police court, brought by a woman who had been manhandled by another woman accused by her of theft after a "trial" by Bible and key.

See BIBLE, BOLTS, DEATH.

KINGFISHER

A kingfisher, hanged by its bill, will foretell the weather.—General.

So long as kingfishers are sitting on their eggs, no storm or tempest will disturb the ocean.—Sailors.

The time referred to in the latter superstition is, of course, that named the Halcyon Days. The halcyon is another name for the kingfisher.

The Halcyon Days was the name given to the period seven days before until seven days after the shortest day, because, according to fable, there were always calms at sea during this time. Pliny wrote: "They (halycons) lay and sit about midwinter, where dais be shortest; and the times whiles they are broodie is called the halcyon dais; for during that season the sea is calm and navigable, especially in the coast of Sicillie."

As regards the first of the superstitions above, Sir Thomas Browne in his *Vulgar Errors* says that it was believed that the bird, "hanged by its beak showeth what quarter the wind is by an occult and secret property converting the breast of the bird to that part of the horizon from whence the wind doth blow."

Shakespeare recalled the superstition in his day:

Disown, affirm and turn their halcyon beaks
With every gale and vary of their masters.

It is a fact that in many cottages in rural areas to-day, there is to be found in a glass case a stuffed kingfisher hanging by its beak—a relic left to the family by great-grandfather, who used the bird as a weather forecast.

KING HERRING

Every herring shoal has a King Herring, which is twice the size of the ordinary herring. It is distinguishable by its size and bloom and the red tip of its fins, from which it is called "the wine-drinker." Bad luck will be experienced by the fishermen who bring the King Herring to port.—West Highlands.

If the King Herring was caught super-stition ordained that it should be detached from the net and given into the care of the oldest member of the crew, who then passed it round the "skudding pole," while the remainder of the crew petitioned Providence for good catches.

The fish must on no account be allowed to touch wood. If the ceremony failed to bring good catches, then the oldest member of the crew was blamed. Either he had allowed the herring to touch the wood of the "skudding pole" or someone else had touched the fish with wood—maybe with his head!

KING'S EVIL

To cure the scrofula, let the patient be touched by the king's hand.—General.

Cut off a hind leg and a fore leg on the contrary side of a toad, and wear them in a silken bag round the neck. The toad should be turned loose. As it pined, wasted and died, so would the distemper pine and die.—Herts.

The latter "cure" seems to have existed only in the neighbourhood of Little Gaddesden, Hemel Hempstead, Herts, where it seems to have been invented by a local farmer.

The greatest belief in a cure for the disease was the touch of the king's hand, from which the disease became known as "The King's Evil."

The practice seems to have begun during the reign of Edward the Confessor. The Jacobites, however, considered that the power of healing did not descend to William III and Anne because the "Divine" hereditary right was not fully possessed by them. The office remained in the Prayer Book till 1719.

Prince Charles Edward, when he claimed to be Prince of Wales, touched a child for the disease in 1745; but the last person officially touched in England was Dr. Johnson, in 1712, by Queen Anne.

The practice was introduced by Henry VII of presenting the person "touched" with a small gold or silver coin, called a touch-piece. The one presented to Dr. Johnson has St. George and the Dragon on one side and a ship on the other side.

Charles II is said to have touched 92,107 people. The smallest number touched in any year was 2,983 in 1669. The largest number was in 1684, when many people were trampled to death in the rush to reach the king's hand. The "touching" ended with the death of Queen Anne.

Scrofula, or struma, is a tubercular affection of the lymphatic gland. It is manifested chiefly in the glands of the neck, which become swollen and thick like those of a pig. The disease is most common in childhood.

KNIFE, FORK AND SPOON
A knife in your pocket will prevent the fairies lifting you at night.—Scotland.

If you toast bread with a knife, you'll have no luck in life.

If you accept a present of a knife (or scissors) you must pay a halfpenny, or bad luck will attend you.—General.

NOTE: This is a superstition still practised to-day.

If a girl receives the gift of a knife, or any pointed instrument, from her suitor, her love affair will be broken off.—Lancashire.

Two spoons in a saucer foretell a wedding.

Knife falls, gentleman calls; fork falls, lady calls; spoon falls, baby calls.—Old domestic servants' superstition.

If a girl, walking backwards, places a knife among the leeks on Hallowe'en, she will see her future husband come pick up the knife and throw it into the middle of the garden.—Wales.

To cross knives at table is bad luck.—General.

To drop a fork when laying the table will break your love affair.—General.

A knife placed under the window sill will keep away the Evil One.—Kent.

Scotland, like Ireland, "ridden" by fairy superstition, had several knife charms.

If a deer was shot and brought home at night, a knife had always to be thrust into the carcase to keep the fairies from lying their weight on it.

Another stated that, whenever you entered a fairy dwelling, you should be sure to remember to stick a knife, or needle, or fish-hook in the door. The elves would not then be able to shut the door until you were safely out again.

The origin of all this was the belief that fairies and pixies, and even witches were helpless against anything iron.

A superstition of the Scottish Highlands was that when on a calm summer day eddies of wind went past whirling dust and straws though not another breath of air was moving, the fairies were in the eddies carrying away men, women and children. A knife or earth from a molehill should be thrown at the eddies to make the fairies loose their booty.

At Croyland Abbey, in allusion to the knife with which St. Bartholomew was flayed alive, little knives were given to all comers to the abbey on St. Bartholomew's Day (24th August). The custom was abolished by the Abbot John de Wisbech, who died in 1476.

KNOCK OF DEATH
Three loud and distinct knocks at the head of a sick person's bed is an omen of death.—General.

In parts of the country it was held that the knocks need not be at the head of the patient's bed, but would also apply if they were heard at the head of the bed in which was sleeping a relative of the person thus doomed to die.

Countless instances have been given in print of alleged warnings thus given which have come true.

The superstition may be traced to the Romans who believed from the earliest times that death announced its coming through a genie who made mysterious and supernatural warnings to those near to the destined victim.

KNOCK SALT
To knock over the salt is to meet trouble.—Yorkshire.

In Yorkshire a man or woman who is always in trouble was called an "awd knock saut" (old knock salt). His misfortunes were held to be due to the fact that he knocked over and spilt too much salt.

KNOTS
If all the knots in a shroud are not

loosed when a body is coffined, the departed spirit will not rest.—Scottish Highlands.

NOTE: It is likely that the real reason behind the unloosing of the knots, however, was the belief, prevalent in other countries, that the knots would prevent the widow or widower from marrying again.

To cure warts, make as many knots in a thread as you have warts, then throw the string away. Whoever picks up the thread will get the warts instead of you. —General.

NOTE: A variation was to place the knotted thread in the spout of a pump before sunrise. The next person to use the pump got the warts.

Immediately before the marriage celebration, every knot about the bride and bridegroom—garters, petticoat, shoe strings, etc.—must be loosened. Then the bridegroom, after the ceremony, should retire with some young men to tie the loosened knots, while the bride, accompanied by some of her sex, should do likewise.—Perthshire.

Knots and all tied things unloosed will give a woman easy childbirth.

With reference to the marriage superstition, in other parts of Scotland it was deemed sufficient that the bridegroom's left shoe should be without buckle or latchet "to prevent witches on the bridal night from depriving him of the power of loosening the virgin zone."

This was, in fact, the reason for the superstition of loosening knots at the wedding ceremony, described above. The same superstition prevailed in Syria, and was actually carried out in the late 1920's.

The Perthshire practice, it should be added, was followed by the bride and groom and all guests leaving the church together and circling the edifice according to the course of the sun.

It was believed in Shetland, Lewis and the Isle of Man, that the wind could be tied in knots, and unloosed by the untying of the knots. The knots were, of course, tied by witches. Shetland seamen bought wind in the shape of knotted handkerchiefs. And there were a considerable number of women in Lerwick who lived by selling wind.

Mr. J. G. Lockhart, in his *Memoirs of the Life of Sir Walter Scott*, wrote of the visit of Sir Walter to one of these women at Stromness. "We climbed by steep and dirty lanes," he wrote, "to an eminence rising above the town. An old hag lives

in a wretched cabin on this height and lives by selling winds. Each captain of a merchantman gives the old woman sixpence, and she boils her kettle to procure a favourable gale."

What is the origin of all this, it is difficult to say. It is hardly likely that the old hags were aware of the receiving of the wind in a leather bag by Ulysses from Æolus, King of the Winds, as described by Homer.

See BOLTS.

LADDER

To pass under a ladder will bring bad luck.—General.

NOTE: In Holland the superstition says that to pass under a ladder is to make sure you will be hanged.

Few people even to-day will pass under a ladder set against a wall. The unbeliever will doubtless say that the ill-luck will probably be something dropped by the man at the top of the ladder! It may well be so; but it is not the origin of the superstition; that goes back very much further.

A ladder leaning against anything forms a triangle. And a triangle has always been symbolical of the Trinity— that mystic number three, which is even more potent when it becomes three times three, or nine. To brave and defy the Trinity has always been held to play into the hands of the Evil One.

However, perhaps it is as well to complete the ladder superstition. Should you inadvertently pass under a ladder, the prospective bad luck can be averted if you cross two fingers, and keep them crossed until you see a dog.

It is probable that the ladder superstition is part and parcel, and the survivor here, of the "head taboo," which was known and practised by the ancient Persians, and is still practised by many native races.

The Siamese, for instance, hold that a spirit called Khuan lives in the human head, of which it is the guardian spirit. The spirit must be protected.

The Burmese consider it an indignity to have anything over their heads, which is why Burmese houses have only one storey.

The Cambodians will pass nowhere where anything whatever is suspended over their heads.

In Polynesia, the head of the Marquesan is taboo, and must never be stepped over by another. The son of a Marquesan high priest has been known to roll on the ground in agony because his head was desecrated by passing under falling water.

So a religious superstition and the necessity of keeping the head unfouled seems to have become associated in some way with the carefulness of the English Christian who will go to any trouble not to walk under a ladder.

LAD'S LOVE

This is one of the many names given to southernwood herb. Others are old man, stalewort, kiss-me-quick, and, in Devonshire. maiden's ruin.

See SOUTHERNWOOD.

LADYBIRD

Bad luck will attend anyone who kills a ladybird.—General.

It is a matter of interest that few people will kill a ladybird even though they have no qualms about killing other insects.

Perhaps one should mention the childish game of catching a ladybird, and holding it on the palm of the hand while a verse is recited which directs the insect to:

Ladybird, ladybird, fly away home,
Your house is on fire and your
children all roam.

The insect invariably flies away; but the reason is not so much the uttered charm, as the fact that the hot and perspiring hand makes it only too glad to get away.

The real superstition of the ladybird is the belief, for some extraordinary reason, that it represents the Virgin Mary— hence its name, lady (our Lady).

LADY'S TREES

Lady's trees will protect the house from fire, if they are dried and fastened in turned wooden stands and set as ornaments on the mantelpiece.—Cornwall.

Lady's trees is the name given in parts of Cornwall to small branches of seaweed, when dried as above. Presumably the "lady" is in honour of the Virgin Mary.

LAMB

If you see your first lamb of the season tail first, you can look for nothing beyond milk and vegetables. But if you see the lamb head foremost, then you will have plenty of meat to eat during the year.—North country.

A black lamb foretells good luck to the flock.—Kent.

NOTE: In Shropshire, however, a black lamb is deemed bad luck to the flock. Should a ewe produce twin black lambs, the ill-luck will be calamitous, unless the throat of the black twins are cut before they can say "baa."

If the lambing season starts with twins good luck will follow the flock throughout the year.—General.

The first lamb born to a flock should be rolled in the snow to bring luck to the flock.—Romney Marshes.

To cure the disease in the sheep fold, a lamb must be burned alive.—Once general.

This sacrifice by burning of one animal to stay a plague in the cattle or among a flock was known as a "Need Fire." Its practice was widespread in all parts of Britain, and is referred to in this work under Need Fire.

In those remote Romney Marshes, in England, and, too, in others parts of rural England, the practice of rolling a new born lamb in the snow is still carried out. Usually it is the first lamb of the flock to be born.

Sir Charles Igglesden tells of a grazier who found one of his shepherds rolling twin lambs in the snow. The result was that both little fellows died. The old shepherd, however, in reply to his employer's recriminations, insisted that it was better to sacrifice the two lambs than have disaster overtake the whole of the flock later on.

A lamb bone figured in a love charm in Shropshire. The maiden was required to take the blade bone of a lamb, prick it with a knife at midnight, and say:

'Tis not this bone I mean to prick
But my love's heart I mean to prick.
If he comes not and speaks to-night
I'll prick and prick till it be light.

On this, the form of her future husband would, it was held, present itself to her gaze.

LAMMAS (AUGUST 1st)

To preserve a cow from the Evil Eye. sprinkle menstruous blood on the animal on Lammas Day.—Scottish Highlands.

On Lammas Day houses can be guarded from harm for the year by sprinkling menstruous liquid on the door posts and all round.—Scottish Highlands.

It was ordained by the superstitions quoted above that the liquid was to be applied by means of a wisp of straw, and the person who discharged the office went round the house in the direction of the sun.

See SUN, WITH THE.

Perhaps the strangest feature of these superstitions is that they are with very rare exceptions against the rule and lore of superstitious fortune.

In all parts of Europe, and in most native races, menstruation is regarded as having ill-luck. The oldest existing encyclopædia is the *Natural History* of Pliny. According to this the touch of a menstruous woman blighted crops, killed seedlings, rusted iron and brass, blasted gardens, killed bees, and did many other misfortunate things.

In Britain, even to-day, it is held that a woman in her courses should she salt down pork, will cause the meat to turn bad; if she makes jam it will not keep. Most of the native races seclude their women from all domestic duties during these periods.

LANTERN

A farmer should never place his lantern on the table, but should put it underneath the table, so as not to cause ill to his cows.—Herefordshire.

The belief is not yet dead. A cowman to whom the authors talked at a lonely farm near Ross-on-Wye in 1945, bemoaning a lost calf, explained: "Reason why the cow calved a month too soon were a'cause master put his lantern on table."

Asked to explain how and why that should affect a cow who couldn't know that the lantern was thus placed, he replied that he didn't know the rights and wrongs of it, being no "skollard," but we could take his word for it that nothing but harm came of putting a lantern on a table.

LAPWING

To see a lapwing is unlucky.—South Scotland.

We find this superstition nowhere else but in South Scotland. It is probably more of a memory than a superstition, for during the persecution of the Covenanters in the reign of Charles II the Covenanters in hiding were frequently discovered to their pursuers by the flight and screaming of the lapwing overhead.

LARK

If you want to know what the lark says, you must lie down on your back in a field and listen.—Scotland, and the North.

A lark will sing more sweetly if it is blinded with a red-hot needle.—General.

Thousands of larks fell victims to this latter vicious belief. They were trapped and blinded and sold in small cages throughout the length and breadth of England. Incidentally, so were other British wild song birds. The law which prevents the catching of wild birds and keeping them in cages has put an end to the belief and the deed.

LAST BREATH

A considerable time elapses between the first semblance of death and the departure of the soul.—General.

It was held that about five minutes after death, to all outward appearance, has taken place "the last breath" may be seen to issue with a vapour or "steam" out of the mouth of the departed.

Sir Kenelm Digby and Jacob Behman, the latter in *The Three Principles,* make reference to this last breath.

LEAD

To cure sore breasts (brestills) go into a church at midnight, and cut off some lead from every diamond pane in the windows. Make a heart from this and let the victim wear it.—Devonshire.

Melt some lead and let it fall into a tub of cold water in drops. From the shape the drops assume in the water, the future destiny of children can be predicted.—Co. Leitrim.

The molten lead prediction was applicable only to Hallowe'en.

See HALLOWE'EN.

LEAF

If you catch a falling leaf in your hand in the autumn, you will be free of colds all the winter.—General.

If the ash is in leaf before the oak, then we get a thorough soak. If the oak is in leaf before the ash, then we only get a splash.—General.

The peculiar belief mentioned in the first of the above superstitions was forcibly brought to the mind of the authors one day in Hyde Park, London, in the autumn of 1946. A man and woman pretty well advanced in years, stood looking up at an oak tree from which leaves were being blown by the wind.

After making several attempts to catch a falling leaf, they at last managed to do so, the man first, and the lady subsequently. They then walked away, apparently satisfied with the game.

A question to them elicited the fact that they expected to be free from colds in the head, by reason of their performance. The authors quoted to them the superstition in which they apparently believed. To this and a further question they announced that they were country bred, in the Shires, and that since coming to London more than 20 years ago, they had regularly caught falling leaves in their hands in the autumn. "And we've never had a cold yet," they concluded.

LEAP YEAR

In leap year broad beans grow the wrong way.—General.

Leap year was never a good sheep year. —Scotland.

The idea is, of course, nonsense. The belief was apparently due to the topsy-turvy idea of courtship—that women may propose during leap year; so the beans grow round the contrary way.

Incidentally, this leap year proposing by the ladies has a condition: the alleged law and statute of the Scottish Parliament enacted that "everie ladie that goes a'wooing must weare a scarlet flannel petticote, the edge of whiche must be clearlie seen: else no man neede paye forfeit."

LEEK

A man with leek or garlic on him will be victorious in any fight, and will suffer no wound.—Wales.

This is a very ancient belief in Wales. Men known for their fighting prowess used to rub their bodies all over with leeks or garlic before meeting their opponents in the ring.

This may be the reason for the adoption of the leek as an unofficial emblem of the Principality—the daffodil is the official emblem.

The authors put it forward as a tentative origin. There are many other suggested origins. But it is an undoubted fact that the earliest Welsh warriors carried the leek as a badge, and it was popular even as late as the nineteenth century.

LEES (FAMILY NAME)
See SEALS.

LEFT FOOT

If you enter a house with the left foot first, you will bring evil to the inhabitants.—General.

If one had carelessly done so, the evil may be averted by at once leaving the house, and re-entering with the right foot first.

This is, again, one of the superstitions

bequeathed to us by our Roman conquerors. In ancient Rome and in Greece it was considered so unlucky to enter a house left foot first that men were specially employed by noble families to see that no visitor so entered.

The men were called footmen, and that is the origin of the term footman for a servant who answers the door.

In the Highlands of Scotland there was a left foot superstition which seems to have been unique, for the authors have found no trace of it elsewhere. It decreed that when a bridal party had left the church and returned to the bride's home, the bridegroom's left shoe should be loosened and left without buckle or latchet, to prevent witches depriving him, on the nuptial night, of the power of loosening the virgin zone.

According to other writers, however, the shoe was occasionally loosened at the church door after the ceremony.

LEFT HANDED

It is unfortunate to meet a left-handed (skir or kir-handed) person on a Tuesday morning. But fortunate to meet one on other mornings of the week. —Durham.

The origin would seem to be connected with the Scandinavian god Tiw, who was left-handed and sacrificed his right hand to the wolf for the good of the people. Durham, it must be remembered, is in the old Danelagh of Britain.

Incidentally, the reason it is unfortunate to meet the left-handed person on a Tuesday is because Tiw was not only the old Scandinavian God of War, but the god who gave us Tuesday, or Tiw's-day.

LETTUCE

Over-much lettuce in the garden will stop a young wife's bearing.—Richmond (Surrey).

No trace of this superstition has been found by the authors anywhere else than the Royal Borough of Richmond.

LICE

Nine lice, eaten on a piece of bread and butter, will cure the jaundice.— Dorsetshire.

This is, without doubt, the most revolting of all the superstitions attached to British folk-lore.

See JAUNDICE.

LIGHT

To give a person a light on Christmas

Day will bring bad luck.—East York-shire.

This would seem to be a superstition peculiar to East Yorkshire on Christmas Day.

Mr. J. Nicholson, in *Folk Lore of East Yorkshire*, relates how one of the last questions before retiring on Christmas Eve in his father's house was: "Is the tinder dry, and are the matches well dipped?"

His father stated that on one occasion in his boyhood days, not having any dry tinder they were unable to light a fire on Christmas morning. They experienced the utmost difficulty in borrowing a light to start a fire, it being considered unlucky to give anyone a light on Christmas morning.

The same superstition, however, was widespread in the North of England *on New Year's Day*. There it was held that the fire should never be allowed to go out on New Year's Eve; and it was regarded as giving all one's luck away for the year, should you give any unwise person who had let out his fire, the wherewithal to rekindle it.

LIGHTNING
The rare coal found under the mug-wort plant at a single hour of a single day (noon or midnight on Midsummer Eve) will, if carried on the person, protect from lightning.—General.

Lightning never strikes the same place twice.—General.

In Shropshire it was believed that a piece of hawthorn, cut on Holy Thurs-day (the Thursday before Good Friday), would protect any house from being struck by lightning.

The origin given for this was that it was under a thorn tree that Jesus Christ was born.

See ADDER SKIN, FIRE.

LILAC
It is unlucky to take lilac into the house.—General.

In some parts of the country this ill-luck applies only to white lilac.

The lilac thus shares the ill-luck with may, ivy and blackthorn, and all flowers taken into a house outside their season.

Yet, the authors cannot remember the time when, in the lilac season, their Surrey country home has not been filled with the fragrance of cut lilac blooms. And they place on record that they have been lucky in nearly everything they have undertaken.

LILY
If a man treads on a lily, he will crush the purity of the womenfolk of his house.—General.

The origin of this is obvious; the lily has been considered always as the emblem of virginity. "Pure as a lily."

LILY-OF-THE-VALLEY
It is unlucky to plant a bed of lilies-of-the-valley. Anyone doing so will die within twelve months.—Devonshire.

LIZARD
A marriage can never be happy if the bridal party on its way to the church sees a lizard cross its path.—General.

This applied, also, to a hare, dog or serpent. But should a spider, toad or wolf (!) cross the path, the lovers will be sure to have happiness.

LOADSTONE
A piece of loadstone carried in the pocket will cure, and keep away, sciatica.—Cornwall and Devon.

The same good deed will be served by carrying the knucklebone of a leg of mutton, or a raw potato in the pocket, or round the neck—at least, so says superstition.

LOAF
To turn a loaf upside down after help-ing oneself from it will bring bad luck.—North Country.

If a loaf parts in the hand while you are cutting it, it bodes dissension in the family.—General.

A loaf, with a little quicksilver in a hole in the top of it, set on water in which a body is suspected to be lying will float to and stand over the place where the body is lying.—General.

The aversion to turning a loaf upside down after cutting was held particularly in North Country fishing villages. There it was held that for every loaf thus turned, a ship will be wrecked.

In Berkshire a large hole in the crumb of the loaf, due, of course, to faulty mixing, was regarded as a grave.

In Nottinghamshire, it was said to be a coffin—which is much the same thing in superstition. It was held to mean that someone in the house would shortly die.

There was a belief that if a person had been drowned in any water, and the body could not be found, that a loaf, in which a hole had been made, and a little quicksilver poured in would, if set afloat, come to a standstill over the spot where the body was lying beneath.

The plan has been tried on several occasions within quite recent years. On all but one it failed to reveal the body.

LOCH MONAR

Persons with any disease if they visit Loch Monar will be cured.—Scottish Highlands.

This superstition is bound up with those of healing stones, such as the Lockerby Penny, and the Black Penny. The story of Loch Monar's healing is as follows:

A woman who came from Ross-shire to live at Strathnaver possessed certain holy or charmed pebbles, which when put into water imparted to it the power of curing disease.

One day when she was walking out, a man assaulted her and tried to steal the stones. She escaped from his hands, ran towards the lake and exclaiming in Gaelic, "Mo nar shaine," flung the pebbles into the water.

The lake was forthwith endowed with healing powers put forth, so the story goes, especially on the first Mondays in February, May, August and November. The Rev. D. Mackenzie, minister of Farr, has recorded that in May and August multitudes of people in his day made pilgrimages to the loch from all over Scotland.

To be healed, the sufferers had to be on the banks at midnight, plunge three times into the water, drink a small quantity, and throw a coin into the lake as a tribute. They must be out of sight of the water before sunrise, else the healing would not work.

See STONES, WELLS.

LOCKERBY PENNY

This was, possibly, the most famous charm known in Britain.

It was—we believe it is still preserved—a piece of silver, and the charm it exercised was that when placed in the end of a forked stick and a well was stirred round with it, the waters would at once cure madness in cattle. Henderson records that on one occasion when on a Northumbrian farm a dog bit an ass and the ass bit a cow, the penny was sent for, and a deposit of £50 was left against its safe return.

The dog was shot, the donkey died, but the cow recovered—a sure sign of the potency of the penny. On the death of the man who had borrowed the penny, several bottles of water were found among his effects, marked "Lockerby Water."

The penny was kept by a family at Lockerby, Dumfriesshire.

There was also a charm against disease and the plague, called the Lee Penny. When the plague raged in Newcastle, in the reign of Charles I, it was lent to the citizens to stay the scourge, £6,000 being pledged for its safe return. There are other minor stone or coin charms, but these are the two most famous.

See LOCH MONAR, STONES, WELLS.

LOCKS

When a person is on a deathbed, all locks in the house should be opened and kept open until after death.—General.

All locks in a house should be opened when the birth of a child is due.—N.W. Argyllshire.

NOTE: If this were not done, then the mother was deemed to have been given a hard delivery.

The openings of locks in a house at death was said to ease the pangs of death, and allow the soul to pass unhindered to its rest. It is an old superstition prevalent in many lands. Virgil mentions it.

The practice is founded on the idea that the ministers of purgatorial pains take the soul as it escapes from the body and flatten it against some closed door (which alone would serve the purpose), afterwards cramming the flattened soul in the hinges and hinge openings. Thus, the soul in torment was likely to be miserably squeezed by the movement of the door on all occasions.

By the superstition of leaving unlocked the doors and all other locked things in the house, the friends of the dead could be assured that they had not been made, unconsciously, the instruments of torturing the departed.

The extent to which the superstition was believed in is evidenced by a case at Taunton, in 1863. A child, sick of scarlatina, was pronounced as on the point of death. A jury of matrons was empanelled to prevent the child dying hard. They ordered that all the doors in the house, all the drawers, and boxes and cupboards should be unlocked and the keys taken out of the locks, in order that the child should have a certain and easy passage to Eternity.

Unfortunately for the matrons, the child declined to accept the facilities for its easy death. It recovered.

There was for many years a belief that

the flower springwort could open, magically, every lock. There was, however, a rather difficult method of securing the flower so that it could exert this magic.

Briefly, you had to mark a hollow in a tree where a woodpecker had built her nest, and hatched her young, and when found, wait for the mother bird to come out. You then had to plug up the hole with a wooden wedge.

The bird on seeing this obstruction would fly away and return with a sprig of springwort in its bill. Fluttering up to the hole it would hold the springwort to the wedge which would then fly out with a bang. At this you must rush from your hiding place nearby and shout. In its fright, the woodpecker would open its bill and drop the springwort. You must catch the sprig in a red or white cloth. This is the sprig which will magically open any lock.

Moreover, the possession of it could make you invisible at will to anybody; and carried in your pocket, would render all steel or lead powerless to wound you.

The superstition was known in Swabia, where when a thief has escaped capture he is said to have had a sprig of springwort.

Another flower said to have had the power of opening all locks was chicory—provided that the flower had been cut with a piece of gold at noon or midnight on St. James's Day, 25th July. The cutting had to be done in perfect silence.

See BOLTS, CORPSE, FEATHERS, KNOTS.

LOOKING BACK
To look back at your house after leaving it for a journey, or to return after having started out, will bring misfortune.—General.

The superstition of looking back or returning is many thousands of years old. It doubtless originated in Lot's wife "having looked back from behind him" when he was led by an angel outside the doomed city of the Plain (Gen. xix, 26).

Mr. Roberts, in *Oriental Illustrations*, remarks that it was considered exceedingly unfortunate in Hindustan for men or women to look back after leaving the house. Accordingly if a man goes out and leaves something behind him which his wife knows he will want, she does not call him, so that he looks back, but takes or sends it after him.

Caffre boys, after a certain ritual,

never look back lest a fearful curse should cling to them.

LOOKING GLASS
To break a looking glass, betokens that the owner will lose his, or her, best friend.—Yorkshire.

To break a looking glass means seven years' bad luck, but not want.—General.

During the time a corpse is lying in the house all looking glasses should be covered over.—Orkneys.

The shadow of a destined bride, or bridegroom, can be seen in a looking glass on St. Agnes Eve.—General.

A bride will have ill-luck who looks at herself in a looking glass after she is fully dressed for her wedding.—General.

NOTE: The misfortune is avoided by leaving off one article such as a glove.

The origin of the last superstition above is doubtful. The bad luck has been traced to those days when there were *no* looking glasses as we know them.

The visitor to Pompeii must have been struck by the presence in the courtyards of nearly all the houses of shallow pools, set in marble surrounds. The purpose of these was neither to bathe in nor as ornament. They were utilized as mirrors, and in the reflection from the still waters would carry out their toilet just as now it is carried out by the operator's reflection in a mirror. A vicious rival had only to toss a pebble into the pool and it was bad luck on the victim's toilet.

On the other hand the superstition may belong to the fact that mirrors in olden times were used by magicians in their diabolical operations.

There was also an ancient kind of divination by looking glass. Potter, in his *Antiquities of Greece*, says: "When divination by water was performed with a looking glass, it was called Catoptromancy. Sometimes they dipped a looking glass into water when they desired to know what was to become of a sick person; for, as he looked well or ill in the glass, accordingly they presumed his future condition."

It may be that the ill-luck relates to the broken appearance a wet glass would give his appearance.

LOOKING UNDER THE BED
It is necessary to look under the bed before you retire in order to ward off the Devil.—Rural belief.

Sir Charles Igglesden in *Those Superstitions*, referring to this superstition, quotes the case of a domestic servant, taken seriously ill. She was to be wrapped up in blankets, kept warm, and on no account to leave her bed.

Her mistress, paying her a visit late at night, found the girl on her knees peering under the bed. She expostulated.

"Well, ma'am," was the reply. "You don't expect anyone to go to sleep without first looking under the bed. I'd rather die than bring bad luck on me and me young man."

Pressed for an explanation, she cited the superstition quoted above, and explained that it was a well-known fact among her people that it was the way to ward off the Devil.

LOVERS

If a courting couple are photographed together, the engagement will be broken off.—General.

To give your sweetheart a knife means that you want to break the engagement. It would be bad luck not to agree.

Should a girl sit on a table while talking to her lover, she will never be married.

If a rose is plucked on Midsummer Day and put away, it will be as fresh as ever on Christmas Day. If then worn at church, the intended partner of a girl will come and pluck it from her breast.—Devonshire.

Lovers should pluck a twig from a laurel tree, break it in two and each preserve a piece. It will keep them lovers.

A girl who fails to look to the north when she leaves the house before breakfast, will remain a spinster.

To know her prospective husband, a girl should go into the churchyard on Valentine Eve, and as the clock strikes twelve should run round the church, saying, "I sow hempseed, hempseed I sow. He that loves me come after me and mow." Her future husband will then appear.

If yarrow is plucked from a man's grave and placed at night under the pillow, a lover will appear in a dream.—Devon.

There are other love divinations connected with verses spoken to the new moon. A common one, still believed in in many places, is that a girl who reads the marriage service all through will never be asked to wed.

If a girl or man looks into the looking glass at midnight on St. Agnes Eve, the shadow of the life partner will appear.

Perhaps two of the quaintest are, firstly, that described by Halliwell. "Two young unmarried girls must sit in a room by themselves from twelve o'clock at night till one o'clock next morning, without speaking a word. During this time each must take as many hairs from her head as she is years old, and having put them in a linen chest with some of the herb true-love, as soon as the clock strikes one she must burn every hair separately, upon which her husband-to-be will appear and walk round the room and then vanish. The same event happens to both girls, but neither sees the other's lover."

The second of the quaint notions was that if any unmarried woman fasted on Midsummer Eve, and at midnight laid a clean cloth with bread, cheese and ale and then sat down as if to eat—the street door being left open—the man whom she is afterwards to marry would come into the room, drink to her with a bow and after filling the glass would leave it on the table, make another bow, and retire.

LUNG DISEASE

To cure the "rising of the lungs," take an egg cup, fill it with gunshot, and make the sufferer swallow the shot. This will sink the lungs.—Sussex.

One would have thought it might very well sink the patient, too! But the remedy was quite well known in Sussex.

LYCH-GATE

If a wedding couple pass through a lych-gate, one of them will die within a year; or, should both survive, the marriage will be unhappy.—Barthomley, Cheshire.

This is the only example of its kind we have come across, and it seems to be peculiar to this town in Cheshire.

The student of folk-lore may see in this a curious lapse, for lych means, of course, a corpse, and a lych-gate is that beneath which a corpse was rested before being headed by the priest and escorted by him into the church for the funeral service.

One would have associated naturally bad fortune to any young couple just starting out on married life who passed through a gate named and devoted to the resting of a corpse.

MACKEREL

Mackerel are not in season and should

not be caught until the lesson of the 23rd and 24th Numbers has been read in Church.—Somerset.

NOTE: The chapters mentioned refer to the story of Balaam and the ass.

In Brighton, the common saying was that mackerel should not be taken until Balaam's ass speaks in church.

Brighton fisher-wives held for very many years a superstition that buns baked on a Good Friday would keep their men from shipwreck. Many buns were baked and the husbands had to take one with them on their journeys for as long as the supply lasted.

See GOOD FRIDAY.

MAD DOG
See HYDROPHOBIA.

MADNESS
A Cornish recipe for the cure of madness, or mental disorder, was to place the disordered on the brink of a square pool filled with water from St. Nun's Well; and giving him no warning precipitate him into the water. There he must be tossed up and down by persons of superior strength till, being quite debilitated, his fury forsook him. He was then carried to church and certain Masses sung over him.

The Cornish called this immersion boossening, from *beuzi* or *bidhzi*, signifying to dip or drown.

It may be as well to state in fairness to the people who practised this superstition, that Pettigrew, in his *Superstitions Connected with Medicine and Surgery*, states that casting mad people into the sea, or immersing them in water until well-nigh drowned have been recommended by high medical authorities as a means of cure.

An Irish charm to cure madness in a person was to give the sufferer three substances not procured by human means. He was to drink them before sunrise in a sane spell.

NOTE: The three substances not procured by human means are honey, milk and salt.

MAGPIE
If a single magpie croak round a house, one of the inhabitants will die.—General.

Always take off your hat to a magpie, or bow respectfully to him, or evil will surely follow.—Somerset.

If you see a magpie and do not cross yourself, you will be unlucky.—N. Lincolnshire.

NOTE: Yorkshire folk had an addition to the above. They also crossed their thumbs and spat over the thumbs in that position.

If a magpie perches on your roof, it is a sign that there is no danger of the house falling down.—General.

If you see two magpies flying together when you are going fishing, you will have good sport.—Lancs.

NOTE: The origin behind this is that in cold and rough weather only one magpie will leave the nest, the other remaining to keep the young warm. If both are out the weather is mild and calm, and, therefore favourable for the art of angling.

It is a death omen should a magpie precede a person going to church.

To see a magpie when going on a journey, means that ill-luck will befall you, unless you return and postpone your business.—General.

The warning in this latter superstition sometimes works out for the benefit of the journeyer.

There is, for instance, the authenticated instance of a county magistrate of Yorkshire, who set out for Challoners' Bank in York to deposit his rents. Hardly had he left his residence when he saw a magpie cross his path.

He hastily turned for home—and stayed there. The following morning he learned that the bank had failed within a few minutes of the time he would have arrived there.

Finally, there is the doggerel superstition about the magpie:

One is for sorrow, two is for mirth;
Three for a wedding, four for a birth, etc.

Now, the "origin" related to explain this magpie superstition of ill-luck, is that the magpie was the only bird that refused to enter the Ark with Noah, preferring to perch itself on the top of the Ark outside and jabber over the perishing world.

MAIDENHAIR (FERN)
To bring maidenhair into a house, will bring bad luck to it.—Norfolk.

MANDRAKE
The person who pulls a mandrake root will fall dead.—General.

The root of the mandrake shrieks and groans when pulled from the earth, and whoever hears the shrieks will die shortly after, or become afflicted with madness.—General.

If you dig up a root of mandrake burn it at once, for anybody who looks at it will go blind.—Sussex.

From earliest times these beliefs existed in connection with the mandrake. Shakespeare refers to them in *Romeo and Juliet:*

"... Torn out of the earth,
That living mortals, hearing them.
   grow mad."

The origin of all these superstitions lies in the name, which is really German, mandragen (resembling man), and is due to the similarity of the shape of the root to a human being. The next stage in the story was the suggestion that the plant had a human heart at its root. Finally, it was said to be watched over by Satan.

It was known, in Shakespeare's day, that the plant's root had opiate properties, and where it was to be used, the plant was pulled out by a device which prevented the actual pulling by man (with the danger of death or madness).

A dog attached to the plant by a rope or string, and then whipped, so that he leapt forward, and up came the mandrake. It was deemed certain that the dog would die.

MAPLE TREE

A child passed through a maple tree will live long.

As late as the nineteenth century, this belief held its ground in many rural areas of the country. The passing had to be through the branches of the maple. And passed through the branches all the babies of the villages were.

There is on record the protest of the mothers of the village of Grinstead (Sussex) when a rumour went round that a maple tree at West Grinstead Park was to be cut down. A petition begging that it should be spared was presented, on the grounds that the lives of children born in the place would be shortened.

The tree had been the favourite "old age giver" of the local populace for two or three generations.

See also RICKETS, RUPTURE, WHOOPING COUGH.

MARBLE HALLS

To play the air "I Dreamt that I dwelt in Marble Halls" in any musical show, except the light opera for which it was written, is regarded by musicians as likely to bring exceedingly bad luck to the orchestra pit, and also to the musical show itself.

See STAGE SUPERSTITIONS.

MARCH

A wet March makes a bad harvest. A dry and cold March never begs its bread.—General.

MARIGOLDS

If you pick marigolds, or even look at them long, you will take to drink.—Devon, Wiltshire.

If marigolds are not open before seven o'clock a.m., there will be rain, or a thunderstorm.—Wales.

The latter is perhaps less a superstition than a horticultural fact, for marigolds close before a storm.

As regards the drunkenness allegation arising from a long looking at the flower, it is for this reason that the popular name for the marigold in Devon and Wiltshire was at one time "The Drunkards."

MARK'S EVE, ST. (APRIL 24th)

On St. Mark's Eve at midnight the Devil's Harvest can be reaped, since at that exact time bracken seed grows, ripens and falls, and can only be caught in the third pewter plate, since it is so strong that it passes through the two above it. If secured, then the Devil will appear and tell the gatherer all he wishes to know.—Horncastle area.

If you watch at midnight on St. Mark's Eve, you will see the ghosts of those who are to die during the year pass into the church.—General.

NOTE: A full description of this superstition appears under the heading Death Watch.

There was, of course, a marriage portent for the Eve of St. Mark's. A maiden had to take three tufts of grass from a churchyard and place them under her pillow, saying:

Let me know my fate, whether weal
   or woe;
Whether my rank's to be high or
   low;
Whether to live single, or be a bride;
And the destiny of my star doth
   provide.

Having carried out these formalities the answer would appear in the maiden's dream that same night.

According to Midlands superstition a girl could be assured of whether she would marry that year, by going on St.

Mark's Eve to the church porch just before midnight and waiting there alone until the clock strikes twelve. She would then see a bridal procession pass into the church. The number of bridesmaids indicated the number of months she has to wait for marriage. If, however, she saw a coffin carried into the church with a white cloth on it, then she would know that she had to die as an old maid.

MARRIAGE

Ill-luck will pursue the married couple who had their banns published at the end of one quarter, and were married at the beginning of another quarter of the year.—Perthshire.

Be sure that on your marriage you do not go in at one door and out at another, or you will always be unlucky.—Yorkshire.

Whichever goes to sleep first on the marriage night will be the first to die.—Yorkshire.

It is unlucky for a pig to cross the path of a wedding party.—Border Counties.

NOTE: South of the Border, the unlucky animal is a hare, or a dog, which passes between the couple.

If a bride is robbed of all the pins about her dress by single women, all who possess one of the pins will be married within a year: unless the pin is a bent one, when she will be doomed to be an old maid.—General.

Wedding after sunset entails a bride to a joyless life, the loss of children, or an early death.—Scotland.

NOTE: Maybe this is what is wrong with some of Hollywood's evening weddings.

The girl who receives from the bride a piece of cheese cut before leaving the table, will be the next bride among the company.—Scottish Lowlands.

Most people know, and respect, the superstition that a bride should neither be married in green, nor wear green at all.

It is not so well known, however, that the original superstition against green was carried right through the wedding; in other words, all green should be taboo in every way—even green vegetables must be eschewed from the breakfast or dinner.

The origin is that the colour green is the fairies' colour and they would resent the wearing of it by humans at a wedding and would destroy the wearer.

A Yorkshire wedding superstition was for a plate of cake to be thrown from an upper window of the bride's parents' house as she entered from the wedding service. If the plate should not be broken, then the wedding would be disastrous. The more pieces of broken plate, the happier the marriage.

A variation in Scotland was the throwing of shortbread from the doorway over the head of the entering bride, the thrower being the oldest inhabitant in the neighbourhood. Good fortune attended whoever secured a portion of the shortbread.

In Yorkshire rural areas it was the custom for a kettle of boiling water to be poured over the doorstep of the bride's old home. If the water dried up, another wedding would follow very soon.

A Scottish superstition to bring good luck to the couple was to pay a visit on the wedding eve to the bride and bridegroom-to-be, stretch each one full length on the floor, bare their feet, which were then smeared with soot and blacking. Why this should bring good luck, the authors are totally unable to say.

A strict Highlands belief for very many years was that a marriage should be avoided on the 3rd May. In point of fact, the Highlander up to the middle of the nineteenth century never began anything of consequence on the day of the week on which the 3rd of May fell. It was styled la sheachanna na bleanagh —the dismal day.

In Herefordshire a girl looked at the new moon reflected in a bucket of water through a silk handkerchief or a piece of smoked glass. As many moons as she saw reflected so many months had she to wait to be wed.

In Lower Peover Church, Cheshire, a large parish chest was for very many years used to test the suitability of a girl to be the wife of a farmer. If she could lift the heavy lid of the chest with one hand, she passed the test; if she could not then she was held not to be strong enough for a farmer's helpmate. And there have been numerous occasions when the lady has been "passed" by a prospective groom as unsuitable.

See BRIDE, SHOE, WEDDING.

MARRIED LIFE

The husband must lock the front door before the family retires for the night. Should the wife perform the task, there will be a quarrel during the night.—North Country.

The authors can well believe that it might have been so—should the husband stay out late and find that his spouse had performed the task!

MARTIN'S DAY, ST.

No woman must spin on St. Martin's Day.—Ireland.

No miller must grind his corn on St. Martin's Day; and no wheel must be turned.—Western Isles.

Blood must be spilled on St. Martin's Day.—Ireland.

If a black cock or a goose could not be obtained for the spilling of blood, it was the custom to cut a finger and let the blood drop on the earth. The blood was sprinkled over the floor of the house and on the threshold.

In the Aran Islands, this day was celebrated with great solemnity. The story behind it is that St. Martin, having given all his goods away, entered a widow's house and asked for food.

Having no meat in the house the woman, in despair, sacrificed her young child, boiled it and set it before the saint for supper.

Having eaten, the saint departed, and the mother went to the cradle to mourn her loss. She found the babe, unharmed, sleeping peacefully.

To commemorate the miracle, and out of gratitude to the saint, the sacrifice of some living thing, or the shedding of blood was made yearly in his honour.

A cock or a goose was thus prepared and boiled, and some of the flesh was given to the first beggar who called at the door. Rich farmers made a practice of sacrificing a kid or a sheep; and the poorer people a black or white hen.

MAY (THE SHRUB)

May in, coffin out.—General.

A reference to the believed ill-luck of bringing the May flower into the house.

To sleep in a room with the white thorn in bloom in it during the month of May will be followed by misfortune.—Suffolk.

If you sweep the house with blossomed broom in May, you're sure to sweep the head of the house away.

May flowers, gathered before sunrise, keep freckles away.—Wales.

There seems to be no good reason why the May blossom should be unlucky. See MAY DAY.

MAY BABY

A May baby is always sickly; you may try but you'll never rear it.—Various rural parts of Britain.

Be that as it may, but a member of the authors' family, born in May, not only enjoyed the rudest of health, and was reared, but has herself reared four children!

MAY CATS

Cats born in the month of May will catch neither mice nor rats, but will bring in snakes and slow worms.—Wiltshire and Devon.

May cats are unlucky, and suck the breath of children.—General.

It will be understood that as a consequence of this, May cats were held in contempt.

MAY DAY

He that would live for aye, must eat sage in May.

To give, either for love or money, a coal of fire or a light of any kind—even for the kindling of a pipe—during May Day, will bring ill-luck on the house.—Ireland.

NOTE: In Britain the same superstition applied to Christmas Day and New Year's Day.

Cattle should be slightly singed with lighted straw on May Day eve to keep away evil spirits.—Ireland.

Cattle should be bled on May Day, and the blood dried and burned.—Ireland.

NOTE: It was believed in Ireland, England and Scotland that cattle were susceptible to evil influences on May Eve and Day.

To ensure good butter and freedom from witches, herbs gathered on May Day should be boiled with some hairs from the cow's tail and preserved in a covered vessel.—Ireland.

A maidservant who brings in a branch of hawthorn in blossom on the 1st May, is entitled to a dish of cream.—Cornwall.

All hares found among the cattle on May Day should be killed. They are old women (witches) who have designs on the milk.—Scotland.

If pieces of rowan are not placed on the doors of the cowhouses on May Day the cattle will be bewitched.—Scotland.

May is proverbially unlucky for marriages, and even to-day, the month is avoided to a great extent by brides. The superstition existed in the days of Ovid; but the British version of it is more likely due to the Roman Catholic

Church's absolute rule forbidding weddings between Rogation and Whit Sunday—since abolished.

There are, of course, the famous May Day revels, more kept in the olden days than at present. They were not superstition, but custom; and they included, as old stagers will remember, the decorating of buildings with boughs, the flower processions and the dancing round the maypole.

These were a survival of the ancient belief, held in all countries, of the power of the Tree Spirits, which is why the Scots put rowan branches to avert the Evil Eye.

At festivals in Lhoosa (S.E. India) on the day corresponding to our May Day, the chief of the tribe goes with his people and fells a large tree. This is carried and set up in the village and danced round—as in Merrie England the people of our villages did.

The keeping of May Day is said by some to have arisen out of the festival of Floralia, introduced into Britain by the Romans. The authors question this origin, for observances were found in places where the Romans never settled.

However, it is true that the festival has a similarity to that of the Roman Floralia.

See MAY DEW.

MAY DEW

If you wash your face with May dew gathered at daybreak on May Day, you will have a good complexion throughout the year.—One of the widest held superstitions of the olden days in Britain. It was believed in by royal ladies and peasants.

May dew sniffed up the nostrils is a cure for the vertigo.—General.

The latter might interest billiards star, Melbourne Inman, if he is not now too uninterested in vertigo! But the dew has to be gathered by the sufferer at daybreak on May Day.

Few superstitions were so widespread among all classes of people at one time as that relating to May Dew. Queens and peasants alike went out in the meadows at daybreak on May Day to wash their faces, or to bathe naked, in the dew of that morning. In 1515 it is recorded that Catharine of Aragon, with twenty-five of her ladies-in-waiting, went into the fields to gather May dew for the preserving of the Queen's complexion.

In 1791 the superstition was still going strong; the *Morning Post* of 2nd May in that year reported that: "Yesterday being the 1st of May, according to annual and superstitious custom, persons went into the fields and bathed their faces with the dew, under the idea that it would render them beautiful."

And the great Pepys records in his diary that his wife and a friend had gone from town on the last day of April to Woolwich . . . . "to lye there and so gather May dew to-morrow morning."

Nor was the belief peculiar to Britain. In the Isle of Man, women washed their faces in dew early on May morning to secure "good luck, a fine complexion, and immunity from witches." Women of Northumberland did the same.

South Slavonian peasants also went out in the fields for dew on this morning. But not for themselves; they did not seem to care whether their complexions were good or not. Their interest in the dew of May Day was to wash their cows with it to preserve the beasts from "the charm of witches."

In Spain, Normandy and Perigord, people were wont to roll naked in the dew in order, they believed, to protect them for the year from skin diseases.

MEASLES

To cure the measles, cut off a cat's left ear and swallow three drops of blood in a wineglassful of water.—Cornwall.

But the old nanna of bygone days had a much nicer and more hygienic cure for measles. It was told by a correspondent in *Notes and Queries*. He wrote:

"My nurse said that I and my brother were cured of the measles by having hair cut from the nape of each of our necks, and then separately placed between two slices of bread and butter. She says she anxiously watched for a strange dog to pass (no other being efficacious). She gave him the bread and butter, and as he ate it without loathing she was sure that we were cured. He then went away, and of course never came back, for He died of the measles."

The authors have found traces of a similar belief in isolated instances in several other counties, but whether they were part and parcel of beliefs in those counties, or whether they were imported by people from Huntingdon; whence the correspondent quoted above came, is a matter we are unable to decide.

See MICE, WHOOPING COUGH.

MEAT

If meat shrinks in the pot when boiling, it is unlucky; if it swells, it is a sign of prosperity.—Weardale, C. Durham.

The authors place on record that this is still fervently believed in by a number of people with whom they have had correspondence during the past two years.

MEDICINE
If you sell bottles which have contained medicine, you will require them to be refilled for yourself.

MICE
When mice swarm into a house hitherto free from them, a member of the household will die.—Northants.

If a mouse runs over a person, it is a sign of that person's approaching death.—South Northants.

If a mouse squeaks behind the bed of an invalid, the sufferer will not recover.—Northants.

If you meet a shrew mouse while on a journey, the journey will be attended by misfortune.

Mice, minced, given to a sufferer, will cure the measles.—General.

To cure the whooping cough, roast a mouse and give it to the patient.—General.

A roast mouse is a certain cure for a child who wets its bed at night.—General, and widely held.

The authors' citation of the old superstition of the roast mouse for bedwetting, made in a periodical not long ago, brought the following letter from Mrs. F. Rowe, Regent's Park, London, N.W.: "This is not so old fashioned after all. A friend of mine with a mite three years old is at present giving her stewed mice for bladder trouble, and it is curing her. Of course, she buys clean, healthy mice from a pet stores. Incidentally, I knew in my youth a lad of fifteen cured by this means of this complaint. And isn't it quite possible that some of us are having mice extract in our present day medicine?" The letter is dated 2nd January, 1945.

Volumes of *Notes and Queries* contain several instances in modern times of the roast mice recipe for whooping cough and bed-wetting.

In his *Compleat History of Animals and Minerals*, Richard Lovell, St. C.C., Oxon, states: "A mouse dissected and applied draweth out reeds, darts and other things that stick in the flesh. Mice bruised and reduced to the consistence of an acopon with old wine cause hairs on the eyebrows. Being eaten by children when roasted, they dry up the spittle. The water in which they have been boiled, helps the quinsey. The fresh blood kills warts. The ashes of the skinne, applied with vinegar, helpe the pains of the head. The liver, roasted in the new moon, trieth the epilepsy."

Mr. Donald A. Mackenzie, M.A., that great authority on myth and superstition, in a letter to *The Times* some considerable time ago, referred as follows to the mouse in Scottish superstition:

"About thirty years ago I saw an old woman taking the liver from a mouse to give to her child *in extremis*. This was at Cromarty. Keats (the article was in relation to Keats's *Cap and Bells*, and a correspondent's reference to the work) may have heard something about the Highland mouse cures. He may have heard that the teeth of mice were worn as charms, and that cattle were cured of various troubles by giving them charmed water into which the skin, backbone, or the teeth of a mouse had been dropped. Mice were supposed to cause certain diseases, including whooping cough, sore throats and measles; and these had to be charmed away by utilizing portions of the bodies of mice.

"Roasted mouse was a folk cure for colds and sore throats."

Now, Pliny refers to the mouse cure; and Professor G. Eliot Smith, in dissecting the naturally mummified bodies of pre-Dynastic Egyptians found in the Sudan, notes "the occasional presence of the remains of mice in the alimentary canals of children." Thus, the mouse cure goes back some sixty centuries. And, as related above in the letter from one of our correspondents, it is still being practised to-day.

It is possible, therefore, that the mouse as a charm is the oldest superstition in British records.

See SHREW ASH.

MICHAELMAS
The common brake flowers only once a year, on Michaelmas Eve at midnight, and the small blue flower disappears at the dawn of day.—Shropshire.

Finding the ring in a Michaelmas pie will ensure the possessor an early marriage.—Ireland.

At Michaelmas the Devil puts his foot on the blackberry.—Ireland, and parts of South England.

NOTE: Many superstitious people still refrain from picking blackberries on this day, though one or two asked the reason why could give none.

So many days old the moon is on Michaelmas Day, so many floods after.—North Country.

If you eat goose on Michaelmas Day, you will never want money all the year round.—General.

The origin of the latter is probably associated with the good harvest—in other words, with the Corn Spirit. In Shropshire the shearing of the last portion of grain of the harvest was referred to as "cutting the gander's neck." In Yorkshire, when all the corn was safely gathered, an entertainment was given by the farmer to his hands, male and female, called "The Innin Goose."

MIDSUMMER EVE (AND DAY)

If it rains on Midsummer Eve, the filberts (nuts) will be spoilt.

Pluck a rose on Midsummer Day and put it away. If it is as fresh on Christmas Day as when it was gathered, and it is worn at church, the person you are to marry will come and take it.—Devonshire.

If an unmarried woman fasts on Midsummer Eve and at midnight lays a clean cloth with bread, cheese and ale and then sits down as though to eat—the street door being open—the person whom she is afterwards to marry will come into the room and drink to her, bowing.—General.

See MIDSUMMER FIRES.

MIDSUMMER FIRES

If fires are not lighted on Midsummer Eve to bless the apples, the crop will be a failure.—Hereford and Somerset.

All over Europe peasants from time immemorial have kindled bonfires on certain days of the year, and have danced or leaped over them. Customs of this kind can be traced back to the Middle Ages, and their analogy to similar recorded customs suggests that their origin goes back to probably centuries before the Christian era.

In Britain, such fires were mostly lit on Beltane, Hallowe'en and Midsummer. Every village celebrated its bonfires on these nights and, although there was more custom than superstition in their lighting, there did creep in, in certain areas, beliefs in the efficacy of the fires to avert disaster or bring luck. The Hereford and Somersetshire superstition quoted above is one of them.

In the Vale of Glamorgan, a cartwheel was thickly swathed with straw.

At a given signal the wheel was lighted and sent rolling down a steep hill. If the "fire wheel" went out before it reached the bottom of the hill, then the harvest was bound to be a poor one. If it kept lighted all the way down, then the harvest would be good; and should it be still alight after it had reached the level, the harvest would be abundant.

In the Isle of Man the bonfires were lit, in country districts, to the windward of the fields, in order that the smoke might pass over the corn, and over the cattle.

To make sure that the cattle were saved from anything evil, they penned them in the folds and carried blazing gorse round them.

Similar practice was followed in Ireland, with the exception that cattle were driven through the smoke as in the case of English Need Fires (q.v.)

On Lettermore Island, South Connemara, ashes from the fires were thrown on the fields to fertilize them, and it was deemed necessary for this purpose that a bone should have been burned in the fires.

In Scotland the fires were not so prevalent as in England, but in the Perthshire Highlands the cowmen were wont on this Midsummer Eve to walk three times round the folds, in the course of the sun, carrying a burning torch. This, it was held, purified the herds and warned away disease.

See NEED FIRES, WASSAILING.

MINCE PIES

For every mince pie you eat in a different house, you will have a month's happiness.—South Country.

That is the tale which has often been told the authors. There is, however, a proviso, not so generally known, if the luck is to work; the pies must be eaten, in the south, for twelve consecutive days. The North Country area, where the charm is also believed, allows a month's extension on this time.

MINERS

To meet or see a woman on the way to the pit in the middle of the night will mean that bad luck will follow.—General.

NOTE: A similar superstition was held by men in the fishing ports. See Fishing.

If a miner washes his back, he will suffer from weakness in the back.—General.

Bad luck of the worst sort will follow

a miner who turns back, and re-enters his house, after he has left for the pit. —General.

If you see a miner going to work, speak up clearly, lest the missing of this civility should send the man to his labours with a poor heart.—Cornwall.

NOTE: It is more likely that the origin of the superstition lies in the fact that a passer-by not speaking would be an "ill-wisher."

An illustration of how strongly was held the seeing of a woman while on the way to work at night as prognosticating bad luck, is a report in the *Oswestry Advertiser* of May, 1874. It reads: "A woman is employed as a messenger at one of the collieries, and as she commences her duties early each morning, meets great numbers of miners going to the pits. Some of them, considering it a bad omen to meet a woman first thing in the morning, and unable to deter her from her work by any other means, visited the pit manager and announced that they would stay away from the shift unless she was dismissed."

Unhappily, we were not told by the paper what eventually happened to the unfortunate woman.

The belief in the ill-luck of turning back once the journey to the pit has been started, exists even to-day in a number of areas. It was, however, generally held even to the end of the nineteenth century. On no account would an old miner re-enter the house, for it was held that the direst of ill-luck would attend him.

He could, however, avert the bad luck and retrieve his forgotten article by knocking at the door and asking that it be given to him. There are records in many mining villages in Scotland and the North of England where a miner, rather even than turn back and ask for his forgotten "snap" has worked all through his shift without food or drink.

Cornwall miners have a superstition all their own—a dread of the cross being made underground.

NOTE: By cross is meant a "x" marking on a wall or other place to mark a spot.

The origin of this lies in the belief that the Little Men (called Trolls) who work, unseen, in the mines, but are to be heard knocking (they are known as the Knockers), are averse to Christianity, and would wreak all their ill-will on any place where the mark of the Cross was displayed.

There is still one other Cornish superstition, the origin of which seems obscure. If miners on the way to work saw a snail they were in the habit of dropping a piece of tallow from their candles by its side. It was unlucky not to do so.

MIRROR

To break a mirror means seven years' bad luck.—General.

For a mirror suddenly to break of its own accord means that the person owning it will lose his, or her, best friend.

For a mirror to fall and break in a house signifies mortality among the family.—General.

To see one's face in a mirror by candlelight is unlucky.

If after a death, a person sees his image reflected in a mirror in the same room as the dead, he will shortly die himself.

No bride must look in a mirror between the time she is fully dressed for the ceremony and the completion of the marriage service. Bad luck will attend her should she do so. But good fortune waits on the couple who, on returning from the ceremony, stand side by side in front of a mirror and view themselves.

No boy or girl should see themselves in a mirror before they are twelve months of age or they will not live to a good age—Durham.

Possibly one of the most widespread superstitions to-day is the bad luck resulting from the breaking of a mirror. Now, to understand this premonition of evil, one should examine the older examples of mirror superstitions.

Father Lambert, in *Moeurs et Superstitions des Neo-Caledoniens* (1900), describes how the old men in New Caledonia hold the opinion that a person's reflection in water, or in a mirror, is his soul.

The Chinese hang brass mirrors over the idols in their houses because it is thought that the evil spirits who might enter the house, seeing themselves in the mirror will be scared.

Thus, in each of these instances the breaking of a mirror would (1) lose a man his soul; whereupon he would, of course, die; and (2) leave evil spirits rife in the house.

With reference to the seeing of one's reflection in a mirror in the room of a dead person: in Scotland folk invariably covered all mirrors in a house after a death, for the very reason given above.

Incidentally, so do the Bombay Sunis, and the Zulus and Basutos of Africa.

The origin of this belief is that the soul projected out of a person in the shape of his reflection in a mirror may be carried off by the ghost of the departed person, and thus, would not go to Paradise.

See LOOKING GLASS.

MISTLETOE

A piece of mistletoe, or a decoction of mistletoe, is a palliative for the epilepsy. —Lincolnshire, and other places.

St. Vitus Dance can be cured by drinking the water in which mistletoe berries have been boiled.—Kirton (Lincs.)

To ensure a good dairy luck, give your Christmas bunch of mistletoe to the first cow that calves after New Year's Day.— England and Wales.

If mistletoe is not burned on Twelfth Night, all the couples who have kissed under it at the Christmas festivities, will be foes before the end of the year.

No mistletoe, no luck. — Welsh farmers.

NOTE: If there was a fine crop of mistletoe at Christmas, then they expected a fine crop of corn.

Perhaps the most interesting of these superstitions of the mistletoe was its alleged remedy for the epilepsy. It was really more than a superstition, for it was recommended by high medical authorities in England and Holland down to the eighteenth century.

The origin seems to be that as mistletoe cannot fall to the ground, it being rooted on a branch of a tree high above the ground, those sufferers from epilepsy (known in those days as the falling sickness) could not fall down while they had on their person, or in their stomach, a fragment of mistletoe. The Druids, it will be recalled, called mistletoe the All-Healer.

In the Scottish shires of Elgin and Moray down almost to the nineteenth century it was held that withes of mistletoe, cut at the full moon of March, and made into circles cured hectics and other troubles.

A Welsh superstition was that if mistletoe is found growing on an ash tree or a hazel, treasure will be found growing underneath the tree's roots.

No identity of the treasure was known later than the sixteenth century, but before that the superstition ran that beneath the roots of such a tree there would be a snake with a ruby jewel in its head. It would seem that, later, the snake was forgotten, and only an unknown treasure survived.

It should be emphasised that in all mistletoe superstition, the charm would not work if the mistletoe was touched by iron or steel. When the Druids went to gather their sacred plant at what is now our Christmas time, they cut its tendrils with a silver knife from the trees in their oak groves. With it they decorated their altars. To-day, mistletoe is entwined with holly berries in our homes at the same season.

Mistletoe was regarded by the Druids as sacred because not only its flowers, but its leaves also, grow in clusters of three united to one stock. It is, however, the one evergreen never included in Church decorations, probably because of its association with the Druids.

The legend of kissing under the mistletoe comes from the Norse mythological story of Balder, one of the gods. He was the son of Odin and of Freya. His mother loved Balder so much that she persuaded all things living to protect him. Unfortunately she forgot mistletoe with the result that Loki, God of Evil, slew Balder with a spear made of mistletoe wood.

The other gods restored Balder to life, and mistletoe promised that it would do no more harm to their favourite, provided it was kept from touching the earth.

The gods accordingly placed mistletoe in the keeping of Freya, the Goddess of Love, hence its association with kissing. Incidentally the pledge that mistletoe should not touch the earth rules to-day; it is, as already stated, a parasite plant sprouting on and living on other trees, with no roots in the ground.

Now, this idea that mistletoe was not only the cause of Balder's death, but also held his life, has a counterpart in Scottish superstition, for it was held for generations that the fate of the family of the Hays of Errol, in Perthshire, was bound up with mistletoe that grew on an oak on the estate, which was near the Firth of Tay. The badge of the Hays was the mistletoe.

When the oak fell, so it was held, the Hays would fall, too. And the two most unlucky things a Hay could do was to shoot a falcon (the oak stood near the Falcon Stone) and cut off any branch of the old oak.

But, it was said, that a sprig of mistletoe cut by a Hay on Hallowe'en with a new dirk, after he had walked round the tree three times sunwise, would be an infallible guard against witches and in battle.

The superstition is recorded in verses by Robert the Rhymer:

> While the mistletoe bats on Errol's aik,
> And that aik stands fast,
> The Hays shall flourish, and their good grey hawk
> Shall nocht flinch before the blast.

> But when the root of the aik decays,
> And the mistletoe dwines on its withered breast,
> The grass shall grow on Errol's hearthstane,
> And the corbie roup in the falcon's nest.

MOLES (ON THE BODY)

A mole on the back of the neck marks out the possessor as in danger of hanging.—Durham and Ireland.

A round mole in the right position will bring good luck, but an oblong mole means always misfortune.

A mole on the left breast of a girl will enable her to choose any man she likes; she is irresistible.

There was much more misfortune and fortune in moles. If in the middle of the forehead, it made a man abound in benefits. If it was warty as well, his good fortune was increased.

A mole on the left side of the face, near the hair, was ominous of ill-luck. (There we have, again, that ominous left side.) One on the forehead a little above the temple, if it appeared red, secured excellent wit and understanding; but black denoted falsehood.

A mole on the chin was lucky, also on the ear and neck; but one on the right breast foretold poverty.

One near the bottom of the nostrils was also lucky, also on the right foot, whereas the left foot was definitely unfortunate. A mole on the eyebrow was lucky, as was also one on the wrist.

Many moles between the elbow and the wrist betokened crosses in middle life, but prosperity at the end.

Misson, in his *Travels in England*, said he found a curious belief—that the hairs that grew out of moles were regarded as tokens of great luck.

MONEY

To make sure that you will always have money in your pocket, put into it a small spider, called a money spider.—General.

An alternative is to keep in one's pocket a bent coin, or one with a hole in it. But only so long as you take it out at every new moon and spit on it.

The latter still lives; the authors have a friend who, on changing his dress on several occasions, has been considerably upset to discover that he had forgotten to put into the new trousers' pocket his coin with a hole in it.

MOON

It is unlucky to look at the new moon for the first time through a window.

A new moon seen over the right shoulder is lucky; but unlucky if seen over the left shoulder.

A new moon seen straight in front prognosticates good fortune to the end of the season.

A housewife seeing the new moon for the first time should run quickly into her bedroom and turn a bed.

If a new moon falls on a Saturday, there will be twenty days of wind and rain.—Worcestershire and Sussex.

If there are two moons in a single month, the weather will be unfavourable till the next new moon.—South Country.

NOTE: In 1946, there were two moons in May, and none in June. An old countryman told the authors that there would be no favourable weather in June, nor any until the new moon in July. And neither was there!

No moon, no man.—Cornwall.

NOTE: Meaning that when a child is born between the interval between the old moon and the appearance of the new moon, it will never grow to puberty, In the same county it is believed that where a boy is born in the wane of the moon, the next birth will be a girl.

You should always show respect to the new moon, by bowing to it, at the same time turning over the silver in your pocket. Then you will be lucky in all your affairs.—General.

Perhaps the most complete description of the early superstitions connected with the moon is that in the Cotton M.S. It cited the following beliefs:

First Day: The moon's first day is the best on which to engage in any new works of any kind. Should you fall ill on the first day of the moon, you will be ill long, and endure much suffering. But a child born on this day will be happy, and live long.

Second Day: An omen for prosperity if you buy and sell, or make a sea journey. Good for garden sowing, and ploughing on the farm.

Third Day: A child born on this day will not live long. Burglars have for many years eschewed their calling on this day, for it is felt that a theft committed on this day will be very quickly detected.

Fourth Day: Is the ideal day for starting building operations. If you go in for politics, it will be a great help to have been born on this day.

Fifth Day: Nothing much in this day.

Sixth Day: Is a hunting man's day.

Seventh Day: Nothing much in this day.

Eighth Day: It is a misfortune to fall ill on this day; you will almost certainly die.

Ninth Day: Nothing.

Tenth Day: One born on this day is destined to be a globe trotter.

Eleven to Twenty: Nothing.

Twenty-First Day: If there is anything in omens, a child born on this day will find robbery a paying profession.

That ends the prognostications.

If you do not like using the barber's shop, you should have your hair cut during the waning of the moon; it will then grow as slowly as it does fast if cut at the waxing of the moon.

If you suffer from corns, cut them on the moon's waning—and they will vanish for good.

A widespread belief, still current, was that certain crops should be planted according to the state of the moon.

A pig should be killed while the moon is waxing. It will swell nicely; while if the pig is slaughtered during the waning of the moon, the pork will cook close and hard.

A Fenland superstition is that public dinners should always be held at the full moon, or tragedy will follow. Knowing the Fenland roads, with the wide ditches on each side, and the total absence of lights, the authors can well believe it. Driving along those roads in the dim light of a waning or waxing moon is an operation fraught with considerable peril—especially after a public dinner, at which the wine has flowed with the generosity of Fenland people.

Wales has a robust stock of moon superstitions. For instance, if you move to a new house, or change from one residence to another at the time of the new moon, then you will have plenty of bread and to spare.

If a member of the family dies at the time of the new moon, three deaths are likely to follow.

Wood cut at the new moon is hard to split; at the full moon it is easily cut.

Grass should be sown at the full of the moon. Then the hay crop will dry quickly.

If lovers cross the moon line together, they will never marry.

Fishermen in the Welsh ports avoided the moon line when setting out to sea; and another moon line superstition is never to cross it without wishing for something.

If you want a comfortable feather bed, then you must make certain that the bed tick was filled with the feathers after the moon has passed the full. The newly plucked feathers will then lie at rest. Otherwise, you are likely to have a lumpy bed.

In many parts of the country the moon was believed to have a magic influence in healing certain types of malady. In Staffordshire, for instance, a cure for chin-cough was to take the child outside and let it look at the new moon. The child's clothes then had to be lifted up, and its stomach rubbed up and down with the right hand while the following words were recited, the reciter's eyes at the same time being kept on the moon:

What I see, may it increase,
What I feel, may it decrease,
In the name of the Father, Son, and
Holy Ghost.—Amen.

Sailors, of course, have their own weather superstition. If the moon, in the first or last quarter, lies in nearly a horizontal position (flat on her back) with the horns upwards, the weather will be fine, as you "may hang your hat on them."

Then, there is the love divination: The first moon of the New Year should be viewed by a young woman through a silk handkerchief, and the number of moons showing through it represents the number of months (moons) she will remain unmarried.

A general superstition of years ago was that it brings bad luck to point at the moon; and that curtseys to the moon will bring a present before the next moon. In Cornwall people always nodded to the new moon and turned the silver in their pockets.

Perhaps the most persistent superstition of the moon held to-day is that should a person sleep with the moon shining on his face, the face will become distorted, and the sleeper may become insane. Although this has been derided by medical authorities, in reply to inquiries, the authors have received so many letters from people of undoubted integrity who vouch for the distortion of face, and who insist that in such circumstances they have awakened with their faces blotched and swollen twice the normal size, that they are of opinion that sleeping with the moon shining on one's face is definitely to be avoided.

Finally, there is the superstition that people's madness is worse with the full moon. The origin of this is, of course, the derivation of the word lunatic from luna, the moon. It was the belief of the ancients; it has no substance in medical fact.

In connection with the new moon being shown respect in being bowed to, the authors, on 3rd September, 1946, received the following letter from a correspondent in Coventry, Warwickshire:

"Dear Wise People,—Having recently been demobbed from the Navy (a Service riddled with superstition), my wife makes me smile at the ritual she practises of bowing to a new moon seven times, and turning over silver coins, to the accompaniment of her wishes and an incantation. She swears that that is why I have had good luck in winning two firsts in the football pools."

So the moon still holds her superstitious spell!

See CROPS, MONEY.

MOP

To lose a mop or a bucket overboard, is a sign of ill-omen.—Sailors' superstition.

The authors once saw a sailor dive overboard to retrieve a dropped mop.

See SAILOR, SEA.

MOTH

If a black moth flies into the house, someone in the house will die within a month.

Night flying white moths are souls of the departed.—Yorks.

In some areas, the time limit for the black moth curse is raised to a year—eleven months' reprieve.

MOUSE

A mouse, roasted and given to a child, will cure the whooping cough.—General.

See MICE.

MUGWORT

If a man wears mugwort in his button-hole, he will never grow tired.—General.

NOTE: The same was said in Wales of the sow-thistle.

Drink nettle tea in March, and mugwort tea in May; And cowslip wine in June, to send decline away.—Wales.

NOTE: By decline in earliest days was meant what we now call consumption.

But the majority of superstitions associated with mugwort concerned the care of the eyes.

Mugwort steeped in water, and the water then used to anoint the eyes would, it was held, either cure bad eyes, or preserve good ones.

In the Midsummer Fires the flames viewed through a bunch of mugwort would guarantee that the sight would be good for a year. This held sway in other countries. In Germany and Bohemia youths wore chaplets of mugwort through which they also glimpsed the Eve of St. John bonfires, this being supposed to keep their eyes in a healthy state for the remainder of the year.

In Prussia, Bavaria, and other parts of Germany a mugwort was used very much as rowan wood was used in Scotland—as a preventive of witchcraft. Prussian farmers stuck the herb on the gates and hedges of fields in which cows grazed, to protect the animals and their milk from the witches.

In Japan, if a house has been robbed at night and the footsteps of the burglar are visible next day, the householder burns mugwort in them, thereby hurting the robber's feet so that he cannot run from the police, and can thus easily be overtaken.

Brand, in his *Popular Antiques*, records the belief held in Britain that a rare coal is to be found under the roots of the mugwort at a single hour of a single day in the year, namely, at noon or midnight on Midsummer Eve. This coal, it was supposed, protected anyone who carried it on his person from carbuncle, lightning, fever or the plague.

MULBERRY TREE

If small shoots are appearing on the branches of the mulberry, there will be no more frosts that year.—Gloucester.

The authors knew an old Gloucestershire gardener who planted his tomatoes—which are most delicate plants—when the mulberry shoots appeared. He never lost any plants by frost, and was generally a week or two ahead with his tomatoes.

MUMPS

To cure the mumps, tie a halter round the neck of the child and lead him to a brook. Bathe him three times three in the name of the Blessed Trinity.—Ireland.

The mumps by this means would be cured. But whether they just vanished, or whether they were transferred to the running water of the brook and were thus carried away, the authors cannot say.

MURRAIN (CATTLE DISEASE)
See NEED FIRE.

MUSHROOM
When the moon is at the full, mushrooms you may safely pull; But when the moon is on the wane, wait ere you think to pluck again.—Essex.

The belief is that the growth of mushrooms is influenced by the change of the moon.

MUSICIANS
One of the most disturbing superstitions of musicians is the playing of "I Dreamt that I Dwelt in Marble Halls" in a musical show except the light opera for which it was written.

It is held that such playing will bring bad luck to the orchestral pit, and also to the musical show on the stage at the time.

Another superstition is against the singing or whistling in a theatre of Tosti's "Goodbye," except in its proper place.

MUTTON BONE
If you throw a mutton bone on the fire, bad luck will attend you.

This omen of ill-luck comes, of course, from the association of lamb with the Lamb of God, and the constant reference by Jesus to His people as sheep; as in "Feed My sheep." There is also, of course, the association of the Good Shepherd, and the shepherds who saw the Star in the East.

MYRTLE
The myrtle is the luckiest plant to have in your window. Water it every morning and be proud of it.—Somerset.

It was held in Somerset, also, that myrtle will not grow unless it is planted by a woman; and not then unless, while planting, the woman spread the skirt of her dress and looked proud.

In Wales, it was held that if myrtle grows on each side of the door of a house, love and peace will never depart from the habitation. But should the myrtle be dug up, then all love and peace in the household would also be uprooted.

NAILS (FINGER)
The finger nails of babies should not be cut until the child is twelve months old. They should be bitten off, or the child will grow up a thief.—General.

To cure epilepsy, nail parings of the patient should be buried with a black cock at midnight at the spot where the epileptic fell.—General.

To cut or pare the finger nails on a Friday or Sunday will bring bad luck.—General.

If the first parings of a child's nails are buried underneath an ash tree, the child will turn out to be a "top singer."—Northumberland.

To cut the nails or hair during a calm, will provoke fierce winds.—Sailors' superstition.

To cure the ague, take parings from nails and clippings from the hair of the sufferer, and place them in a bag under the threshold of a neighbour. He will then get the ague instead of you.—Devonshire.

It is interesting to compare with the Devonshire "cure" for ague given above, the ancient Roman cure for the "fever" —which was ague.

The Romans, then, pared the nails of the person with fever, and stuck them with wax on a neighbour's door before sunrise. The fever then passed from the sick man to the neighbour. And that was a few generations before Devonshire was even dreamed of!

See EPILEPSY, FINGER NAILS.

NAILS (IRON)
To cure the ague, nail a lock of the patient's hair to an oak tree. Then let the patient wrench the lock from his head by a sudden pull, and he will leave the ague behind him in the tree.—Herts.

NOTE: At Berkhamsted, in Herts, there were for many years a row of oak trees which were celebrated for this cure of the ague. Their trunks were dotted with hundreds of nails.

An ague sufferer should go alone to a cross-roads at midnight and as the clock begins to strike, turn himself round thrice and drive a tenpenny nail into the ground. Then walk backwards away from the spot before the clock has finished the twelfth note. He will miss the ague.—Suffolk.

This Nailing of Evils is one of the oldest and most widespread superstitions in the world. There is hardly a country, civilized or uncivilized, in which it was not practised in one form or another.

The evil—by which is meant, of course, the illness—could be nailed to the ground, a tree, a door or any other substance into which it could be nailed and thus secured from getting back to the patient as he walked away.

At Blida, in Algeria, women knocked nails into a celebrated sacred tree, in order to rid themselves of their ailments. In Persia, an aching tooth was scraped until it bled, and the bloody nail was then hammered into a tree—with the toothache. If anyone was so unwise as to draw out the nail, then he acquired the toothache.

At Port Charlotte, in Brunswick, in North Africa, in Mogador, Tunis, and in Egypt, the story is the same. In Cairo, even in recent times, sufferers knocked a nail into the wooden doors of the South Gate to rid themselves of a head-ache.

Thus, once again is evidenced the identical superstition in world-wide practice without any linking medium of association. It is possible, however, that the Suffolk superstitious cure for the ague came here with the Romans, for the Roman method of curing the epilepsy was, according to Pliny, to drive a nail into the ground on the spot where the patient fell.

NAME

*If a child is named after one which has died in the family, the dead child will come and call the living away.—*General in rural areas.

*A woman who has had two successive, but unrelated, husbands bearing the same surname, can cure the whooping cough and other illnesses by cutting bread and butter and giving it to the patient.—*Herefordshire.

The former of the above two super-stitions is still widely believed in in many rural areas, and the utmost care is taken that no name of any dead person in the family be given to a newly born member of it.

The belief goes still further in other parts, where it is held that if a parent gives to a child the name of a favourite pet animal, misfortune will overtake the child and the animal.

There are a number of recorded instances where fatalities have occurred after such namings, but no guarantee, of course, that they would not have happened if the name had not been given.

Up to a few years ago the bread and butter cure for whooping cough men-tioned above was still in operation in some parts of Lincolnshire, and the authors recall an old village woman who was in great demand as a curer of the cough because she had married two husbands with the same surname. We should point out that the coughs in each case were cured—as they would have been, in any case, in due course!

For the calling of things other than by their proper name, see FISHING (SEA).

See PARSON.

NAPKINS

*A guest who folds his napkin after a first meal in any house, will never go to the house again.—*General.

From this superstition a certain etiquette in table napkins has grown up, and is rigidly adhered to by those people who move in country house circles.

According to this a casual visitor, who is taking but a single meal in the house, should leave his napkin crumpled up on the table. Only those who are staying for a period should fold the napkin and lay it by the side of the plate.

NEED FIRE.

*To cure murrain (disease) among cattle, rub two pieces of wood together, thereby causing them to ignite. Kindle a bonfire with the flame and drive cattle through the smoke, keeping them there for some time.—*Stamfordham (North-umberland), Yorks, and Scotland.

The wording of the superstition given above is that of the areas named, only because of its briefness for tabulation. It by no means covers the extent of the belief.

Not only in England, Scotland and Wales, but throughout Europe this charm for the disease of cattle was fervently held in superstitious respect.

In England the earliest notice of need fires is contained in the Chronicles of Lanercost, 1268, where is described how when an epidemic was raging among cattle that year, "certain beastly men, monks in garb but not in mind, taught the idots of their country to make fire by the friction of wood, and to set up an image of Priapus, whereby they thought to succour the animals."

From that the custom spread until there was no part of rural England or Scotland, where the need fire was not resorted to.

At Ingleton, a small town in West Yorkshire, the method was to rub two pieces of wood together and setting fire to a large bonfire of faggots and brushwood. These were then dispersed, and the cattle driven among the burning embers.

In Northumberland even down to the nineteenth century, the practice was first to extinguish all fires of any kind in the area, in houses as well as other places. Two pieces of dried wood were then rubbed together until they ignited, and with this straw and brushwood was lit, juniper thrown into the flames, and the cattle driven through the smoke.

Lighting from the forced fire was passed to neighbours who with it lighted other fires in their area, so that within an hour there was a ring of need fires throughout the stricken area. Such fires have been placed on record by the vicar of Stamfordham, in Northumberland, as late as the first half of the nineteenth century.

In the Island of Mull, Hebrides, the people carried a wheel and nine spindles of oak wood to the top of Carnmoor. Every fire in every house within sight of the hill was extinguished, and the wheel was then turned rapidly over the nine spindles until fire was produced by the friction. The same procedure was adopted in Caithness.

In other parts of Scotland, the northeast of Aberdeenshire, for instance, the fire was produced on the "muckle wheel," a cartwheel set on a spindle which had never before been used. It was turned rapidly until friction fire resulted. From this "virgin flame" fires were kindled in all the cattle byres.

In County Leitrim, Ireland, in the event of a cattle plague, all the fires on the townland, and the two adjoining (one on each side) were extinguished. In this area, the fire was produced not by a wheel or by rubbing two small pieces of dry wood, but by setting one large block of wood on the ground and fitting an upper block with handles by which it was drawn backwards and forwards over the lower block. From the fire thus produced, the extinguished fires in the townland were again ignited.

In some cases it was necessary, in the view of the populace, that an animal should be sacrificed in the fire. Thus, in the Hebrides, one of the stricken cattle, usually a heifer, was cut in pieces, the diseased part burned, and the remainder eaten in feasting after the completion of the need fire ceremony. In other areas, particularly the Isle of Man, the animal was a calf, or a pig, or a sheep.

The origin of the sacrifice to God of the killed animal would seem to have its origin in the sacrifice by Abraham of the ram after his son, Isaac, had been spared.

See CALF.

NEW YEAR

Empty pockets or empty cupboards on New Year's Eve portend a year of poverty.—General.

NOTE: Burns referred to this as well known in his day, in a letter to Colonel de Payster from whom he borrowed a small sum at this time of the year, "To make the old year go out groaning; and keep the New Year from coming in groaning."

If a new suit or dress has money in the pockets, they will not be empty throughout the year.—Scotland, and England.

To let the fire die out on New Year's Eve is decidedly bad luck.—General.

No iron, no light, and nothing else should be taken out of a house on New Year's Day, or ill-fortune will attend the household.—North of England, and, particularly, in Scotland.

Remarkable precautions were taken by the Celts, particularly, to ensure that there was no chance of the fire going out in their homes on New Year's Eve. Because, if the calamity happened, it was impossible for them to obtain a light from any neighbour. (It must be remembered that in the early days of this superstition there were no such things as matches.)

A neighbour who gave a light to such a household would, it was superstitiously believed, be giving away her luck for a year. If a family, deprived by its own negligence, sought to remedy their fireless home by stealing a light, their ill-luck would be increased since the light stolen was not "holy."

The origin of the superstition undoubtedly came to us from the Romans, for Hospinian has recorded that in Rome no one would suffer another to take fire out of his house on New Year's Eve or Day, or anything made of iron.

The custom died hard, for a great-grandfather of one of the authors on the last night of the old year called his staff together and warned them against allowing *anything* to be carried out of the house on New Year's Day under pain of instant dismissal. Thus, even the fire ashes of the night, and the waste vegetables, etc., were kept indoors until 2nd January. And that was as late as 1870.

It would seem that anxiety over the incomings and outgoings of the coming year was at the root of the superstition since anything might be *brought into* the house, but not taken out.

From a well-wisher in Surrey on December 28, 1946, we received a letter which read:

"If you want money to come to your house during 1947, put some out of doors as the last thing you do on New Year's Eve, and the first thing on New Year's Day go out and fetch it in."

See FIRST FOOTING.

NEW YEAR DRINKS

The last drink drained from a bottle on New Year's Eve will bring good fortune to whoever comes in for it.

NEW YEAR WIND

In the rural areas of both Scotland and England superstition in weather ran high. One such concerned the state of the wind on New Year's Eve. The lore was in rhyme, now, we fear, almost forgotten:

If New Year Eve night wind blow south,
It betokeneth warmth and growth.
If west, much milk and fish in the sea.
If north, much cold and storms there will be.
If east, the trees will bear much fruit.
If north-east, flee it, man and brute.

Another, a couplet, current in Bucks, about the same time as the verses above went:

If the calends of January be smiling and gay,
You'll have wintry weather till the calends of May.

NIGHTMARE

To cure the nightmare, hang your stockings crosswise at the foot of the bed with a pin stuck in them.

A stone, having a natural hole through it; hung in the cowhouse will prevent nightmare among the cattle; and hung in a bedroom will be of equal service to the sleeper.—Orkneys.

In Lancashire, the peasantry placed their shoes under the bed with the toes pointing outwards as a preventive of nightmare.

Another method in vogue in the early nineteenth century, was to lay a knife, or any other steel article under the foot of the bed. Or it could be a piece of iron.

The origin of nightmare is related to the nightmare of the olden days, which was not quite the same as the modern nightmare.

The original nightmare was supposed to be a female spirit (hence "mare") supposed to beset people and animals at night by settling upon them when they were asleep and producing a feeling of suffocation by its weight. It was at one time thought to be an incubus.

From this, the telling effect of iron or steel in keeping the nightmare away is apparent; witches and evil spirits cannot, according to superstition, abide iron. Hence the horseshoe, and the knife stuck beneath a window to keep away witches.

NOSE

The moss of a dead man's skull applied so as just to touch the skin is the most effective cure in stopping nose bleeding.—Eighteenth century.

A cold key pushed down the back will stop the nose bleeding.—Twentieth century.

To stop the nose bleeding, transfix a toad with a sharp-pointed instrument, enclose it when dead in a little bag, and suspend it round the neck.—North Country.

There was an even more incredible cure: "If he be a man who suffers, he asks a female to bring him a lace (if a female, she asks a man) without giving money, saying why it is wanted, or returning thanks when received. The lace must be worn round the neck for the space of nine days, at the expiration of which the patient will experience no return of the disorder.

A Devonshire remedy for nose bleeding was to put two large toads into a cold oven and increase the heat until the toads were cooked to a crisp mass. They were then beaten to powder in a stone mortar, and the powder was stored in a box and used as snuff.

The Shropshire "charm" was to tie the patient's left garter round the family Bible, and then put a key at the back of the neck of the patient.

Just one more superstition relating to noses; if you possess a blue vein across your nose, you will not live long—according to the good people of Cornwall.

And if your eyebrows meet across your nose, you are either deceitful, or in for a very bad spell of misfortune.

NUMBERS

If the date of your birth can be divisible by seven, you will be lucky on earth.

The seventh son of a seventh son possesses second sight, and can foretell the future.—General.

The seventh son is destined to be an infallible physician.—Scotland.

There is luck in odd numbers.—General.

Throughout generations the fortune in odd numbers has been a matter of superstitious belief. Particularly if the odd number be seven or three, or three times three, which is the number nine.

Note how the odd numbers occur in everyday life: A sitting of eggs is always thirteen; our names are called three times when our services are required in a court of law; the banns of marriage are called three times; demands for money are always made three times before any unpleasant results are started; we give three cheers for any joyful occasion.

On the sacred side, there were three churches of Asia; man is threefold (the world, the flesh and the devil); the Christian graces are three; the cardinal colours are three; the Trinity is three.

Of the number seven, there were seven days in Creation; the Hebrew word to swear means, literally, to come under the influence of the seven things; and all through the Old Testament, the number seven predominates.

The unlucky odd number thirteen is, perhaps, the best known instance of misfortune.

NUN'S WELL, ST.

See MADNESS, WELLS.

NURSING

If a nurse in hospital knocks over a chair, it is a sure sign that a new patient will shortly arrive.

Should a nurse, while dressing, twist her apron strings, she will soon be taking over new work.

NUTS

If children go nutting on a Sunday, the Devil will hold down the branches for them, and misfortune will follow them all through life.—Sussex.

NOTE: This superstition sounds to the authors very like a Sunday School teachers' invention! But it is credited with the Sussex simile, "As black as the Devil's nutting bag."

A bride who receives a bag of hazel nuts as she leaves the church will be fruitful.—Devonshire.

The nuts had to be presented to the bride by an old woman, preferably a married one who had had a family of children.

This was before the introduction of rice at a wedding. Rice is prolific, like orange trees—hence orange blossom for a bride—and hazel nuts are equally known as prolific croppers.

A love divination ritual with nuts was for ladies only. The seeker after knowledge had to place as many nuts on the top bar of the grate as there were women present in the company, and an equal number for their sweethearts. They must have been placed in pairs, side by side. If the nuts remained together and were consumed, all was well. If any of the pairs flew apart, the marriage, as the present announcements have it, "will not take place."

OAK TREE

A nail driven into an oak tree will cure the toothache.—Cornwall.

To cure the rupture in a child, it should be passed through a cleft oak sapling. The opening should then be closed up and bound; and as the cleft in the tree heals and the parts come together again, so the rupture in the child will be healed.—Sussex.

NOTE: An ash tree sapling could also be employed for this healing.

The oak tree blooms only on Midsummer Eve at midnight, and the flowers wither before daybreak. If a maiden spreads a white cloth under the tree at night, and in the morning gathers the little dust which is all that is left of the blossom, and places it under her pillow, her future husband will appear in her dreams.—Shropshire.

Rub a piece of oak on the left hand in silence on Midsummer Day, and the oak will afterwards heal all your sores.—Wales.

But the real superstition of the oak in Britain laid in its sacredness. At one time it was considered a fatal sin to cut down an oak, though any other tree could be hewn by the common people.

It was invariably the wood of the oak

with which the healing fires of the countryside were ignited. And so it was throughout Europe.

The Druids esteemed nothing more sacred than the oak, and performed few rites without oak leaves, and the mistletoe. It is supposed in Wales that if the leaves of the oak curl, heat is foretold. A worm in an oak apple denotes poverty for the finder, and a spider in the oak apple, illness for the finder.

The acorn of the oak was a love denoter. If two were taken and named, one for oneself and the other for the sweetheart, and were then set to float in a basin of water, should they come together a marriage was certain; should they float apart there would be no wedding bells.

Incidentally, the same "charm" was said to work with two wisps of straw or two pieces of stick.
See NEED FIRES, RICKETS, RUPTURE.

OMENS
See under separate headings of animals and things.

ONIONS
In buying onions always choose a shop with two doors, go in by one door and out at another.

NOTE: The authors cannot trace what are the suggested consequences of not following this advice.

*Onions, placed under your pillow on St. Thomas's Eve, are sure to bring visions of your future husband.—*London.

Onions are good in a sick room.

The last, though long counted as a superstition, is really a sound hygienic principle.

Skinned onions should not be placed in a larder even for a few hours. They become impregnated with germs. If the whole onion is not cooked after being peeled it should be thrown away. Thus, in a sickroom, they would, undoubtedly, attract the germs of the illness, and in that way probably would be a good thing in the sickroom.

Here is a love divination with onions, the origin of which the authors cannot place: Take four to eight onions and scratch on each the name of those most fancied for a husband. Set them in the chimney corner, and whichever be the first to sprout the name on it will be your future husband.

ORANGE BLOSSOM
The bride who wears orange blossom will have good luck.—General.

It depends, of course, on what the bride considers to be good luck. For the accepted origin of the orange blossom for the bride is that she may be fruitful, the orange being a prolific fruiting plant.

With this as the origin, the wearing of orange blossom by a bride is part of world-wide propitiation of the beneficent Tree Spirits, of which instances have already been given in this volume.

The orange blossom is, by impute, an appeal to the tree spirit that the bride shall not be barren.

Among the Maoris, the power of making women fruitful is ascribed to trees. A barren woman who embraced a fruitful tree would, it was held, bear a male or female child, according to whether she embraced the tree on the west or east side.

A south Slav woman, desiring a child, placed a chemise upon a fruitful tree. The women of Kara-Kirghiz roll on the ground under an apple tree in order to ensure offspring. And there are other similar examples among native races.

There is not so much difference, really, between these brides and the British bride who wears the orange blossom.

ORPINE
Plant slips (cuttings) of orpine in pairs on Midsummer Eve, one slip standing for a young man and the other for a young woman. If the plants, as they grow up, bend towards each other the couple will marry; if either of them wither, he or she whom it represents will die.

This was widely held in rural England for many years. Perhaps country people will recognize orpine better by its popular name of midsummer men.

The plant grows on a gravelly or chalky soil near hedges, on the borders of fields and on bushy hills. The flowers, clustered tufts of crimson or purple petals, come in August.

Exactly the same superstition as that given above was practised in Switzerland and in Westphalia.

OVERLOOKING
See EVIL EYE.

OWL
To see an owl in the sunlight is a bad

fortune for the beholder.—Scotland and general.

To cure the whooping cough in a child, give him owl broth.—Yorkshire.

Who looks into the nest of an owl will become morose and melancholy for the rest of his life.—Cheshire.

When an owl hoots among houses, a maiden will lose her chastity.—Wales.

From ancient times the owl has been regarded as an unlucky bird.

Reference is made above to the Scottish superstition of the ill-luck of seeing an owl in the daylight hours. The Romans held the owl in abhorrence, and when it was seen and caught in the city in the daylight hours, it was burnt and its ashes publicly scattered in the Tiber.

Yet, the owl is regarded in Britain as a wise bird—"a wise old owl."

It is probable that it owes its bad name, both now and in the days of Rome, to being a tenant of the night, amidst silence, solitude; and because of its melancholy hoot.

Pliny denominated the owl as "the funeral bird of the night," and Spenser in his *Fairie Queene* as "death's dreadful messenger."

In *The Book of Days*, it is recorded that two owls "of enormous size" warn the family of Arundel of death among them. Whenever they were seen perched on the battlements of the family mansion, it was held that a member of the family was about to die.

A word on the Welsh superstition recorded above. This was held even more firmly in the village of Llangynwyd, near Maesteg, Bridgend, Glamorgan. There it was maintained as a positive fact that should an owl hoot in the early night from one of the churchyard yews, it was a sign that an unmarried girl of the village had surrendered her chastity.

T. C. Evans, in his *History of Llangynwyd*, states that "even now (1908) there are people in the village who maintain the trustworthiness of this sign."

And a tentative inquiry by the authors of an old resident in the place suggests that there are still people who mourn the passing of chastity at the hooting of the churchyard owl.

PALM SUNDAY

From whatever quarter the wind blows for the greater part of Palm Sunday, it will continue to blow from the same quarter during the most part of the ensuing summer.—Winchester.

Another weather superstition relating to Palm Sunday is that if the sun shines clear on that day, there will be great store of fine weather, plenty of corn and other fruits of the earth.

PANCAKE

If on pancake day, a pancake is thrown to a cock, and he eats it himself, bad luck will follow the household. If he pecks at it, and leaves it for his hens to finish, it is a sign of good luck.—Horncastle district.

Eat pancakes on Shrove Tuesday and grey peas on Ash Wednesday, and you will have money in your pocket all the year round.—General.

This luck associated with pancakes, is not peculiar to Britain, neither are pancakes, which may come as a surprise to most people.

In Estonia, when a peasant woman plants her cabbages she makes a large pancake, in order that her cabbages shall have big, broad leaves; and at the time of planting wears a dazzling white headdress, believing that this will give the cabbages good white hearts.

The origin of the pancake tradition for Shrove Tuesday has two sources. The authors incline to the idea that it was prepared to sustain the unfortunate people who on Shrove Tuesday had long waits at the church (Roman Catholic in those days, of course), and took the pancake for sustenance while waiting their turn to be shriven of their sins.

The other suggestion is that the making of pancakes was a convenient way for the housewife to get rid of all the fats she possessed in the house, and which she must not use during the season of Lent, which began the following day. Meat, and all appertaining to it or coming from it, was, of course, forbidden by the Church during Lent.

PANSIES

If you pick pansies on a fine day, it will rain before long.

PARSLEY

If parsley is grown in the garden, there will be a death in the family before the year is out.—London and Surrey.

If parsley is sown on any day other than Good Friday, it will not grow double.—Cobham (Surrey).

To give away parsley is to give away your luck.—South Hampshire.

To transplant parsley, puts the whole of one's garden into the hands of the Evil One, and the crops will fail.—Oxfordshire.

Who wants to transplant parsley, anyway?

The origin of this death and evil fortune associated with parsley, would seem to have its origin, once again, in our Roman conquerors. The Romans used to line all their graves with parsley, the herb being of the evergreen variety.

In the Nemean Games the victors' crowns were made of parsley, as the Greek heroes' crowns of victory were of laurel.

Bartholomeus, in *De Proprietatibus Rerum*, relates that "Hercules made him fyrste garlondes of this herb."

PARSON

To mention the name parson, or clergyman, will bring bad luck to the fishing.—Northern fishing ports.

A parson on board a ship will bring bad luck.—Seamen's superstition, many centuries old.

This is one of the several superstitions of fishermen round the small British ports against calling people or things by their proper names when out fishing, or on the point of starting out with their nets.

The parson, if he had to be mentioned at all, was called "the upstander." Similarly a pig and a rabbit, if it was necessary to refer to them, were given altogether different names.

The origin is a mystery; but it is an interesting fact that it exists in many places in the world. On Scotland's northeast coast, the word "kirk" must never be mentioned by fishermen; it is the "bell hoose." The minister is "the man wi' the black quyte." A brewer in some districts of Scotland thinks that to mention the word water would spoil the brewing. In the Outer Hebrides, a kiln is called not teine (fire) but aingeal.

Manx fishermen think it unlucky to mention by their names a horse or a mouse.

Illustrating the point, in Prussia and Lithuania a wolf must not be called that in the month of December; it should be referred to as the vermin (das Gewurm), or you will be torn to pieces by werewolves.

In Mecklenberg there lived at one time a Mr. Wolf. During December, when the word wolf was taboo, he was referred to as Mr. Monster.

Throughout Europe there are numerous animals which during certain parts of the year may only be mentioned by some euphemism on their name.

Among many native races—the hill tribes of Assam are an illustration—each person has a private name which must never be revealed. The whole village was tabooed for two days if any dweller in it revealed his private name.

A Bagobo man of Mindanao, in the Philippines, never at any time speaks his own name lest he should be turned into a raven, because the raven croaks out its own name.

Similar taboos on names exist in the South and Central American Indians, in Chili, in Guiana, and Colombia. The Indians of Darien, asked for their names, reply, "I have none." So it is, also, with the Navajoes of New Mexico and the Tonkawe Indians of Texas. The North American Indians will tell their American titles readily enough, but not their own or their squaws' Indian names.

There are various reasons for the reluctance to tell their names, or use them. One is that an enemy, once he knows the name, can work havoc by the use of it; another that he would lose his soul if his name was known, his name being a part of himself.

All this, however, does not explain satisfactorily why fishermen in the North of England and in Scotland cannot call a pig a pig or a parson a parson. Nor does there seem to be any known explanation of the superstition.

It is interesting, *en passant*, to note that several weeks after they had written the above, the authors, browsing through an old book on Egypt, came across a description of the naming of the children of ancient Egypt. According to this, each child received two names, which were known, respectively, as the true name and the good name, or the great name and the little name. While the good, or little, name was made public, the true, or great, name was concealed.

It should be explained that this parson superstition is one which has not altogether died out in many parts of Cornwall. The authors have knowledge of one party of old Cornish fishermen who as they put to sea saw a clergyman visitor come to the harbour to watch them. There was much grumbling among the older men of "no fish for us to-night." They would not, in fact, have put to sea at all except for the younger and non-superstitious men on board, who insisted on the foolishness of such beliefs.

As late as 1932, at St. Ives, a fisherman set off to visit friends. Standing beside a steamer at Penzance he was greeted by a minister of the St. Ives chapel, who chanced to be passing. The fisherman acknowledged the greeting, and added: "I'm sorry to see you this morning. I'd been thinking of going over to Scilly, but, of course, I can't go now I've met you." Failing to persuade the man that such a superstition was nonsense the pair got together into the train for St. Ives.

See FISHING, NAMES, PIG.

PASSING BELL

If the clock strikes while the passing bell is ringing, there will be a second death within a week.—Buckinghamshire.

If the cathedral bell tolls once, it will toll thrice.—Durham.

The passing bell is sounded to-day, of course, as a sign of mourning and respect to the dead person. But its original purpose seems to have been to drive away the evil spirits which were believed always to be hovering around ready to seize the soul of the departed. For that reason it was more readily called, in those old days, the soul bell. It was so referred to by Shakespeare in *Henry IV*, part ii.

Henderson recalls, in this respect, the incident when a clergyman, having made a rule that the passing bell should be tolled only in the daylight hours, had a tolling stopped at five a.m. after one or two notes had been sounded. The dead man was a farmer, and the widow afterwards complained bitterly at the delay in tolling. "It was cruel," she said, "to keep the poor soul all those hours a'waiting."

PEACH

The falling of the leaves of a peach tree before the autumn presages a murrain (cattle disease).—North Country.

The same belief attached itself to the falling leaves of the elm tree.

See NEED FIRE.

PEACOCK

To have a peacock's feather in the house will bring misfortune to the owner and his family.—General.

A peacock's feather on the stage, or in the theatre, will mean disaster to the play.—Stage superstition, and very much in vogue even to-day.

The stage aversion to the peacock's feather has lost nothing of its menace with the passing of the years. Nor is it confined to the younger section of chorus girls.

Some years ago, at the end of the first act of *Othello*, the late Sir Henry Irving sent a note to a woman who was in the second row of stalls. It read: "For heaven's sake take your peacock feather fan out of the theatre to save disaster."

The attendant whom the woman called and handed her fan, refused to take it, and showed every sign of great agitation. Eventually, the woman herself went to the entrance, and threw the fan into the street.

Two origins are given for this evil superstition of the peacock feather. One is the Mohammedan belief that it was a peacock which opened the wicket gate of Paradise to admit the Devil.

The other, and more likely, is that the bird was sacred among the Greeks and the Romans to Hero or Juno. In later years they were used to adorn the Holy Temples, and none but the priest was allowed to touch them. To do so was sacrilege — when sacrilege was punishable by death.

In the same way it was sacrilege for a layman to light three candles from one taper—the most likely origin of to-day's superstition of the ill-luck of lighting three cigarettes from one match.

PEAS

If, in shelling peas, you find a pod containing nine peas, you must throw it over your shoulder and wish—and your wish will come true.—General.

There is, however—or perhaps it should be "was"—a similar superstition for young women. A maiden shelling peas and finding a pod in which were the requisite nine peas, if she then placed the pod on the lintel of the kitchen door, the first man to enter afterwards would be her future husband. Shakespeare refers to this where he makes mention of "I remember the wooing of a peascod instead of her."

Incidentally, it was the habit in Cumberland, for a girl whose lover had been faithless to her, to be rubbed over with pea straw by the neighbouring lads—for what reason, the authors cannot say.

PENNY

Heave a penny over the ship's bows

when going out of dock if you would have a successful voyage.—Welsh sailors.

PERIWINKLE
If you uproot a plant of periwinkle from a grave, the dead person beneath will appear to you, and you will have terrible dreams for twelve months.—Wales.

PETER'S DAY, ST.
Unless orchards are christened on St. Peter's Day, the crop will not be good.—Herefordshire.

The christening was done, of course, with cider.

St. Peter's Eve was also the date of the Midsummer Fire festival, referred to elsewhere.

See APPLE TREES, WASSAILING.

PHOTOGRAPH
If a betrothed couple are photographed together, they will never marry.—General.

Which seems to the authors a very handy way of one of the parties getting out of the engagement—if the other can be induced for one occasion to be snapped side by side by a beach photographer.

The authors have at various times over the years come across a number of old people who steadfastly refused to have their photographs taken. They were bound to no particular county, but have been encountered in Lincolnshire, Suffolk, Yorkshire, and Cornwall.

The only reason they gave for the refusal was that it would bring them ill-luck. They could not say why, only that it would bring about misfortune.

Now, some years ago while travelling in the country around Tangier we were entertained by an Arab chieftain who had been educated and spent some years in England, and had imbibed a good deal of modern knowledge. After a luncheon, at which all the other guests were Arabs, we produced a miniature camera, and asked that we might have a photograph of the gathering. At once there was a sibilant hiss and every face in the company was covered. The host gravely explained that no Arab would be photographed.

Similarly in the streets of the villages we afterwards visited, every time the camera was raised to register a snapshot of some scene, the result showed that any Arab who chanced to be facing the camera had his face covered.

None of them would vouchsafe any explanation. But, the authors were told, the belief is that a face is a man or woman's personal property, and anyone taking it from them takes away the soul of the person. This belief also rules in many of the native tribes of other Eastern countries.

It may possibly be that the objection we found among the old people in England mentioned above, has, in some way, the same superstitious idea behind it.

PICTURE
If a picture falls in the house, someone in the house will die within a month.—General.

If a portrait of a person falls, that person's death will follow within a month.—General.

Both these superstitions flourish today. It is not many months since that the authors were written to by a terrified woman. A picture had fallen and broken in her home, she explained. Her husband was serving in the army abroad. Did it mean that he was dead?

It was of no use telling the woman that such superstition was absurd; she would not have believed it anyway. There was, however, a way out. Our reply was that he was not concerned in the business at all since the fall of a picture in the house foretold, according to the superstition, only the death of someone in the house. All was eventually well, because the husband was home on leave within a few weeks.

There is a proviso in the falling portrait superstition quoted above; the glass of the portrait must be broken in the fall, otherwise the portent is robbed of its import.

The origin is much the same as that governing the hiding of names, or the calling of things by names other than their real names—see Parson, above.

A portrait was held to contain the soul of the person portrayed. Therefore, *ipso facto*, if the portrait fell down and was smashed, then the soul of the person had fallen and was broken.

Nelson relates in *The Eskimo about Behring Straits* how in the Lower Yukon River an explorer had set up a camera to obtain pictures of the Esquimeaux moving about among their houses. While he was focusing, one of the headmen came along and insisted on peeping under the cloth.

For a moment he gazed intently at the moving figures on the ground glass, and then emerged to shout, "He has all of your shades in this box." A minute later there was not a solitary soul on the scene except the photographer.

PIEBALD HORSE

To cure the whooping cough, inquire of anyone riding a piebald horse for a remedy. Whatever may be named will be an infallible cure.

PIES

It is lucky to see two pies; but unlucky to see only one.—Ireland.

This would seem to belong to the species that there is only one thing better than a glass of beer, and that is two glasses of beer!

PIG

A pig must be killed during the increase of the moon, or the bacon will sink with the boiling and waste away in the pot.—Most rural areas, even to-day.

It is unlucky to see a pig cross your path.—Scotland.

NOTE: This is particularly so in the case of fishermen going to their nets. They turn their backs on any pig which may be approaching. It rules also throughout Yorkshire.

It is unlucky to mention the word pig during the preparations for, or during the actual, fishing trip.—Whitby, and Scotland.

If pigs run about the farmyard with straws in their mouth, a storm is approaching.—Ireland.

If anybody mentions pig while fishing lines are being baited the haul will be a poor one.—Flamborough, and other fishing ports.

A pig gives its master warning of his approaching death by giving utterance to a certain peculiar whine.—South Northants.

NOTE: Gaule explains, however, that the particular whine is understood only by those initiated in such matters.

Pigs bathed in water in which killed swine have been scalded, will thrive better and grow well.—Wales.

Pigs can see the wind.—General.

Should a woman touch a pig during the process of curing, the resulting bacon will turn bad.—General rural belief.

Take the last-mentioned superstition first. On 7th January, 1945, the authors received from a resident in Stonelane, Kinver, Worcestershire, the following inquiry: "Is it an old wives' tale that they tell me here—that if a woman touches a side of a pig while it is being cured, the bacon will go bad?"

So the old story of a hundred years lives on even in these times. It exists, still, in Lincolnshire, which is a great pig country. But there, and in other parts of the country, it is regarded not as a superstition, but as a positive fact.

There is, however, an addition to the wording of the superstition as given above, and that is, that it is a woman *during menstruation,* or who is about to become a mother, who must not touch a pig while it is being cured, else it will go bad.

Moreover, this is said to apply not only to bacon, but to making jam, bottling fruit, beans, and so on—all of which, it is claimed, will "go wrong."

Now, all this is of peculiar interest, for it exists in many parts of the world, north, south, east and west, among civilized and uncivilized peoples.

In Syria, to this day, a woman who has her courses on her may neither salt nor pickle, for it is held that should she do so, the product would turn bad.

The Kharwars, an Indian tribe, exclude a menstruous woman from the kitchen. Hindu women must seclude themselves, and not even use the common footpaths. In Annam, a menstruous woman must not touch food, or it would, they say, putrefy.

The Guayquiries, of the Orinoco, think that everything a woman in that condition touches will die. So do the Guaraunos. Among the North American Indians, not even a plate or a cup or other vessel used by a woman in her courses might be admitted at that or any other time to the house; they were kept in a separate place to where she was banished.

The aborigines of Victoria, the women of Carrier, the St. Seelis Indians of British Columbia, also have the same strict seclusion, and exclusion of their women at these times.

How old the superstition—or fact—may be is evidenced by the fact that Pliny held that the touch of a menstruous woman turned wine to vinegar, blighted crops, killed seedlings, brought down fruit from trees, dimmed mirrors, blunted razors, and did many other things. And Pliny died in A.D. 79.

To return, now, to the pig and its superstitions. If fishermen found it necessary to make mention of the animal, another name was always used for it, as they did for the parson (q.v.) and for a rabbit.

At the same time fishermen in York-shire and in Scotland desisted from the task they were engaged on when the name was mentioned, hoping thus to avert any ill-luck. As an instance, if mention of an egg had to be made, it was referred to as a "roundabout."

PIGEON

Nobody can die on pigeons' feathers. General.

If a white pigeon alights on the chimney, it is a sign of death in the house.

If a pigeon settles on a table, it means sickness.

If a pigeon is seen sitting in a tree, or comes into a house, or from being wild suddenly becomes tame, it is a sign of death.—Lincolnshire.

If pigeons congregate on the ridge of a house roof, it foretells a storm of rain.

Living pigeons cut in half and applied to the feet of a man in fever will cure him.

Now, the last was mentioned, if the authors' recollection is correct, by Pepys, and certainly by Jeremy Taylor, as being a superstition in 1660.

One would not expect it to be flourishing in this age of medical know-ledge. Yet, shortly before the last war, a Cornish doctor attending a woman gravely ill after childbirth became con-vinced that there was little hope for her recovery. He had, in fact, decided that she was actually on the point of death.

To his surprise on visiting the house next morning, he found the patient remarkably improved. On making inquiries, he elicited the fact that after his visit the previous night, the members of her family had obtained a pigeon, cut it in half without killing it, and had applied the bleeding portions to her feet. The woman completely recovered.

In the more remote parts of the country, the belief that a person cannot die easily on a pillow or in a bed stuffed with pigeon feathers still exists to-day.

If it was seen that a person was dying hardly, the onlookers invariably sus-pected that there were pigeon feathers in the bed, it was the practice to remove him from the bed and lay him, instead, on the floor, in order that the hindrance might be removed, and death might come "easily."

The authors have been told of instances where a bag of pigeon feathers has been deliberately put under a dying person's head for a pillow to "hold him back" until an expected relative could arrive.

See DEATH.

PILCHARDS

It is unlucky to begin eating pilchards, or any kind of fish, from the head down-wards.—Cornwall.

The origin of this is the belief of Cornish fishermen that to eat a fish that way will turn the heads of fish away from the coast, and thus take from fishermen their living.

Fish, it is insisted, should be eaten from the tail towards the head. This brings the fish to the shore—and the fishermen's nets.

PIN

See a pin, pick it up; all the day you'll have good luck.

See a pin, let it lie; you'll have bad luck all the day.

It is lucky for a bridesmaid to throw away pins on the wedding dress.

If a bride has a single pin left about her when she goes to the altar, nothing will go right with her.

Never lend a pin.—North Country.

Never have a pin with you on board ship.—Yorkshire.

Probably the only one of these super-stitions left to-day is the never lend a pin one. It is still rigidly held in the North Country, where a request for a pin is, more often than not, "You can take one, but I haven't given it to you." Where the "ill-luck" lies we have not been able to fathom.

The rhyme concerning the seeing of a pin has a certain "condition." Should you see a pin it is best to ascertain first, before you pick it up, how it is lying. Should the point be towards you, it would bring you bad luck to pick it up. There is nothing, of course, to stop you turning back and seeing it again—with the point away from you!

It is difficult to understand the ill-luck of the presence of a pin in a bride's dress. But Misson, in his *Travels*, wrote: "Woe to the bride if a single pin is left about her. Nothing will go right. Woe, also, to the bridesmaids if they keep one of them, for they will not be married before Whitsuntide."

Which seems to coincide with the superstition that a bridesmaid should throw away the pins on the wedding dress and be lucky.

There is a curious reference to pins in the wedding dress of Mary, Queen of Scots, when she married Darnley. Randolph, in his *Letters*, says that when the queen after the marriage went to her chamber to change her clothes, she "suffered them that stood by, every man that could approach, to take a pin."

An old superstition, anent pins, was that if you desired to bring about the death of an enemy, you should make a waxen image in his likeness and then stick pins around the heart. This was, of course, the practice adopted by witches towards those they wished to injure.

It was also a practice of women at one time to bring to them their erring lovers. A figure was made of the lover and pins were stuck in, in the sure belief that the lover, suffering some pain, would come along to see what the lady was up to, being quite certain that she was the cause of his pain.

In the Isle of Oxney, Romney Marshes, after a funeral it was the habit of mourners as they left the churchyard to stick a pin into the churchyard gate through which the body had passed. They believed that it guarded them against evil which might befall them.

The same practice was performed by a gamekeeper who, should there have been a shooting accident, stuck a pin into any fence or stile over which the body had been lifted. The superstition seems to have some alliance with that of nailing evil.

See NAIL.

PIXIES

It was usual in olden days in Cornwall always to leave a hole in one corner of the wall of a house for the "piskies," the Cornish name for pixies, to come in and out.

Such an instance, in comparatively modern times, is recorded in *Notes and Queries*, vol. 5, page 173.

PLAYING CARDS

To drop a card on the floor during a game, is a bad omen.

If you sing while playing cards, you and your partner will lose the game.

To play with a cross-eyed man at the table, will be unlucky for you.

If you are angry while playing cards you will lose. The demon of bad luck always follows a passionate player.

He who lends money at play will lose; he who borrows money will win.

Of these superstitions, the one most in use to-day is that relating to borrowed money winning. The barman in the International Sporting Club at Monte Carlo, makes an excellent side line fortune from lending money at good interest to English and American gamblers who have a sublime faith in the winning power of borrowed money.

As a humorous comment the authors place on record that on the only occasion that they incurred serious losses at Monte Carlo, in a night of consistent bad luck, when their funds were exhausted, they borrowed two thousand francs from the barman in the sporting club, returned to the table at which they had been playing roulette all the evening—and promptly won back all their night's losses, and nearly four thousand francs in addition!

PLOUGHING

To avert the Evil Eye from the land when horses are put into the plough for the first time in the year, take a bucket of chemerly, put some hen dung into it, and stir for some time. Then sprinkle the mixture over the horses and the plough.—Isle of Man.

PLOVER

To see seven plovers together is a portent of coming misfortune.—Lancashire.

The origin of this is that the plovers are believed to be wandering Jews and the tradition is that they contain the souls of the Jews who assisted at the Crucifixion. In consequence they are doomed to float in the air for ever.

PLUM

When plum trees blossom in December, it is a sure sign of death in the house of the owner of the trees.—Wales.

This is a further instance of the "omen" of plants blossoming at times other than their natural blossom time, reference to which has been made earlier.

For instance, geraniums blooming in the house in the winter time—that is out of the summer for which they are normally grown—is said to mean a death in the family.

PNEUMONIA

To cure pneumonia, tie the lungs of a sheep, or a bullock's milt, to the soles of the feet of the patient, and bury them afterwards. This is a certain cure for the pneumonia.—Cheshire, Lancs.

This, again, is a superstitious cure still resorted to in parts of Cheshire. Miss Christina Hole, in one of her excellent folk-lore books, records that it was done with success to her knowledge as recently as 1932.

POINTING AT A SHIP

If you point at a ship, you will bring bad luck to it.—Norfolk coast.

POKER

To make a dying fire pull up, place a poker standing upright against the bars of the grate. It will then draw up.—General.

To put the poker and tongs on the same side of the fireplace, will mean a quarrel in the house.

For years now, the authors have been called upon by wives to confirm that the first of these "charms" is a certain way of making the fire draw; and by husbands to convince their wives that it is purely a stupid superstition. The argument has appeared in every book of fallacies the authors have read.

The origin given for the belief is the old one of the Evil Eye. It was held that should a fire smoke, or refuse to draw for no apparent reason, then the Devil or an agent of the Devil, such as a witch, was at work, and could only be circumvented by the Sign of the Cross. The placing of a poker upright against the grate formed a cross with the bars of the grate, hence it would remove the Devil's spell and the fire would draw.

But the origin has been forgotten, and the housewife of to-day holds that by placing the poker thus, a draught is created, which has the effect, of course, of making the fire pull up. Scientific gentlemen have ridiculed the idea, and affirm that the poker is a superstitious myth.

This view of the authors, which appeared in their *Encyclopædia of Phrases and Origins*, brought a response from Mr. H. C. Bartholomew, of London, a suggestion which may well contain the truth of the matter. He suggested that certainly the poker of itself, so placed, could not induce a draught. But supposing that the poker had been taken from the fire where it had laid to lift the fire embers in an endeavour to induce the fire to burn, and supposing that as a result the poker was red hot, then placed ·against the bars in the manner described, the heated poker would undoubtedly attract a draught which, drawing up the chimney,

would have the effect of causing the embers to pull up. This seems to be a sound scientific reasoning missed by learned gentlemen and folk-lore people alike. It is, of course, a fact that heat will engender a draught.

POPPIES

In Derbyshire and Nottinghamshire, poppies were called "earaches," because it was said that if they were gathered and placed to the ear of the person picking them, they would cause violent earache.

In parts of Yorkshire their local name was "blind-buff."

It was also held that a poppy placed to the eye would blind the person doing so.

PORK

If a pig is killed after the waxing of the moon, the pork will be ruined.—General in rural areas.

See PIG.

POSTHUMOUS CHILD

A posthumous child has magical gifts of healing, and if he or she breathes into the mouth of a child suffering from the thrush, will cure it.—North Country.

In many rural villages the services of a posthumous child are still sought for this complaint and for others. It is much the same belief as that which holds that the seventh son can heal the sick.

POT

If the meat shrinks in the pot, you will have a downfall in life. If it swells to a large size, the master of the house will be prosperous in all his undertakings.—Border Counties.

When a pot is taken off the hook hanging from the chimney the vibration of the chain must be stopped as soon as possible, for whilst it is in motion the Virgin weeps.—Yorkshire.

POTATO

When new potatoes are first dug in the year, all the family must taste them, or the spirits in them (the potatoes) will take offence and they will not keep.—Sutherlandshire.

If potatoes are dibbled in on Good Friday, a bad crop will follow.

A potato carried in a trouser pocket is an infallible cure for rheumatism.—General.

The latter superstition is still widely held. The authors have knowledge of a score of their friends who still swear by it as a preventive.

Perhaps the most remarkable potato superstition of the country at any time was that affected in Scotland, where, when the potato crop was in danger of failing the farming populace called for the showing of the "Macleod's Fairy Banner."

This was the banner of the laird of Dunvegan, who is chief of the clan of the MacLeods. To it are ascribed strange supernatural powers. When it is unfurled victory in war attends it. Every woman with child who sees it, is taken with premature labour, and every cow casts her calf.

POULTRY

The crowing of a hen bodes evil.— General.

*Before the death of a farmer, his poultry will go to roost at midday, instead of at the usual time,—*Northants.

*When the cock struts up to the door and crows, the housewife may expect a stranger to call.—*General rural.

*If an even number of eggs are set under a hen, the chickens will not prosper.—*General farm belief.

*The last egg of a hen should be preserved; it is a charm upon the well-doing of the poultry.—*Northants.

An egg laid on Good Friday, if preserved, will ensure luck with one's poultry.

Of this series of superstitions, the one most observed to-day is that of the odd number of eggs put under a hen. No farmer's wife, and no back-yard poultry keeper, would think of setting fewer than thirteen eggs.

To carry the superstition to its full extent, each of the eggs thus set should be marked in black with a small cross. This, it is held, will be instrumental in securing good chickens, and also prevent any attack by weasels or other farmyard marauders.

In the South Northampton area it was customary for the first egg laid by a pullet to be secured by the shepherd to present to his sweetheart. It was held to be the luckiest gift he could give her.

PRAYER BOOK

When you go to bed, place under your pillow a prayer book open at the part of the marriage service, where the line "with this ring I thee wed" occurs. Place on it a ring, a key, a flower, a sprig of willow, a small heart cake, a crust of bread, and the following cards—ten of clubs, nine of hearts, ace of spades and the ace of diamonds.

To complete the formula, you must say as you get into bed:

Luna, every woman's friend,
To me thy goodness condescend.
Let me this night in visions see,
Emblems of my destiny.

Now, if after this, you should dream of storms, trouble betides you. If of the ring, or the ace of diamonds, marriage is your portion. A dream of the piece of cake portends 'a prosperous life; of the flowers, joy; of the willow, treachery in your love affair; of the ace of spades, death; of the ace of diamonds, money; of the clubs, a visit to a foreign land; of the keys, that you will rise to trust and power and never know the need for money.

All this must occur at the period of the harvest moon only.

PRIDE

To tell the pride of anyone, take a hair belonging to that person, and pull it smartly between the nails of thumb and finger. The pride is in accordance with the curled appearance of the hair after that operation.

PRIMROSE

To take less than a handful of primroses into a farmer's house will bring him bad luck. It will bring destruction on his broods of chickens and ducklings. —Worcestershire.

Let a youth or a maiden pull the primrose and after cutting off the tops of the stamens with a pair of scissors, lay it in a secret place where no human eye can see it. Let him think throughout the day, and dream throughout the night, of his sweetheart, and then, on looking at the primrose the next day, if he finds the stamens shot to their former height, success will attend him in love; if not, he can only expect disappointment.— Northern Counties.

Considerable trouble has from time to time been reported over the handful of primroses. The gift of less than the necessary number has been interpreted as a sign of bad will from one neighbour to another.

And, in one case reported in a newspaper of the day, a charge of assault followed such a gift deficient in quantity; it chanced that the gift through a child of one primrose, was actually followed by the hatching from one setting of eggs of a single chick.

A mid-Wales superstition is that if the primrose blooms in June it will bring bad luck. The same locality eyes with equal misgiving the blooming of a summer rose in November or December.

PROVERBS (BOOK OF)

To choose a wife, ascertain the date of the young woman's birth, and refer to the first chapter of Proverbs.—West Country.

Each of the verses one to thirty-one is supposed to indicate, either directly or indirectly, the character of your tentative choice. The verse corresponding to the woman's age is an index of her character.

PUPPY

Bury three puppies brandwise in a field, and you will rid the field of weeds. —Devon.

This is part of the sacrifice of animals superstition that was at one time widespread in Britain, and was held to save the remainder of the animals.

　　See CALF, NEED FIRE, SACRIFICE, TOAD.

QUARRY

If work is carried out in a quarry on Ascension Day an accident will be sure to occur.—Penrhyn.

So strong was this superstition that for a great number of years, the extensive slate quarries at Penrhyn, belonging to Lord Penrhyn were always kept idle on this day.

After considerable effort work was performed one year, and sure enough there was an accident. The result was that the following year the men refused once more to enter the quarries on Ascension Day.

The authors do not know whether at the moment the superstition holds, but it was observed up to a few years before the 1939-45 war.

QUARTER-DECK

Saluting the quarter-deck was, originally, an appeal to Ishtar to help the quarter-master. The quarter-deck was a shrine to Ishtar.

Wine used on the bows of a ship at the christening was originally regarded as blood cast on the figurehead of the ship to give it life.

RABBIT

To see a rabbit while on the way to the pit is an omen of misfortune.—Cornish miners.

To dream of your sweetheart, take the blade-bone of a rabbit, stick nine pins into it, and put it under your pillow. You will be sure to see the object of your affections.—Hull and Yorkshire in part.

Bad luck will follow any fisherman who mentions the word rabbit.—East coast and south coast fishing ports, also Scotland.

The third belief still continues even to-day.

In the *Morning Post* of 9th June, 1919, Mr. Edward Lovett mentioned the case of a fisherman on one of the Norfolk boats who was present at a drinking party. The talk came round to rabbits, and the fisherman, on hearing the word, became so frightened that he at once left the party—*and left, also, his beer.*

Mr. Lovett was a distinguished writer on folk-lore, and he spent many years endeavouring to trace this superstition to some source, without success.

In Brighton and other parts of Sussex, as late as 1934, the superstition was rife, and the authors were assured that it was in the year of grace 1946. In all cases, if the rabbit has to be mentioned it is referred to by the name "coney."

A friend related to us only a few months ago that the casual mention of "rabbit" in a gathering in a prominent cruising club in Sussex provoked an uproar among the members.

Some extent of the trouble that can be caused in fishing circles by the rabbit is evidenced in the story related by Mr. Lovett in *Magic in Modern London.* Two families of fisher-folk, who owned small boats, fell out. One night, the men of the offended family, having obtained a pound of iron tacks and a rabbit skin, used the whole of the tacks in pinning the skin securely to the mast of the boat belonging to the other family.

Almost every inch of the skin was tacked down, making the job of getting it clean off a long one. This put the opposing boat out of action for a considerable time, for the men would not put to sea so long as there was even a trace of the skin on the mast.

Possibly the rabbit superstition is associated with the moon, which, of course, affects the tides, and in that case affects fishermen. In old Sanskrit literature the rabbit and the hare (which also figures in many superstitions) were the ambassadors of, and the symbol of, the god Chandra (the moon), and rabbits and hares were appointed to guard the fountain consecrated to that deity. In Burmese mythology, the hare is also the symbol of the moon.

In association with this, it is of interest to note the custom of certain tribes of natives in South Africa when too much rain has fallen. The wizard visits with a crowd the house of a family in which there has been no death for a long time, and there burns the skin of a rabbit. As it burns, he shouts: "The rabbit is burning," and the cry is repeated by the crowd in shouts until they are exhausted. The effect, so it is believed, is to stop the rain. Here, again, the moon and rain are associated.

A superstition still in force in most parts of Britain to-day is that which entails the calling of "rabbits" on the first day of a new month. It should really be said three times in rapid succession if fortune is to be kind to the caller throughout the month.

At New Biggin, Richmond, Yorkshire, a white rabbit figured in a death superstition for many years. According to this, when a white rabbit was seen in New Biggin, death would visit the inhabitants. The rabbit apparently was seen at dusk. Soane recorded in 1849: "It is not twenty years since the doomed or dooming rabbit appeared to the wife of a brazier, by name Hayward, who had always been a heretic in such matters. His death convinced his neighbours how much he had been in error."

See HARE.

RABBIT'S FOOT

A child should be brushed at birth with a rabbit's foot.—Widespread.

An actor or actress must never lose the rabbit's foot from their make-up box, or ill-luck will follow them.—Stage superstition.

Let us start by saying that a rabbit's foot is the most potent charm of the American negroes, who, it is said, turn white with fright at the loss of one. We can then turn to the enlightened men and women of Britain.

"I am told," says Sir Charles Igglesden, in one of his works on folk-lore, "that hundreds of mothers, even to-day, place a rabbit's foot in the perambulator when a child is taken out by a nurse."

The superstition behind this is that it prevents any kind of accident happening to the child.

It was the custom on the stage, at least up to twenty years ago, to present to a person entering upon the Boards as a profession, a rabbit's foot, to be placed in her, or his, first make up box. Its use was to apply rouge to the face.

It also guaranteed success to the person. But should the foot be lost, then disaster would overtake the loser, and no success or talent would accrue.

The practice would seem to have died out—judging by the remarkable lack of talent and ability on the part of so many of the younger people playing on the stage to-day!

The origin of the superstitions concerning the luck of the rabbit's foot lies in the belief that young rabbits are born with their eyes open, and thus have the power of the Evil Eye, and can shoo away the Evil One.

RACING

The superstitions accredited to racing and jockeys are numerous, but exceedingly difficult to get hold of.

Mention to any jockey the word superstitions, and he will walk away. The very mention of the word, he maintains, is in itself an omen of bad luck.

However, here are one or two.

No jockey will willingly have his photograph taken on his mount *before* the race. If circumstances compel him to do so, he rides in the certainty that he is not likely to win.

To drop his whip before or during the race is a sign of bad luck in the race; and there are a number of jockeys who hold that their favourite whip is a mascot, without which they will not be in the first three.

Another superstition relates to boots, and it is of considerable moment. A jockey's boots should never be placed on the floor in his dressing room.

There is on record the case of one jockey whose valet placed his boots on the floor. With an oath he rose quickly from his seat, walked solemnly round the boots three times, and then motioned to the valet to replace the boots on the shelf from which they had been taken.

This done, they were taken down and at once put on by the jockey before they had again touched the floor. But the rider was still exceedingly unhappy about the incident.

RAIN

If you burn ferns, you will bring down rain.

Burning the heather brings rain.—Melrose area.

If it rains while a wedding party is on

their way to or from the church, they will have a life of unhappiness.

Rain which falls on Holy Thursday, if caught, and preserved in a bottle, is a sovereign remedy for sore eyes.—Banbury district of Oxon.

If rain falls on a coffin, the soul of the departed has arrived safely.—Cornwall.

As the superstition of the efficacy of May dew was held not only by peasants, but by a Queen of England (see Dew), so likewise, the burning of ferns as inducing rain was held by a King of England, as well as by his peasants.

In 1636, the King, Charles I, was contemplating paying a visit to Staffordshire. Accordingly, the Lord Chamberlain (the third Earl of Pembroke) wrote the following letter to the Sheriff of Staffordshire:

"Sir,—His Majesty, taking notice of an opinion entertained in Staffordshire, that the burning of ferne doth drawe downe rain, and being desirous that the country and himself may enjoy fair weather so long as he remains in these parts, His Majesty has commanded me to write to you, to cause all burning of ferne to be forbidden until His Majesty be passed the country."

The letter is preserved in the British Museum. It is a pity that no record is contained with it as to whether it did or did not rain during the visit, despite the ban on burning fern.

It should be added that the burning of fern as a rainmaker was by no means confined to Staffordshire, but was prevalent up and down England, and in Scotland.

On Snowdon a tarn called the Black Lake (Dulyn) has a row of stepping-stones running out into its waters. It is held that if anyone goes as far as possible along the row and throws water so as to wet the farthest stone rain will come before night, even in the hottest weather.

Now, this stone is known as the Red Altar; and it is probable from this that it had some sacred association at some time or other.

If so, then the origin of the rain-making becomes plain, for a method largely in use in many places to procure rain was to dip a holy cross in water. Either that or some holy relic.

In many parts of France there used to be a custom of dipping an image of a saint in water for that purpose. In Navarre, for instance, where it was the custom to pray to St. Peter for rain, when on one occasion nothing happened

the inhabitants of one village carried the image of the saint to the river, and, despite the remonstrance of the outraged clergymen, dipped it completely in the water.

It was not, by the way, the superstition to which the clergy objected, but the dipping of the saint; they urged that a simple caution, or admonition, addressed to the image would have done just as well!

In the Island of Uist, in the Outer Hebrides, opposite St. Mary's Church, there stood a cross known locally as the Water Cross. When rain was wanted, the cross was set up on high; when enough rain had fallen, it was laid flat on the ground.

The monks of Iona, to procure rain, shook the tunic wherein their patron saint, Columba, had expired, thrice in the air, while reading books written by his hand. "Abundance fell," it is recorded, "to refresh the arid earth and produce a luxurious harvest."

RAINBOW

Saturday rainbow is sure to be followed by a week of rainy weather.—Ireland.

If you dig at the end of a rainbow where it touches the ground, you will find a bag of gold.—General.

Rainbow at morn, put your hook in the corn; rainbow at eve, put your head in the sheave.—Cornwall.

It has, of course, been a matter of weather lore for generations that a rainbow seen during rain means that the rain is giving way to sunshine.

There is another which says that a rainbow seen in evening betokens a fine day, but one seen in the morning a wet to-morrow. A German superstition follows exactly the same lines.

In Wiltshire there was recited a verse curious for its old Saxon language, interpolated with a much more modern reference to a "great coat." It ran:

The rainbow in th' marnin'
Gies the shepherd warnin'
To car' his girt cwoat on his back.
The rainbow at night
Is the shepherd's delight,
For then no girt cwoat will be lack.

There seems little doubt that the verse, and the morning and evening rainbow superstition, were born of the fact that in the morning the rainbow is seen in the clouds in the west, the quarter from which Britain gets most rain, and in the evening from the east, whence comes the finer weather.

There is in many countries with native populations a dread of the rainbow. The natives of Nias, for instance, are terrified at the sight of the rainbow, being under the belief that it is a huge net set by a powerful spirit to catch their shadows. To them a shadow is their soul.

Now, this interested us, from the fact that while on a visit to a North Country town some years ago, the appearance of a rainbow was at once followed by a little group of children making a cross on the ground with two pieces of stick. Asked what was the idea they replied, simply: "To cross the rainbow out."

Delvers into strange beliefs and customs as we are, we made further inquiries. The town was Leeds, in the West Riding of Yorkshire, and our search discovered that there was among the old people this recipe for "driving away a rainbow": Make a cross of two sticks and lay four pebbles on it, one at each end of the cross.

But why desire to drive away a rainbow? The old people who practised it could not tell us; they knew the sign; they knew that the bow should be dispersed, because their parents had told them so, and the grandparents had told their parents so. But why it should be dispersed they neither knew, nor were they interested in it.

The clue came to us, we think, from the sky itself. In the old mythology the sky was the Road of the Gods; that is perfectly well known. After Odin, the Norse god of mythology, had prepared his heavenly palace, he reared to it the bridge Bifrost, by which the palace could be reached. His Bifrost was of three colours: in the centre was red, for it was of fire, and this pathway on the bridge was intended to consume souls unworthy to enter the palace. Thus, from mythology the Bifrost, or the Road of the Gods, became the Road of Souls, which they took to ascend to Heaven.

Now, let us take you to Norway, and to Denmark, where a runic gravestone frequently would bear such an inscription as this: "Nageilfr had this bridge built for Anund, his son."

What does that mean but that the son, in dying, had passed over the bridge to Heaven? Thus, the Bifrost of Odin, the bridge of souls to Heaven through the Milky Way is the rainbow, which the souls of the dead traverse to the goal of their rest.

The Norse influence on the northern counties of England was very great; many of the names given to places and events in the North are of Norse origin. What more likely, therefore, that the legend persists to this day that the rainbow is a bridge for the souls to ascend; in other words, the appearance of a rainbow is the sign for a death, for a soul to be provided with the bridge to Heaven. To drive the rainbow away would be to prolong a life, since there would be no bridge for the soul to cross. And that, we think, is why, even to-day, children in the northern counties follow still the sign of the cross to "drive away the rainbow."

There are places in Austria and in parts of Germany where the belief is still fervently held that the souls of children ascend the rainbow to Heaven.

Follow the idea of the bridge farther back into antiquity. The goddess of death of the Ancients, Demeter, had among her priestesses an Order of the Bridge; and Demeter herself was known as the Lady of the Bridge. In Rome the priest was a bridge builder, pontifex, as he undertook the care and charge of souls.

RAIN WATER

Pure rain water is an infallible cure for sore eyes.—Lincolnshire.

But there is a formula to work the miracle. The rain water must be collected in a clean, open vessel in the month of June, and must not have been contaminated by being previously collected by any other means. It will then remain always pure if preserved in a bottle.

The Welsh had two superstitions connected with rain water. The first maintained that rain water baths would make babies talk earlier; and the second that money washed in clear rain water could not be stolen.

The former of the two is still practised to-day.

RALEIGH BELLS

If you go on Christmas morning and put your ear to the ground, you will hear the Raleigh bells ringing deep down in the ground.—Nottingham.

The legend attached to this is that many centuries ago the village of Raleigh, Nottinghamshire, together with the church, was swallowed up by an earthquake. But every Christmas morning the bells ring out as they did when the church stood above the ground. It was a Christmas morning custom at one time for people to go out to the valley and, ears to the ground, listen for the pealing of the bells.

RATS

The sudden departure of rats from a house betokens the death of someone in the household.

Dried rat's tails will cure a cold.— General.

A friend who is wise in the ways of country people, tells us that there was a superstition in his father's childhood, told to him by his father, that when a child's tooth came out, or was knocked out, the tooth was thrown away with the adjuration: Rats, send me a stronger tooth (the idea being apparently that the teeth of rats, which can gnaw through almost anything, are strong).

This, although we are unable to trace the area in Britain where it was customary, interested us intensely, because Jewish children in the south of Russia had a similar superstition. When a tooth came out, it was thrown up on to the roof with the request to mice or rats to give an "iron tooth" in exchange for the one of bone. And at Raratonga, in the Pacific, when a child's tooth has to be extracted the following verse was recited:

Big rat, little rat,
Here is my old tooth.
Pray give me a new one.

The tooth was then thrown away on to the thatched roof of the dwelling. The origin in both cases was the same as the British one—to gain a tooth of iron that would not fall out, or have to come out.

A Welsh superstition for getting rid of rats in a house, or on property, was to write out the following:

r.a.t.s.
a.r.s.t.
t.s.r.a.
s.t.a.r.

The paper had then to be placed in the mouth of King Rat. Unfortunately, the old Welsh people forgot to leave on record how to catch the King Rat, or how to recognize one as such when it was caught. But the "charm" is interesting because an ancient Greek treatise on farming advises a farmer who would rid his land of rats to:

"Take a piece of paper and write on it as follows:

" 'I adjure you, ye mice or rats here present, that ye neither injure me, nor suffer another mouse or rat to do so. I give you yonder field (a particular field is indicated), but if I ever catch you here again by the Mother of the Gods I will rend you in seven pieces.'

"Write this and stick the paper on an unhewn stone before sunrise, taking care to keep the written side up."

In the Ardennes, peasants repeat, "Erat verbum apud Deum vestrum. Male rats and female rats, I conjure you by the great God, to go out of my house and all my habitations, and to betake yourselves to such and such a place there to end your days."

The words were then written on pieces of paper, the papers were folded up and placed, one under the door by which the rats are to leave, and the other on the road which they are to take. This must be performed at sunrise.

Now all this was long years ago. But, believe it or not, a few years ago an American farmer wrote a letter to the rats which infested his farm telling them that his harvest had been a poor one and that he could not afford to keep them through the winter. He had, he said, been kind to them and now, for their own well being, he thought they had better leave him and go to his neighbours who had more grain. This letter he pinned to a door in his barn for the rats to read.

In all these cases the place specified for the rats to take their fill can be, if thought necessary, a neighbour's barn or field.

RAVEN

If a raven croaks when there is illness in the house, it is an inauspicious omen. —General.

A raven croaking over a house bodes ill to some member of the family.— Cornwall.

To shoot a raven is to shoot King Arthur.—Cornwall.

If blind people are kind to ravens they will learn how to regain their sight.— Wales.

For generations the legend has persisted that the raven is a bird of ill omen. Cicero, it is stated, was warned of his approaching death by a number of ravens flying round him.

When Alexander entered Babylon, a large number of ravens flew round his victorious forces. After his death it was held that the ravens, appearing in such large numbers, had presaged it.

So from Cicero and Alexander we get the superstition in England that the croak of a raven over a house also presages death.

In this connection Dr. Wren wrote: "The raven, by his acute sense of smell ing, discerns the savour of dying bodies from the tops of chimneys and that makes it flutter about the windows as they used to do in search of a carcase."

As they did, for instance, when they congregated and fought with kites in the fields beside Beneventum and Apicium, thus, according to Jovianus Pontanus, prognosticating the great battle that was to be fought in those fields. And Nicetas spoke of "a skirmish between the crowes and the ravens presignifying the irruption of the Scythians into Thracia."

The raven was accorded great respect by the Greeks as being sacred to Apollo, patron of the Augurs, and the bird was regarded as the attendant on that god. The Augurs looked upon the bird as possessing a preternatural sagacity in predicting events.

The Norse looked upon the raven as dedicated to Odin. The god, it was held, possessed two ravens whom he let loose every morning to collect intelligence of what was going on in the world, and they, on returning in the evening, perched upon Odin's shoulder to whisper whatever they had collected. According to tradition the raven was white formerly, but was changed into black for babbling. So something must have happened between them and Odin.

The ban on shooting a raven concerned in the Cornish superstition is due to a belief that King Arthur is still alive in the form of a raven. Hence, superstitious people refused to shoot ravens, from a fear that they might thus destroy the mythical warrior.

This is more than usually interesting, because the Bororos of Brazil believe that the human soul has the shape of a bird, and passes out of the body in that form—and they favour ravens.

And the soul of Aristeas of Proconnesus, according to Pliny, was seen to issue from his mouth in the form of a raven. Thus, once more, is a round-the-world link-up of the same superstition without any apparent connecting link.

In all this bad omen of the raven there is just one good deed. The story goes that a Cornish quarry man was working under a large block of stone which was on the point of falling. A raven, seeing the danger, picked up a pebble and dropped it on the man's head. The man cursed the bird for a foul creature, and continued working.

Again the raven dropped a stone, and the man took no notice. Thereupon, the bird flew to the beach and returned with a piece from a wrecked ship, dropping it in front of the quarryman. "Hallo," said the quarryman, "where did that come from? There is more to be got," and dashed off to the beach. The rock crashed down a moment later.

Incidentally, the Welsh, as well as the Cornish folk, regarded the killing of a raven as unlucky because the soul of King Arthur was supposed by them to hover in raven's form over his favourite spots.

RED THREAD

It was a common device of Scottish housewives on farms in olden days to tie a piece of red thread round the tails of cows the first time they were turned out to grass in the spring.

This, they said, secured the cattle from the Evil Eye, and from being elf-shot by fairies.

RETURNING

See LOOKING BACK.

RHEUMATISM

A potato, begged or stolen, is a preservative from rheumatism.—General.

NOTE: To our many friends who carry a potato in their pockets we emphasize the condition—begged or stolen.

To be free of rheumatism the right forefoot of a hare should be worn continuously in a pocket.—Northants.

Silver rings made from coffin hinges will prevent and cure rheumatism, fits or the cramp.—Lancashire.

A piece of mountain ash carried, will cure rheumatism.—Cornwall.

NOTE: Mountain ash (care in Cornwall, rowan in Scotland) was dreaded by evil spirits, rendered nil the power of witches, and had, it was claimed, many other wonderful properties.

To cure the rheumatism, get a woman who has been delivered of a child feet foremost to treat the patient.—Cornwall.

In Cheshire there existed, and we believe still exists in country areas, a belief that the best cure for rheumatism, was to have the affected part stung by bees.

A year or two ago, the authors came across the same belief in a family in Lincolnshire.

It may be not without interest to state that in Java, a popular rheumatic cure is to rub Spanish pepper into the nails of the fingers and toes of the sufferers. It is held that the pungency of the pepper is too much for the rheumatism, which goes away quickly. (It must be remember that illness in these races is caused by a demon—the demon of disease.) Maybe the sting of the bees works the same way.

On the Slave Coast of Africa, if a child was sick the mother was wont to make small cuts on various parts of the body, and insert into the wounds green pepper or spice, thereby causing the demon so much pain that he left the child. Again, not very much different from the bees of Cheshire and Lancashire.

On the other hand, in some parts of England, and in Wales, the cure for rheumatism is to interpose a barrier between it and the sufferer. So the patient crawled under a bramble which had formed into an arch by sending down a second root into the ground. As he emerged on the other side, it was held that he had left the rheumatism behind.

There are few tribal races who do not hold the same belief in the efficacy of leaving disease behind after crawling through an archway of some kind or other.

Possibly the most extravagant superstition of all was that practised in an area of Yorkshire, that to effect a cure of rheumatism, the patient should be wrapped in a blanket and laid in a running stream for a quarter of an hour. The effect in a number of recorded cases was certainly a cure for rheumatism. The patient was sent beyond the reach of that or any other complaint!

An Irish superstition for the cure of rheumatism was to carry in the pocket the bone of a haddock that lies under the marks of Christ's fingers. This is a curious remedy, for the marks on the haddock are usually ascribed to the fingers of St. Peter, as he extracted the money from the mouth of the fish. Never before have the authors seen the marks ascribed to Christ's fingers. Incidentally, the charm would not work if the bone was exhibited at any time, or was lent, or touched, except by the wearer.

In Leicestershire, a popular cure was to bury the patient up to the neck in a churchyard for two hours.

Wales improved on this considerably. There, the patient was stripped and buried in a standing position up to the neck for two hours. If the pain of the ailment had not vanished at the end of that time, the burying was repeated at the same time and place the next day— and for nine days. If the pain still remained, a three days' rest was ordered,

after which the burying was once more practised.

RICKETS

Split a young ash tree longitudinally for a few feet, and pass the child naked, either three times or three times three, through the fissure at sunrise. Bind up the tree and as it heals so will the rickets in the child be cured.—General.

NOTE: This was also the cure for rupture in a child.

Pass a child through the Men-an-tol (Holed Stone) and the rickets will be cured.—Madron (Cornwall).

Rickets will be cured if the child is passed through the Shargar stone.—Fyvie (Aberdeenshire).

NOTE: Shargar means a weakly child.

Give the child a laying.—Banff, North-east Scotland.

Few superstitions had a greater hold than the passing through a split ash or oak tree for the cure of rickets or rupture in a child. There was no part of Britain where it was not practised.

In some parts of the country, it was asserted that the only tree that would prove effective was a maiden tree that had never been topped or cut. It was demanded that the split should be made east and west, and that the child should be passed through by a maiden and taken out at the other side by a boy; and the passing must be feet foremost.

Incredible though it may sound this remedy was in use at Fittleworth, Sussex, and other places in the same county down to the second half of the nineteenth century.

The method of the passing varies, some taking place on the one morning, and in other places, the passing taking place on each morning of nine days— the three times three.

For rupture the tree after binding up had to be plastered with clay or mud; and as the tree knit itself together again, so did the rupture knit in the child.

There was, however, a vicious addendum to the remedy. It was held that once the child had passed through a tree, its life depended on the life of the tree; and should the tree die or be cut down at any time in the near or distant future, the disease, or the rupture, would return, and the child, though now grown to a man's estate, and wherever he may be, even in another land, would die.

There was, at one time, an ash tree growing at Shirley Heath, near Birmingham, which the owner of an adjoining farm tended with such great care that he would not allow a branch of it to be touched with a knife or axe. He had been passed through the tree thirty-two years before and held that his life lay in the tree.

There was a row of ash trees at Petworth, which had for years been used for rickets and rupture. In 1868, one of these was purchased by a stranger for cutting down for timber. He was visited by the father of a child who had been passed through it, and assured with great conviction that if he followed his design and cut down the tree, his (the father's) child would have a return of the disease. The tree was allowed to continue standing.

This tree cure was prevalent all over Europe. In Armenia and in Nias, children are made by their parents to crawl through certain sacred trees to put a stop to the evil spirits which had made, or were making, them ill and weakly.

The origin of the superstition is difficult accurately to define. It was held at one time that it signified the new birth, in perfect health and physical fitness, of the passed child; in other words by the passing of the illness to the tree, as in the case of the nailing of evils (see Toothache). But in that case the tree, having caught the disease, should properly decline and die. It doesn't.

On the other hand, the Cornish and Scottish "cure" of passing a child through a holed stone, would suggest that the object was, as has been stated in other superstitions mentioned earlier, to interpose a barrier between the illness and the patient. In other words, that in passing through the opening, he scraped the evil from him, and left it on the other side of the passage.

It is significant, and not uninteresting, in this connection to note that certain Borneo tribes, when a death occurs, after the funeral, make an arch of a bough bent double and insert each end into the ground. Through this they pass, and then lock it by tying the two ends together. They regard this as making certain that the ghost of the dead man cannot come back to them. In the same way, the authors think that the origin of the split trees and the holed stone, is contained in some earlier and primitive idea of "giving the slip" to the evil spirit, which was contained in the illness of the child.

The Banff charm of "laying" a child referred to above consisted of taking the child before sunrise to the forge of a blacksmith in which three men of the same name worked. One of these laid the child in the water trough of the smithy, and then on the anvil. All the tools of the smithy were then passed over the child, who was then given back to the parents and once more washed in the water trough.

"Laying" was also a treatment in Northumberland for a puny child, supposed to be a victim of "overlooking" by a witch. The smith in this case, however, had to be the seventh generation of smiths in an unbroken line.

RIGHT-HAND TURN

Nothing is, or has been, so widespread in superstition as this rule of doing everything with a motion corresponding to the course of the sun. It is often referred to as "sunwise," less seldom in England, but more often in Scotland, as "deiseal."

With rare exceptions the charms of "passing" of any kind, such as passing children through a cleft ash sapling for the rickets, are useless unless done sunwise.

To take a body to its funeral in a churchyard in a route against the sun would, it was held, hand over the dead man to the Devil.

Boats were always turned to sea deiseal. A fiery circle round a house should always be made by a man with a torch going sunwise.

Infants are "sained" sunwise or deiseal, else the saining might as well not take place at all; in fact it were better for the infant that it did not take place.

After milking a cow, a dairymaid was under orders, in olden days, to strike it deiseal with the shackle, saying "out and home," which would secure its safe return.

The origin, of course, lies in the belief in the evil of the left.

A morganatic marriage was called a left-hand marriage.

A man who gets up in a bad temper is said, even to-day, to have got out of the wrong side of the bed—he left the bed by the left-hand side.

To step over the threshold of a house with the left foot is to bring ill-luck upon the residence and upon the inmates of it.

Strangely enough, although deiseal and sunwise mean one and the same, the word deiseal has nothing actually to do with the sun. The word is from

deas, right hand, and *iul,* direction.
See FOOT, SUNWISE.

RINGING GLASS
*Should a glass tumbler be hit, and
because of it emit a ringing sound, it
is the cry of a drowning sailor.—Sailors'*
general superstition.

Fortunately, the evil can be avoided
by the person who has struck the glass
putting his finger on the brim, and thus
stopping the ring. It also absolves him
from having the death of the sailor on
his conscience.

RING FINGER
*The ring finger, stroked along any
sore or wound, will soon heal it.—*
Somerset.

The point of this is that it was held
in the same county, and, we believe,
elsewhere, that this was the only healing finger, all the other fingers being
venomous, especially the forefingers.

Much the same belief was held in
Lancashire as regards the other fingers,
for it was supposed that no medical
man would dare rub ointment on a
wound with the forefinger of his right
hand, for the wound would never again
heal.

RINGWORM
The Shetland Isles formula for the
curing of ringworm was to take some
ashes between the forefinger and thumb
on each of three successive mornings,
and before taking any food. The ashes
had to be held to the part affected, and
the following words recited:

Ringworm, ringworm red, never
mayst thou speed or spread. But aye
grow less and less. And dee away
among the ashes.

There was at one time an old man in
the village of Stamfordham, Northumberland, who cured ringworm with an
earth and word charm. The patient was
obliged to go to him before sunrise. He
would then take a small quantity of
earth from his garden and rub the
affected part, the while he mumbled
some words, the tenure of which were
not known.

He averred that he was given the
charm from his father, and added that
the secret might be communicated by a
man to a woman or vice versa, but it
would be broken if a man told it to a
man or a woman to a woman. The fact
that he did in fact cure ringworm by
this charm is vouched for by the then
very puzzled vicar of the village.

RIVER (LIFE EVERY YEAR)
*The Eager must have three lives every
year.—Gainsborough.*

*The Ribble claims one life every seven
years unless a cock, or some animal, is
offered to her instead.—Cheshire.*

The Eager is the name given to a
strong spring tide which rushes up the
lower reaches of the River Trent, and
makes the river very dangerous. The
name, undoubtedly, comes from the
Scandinavian god Ægir, once worshipped
in northern England.

As for the three lives superstition
demanded by the Eager, it was still
firmly believed in by old people in the
neighbourhood as late as 1938.

Another Cheshire river superstition
was that if any Christian were drowned
in the River Dee and the body needed to
be recovered for Christian burial a light
would appear over the spot where it
was lying beneath the water.

This belief that a river requires
human lives has existed since Pagan
times, and it still rules in many parts of
the Continent as well as in Britain.

The Saale and the Spree, in Germany,
are believed still to require a victim on
Midsummer Day, and the utmost care is
taken by superstitious people not to
bathe in either of those rivers on that
day.

It is believed, too, that the Neckar,
below Heidelberg Castle, requires one
life on Midsummer Eve, another on
Midsummer Day, and a third the day
after. On these days if a call from a
drowning person is heard from the river,
the superstitious take no notice of it,
holding that it is only a water demon,
or a fairy, seeking to lure a life to its
doom.

Up to a few years ago, no fisherman
would launch a boat on the Elbe on
Midsummer Day, because a victim is
demanded by the waters.

Swabian peasants on the waters of
Lake Constance will neither go swimming nor climb a tree on St. John's Day,
for it is held that the Angel of St. John
must on that day have a swimmer and a
climber. The same belief exists at Schaff-
hausen, and at Cologne.

For other river death superstitions
see DROWNING.

ROBIN
*If you kill a robin, a large lump will
form on your right hand, preventing
you from working, or from hurling.—*
Ireland.

If a robin dies on your hand, the hand will always shake.—General.

If a robin is killed, one of the cows belonging to the person, or family of the person who killed the bird, will give bloody milk.—Yorkshire rural superstition.

NOTE: It was held that the same effect would follow if a farmer killed a swallow. But the authors cannot find trace of this other than at Walton-le-Dale.

Should a robin go about a hedge chirping mournfully, though the day be bright and the sky cloudless, it will rain before long. When he is singing cheerfully on a topmost twig, it will soon be fine, though it might then be raining.—General, rurally.

Should a cat catch and eat a robin, the cat will lose a limb.—Herts.

NOTE: This superstition was prevalent in the county as late as 1944, when it was confidently told to the authors by a countryman.

Should a person in the country be about to die, a robin will tap three times on the window with its beak.—General.

For a robin to fly into a room through the open window, is a sure sign of death in the house.—General.

Belief in the robin's visit as a harbinger of death is still widely held in country areas of Britain. The authors have come across it on a number of occasions.

Possibly one of the coincidences—we will not put it higher than that—was an incident which occurred at St. John's College, Hurstpierpoint, experienced and related by the Rev. S. Baring-Gould, that great authority on folk-lore. There was a superstition at the college that when a death took place, or was about to take place in the college, a robin would enter the chapel, alight on the altar and sing.

One evening at six o'clock the Rev. Mr. Baring-Gould chanced to be in the chapel when a robin entered at an open circular window and, alighting upon the altar, twittered a few notes. "A few moments later," said Mr. Gould, "the passing bell began to toll for a boy who had just died."

On the other hand, there is a story from West Cornwall of a vicar who was sitting by the bedside of one of his parishioners thought to be dying. The windows were standing open in order to give the sick man air, when a robin made its appearance in the room.

Roused by the fluttering of its wings, the dying man started up, and shaking his fists in a fury shouted, "Get out, you ——. I ain't going to die yet—with the prettiest field of broccoli that ever was seen on this farm waiting to be cropped." What is more, the farmer made a remarkable recovery!

The Yorkshire belief that death or the direst ill-luck will attend anyone killing a robin, brought to *Notes and Queries* (vol. viii, page 504) this story from a Yorkshire miner:

"My father killed a robin and had terrible bad luck after it. He had a pig which was nearly ready for pigging. She had a litter of seven, but all died. When the pig was killed the hams all went bad. Three of my family had a fever, and my father himself died of a fever. The neighbours said it all came about through killing that robin."

The robin ill-luck extends even to its nest. In Derbyshire, it was held that to take eggs from a robin's nest will be followed by misfortune.

The origin of all this lies, of course, in the sacred associations of the bird and its red breast. Most people know the tradition that the red came from the bird trying to pull the thorns out of the crown of the Saviour on the Cross. In Scotland, however, they have another belief, a pleasing one, that the bird is thus protected because each day it is supposed to carry a drop of water in its beak to the place of torment, in order to extinguish the flames.

This latter idea exists also in Wales. In Carmarthenshire, for instance, the following story used to be told of the red breast of the robin:

"Far, far away, in a land of woe, darkness, spirits of evil and fire, day by day the little bird bears in its bill a drop of water to quench the flames. So near to the burning stream does he fly, that his dear little feathers are scorched, and hence he is named *bron-ruddyn* (in Welsh 'breast-burned' or 'breast-scorched'). To serve little children the robin dares approach the Infernal Pit. No good child will hurt this benefactor of man. The robin returns from the land of fire, and therefore feels the cold of winter far more than his brother birds. He shivers in the brumal blast; hungry, he chirps before your door. So, in gratitude, throw a few crumbs to poor redbreast."

According to another notion, the robin and the wren are said to cover with moss and leaves any dead bodies they may chance to find unburied. Whether this is due to the fairy story of *The Babes in the Wood*, or to the story in Reed's *Old Plays*, the authors cannot say. The reference in Reed's *Old Plays* is contained in the words:

Call for the robin redbreast and the wren,
Since o'er shady groves they hover,
And with leaves and flowers to cover
The friendless bodies of unburied men.

And Drayton says, pathetically:

Cov'ring with moss the dead's unclosed eyes,
The little redbreast teacheth charitie.

In the mining areas of Wales a robin flying over a pit is regarded as an omen of disaster. The *South Wales Weekly News* of 14th September, 1901, referring to the explosion at Llanbradach colliery, mentioned that miners asserted that, some days before, a robin was found in the pump house underground where it had made its home.

This it was held was an omen, for a similar bird had been seen in the Senghenydd pit before the explosion there. Also a dove and two blackbirds had been noticed overhead.

See DOVE.

ROCKING A CRADLE

If a cradle is rocked when it is empty, it will be filled with another baby within a year.—General.

In some parts of the country, however, the belief is that the rocking will result in the death of the present baby within a month. This is the belief in Scotland (particularly in Selkirkshire), and in Durham and Yorkshire, where the maxim "Soon teeth, soon toes" is another belief, meaning that if a baby's teeth come early there will soon be fresh toes, i.e., another baby.

In Holland the same belief in the death of the child if an empty cradle is rocked also obtains.

ROOKS

If rooks leave a rookery, misfortune may be looked for.—General.

The misfortune threatened was of diverse nature. Should the rookery be on an estate, it presaged the downfall of the family. There is a Northumbrian saying that after rooks deserted the rookery at Chipchase, the family of Reed lost the property.

A Kentish superstition held that if rooks left the rookery of an estate it

meant that there would be no heir born to the family.

In connection with this, the story is related of the Chilham Castle in that county. It was at one time purchased by a family named Heron. When the family entered into possession a number of heron birds appeared and drove away the colony of rooks that had been established there for many years. The Kentish superstition of no heir for the family was spoken of. And no heir was, in fact, born.

After Cosmo di Medici, later the Grand Duke of Tuscany, had visited England (in the reign of Charles II), he wrote, in an account of his travels, of the rooks which the nobles of England prided themselves on attaching to their castles, because they were regarded as "fowls of good omen." He added that "no one was permitted to kill them, under severe penalties."

There was an eccentric vicar of Morwenstow, who endeavoured with great trouble to form a rookery in the trees around his vicarage. He even made the endeavour the subject of special prayers in the church on sustained occasions. Maybe he wanted di Medici's "fowls of good omen."

Finally, we may refer again to the superstition quoted at the head of this article that the desertion by rooks of a rookery means misfortune for everybody. According to the Wilkie MS., when rooks haunt a town or a village, mortality awaits its inhabitants. The rook seemed a bird of ill omen either way!

ROSE

To scatter the petals of the red rose on the ground is an evil omen.—General.

NOTE: In some parts of Britain the scattering of *any* rose leaves, of any colour, was so regarded.

If roses and violets flourish in the autumn, there will be an epidemic of disease the following year.

If the Burnet Rose blossoms out of its proper season, it is an omen of shipwreck.—Bristol Channel Islands.

On 7th April, 1779, a Miss Reay was murdered at the piazza entrance of Covent Garden Theatre, by a man named Hackman. With her at the time was Mrs. M. G. Lewis.

In the *Life and Correspondence of M. G. Lewis,* the following account of an incident before the murder is recorded:

"When the carriage was announced (to take Mrs. Lewis and Miss Reay to the theatre) Mrs. Lewis chanced to remark on the beautiful rose which Miss Reay was wearing in the dress which she was then adjusting. As the words were uttered the flower fell to the ground. As she stooped to retrieve it, the petals fell apart, and the stalk alone remained in her hand. The poor girl, who had been in good spirits before, was very affected by the incident, and said, in a slightly faltering voice, 'I trust I am not to consider this is an evil omen.' But soon rallying, she expressed to Mrs. Lewis, in a cheerful tone, her hope that they would meet again after the theatre— a hope, alas, which it was decreed should not be realized."

It was likely, again, that the rose's association with ill-luck and mortality came to us with the Romans.

The flower figured largely both in Roman and Greek funereal purposes. The tombs of the Greek dead were frequently decorated with the rose under the superstition that it protected the deceased. Romans frequently left legacies in their wills so that their tombs might be lined with roses. This, of course, entailed the scattering of rose petals on the ground.

In Britain, Aubrey, Camden and Evelyn all speak of the custom in their day of maidens planting rose trees on the graves of their dead sweethearts.

In Wales, it was usual to plant a white rose on the graves of young and unmarried females, and a red rose on the grave of any person who had shown benevolence and charity.

There was, of course, a love divination related to a rose. The rose had to be plucked on Midsummer Eve, and kept in a clean sheet of paper. If it was as fresh on Christmas Day as it was when it was plucked, and the lady wore it in her bosom to church on Christmas Day, the man who was to be her intended husband would come up and pluck it out.

The superstition of the rose on graves has a counterpart among the Thompson Indians of British Columbia, where, on a death, the widow (or widower) is made to pass through a patch of rose bushes four times in order to rid herself of the ghost of the dead man, which is supposed to stick on a thorn of the bushes as the passage through is made.

In Transylvania it is held that witches will ride on the backs of cows unless wild rose bushes are placed over the gate of the field.

Incidentally, the legend attached to the colour of the red rose, is that Aphrodite, while hastening to her wounded lover, Adonis, trod on a bush of white roses. The thorns tore her feet and the sacred blood dyed the white rose for ever red.

ROSEMARY

Rosemary worn about the body strengthens the memory, and adds to the success of the wearer in anything he may undertake.—North of England.

Rosemary grows only where the missus is master.—Herts.

Rosemary, placed on the door and lintels, will keep witches away from the house.

This belief obtains also in Germany, and in the Tyrol, where on May Day the ceremony of "Burning out the Witches" was performed. It included the gathering of various herbs, among them rosemary, making them into bundles with resinous splinters and burning them to the refrain:

Witch flee, flee from here,
Or it will go ill with thee.

The buildings were encompassed seven times, to the accompaniment of shouting crowds and the beating of pots and pans. Thus were the witches smoked out of their strongholds.

The Welsh had a belief that spoons made from rosemary wood make all food picked up by them nutritious.

It was also held in the principality that rosemary was a remedy against drunkenness; and it was the practice of housewives in the good old days, when a barrel of beer was kept in most homes, to put a decoction of rosemary into the barrels, secretly.

ROWAN WOOD

If you do not hang up on Rood Day branches of rowan wood (mountain ash) above the floors of the cowhouses, and tie them round the tails of the cattle with red thread, the witches will be at work milking the tether.—Scotland and the Hebrides.

Probably the most potent and general charm throughout Scotland was the rowan wood. It kept the Evil Eye from cattle, people and homes; it kept witches and fairies from the cattle. It kept disease from the cattle and the sheep, and figured in most customs and celebrations.

In the North of Scotland, it was held that herdsmen should cut rowan wood on Maundy Thursday, and fix the pieces of wood or leaves into a stave. The stave should be kept until next May Day, when, fixed over the doors of the sheep cots, they would preserve the sheep from disease until the following May.

The superstitious Scots had good tutors for their superstition, for this belief was practised by the ancient Greeks.

It was on Beltane that the Scots made the most use of the rowan wood. It was believed that on that evening witches were abroad casting spells on cattle and stealing the milk of cows.

To counteract the bewitching, pieces of rowan wood were placed over the doors of cowhouses, and fires—the Beltane fires—were kindled by every farmer and cottar.

For the same reason, Highlanders of Scotland insisted that the peg of the cow shackle and the handle and cross of the churn staff should always be made of rowan wood as a charm against the butter being bewitched and not coming in the churn.

In the Isle of Man, people carried rowan crosses, and tied crosses of rowan to the tails of the cattle. This was performed on May Day.

Now, come for a moment to Estonia. There the cattle, after wintering in the houses during the bleak months, are turned out in the fields for the first time on St. George's Day. The herdsmen, after receiving a sum of money, called "tail-money" set their crooks in the ground, muttering prayers as they do so.

It is regarded as essential that the crook shall be of rowan wood and carved by a "wise man," who also consecrated it. In Sweden the same ceremony is performed on the same day, the herdsman providing himself with a wand of rowan wood.

In Sweden, too, the "flying rowan" is used to make a divining rod with which it was supposed hidden treasure could be discovered. The "flying rowan" was that which had grown from a seed dropped by a bird from its bill, and which was growing on a wall or a high mountain.

But to be effective it had to be cut in .the twilight between the third day and the night after Lady Day, and neither iron nor steel was used to gather it. Also, it must not have fallen at any time to the ground.

In Westphalia and in Germany, too, rowan was a potent weapon against witchcraft, not only for the farmer, but for the ordinary citizen. In Norway, sailors and fishermen carried a piece of it in their boats for luck.

RUPTURE

Cleft a long ash sapling longitudinally for a few feet, and pass the ruptured child, naked, through it either three times or three times three, at sunrise. Then bind up the tree tightly again, and plaster the fissure over with clay or mud. As the cleft in the tree heals, so will the child's rupture heal.—General.

Take a snail, thrust it at sunset into a hollow tree, and stop up the hole with clay. Then, as the snail perishes, the child recovers.—Old Saxon remedy.

NOTE: There was, however, a secret and proper form of words which had to accompany the ceremony.

The utmost care had to be taken to see that the tree was properly bound up and plastered after the operation, for it was part of the superstition that if the tree cleft did not heal, or knit, neither would the rupture. And if the tree were to die, so would the child die.

It is surprising that down to the middle of the nineteenth century this absurd cure for rupture was still being practised in Sussex.

There were trees at Fittleworth in that county which were kept for the purpose of curing rupture.

Certain ash trees, once standing in a farmyard at Selborne, showed for many years long cicatrices down their sides, due to the number of times they had been split.

An old ash tree in Richmond Park, Surrey, was another favourite curer; it was known as the Sheen Tree.

An ash tree which had been used for this purpose grew at the edge of Shirley Heath, near Birmingham. Not a branch of it was allowed to be touched; it was never trimmed in any way, by order of its owner, Thomas Chillingworth, who was passed through it for rupture when a small child.

He believed in the superstition that his life and his health were bound up in the tree, and that if it died, he would die, though it was more than thirty years since he had passed through its trunk.

But in all these cures, there had to be certain conditions. The ash sapling, it was held, must be sound at heart, and the cleft must be made in one stroke with an axe. The child on being taken to the tree must be accompanied by nine persons, each of whom must pass it through the cleft from west to east. (In some cases the passing had to be "sunwise.")

In Germany, similar rites were observed for the curing of rupture, except that the tree in this case was sometimes an oak, and the ceremony had to be conducted at sunrise in complete silence.

In Oldenburg and Mecklenberg, the cure was regarded as only effective if carried out on St. John's Eve (Midsummer Eve) by three men named John, who assisted in holding open the cleft and passing the child through it. There, too, the affinity between the child and the tree was implicitly believed in.

In the island of Rugen, the belief went further; it was held that when a person thus cured of rupture died, his soul passed into the tree through which his body had been thus passed in childhood.

In the Vosges, rupture was held to be curable by taking a coffin nail, touching the child with it, and then while the child stood barefooted beside an oak tree, driving the nail into the trunk above his head.

All these instances of supposed cures belong, of course, to the belief in the transference of evil, which has existed for many centuries. It still exists to-day among thousands of native tribes.

In South Mirzapur, for instance, the Majhwars believe that all illness is due to ghosts, and if the ghost can be shut up in a tree the illness will depart.

At Blidar, in Algeria, there was, when the authors last saw it, an old olive tree regarded as sacred, in which women knocked nails for the purpose of ridding themselves of their ills and ailments— exactly as did people in the south gate of Cairo, and in the temples of ancient Rome.

NOTE: Some months after completing the rupture section of this volume, the authors, browsing through the intensely interesting *Rustic Speech and Lore*, by Elizabeth Mary Wright, came across the following: "An instance of these practices of passing a child suffering from rupture through the split trunk of a young ash tree was reported to me from Devonshire last summer." The book was dated 1913.

So the superstition, strange and unbelievable though it may seem, was credited in recent times.

A publisher's reader who ploughed through this volume placed a query at the foot of this section: "Why an ash tree for the cure? Why not any other tree?"

The answer is the belief that the infant Jesus was first washed and dressed in front of a fire of ash wood.

See ASH, NAIL, TREE.

RUST

If, without any neglect on your part, articles made of iron or steel, such as keys, knives, etc., continually become rusty, somebody is laying up money for you.—Wales.

SACRIFICE

In North Wales, in the seventeenth century, when disease broke out among cattle, farmers clubbed together to buy a bullock, which was then taken, with certain formalities, to the top of a precipice, from which it was hurled as a propitiatory offering. The superstition was called "Casting a captive to the Devil." It was said to have continued well into the nineteenth century; and was known also to have been practised in Lanarkshire and in West Lothian.

In Kingsteignton, Devon, there was on Whit Monday the sacrifice of a lamb. The animal was first drawn to a decided spot in a garlanded cart, and then killed and roasted in the middle of the village, the carcase being sold to the poor at a cheap rate. The origin is stated to be that, way back in history, the village suffered a dearth of water, and the inhabitants prayed to their pagan gods for the liquid. A spring welled up in reply and ever afterwards supplied all the needs of the villagers. So the lamb was annually sacrificed. But why a lamb?

Even St. Paul's Cathedral had its sacrifice. Dugdale records the annual grant of a doe yearly in winter on the day of the conversion of St. Paul and a fat buck in the summer upon the day of commemoration of the same saint, to be offered at the altar. Many suggestions for the sacrifice have been given which the authors regret they cannot accept. It is more likely that it is a relic of more ancient times, and was an offering to Diana, huntress goddess, whose shrine once occupied the site of St. Paul's Cathedral.

Sacrifices associated with calves, dogs, and other animals are given in this volume under their respective headings.

SAGE

He who would live aye, must eat sage in May.—General.

The sage plant must never bloom, for the flower brings misfortune.—General.

If a girl plucks twelve sage leaves as

the clock strikes twelve at midday on St. Mark's Day, one leaf for each and at each stroke of the clock, she will see her husband, if she is to have one.—Horncastle area.

A story is related by the Rev. J. H. Penny, in one of his books, of a mistress who induced her servant to try the experiment. At the last stroke of the hour she exclaimed: "Now look up and see if you can see your husband."

The girl glanced up and replied: "No, I can't see anybody except master coming up the drive."

At that the mistress fell down in a dead faint, for she herself could see nothing of her husband. In fact, he did not return to the house until an hour later. Subsequently, it is recorded the mistress died, and the master did actually marry the maid.

Sage, like all succulent plants, is very tenacious of life long after it has been torn from the earth. In Norfolk, it is believed that if it is hung up in a house, it will tell truly the health of absent friends or relatives.

According to Brand red sage placed in a bowl of rose water on Midsummer Eve will divine the course of love.

SAIL
It will bring bad luck to stitch or mend sails on the quarter-deck.—Wales.

We should say it would be indeed decidedly unlucky for any sailor who "tried it on."

SAILORS
A ship with a dead body on board cannot make any way.—Seamen's belief.

To lose a mop or bucket overboard, is a sign of ill omen.—General.

Should a glass tumbler be hit, the ring which it emits is the cry of a drowning sailor, unless the person who hit the tumbler places a finger on the rim and stops the ring.

Touch a sailor's collar for luck.—General, even to-day.

Disaster will overtake a ship, the name of which has been changed.—General.

Misfortune will follow any ship that sails on a Friday.—General, with passengers as well as sailors.

Two incidents, or rather sets of incidents, a few years ago, revived the superstition of the ill-luck attached to the changing of the name of a ship.

An Englishman who purchased the last half-dozen windjammers remain-ing, renamed them all so that the last syllable of the name should be that of the ending of his name. Every ship was lost within a year.

A year or two later, just before the 1939-45 war, the submarine Thetis, while undergoing her trials, was sunk with the loss of most hands. She was raised and some time later renamed the Thunderbolt, and put into service. There was an outcry by some of the men drafted to the crew. The Thunderbolt was lost, again with all hands.

To touch a sailor's collar for luck is not so much a superstition of sailors as their lady friends ashore. There are few girls to-day who, passing a sailor, do not surreptiously touch the collar.

There is, however, a sound origin for the phrase. It dates to the old days. Port "harpies" made it a practice to meet all ships coming into port from a long voyage. The sailors were always paid off on reaching port, and frequently received sums ranging up to £30 or £40. They were pounced upon by these women, and induced to drink heavily. In most cases the drink was drugged, but in any case, when they were either securely drugged, or "under the table," their money was stolen from them. "Touching" sailors was certainly lucky for the harpies.

Incidentally, let us remove once and for all the belief that the three stripes round a sailor's collar commemorate the three victories of Nelson. They do not. The three stripes are merely ornamental. Neither the French, the Germans, nor the Americans have any occasion to remember Nelson's victories—and their sailors wear the same stripes.

A Cornish superstition of sailors was that it was bad luck to walk at night on those parts of the shore where there had been wrecks. The souls of dead sailors, they held, haunted the spots, and any sailor passing would hear the "calling of the dead" hailing their own names.

Most people at times have noticed the sea to be phosphorescent. Old fishermen and sailors say that at such a time a plaintive sound is often heard coming from the waves. This, they suppose, proceeds from the souls of the drowned suffering in hell the fire of which the phosphorescence is the reflection.

See BODY, FISHING, SEA.

SAINING A BABY
In the Highlands of Scotland, the Orkneys and in parts of the North of England, it was deemed very necessary that a baby should be "sained" shortly

after birth. Fir candles were lighted and whirled round the bed on which mother and infant were lying. The whirling had to be done three times, and sunwise (in the direction in which the sun moves round the house).

Later, the "saining" was performed by drawing the bed into the centre of the room, after which the midwife or nurse waved round the bed an open Bible, three times three times, each three for the persons of the Trinity.

NOTE: "Sain"—from the old English *segnian*, and Old Norse *signa*, to sign with the cross. To secure by prayer or enchantment from evil influence.

SAINING A CORPSE

In the same area as those given above, a corpse was also sained. The rites are given at some length in the Wilkie MS., as practised in the Scottish Lowlands.

After the body has been washed and laid out, one of the oldest women present must light a candle and wave it three times round the corpse. Then she must measure out three handfuls of common salt into an earthenware plate, and lay it on the breast of the corpse. Lastly, she arranges three empty dishes on the hearth, as near the fire as possible; and all attendants going out of the room return to it backwards, repeating a rhyme, beginning "Thrice the torchie, thrice the saltie. . . ."

Sometimes a sieve was placed between the dishes, and the person who was so fortunate as to place her hand in the sieve, was held to have done most for the dead man's soul.

Meanwhile, all the windows in the house were opened, to give the soul free egress. The dishes were placed near the fire for the reason that the soul was said to resemble a flame, and to hover round the heart for a certain period after death.

In some areas, the dishes were, however, set upon a table close to the deathbed, and in later years, the saining became something of an orgy, with the attendants sitting with their hands in the dishes, and singing songs or repeating rhymes and telling fortunes.

There are stories—and we expect they *are* stories—of the corpse, angered by this display, rising up and placing his cold hand in one of the dishes. This, it may be as well to add, presaged death to the person whose hand was already in the dish. It would appear as though the whisky bottle was also present at the saining on these occasions.

It was held in the very superstitious Highlands that the candle for saining should be procured from a suspected witch, or from a person with flat feet or ringlet eyed. The old mosstroopers held that it ought to have been made from the fat of a slaughtered enemy

However this may be, the conclusions of the saining obliged the saining candle to be kept burning all night, and the table covered with a cloth so long as the body remained in the house.

The corpse, too, had to be watched all night by one of its kindred and a stranger, who could only be relieved by another kinsman or kinswoman and another stranger.

ST. ANTHONY'S FIRE

To cure the complaint, boil a handful of sage, two handfuls of elder leaves and an ounce of alum, in two quarts of forge water. Anoint with this.

In Germany, a cure for St. Anthony's Fire was to carry round a stick of red sealing wax.

ST. JOHN'S EVE

See MIDSUMMER FIRES.

ST. MARK'S EVE

See DEATH WATCH, MARK'S EVE, ST.

ST. PAUL'S DAY

On this day the husbandman prognosticates the whole year.—Lloyd, in *Dial of Daies.*

If St. Paul's Day be windy, there will be wars. If it be cloudy, it foreshadows the plague. If it be fair, it will be a pleasant year.

If the sun shine, it betokens a good year. If it rain or snow, indifferent. If misty, it predicts great dearth. If it thunders, great winds and deaths of people that year.—Shepherd's *Almanack* 1676.

In France and in Germany, also, it was held that the weather on this day, 26th January, prognosticated the year. In the Harleian MSS. (No. 593), in the British Museum, is an old French rhyme concerning it.

Bishop Hall, in his *Characters of Virtue*, observes that St. Paul's Day and St. Swithin's Day are his oracles (by this he means man's), which he dares believe against the almanack.

Schenkius, in his treatise on images (chap. 13), relates that it was the custom in Germany if the day chanced to be a foul one, to drag the image of St. Paul to the river, and there immerse it.

Why this day, and why St. Paul?

Well, Bourne, in his *Antiquities*, observes: "How the day came to have this knack of foretelling good and evil fortune of the full year is no easy matter to find out. The monks who were the first to make the observation, took care that it should be handed down to posterity, but why, or for what reason, they took good care to conceal."

St. Paul did, indeed, labour more abundantly than the other apostles but never, that the authors heard, in science or astrology.

ST. SWITHUN'S DAY

On St. Swithun's Day, if it should rain; for forty days it will remain.—General.

Absurd, of course, and not supported by fact. But the superstition must have gained much impetus from the weather which followed the rainy St. Swithun's Day of 1946; it rained for forty-two days.

St. Swithun was Bishop of Winchester. When he was dying, in 862, he expressed a wish to be buried not inside his church, but outside in the churchyard "that the sweet rain of Heaven might fall upon my grave."

This was done, but when he was canonised, the monks felt that a saint should really be buried inside the holy building. They accordingly made arrangements to move the body on 15th July.

But it poured with rain on that day (so the story goes) and continued to rain for forty days, "so that the monks saw that the saint was averse to the plan, and abandoned it." Then the rain ceased.

The Duke of Monmouth, who was exceedingly superstitious, placed considerable faith in the prediction of a fortune teller that, should he outlive St. Swithun's Day, he would be a great man. It is singular that he died on that day.

NOTE: The records of the past twenty-five years are against the accuracy of the St. Swithun's Day tradition.

ST. VITUS'S DANCE

For the cure of St. Vitus's dance, old people in Devonshire carried on their persons a charm obtained from a wise woman.

It consisted of a piece of parchment, on which was written:

Shake her, good Devil,
Shake her once more;
Then shake her no more,
Till you shake her in hell.

At Kirton-in-Lindsey, Lincolnshire, a remedy for St. Vitus's dance was the boiling in water of the berries of the mistletoe, the liquid then being given to the patient to drink.

In the Central Provinces of India, the "dance" is traced either to the possession of a demon, or to the shadow of an enemy which has fallen across the sufferer at some time.

Whether this has something to do with the European adoption of the name St. Vitus's dance, the reader will be able to judge for himself, when the origin of that name is explained.

St. Vitus had no predilection for dancing, and far from giving his name to any such recreation, was a devout youth of Sicily who, during the Diocletian persecution, in the year 303, was martyred, together with his nurse and his tutor.

It was more than twelve hundred years later that his name became associated with the "dance." Then, for no known reason, the remarkable superstition arose throughout Germany that anyone who danced before the statue of St. Vitus on his feast day (15th June) would be assured of good health for a year.

Thousands of people thronged round figures of the saint on this day and the dancing became almost a mania. So much so that it became confused with chorea (a nervous disease characterized by convulsive movements), and chorea came to be called St. Vitus's dance.

Eventually the aid of the saint was evoked against the dance.

SALT

Help to salt, help to sorrow.—General.

Give a baby, when it first goes out of the house, an egg, some salt, a little bread and a small piece of money, and it will never want the necessities of life.—North.

Bad luck will follow the spilling of salt, unless a pinch is picked up and thrown over the left shoulder.—General.

If you do not put a pinch of salt in the churn before beginning churning, the butter will not come.—Lincolnshire.

Put a small heap of salt on the table on Christmas Eve. If it melts during the night, you will die within a year. If it remains dry and undiminished, you will live to a ripe old age.—Wales.

In the Isle of Man, stated Waldron, in his description of the island, nobody would go out on any important business without taking salt in his pocket, much less remove from one house to another. Many, too, will not put out a child to nurse, or take one in, without salt being mutually exchanged. And a poor beggar in the street would not accept food unless it was accompanied by salt.

Brand, in *Antiquities,* commenting on this says that the origin and the reason given for this, is an account given by a pilgrim of the dissolution of an enchanted· island occasioned by salt spilled on the ground.

The bad luck of spilling salt is, of course, one of the major superstitions of the present day; and very few people are there who do not apply the remedy of casting a little of the spilled salt over the shoulder.

The putting of salt on another person's plate, which gives rise to the proverb, "Help me to salt, help me to sorrow," can be overcome by giving the person a second helping. Why that should not increase the bad luck a hundredfold is one of the little mysteries of superstition.

It is not without interest that the authors, in September, 1946, were asked by a young wife in the North of England, why a neighbour had sent her baby a gift of salt, an egg, and a silver coin.

So *that* superstition still lives, as well.

A curious salt superstition was practised in the Isle of Man at Hallowe'en, not noted anywhere else. Each member of the household before going to bed was given a thimbleful of salt. The contents of the thimbles were then turned out in neat piles on a plate and left there overnight. Next morning the piles were examined, and if any of them had fallen down, he or she, whom it represented would die within a year.

The overturning of a salt-cellar betokens the breaking of a friendship, except when it happens in the house of a fishing village; there it signifies the sinking of a ship.

The suggested origins of the superstitions on salt are nearly as varied as the superstitions themselves. Leonardo's picture of *The Last Supper* depicts Judas in the act of overturning the salt, and this, it is claimed by many etymologists, is the real reason for the salt superstitions.

But salt figured in religious rites and ceremonies many centuries before Judas. The Greeks and Romans used salt in their sacrificial cakes.

In Biblical days, salt was precious, and a sign of friendship. In ancient Egypt salt was regarded as a sacred symbol.

The origin of salt in superstition, the authors would say, lies back in the days of ancient Egypt.

In South Uist and Eriskay, two of the Outer Hebrides, a maiden's dream of the future was induced by the eating of bonnach salainn, a salt cake. It was made of common meal, but with a great deal of salt added. After the cake had been eaten the maiden might not drink water or utter a word to anyone; in fact, prayers might not be said.

SATURDAY

A Saturday moon if it comes once in seven years, comes too soon.—General.

The sun shines, if only for a minute, on every Saturday in the year.—Northants.

NOTE: The Spaniards have a similar belief.

Always baptize children on a Saturday; if on any other day they will die.—A superstition in St. Kilda recorded by Martin in his *History of St. Kilda.*

Saturday no luck at all.—In marriage.

Friday's dream on Saturday told, is bound to come true, be it never so old.—Lancashire.

Persons born on a Saturday can see ghosts.—Highlands.

A Saturday rainbow is sure to be followed by a week of rainy ("rotten") weather.—Ireland.

Saturday and Sunday were considered in the country up to a very few years ago as unlucky days for servants to go to new situations. In Northamptonshire there was a rhyme: "Saturday servants never stay; Sunday servants run away."

Saturday, in fact, seems to have been an unlucky day from time immemorial, for in extracts from Saxon manuscripts, published by Dr. Hicks, is the following:

"If on entering the year the first thunder happens on a Sunday, then it denotes mortality in royal families; if on a Saturday, then it will be mortality of judges and governors."

Apropos the belief in the Highlands that people born on a Saturday can see ghosts, is the Bulgarian peasants' belief that a Saturday-born person can see the vampires that harass their cattle; and also that they can see once a week the ghosts of those whose shadows have been buried in buildings.

The latter requires some explaining. It was an old Bulgarian belief that if a man was buried under a new building, the edifice would gain in stability. Since no man was usually willing to make such a contribution, the next best thing was to get a man's shadow.

The practice was for a mason to measure a man's shadow with a piece of string, place the string in a box and then build the box into the wall of the edifice.

It was supposed that within forty days the man whose shadow had been measured would be dead and his soul in the box beside the string. His ghost was permitted to come out on a Saturday, and this was the ghost that those born on a Saturday were fabled to be able to see.

As a result of this, it was seldom that anybody would walk anywhere near a building in the course of erection, and if someone approached, there were those who called out: "Beware lest they take thy shadow."

We have stated that it was considered that a building would acquire stability by the presence of a man buried in the foundations. This did not only apply to Bulgaria, and other mid-European states, but also to Britain. It is dealt with in this volume under Christening.

Bourne observes that in his time it was usual in country villages in Britain to pay a greater deference to Saturday afternoons than to any of the other working days of the week; and in Jacob's *History of Faversham* we find this confirmed, for in the list of expenses given appears: "The . . . . sexton, or his deputy, every Saint's Even and Principal Feast and *every Saturday noon* shall ring noon with as many bells as shall be convenient."

SCALDS

For a scald or burn, gather nine bramble leaves, and put them into a vessel of clear spring water. Pass each leaf over the scald and repeat three times to each leaf: Three ladies came from the east; one with fire and two with frost. Out with thee, fire; and in with thee, frost. In the name of the Father, Son and Holy Ghost.—Sussex, Devon, Cornwall, and also in Norfolk, with a slight change of wording.

The pain was finally dispelled by taking a stick of fire from the hearth and passing it over and round the scald nine times (three times three). The words, however, had to be said quietly without being heard by anyone, and in the presence of the patient only.

The *Pall Mall Gazette* of 23rd November, 1868, records an inquest on the child of a Devonshire labourer, who had died from scalds, and a witness named Ann Manley was reported as saying:

"I met Sarah Sheppard (mother of the child) coming on the road with a child in her arms, wrapt in the tail of her skirt. She said her child was scalded. Then I charmed it, as I charmed before, when a stone hopped out of the fire last Honiton Fair and scalded its eye. I charmed it by saying to myself: There were two angels come from the north. One of them brought fire and the other frost. Out fire, in frost, etc. I repeated this three times. This is good for a scald. I can't say it is good for anything else. Old John Sparway told me this charm many years ago. A man may tell a woman the charm, or a woman may tell a man. But if a woman tells a woman, or a man a man, I consider it won't do any good at all."

In the Shetland Isles, to cure a burn or a scald, the words used were: Here come I to cure a burnt sore; if the dead knew what the living endure, the burnt sore would burn no more. The reciter then blew three times upon the burnt place—and the pain went.

SCARLET FEVER

Cut off some of the hair of a person ill with scarlet fever, and put it down the throat of the ass.—Ireland.

The patient loses the scarlet fever, and the ass gets it—another instance of the belief (world-wide) of the transference of evil.

SCIATICA

The knuckle bone of a leg of mutton carried on the person will cure, and prevent, the sciatica.—Devon and Cornwall.

NOTE: A raw potato or a piece of loadstone will have the same effect.

But the most potent charm for sciatica, in the counties mentioned, and in others. was the boneshave.

Halliwell's Dictionary, 1865, states: "Boneshave: a noted charm for sciatica."

The patient was laid on his back on the bank of a brook or stream, and between his body and the stream was placed a straight stick or staff. While in this position the following lines were repeated by way of incantation:

Boneshave right,
Boneshave straight.
As the water runs by the stave.
Good for the boneshave.

The utmost reliance was placed upon this peculiar charm-cure.

Cornish superstition was able to cure sciatica by the simple expedient of wetting the forefinger of the right hand with spittle, crossing the front of the left shoe or boot three times, at the same time repeating the Lord's Prayer backwards.

Another Cornish cure was to keep a piece of loadstone in a pocket of the clothes you wore. Alas, this was one of the few superstitions one of the authors has tried. But he still suffered from sciatica.

SCISSORS

If a dressmaker drops a pair of scissors accidentally, she will shortly have a mourning order.

Never accept a pair of scissors for a present without giving a coin in exchange; they will bring you bad luck.

It is unlucky to pick up yourself a pair of scissors which you have dropped. Someone else should be called to perform the service.

NOTE: This applies also to a dropped umbrella.

Supposing, however, there is no one within hearing, then the ill-luck that would come from picking up the scissors yourself can be averted by warming the scissors in the hand before they are again used.

Scissors appear in a curious superstition to this day throughout North Africa. It tells how an ill-wisher of a bridegroom might stand behind the happy man, when he is on horseback, holding an open pair of scissors, and call the bridegroom by name. Should the bridegroom answer, the scissors are snapped shut, whereupon the bridegroom is rendered impotent to consummate the marriage.

SCYTHE

A scythe, placed on top of a haystack, and left until it shows signs of rust, will keep away overheating.

A better way, to the authors' thinking, is to have the stock properly "laid," and then properly thatched.

SEA

Bad luck will attend a ship that sails on a Friday.—General.

To put to sea after you have seen a pig first thing in the morning, will bring misfortune on the voyage.—Scotland and the North.

To see a woman with a white apron while on the way to a fishing boat, is an omen of misfortune.—Scotland and the North.

Misfortune will attend you if you put to sea after finding your earthenware basin turned upside down in the morning.—Scarborough and Yorkshire.

A fisherman's sea-boots must never be carried on the shoulder, but under the arm when taken to the ship.—Whitby.

If anything from one ship is lent to another, luck goes with it, unless some portion of the article is first deliberately though slightly damaged.—Wales.

No old Yorkshire fisherman, especially if he comes from Whitby, would think of going out in his boat if his boots had been carried on the shoulder of a boy. He would not venture on board his ship until the following morning.

The upside down earthenware basin superstition was made considerable use of by apprentices who wanted a day's holiday. They had a habit of deliberately turning their basins upside down!

The Friday sailing of ships as an omen is still held my many people. Only a few years before the 1939-45 war the sailings of two large liners from Southampton were postponed until a minute after midnight, following loud and concerted protests at a Friday sailing from a considerable section of the passengers.

Yorkshire sailors and fishermen who chanced to see a woman in a white apron as they went down to the quay early in the morning would without fail turn back, and not set foot on the quay during the day.

Among Welsh seafaring men the utmost perturbation was felt if anything was stolen from their ship. It was held that the ship's luck has gone with the stolen article, and it must be brought back, whatever the price asked for it, or the luck would never return.

A Scottish superstition of the sea was that if the song of the sea is heard from the west, the weather will turn and continue fine.

To return to Wales, it is held that the bells of the Squire of Bottreaux, if heard coming from the sea, announce an approaching storm. The legend attached to this is that the Squire of Bottreaux, once upon a time, wanted to make a present to the people of Boscastle of bells as large as those of Tintagel. He shipped the bells on a vessel. When the ship was in sight of Boscastle, the pilot wanted to sound the chimes, as a thanksgiving for the happily accomplished voyage.

The captain, however, said that thanks were due rather to the solidity of the vessel, and as for ringing the bells there would be plenty of time when they had been safely landed. Immediately a fierce storm arose, and the ship sank with the crew, all except the pilot.

In the western parts of Ireland, it is still believed that there is everything in the sea the same as on land—in other words, horses, cows, etc. As late as 1920, stories were told of horses that came out of the sea at night, cows, too, and men and women. These latter are, of course, mermen and mermaids.

One such story, told in Connemara by a woman, said: "I was told that there was a mare that had a foal, and it had never had a horse. And one day the mare and foal were down by the sea, and a horse put up its head and neighed, and away went the foal and was seen no more.

"And there was a man in this island watched his field one night where he thought his neighbour's cattle were eating his grass, and what he saw was horses and foals coming out of the sea. And he caught a foal, and kept it, and set it racing, and no horse or pony could ever come near it for speed, till one day the race was on the sands, and away it went into the sea, and the jockey with it, and they were never seen again."

The reader who would like to read more of these strange stories of the sea, could not do better than obtain a copy of *Visions and Beliefs*, by Lady Gregory.

See GULLS, SAILORS.

SEAGULLS

Three seagulls flying together overhead are a sign of death.—Sailors' superstition.

It is unlucky to kill a seagull.—General superstition of the sea.

It is certainly unlucky to shoot seagulls to-day, for the birds are protected in certain places by law. In earlier days, however, it was only superstition that preserved their lives.

The origin of the superstition lies in the fact that the seagull is a useful scavenger of the beach, devouring dead fish and offal, which, if left to rot, might very easily start an epidemic.

In the Rye area many years ago, the shooting of a seagull superstition gained strong support from the tragedy of a coastguardman, who, in a moment of forgetfulness, shot one of the birds.

Sir Charles Igglesden tells the story as it was told to him by a woman witness of the affair. Immediately, she said, hundreds of seagulls flew screaming round the head of the gunman. Terrified he ran inside his house and shut the door.

But the gulls continued to fly, screaming, round the house. Next morning the coastguardman was found with his throat cut, and quite dead, in a hollow in the sand dunes. Looking down on him from the crests of neighbouring dunes were hundreds of seagulls, silent and still.

See GULLS.

SEALS

None of the Lees will ever be drowned; they are related to the seals.—Said in Tralee.

None of the Clan Coneely will shoot a seal, lest it bring them bad luck.

It was asserted that some of the Clan Coneely were changed by magic art into seals, hence the non-shooting of seals. Many of the clan because of this legend changed their name to Connolly.

The Scottish Mackays are said to be descended from seals, and are known, says Sir J. D. Frazer, in the *Golden Bough*, as "the descendants of the seal."

The clan stands in Sutherland, and the story as related is that the laird of Borgie used to go down to the rocks below his castle to bathe. One day he saw a mermaid close in shore, swimming around as if anxious to land. After watching her for some time the laird saw that her cowl was on the rocks beside him. Knowing that she could not go to sea without it he carried it up to his castle in the hope that she would follow him. She did, in fact, follow, but he refused to give up the cowl, detained the sea-woman and married her.

She consented to the wedding with great reluctance, telling him that her life was bound up in the cowl, and that if it was destroyed, or if it rotted, she would instantly die.

For safety, the cowl was placed in the centre of a large haystack, where it laid for years. Until one unfortunate day, while the laird was away from home, labourers on the estate who were getting hay from the stack found the cowl, and in order to discover what it was, showed it to their lady.

The sight of it aroused old memories of her life in the depths of the sea. She took the cowl, left her child in its cot, plunged into the sea, and never returned.

Sometimes, it is recorded, she would swim close in-shore to see her boy, and then she wept because he was not of her kind, and she could not take him to sea with her. But all the descendants of him are famous swimmers, and cannot drown; "and," says the story, "they are known in the neighbourhood to this day, as Sliochd an roin, that is descendants of the seal."

SEAWATER
If you begin in childhood by taking a dose of seawater immediately on getting out of bed in the morning, you will live to a ripe old age.—Wales.

SEAWEED
Dried seaweed (known as Lady's Trees) if kept in vases on the mantelpiece, will prevent the house catching fire.—Devon fishing villages.

This is another superstition which is still held in the Devon fishing villages among the older people. The authors have visited many houses where the sea-weed has a place of honour over the chimney-piece.

It was held in Wales that a bunch of seaweed kept hanging in the back kitchen would keep away all evil spirits.

SEED (TIME AND SOWING)
If a seed drill goes from one end of the field to the other without dropping any seed, some person connected with the farm will die before the year is out.

In many parts of the world the sowing of seeds is accompanied by certain rites and services, all designed to propitiate the Spirit of the Corn.

In the Rye (Sussex) area, every day during sowing a seed cake and a bottle of wine were taken to the field with orders to the sowers to wet both eyes and to cut, not sparingly, from the cake.

In Herefordshire, and in Gloucestershire, on Twelfth Day, the seed was "wassailed." Twelve small fires and one large fire were lighted in a field sown with corn, and these were danced round by the farmer's men and their women-folk.

Mrs. Ella Mary Leather, in her *Folk-lore of Herefordshire*, states that "without this festival they think they would have no crop."

Ceremonies similar to the above were also held in several other shires, but not, as a rule, in the fields.

Now this is of some interest, because in Courland, when seeds are being sown the farmer's wife was wont to boil a chine of pork, with the tail attached. This was then sent to the fields.

The sower ate the chine, but stuck the tail into the ground in a part of the field, thus ensuring, according to the old belief, that the ears of corn would be as long as the tail.

In Germany, at seed sowing, barley and flax were sown over weakly and stunted children in the belief that this would make them grow with the growth and strength of the flax or barley.

In Estonia, at seed setting time, a child is set in the middle of the land to be sown, and is left there until the seed is sown. After that it is supposed that the child will shoot up in stature like the seed that has been sown. We give the superstition because it is the only one we know of in reverse, so to speak.

From time immemorial the sowing of crops has been accompanied by ceremonies designed to placate the corn spirit, or the corn mother. And in most countries, Britain included, the method has been to link up a harvest with the new seed.

For instance, in some parts of England, the last sheaf of corn harvested on a farm is kept until the following spring, and its grain is then mixed with the new seed.

In other cases, a part of the ash from the Midsummer Fires is carefully put away and this, too, at the next sowing time is mixed with the first seed to be sown. In this way, it was held that a plentiful harvest would be secured.

In Saxony and among the Slavs, exactly the same superstition was carried out. In Transylvania, a live cock is bound up with the last sheaf, and is then killed. The flesh is thrown away, but the skin and feathers are retained and scattered over the ground to be tilled just before the proper tilling commences in the spring.

How far back lies the origin of this worship of the corn mother, it is not easy to ascertain. The corn mother of the ancient Greeks, who had some similar kind of ceremony, was Demeter, one of the Olympian deities, and the goddess of fruit, crops and vegetation generally. The Cretan name for Demeter was corn mother. Yet it is likely that there existed a Scottish, or rather Gaelic, corn mother even before Demeter.

There is, of course, a marriage superstition connected with sowing. This is Scottish and Irish, and entails a maiden going out in the darkness of Hallowe'en and sowing hempseed over nine ridges of ploughed land, saying as she does so: "I sow hempseed, and he who is my husband to be let him come and harrow it." If she then turns her head over her left shoulder, she will see the form of her future husband in the darkness.

For superstitions on the time for sowing seeds, see BEANS, PEAS, etc.

SELLING

It is unlucky to bid a price for an animal (a cow, pig, or horse) when it is not for sale. If it is done, the animal will surely die.—Rustic belief.

It was a widely held superstition in markets that the first money taken at the opening of the day, a piece should be returned to the buyer, in order to "handsel" the day—to ensure that it should be a good day.

The practice still rules among many of the hucksters, who travel with a stall from market to market these days.

SERMON

One of the most stupid superstitions the authors have come across is that held in various parts of Somerset, that all texts of sermons heard in a church should be remembered by the congregation, for they must be repeated at the Day of Judgment.

On a par with it, however, was the belief of two old ladies that they must keep all their hair clippings and nail parings, since they would be expected to produce them on the Day of Judgment.

See HAIR.

SERVANTS' SUPERSTITIONS

If you place cold boiled water in a bedroom, it will bring bad luck.

To sweep out a bedroom of a departed guest before the guest has been gone for one hour, will bring bad luck to a friend of the family.

If a newly lighted fire breaks into two parts, the housemaid will lose her situation.

If a fire burns without blowing, you will have company without knowing.

Knife falls, gentleman calls; fork falls, lady calls; spoon falls, baby calls.

Perhaps the most curious superstitions that ruled the lives of domestic servants in olden days was that which decreed that if she entered the house of a new mistress before midday, she would bring ill-luck on the family.

The authors have record of one instance where a girl having been brought, with her box, some distance by a cart, and arriving at the house in the early hours, refused to enter, or to partake of any food or drink until after the midday hour. She sat in the front drive, on her box.

SEVEN YEARS

A curious superstition general in Britain, which existed for a great many years, and of which the authors have found traces at the present time, is that the body and the mind of every person undergoes a complete change every seven years.

Because of this, ailing or recalcitrant children were not unduly worried over, it being believed that they "would be quite different" when they reached the age of seven years, and similarly in older children when they reached the age of fourteen years.

Miss Christina Hole relates in one of her books in this connection how in Reading (Berks) two brothers, both aged twenty, suffering from bone disease which necessitated them wearing leg irons, told the secretary of their guild that they would know definitely within a few months whether they would get better or not. They were waiting, they explained, for their twenty-first birthday, on which date they were expecting to wake up completely cured.

SEVENTH SON

A seventh son can cure diseases.—South coast.

The seventh child of a family is always lucky.

NOTE: The seventh child of the family of one of the authors was killed in a motor accident—the only one to be killed.

The seventh son of a seventh son is a born doctor.—Somerset.

The seventh son of a seventh child is possessed of second sight.—Scotland, and the Border Counties.

The origin for all these beliefs lies, of course, in the mystic number seven; and the fact that seven of seven is the acme of the mystery.

Both in Scotland and in Cornwall, it was held—and in fact is still held in the outlying districts—that a seventh child, particularly if the child is a girl, has curative powers and by laying her hand on a burn can stop all pain. She has also the power of curing the King's Evil (q.v.).

In Somerset, "the doctor" is a recognized name for a seventh son; and it is commonly held that he should be trained for the medical profession as a matter of course.

In Scotland chiefly lies the belief that a seventh son of a seventh son or the seventh child of a seventh child possesses second sight, and is able to foretell the future. The same view is held in France, where such a child is called a Marcou.

How widespread was the belief in Scotland that the seventh son could heal the King's Evil in the seventeenth century that the saying was: "In England the King cures the struma by stroaking; and the seventh son in Scotland."

SHEEP, SHEPHERD

It is lucky to meet a flock of sheep on the road when making a journey.

NOTE: Except, perhaps, if you are cycling or motoring.

A small bone taken from the head of a sheep and carried on the person, will bring good luck.—Northants, Notts, Yorks and Lancs.

A farmer who sees his first lamb of the season, with its tail towards him, will have bad luck with the lambing; but if the head is towards him, the season will be good.—General.

black lamb foretells good luck to the fl k.—Kent.

NOTE: In Shropshire, however, a black lamb is accounted unlucky. See below.

If the lambing season starts with white twins, it will be a good lambing year.—Widely held by shepherds.

At Christmas, all sheep rise at dawn, turn towards the east, and bow three times.—Old belief in Romney Marshes.

Sheep should be driven under hoops of rowan tree on All Saints' Day and Beltane (1st November and 1st May).—Scotland.

The difference in the viewing of a black lamb between Kent and Shropshire is rather remarkable, for superstition among shepherds is usually what might be called basic.

Shropshire, however, took a very strong line on the black lamb in olden days. As recently as 1932 even, if a black lamb was born first of the flock of a Shropshire farmer, the unfortunate creature had its throat cut. If the first birth were black twins, the only way to save the remainder of the lambs to come was, so it was held, to cut the throats of the twins before they could say "baa."

An addition to the Romney Marshes belief of the bowing sheep is an equally firmly held idea that on any morning at dawn ewes turn towards the east and stand in rows. The origin is, of course, the association with the Lamb of God.

The Marshmen are soaked in tradition, as they were at one time soaked in smuggling. The authors meeting stubborn resistance from an old shepherd to the suggestion that the standing-in-rows ewes was a superstition, offered to go with him at dawn and investigate it. The old man was horrified. To do so, he insisted, would be an insult to God and would bring ill-luck to his flock. There is no way of getting round these superstitious gentlemen of the marshes!

Apropos the superstition, Sir Charles Igglesden, in *Those Superstitions*, relates how a parson, visiting an old shepherd of his flock, fallen sick, was requested to read the old man's favourite hymn, which begins with the line:

"The roseate hues of early dawn."

The old man was staggered by the parson's rendering; he could not read, he explained, and had always understood the words to be

"The rows of ewes at early dawn."

The story sounds to the authors as though it may well illustrate how, in the day of some illiterate shepherd, the superstition of the rows of ewes may have arisen.

Another firm belief in the Romney Marshes was that unless the first lamb to be born was rolled in the snow, disaster would overtake the rest of the flock. Many a good lamb has died from the treatment.

Of shepherds, old lore of the countryside made it a custom to place a tuft of sheep's wool in the coffin of a shepherd, before it was closed for the burial.

This was in order that, on the Day of Judgment, God would know him for a shepherd, and excuse his non-attendance at church, since a shepherd is unable to leave his flock.

In Somerset, a cure for any affliction of the respiratory organs was to carry the child sufferer through a flock of sheep as they were let out of the fold in the morning. The time was considered of great importance in the cure.

Lest it should be thought that only the ignorant held to this superstition, we hasten to add that an Archbishop of Dublin practised it when young, and it was fervently believed in by his parents.

A cure of some similarity was for whooping cough, for which a child was laid in the place from which a sheep had just risen in the morning. And even to-day, to carry a child through a gas works will, it is believed, cure respiratory trouble.

SHOE (THROWN FOR LUCK)

Throwing an old shoe after a bride, will bring her and her husband luck.—General.

The right foot bridal shoe of a bride should be thrown among the unmarried guests from the head of the staircase. The one who catches it will be the next to wed.

To burn an old shoe prevents infection.—Nottingham.

It is lucky to burn old boots before starting out on a journey.—Herefordshire.

Here, again, is another of the old superstitions which is still practised with great regularity. Few weddings are celebrated to-day without the old shoe, either thrown after the car, or fastened to the back of the car.

Curiously enough, however, the old shoe for luck is now used only at weddings. It was originally used for luck on all kinds of occasions. Perusal of the many volumes of that indispensable publication *Notes and Queries* reveals many instances.

At Swansea are records of old shoes thus thrown at a sailor leaving home to embark upon a voyage. There is a recorded instance in Norfolk of a cattle dealer, who, desirous of purchasing a lottery ticket—they were being sold in Norwich—ordered his wife to "trull her left-off shoe arter him." He bought a ticket, and with it won £600—evermore attributed to the old shoe trailing after him.

It is more difficult to account for the luck in the old shoe, than it is to subscribe the probable reason for the old shoe's appearance at a wedding. The latter has a most ancient lineage.

To understand it, one should, perhaps, start with Psalm lx, in which occurs: "Moab is my washpot! over Edom will I cast out my shoe." Immediately afterwards occurs the sentence: "O God, who hast cast us off." Now, if it means anything, it means that the threat to cast off Edom was contained in the words, "Over Edom have I cast out my shoe." Among the Jews, the brother of a childless man, in Biblical days, was bound to marry his widow, or, at least he had the refusal of her, and she could not marry again until her husband's brother had formally rejected her. This rejection ceremony took place publicly, and is mentioned in Deut. xxv. If the brother publicly refused her, she loosed his shoe from off his foot and spat before him. His giving up of the shoe was a symbol that he abandoned all authority over her.

Similarly with Ruth and Boaz. The Bible states that "as it was the custom in Israel concerning changing, that a man plucked off his shoe and delivered it to his neighbour." Ruth's kinsman, refusing to marry her, plucked off his shoe and delivered it to Boaz as a public renunciation of Ruth, and all dominion over her.

That this was also known to the early Christians is evidenced by the fact that when the Emperor Wladimir desired to wed the daughter of Raguald, her retort to him was, "I will not take off my shoe to the son of a slave."

Martin Luther, a guest at a wedding, after the ceremony, conducted the bride to bed, and told the bridegroom that he ought to be master in his own house, and for a symbol took off the bridegroom's shoe and placed it at the head of the bed.

From all this, the authors would suggest that the throwing of the shoe after the bride was not a symbol of luck, such as was known, and practised in the case of the Norfolk cattle dealer, but was a survival of the Biblical act; in other words that the shoe was a symbol of the renunciation of authority over her by her parents or guardians.

To support this, there is an ancient rhyme—we cannot now remember whence it comes—which went:

When Britons bold
Wedded of old.
Sandals were backwards thrown
The pair to tell
That, ill or well,
The act was all their own.

SHOOTING STARS

You must express a wish when a star shoots over you, or you will be unlucky all the year.—Wales.

Shooting stars are souls coming from Heaven to animate new-born children.—Yorks.

Throughout the world, and all races, these falling stars are associated in some way—sometimes entirely different ways —with souls.

Amongst the oldest of the present civilized races on earth are the Chinese. The Lolos, a tribe of Chinese, hold that for every person on earth there is a corresponding star in the sky. Therefore, when a man was ill they sacrificed wine to his star. When the man died, they dug a hole in the chamber of death and prayed that the dead man's star, which must fall or shoot on his death, might descend and be buried in the hole. Otherwise in its fall the star might injure someone on earth.

Similarly in Brittany, in Transylvania, Bohemia, the Abruzzi, the Romagna, and in Oesel, it is also held that each man has his star in the sky, which falls or shoots to earth on his death.

Coincidental with the Yorkshire belief that shooting stars are souls coming from Heaven to animate new-born children, is a legend of the Irish saints, in which the mother of one dreams that a spark has fallen into her mouth from a star, which she recognizes as the soul of her unborn child come to her; and that of the Mandans, of North America, who hold that when a woman is brought to bed for childbirth, a star falls from Heaven and, entering her, is born as a child.

A shooting star to the Maoris of New Zealand is a soul leaving the body of a man or woman, and going to the nether world. This same belief was held for many years in Belgium and parts of France.

We have taken here only those beliefs in shooting stars which correspond to superstitions here that they are related to human souls; there are many others, in various countries, which view such stars as evil spirits hurled from the celestial vaults. Included among these are some of the Estonians and most Mohammedans.

The Tarahumares of Mexico view a shooting star as a dead sorcerer coming to harm a man who had harmed him in life; and the Bororos, of Central Brazil, think him to be a dead medicine man announcing that he wanted meat, on which someone of the tribe would die.

SHREW ASH

The twigs and branches of the shrew ash will cure the pains of a beast suffering from the running of a shrew mouse over its limbs.—Old belief.

It was supposed, in those days, that if a shrew mouse crept over any beast— horse, cow or sheep—the animal was afflicted with cruel anguish, and was even threatened with the loss of the limb. Against this, farmers kept a shrew ash.

The shrew ash was made by boring a hole in an ash tree, inserting therein a shrew mouse, alive, and then plugging up the hole. The ash tree was then transformed into a shrew ash, with the remarkable qualities already described.

The practice was well known in Warwickshire.

SICKLE

Unless a shearer cuts himself with a sickle the first time he uses it, he will never be an expert with the implement.

SIN EATING

Most popular and common in Wales, but practised also in the Northern Counties, this superstition was designed to ensure that a dead person might go untrammelled and certain to Heaven, by the simple method of having all the sins of which he had been guilty, transferred to somebody else, willing to have them.

The method can, perhaps, be told in the words of Aubrey, who was alive at the time it was practised in Hereford:

"When a corps was brought out of the house and lays on the Biere, a Loafe of bread was brought out and delivered to the Sinne-eater over the corps, as also a Mazar-bowle of maple full of beer, which he was to drinke up, and sixpence in money, in consideration whereof he took upon him (*ipso facto*) all the sinnes of the Defunct and freed him (or her) from walking after they were dead."

There seems from the records to have been an "old sire," who followed the calling of a sin eater for a living in the various places where the superstition was practised.

Bagford (referring to Shropshire) describes how on a death the "old sire" was informed, who "presently repaired before the door of the house, when some of the family came out and furnished him with a cricket (a three-legged stool), on which he sat down facing the door. Then they gave him a groat, which he put into his pocket; a full bowle of ale, which he drank off at a draught. After this, he got up from the cricket stool and pronounced with a composed gesture the ease and rest of the soul departed."

The old sire must have been by the time he died the most sinful man in the world!

Now, in Travancore, when a rajah is dying, a Holy Brahman is sought who, for a large sum of money, consents to take upon himself the sins of the dying man.

In Tahiti, when a person of rank died a priest who bore the title of the "corpse-praying priest," was engaged. He prayed to the god by whom it was supposed that the soul of the deceased had been called away. The prayer asked that all the dead man's sins, especially that one for which his soul had been required of him, might be deposited in a hole which he (the priest) had dug.

Travancore, Tahiti, Wales, Hereford, and Shropshire—all bound together in this single superstition.

There was another kind of sin eating (or rather drinking) in Hereford. Attending the funeral of a farmer, a chance acquaintance was invited upstairs where the body was lying. On a table near the bedside were a bottle of port and a number of glasses. Asked to drink, he politely refused on the ground that he never took any wine.

"Oh, but you must drink, sir," was the reply. "It is like the Sacrament. It is to kill the sins of my sister."

Adverting to the "old sire" sin eater, Bishop Kennet added a note to Aubrey's MS., relating to a much later date. "It seems a reminder of this custom (he wrote) which lately obtained at Ambrosden, in the county of Oxford, where at the burial of every corpse, one cake and one flagon of wine, just after the interment, were brought to the minister in the church porch."

The very best man, undoubtedly, upon whom to load the sins of the dead!

SKULL

If a man swears on a skull and tells a lie, he will be struck dead.—Ireland.

The main point of this superstition is that the dire penalty attached to lying evidence, acted as a tribute to the truth of anyone who swore on the skull of the dead.

Now, a skull had to be obtained, of course. In April, 1851, a man was sent

to prison at Mayo for cutting off the head of a corpse only a few days buried. His defence was that he only wanted the head on which to swear in order to clear himself of a crime imputed to him.

In Wales, it was at one time believed that a portion of a human skull, grated as one grates ginger, and mixed with a liquid, was a remedy against fits.

For pains in the head, great stress was laid on the efficacy of moss growing upon a human skull. It was dried and powdered, and taken as snuff.

SLEEP

The head of a sleeper should face the church. If this is not possible because of the size of the room, then the head should face south.—General.

This superstition was widely held just over a hundred years ago. It was held to give more restful sleep to the person thus lying. And hostesses with the welfare of their guests at heart did their utmost to arrange their sleeping accommodation on these lines.

Some ten years ago, the medical profession in Britain became involved in a debate on which position the body found most beneficial to lie in for sleep. It was agreed by the majority that the most restful position was to lie facing south.

Perhaps there *is* a little something in superstition after all!

SLIPPERS

To cross a pair of slippers in the house, is unlucky.

This goes also with crossing knives at table.

SLUG

To find the name of your future husband, take a slug (or shell-less snail) which has been accidentally found, and not searched for. Place it upon a table which has been sprinkled with flour or ashes, and cover it with a wooden bowl.

In the morning, in the slimy track of the snail's wanderings, will be the initial of your husband to be.—Ireland.

SMALLPOX

To cure the smallpox, take a bun from the shop of a person who, when she was married, did not change her name. It must not be paid for, nor must the person be thanked for it. Give it to the patient to eat, and the smallpox will be cured.—Cheshire.

To prevent or cure the smallpox, open the windows of the sick room at sunset in order to admit the gnats. They will load themselves with the infection, and then fly forth and die.—Huntingdonshire.

It was also held that whooping cough could be cured by the method described in the first of these "charms."

It may be mentioned of the gnats impregnated with the germs of smallpox, that in Murzapur, smallpox is cured by taking some of the scabs or scars from the patient and burying them with flowers in a little heap of earth in the roadway.

The savages of Formosa "drive" the smallpox demon into a sow, which is then burned. In Buru (East Indian Islands) the patient is struck lightly with branches, which are then thrown into a proa (boat). The proa is then rowed to sea and abandoned with the farewell: "Grandfather Smallpox go away. Go willingly away. We have put food and drink for you."

The same "charm" is carried out by the Yabim, of New Guinea.

The point of all this is that in each case, including the old Huntingdonshire gnats, the disease is "transferred" to some scapegoat—the ancient and worldwide belief in the transference of evil.

SNAIL

If a child is coughing in the night, two or three snails boiled in barley water, or tea water, will cure the malady.

If a miner on the way to work meets in his path a snail (bullhorns in Cornwall), he must propitiate it with a few drops of tallow dropped from his candle.—Cornwall.

To cure the ague, sew up in a bag a common garden snail, and wear it round the neck for nine days. Open the bag, and throw the snail into the fire. It will shake like the ague, and you will never be troubled with shaking again.—Gloucestershire.

In South Glamorgan and West Pembrokeshire, snails were used to get rid of warts. A black snail was rubbed on each wart, to the accompaniment of the following rhyme:

Wart, wart, on the snail's shell black.
Go away soon, and never come back.

The snail was then put on the branch of a tree or bramble, and nailed down with as many thorns as there were warts. When the snail had rotted away on the branch, the warts disappeared.

A North Country superstition was that if a black snail was seized by the horns and thrown over the left shoulder, good luck would come to the performer.

If anybody is sufficiently quick to seize any kind of snail by the horns, he's entitled to all the good luck there is going!

Incidentally, this luck charm holds that should it be carried out by a person who had within the last three days become engaged to be married, his course of love will run much smoother than otherwise would have been the case.

See AGUE, WARTS.

SNAKE

If you wear a snake skin round your head, you will never have a headache. North Lincolnshire.

A dead snake bruised on the wound it has occasioned, is an infallible remedy for its bite.—Cornwall.

Should a snake cross the path of a bridal party on their way to the church, the union will not be a happy one.—General.

Snakes never die until the sun goes down, however much they may be cut in pieces.—General.

NOTE: The same thing is said of eels.

To cure the "large neck" (goitre), draw a common snake held by its head and tail nine times slowly across the swelling, the reptile being allowed after every third time to crawl around for a time. Afterwards put the snake alive in a bottle, and bury it in the ground. As the snake decays so will the goitre vanish.—Sussex.

One of the oldest snake superstitions in the country was that if you ate snake you would keep young. Massinger, in *Old Law* (act 5, sc. 1), makes one of his characters say:

He hath left off, o' late to feed on snakes.
His beard's turned white again.

Another belief was that if a tongue was torn out of a live snake on St. George's Day, put into a ball of wax, and the ball laid under the tongue of a person, that person would be able to talk anybody down. The same thing was said in Bohemia.

A Cornish superstition is that no snake is ever found near an ash tree, and that a branch of an ash tree will prevent a snake approaching a person.

A queer story anent this is contained in Cornish literature. It relates how a child was in the habit of sharing its bread and milk, served to it at the cottage door, with a snake—a poisonous adder. The reptile came each morning, and the child, pleased with the beauty and the markings of its companion, encouraged the visits.

The mother, discovering this and finding it impossible to keep the snake away from the child when it was left alone, during working hours, adopted the precaution of binding an ash twig around the child's body. The adder no longer came near the child, says the story. But from that day the child pined, and eventually died of grief at having lost its companion.

See ADDER STONES.

SNEEZE

Should a sailor sneeze on the right side of the ship when embarking, the vessel will have a lucky voyage; if on the left side, there will be foul weather.—General.

A new-born baby is in the spell of the fairies until it sneezes, after which it is safe.—Scotland.

No idiot child ever sneezed, or could sneeze.—Scotland.

If you sneeze in the morning before breakfast, it is a sign that you will have a present before the week is out.—East Anglia.

It should be borne in mind that all these sneezing beliefs were dependent for their potency on the sneeze being purly an accidental one. A cold in the head, or a sniff of pepper or snuff, did not count.

Bearing this in mind, a sneezing rhyme of luck generally held (with one or two local differences) was:

Sneeze on a Monday, sneeze for danger.
Sneeze on a Tuesday, kiss a stranger.
Sneeze on a Wednesday, get a letter.
Sneeze on a Thursday, something better.
Sneeze on a Friday, sneeze for sorrow.
Saturday—see your true love tomorrow.

With regard to the Scottish belief in the fairy spell being broken when the newly born child sneezed: every good midwife of the day included in her bag a supply of snuff—to ensure that the child did sneeze; the ban on non-accidental sneezes apparently having no hold in Scotland. Or maybe it was

deemed that any kind of a sneeze was better than none at all.

The ejaculation "God bless you," still used on hearing a person sneeze, is not a superstition. Its origin was in the great Athenian plague, a sneeze being so frequently the first indication that a person had contracted plague.

The Romans practised the "blessing" and brought it to Britain. Here it was used extensively in the plague, for the same reason that the Athenians of old had used it—an invocation to the Deity for a person who was like to die.

There is some sort of foundation for the blessing, in the fact, vouched for to the authors by a famous doctor, that one is never so near to death as during a sneeze.

SNOWDROP

If a snowdrop be taken into a house, some member of the household will die before the snowdrops come again.

NOTE: This is said also of the hawthorn.

Miss Elizabeth Wright, in her *Rustic Speech and Folk Lore,* records that the death of a school companion in a boarding house was blamed on her (Wright's) parents for sending a box of snowdrops from their garden to the school.

SNUFF

A strange practice in parts of Ireland was to place a plate of snuff on the body of a dead person. Etiquette demanded that all invited to the funeral should take a pinch of the snuff on arriving in the house of mourning.

Just what it meant to the dead is not clear; but the practice is the origin of the phrase:

"I'll get a pinch off your belly yet," as a retort to a threat.

SOAP

It is unlucky if soap slips out of your hand.—Highlands.

A correspondent of *Notes and Queries* has described an anecdote illustrative of this superstition.

A Highlands woman named Kate Elshender, going to a quarry hole to wash clothes, called in at a village shop, and bought half a pound of soap. Shortly afterwards, while washing, the soap slipped from her hand and into the deep quarry hole. Going back to the shop, she purchased another half-pound. The shopkeeper warned her to take care, as the fact that the soap had slipped and been lost was a warning.

She laughed and returned to her washing.

Once again the soap slipped away, and again she returned for another piece. The shopkeeper, now quite frightened, begged her not to try the washing again. But again the woman laughed, and returned to the quarry. And in the quarry, some time later, she was found drowned.

SOOT

If during a wedding breakfast, a clot of soot should come down the chimney, it is a sign of bad luck for those married. —Scotland.

SORE EYES

Rain which fell on Holy Thursday and was bottled, is a cure for sore eyes. —General.

A more potent, and certain, "cure" was that employed in many parts of the country, but especially in Devonshire.

It necessitated a house-to-house visit begging for pennies, until four shillings and sixpence worth had been obtained. If a woman was the collector, she must take pennies only from males, and must not say please or thank you for the gifts. If a man, then the collection, again with no thanks, must be from women. With the four and sixpence a pair of earrings would be purchased and these, it was certain, would do the eyes good.

SORES

North Country people, fifty years ago, had a sovereign remedy for arms covered with sores.

They attended at a slaughter-house on killing day, and for a consideration, the butcher, as soon as an animal had been killed, cut a slit in the stomach.

Into this the sufferer thrust his arm, and kept it there until the stomach had cooled down.

A few applications of this treatment was said to cure the most stubborn case of sores.

Infants, whose skin was affected with sores, were also inserted partly into the slit thus cut in the animal's stomach.

SOUL

Night flying white moths are the souls of the departed. —Yorkshire.

Sparrows carry the souls of the dead.

It was held in parts of Yorkshire that the souls of new born children came to them in the form of shooting stars. In other parts of Europe and among many native races, the belief obtained that every soul of a living person had its own star in the sky.

See BOLTS, CORPSE, DEATH, LOCKS, SPARROWS.

SOULING BELL

Name given in the North of England to the passing bell, because it was thought to drive away lurking spirits that might be lying in wait to seize the soul of the departed person.

SOULING DAY

See ALL SOULS' DAY.

SOWING

It is unlucky to sow any seeds during the last three days of March. —Devonshire.

The superstition, widespread throughout Devonshire, led to the last three days of March being called "The Blind Days."

See SEEDS.

SOW THISTLE

If a leaf of the sow thistle is carried by anyone, he will be able to run and never grow tired. —Wales.

However, the superstition adds that should he have a companion, it will take the vitality from him; and should the wearer of the sow thistle give a leaf to his wife, one of them will waste away and die.

SPARROW

It is unlucky to destroy sparrows. —General.

To catch a sparrow, and keep it, forebodes death in the house. —Kent.

Sparrows carry the souls of the dead.

A story is told of the belief of the last of the above superstitions, not from the rural countryside, but in the heart of crowded London.

A sparrow dashed its bill against a London house window. "Oh," declared the housewife, "something is the matter with poor Edward" (her brother). Hardly had she spoken the words when a man rode up on horseback with the news of the death of Edward.

The relater of the incident said that the family were convinced that the sparrow had carried the soul of the dead Edward to his house.

The probable origin of the superstition against killing sparrows is the belief of the ancients, who consecrated the little bird to the Penates.

NOTE: Dii Penates were the gods of the household.

SPIDER
Good luck will attend anyone upon whose face a spider falls from the ceiling.

If a spider is met with in the path of a bridal party on its way to the church, the bridal couple cannot have happiness and prosperity.

If you have the ague, catch a spider and shut it into a box. As it pines away, so in proportion will the ague wear itself out.—Somerset.

The spider was also an excellent cure for whooping cough and asthma, according to the superstitions in Cornwall.

For whooping cough, a muslin bag— no size stated—filled with spiders, was hung around the sufferer's neck; there it had to be worn night and day.

For asthma, spiders' webs were collected, and rolled into a ball in the palm of the hand. They then had to be swallowed.

If a spider is found upon your clothes, or about your person, you will shortly receive some money, is a South Northampton belief.

A spider is used by the Toradjas, of Central Celebes, to cure thieving. A "wise woman" places a bag containing spiders and crabs on the hands of the person addicted to thieving, calculating that the prehensile claws of these creatures, so suggestive of the hand of a thief closing on its prey, will seize the vicious propensity in a young woman's mind, and extract it as a pair of forceps would extract a thorn from the flesh. It might be an idea to try on our present shoplifters.

SPILLING SALT
To spill salt at the table will bring bad luck, unless you pick up a pinch between finger and thumb, and throw it behind you over your left shoulder.—General.

This is, of course, one of the most prevalent superstitions of to-day. Even those persons who laugh at superstition will seldom upset salt without throwing a pinch away.

Many do so, of course, out of deference to the feelings of people present who may be superstitious, and would see in the spilling an omen sufficient to disturb them. But the majority of the disbelievers, we fear, do it "just in case."

The authors cannot understand the reason for the superstition of spilling salt, for the taking of salt has been throughout the ages a sign of friendship and hospitality. To break salt was old even in Biblical days; and was a sign of friendly relations and of peace.

It is shared by the "barbaric" races, even to-day. There was reported not so many years ago, the case of a man captured by an Arab bandit in the desert behind Morocco. No ransom had been paid, and the man was about to be executed when, suddenly, he slipped from the grasp of the chieftain's men, dashed to the table, put finger and thumb in the vessel containing salt, and slipped the salt into his mouth.

"Let him go," ordered the bandit chief. "He has broken salt with us. Illluck will attend us should he die."

We never heard of a clearer case of spilling salt.

See SALT.

SPITTING
The first money taken at the start of the day's business, should be spat on to ensure ready sales and good luck.—Market square superstition.

NOTE: The saying is, or at any rate was, " Handsel (q.v.) is always lucky when well wet."

If two persons wash in the same water, it produces bad luck, unless one of them spits into the water.—General.

NOTE: Or makes the sign of the cross over the water afterwards.

Spit in your boat for luck.—Yorks fishermen.

Always spit into the trawl or dredger before lowering it into the sea.—Fishing ports.

In Scotland in older days—and in one or two places in England at the present day—it was the custom of the priest at a christening to moisten with spittle the nostrils and behind the ears of the child, before touching it with holy water on the forehead as is usual.

The theory of the Canonists behind this superstition—for it was nothing else but superstition—was expressed thusly: "Let the nostrils and the ears be touched with spittle, that the nostrils may be opened to receive the odour of God, and the ears to hear His mandates."

In the village of Buckie, Scotland, there were some family names, especially Ross and Coull, which fishermen would never pronounce. If any one of the names was mentioned in the hearing of a fisherman, he spat (chiffed).

A similar habit was associated with other names. The holders of the names had a difficult task to secure a livelihood in the fishing industry; they, in any case, had to pass under some other cognomen.

The Yorkshire—and other northern fishing folk—habit of spitting into the boat and the trawl before the net was dropped overboard is an age old superstition of men who have followed the sea. It was of great antiquity even in Pliny's day. Probably few fishermen on our coasts who faithfully carry out the practice to-day know that the origin lies in the belief held that saliva represented a man's soul; and to spit, therefore, was to make an offering to the gods.

There is hardly a native race in which does not exist the custom of spitting for luck, or to ward off evil. In fact, the authors doubt whether there is a more universal superstition.

The Watchandie people, of Australia, if a dead man's name is mentioned, spit thrice to counteract the evil effect of having taken a dead man's name into the lips.

When the Baronga, of South Africa, see a shooting star, they spit on the ground and call, "Go away. Go away alone," by which they mean that the light, which they know will soon be extinguished, is not to take their souls with it, but die by itself.

In sickness, the Sihanaki, of Madagascar, exorcise the devil that is in the patient, and all the relatives, waiting at the door, and also the sick man, spit towards the door to expedite the departure of the evil.

In Guatemala, big piles of stones stand at the parting of the ways, and on mountain and cliff tops. Every Indian passing them gathers a handful of grass, rubs his legs with it, spits on the grass, and lays it on a flat stone on top of the pile. Thus, he believes, he will restore the flagging vigour of his legs.

There are many other instances of the kind, but these will suffice to illustrate again the affinity of superstition the world over.

What is the origin of this use of spittle? Who can say? The properties of the human saliva have received notice in history, sacred and profane.

Among the ancient Pagans, Pliny, no less, recorded it as an antidote to fascination, a preservative from contagion in that it was held to counteract poisons; he also averred that in pugilistic encounters it aggravated the vehemence of the blow. Illustrating this, it is a very curious thing that to-day when two men, or even boys, prepare to engage in a bout of fisticuffs, they invariably, and automatically, begin by spitting on their hands. We leave the reader to suggest the reason why.

In Scotland, the "skilful" were engaged to spit on distempered animals. If cows fell sick, or their milk dried up, the wise person's spit would instantly put the contretemps right.

The ancients were said to have cured blindness, and restored sight by spitting on the closed eyes; there are stories of old Scotland of sight similarly restored.

See NAMES, PARSON, PIG.

SPOON

To pour gravy out of a spoon backhanded, will lead to quarrels in the house.—Cornwall.

Two spoons in one saucer foretell a wedding.—General.

Scottish nurses always noted with which hand a child first took up a spoon to sup. If it was taken with the left hand, then the unfortunate infant was deemed to be unlucky for life. The belief is recorded in the Wilkie MS.

SPRAIN

It was usual in Scotland, if one sprained a limb, to call in a person experienced in casting the wrested thread.

The thread consisted of a piece of spun black wool. On this was cast nine knots, and it was tied round the sprained limb. As the operator was engaged in the winding he spoke inaudibly to bystanders these words:

The Lord rade (rode) and the foal slade (slipped).
He lighted
And she righted.
Bone to bone,
And sinew to sinew.
Heal in the Holy Ghost's name.

That was the cure.

The same charm was followed in the Shetland Islands.

A charm used in other parts of the country consisted in saying over the injured limb these words:

Bone to bone and vein to vein.
Oh, vein, turn to thy rest again. . .
In the name of the Father, Son and Holy Ghost.

In Devonshire the verse recited, always in tones so low that the words could not be heard was:

As our Blessed Lord and Saviour was riding into Jerusalem, his horse slipped and sprained a leg. Our Blessed Lord and Saviour blessed it, and said, Bone to bone and vein to vein. O vein, turn to thy rest again. So shall thine, in the name, etc.

A curious superstition for curing sprains was at one time extensively practised in the North of England. The injured person laid his strained leg, or other injured limb, on the ground, whereupon a "stamp-strainer" stamped on it with his feet. The limb was then bound up in the skin of an eel.

It was said to be greatly efficient, and to effect a painless cure after the first twinge of the stamp. There were at one time a large number of people scattered in villages and hamlets all over the country who earned an income from "stamp-straining."

SPRING
Spring arrives when you can set your foot on twelve daisies at once.—Durham.

They had no truck with the calendar in Durham County!

SPRING CLEANING
It is unlucky to spring clean a house after the month of May.—General.

This is another of the superstitions still in force among housewives. Its origin would appear to lie in the survival of the Jewish insistence of the cleansing of their houses being concluded each year before the Passover Feast.

SPRINGWORT
The springwort is a magic plant, and will open any lock, and render the possessor of it invisible.—Very old country belief.

However, there was a special means of obtaining the necessary sprig of the plant, without which the magic could not be engendered. Briefly, you had to mark a hollow in a tree in which a woodpecker had built a nest and hatched young birds. When the woodpecker left the nest in search of food, you had to plug up the hole with a wooden wedge, and hide close at hand until the bird returned. Finding the wedge, the woodpecker would at once fly away and return with a sprig of springwort in its bill. It would flutter up to the tree, and hold the springwort to the wedge, whereupon the wedge would shoot out of the hole with a bang.

You now rushed from your hiding place, shouting loudly, and in its fright the woodpecker would open its bill and

drop the springwort. As it fell you caught it in a red or a white cloth. Henceforth the springwort would open any lock or door, and make you invisible at will.

There was another flower credited with the same magic—chicory. But this had to be cut with a piece of gold at either noon or midnight on St. James's Day (25th July).

The cutting had to be done in perfect silence; if you spoke you would, so it was believed, die almost at once.

SQUINT
If you meet a squint-eyed person, you must spit three times, or bad fortune will attend you.

Or, should you meet the squint-eyed person when you are going on business, the ill-luck can be averted by returning home, eating a meal, and setting off again later.

See SPIT.

SQUIRREL
To shoot a squirrel, will bring bad luck on the person doing the shooting.

No sportsman who shoots a squirrel will have any more luck with game.

The origin of the bad luck in shooting squirrels is obscure, but is probably related to the legend that the animal was the only witness of the eating of the Forbidden Fruit by Adam and Eve in the Garden of Eden.

The squirrel had the tail of a rat in those days, so the legend goes, and was so horror struck that he drew his tail across his eyes to shut out the sight. As a reward, all squirrels were given the thick brush of a tail.

STAGE
The "tag" (last line of the play) should never be spoken at rehearsals.

Whistling in the theatre anywhere will bring bad luck.

The air of Tosti's "Goodbye," hummed in a theatre, will lead to bad luck.

Peacock's feathers anywhere in a theatre are dreadfully unlucky to the play.

These are four of the principal superstitions attached to the theatre and theatre people. There are many more.

For instance, Friday is regarded as a disastrous day on which to open with a new play.

The dressing room should always be left left foot first.

Pictures should never hang on a dressing room door.

Soap must not be left in the dressing room.

Macbeth music should not be hummed during rehearsal.

Thirteen is very unlucky. (There is never a No. 13 dressing room in a theatre.)

Real flowers should not be worn on the stage; only artificial ones.

To fall *naturally* on the stage is taken as a sure and certain sign that you will have a return date at the theatre.

A cross-eyed chorus girl will bring bad luck to the play. Not that there is much danger of this, since a cross-eyed chorus girl would have little chance of getting past the audition, let alone get on to the stage.

The late Sir Henry Irving, when playing in *Othello*, noticing a woman in the stalls with a peacock's feather fan, at the end of the first act sent her a note, which read: "For God's sake, take that peacock fan out of the theatre to prevent a disaster."

The unluckiest play to put on the stage is *Macbeth*. The belief in this connection is that the Witches' Song has the power of raising evil. Hundreds of instances have been told of the misfortunes which have followed theatres or members of the cast in the play. Incidentally, one of the latest to be noted is that Miss Lilian Baylis, the fairy godmother of the Old Vic Theatre, London, died while *Macbeth* was being played in her theatre.

Robin Hood and the *Babes in the Wood* are accounted unlucky pantomimes; and *Cinderella* as one of the luckiest.

It is held that should an actor's shoes squeak as he makes his first entrance in a play, he will be lucky in the run of the piece. Should he, however, catch a portion of his clothing on any scenery as he makes his first entrance, he should go back—despite what the stage manager is likely to say about it—and make his entrance again, or he will have bad luck.

To stumble on making a first entrance is accounted a sign that some time in the evening the actor will miss a cue, or "fluff" his lines. Yellow in a theatre is unlucky.

But unluckiest thing of all to happen to an actor or actress inside a theatre, is for another of the company to look over his or her shoulder into a mirror. The one so overlooked is bound to meet with misfortune.

Outside the theatre "luck" still awaits the actor; should he try the handle of the wrong door when going to see a manager or an agent, he will be unsuccessful in his quest for a part.

Finally, let us mention a cat. If one walks across the stage at rehearsal, then the show being rehearsed will be a success.

STAIRS

It is unlucky to meet on the stairs.—General.

If you trip going upstairs, it means a wedding in the house.

Should you trip going downstairs, you will have bad luck.—General.

NOTE: The authors think this quite likely; the tripper would stand a good chance of breaking his, or her, neck.

The ill-luck of meeting, or of passing, on the stairs is still potent at the present day. Few, even of the moderns, will attempt it, the person ascending generally retracing his steps to the bottom again.

A curious staircase superstition which ruled in the Tudor mansion of a Staffordshire family is worth mentioning, although it is a single instance of its kind. It is related thusly, by Sir Charles Igglesden:

The bridegroom took his wife in his arms, and together they slid, astride, down the handrail of the ancient staircase. In the hall stood the best man whose duty it was to catch the couple as they ended the journey.

Until the Tudor mansion was burned to the ground a short time ago, the custom was carried out on the wedding day of sons of the house for generation after generation, and the polished oak staircase was treated with the greatest reverence.

The fact that no children have been born to the last two male descendants of the family is attributed to the fire which consumed the staircase and prevented the ancient custom from being carried out on their wedding day.

STEALING

If you wear a toad's heart concealed about your person, you can steal without being found out.—Herefordshire.

This belief was at one time pretty widespread around Herefordshire.

Mrs. Leather, in her *Folklore*, states that a suspected thief was on one occasion heard boasting: "They never catches me. I allus wears a toad's heart round my neck, I does."

See HAND OF GLORY.

STILE

Never place a stile in a footpath leading to the sea. It is unlucky.—Seamen's superstition.

According to the superstition, a stile thus placed meant death to sailors. With it went a repugnance to fences or railings on all parts leading to the sea. If they *must* be erected, then there should be left large gaps here and there.

On one occasion when such wire fences were erected at Hythe, the wives of the Hythe fishermen tore down all the wire that had been fixed opposite the beach, with cries of "It's murder."

The authors suggest that the origin of this may quite easily have been the necessity for leaving the coastline open for the launching of a lifeboat to men in distress. A stile or fencing of any kind would present an obstacle which would waste much time in getting the boat on the water.

See PINS.

STILLBORN CHILD

It is lucky to have a stillborn child put into an open grave, as it is a sure passport to Heaven for the next person buried therein.—General.

See CORPSE, DEATH, GRAVEYARD.

STOCKING

Good luck will attend anyone throughout the day, who puts on the left stocking first.—General.

This is a remarkable superstition in that it brings luck from the "left" mostly regarded as the unlucky side.

See RIGHT-HAND TURN, RIGHT FOOT, SUNWISE.

STONECROP

Stonecrop placed on the roof of a cottage, will protect it from lightning and witches.—Wales.

See ADDER, HOUSE LEEK.

STONES

Stones have always been held, in certain circumstances, to possess great powers of healing, and they figure largely in medicine charms. Most fortunate of all stones are those with a natural hole through the centre of them.

It was considered lucky in the Isle of Sheppey to possess such a stone. For many years it was the custom of parents in the Isle to hang such a stone, or even a beach stone, round the neck of every child until it reached its first birthday— but never afterwards.

The Irish also held, and in many parts still hold, that the stone with a hole through it is a natural talisman.

The water of Loch Monar, near the Strath in the Highlands, was renowned for healing, said to be due to holy stones. According to tradition, a woman of Ross-shire, who went to live at Strathnaver, possessed some holy and charmed stones. One day a man attempted to rob her of the stones. She ran towards Loch Monar, and saying in Gaelic "Mo nar shaine," she flung the pebbles into the water, whence the lake became endowed with healing properties, particularly (reason not revealed) on the first Mondays in February, May, August and November.

There were, however, certain conditions for healing. The sufferers had to be on the banks of the loch at midnight, plunge thrice into the water, drink a small quantity and throw a coin into the loch. If the sufferer remained in sight of the loch after sunrise, the cure failed.

In Lewis, diseases of cattle were invariably attributed to the bite of serpents, and suffering animals were made to drink water into which "charm stones" had been put. Two such stones are preserved in the Museum of Antiquities.

There was at one time a famous charm stone in Kyloe House, near Stamfordham, which was most in demand for healing wounds. The stone had been brought from Ireland, and was never permitted to touch English soil. It was placed in a basket and carried to the patient, and there rubbed on the wound to be healed.

Irish stones were popular as charms in the Northumbrian dales, to keep frogs and vermin from entering the homes of the possessors. One such belonged to Mr. Thomas Hedley, of Woolaw, Redesdale. Pale blue in colour and three and a quarter inches in diameter and three-quarters of an inch thick, it was not perforated. This fact was unusual, for self-bored stones were those regarded as charms against witchcraft and against nightmare. For this reason they were usually suspended at the head of the bed and in the stables of animals. The practice was widespread throughout Scotland, and down to Cornwall.

Here are some of the more famous of the healing stones:

The Murrain stone, which had been in the FitzGerald family for generations. Water into which it was dipped was held to be a cure for cattle murrain and for hydrophobia. Even as late as 1890, the family received applications for the stone.

The Red Stone, which was held by the Stewarts of Ardvoirlich (Perthshire). It was noted for curing distempers.

The Lee Stone, for which during the Plague, the citizens of Newcastle sent £6,000 security for the loan of it. It was held that the stone would stay the plague. It was said to have been brought home by the Earl of Douglas, when he went to the Holy Land to carry the heart of Robert Bruce, and the legend is that it cannot be lost.

The Lockerby Penny, preserved at Lockerby, in Dumfriesshire. It is a piece of silver, and was used in the curing of madness in cattle. The penny was put into a cleft stick, and a well stirred round with it, after which water was bottled off and given to the animal affected.

In 1860, on a Northumbrian farm a dog bit an ass and the ass bit a cow. The penny was sent for, and a deposit of £50 left against its restoration. The dog was shot, the ass died, but the cow was saved "through the miraculous virtue of the penny." On the death of the man who had borrowed the penny several bottles of water were found in his house labelled "Lockerby Water."

The Black Penny was owned by a family of Hume-byers. It was a little larger than a penny and was probably a Roman coin. When dipped in a well, the waters of which ran to the south (this was indispensable), water afterwards drawn from the well given to animals cured the madness.

Burbeck's Bonca tablet of ivory, long preserved by the family of Campbell, of Burbeck, was regarded as a complete remedy for madness, and a deposit of £100 was demanded against its return from any borrower.

Another famous superstitious article was that known as "The Luck of Eden Hall," which was owned for generations by the family of Musgrave, near Penrith. It was apparently an old chalice of stone —anciently chalices were on occasion made of stone or horn—and was a thing of great beauty.

The legend regarding it is that the butler of the family, having gone one night to draw water at the well of St.

Cuthbert, a copious spring in the garden of the mansion of Edenhall, surprised a group of fairies disporting themselves beside the well, at the margin of which stood the chalice. He seized hold of it, and a struggle ensued between them. The elves were worsted, and thereupon took to flight, calling as they went:

If this glass do break or fall,
Farewell the luck of Edenhall.

Thereupon, the superstitious family took the greatest care of their "luck." The wild Duke of Wharton is said on one occasion to have nearly destroyed the luck by letting it drop from his hands; but it was saved by the presence of mind of his butler, who caught it in a napkin. The Edenhall mansion is now destroyed.

Late in 1946, the "Luck of Eden Hall" came under the auction hammer, and is now in a museum.

But there were other stones, quite ordinary ones, which, given certain circumstances, also possessed great powers in superstition. On the coast of Morven and Mull are thin ledges of rock pierced with large holes near the sea.

To these, consumptive patients were brought, and after the tops of nine waves had been caught in a dish and thrown over the head of the sufferer he was made to pass through the rifts in the direction of the sun.

Consumptive patients were also treated at Crossapol, in Coll, Scotland, by being passed through the Hole Stone (Clach Thuill); and there are several stones so used on other islands in the North.

At Cambus O' May, near Ballater, is a rock standing in the Aberdeenshire River Dee. It is large enough for an adult person to squeeze through—and through it went childless women who desired the blessings of a child. Now this is of interest when it is mentioned that Cypriot women to remove their barrenness pass through perforated stones.

Elsewhere mention has been made of passing between stones or through arches to cure children of the rickets, or to scrape off diseases which adults might have contracted.

In Scotland on Hallow Eve, people lit bonfires, and around them placed a circle of stones, one for each person in the families to whom the fires belonged. Next morning the positions of the stones were examined with great attention; if one were displaced, the person it represented was regarded as "fey" and would not live beyond the year. There were similar beliefs in parts of England, and in Wales.

A Brahman (India) boy, when he reaches the age of discretion, is made to tread with his right foot on a stone while the words are repeated: "Tread on this stone; like a stone be firm." In Cos (Greece), at the midsummer fires, boys danced round the blaze, each with a stone tied to his head, so that he might become as strong as a stone.

See ADDER STONES.

STOOL

To throw a child's stooling on the fire, will give the child constipation.—Devon and Somerset.

STORMS

To cut the nails and hair during a calm at sea, will provoke fierce winds.—Seamen's superstition.

If a marigold flower does not open before seven a.m., there will be a storm.

In the Highlands of Scotland, it was said that no sister should comb her hair at night if she had a brother at sea. It would raise storms and imperil his life.

Both these superstitions are of passing interest, because the Romans held that no person at sea should cut his hair or nails except when a storm was in progress.

The Thlinkeet Indians attributed stormy weather to the fact that some woman must have combed her hair outside her house.

In some Victoria tribes, the sorcerer burns hair during a drought, because it is held that that act will bring rain.

In the Tyrol, people burnt their hair lest witches should use it to raise thunderstorms.

A Welsh superstition along the Gower coast, is that before a storm the Lord and Lady of Rhosilly, seated in a coach drawn by four headless horses, drive madly along the sands at the Worm's Head.

See SAILORS, SEA.

STUMBLING

If a man stumbles in the morning, as soon as he leaves the house, it is a sign of ill-luck during the day.

If a horse stumbles on the highway, bad luck will follow.

To stumble upstairs is a sure sign of a wedding. But if the same night you dream of a wedding, you will change the omen into death.—General.

To stumble downstairs is a sign of bad luck.—General.

To stumble at a grave is ominous.—General.

Shakespeare refers to the last superstition, as prevalent in his time, in the lines:

> How oft to-night
> Have my old feet stumbled at graves.

And, again:

> For many men that stumble at the threshold
> Are well foretold that danger lurks therein.

The origin of the ill-luck of stumbling lies hidden in antiquity. Cicero mentions it as among the omens at which weak minds are terrified.

Tiberius Gracchus stumbled upon the threshold of his house, and died the same day.

Antigonus on the battlefield stumbled on leaving his tent. It was taken by his men as a bad augury. He was killed soon afterwards.

Crassus and his son had a similar warning. The son stumbled on the way to encounter the Parthians, and the father fell on top of him. The son was killed at the battle of Balissus, and the father was murdered soon afterwards.

Protesilaus stumbled as he left his father's house to conduct his Thessalian warriors to the siege of Troy. Laodamia marked the omen, and trembled for the fate of her lover. With a good cause, apparently; he fell in the siege.

See STAIRS.

STY (IN THE EYE)

On the first night of the new moon, procure the tail of a black cat, and after pulling from it one hair, rub the tip nine times over the sty on the eye, and it will be cured.

If you rub a sty nine times with a gold wedding ring, or the finger ring of an unmarried lady, it will be cured.—General.

NOTE: In other parts of the country, notably in Lincolnshire, it is claimed that the wedding ring, to be effective, must belong to the patient's mother.

Beaumont and Fletcher, the great writers of comedy in the seventeenth century, testify to the currency of this superstition in their day. In *Mad Lover*, produced about 1619, appear the lines:

> .... I have a sty here, Chilax.
> Chilax: I have no gold to cure it—
> not a penny.

The superstition is perpetuated even to-day by the name golden ointment for any ointment meant to be used on the eyes.

Incidentally, the authors know of at least two persons personally who still rub a sty in the eye with a wedding ring. And far from being persons of weak intellect, one of them is a B.A. of Oxford.

An Irish charm for the sty is to point nine thorns in succession at the eye without touching it, and throw each away after use over the left shoulder.

SUN

The sun hides his face before any great sorrow or national disaster.—Wales.

NOTE: It was for this reason that eclipses of the sun were regarded with concern by the Welsh of days gone by.

People born at sunrise, will be clever; those in the afternoon or at sunset, will be lazy.—Wales.

Mayflowers gathered just before sunrise, keep freckles away.—General.

The sun never shines on the perjurer.—Cornwall.

The Cornwall superstition goes that though the sun may be shining and everyone sees and feels the warmth of it, a man who has perjured himself, neither sees nor feels its heat.

Robert Hunt, in his *Popular Romances*, tells of a man in the west of Cornwall, known to have given false evidence.

"The face of this false witness," says the description, "is the colour of one long in the tomb, and he has never, since the death of the victim of his forswearing, seen the sun." It must be remembered that the man was not blind.

Welsh people held that all magical herbs—by which was meant those that were to be used as charms—should be gathered before sunrise. And all healing waters should be drawn and quaffed before sunrise.

SUNDAY

It is unlucky to turn a feather bed on Sunday.—Devon.

If a child with the whooping cough is carried fasting on a Sunday morning into three parishes, he will soon be much better.—Devon.

Who on Sunday pares his horn (nails), 'twere better for him he had ne'er been born.—General.

After an open grave on a Sunday, a death is sure to take place within a month.—Gloucestershire.

Sneeze on Sunday morning, fasting; you'll enjoy your own true love for everlasting.—Devonshire.

NOTE: For the purpose of the charm, the sneeze must be an accidental one, not caused by a cold or any irritation.

In fevers, the illness is expected to be more severe on Sunday than on any other day of the week; if easier on Sunday, a relapse is feared.—Perthshire.

The fever superstition quoted above is taken from the evidence given by the minister of Logierait, Perthshire, appearing in Sinclair's *Statistical Account of Scotland*.

From early ages Sunday's child has been picked out as possessing special birth rights: though why, superstition does not tell us, nor is there any clue at this time.

In Yorkshire, Sunday children were regarded as safe from ill-wishing or "overlooking." Nor could witches harm them.

In Germany they were regarded as privileged beings. In Denmark, the Sunday child is credited with the faculty of seeing things hidden from others.

Thorpe, in his *Mythology*, records that in Fyen a woman who had been born on a Sunday could not pass by her village church at night without seeing a hearse or a spectre. Seeking the advice of a man skilled in these matters, she was told that whenever she saw a spectre in future she should say, "Go to Heaven," but to a hearse, she should say, "Hang on."

Meeting a hearse some time later, and momentarily upset, she said "Go to Heaven," whereupon the hearse rose in the air, and vanished. Depressed by this unfortunate circumstance, she then, meeting a spectre, commanded him to "Hang on." Whereupon it clung round her neck, hung on and drove her down into the ground before it. For three days and nights her shrieks were heard before, finally, the spectre ended her life.

The weakness of this is, of course, how the story-teller knew what the woman met and what she said.

In Transylvania, treasures are said sometimes to bloom or burn in the earth, or to reveal their presence by a bluish flame. But only children born on a Sunday can see them.

In East Anglia, England, Sunday was regarded as a day for good beginnings, and even to-day mother and new born child will come downstairs for the first time together on a Sunday, if it is at all possible.

See WHOOPING COUGH.

SUNWISE

The dead must be buried with the sun.—General.

The practice of performing all important ceremonies by way of the sun's course has existed from the most ancient times, and has not died out, even to-day. It persists in many rural areas of Scotland and Southern England.

It was perhaps more commonly used at the burial of the dead. In one Devonshire churchyard, the vicar had a cross broken up because parishioners insisted at funerals in carrying the coffin thrice round it with the sun before entering the church. His refusal to permit the custom had been ignored.

At Brilley (Herefordshire) coffins were carried three times round the funeral stone which stood in an open space outside the churchyard. It prevented the Devil from obtaining the soul of the dead, said the locals. It had, of course, to be carried round with the direction of the sun.

At the village of Stranton, near West Hartlepool, a vicar, new to the countryside, while waiting at the church gate to receive a funeral, was surprised when the cortege had arrived within a few yards of him to see it wheel round and make a circuit of the churchyard wall, traversing its west, north and east boundaries, and making the distance to carry the body some five or six times more than was necessary.

The vicar sought from the sexton an explanation.

"Why, ze wad no hae them carry the dead again the sun," was the astonished reply. "The dead maun aye go wi' the sun."

In Lewis Island, it was the practice to make a complete circle about the house, the corn and the cattle at certain seasons, or days. A man carried a lighted torch in his right hand, and went round the places named, sunwise. In that way he believed that he had preserved the house, cattle and crops from disease for a year.

In Scotland, the same procedure was carried out—the authors have heard rumours that in the more remote parts of the Highlands it is, indeed, still a rite. To walk round a churchyard, or a house, anti-sunwise (witherskins) was an evil incantation.

The origin? Well, there was an ancient British, or Celtic, custom of walking three times round a dead person, according to the course of the sun. And it may be borne in mind that sunwise is *right* handed; and readers will have noted earlier in this volume the numerous superstitions related in which evil was held to come always from the *left.*

It might finally be added that no fisherman would willingly turn his boat in a direction contrary to the sun's course.

Far away to the east, the Llama monk whirls his praying cylinder in the way of the sun and fears lest a stranger should get at it and turn it contrary which would take from it, he believes, all the virtue which it had acquired.

The monks, too, build piles of stones and pass them on one side and return on the other, so as to make the circuit of the sun.

Mohammedans make a circuit of the Caaba in the same way; and the ancient Dagohas of India and Ceylon were also traversed round the same direction.

The Irish and Scottish way has been always to make all movements deiseal, or sunwise, round houses or graves.

See RIGHT HAND.

SUPERSTITION

One story will be sufficient here to illustrate the word superstition. Here it is:

An old woman one day went to Flamsteed, the Astronomer Royal, to ask him the whereabouts of a bundle of linen which she had lost. Flamsteed, determined to show the woman the folly of that belief in astrology which had led her to Greenwich Observatory (under some misapprehension as to the duties of an Astronomer Royal), asked her a few questions, and then drew a circle, put a square into it, and gravely pointed out what he said was a ditch near her cottage where the washing would be found.

He then waited until she should come back, disappointed, and in a fit state of mind for rebuke from him.

She, however, came back in great delight, with the bundle in her hand—found in that very place!

SWALLOW

If a swallow builds a nest on your house, it is a sign of luck.—General.

It is unlucky if a swallow starts to build a nest on a house, and then deserts it.

If a swallow's nest is disturbed, the crops will go wrong.—Farmers' wives' belief.

If a farmer kills a swallow, his cows will yield blood instead of milk.—Walton-le-Dale old belief.

NOTE: This belief was also widely held throughout Switzerland.

If a swallow alights on your shoulder, it is a sure sign of your death.

Bad luck will follow the pulling down of a swallow's nest from a house.—General.

The belief in the misfortune that will come if a swallow's nest is pulled down persists to-day in rural areas, and very few are disturbed.

Apropos this, is a story told of a Yorkshire banking family. The sons of the house bought an old farmhouse, and at once pulled down a row of nests, which they said made the place look untidy. The swallows had built there for many years. Shortly afterwards, the bank had to close its doors, and, went the tale told by a neighbouring farmer's wife, "the family have had nought but trouble ever since."

In Germany, the swallow, as the harbinger of spring, has always been held as a sacred bird. It is believed to preserve from fire and storm any house on which it builds its nest.

Strangely enough in Ireland, according to Archbishop Swateley, the swallow was regarded as the Devil's Bird, and it was held that there was a certain hair on the head of every man and woman which, if a swallow picked it off, would doom that person to perdition.

Another Irish saying of the bird is that "every swallow has in him three drops of the Devil's blood."

SWAN

Swans are hatched during a thunderstorm.—Hampshire.

Swans sing just before their death.—General.

Swans do not, of course, sing before their death, or at any other time. But the belief goes back to very ancient days.

It is said that Orpheus, the musician, became a swan. Perhaps the origin of the song lies in that. Or maybe, in the theory of Plato, who held that the transmigration of souls in the bodies of

animals is a punishment and degradation entailed on the souls by the weaknesses to which they had been subject in life, or the vices to which they had been addicted; and that the kind of animal into which the soul migrates is appropriate to the degree of the weakness or the vice. Thus, added Plato, a bad poet *or a bad musician* turns at death into a swan. Maybe Plato classed Orpheus as a bad musician.

Lord Northampton, in his *Defensative Against the Poyson of Supposed Prophecies* (1583), dealing with the idea that swans are hatched during thunderstorms, says: "It chaunceth sometimes to thunder about that time and season of the yeare when swannes hatch their young; and yet no doubte it is a paradox of simple men to thinke that a swanne cannot hatch without a cracke of thunder."

SWARM (OF BEES)

If a stray swarm of bees settle on a person's premises and are not claimed by their owner, there will be death within the year in the family on whose land they have settled.—Suffolk.

If bees swarm on dead wood, the owner will die.—General.

The authors have been able to trace, personally, only one case in which there was a death in a family in such circumstances. It was taken to prove the old saying, which is still held in parts of Suffolk.

However, since the death was of a man who had an incurable disease, and would have died in any case, the incident does not prove much.

See BEES.

SWEEP

If you meet a sweep and bow to him three times, good luck will attend you.—General.

It is lucky for a bride to meet a sweep on coming out of church, if she kisses him.—General.

The former of these superstitions still exists to a marked degree. On 14th February, 1947, a Miss Norma Simpson, daughter of a Kensington (London) artist, was chosen from 3,000 girls for a leading part in a British film. She explained that she attributed her fortune to the fact that a few hours before she had met a sweep and had duly bowed to him three times!

SWEEPING

To sweep the dust out of your house,

is to sweep away the good fortune from your family.—Borders, and General.

The correct way, to preserve the luck, is to sweep all dust inwards, and carry it out of the house in a shovel or a bucket. Then, no harm will follow.

Perhaps the strangest thing about this superstition is that it is one of the few which is at variance with other races. The Dyak priestesses sweep *misfortune* out of the house—with brooms made of the leaves of certain plants, and sprinkled with rice water and blood. Having swept the misfortune out, they gather up its dust and put it into a little toy house made of bamboo, and set, in this way, misfortune adrift in the river, whence it flows out to sea.

Similarly, the Hos of Togoland (West Africa) sweep bad luck out of their towns by dragging a toad fastened to a palm leaf through the town.

In country houses it was considered bad luck for a housemaid to sweep out a bedroom until the guest had departed at least an hour. Doing so would, it was held, bring misfortune to a friend of the family.

SWEETHEARTS (CALLING)

If you stick pins through the end of a tallow candle and at the same time repeat a rhyme, your sweetheart will come to you.

Henderson, in his *Folk Lore of the Northern Counties*, quotes two instances of this charm.

One in the City of Durham, communicated to him by a clergyman, concerned two servant girls. One peeped into the box of the other and saw a candle end stuck all over with pins. She asked the reason.

"Oh, that's to bring my sweetheart," was the reply. "Thou seest, sometimes he's slow a-coming, and if I stick the pins in the candle it always fetches him."

In Buckinghamshire, within no more than sixty years, the charm was being used. The method there was to stick two pins through the candle, making sure that the pins passed through the wick. While doing this, the following rhyme had to be recited:

It's not this candle alone I stick,
But ———'s I mean to prick;
Whether he be asleep or awake,
I'd have him come to me and speak.

A nurse has placed it on record that she knew personally of three cases in which the charm had worked, so far as the appearance of the lover was concerned.

One of the girls married, but her married life turned out unhappy. Another was greeted by the lover with the words: "I know you've been up to some devilment or other. No tongue can tell what you've made me suffer." And the marriage was off.

SWELLINGS

Of all the vicious superstitious remedies the authors have come across in the years of research spent in compiling this volume, none is more horrifying as a remedy than the following one for a swollen knee. It was in vogue in the North under seventy years ago.

Kill a cat, split the body lengthwise, and apply it, while warm, to the knee, binding it thereon, and let it stay there till the cure is complete.

It was added by the supporters of this "remedy" that in the absence of a cat, a fowl would do.

See FEVER, GOITRE, MAY DEW.

SYMPATHY POWDER

Sympathy powder cure for wounds was the invention of Sir Kenelm Digby, and was a celebrated and widespread remedy in the middle of the seventeenth century. It derived its virtues not from its composition, but from the mode of its application; for it was applied not to the wound, but to the weapon by which the wound had been caused.

After the weapon had been so doctored, the wound was ordered to be closed up, and then no further attention was given to it.

The treatment was, of course, ridiculed, but after being pretty fully tried, it was found that the treatment was, on the whole, more successful than the scientific treatment by doctors.

It continued to gain ground in the public estimation until some bright innovator ventured to try the experiment of *closing the wound without applying the sympathetic powder to the weapon*. And this was equally efficacious. Which killed Sympathy Powder.

Blagrave, in his *Astrological Practice of Physic*, gave the recipe for Digby's Sympathetic Powder as: Take Roman vitriol six or eight ounces, beat it very small in a mortar, sift it through a fine sieve when the sun enters Leo. Keep it in the heat of the sun by day, and dry by night."

TABLECLOTH

If a tablecloth, when unfolded, has a

diamond-shaped crease in the middle, it portends death.

In January, 1947, the authors received from a young woman in the North an inquiry as to what a diamond-shaped crease meant. Thus, apparently, the "omen" has not died out.

TALKING UNDER RAILWAY BRIDGE

To talk when passing under a railway bridge, brings bad luck.—Wales.

It is an interesting fact that this superstition was generally observed during the 1914-18 war by the Welsh regiments.

There is a possibility that this superstition, which is peculiar to Wales, is connected in some way with the fear of being "over-headed," which is a potent superstition of many races allied to the Welsh in superstitious feelings and fear of witchcraft.

There are a number of native tribes among whom terror was stricken at the thought of anything over their heads. Even the shadow of something crossing their bodies meant that some dire misfortune was about to come upon them.

TEA

For two people to pour out tea from the same pot, will bring bad luck.—Kent.

If a girl lets a man in her company pour her out a second cup of tea, she will succumb, to her misfortune, to his own designs.

By putting milk or cream into your tea before sugar, you run the risk of losing your sweetheart.

To stir the tea in the teapot, is to stir up strife.

Bubbles on tea denote that kisses are coming.

If a man and a woman pour out tea together, they will have a baby.—Romney.

Everyone knows, even to-day, that a tea-leaf floating on the tea in a cup "foretells" that a stranger will be paying the house a visit. But the custom of old wives went further than that. The tea-leaf was taken from the cup, placed on the back of the left hand, and tapped with the other hand until the tea-leaf ceased to adhere to the back of the hand. The number of taps necessary before this result, represented the number of days which would elapse before the right stranger appeared

TEACHER'S CANE

Still widespread among school children is the idea that if a horsehair is wrapped round the bole of the hand, not only will the teacher's cane be not felt, but the cane will split from top to bottom.

Another "belief" in the power to take away the sting from the cane, is to rub the hand in advance with an onion or a green walnut shell.

TEARS

If the dying are wept over, or tears allowed to fall on them, they will be hindered from resting peacefully in the grave.—General.

See CORPSE, DEATH.

TEETH

If your teeth are set wide apart, you will be lucky and travel.—Northumberland.

When a child first loses a tooth, the molar should be thrown on the fire to burn evil that may be hiding in the body.

To dream that your teeth are falling out, is a bad sign, foretelling some dreadful, though unknown, thing.

If a baby's teeth come early there will soon be fresh toes.—Durham and Yorkshire.

If a child's first tooth is in the upper jaw, it betokens death in infancy.

Another rendering of "fresh toes if teeth come early" is "Soon teeth, soon toes," the implication being that another baby will come and the present one die.

There seems no origin of this senseless idea; nor of the equally foolish notion that a tooth appearing in the upper jaw first, dooms the possessor to die in infancy.

If a child's tooth fell out, it was the usual practice to throw it on the roof, with the request to a rat, or a squirrel, to supply a stronger tooth—the idea being, of course, that the teeth of a rat, which will gnaw through almost anything, will be stronger than the tooth of the child which has "crocked" up.

There is an odd connection between the British superstition of the growing of teeth by a baby in the upper jaw before the lower jaw and certain tribes in Central Asia. There, children whose upper teeth appear before those in the lower jaw are exposed to the hyenas, and thus eaten, and the mother is declared unclean for having given birth to such a child.

Thus the superstition here that the child's death in infancy is prognosticated is, in Central Asia, an actual fact.

TENCH

Eat a tench to cure the jaundice.

This was an old superstition, which was once very prevalent. The origin is, undoubtedly, from the era of the "Doctrine of Signatures."

This doctrine existed for a considerable time among medical men, and gave rise to the names of several plants, from the resemblance of the leaves and roots to the form of the human body. Instances are: Lung-wort, liver-wort, spleen-wort, and so on.

The tench, in the same way, was recommended under the ægis of the doctrine as a sovereign cure for jaundice, because of the *golden* colour of the fish when in high season. It matched the colour of the skin of a person with jaundice.

The efficacy of a tench to cure jaundice extended to Bohemia, only the fish was not eaten. The remedy ran as follows: Take a living tench, and tie it to your bare back. Carry it about with you for a whole day. When the tench has turned yellow and died, throw it into running water, and your jaundice will depart with it.

This is, of course, a further belief in the transference of evils.

See SYMPATHY.

TENNIS

To hold three balls in one hand while serving, will bring bad luck.

The superstition does not say to whom the bad luck will come, but it apparently is not bad luck to the person holding the three balls, but to his, or her, opponent. The authors knew of a ranking star, who, at a Riviera tournament, refused to continue to play in a vital match of a French Riviera tournament, unless his opponent ceased to hold the three balls in his left hand, preparatory to serving!

THIEF

If a robbery has been committed, pluck six leaves of grass from the spot, and take them to a white witch. As many scratches as she makes with a pin in the grass blades, so many rents will there be in the face of the thief.—Devonshire.

Potter's *Grecian Antiquities* (1697) records that "the vulgar in many parts of England have an abominable practice of using a riddle and a pair of shears in divination."

The practice was to stick the open points of the shears, or scissors, into the rim of the sieve so that they supported the measure. Two persons, of opposite sex, then took the sieve into a dark place, and held the middle finger of each right hand under the ring of the scissors so as to hold up the sieve. One of the pair then inquired: "In the name of God the Father, God the Son, and God the Holy Ghost, I ask thee—tell me truly has —— done it" (naming a suspect). When the right name was called, the sieve fell to the ground.

At a later date a Bible and key were substituted for the sieve. The key was fastened with string to the Bible. A portion of Scripture was then read while a person supported the key on the tips of the fingers of one hand. The names of all the suspected persons were then called out aloud. When the key "turned"—fell off the fingers—the name last mentioned was presumed to be the guilty party. The practice was at one time widespread throughout Britain.

In 1832, at the Thames Police Court, London, an instance of this proof of guilt was recited when a woman thus found guilty attacked her accuser, and was summoned for assault.

In Herefordshire, it was held that if you wore a toad's heart concealed on your body, you could steal to your heart's content without being found out. A suspected thief was once heard to be boasting: "They never catches me, and they never will, either. I allus wears a toad's heart round my neck, I does."

It was regarded by thieves as very unlucky to find among their loot a pack of playing cards. Misfortune would fall upon them. This was active, even though they had no idea that cards were in, say, a box which they had taken away.

A further warning to thieves was the robbing of a hunchback, whether wilfully or accidentally. He would be an unlucky thief for the rest of his life.

And, finally, misfortune all his life attended a thief who robbed a church, particularly if he got away with the chalice.

See HAND OF GLORY.

THIRTEEN

If thirteen people meet in a room, one of them will die before the year is out.—General.

One of the most common of superstitions still practised to-day is that connected with the number thirteen.

Thirteen at table is, perhaps, the most common form. And hostesses are at great pains to ensure that the number is avoided at any party. At the best it is regarded as bringing bad luck to the hostess or her family; at the worst it means that one of the thirteen will die before the year is out. In some parts of the country it is held that death will overtake the first member of the party to rise from the table; but in Yorkshire it is held to be the last to rise.

The ill-luck of thirteen is heightened if by chance the thirteenth of the month should fall on a Friday.

It is, therefore, surprising to find in this welter of thirteen ill-luck, the superstitious belief that any child born on the thirteenth of the month will be lucky in all his ventures started in after life on this day.

The thirteen superstition exists all through Europe. It is impossible in any French city or town to find a house numbered thirteen. Nor to find room thirteen in any French hotel. And not many British hotels will have the number marked on a door.

Many years ago in an English country town, there took place an official renumbering of houses in a certain street. Number thirteen was placed on the door of a house belonging to a woman.

She protested against the number, and when leave to change it was refused, took the matter to the High Court. House agents, called in evidence, declared that number thirteen was definitely damaging to her property, since they would find it practically impossible to let a house so numbered to any tenant.

The woman won her case—but here is the sequel: she died from a heart attack the following day.

Despite the fact that the number of the house was changed to 12a, it remained untenanted for many months.

As evidence that the superstition was not confined to the less intelligent of the population, there may be cited the case of Mr. Justice Luxmore, an English High Court Judge, who held very strongly by the superstition. When practising at the Bar, he would never accept any brief marked thirteen guineas. One solicitor, who knew this, sent him on one occasion a brief marked "Twelve and another." It was returned to him.

On Friday, November 13, 1931, Mr. J. A. Mollison, the airman, left Lympne in an attempt to beat Miss Salaman's record for a flight to the Cape and back. He failed. On the same day the liner Aquitania was due to leave New York for England; the sailing was postponed until after midnight in response to the protests of many passengers.

Now for the other side of the story. Lord ("Bobs") Roberts was fond of relating how twelve other officers and himself dined together shortly before the Afghan War. They fought all through the campaign, and all came through without a scratch.

There have been thousands of death-defying brides who have been married on the thirteenth of the month, have worn green, and have even had thirteen attendants—without ill effect.

There are Thirteen Clubs, which meet to the number of thirteen on the Friday the thirteenth of the month, also without tragedy following. Miss Peggy Salaman left Capetown on her return to England in her record flight on a Friday, which was also the thirteenth—and she set up a record.

As to the origin of the thirteen superstition, religious circles ascribe it to the Last Supper, at which were Christ and the twelve Disciples—thirteen in all. But this would hardly account for the dislike of the Romans and Greeks for the number thirteen.

It is more accountable in this case by the story of the Valhalla banquet in Greek mythology, to which twelve of the gods were invited. Loki, the Spirit of Strife and Mischief, intruded, making thirteen, and Balder, the favourite of the gods, was killed.

The *Gentleman's Magazine*, in 1798, in attempting to find an origin of the superstition that if thirteen people gather in a room, one of them will die within twelve months, stated: "The superstition seems to be founded on calculations adhered to by insurance offices, which presume that out of thirteen people, taken indiscriminately, one will die within a year."

But this, too, was long after Balder and the Last Supper!

See FRIDAY.

THORN

Never pick holy thorn on Christmas Eve, when you hear the cracking of the buds, or you will receive a curse.—Somerset.

NOTE: It should be noted that this refers to *old* Christmas Eve, 5th January.

To sleep in a room with the white thorn in bloom in it during the month of May, will be followed by some great misfortune.—Suffolk.

To cure a wound caused by the prick of a thorn say: "Christ was of a Virgin born. And He was pricked by a thorn. And it never did bell (fester) or swell. As I trust in Jesus, this one never will."—Cornwall.

NOTE: The same verse with minor variations was used in Yorkshire, Lancashire and Northampton.

A Devonshire superstition held that the skin of a snake was unfailing in extracting thorns, etc., from the body. But unlike other remedies, the snake skin was repellant, not attractive. Accordingly, it had to be applied on the opposite side to that on which the thorn entered.

If applied on the same side, it was the belief that the thorn would be forced right through the part of the body into which it had entered.

Mention has been made elsewhere of the value of thorn in driving away witches. On Beltane night in Scotland, and All Hallowe'en in all parts of England, branches of thorn were hung over the doors of cowhouses, in order to keep away witches, who might otherwise suck the milk of the cows.

This practice was widespread, too, throughout Eastern Europe. Transylvanian and Rumanian locals set thorn bushes in the doorways of their cowhouses on St. George's Eve for the same reason.

THREAD

Steal alone at night to the nearest lime-kiln, and throw in a ball of blue yarn, winding off in a fresh clew as you come near the edge. Grasp hold of the thread lying in the kiln. You must then ask who holds the other end, and the name of your future life partner will be uttered.—Scottish Lowlands.

Red thread was regarded as a powerful charm for cattle for protection against witches, when the cattle were turned into the fields for the first time, or on May Day, when witches might be expected to suck the milk from the animals. This, too, was a Scottish belief, both in the Highlands and the Lowlands.

THREE

Another widespread superstition in belief at the present day is that should one accident of any kind occur, there will be three before the ill-luck is ended.

A break of crockery in a home will, it is asserted be followed by two more; and the anxious housewife hails the breaking of the third with relief.

If there is one death in a village, there will be two others. So it goes on. Strength was given to the legend in September, 1946, when a passenger plane crashed in France, and the crew and passengers were lost. A second occurred within a few hours, and a third in America a few days later.

Nothing was said, however, of the various single plane crashes which have occurred on a number of occasions without the accompanying two others.

It is, also, a point to be remembered that in practically every superstition in which some ritual had to be performed, the ritual was in threes, or multiples of three.

Thus, a child who was passed through a cleft ash sapling as a cure for rickets, had to be passed through either three times, or three times three.

Those wishing to see who in their parish were to die during the year, must watch the church door on St. Mark's Eve for three years in succession; and the prophecy would be vouchsafed on the third of the ordeals.

The person who would be cured of ague must undergo a three times ritual.

No charm of words was held to have a chance of success unless it was ended with "In the name of the Father, Son, and Holy Ghost," the Three-in-One, or Trinity.

THREE CIGARETTES

A popular superstition in force to-day refers to the bad luck which will follow from lighting three cigarettes from a single match, or light of any kind. It is widespread.

Various origins have been tacked on to the belief. The most popular is that it was born during the Boer War, from the fact that the time spent in lighting the three cigarettes from the one match gave the Boer sharpshooters on the veldt time to spot the light, take an aim, and fire—with likely bad luck to one of the three.

But three is the symbol of the Trinity. To transgress against the Holy law was to invite the worst of the future—to put oneself in the hands of the Evil One. This is the origin of all superstition connected with the number three.

There is good reason to believe that the three lights ill-luck was actually originated among British troops during the Crimean War, from Russian captives. For it was a sacred rule in Russian churches that the three candles on the altar might not be lighted from one taper except by one person—the High Priest.

THREE-LEGGED STOOL

If you take a three-legged stool and sit at the junction of three cross-roads as the clock is striking midnight on All Hallows' Eve, you will hear proclaimed aloud the names of people in the parish to die during the ensuing twelve months.—Scottish Highlands.

You, of course, took the risk of hearing your own name "proclaimed aloud."

See DEATH WATCH, ST. MARK'S EVE.

THRUSH (COMPLAINT)

To cure the thrush in a child take it, fasting, on three following mornings to have its mouth blown into by a person who never knew his father.—Cornwall.

NOTE: A person who never knew his father refers to a posthumous child.

Take three rushes from any running stream, and pass them separately through the mouth of the infant suffering from thrush. Then plunge the rushes into the stream, and as the current bears them away, so will the thrush leave the child.—Devon and Cornwall.

A Devonshire vicar records in *Notes and Queries* (vol. viii, 146) that, finding the child of one of his parishioners suffering from thrush, he inquired what medicine she had given the child. The reply was that she had done nothing except say the eighth Psalm over it, three times three days running. It had, she affirmed, cured one of her other children.

It is in this Psalm that there occurs the phrase "Out of the mouths of very babes and sucklings."

Now, if either of these remedies for the thrush should not effect the desired cure, there is still another—from Devonshire.

The local captured the nearest duck that could be met with, and placed its mouth wide open within the mouth of the sufferer. The cold breath of the duck would be inhaled by the child, and the disease as a result gradually disappeared.

NOTE: Thrush is a throat disease peculiar to children.

THUNDER

When there is thunder about, a bar of iron should be put on the barrels of beer to keep them from souring.—Hereford and Kent.

If thunder is heard and lightning seen between November and 31st January, the most important person in the village will die.—Rural Wales.

Church bells, if rung, will keep thunder and lightning away.—Wales, and General.

If the windows and doors of your house are left open, the house will be safe from a thunderbolt, as it will go straight through the house; if the doors are shut the house will be blasted.—Bedfordshire.

In parts of Wales it was the general practice to ring the church bells when a thunderstorm threatened. The superstition was continued into the nineteenth century.

Moreover, it enjoyed a wide popularity in the North Country during times of storm; and in remembrance of the escape of one cathedral, a service was held once a year at the top of the cathedral, with the choristers, robed, taking part in the singing.

Wynkyn de Worde tells us that: "Bells are rung during thunderstorms, to the end that the fiends and wicked spirits should be abashed and flee, and cease the moving of the tempest."

The belief is world-wide; the Teso people, of the plains between Mount Elgon and Lake Kioga, make use of bells to exorcise the storm fiend.

Another safeguard against thunder damage was a charred stick taken from the Midsummer Fires. This, kept in the house, was, in the sixteenth and seventeenth centuries, a powerful guarantee that the house would not suffer from damage by thunderstorms—and that, of course, included lightning.

So, too, with the charred sticks from the great bonfires. In Brittany, charred sticks were retrieved from the Summer Fires, and taken home. They were placed near the bed of the head of the household, between a bit of Twelfth Night cake and a sprig of boxwood, which had been blessed on Palm Sunday. (You will note how the priests, seemingly, helped in the superstition.) From that moment, the house was regarded as safe from all damage by storm.

In Westphalia, a piece of the Yule log was withdrawn from the fire as soon as it was scorched. It was kept carefully and replaced on the fire whenever a thunderstorm broke. It was held that no thunderbolt could strike a house where the Yule log was smouldering.

A final superstition. A Saxon manuscript, which was translated by Dr. Hicks, tells us: "If, on the entering year, the first thunder happens on a Sunday, then it denotes mortality in royal families; if it thunder on a Saturday, then it will be mortality of judges and governors."

THURSDAY

Thursday has one lucky hour—the hour before the sun rises.—Devonshire.

Thursday for crosses.

Unfortunately, nobody seems to have any reference as to how the one hour before the sun rises is lucky. Stow mentions it without reference to the kind of luck that may be expected; but he does add that Thursday was noted as a fatal day for Henry VIII and his posterity.

It is passing strange that there is not in British superstition any one for Thursday referring to protection from thunder, for the day is named after Thor, who is identified with the German god Thunar and the Italian Jupiter, all being the God of Thunder.

There is one Thursday custom which may be not generally known to delvers into folklore. In Catholic countries (and England was at one time a Catholic country), all church bells were silenced at noon on Maundy Thursday, and were kept silent until noon on Easter Saturday, wooden rattles being used in the interim.

TICKLING

From a correspondent in St. Budeaux, Plymouth, Devonshire, on 1st January, 1947, the authors received this letter: "Since being presented with a baby daughter, I have heard yarns and superstitions of various kinds. But this one beats the lot—if a baby's feet are tickled, it will stammer in later years."

So *that* superstition still lingers on in Devon. It was known many years ago in the South and the North.

TIDE

No one can die till the tide is on the ebb.—General coastal belief.

Births occur at the flow of the tide.
See DEATH WITH THE TIDE.

TOAD

If a toad crosses the path of a bridal party on the way to church, the couple will have prosperity and happiness.—General.

If you wear a toad's heart concealed on your person, you can steal to your heart's content without being found out. —Herefordshire.

If you have trouble with your cows, take a living toad at midnight, and, keeping silence, roast it to death on the "brandis." As midnight strikes, the "ill-wisher" will appear.—Cornwall.

Throughout rural England, in the sixteenth century, witchcraft was an article of current faith, and a toad was regarded as an emissary of the Evil One, and was burnt in the flames. The Cornwall superstition, cited above, is one example.

Now, this is strange, for the reason that it is one of the few superstitions that run counter to the beliefs held in other parts of the world. There, the toad is something of a beneficent being.

In his *History of the New World Called America*, Payne observes: "Throughout the New World, from Florida to Chili, the worshipping of the toad or frog as the offspring of water, and the symbol of the water spirit, accompanied the cultivation of maize."

A species of the water toad was called by the Araucanians, of Chili, *genco*, which signifies Lord of the Water, and they believed that the toad watches over the preservation, and contributes to the salubrity of the waters.

(*En passant*, in the authors' childhood days in Lincolnshire, it was considered that a toad in the household well was a guarantee that the water would remain pure, and the utmost effort was made to ensure that the toad did not get out of the well.)

The Orinoco Indians regarded the toad as Lord of the Waters, and for that reason never killed the animal, even when ordered to do so.

In Kumaon, a district of North-West India, one way of obtaining rain was to hang a toad by the mouth to the top of a long bamboo pole, or a tree, for a day or two. The idea was that as the toad was a water spirit, the God of Rain, seeing him hanging there would, in pity, send down rain.

An ancient Eastern charm for preventing storms from damaging the crops, was to bury a toad in a new earthenware vessel in the middle of the field. The argument seemed to be that the God of Rain would not drown the toad.

On the other hand, the folk of Norrland held the toad, as in England, to be in league with the Evil One, and on St. John's Eve, after they had danced round and jumped over bonfires, a toad was cast into the flames to counteract the power of the Trolls and other evil spirits believed to be abroad on that night.

When a severe epidemic of 'flu broke out among the natives of Togoland, in 1892, the natives blamed it on the machinations of evil spirits which must be expelled. So they dragged a toad through the streets, followed by an elder scattering holy water. By this means the epidemic was concentrated in the toad, which was then cast into the nearby forest.

For three hundred years the superstition prevailed in England until the end of the sixteenth century, that luck would follow the wearing of a toad stone ring. The stone, said to have been found in the head of an aged toad, was believed to indicate to the wearer the presence of poison by sweating.and changing colour —a very desirable guide in those days.

There is no known origin for this belief, but, strangely enough, there was, much earlier, a belief in India that when the shesh nag (a variety of snake) reached the age of a thousand years, a precious jewel formed in its head. The stone had the quality of soaking up and rendering harmless the poison of any reptile when applied to the part. It is most likely that the superstition permeated to this country, and reappeared in the old toad stone.

In Scotland the toad stone was preserved to prevent the burning of a house, or the sinking of a boat; and if a commander in the field had one about him, he was sure to win the day. The authors would like to know what would have happened if each of two opposing commanders possessed a toad stone.

An old Scottish legend stated that the toad stone might be procured by burying a toad in an ant hill to consume its flesh, and the genuineness of any supposed stone could be ascertained by placing it within reach of a toad, who would rise on its legs and snatch at a genuine stone.

See STEALING, SWEEPING.

TOES

To have lucken toes, will give you luck all your life.—Scotland.

Lucken toes are toes joined by a web, or film.

TONGUE

If you bite your tongue while eating, it is because you have told a falsehood. —General.

A piece of a cat's tongue carried in the pocket, will save a man from a chattering wife.—Thames bargees' belief.

Keep a tip of a human tongue in your pocket, and the pocket will never be empty.

Another belief in the tip of a human tongue was that it would keep bad luck away from the possessor. Sir Charles Igglesden has recorded that a famous Harley Street surgeon treasured a tip of a human tongue and had the greatest belief in it.

He had acquired it during his early days as a medical student, and carried it in his pocket every day of his life.

TOOTH

If when a tooth falls out it is not burned, the one which grows in its place will be a dog's tooth.

If a bairn teeths odd, it'll seean gan to God.—East Yorkshire and Scotland.

If a babe cuts its first tooth in the upper jaw, it means that it will die in infancy.

The "teething odd" referred to irregularly spaced teeth. But a gap between two front teeth wide enough to allow a sovereign to pass through was accounted an omen of luck or wealth.

Throughout Yorkshire, and the authors believe in Lancashire, the belief was held that when a child's tooth drops out, it must be dropped in the fire and a rhyme recited. Otherwise the child would have to seek the tooth after death.

The more probable danger, however, was not the seeking after the tooth in Eternity, but the tooth getting into the hands of a witch, who would thus gain power over the child.

The necessary rhyme mentioned above was: "Fire, fire, tak' a beean. And send our —— a good teeath ageean."

In the Lakeland district, and in London too, salt was placed on a tooth which had fallen from its setting naturally (without being pulled out), and it was then thrown into the fire with the phrase, "God, send my tooth again."

TOOTHACHE

A nail driven into an oak tree, will cure the pain of toothache.

Take a tooth from the mouth of a corpse, envelop it in a little bag, and hang it round your neck. You will never have the toothache.—Northants and Sussex.

Wear a double nut in your pocket to prevent the toothache.—Northants.

Take the forelegs of a mole and one of the hind legs, and put them into a bag. Wear it round your neck, and you will never have the toothache.—Stafford-shire.

Bite from the ground the first fern that appears in spring, and you will cure the toothache, and never have it again during the year.—Cornwall.

If you clothe your right leg first (i.e., put your right stocking on first, and your right leg into your trousers first), you will never have the toothache.—Wales and Sussex.

The people of Stamfordham some eighty years ago, had an "excellent" recipe for the curing, and prevention, of toothache. They walked to Winters Gibbet, on Elsdon Moor, some twelve miles away, for a splinter of wood from the gibbet. This, applied to the tooth, disposed of the ache in a jiffy!

Something similar was practised at Tavistock, in Devonshire. The cure in this case was to bite a tooth out of a skull in the churchyard, and then carry the tooth in a pocket always.

At Horsham, Sussex, in 1734, Jacob Harris, a Jew pedlar, was executed, and his body was hung in chains on Ditchling Common. It was believed in the area that a chip of the post on which the murderer's remains hung would, if carried in the pocket, cure the toothache. The "cure" was so popular that the original post was gradually reduced to a mere fragment, and had to be replaced by another.

Now, the oldest of all these remedies was the nailing of the toothache into a tree. There is little doubt that it came here with the Romans. The practice was to take a few clippings of the sufferer's hair and a few parings of his nails, make them into a small parcel, and nail the parcel to the tree.

In Germany, the procedure differed a little. The parcel was put into a hole bored in the tree, and the hole had then to be stopped up with a piece of wood taken from a tree that had been struck by lightning. If the hole was not stopped up, the toothache got out again, and back to the unfortunate sufferer.

In Brunswick, the toothache could be nailed into a tree or wall—it didn't really matter which.

At the head of Glen Mor, near Port Charlotte, in Islay, there stood, and probably still stands, a large boulder. Anyone who drove a nail into this piece of stone, was deemed ever afterwards to be free of the toothache.

Now, look at the "cure" in North Africa. There, Arabic letters were written on a wall. While the patient held a finger to his aching molar, a friend lightly tapped a nail into the first of the letters. If the ache went, the nail was pulled out completely. If, on the other hand, the ache remained, the nail was removed, and tapped into the next letter, and so on until the pain did vanish.

In Japan, a toothache sufferer stuck needles into a willow tree. His belief was that the pain thus caused to the Tree Spirit would be so great that it would be compelled to exercise its power to cure the human's pain.

As it was in these places, so it was in Britain. Now, when Britain was covered with forests, which were the haunts of savage beasts, the highest magistrate in Rome knocked a nail in a wall of his capital to avert pestilence or disaster to the city.

Another cure for the toothache practised in Devon and Cornwall, was to catch a frog, open its mouth, spit into it, and cast the frog away. It took the toothache with it. Marcellus, who died in 23 B.C., wrote in *De Medicamentis:* "Stand under the open sky on the ground, catch a frog, spit into its mouth, request it to go away, carrying the toothache with it—and let it go."

Mention is made above of a mole's forelegs and a hindleg as a toothache preventive. The mole had thus to be mutilated while it was still alive, and so long as the person carried the feet, he would be safe from the ache. There is on record a death bequest of a mole's foot, made by Master Thomas Loten, a Sussex noteworthy. He bequeathed it to his vicar.

Ireland had two popular superstitions for this unpleasant ache. The first one entailed either the drinking of water from a human skull, or the taking of a pinch of clay from the grave of a priest, and putting it into your mouth. You then had to kneel down, say a Paternoster and an Ave, following which it was credibly supposed that you would never again have toothache so long as you lived.

The second "cure" was to take the tooth to a dead horse, or the hand of a dead man, and rub it over the aching jaw. In regard to this, it might be mentioned that the Cholones, of Eastern Peru, rub the aching place with the tooth of an Ounce.

A German method, in addition to those above mentioned, was to go in silence before sunrise to a tree, especially a willow tree, make a slit in the bark on the north side of the trunk, cut out a splinter from the place, poke the splinter into the aching tooth, then put the splinter back into the place it was taken from, fold the bark over it, and tie it round with string, so that the splinter might grow back into the tree. As it grew so your pain would vanish.

Quaintest superstition, however, was that current in Derbyshire, where it was supposed that the ache in the tooth was caused by a worm. A small quantity of a mixture of powdered herbs was placed in a vessel, and a live coal from the fire was dropped into it. The patient then held his, or her, mouth open over the cup, and inhaled the vapour so long as he could stand it.

The cup was then taken away, and a glass of water was placed before the patient. Into this the person breathed hard for a few moments. Then, it was supposed, the unseen worm had been breathed out into the water—so there could be no more toothache!

In the Orkney Islands, too, toothache was supposed to be due to a worm. The remedy was simple. The patient carried with him the "Wormy Lines," and the ache vanished.

The "Wormy Lines" were as follows:
Peter sat on a marble stone, weeping;
Christ came past and said: What ails thee, Peter?
O my Lord, my God, my tooth doth ache.
Arise, O Peter. Go thy way. Thy tooth shall ache no more.

See HEAD, WELLS (St. Servans).

TOUCH WOOD

From boyhood days to manhood most people in Britain have added to the announcement of their good health, or good fortune, the phrase "touch wood," at the same time touching with the forefinger of the right hand an object made of wood. The meaning, in superstition, is that we are challenging our fate, but at the same time seeking the protection of things holy.

The origin of the superstition is usually given as the protection of the Cross; and it seems to have arisen in this connection from the old-time practice of sanctuary. That is, the sanctuary provided by a hunted person touching the door of a church, when it was regarded as sacrilege for any of his pursuers to continue efforts to apprehend him; he was regarded as under the protection of the church, and the Holy Cross, which the church signified.

That, however, is a very modern application of "touch wood." To discover the real origin of the superstition, we have to go back to those early circumstances in which man paid reverence to trees of various species; in other words to the days of the worship of the beneficent Tree Spirits.

Certain trees were identified with certain deities. In Greece, for instance, the oak was sacred to Zeus, while in Britain, it was dedicated to a Celtic deity, the identity of which is a matter of conjecture. The ash tree was sacred to Thor, the Norse God of Thunder, and the sycamore to the Egyptian goddess Hathor.

The cult of the oak tree later became universal throughout Europe, and it became associated with the European Sky God. Men observed that the oak was the tree most commonly struck by lightning. From this it was assumed that the oak was the dwelling place of the Sky- and Thunder God. The parasites of the oak tree, it was believed, at the same time partook of the attributes of the tree on which they lived, and so did the birds which sang in its branches; and it was held, in addition, that the breeze conveyed the thoughts of men to the leaves of the oak, which thereupon communicated the secrets to the spirit in the oak.

Thus, to avert evil through boasting, what we now call sympathetic magic had to be employed, and to touch the oak, or other sacred tree, meant that one would be rendered immune from the vengeful essence or emanation of the irritable Sky God, who punished boasters either with the lightning stroke or by sending down some dire influence.

Thus, from the touching of the oak, the old superstition came, in the course of time, to the belief that the touching of any piece of wood was sufficient to ward off or neutralize any possible evil from a boasting assertion.

Only in certain pagan countries is the superstition still confined to the oak. For instance, in the Tonga Islands, leaves of the sacred tree are worn round the neck by the priests as a mark of submission to the god who dwells in the tree; and on the Calabar River the natives pluck a leaf from their sacred tree, and rub it on their foreheads to avert danger from crocodiles when about to cross one of the fords. In the Nicobar Islands, people thought to be possessed of a devil are beaten with the branches of the sacred tree.

Touching Iron. Similar origin accounts for the touching of iron in certain circumstances, for instance when the word pig, or priest, or church is used on board a fishing trawler manned by Scottish Highlanders, or fishermen of the Orkneys. To touch iron was to place oneself under the protection of the gods presiding over that metal; Vulcan and Thor cultivated the art of the black-smith, and made and cast thunderbolts.

See APPLE TREE, FISHING (SEA).

TOUCHING THE CORPSE

It was regarded as a sign of friendship among the poorer classes in Co. Durham for friends and acquaintances of a bereaved family to visit the house and "touch the corpse."

The touching was a sign and a symbol that the toucher wishes no harm to the dead, but is in peace and amity with him.

To the mind of the antiquarian and delve into superstition and folklore, the custom will be·associated with the old belief of two centuries before, that a corpse would bleed at the touch of its murderer.

This, in fact, one of the Trials by Ordeal, is mentioned in the *Daemon-ology* of James I:

"In a secret murder, if the dead carkasse be at any time thereafter handled by the murderer, it will quick gush out blood, as if the blood was cry-ing to Heaven for revenge on the murderer."

This bleeding of the corpse was held as evidence of guilt of murder in the High Court of Justiciary in Edinburgh, and was common also in England in the medieval ages.

TREES

If you look at trees in front of your house in the morning on an empty stomach, they will not thrive.—Dorset.

Mr. Thomas Hardy, the eminent writer, has placed on record that this belief was conveyed to him by a garden-ing authority, of whom he inquired why the trees in front of his house, near Weymouth, did not appear to be doing well.

It is interesting by reason of the fact that this is the only instance in Britain of the belief that the authors have been able to find.

They take the view that it was not so much the looking at the trees in the early morning that was in the mind of the old gardener, as the looking on them *with an empty stomach.*

For there are a number of supersti-tions, East and West, regarding this. It is a Malay maxim that maize should only be planted when the stomachs of the planters were full. And Skeat, in *Malay Magic,* says the same thing in regard to planting rice. An Estonian peasant, planting cabbages, bakes large pancakes, in order that the cabbages shall have broad leaves.

But trees have been bound up with men's health and lives from the earliest days, both in this country and in others, civilized and savage. There was a time in Britain when it was a death offence to cut down a tree, for it was held to offend the Tree Spirits, which were wor-shipped (and of which, incidentally, the May Day revels are a survival). A man who cut off a branch of a tree, it was believed, would lose a limb of his body.

Of more recent times were the beliefs that a person's health was bound up with certain trees. Mention has already been made of children passed through a cleft ash to cure them of rupture; and of the belief that ever afterwards their life was bound up in the tree; if it withered and died, they died; if the cleft refused to heal, their rupture would not heal.

Near the castle of Dalhousie, close to Edinburgh, there stood what was known as the Edgewell Oak, with which it was said the fate of the family was linked. If one of the family was about to die, so ran the legend, a branch fell off the tree.

In July, 1874, an old forester passing the tree saw a branch fall. "The laird's deid noo," he said, and within half an hour Fox Maule, eleventh Earl of Dal-housie was dead.

Similarly it was held that an old tree at Howth Castle, Ireland, held the fate of the St. Lawrence family. The legend ran that when the tree fell, the direct line of the Earls of Howth would become extinct. In 1913, the tree was propped up by strong supports round the base.

There used to stand at the village of Oster-Kappeln, an old oak. It was sup-posed to be the life tree of the royal Guelph family of Germany. In 1866 the tree, without any visible reason, crashed to the ground. Hanover's King George

V ordered it to be raised again, and had it chained to the neighbouring trees to keep it in position. A few months later, however, Hanover became part of the Prussian monarchy.

In the private garden of the Emperors of China, set in the centre of the Forbidden City of Peking, there stood one, and only one, natural tree amidst artificial rockeries and strangely clipped bushes. It was known as the Life Tree of the Dynasty.

According to the legend, the welfare of the reigning house went with the life or death of the tree. In 1901, despite all the care and attention lavished upon it, it was practically dead, being propped up to give it a semblance of still standing. In 1902, the dynasty came to an end.

So, too, did the two myrtle trees in Rome grow and fade with the change from Patrician to Plebeian rule. Those were the names given to the two trees. It was said that so long as the Patricians were in power, their Patrician tree flourished and the Plebeian tree withered, but after the Marsian war, when the Plebeians began to gain ascendancy, their tree picked up a new lease of life, and the Patrician tree withered.

TUMOURS

Placing on them the hand of a man who has committed suicide will cure tumours on the skin.—Cornwall.

This is a variation of the belief that the touch of the hand of a man who has been hanged on the scaffold will cure the goitre or a wen.

See GOITRE, SWELLING.

TURNING BACK

To turn back after leaving on a journey will bring bad luck.—General.

This superstition is, again, one of those still held to-day, even by the most unsuperstitious people. However, it may bring relief to know that the "bad luck" is only part of the old belief. If, after turning back, you ask for bread and meat, and partake of it, all will be well.

The origin of this turning back, or looking back, doubtless dates to the story of Lot's wife in the Bible; but the English tradition belongs to the days of swords over here. To leave one's residence was to face any attack from any quarter; to turn one's unprotected back to a thrust from an enemy.

It was this same fear that ordained that a lady should precede a gentleman —whose sword protected her until she had reached safety. It was also the origin of the lady walking on the left of the man—leaving his sword arm unfettered.

See LOOKING BACK.

TWELFTH DAY

Anyone who rides or drives a horse on this day is certain to meet with an accident, as this day is the horse's special holiday.—Somerset.

NOTE: The authors have been unable to trace why, and since when, Twelfth Day became a horse holiday. It is, however, possible that the origin lies in the fact that Twelfth Day was regarded in Somerset as Old Christmas Day.

If apples are not wassailed on Twelfth Day, the cider crop will not be a good one.—Hereford, Somerset.

Bad fortune will attend any house where the Christmas decorations are not taken down on Twelfth Night.

The practice in Herefordshire and Somerset was to proceed to the field or orchard, make twelve fires of straw and one larger one "to burn the old witch." Singing and dancing took place round the fires, and then the company repaired to the farmer's house, where the night was spent in revelry.

Similar practices took place for the wheat and other corn crops in most parts of the country.

This "firing" on Twelfth Night was a widespread custom. They were often kindled on the tops of hills, and it was possible to see a ring of sixty fires blazing in the sky at one time.

The origin seems to have been in the belief that during the twelve days between Christmas and the Twelfth Day witches and fiends of all kinds were let loose. By the fires they were formally driven away, and the crops, and people, saved from their intentions. Ireland, also, had its fires.

See APPLE TREES.

TWINS

If one of twins dies, and the limbs do not stiffen rapidly, the dead one is waiting for the other.—Dorset.

In such cases, the funeral of the dead child was invariably delayed, in order to see whether the second would, indeed, die.

UMBRELLA

To open an umbrella into the house will bring bad luck.—General.

If you drop an umbrella, and pick it up yourself, you will have bad luck.— General.

Both these very old superstitions are still in vogue to-day. No particular form of bad luck has ever been attributed to them; just the usual ill-fortune of so many of these absurd superstitions.

UNBAPTIZED CHILD
*If you tread on the grave of an unbaptized child (unconsecrated ground), you will contract grave-scab.—*Northern Counties.

An unbaptized child cannot die.— Northern Counties.

It is lucky to have a stillborn or an unbaptized child put into an open grave, for it is a sure passport to Heaven for the person finally buried in that grave. —Southern Counties.

Grave-scab was a complaint, in which all the limbs began to tremble, breathing became hard, and the skin was afflicted with a burning sensation. Contracted by walking over the grave of an unbaptized child, it could be "cured," said superstition—but at considerable trouble.

The sufferer must wear a sack made of lint grown in a field which had been manured from a farmyard heap that had not been disturbed for forty years. It must have been bleached by an honest bleacher, in an honest miller's mill dam, and sewed by an honest tailor.

The superstition that an unbaptized child cannot die, was reflected in a case reported in the *Morning Herald* of 18th June, 1860, where a woman was accused of the attempted infanticide of her child. She had apparently laid the child in the grounds of a gentleman's residence near Liverpool.

Confessing to her guilt, the woman said she had previously succeeded in having the child baptized, as she believed that otherwise it could not have died. In point of fact the child was found, and it recovered.

UNDER THE BED
It takes only a comedian in a stage play to look under the bed to raise a howl of laughter. So perhaps the superstition given below may also raise a laugh.

Every single or "walking out" girl in the country areas was in honour bound to look under the bed each night, lest she brought bad luck and shame to her "young man."

Sir Charles Igglesden recalls a case in which a servant girl had fallen seriously ill. The doctor ordered that she should be wrapped up in warm blankets and on no account be allowed to leave her bed. Her mistress, a little later, going to the room, found the girl on her knees peering under the bedstead.

To her protest, she received the reply: "Well, ma'am, you don't expect me to go to sleep without first looking under the bed. I'd rather die than bring bad luck upon me and my young man."

She explained further that it was a well-known fact that to ward off the Devil, it was necessary for everyone to look under the bed at night.

UNLUCKY DAY
The unluckiest day in the year is Childermass (Holy Innocents') Day.— 28th December.

Of old no fisherman would go to sea on this day, nor would any business man begin an undertaking of any importance.

It is stated that the coronation of Edward IV, set by mischance on this day, was postponed until 29th December. Louis XI always declined to transact any business on Holy Innocents' Day.

URINE
*Children who cannot retain their water, can be cured by eating three roasted mice.—*General.

Incredible though it may appear this superstition was still practised in 1946. The authors in that year, in the course of an answer to a correspondent concerning superstitions, mentioned the above as an instance of absurdity.

The sequel was astounding; nearly a dozen mothers, or their friends, wrote to say that not only were they giving their children roasted mice to cure them of bed wetting, but it was, in fact, curing them, and had cured their older children.

One friend explained: "Of course, she gets the best and cleanest tame mice from a pet shop."

VALERIAN
*If a maiden wears valerian in her girdle or her corsets, she will attract the opposite sex.—*Wales.

Well, it seems worth a try—for there are in Britain nearly two million surplus women!

VEIN
If you show a blue vein on the bridge

of your nose, you will never survive to wear wedding clothes.

VERTIGO
Go out early as dawn on the 1st of May, and snuff May dew from the grass up your nostrils, and you will never have vertigo again.—Southern Counties.

"V" FINGERS "V" SIGN
During the time that Mr. Winston Churchill was making a habit of giving the "V" for victory sign, with the first and second fingers of his right hand, the authors received a vigorous letter of protest from a Cornish woman. It was, she insisted, a sign of Satan, and indicative of the fact that while it was persisted in, the Devil would be in the ascendant.

Unfortunately, she gave no indication of her address, so inquiry into the reason for her belief was impossible. It was not till many months afterwards that the authors' search into this strange story was rewarded. They then discovered that in Spanish and Italian religious circles, the fingers thus presented was regarded by some as emblematical of the horns of Satan. Pointing downwards indicated that Satan was being kept in the infernal regions below, where he could not effect any mischief. But pointed upwards, as in the "V" sign, they placed the Devil in the position of triumphing evil over good.

Many of the Cornish people have traces of Spanish blood in their ancestry. There is no doubt that the woman's letter to us was born of a story passed down from her Spanish ancestors, for a devout Spanish Roman Catholic even to-day, we are informed, will point two fingers downwards on first rising in the morning.

VIOLETS
To take less than a handful of violets into the house of a farmer, will spell death to his broods of chickens and ducklings.—Worcestershire.
See PRIMROSE.

VIPER
If a viper bites you, kill it and apply the fat from the serpent to the wound. This will stop the poison.—Devon.

VISITOR
It is unlucky to watch a departing visitor completely OUT of sight.—General.

WALKING UNDER LADDER
It will bring bad luck if you walk under a ladder.—General.

Apart from the fact that you are as likely as not to have the exceedingly bad luck of having a blob of paint dropped on you, or even, perhaps, something heavier, the real reason for the superstition lies in the fear of sacrilege.

A ladder leaning against a wall forms a triangle; and a triangle is symbolical of the Trinity. To walk under it was, therefore, practically a defiance of things sacred, and thus bound to bring ill-luck on the offender. That was the argument.

It is analogous to the lighting of three things from one light; in the Russian Church, none but the High Priest could light the three candles on the High Altar with a single light.
See LADDER.

WALNUT TREE
A woman, a spaniel, and a walnut tree,
The more you whip them, the better they be.—General.

Long before Halliwell's time it was a common persuasion among country people that whipping a walnut tree tended to increase the produce and improve the quality of the fruit.

In the authors' childhood it was invariably resorted to in the early spring. We have no doubt that in some rural parts the trees are still whipped.

The origin of it we do not know; despite all research, it remains a mystery.

WARTS
Take a large black snail, rub it over the wart and hang it on a thorn. Do this nine nights successively, at the end of which time, the wart will disappear.—Northampton, Gloucestershire.

Steal a piece of meat, rub it over the warts, and then bury it. As the meat decays, the warts will vanish.—Cornwall, Yorks, Lancs., and Devon.

When a funeral is passing, rub the warts and say, three times: May these warts and this corpse pass away and nevermore return.—South Ireland.

Now, these are only three of a large number of ways of getting rid of warts, which were practised by the people of Britain a century ago. Whether any of them exist to-day, is mentioned below.

There was a Cornwall tradition, which also was known in other parts of the country, to the effect that you must take as many pebbles as you have warts, and touch each wart with its corresponding pebble. Wrap the stones, afterwards, in either a paper or a piece of cloth and throw them away in the roadway, or, better still, "lose" them on the way to church. Whoever picks up the parcel of pebbles, will get your warts, and you will lose them.

Up and down Britain, there ruled a similar cure, with such trifling substitutions for pebbles as nodules of corn (Scotland), a bottle of pins to be dropped in an open grave (Cornwall), and peas (general).

The same superstition was rife, too, in Germany, Austria and France. In Brittany, they were practised at the waning of the moon, because the people there thought that the moon had something to do with warts, which grew at the waxing, and vanished at the waning.

In each case, the person picking up the discarded ingredients contracted the warts, and you lost them. All these devices were, of course, a version of the transference of evils, of which mention has been made elsewhere in this volume.

Whence did they come?

In the fourth century, Marcellus, of Bordeaux, prescribed the pebbles charm (he called them "little stones") in his *De Mendicamentis*. The other ingredients—the pins and the corn nodules—have grown out of Marcellus's "little stones."

But before Marcellus, there was Pliny (A.D. 23-79), who had declared in his *Natural History* (22,149): "You are to touch the warts with chick peas on the first day of the moon, wrap the peas in cloth and throw them away behind you." But Pliny did not say that the warts would be transferred to the person who picked up the chick peas. Somebody put in that bit later.

Another wart remedy—and still another transference of evil—concerned decay. In parts of Lancashire, including Manchester, a piece of string was tied in as many knots as there were warts on the sufferer. Each wart was then touched with the appropriate knot. The string was then buried in a damp place with the admonition: "There is none to redeem it save thee." As the string rotted away, so did the warts.

The stolen meat, in the superstition quoted above, was a variation of the knotted string. In some areas, however, the knotted string was not thrown away or buried, but was placed before sunrise

in the spout of a pump; and the next person to use the pump handle got the warts.

Still another method was to rub the warts with fat bacon rind, or bleed them on a rag, and then throw whichever was used away. The warts were, again, transferred to the person so unwise as to pick up the article.

There is, however, a variant of the bacon remedy. Lord St. Albans, in his *Natural History*, says: "I had from my childhood a wart upon one of my fingers; afterwards, when I was about sixteen years old, being then in Paris, there grew upon both my hands a number of warts, at the least a hundred in a month's space.

"The English Ambassador's lady, who was a woman far from superstitious, told me one day she would help me with my warts; whereupon she got a piece of lard with the skin on, and rubbed the warts all over with the fat side, among the rest the wart which I had had from childhood. Then she nailed the piece of lard with the fat toward the sun, upon the post of her chamber window, which was to the south. The success was that within five weeks' space all the warts went away."

Now the queer thing about this story is that Bacon, in his *Sylvia Sylvarium*, tells exactly the same story as happening to himself, and almost in the same words, except that it was not a piece of lard that the English Ambassador's lady used, but a piece of bacon rind.

To return to the warts: Another way of ridding oneself of them was to apply an eel's skin to the warts, and they went. Or you could take a new pin, cross the warts with it nine times (this is the old three times three idea again), and fling the pin over the left shoulder. Again, an apple could be cut in two parts, and the warts rubbed with each part in turn. Then the apple had to be joined together again, and buried. As the apple decayed, so did the warts.

An easier way was to rub the afflictions with a green elder stick, and then bury the stick to rot in muck.

A Welsh cure was to impale a frog on a stake, and then rub the warts with the creature. As the frog died, the warts died. In Glamorgan and Pembrokeshire, a snail was gathered (a black one for preference), and its shell was rubbed on each of the warts with the accompanying words:

Wart, wart, on the snail's shell black,
Go away soon, and never come back.

The snail was then placed on a branch or bramble, and secured with as many thorns as the sufferer had warts. As the snail rotted, the warts vanished.

Although the authors can find no actual evidence, they think it likely that the snail cure is still practised in Wales. While fishing at Ross-on-Wye, two years ago, we found two snails impaled by a pin on a tall bramble bush along the banks of the river in front of the Royal Hotel. They could not have got there by themselves, much less have stuck themselves through with a pin. There is no doubt in our minds that they had been used to charm away somebody's warts.

Staffordshire seems to have had a wart lore of its own. It was held in that county, that if a person suffering with warts rubbed them over with the hand of a dead man, they would disappear. And another Staffordshire "cure" was to rub them with the tail of a tortoiseshell tom·cat in May.

In Ireland, it was considered sufficient to prick each wart with a gooseberry thorn *through a golden wedding ring*.

A common remedy, still used to-day, is to tie a hair round each wart, and leave it there until the wart went. It is likely, however, that there may be a sound medical explanation of this.

Miss Christina Hole, in her *Witchcraft in England*, tells of her own maid's action in sticking pins into a mountain ash tree in Miss Hole's garden. The warts, she said, disappeared within a week.

But let us now come to an ultra-modern superstition. The authors, a few months ago, received the following letter: "I am sure you will be interested to know that the easiest way to remove a wart is to *rub it with the inside of a banana skin*. I had a 'vascular' wart on a hand, and each time I had a banana I rubbed the wart with it. The wart got smaller and smaller, until, one day, there was no more sign of it. I have never had one since."

WASHING

If you spurt or scatter water from your hands first thing in the morning, you scatter your good luck for the day. —Wales.

To wash your hands in water in which eggs have been boiled, is a certain way to get warts.—General.

NOTE: This is still widely believed to-day.

If two persons wash in the same water at the same time, it means bad luck unless one of them spits in the water.—General.

NOTE: A variation of this is for one of them to make the Sign of the Cross over the water.

To wash clothes on New Year's Day, is to "wash someone out of the family." —Scotland and North of England.

NOTE: To cause their death.

Welsh people had a wealth of superstition concerning washing operations. It was held that if a new garment was washed for the first time when the moon was new, it would never wear well. Or, if a washerwoman pulled any garment out of the dolly-tub upside down, or to the left, the wearer of the article could never be bewitched. It should be emphasized that it was no good the lady peeping to make sure that she had got the article upside down before pulling it out of the tub; it had to be drawn that way accidentally, or the charm did not work.

Another Welsh superstition was that the woman who wet her apron over-much in washing, or who splashed water about, would be cursed with a drunken husband. And to spill water while carrying it from the spring or brook is an omen of sorrow.

People in the Orkney Islands will sometimes wash a sick man and throw the water afterwards down at a gateway, in the belief that the sickness will leave the gateway, and be transferred to the first person who passes through the gate.

In the North of England, great attention was paid to the day on which to do the family washing. It was expressed this way:

They that wash on Monday, have the whole week to dry.
They that wash on Tuesday, are not so much arye.
They that wash on Wednesday, may get their clothes clean.
They that wash on Thursday, are not so much to mean.
They that wash on Friday, wash for their need.
But they that wash on Saturday, are clarty-paps indeed.

NOTE: Clarty-paps means dirty sluts.

A Northumberland superstition maintained that a child's right hand should not be washed for the first twelve months of its life, so that it will gather riches quicker in later life. It sounds to the authors like dooming the child to "dirty" money, which probably would be gathered quickly.

WASPS

If you kill the first wasp seen in any season, you will secure good luck and freedom from enemies throughout the year.—South Northampton.

WATER

Spring water drawn between eleven o'clock and midnight on Christmas and Easter night, turns into wine.—Wales.

Boiled water should never be left in a bedroom. It will bring bad luck.—General.

NOTE: The remarkable explanation of this is that boiled water, it was said, will not freeze, and should the Evil One want it to freeze, and it wouldn't, he would get angry, and put bad luck upon the house. The fallacy, of course, is that boiled water will freeze equally with unboiled.

Water drawn from downstream before sunrise, and in silence, on any Sunday morning, in one jug from three separate and flowing springs, is magical in its use and influence.—Wales.

Running water drawn at midnight from any important spring on St. John's Eve, will remain fresh and pure for a year, and has healing propensities.—Wales.

In this latter superstition is a relic of the old Celtic worship of the Water Spirit, as they also worshipped the Tree Spirit.

A generation ago it was still practised in Wales. Even as late as the early nineteenth century, it was the custom in Glamorgan and Carmarthenshire for young men and women to walk to the nearest spring on Easter morning, draw water in jugs, and throw showers on the surrounding flowers, herbs and shrubs. By doing so they believed that they would have good luck during the year.

There was also a belief in many parts of Wales, that if a man wrapped in the skin of an animal just killed, was laid alone beside a waterfall, he would have the future revealed to him by the sound of the waters.

In Ireland, too, water was held to acquire mystical value at midsummer. For instance, at Stoole, near Downpatrick, where there are three wells, there was held, on Midsummer Eve, various penance services, after which crowds of halt, maimed and blind people thronged the wells and streams issuing from them, pressing to wash away their infirmities with the water consecrated to St. Patrick, whose chair was set in a mount high above on the hills overlooking the wells.

Now, all this is interesting as showing the belief in water magic. The same idea prevailed in Sweden, where springs were supposed to be endowed with wonderful medicinal value on St. John's Eve.

In the Andjra district of Morocco, and in Oran, people bathed themselves in the sea or rivers at this time, and washed their cattle in the waters, believing that on this day the waters possess a special virtue, which dispels sickness and ill-luck.

A Scottish water superstition among Scottish brewers was that the word should never be mentioned in connection with their calling. It was supposed that to speak the word "water" to the brew would spoil the brewing.

Some German rivers, such as the Saale and Spree, are believed to require a victim on Midsummer Day, a relic of pagan belief in Europe.

Not only there, but in Scotland itself, it is still believed that a person a year must be drowned as the river's yearly toll. One river thus designated is the Ross. A similar belief existed, and probably still does among the older people, in Ireland.

Wales had a spate of superstitions concerning water. It was held that money washed in clear rain water could not be stolen, and that water in which a babe was washed for the first three months of its life should be thrown under a green tree or the babe would not thrive. Another baby belief was that rain water baths made them talk earlier than they would otherwise do.

Pigs bathed in water in which killed swine had been scalded would, it was held, thrive better and grow well.

Finally, the Welsh country people believed that if water took a long time to get to the boil, it was bewitched, and to make it boil, three different kinds of wood would have to be used on the fire underneath it.

In North Taunton, near a house which was called Bath, there was a pit, or pool, not maintained by any spring, and usually dry in summer.

Of this pool, it was said, that before the death of any prince it would, though it might be a hot and dry season, overflow its banks, and so continue until that which was prognosticated was fulfilled.

This story is told in Burton's *Admirable Curiosities.* Unfortunately, he did not include any information as to whether such a phenomenon had at any time been fulfilled.

See DROWNING.

WATER, HOT—AT WEDDINGS

In Yorkshire, hot water was poured over the doorstep as a bride and bridegroom drove away. The practice was known as "keeping the threshold warm for another bride," it being held that before the hot water dried up another wedding would be fixed from among the young folk who had gathered to send-off the bride.

WAVE GOODBYE

Ill-luck will follow if a hand is waved at a parting friend until he is out of sight.—Berkshire.

This superstition was at one time widely held throughout the county; and is still believed in even to-day in one or two of the remote villages.

WAVES

To cure consumption, catch the tops of nine waves in a dish, and throw the water on the head of the patient, afterwards passing him through a rifted rock in the direction of the sun.—Scotland.

At Christmas and Easter and All Hallows Eve, all those who have been drowned at sea come up to ride over the waves on "white horses," and hold their revels.—Welsh coastal.

It was from the latter superstition that there was born the name "The Merry Dancers" for the white waves round the sands of Nash, South Glamorgan. White waves were watched with awe by the old people of Wales.

On the coast of Morven and Mull are a number of rock ledges, many of which are pierced with large holes near the sea. These are the rifted rocks referred to above in the superstitious cure for consumption.

See HOLES (PASSING THROUGH).

WEAK EYES

Club moss, if properly gathered, is good for all diseases of the eyes.—Cornwall.

Pure rain water is an infallible cure for sore and weak eyes.—Lincolnshire.

Rain which happens to fall on Holy Thursday (the Thursday before Good Friday), if bottled and preserved, is a remedy for sore eyes.—Oxfordshire.

The proper way to gather club moss, as an eye charm, was as follows:

"On the third day of the moon, when the thin crescent is seen for the first time, show it the knife with which the moss is to be cut, and repeat:

As Christ heal'd the issue of blood,
Do thou cut what thou cuttest for good.

"At sundown, having carefully washed your hands, the club moss is to be cut kneeling. It is to be carefully wrapped in a white cloth, and subsequently boiled in water taken from the spring nearest to the place of cutting. This may be used as a fomentation. Or the club moss may be made into an ointment with butter from the milk of a new cow."

A Devonshire charm for weak eyes was to pay a house-to-house visit begging penny pieces. A woman had to seek the pennies only from males, and had not to say please or thank you, or the spell would be broken. A man was under the same obligation in begging only from women.

When the amount collected reached four shillings and sixpence, a pair of earrings had to be purchased, and these when worn would cure the weak eyes. It is this silly superstition which is responsible to-day for the belief that pierced ears help the eyesight.

As regards the pure rain water remedy, it had to be collected in a clean open vessel in the month of June, and must not have been contaminated by being previously collected by other means. It would then remain pure for any length of time, if preserved in a bottle.

There lived on Tweedside some eighty years ago, an old woman who was famed for her curing of weak eyes, inflamed eyes or sprained limbs. She applied a talisman or charm to the affected parts.

This charm was called a lammerbead, lammer being the Scottish for amber, from the French l'ambre. It was apparently an amber stone dug out of an ancient British barrow, or grave.

Similarly, in Devonshire there lived about the same period a Miss Soaper, in the village of Thurshelton. She possessed a blue-coloured stone, which, rubbed over weak or sore eyes, was believed to, and in fact did, cure eyes.

See EYES.

WEASEL

If a white weasel crosses your path, it presages death or misfortune; but if one runs in front of you, you will be able to beat all your enemies.—Wales.

The omen, however, had to be observed a little more closely than the quotation above supposes. Should the weasel run in front of you to the left, you are warned that you have enemies within your house. (Note that disastrous left side again.) If the weasel suddenly turned backwards along its path, it was a portend of sudden death; while a zig-zag course forward meant success.

The same was said of a white hare.

WEATHER

If spiders desert their webs for sheltered crevices, rain is coming.—General.

If swallows fly low, the weather will be bad.—General.

If soot falls down a high chimney, the weather is going to be bad.

Now, there are scores of weather superstitions, the majority of which are just rhyming verses and proverbs, and as such are too well known to be needed in this volume. But there are others which have a very considerable interest, and three of them are those given above.

All these were known a hundred and fifty years ago, before science had made much progress with meteorological fore-casting. They are, therefore, genuine superstitions, for they were implicitly believed in, and invariably came right.

Look into them in the light of present-day knowledge of atmosphere. If swallows fly low, the weather will be bad. We know now, that the reason the swallow flies low is due to their being affected, as are most birds and insects, by air pressure, and it is air pressure that affects the state of the weather. The swallow, when the pressure shows good weather, flies high, and so do the natural food of the bird—insects. Pressure before wet weather affects the sensitive ears of the swallow, so it flies low.

Spiders, too, are very sensitive to air pressure, which explains the old super-stition that when there is rain about, they get out of the air into the shelter of a crevice.

The same explanation can be given of falling soot in a high chimney. The soot is held in place by air pressure.

Another weather superstition, still held to-day, is that if the badger in January comes out of hibernation, and finds his shadow on the snow he will come out for the year. But if the sun is not shining, he will return to his hiber-nating for a further spell, knowing that the worst of the winter's weather is still to come.

If rooks in January or early February begin to build high in elm trees, a fine summer may be looked for, say the old country people. It is held that should they build lower down it means that they know they are likely to need thicker foliage to shelter their eggs and young, and a cold summer is in store. Also, if on a summer's day, the rooks leave their nests in the rookery, the rest of the day will be fine. Should there be rain in the offing, they will stay at home. That is a very old country super-stition.

Now there are certain prognostications which are not properly understood at the present day. One of them is "A green Christmas makes a fat churchyard." Another is the old superstition that appeared in *The English Husbandman*, which reads:

"You shall understand that what weather shall fall at Christmas shall fall again in the following month."

Then there are others all referring to what the weather is like at Christmas. The extract from *The English Husband-man*, 1635, and the others are also round about that period. They have all been made as naught by the change in the calendar, which came into being in the year 1752. Before that Christmas Day in England was the present 6th January. Thus all these weather conditions if they mean anything at all, should be looked for on 6th January.

Here are some more of the lesser known weather "omens": "If the ice bear a man before Christmas, it will not bear a mouse again," meaning that ice and cold in November predicts warm weather about Christmas and in the early new year.

" 'Tween Martinmas and Yule, water's wine in every pool," as showing the value of rain in the North of England during those times.

In the Border Counties and the North it was held that the first twelve days of the new year epitomized the weather for the next twelve months. Here is the superstition attached to it:

If New Year's Eve night wind blow south,
It betokeneth warmth and growth.
If west, much milk and fish in the sea.
If north, much cold and storms there will be.
If east, the trees will bear much fruit.
If north-east, flee it, man and brute.

A final one: "Water in May is bread all the year."

Other weather superstitions of note are dealt with under the various months associated with them.

WEDDING

If a marriage takes place while there is an open grave in the churchyard, it is a bad omen for the couple.—North of England.

If a cat sneezes in the home of the bride-to-be on the eve of her wedding, it is a lucky omen.

It is unlucky for a bride to look in the glass after she is completely dressed before she goes to church.—General.

If a hen is taken into the couple's new home, and made to cackle, after the wedding, it will bring good luck.—West Riding, Yorks.

It is unlucky if the bride does not weep bitterly on the wedding day.—Former strong superstition.

Should a dog pass between a couple on their wedding day, it means bad luck for the wedding.—Highlands.

The last thing in the world the bride of to-day would think of doing is to wear a pair of old shoes at her wedding; yet in older days it was considered lucky for any bride to marry in old shoes.

In Berkshire, it was considered that whichever of the newly married pair stepped out of the church first will be master in the house. The belief frequently led to an undignified scurrying on the part of the bridal couple as they left the church; and to very keen observation by the bride's mother, and subsequent grim satisfaction, should her daughter manage to make the threshold first. In Yorkshire, however, the master of the house was regarded as the one who first stepped across the threshold of the new home.

In the west of Scotland, it was held unlucky if either the bride or groom separately, or together, met a funeral on the way to or from the church. If the funeral was that of a female then it was held that the bride would not live long; if that of a man, then the bridegroom would die before long.

It was generally held that should the younger daughter of the house wed before her elder sisters, the sisters must all dance at her wedding without shoes, otherwise they will never gain husbands. This was an old belief, for Grose mentions it.

One of the oldest superstitions connected with marriage is that marriages in May are unlucky. It is said of this month: "From marriages in May all the bairns die and decay"; and "Who marries between the sickle and the scythe will never thrive."

This foretold ill-luck of May weddings was old in the time of Ovid. He tells, in *Fasti*:

> Nec viduae taldis eadem, nec virginis apta.
> Tempora quae nuptsit non diunturna fait.
> Hoec quoque de causa (si te proverbia tangunt)
> Mense malas Maio nubere vulgas ait.

The last line was fixed over the gate of Holyrood on the morning of 16th May, 1567, after the marriage of Mary, Queen of Scots and Bothwell.

Plutarch assigns the reason for the ill-luck of May weddings as because May was the month of old men, and June, that of young men. Juno, it should be remembered was, in Rome, the goddess of the young.

A Yorkshire wedding custom was that as the bride arrived at the door of her father's house, after the ceremony at church, a plate covered with morsels of bride cake was flung from an upstairs window upon the heads of the people below.

If it reached the ground in safety, without being broken, the omen was a most unsatisfactory one. If, on the other hand, the plate was shattered into pieces, the marriage was likely to turn out most happy. Very much the same superstition prevailed, with trifling variations, in Northumberland and Scotland.

In Durham, a superstition existed that it was unlucky for a woman to marry a man whose surname began with the initial letter of her own. The rhyme ran:

> If you change the name and not the letter,
> You change for the worse and not for the better.

In the Leeds area of Yorkshire, it was held that there was no chance of a family for the couple unless, before she retires on her wedding night, her bridesmaids lay her stockings in cross form on the bed. And, in the Durham area, it was held that the first of the bridal pair to go to sleep on the wedding night would be the first to die.

The Celtic wedding superstitions were, and still are, many. If a woman bursts a wedding glove, or a shoe, or splits any part of her bridal array, she will be ill-treated by her husband. A woman should always be married with the new moon; to be wed on the wane of the moon, means that the luck of the marriage will also wane.

Unless a Welsh bride takes out any pin used in her wedding dress and throws it over her left shoulder, or into the fire, she will be unlucky in her married life.

Should she lose her wedding ring, or break it, or have it fall from her finger, a Welsh bride will lose her husband's affection. This, by the way, is a pretty general superstition.

Also general, as well as proverbial in Wales, is the fact that a silver sixpence in a shoe will ensure the bride a happy and prosperous life. In olden days, both bride and groom were accustomed, in country areas, to ride to the wedding on horseback. Should the bridegroom ride to the church on a mare, his wife would have daughters but no sons. It was singularly fortunate that there was no similar superstition about riding to the wedding on a male animal.

At Welsh weddings it was a practice to cut several pieces of bread and butter. One of these was given by the best man to the bride to eat before the wedding cake was cut; it ensured, by its smallness and daintiness, that the children born to the bride in subsequent years would have pretty and small mouths.

It was unlucky for a stone to roll across the pathway of a newly married pair.

See BRIDE, MARRIAGE.

WEDDING CAKE

A slice of wedding cake, thrice drawn through the bride's wedding ring, and laid under the head of an unmarried man or woman, will make him or her dream of future wife or husband.

A Yorkshire superstition had it that unless the bride cut her wedding cake herself, she would go through her married life childless.

It is, of course, a fact that all brides in all counties, cut their own cake—helped by the left hand of the bridegroom.

WEDDING RING

*If a married woman loses her wedding ring, she will lose her husband.—*General.

*If a wedding ring has worn so thin as to come to pieces, or if it breaks, she or her husband will die.—*General.

NOTE: The idea seems to have been that if the ring wears thin, so has the marriage.

To cure warts, prick them with a gooseberry thorn through a golden wedding ring.

Apropos the losing of a wedding ring, followed, as a matter of superstition, *Notes and Queries* contains a story of a murder in North Essex, which deprived a family of its head. Condoled with by a friend of the family, some time later, the widow replied: "Ah, I thought I'd soon lose him, for I broke my wedding ring a few days before, and my sister lost *her* husband soon after breaking her wedding ring. It is a sure sign."

It is a common superstition in Ireland, that a marriage is not legal unless solemnized with a gold ring. At many towns in the poorer areas of Ireland, it was the custom of the priest, or the registrar to loan, for a small fee, a golden wedding ring for those who could not afford to purchase the gold circlet. The ring was returned immediately after the ceremony.

A wedding ring was also used in divination. For a girl to know whether she was to be married or not, it was necessary for her to take a tumbler of south running water—that is, water from a stream running southwards—borrow the wedding ring of a happily married woman, and suspend it by a hair from her own head over the glass of water, holding the hair between a finger and thumb of the left hand. If the ring hit itself against the rim of the glass, the holder was doomed to die an old maid. If, on the other hand, the ring turned quickly round, she would be married. Should it turn slowly round, she would be blessed with two husbands —at different times, of course.

A common superstition is that the wedding ring is worn on the third finger of the left hand, because from that finger a vein runs direct to the heart. There is no such vein.

The belief was mentioned, however, by Sir Thomas Browne, that old authority on curious things. But long before Browne, Appianus asserted that a very delicate *nerve* runs from that finger to the heart. Swinburne, in his *Treatise of Spousals*, wrote that "by the received opinions of the learned, in ripping up and anatomising men's bodies, there is a vein of blood, called Vena Amoris, which passeth from that finger to the heart."

We have stated above that there is

neither vein nor nerve so running. The explanation of the use of that finger is fairly obvious, and was put forward in the *British Apollo* in 1788—it is the safest finger of the two hands. Why? Because it has the peculiar advantage for a ring that it cannot be extended full out except in company with another finger, whereas every other finger can be stretched independently. A ring cannot easily fall off a crooked finger.

WELLS

A child baptized with water from the well of St. Ludgvan, is secure from being hanged.—Cornwall.

NOTE: Is it a reflection on the mothers of the county that water from the well was duly supplied on request for christenings.

If you ask at Gulval Well: "Water, water, tell me truly. Is the man I love duly, on the earth or under the sod. Sick or well—in the name of God," the water will bubble and boil if he (or she) is well. If the water shows no movement, the worst can be expected.—Cornwall.

NOTE: The question had to be asked leaning over the water on St. Peter's Eve.

These are but two of the many superstitions attached to holy wells up and down Britain, and in Europe, superstitions which have existed for ages, in fact from the ancient days of belief in the Water Spirit.

Cornwall abounds in this healing belief in waters, or in divination by water. If a cross of palm is thrown into the holy well at Little Conan, and it floats, then the thrower was assured that he, or she, would outlive the year; if it sank, he, or she, would die within twelve months.

Lunatics might be cured of their frenzy, so it was believed, by being tossed by strong men in the waters of St. Nun's Well, at Altarnum. They were tossed until the frenzy left them—a reading of the treatment might lead one to suppose that the frenzy left them through sheer exhaustion of the patient. Bathing in St. Tecla's Well was believed to be a certain cure for the falling sickness (epilepsy).

If you repaired to Eglwys Well, in Lleyn, descended the steps, filled your mouth full of water, ascended the steps and walked round the church once without spilling any of the water, your wish would be gratified. The ladies in the neighbourhood (opposite Bardsey Island) were still seeking this fulfilment

as lately as 1912 to the knowledge of the authors. The legend of this superstition is that a very beautiful lady, who had a wish she desired to obtain, was visited at sunset one day by a strange woman, who gave her the recipe detailed above.

The Silver Well at Llanblethian, Glamorgan, was a resort of youths and maidens in order to test the fidelity of their sweethearts. Blackthorn points were broken off, and one was thrown into the well. If it floated, the lover was faithful; if it sank out of sight, he was unfaithful. If the point whirled round, the lover would make a cheerful husband; if it just stayed put, he would be sullen. Suppose by chance you let a number of the thorns fall into the well, accidentally, then your lover would be a great flirt.

St. Servan's Well was good for the eyes and the toothache. The suppliant had to wash in the water, go into the chapel, and sleep on the stone of the saint, which formed the floor of the little church. The Chapel Farm Well, at St. Breward, Joan's Pitcher, in Lewannick, and the Castle Horneck Well, in Madron, were also considered excellent for sore eyes.

In the well at St. Peris, at Llanberis, North Wales, there was a large eel, which was carefully protected. If it coiled round a person who bathed in the water, that person would be healed of his infirmity. However, one person, a girl, is said to have died of fright on feeling the cold eel on her skin.

Gwyned Well, at Abererch, was another Welsh well, which, it was held, prognosticated the result of a friend's or relation's illness. In this case, a garment of the sick person was thrown into the water. Should it sink to the right the person would recover.

The waters of St. Fegla's Well, Caernarvonshire, was used to cure the falling sickness (epilepsy). Sufferers washed their hands in the water, and then dropped in a fourpenny piece. Then, repeating the Lord's Prayer, they walked round the well three times. Each male patient had to carry a cock and the female a hen in a basket. After the perambulation, the patient went into the church and laid down beside the altar, with a Bible under his head. At daybreak he rose and left the fowl in the church. If the bird died, it was gathered that the epilepsy had left the human and entered the fowl. This was probably the most elaborate ritual in Britain for the transference of evil.

A well at Llanbedrog, in Lleyn, was

supposed to give the name of thieves. If you threw into the water a piece of bread, and spoke the names of persons you suspected, the bread would sink at the name of the thief.

Returning to Cornwall, there were Alsia Well, in Buryan, and St. Piran's Well, in Perranzabuloe, which was famed for its cure of rickets, and Menacuddle Well, at St. Austell, for weakly children. The well of St. Keyne and St. Martin's Well, at Liskeard, were supposed to influence married life.

But the most famous of the Cornish wells, was that of St. Madron, near Penzance. Here, on the first three Wednesdays in May, children afflicted with shingles, wild fire, and all skin complaints, were plunged under the water three times against the sun, and carried nine times round the spring, going from east to west. After this, a piece of the child's clothing was torn from a garment and hung on the thorn tree which grew near the baptistry or left between stones.

WEN
To cure a wen, you should go to an execution, and after the criminal is dead, but still hanging, one of his hands must be rubbed thrice over the wen.—General.

This ghoulish charm was so believed in at the time of public executions in England, that the money paid by sufferers was a lucrative source of perquisites for the hangman. The fees demanded were by no means small, yet the hangman, especially in the County of Northamptonshire, had usually a ring of applicants waiting at the foot of the gallows for the touch of the dead man's hand.

See CORPSE, DEAD MAN'S HAND, GOITRE.

WHILKS
To cure a whilk on a child's eye, you must pass the tail of a black cat nine times over the place.

It is added that if the tail is of a ram cat, then the cure is more certain.

WHINNEY MOOR
In Yorkshire, as late as Aubrey's time, it was held by country people that upon the death of anyone his soul went over Whinney Moor. Women at the time were sometimes hired to chant a lament and sing a funeral song. One verse of this went:

From Whinney Moor that thou mayst pass

Every night and awle.
To Brig of dread thou comest at last,
And Christ receive thy saule.

There were about twenty verses of this, and each verse ended with the line given above.

The point of the superstition is that Whinney Moor had its name from the abundance of whins (furze) growing on it, by which it was particularly calculated to test the quality of a soul on its pilgrimage.

WHIPPING A DOG
It was held in all parts of the country, sacrilegious for a dog to enter a church; and should such an animal enter during divine service, it was at one time incumbent on the priest to restart the ritual from the beginning. The belief existed to comparatively modern times, and one of the duties of the beadle of a church was to whip dogs out of the church.

In many old churchwardens' accounts will be found repeated expenses given as "payment to dog whippers." This was one of the posts held by a beadle.

There was one exception to the general rule. At the consecration of a new church, a dog was driven into the building through the main door before any human entered. This was a concession to the old superstition that the first living thing to enter a church on its consecration was claimed by the Devil. Thus, the dog was sacrificed.

One other superstition attached to a dog concerns its howling. Should he howl at night, a death is presaged.

En passant—and a little out of superstition—most dog owners know that a dog's health can be judged by the coldness and wetness of its nose. The legend of this cold and wet nose runs thus: One of the two dogs which Noah took with him into the Ark discovered a leak in the Ark during the voyage. Noah, in his extremity, pushed the dog's nose into the leak, but realizing that the animal would die before long, then took his wife by the arm and pushed one of her elbows into the hole. For this reason, ever since a dog's nose and a woman's elbow have been cold; and a dog's nose, also wet.

WHISTLING
If a miner whistles in a mine, there will be an explosion.—General pit superstition.

Whistling on board a ship, will bring up a gale.—Sailors.

To whistle in a theatre, or in the dressing rooms, prognosticates the failure of the play.—Stage superstition.

The authors were told by a reliable person of an instance where the captain of a vessel refused to allow a woman passenger to come aboard in order to see a friend off on a voyage.

"She whistles," he insisted. The ship never reached its destination; and it was probably fortunate for the woman that she had not set foot on board, else the blame would most certainly have been laid on her head—or whistle.

WHITE HARE
When a maiden, who has loved not wisely, but too well, dies forsaken and broken-hearted, she comes back to haunt her deceiver in the shape of a white hare.—West Country.

It was held that the phantom hare followed the false one everywhere he went, but was invisible to all save he. It frequently saved him from danger, but in the end always encompassed his death.

WHITE HORSE
It is bad luck to meet a white horse.—Midlands.

The ill-fortune can, however, be averted if you spit at the unfortunate animal.

WHITE PIGEON
A white pigeon fluttering round a house, is an omen of death.—Yorkshire.

A Methodist preacher had fallen dead in the pulpit at, the authors think, Fishlake, in Yorkshire. "And not many hours afore," said one of his flock afterwards, "I had seen a white pigeon light on a tree nearby. I said as 'ow summat was going to happen."

A Lincolnshire superstition holds that if a pigeon is seen sitting in a tree, or comes into the house, or from being wild suddenly becomes tame, it is a sign of death.

WHITE THORN
To sleep in a room with the white thorn in bloom in the month of May will be followed by great misfortune.—Suffolk.

See HAWTHORN, MAY.

WHITLOW
To cure a whitlow, place a large black slug on a piece of clean rag, and stab it all over with a needle. Then wrap the offending finger in the rag.

A gipsy cure for whitlows is recorded in a reader's letter to the *Sussex Magazine*. According to this, when Mrs. "H" was servant girl to the Squire of Waldron, she suffered terribly from whitlows. One morning she was crying with pain when a tap came at the front door. A gipsy woman stood there with pegs for sale. She asked why Mrs. "H" was crying, and was told that the whitlows were so terribly painful, that nobody could help crying.

Said the gipsy: "There's no need to suffer pain any longer, my dear. Get the poker, make it red-hot and push it down in the ground. Then take it out, and put your finger in the hole for a few minutes, and you will have no more whitlows."

The account adds: "Mrs. 'H' did this, her whitlows were cured, and she had no more."

It is added that this remedy had never been known to fail. *The author is speaking of the year* 1944.

WHOOPING COUGH
Crushed snails and minced mice, given to children, will cure the whooping cough.—General.

Get a saucerful of brown sugar, and then obtain a black snail. Let the snail crawl over the sugar until the sugar goes slimy. Then feed the sugar to the child.—Gipsy cure.

Tie a hairy caterpillar in a bag round the child's neck. As the insect dies the cough will vanish.—General.

Put a hair from the head of the patient between two pieces of buttered toast, and give the sandwich to a dog. The dog will get the cough, and the patient will be free of it.—Devonshire.

Whooping cough will never be taken by a child who has ridden upon a bear.—Lancashire.

Pass a child with the whooping cough under the belly of an ass or a piebald pony, and it will be cured.—General.

If a child with the whoop is dragged along the earth at four lanes' end, it will be cured.—Lancashire.

To rid a patient of the whooping cough, fill a muslin bag full of spiders, and tie it round the neck of the patient, who must wear it night and day till the cough is better.—Cornwall.

If these strange remedies sound like the

nonsense of an unenlightened age, consider the following letter received in this enlightened age of 1946. The authors had been inquiring into the existence of superstitions at the present day, and the following letter was received from a mother at Basingstoke, Hants:

"In 1917, my children were down with whooping cough, very ill. An old neighbour came in to see them. She said to me: 'Put a nail up the chimney as high as you can get. I'll be back in a moment.' She came back with twelve snails, live ones. She threaded the snails on a piece of grey wool. 'There,' she said, 'let me hang these on the nail, and as they die so will the whooping cough.' Strange, but true, my children were soon able to go back to school. The twelve snails did what the doctors had been trying to do for weeks. And am I thankful for knowing it."

Only a few weeks before, the authors had received a letter from a woman that she was feeding roast mice to her child to cure its bed wetting habit, and also had cured the same child with minced mice for whooping cough.

In 1945, the authors received a letter from Alvenstoke, Gosport, as follows:

"Another cure we know of for whooping cough, is to place a frog in the child's mouth, but hang on to its (the frog's) hind part. It inhales the complaint, and so cures the child."

This remedy was a popular one in Cheshire, with the exception that a toad was the favoured animal—or, rather, victim. Several instances of the remedy in recent years have appeared in *Notes and Queries*.

A curious "cure" in Cornwall, was for the patient to eat a piece of cake belonging to a married couple whose Christian names are John and Joan. Why John and Joan, and not Jim and Jennie, or any other couplet, the authors have been unable to discover.

In Devonshire, one remedy was to carry the child fasting into three parishes on a Sunday morning. This, it was held, invariably effected a complete cure.

A popular superstition in the North of England, was to get a basin of new milk, let someone's ferret drink half of it, and then give the other half to the patient with the whooping cough, whereupon he would be cured.

Another Devon remedy was to carry the child to a sheepfold, and let the sheep breathe on its face. Then the child had to be laid on the spot of ground from which a sheep had just risen. After this performance had been carried out seven mornings in succession the child would be cured.

This "cure" is still carried on in Somersetshire. The authors have authenticated instances where three children had thus been laid since 1940.

In Norfolk, the house was hunted for a dark spider, which was then held over the child's head, while the following doggerel was recited:

Spider, as you waste away, whooping cough no longer stay.

The spider was then hung in a bag on the mantelpiece, and when it had dried up the cough would have gone.

In Shropshire, the only treatment deemed necessary was to put a stay lace of the child's godmother round the throat.

One Cornish treatment was to gather nine stones from the bed of a running stream, taking care not to interrupt the free flow of the water in doing so. Then a quart of water had to be taken from the stream using the vehicle in the direction of the flow of the water. By no means must the vessel have been dipped against the flow. The stones had then to be made red hot, and put into the quart of water, which was afterwards bottled and given to the child in doses of a wineglassful for nine mornings following. It was added that if this did not cure the whooping, then nothing would.

Another Cornish practice was to find a female donkey three years old, and draw the child, naked, nine times over the animal's back and under its belly. Three spoonfuls of milk were then drawn from the donkey's teats, and three hairs cut each from the back and the belly and placed in the milk, which, after it had stood for three hours to acquire the proper virtue, was given to the child to drink. The process had to be carried out for three successive mornings, when the child would be free of the cough.

This passing under the belly of a donkey is of more than passing interest, for a very common superstition for whooping cough and for rickets and rupture, was to pass the patient *underneath* an archway formed by a bramble which had made an archway by reason of the fact that one end of it had formed a root after contact with the ground. This crawling, or passing, under an arch was one of the most common superstitious cures in this country, and not only in this country, but in nearly every other country, civilized and uncivilized.

For instance, a native of the Kawars, in the Central Provinces of India, suffering from fever, will walk through a narrow passage between houses, and under the eaves, to rid himself of his complaint.

In Denmark, even as late as the nineteenth century, the cure for many childish ailments was to dig up several sods of earth, arrange them in the form of a tunnel, and pass a child through. The Hindus of the Punjab, to avert ill-luck to a son born after daughters, break the centre of a bronze plate, remove all the inside of the rim, and then drag the child through the opening.

In the ruined church of St. Brandon, ten miles from Dingle, West Ireland, was a narrow window, through which sick women were passed three times in order to be cured.

St. Eloi, Bishop of Noyon, in the sixth century, had to forbid the faithful to drive their sheep and children through holes in the ground and through hollow trees.

Among the Corannas, of the Orange River, the recovery of a child from illness was celebrated by digging a trench in the ground, across which an arch was built, and on the arch an ox made to stand. The child was then dragged underneath the arch. Always, in many lands with various tongues and various deities, was there the same "something" through which a sufferer must be passed to effect the cure of his illness or ill-luck.

When whooping cough is prevalent in a Bulgarian village, an old woman will scrape the earth from under the roots of a willow tree. Then the children of the village creep through the opening thus made, and a thread from the garment of each is hung on the willow. When sickness is rife in villages of Lake Nyassa, the entire population crawl through an arch formed by bending a wand and inserting the two ends in the ground.

In some parts of the West of England, people suffering with boils crawl through a natural arch nine times with the sun; so they did in Perigord, and other parts of France for the same complaint.

The Romans used the arch as a healer; so did the Greeks.

The superstition seems to have been founded on the age-old belief in putting a barrier between the illness and the sufferer. By passing through the arch, with its downward parts inserted in the ground, it was believed that the illness was brushed off the victim, or left behind. All that remained was to ensure that it did not escape through the opening, and so again attack the sufferer, who had just lost it. For that reason it was the practice to leave either some small part of the sufferer behind, a thread of his clothing, for instance, or for him to wash himself after the crawl.

Returning to Britain, a Sunderland cure was to shave the head of the sufferer from whooping cough, and to hang the hair on a bush or tree. Birds who would carry the hair to their nest for lining would, at the same time, take the cough with it.

A cure much practised, even to-day, is to carry the child to a lime kiln, or a gasworks, and let it breathe the smoke or the gas fumes—or, as it was put, the "harmonious air." No doubt "harmonious" was a phonetic corruption of ammonia.

Ireland had a variation of the Gosport remedy, except that the frog or toad becomes a trout, which was taken from a stream, held with its head in the child's mouth, and then put back in the stream where, as may be supposed, it darted off upstream carrying with it, of course, the whooping cough.

Another Irish method was to take a mug of water from a running stream *against* the current. After the child had drunk from it, the water was poured back into the stream, but *downstream*. After this had been repeated on three mornings, the cure could be regarded as complete.

Still another method of the distressful Isle was to take a lock of hair from the head of a person who never saw his father (a posthumous child) tie it in a piece of red cloth and put it round the neck of the patient. This may well have been the best of them all, for the warmth of red cloth is a well-recognized medical fact.

In Cheshire, the popular cure for the whooping cough was to take some of the hair of the patient, bore a hole in a rowan tree and insert the hair in the hole, afterwards plugging up the hole. It was supposed that as the hair decayed in the tree, so would the cough vanish.

WIDOW

If a woman's hair grows in a low point in the centre of her forehead, it presages widowhood.—North Country.

The formation of the hair thus described, is generally known as a widow's peak; and in Warwickshire as a widow's lock.

WILL

A man who makes a will, will soon afterwards die.—Cheshire.

A stupid superstition still implicitly believed in by large numbers of people. The authors know of a score of their friends, who have made no will through a belief that it would hasten their death.

In two cases the lack of such a document has, after death, led to family quarrels, and in two other cases to litigation, in which most of the money of the estate went in costs.

WILL OF THE WISP

See CANDLE, CORPSE.

WILLOW HERB

The willow herb will stop bleeding, heal wounds, and drive away snakes, gnats and flies.

WINDOW

All windows should be opened at the moment of death, so that the soul can have free access.—Scotland and the North.

If a robin taps at the window of a sick room, it is a sign that the sick person will die.—General.

A robin singing close to a window means sorrow.—Wales.

See BOLTS, CORPSE, DEATH, LOCKS.

WINE

An ailing or weakly child will be cured with a drop of Sacramental wine.—Surrey.

WINTER

A green winter makes a fat churchyard.—General.

A January spring is worth naething.—Scotland.

This piece of weather superstition has a history of many centuries. Before Britain was discovered, the Chinese had a belief which ran: A mild winter makes a full churchyard," to give the English translation.

The origin is probably to be found in the fact that a mild winter usually has an intermission of mild and then very cold weather, and the cold spell, following the mild conditions, accounts for many deaths among the older people

An illustration in modern times were the years 1933 and 1937, which in Britain were peak years of influenza deaths. The year 1933 had an exceedingly mild January, which later changed to a cold spell. The year 1937 had a green January, a mild February, and a bitterly cold March.

WITCHES

Throughout the sixteenth and seventeenth centuries witchcraft was rife all over Britain, and almost every illness and especially of cattle was put down to "overlooking," or the spite of witches.

Witchcraft was born in superstition, lived in superstition and—we were going to say—died in superstition; but it still lives in parts of the country, and in illiterate minds.

In 1939, a gipsy was convicted at Portsmouth for unlawfully undertaking to tell fortunes and "remove a spell." She had told a half-witted woman that troubles she had were due to a spell cast upon her by a certain ring she was wearing, and that the remedy was to bury a human hair and a pound of steak in the ground, and also to burn a glove with a needle and pin in it. And the woman did it.

There was, also, if the authors remember correctly, a charge of witchcraft at a date later by some three or four years.

To detail in full the superstitions allied to witches would be impossible in a book of this size. The reader is recommended to read *Witchcraft in England*, by Christina Hole, than which we know none better.

Below, however, are some of the spells and the remedies which were household knowledge in Britain.

Most of the spells cast by witches were done with the aid of a wax image of the destined victim. Needles or pins were stuck in the image at spots and, it was said, the person in whose image the wax had been moulded, would at once feel the pain at the particular spot, and continue to suffer pain so long as the pin remained in the wax.

But it was held, that should the victim hang a bullock's heart, stuck all over with pins, in his chimney, this would reverse the process, and give the witch such pains that she would, to ease herself, remove the spell she had cast.

Such hearts almost petrified have been found on many occasions by workmen pulling down, or reconstructing, old houses.

In the County Museum at Taunton, Somerset, there may still be seen pigs' hearts full of pins. The superstition behind this was the belief that the pigs had been killed by the Evil Eye of an "overlooker," or witch. The heart of the pig, which died under the spell, was taken out of the body, stuck all over with the pins, and placed on the ledge inside the wide chimney which was then customary in most rural houses, in the belief that as it dried up and withered, so would the heart of the person who had betwitched the pigs, thus removing the danger of any further animals suffering the same way.

A bunch of ash-keys carried in the hand, or in the left stocking, were regarded as personal safeguards against harm by witches; but the more potent and common were horse shoes, silver, spittle and the sign of the Cross in England, and rowan wood in Scotland.

It was believed that witches changed themselves into hares, and that these hares could be shot only with a silver bullet or a silver crooked sixpence.

If butter would not come from a churn, it was regarded as bewitched. A silver coin, or a silver spoon, dropped in the churn would at once produce the butter.

No Banffshire farmer or dairymaid thinks of milking a cow for the first time after calving, except over a "crossiecroon shilling" to protect the animal from the Evil Eye.

Steel was another protection against witches and the Evil Eye; and it exists even down to the present day. The grandmother of one of the authors when she had kneaded the dough for the week's baking, never failed to make a long cross on the top of it, as it stood in the earthenware vessel to rise. The cross had to be cut with a steel knife. The practice was followed by her daughter, the mother of one of the authors. We remember asking her as children why she did it. She did not know, but added that it must always be done. We can tell her now: it was to avert the Evil Eye from the bread. Or, as Henrich put it in his *Hesperides*:

Cross your dough and your despatch
Will be better for your batch.

Another charm to keep away the Evil Eye was an adder stone (q.v.).

Rowan wood was the great Scottish charm against witches, as it was also throughout Europe. On Midsummer Eve, on All Hallows, and on other "evil" days, the wood was gathered and placed over the doors of cattle houses and byres to protect the inmates.

It was regarded as essential to place a knife or a piece of iron under the doorstep of the house to keep witches at bay.

When carters passed the cottage of a known or suspected witch, they were in the habit of running the blade of a pocket knife round the iron tyres of their wagon wheels. This, it was held, so affected the witch that she screamed in agony, and was unable to harm them.

In the *Mirror of Literature* of Saturday, 4th March, 1780, there was given this recipe for combating the effect of witchcraft: "Dog's grease, well dissolved and cleaned, four ounces; bear's grease, eight ounces; capon's grease, twentyfour ounces. Three trunks of the mistletoe, of hazel while green—cut it in pieces and pound it small till it becomes moist. Bruise it together, and mix all up in a phial, and expose it to the sun for nine weeks, wherewith if you anoint the body of the bewitched, especially the part most affected, they will certainly be cured."

It was added by the paper that the recipe had been tried with amazing success in the case of a young girl, whose condition was truly deplorable, for she vomited feathers, bundles of straw and a row of pins stuck in blue paper as fresh and new as any on the pedlars' stalls, pieces of glass windows and the nails of a cart wheel.

See EVIL EYE, ROWAN WOOD.

WOMAN
To meet a woman when setting out on an expedition, is a bad omen.

If a woman is the first to cross the threshold on New Year's morning, bad luck will attend the person who meets her.

The ill-fortune at meeting a woman was held particularly by fishermen and miners. None of the men of these callings would go to the day's work, if a woman crossed their paths.

In the case of fishermen, the ill-luck was intensified if the woman was wearing a white apron.

There are a large number of sayings about women, which are more in the nature of proverbs than anything else, but among them are a number which can be accounted as superstitions applicable only to women. Here are a few of them:

If you have your clothes mended on your back, you will be ill-spoken of. (In Sussex, they say that such a practice will lead you to want.)

To have good luck with any article of

dress, you must wear it the first time to church.

To put on an article of dress the first thing in the morning inside out, is an omen of success. But it is emphasized that the mistake must be an accidental one.

Curiously enough, to put a wrong hook or button into a hole presages misfortune.

If you do not appear in new things on Whit Sunday, you forfeit all your good luck for the next twelve months.

If a young woman's petticoat is longer than her dress, it means that her mother does not love her as much as her father.

When a married woman's apron falls off, it is a sign that something is coming along to vex her; but should an apron fall from an unmarried woman it is a sign to her companions that she is thinking of her sweetheart.

Suffolk women used to wear a large apron called a "mantle." It was blue in colour. If it accidentally fell off, it was regarded as a bad omen.

A woman must not give another woman a pin, but can allow her to take one, provided she says, "Mind, I do not give it to you." This is a North Country superstition.

Woman's gift for talking is said to have arisen this way: Woman was created without a tongue. But Adam one day put an aspen leaf under her palate, which grew into a tongue. The meaning is obvious when it is remembered that the aspen leaf is never entirely still, being moved by even the slightest of breezes. However, we can come to the aid of the ladies in this connection, for the legend of the trembling of the aspen leaf is generally held to be due to the fact that the Cross of Christ was made of the wood of the tree, and the leaves have shivered in horror ever since. So the Adam story cannot bear talking about.

Then, there is the sentence: "A whistling woman and a crowing hen, are neither good for God nor men." The origin of the whistling woman part is supposed to be due to the fact that a woman stood by and whistled as she watched the nails being forged for the Cross. As a result, every time a woman whistles, the heart of the Virgin Mary bleeds. Incidentally, a crowing hen used to be instantly killed by farmers in this country; and is still killed in China, Persia, Portugal and Italy.

Another couplet goes: "A woman, a dog and a walnut tree, the more you whip them, the better they be." The origin is unknown; but in many rural areas of the country, it is still regarded as essential to whip the trunk of a walnut tree in the spring, in order to improve the flavour and quality of the fruit.

"He that tells his wife news, is but newly married," is another saying, meaning that he has yet to learn that a woman cannot keep a secret.

In Cheshire, a good looking girl was always referred to as being "as fair as Lady Done." Pennant explains the phrase in his *Journey from Preston to London,* in 1793: "Sir John Done, Knight, Hereditary Forester and Keeper of the Forest of Delamere, Cheshire, died in 1629. When James I made a progress in the year 1607, he was entertained by this gentleman at Utkinton. He married Dorothy, daughter of Thomas Wilbraham, Esqr., of Woodhey, who left behind her so admirable a character that to this day when a Cheshire man would express some excellence in one of the fair sex, he would say: 'There is Lady Done for you.' "

See FISHING, MINE.

WORM CURE (FOR WOUNDS)

Among the superstitious "cures" round the 1870s, was the worm cure for the treatment of injuries.

Reference has been made elsewhere to the stringing of a wriggling worm round the neck of a child to cure the whooping cough, or a sore throat.

In Cornwall, should a fisherman cut himself, he at once lifted from his bait a large lobworm, pressed it upon the wound, and then threw the worm into the water. The cut was then washed in the water.

The superstition behind this was that the worm had taken the evil out of the wound, and the water had afterwards cleaned it.

WORMS CURE

To cure the worms in children, take wormwood, rue (gathered at midnight), bull's gall and hog's grease. Fry all together, and apply to the child's navel, and anoint the stomach with the same.

Boil a number of earthworms in water, and give the child of the liquid to drink. This is an infallible cure.— Tweedside.

In Cleveland, great reliance was placed on catching a "wick" trout (a quick or live trout), and laying it on the stomach of the child.

WOUNDS

If you clean and polish the article which has inflicted the wound, the wound will not fester, but will heal cleanly.—Northumberland and the Eastern Counties, particularly.

This was a belief which came long after the famous Sympathy powder remedy of Sir Kenelm Digby (q.v.). It was widespread, but more so in the Eastern Counties than elsewhere. It was also widespread in pagan countries.

In Suffolk, if a hedger cut himself with his billhook, he at once took care to see that the hook was kept polished and bright, in order to ensure that his wound would not fester. In the same county, Frazer records the case of a man who went to the doctor with a badly inflamed hand, he having some time previously run a thorn into it. Being told that the hand was festering, he avowed that that could not be, for he had greased the bush well after he had pulled the thorn out of his hand.

As recently as 1902, a Norfolk woman, who had run a nail into her foot, without taking the trouble to examine the foot, or even remove her stocking, told her daughter to grease the nail. If this was done, she said, no harm would come to her foot. Unfortunately, harm did come to it.

The same belief extended even to animals. Cambridgeshire farm horsemen, if their horse ran a nail into its foot, thought it vitally necessary to grease the nail with fat or oil, and put it away in some place, or the horse would not recover.

A veterinary surgeon was called some years ago to attend a horse which had ripped a side open on the hinge of a gatepost. On arriving he found that nothing whatever had been done in the way of attending to the horse's wound, but the men were endeavouring to prise the hinge off the post in order that it might be greased and put away.

Now compare these beliefs with the following: Pliny recorded the conviction in his day that if you have wounded a man, and are sorry for it you have only to spit on the hand that inflicted the wound, and the pain will vanish.

In Melanesia, natives get possession of the arrow that has wounded one of them and keep it in a cool, damp place, so that the wounded man's inflammation will subside. The enemy, on the other hand, drink hot juices in order to inflame the wound in their victim.

It has been conjectured that the idea behind the man and the weapon is that the blood on the weapon continues to feel the blood in the body. Bacon records that "It is constantly avouched that the anointing of the weapon that maketh the wound will heal the wound itself."

Perhaps a more simple cure(!) is that which was usual on Dartmoor. Here it is: "Say three times, 'When our Lord Jesus Christ was on earth he pricked himself with a—here name the cause of your injury—and the blood sprang up to Heaven. Yet His flesh did·neither canker, mould or corrupt, no more shall thine. I put my trust in God. In the name of the, etc.'"

After this the Lord's Prayer had to be recited.

See SYMPATHY POWDER.

WRONG SIDE

To put an article of clothing on wrong side out, will bring you luck—General.

But only so long as it was thus put on accidentally, and is not changed throughout the day.

YARROW

The superstitious use of the yarrow as an article of love divination was as follows:

Go on May Day eve to a bank, on which the yarrow grows and gather nine sprigs, saying: "Good morrow, fair yarrow, and thrice good morning to thee. Come tell me before to-morrow, who my true love shall be." Bring the yarrow home, and put into the right foot stocking, which you should then place under your pillow. Your husband-to be will be seen in a dream.

There was one snag; if the lady opened her mouth to speak to anyone after pulling the yarrow, the spell would be broken.

YELLOWHAMMER

The yellowhammer drinks a drop—some say three drops—of the Devil's blood each May morning.—Scottish peasantry.

For this reason, the nest of this pretty and harmless little bird was regarded as fair game.

In Scotland the boys used to address it with this reproachful rhyme:

Half a paddock, half a toad,
Half a yellow yorling;
Drink a drap o' the de'il's bluid,
Every May morning.

YEW TREE

It was held that anyone who had the temerity to pluck a branch of a yew tree, which grew in the cloisters of Muckross Abbey, would die within the next twelve months.

The yew has been for generations regarded as the gentle guardian of the dead, which is why it is found in most churchyards.

In Wales it was so revered, that to cut it down was regarded as an act of desecration, and to burn any part of the tree as sacrilege.

Because of its association with the dead, it was regarded as unlucky to have yew in the house, and it was never included in any decorations.

YOUTHFULNESS

If you would regain your youthfulness, or youthful appearance, you should eat snakes.

The extent or the area of this quaint superstition is unknown to the authors, but it is mentioned by Fuller, who wrote in *The Holy State and the Profane State* (1641): "A gentlewoman told an ancient bachelor, who looked very young, that she thought he must have eaten snakes; and received the reply: 'No mistris, it is because I never meddled with snakes that maketh me look so young.'"

BIBLIOGRAPHY

The following books have been read or consulted during the preparation of the *Encyclopædia of Superstitions*:

A Book of Folklore	S. Baring-Gould
Accounts of the Religion, Manners and Learning of the People of Malabar	J. T. Phillips
A Journey to the Western Islands of Scotland	Dr. S. Johnson
American Journal of Folklore, 1898.	
Among Congo Cannibals	Rev. J. H. Weeks
Among the Indians of Guiana.	
Anatomie of the Elder	Blochurch
A Naturalist in North Celebes	J. Hickson
Ancient Cures, Charms and Usages of Ireland	Lady Wilde
Ancient Legends, Mystic Charms and Superstitions of Ireland	Lady Wilde
Ancient Legends and Superstitions of Ireland	Lady Wilde
Archaic England	Bayley
Authority and Archæology, Sacred and Profane	Edited, D. G. Hogarth
Book of Days	Chambers
Book of Days	Hone
Borders of the Tamar and the Tavy	Anna E. Stotherd
Britannic	Camden
British Calendar Customs	Edited, T. E. Lones, M.A., LL.D.
British Popular Customs	T. T. Dyer
Bygone Beliefs	George Long
Bygones Relating to Wales and Border Counties.	
Celtæ and Galli	Sir John Rhys
Celtic Folklore	Sir John Rhys
Celtic Heathendom	Sir John Rhys
Celtic Scotland	Skene
Census of India, 1911	Pandit H. Kaul
Characters of Vices and Virtues	Hall
Choice Notes	from *Notes and Queries*
Complete History of Animals and Minerals	R. Lovell
Cornwall and its People	A. K. H. Jenkin
County Folklore, printed Extracts, Leicestershire and Rutlandshire	Edited, C. J. Billson
County Folklore of Lincolnshire	Mrs. Gutch, Mrs. Peacock
County Folklore, North Riding of Yorkshire	Edited, Mrs. Gutch
County Folklore of Suffolk	Lady Gurdon
Coutumes, Mythes et Traditions des Provinces de France	A. de Nore
Curiosities of Indo-European Tradition and Folklore	W. K. Kelly
Custom and Myth	Andrew Lang

(Also a number of Articles contributed to *Folklore* by Sir John Rhys.)

Darker Superstitions of Scotland	T. Graham Dallyell
David Copperfield	Charles Dickens
De Borussias Antiquitatibus	Erasmus Stella

De Mendicamentis · · · · · · · · · Marcellus
Dictionary of Greek and Roman Antiquities · · · · · W. Smith
Die Deutsch-Russischen Ostseeprovinzen · · · · · · J. G. Kohl
Discourse on Sympathy · · · · · · · · Sir K. Digby
Discovery of Witchcraft · · · · · · · · · R. Scott

Egyptian Myth and Legend · · · · · Donald A. Mackenzie, M.A.
Encyclopædia Britannica, 14th Edition.
Encyclopædia of Religion and Ethics · · · · · J. H. MacCulloch
England's Antiphon · · · · · · · · · G. Macdonald
Eskimo about Behring's Strait · · · · · · · E. W. Nelson
Essays on Natural History · · · · · · · · Waterton
Evolution of the English Town · · · · · · · Pickering

Fetishism in West Africa · · · · · · · · R. H. Nassau
Finger-ring Lore · · · · · · · · · · W. Jones
Flowers of Folklore · · · · · · · · Rev. H. Friend
Folklore of British Isles · · · · · · · · Eleanor Hill
Folklore of the British Isles.
Folklore of East Yorkshire · · · · · · · J. Nicholson
Folklore of Herefordshire. · · · · · · Mrs. E. M. Leather
Folklore of Lowland Scotland · · · · · · · Eve Simpson
Folklore Medicine · · · · · · · · · W. Black
Folklore of Mid Wales · · · · · · · · J. C. Davies
Folklore of the North of Scotland · · · · · · W. Gregor
Folklore Round Horncastle · · · · · · J. A. Penny, M.A.
Folklore Stories of Wales · · · · · · Marie Trevelyan
Folklore of West and Midlands.
Folklore of the West of Scotland · · · · · · · W. Gregor
Forest of Varieties · · · · · · · · Lord North

Geoponica.
Glimpses of Unfamiliar Japan · · · · · · · L. Hearn
Grecian Antiquities · · · · · · · · · Potter

Halliwell's Dictionary.
Handbook of Folklore · · · · · · Charlotte Sophia Burne
Hereford Folklore · · · · · · · · E. M. Leather
Het Nederlands · · · · · · · · · J. H. Letteboer
Highlands and Islands of Scotland · · · · · J. G. Campbell
Historie Critique des Pratiques Superstitieuses · · · · · Le Brun
History of the American Indians · · · · · · James Adair
History of Antiquities of Kingston-on-Thames · · · · W. D. Biden
History of Cornwall · · · · · · · · · Hitchen
History of Remarkable Providences · · · · · · · Turner
Household Tales · · · · · · · · · S. O. Addy

In Central Borneo · · · · · · Dr. A. W. Nieuwenhuis
Indian Notes and Queries.

John O' London's Weekly · · · · · Edited, Wilson Midgley
Journal of the Anthropological Institute (A. Simpson).

Kaffir Folklore · · · · · · · · · G. M. Theal
Kaffirs of Natal and the Zulu Country · · · · · Rev. J. Shooter

Lancashire Folklore - - - - - - - - - - T. F. Dyer
Lancashire Notes and Queries.
Lapponia - - - - - - - - - - - J. Scheffer
Le Folklore des Hautes-Vosges - - - - - - - L. F. Sauve
Le Folklore du Poiton - - - - - - - - L. Pineau
Leicestershire and Rutlandshire Folklore - - - - - C. J. Billson
Letters on Demonology and Witchcraft - - - - - Sir Walter Scott
Literature of the Middle Ages - - - - - - - - Wright
"Live Letters" of the Daily Mirror, London. - - - Edited, E. Radford
Lucks and Talismans - - - - - - - - - C. R. Beard

Mabinogion - - - - - - - - - Lady C. E. Guest
Mag-Astronomers Posed and Puzzled - - - - - - Gaule
Magic in Modern India - - - - - - - - E. Lovett
Magic in Modern London - - - - - - - - E. Lovett
Magic, Religion and Mythology - - - - - - - E. Shortlands
Magic et Religions et Folklore of India - - - - - E. Doutte
Malay Beliefs - - - - - - - - - R. J. Wilkinson
Malay Magic - - - - - - - - - W. W. Skeat
Malay Poisons and Charm Cures - - - - - - Gimlette
Manners and Customs of Mankind - - - - Sir John Hammerton
Mededeelingen van Wege.
Medical Superstitions.
Memorials of London, 1868.
Mirror of Literature, 1823 (Volume I).
Miscellaneous Remains - - - - - - Archbishop Whateley
Miscellanies - - - - - - - - - - Aubrey
Modern Greek Folklore and Ancient Greek Religion - - - J. C. Lawson
Mores Leges et Ritus Omnium Sentium - - - - - J. Boemus
My School and Schoolmasters - - - - - - Hugh Miller
Myth, Ritual and Religion - - - - - - - Andrew Lang
Myths of the Cherokees - - - - - - - J. Mooney

Native Tribes of Central Australia - - - - - Spencer and Gillen
Native Tribes of South Australia - - - - - H. E. A. Meyer
Natural History - - - - - - - - - . Bacon
Natural History - - - - - - - - - Pliny
Natural and Moral History of the Indies - - - - J. de Costa
Natural History of Cornwall - - - - - - - Borlase
Natural History of North Wales - - - - - - Aubrey
New Book of Knowledge - - - - Edited, Sir John Hammerton
Northern Mythology - - - - - - - - B. Thorpe
North Riding, Yorkshire - - - From County Folklore by Mrs. Gutch
Notable Things - - - - - - - - - Lupton
Notes on Ancient Britain - - - - - - - W. Barnes
Notes on the Folklore of the N.E. Scotland - - - Rev. W. Gregor
Notes on Folklore Objects Collected in Argyllshire - - R. G. Maclagen
Notes and Queries.
Notes sur les Coutumes et Croyances Superstiteuses des Camborgies   E. Aymonier

Old Church Life - - - - - - - William Andrews
Old Scottish Customs - - - - - - - Miss E. J. Guthrie
On Superstitions Connected with the History and Practice of Medicine
    and Surgery - - - - - - - - T. J. Pettigrew

Origins of Popular Superstitions and Customs - - - - T. S. Knowles
Orkney and Shetland Folklore - - - - - - - G. F. Black
Orkney and Shetland Islands Folklore - - - - - N. W. Thomas

Pagan Races of the Malay Peninsula - - - - Skeat and Blagdon
Pagan Tribes of Borneo - - - - - C. H. Hose and W. McDougall
Pictorial Calendar of the Seasons - - - - - - - Howitt
Popular Antiquities - - - - - - - - - Brand
Popular Religions and Folklore of North India - - - - W. Crooke
Popular Romances - - - - - - - - Hunt
Popular Romances of the West of England - - - - - R. Hunt
Popular "ales from the Norse - - - - - - G. W. Dasent
Primitive Physic - - - - - . - - - John Wesley

Ramblings and Recollections of an Indian Official Major-General Sir W. H. Sleeman
Religion and Myth - - - - - - - James Macdonald
Remains of Gentilisme and Judaisme - - - - - John Aubrey
Revue des Traditions Populaires (1899).
Rural Economy - - - - - - - - - - Best

Savage Life and Scenes in Australia and New Zealand - - - G. F. Angas
Scenes and Legends of the North of Scotland - - - - Hugh Miller
Scenes and Studies of Savage Life - - - - - - G. M. Stroat
Science and Superstition - - - - - - - P. Shorr
Shropshire Folklore - - - - - C. E. Burne and G. F. Jackson
Social History of Ancient Ireland - - - - - - P. W. Joyce
Social Life in Scotland - - - - - - - Charles Rogers
Speculum Mundi - - - - - - - - - Swan
Sports and Pastimes of the People of England - - - - J. Strutt
Statistical Account of Scotland - - - - - Edited, Sir John Sinclair
Strange Survivals - - - - - - - S. Baring-Gould
Suffolk Folklore - - - - - - Lady Eveline C. Gurdon
Superstitions of Sailors - - - - - - Dr. A. S. Rappenport
Superstitious Man - - - - - - - - Theophrastus

Tales of the Munster Fairies - - - - - - - T. Curtin
The Craven and North-West Yorkshire Highlands - - - Harry Speight
The Cochin Tribes and Castes - - - - - - L. K. Iyer
The Evil Eye - - - - - - - - F. T. Elsworthy
The Folklore of the Magyar - - - - W. H. Jones and L. L. Kropf
The Folklore of the Northern Counties of England - - - W. Henderson
The Golden Bough - - - - - - - - Sir J. Frazer
The Heart of Africa - - - - - - - G. Schweinfurth
The Land of the Lamas - - - - - - - W. W. Rockhill
The Saxons in England - - - - - - - J. M. Kemble
Thorpe's Mythology.
Three Years in Savage Africa - - - - - - - L. Decle
Those Superstitions - - - - - - Sir Charles Igglesden
Tour of Scotland - - - - - - - - John Pennant
Traces of the Elder Faiths of Ireland - - - - G. Wood-Martin
Traditional and Hearthside Stories of West Cornwall - - - W. Bottrell
Traditions and Customs of Cheshire - - - - - Christina Hole
Traditions and Superstitions of the New Zealander - - - E. Shortland
Traditions, Coutumes, Legendes et Contes des Ardennes - - - A. Meyrac
Traditions et Superstitions de la Haute-Bretagne - - - - P. Sebillot

Traite des Superstitions - - - - - - - - J. B. Thiers
Tramps and Drives in the Craven Highlands - - - - Harry Speight
Travels - - - - - - - - - - Boullage le Gunz
Travels in the Interior Districts of Africa - - - - - Mungo Park
Travels through Sweden, Finland and Lapland - - - - - J. Acerbi

Voyages and Travels - - - - - - - - - Pinkerton
Vulgar Errors - - - - - - - - Sir Thomas Browne

Welsh Folklore - - - - - - - - - Elias Owen
Whitby Lore and Legend - - - - - - - - S. Jeffrey
Witchcraft in England - - - - - - - Christina Hole
Witchcraft and Second Sight in the Highlands - - - J. G. Campbell

Yorkshire Folklore Journal.
Yorkshire Legend and Tradition - - - - - - T. K. Parkinson

In addition, the authors acknowledge with thanks the assistance, always so courteously given, of the staff of the London Library; the Library of the Royal Society of Arts; and the assistance of a large number of interested people, including Mr. C. E. Leese, B.Sc., of Sir James Smith's Grammar School, Camelford, who delved into many of the old Cornish beliefs for us.

ISBN 0-8371-2115-9

90000>

EAN

9 780837 121154

HARDCOVER BAR CODE